D1084693

AMERICAN FOREIGN RELATIONS
1978
A DOCUMENTARY RECORD

COUNCIL ON FOREIGN RELATIONS BOOKS

The Council on Foreign Relations, Inc., is a non-profit and non-partisan organization devoted to promoting improved understanding of international affairs through the free exchange of ideas. Its membership of about 1,700 persons throughout the United States is made up of individuals with special interest and experience in international affairs. The Council has no affiliation with, and receives no funding from, the United States government. The Council does not take any position on questions of foreign policy.

The Council publishes the quarterly journal, *Foreign Affairs.* In addition, from time to time, books and monographs written by members of the Council's research staff or visiting fellows, or commissioned by the Council, or written by independent authors with critical review contributed by a Council study group, are published with the designation "Council Paper on International Affairs." Any book or monograph bearing that designation is, in the judgment of the Committee on Studies of the Council's board of directors, a responsible treatment of a significant international topic worthy of presentation to the public. All statements of fact and expressions of opinion contained in Council books, monographs, and *Foreign Affairs* articles are, however, the sole responsibility of their authors.

AMERICAN FOREIGN RELATIONS 1978

A DOCUMENTARY RECORD

Continuing the Series
DOCUMENTS ON AMERICAN FOREIGN RELATIONS
THE UNITED STATES IN WORLD AFFAIRS

Edited by **ELAINE P. ADAM**
with an introduction by
RICHARD P. STEBBINS

A Council on Foreign Relations Book
Published by
New York University Press • New York • 1979

PREFACE

This volume offers a condensed historical narrative together with a selection of documents reflecting salient aspects of the foreign relations of the United States in 1978. Continuing the series of foreign policy surveys initiated by the Council on Foreign Relations in 1931 under the title *The United States in World Affairs*, the volume also maintains the service provided annually for more than three decades by the separate *Documents on American Foreign Relations* series, inaugurated by the World Peace Foundation in 1939 and taken over by the Council on Foreign Relations in 1952. The fusion of narrative and documentation, commenced on a trial basis with the inception of the present series in 1971, was designed to provide a single, comprehensive, and nonpartisan record of American foreign policy during the bicentennial decade and beyond. In view of the feebleness of public response, however, the series is being discontinued with this volume.

The interests of orderly presentation have appeared to be best served by the inclusion of a fairly detailed historical essay that reviews the year's main foreign policy developments and serves as introduction to the accompanying documentary material, which is presented in a parallel sequence to facilitate cross referencing between the two parts of the volume. Some readers will no doubt be satisfied to stop with the Introduction; others may wish to go directly to the documents, which are presented in authoritative texts and accompanied by whatever editorial apparatus seemed necessary for independent reference use.

A key to certain abbreviations used in footnotes throughout the volume appears at the end of the Table of Contents, and organizational abbreviations and acronyms are listed and explained in the alphabetical Index. The Appendix presents a selected checklist of historical documents referred to in the volume. The spelling of proper names reflects contemporary American usage. In quoted matter in the Introduction, paragraph divisions have occasionally been disregarded. All dates refer to the year 1978 unless a different year is specifically indicated.

The editorial procedure described above admittedly involves the exercise of a substantial measure of individual judgment and demands all possible objectivity in the handling of controversial events and data. While hopeful that the volume will not be found wanting in this regard, the editors wish to emphasize that the editorial viewpoint is of necessity a personal one and in no way seeks to reflect the outlook of the Council on Foreign Relations or any of its officers and directors, members, or staff.

Among their immediate associates, the editors would note their special indebtedness to Winston Lord, President; John Temple

Swing, Vice President and Secretary; Grace Darling Griffin, Publications Manager; and Janet Rigney, Librarian, of the Council on Foreign Relations; and to Despina Papazoglou, Associate Managing Editor, and other friends at NYU Press. They are also indebted to various official agencies which have provided documentary material, and to *The New York Times* for permission to reprint texts or excerpts of documents appearing in its pages. As always, the editors themselves are responsible for the choice and presentation of the documents as well as the form and content of the editorial matter.

June 28, 1979

CONTENTS

vii

PART TWO: DOCUMENTS

KEY TO ABBREVIATED REFERENCES

(The abbreviation GPO refers to
the U.S. Government Printing Office)

"AFR": American Foreign Relations: A Documentary Record (New York: New York University Press, for the Council on Foreign Relations; annual vols., 1971–78).

"Bulletin": U.S. Department of State, *The Department of State Bulletin* (Washington: GPO, weekly through 1977, monthly thereafter). Most references are to vols. 78 (Jan.–Dec. 1978) and 79 (Jan–Feb. 1979).

"Documents": Documents on American Foreign Relations (annual vols., 1939–70). Volumes prior to 1952 published by Princeton University Press for the World Peace Foundation; volumes for 1952-66 published by Harper & Row for the Council on Foreign Relations; volumes for 1967–70 published by Simon and Schuster for the Council on Foreign Relations.

"Keesing's": Keesing's Contemporary Archives (Bristol: Keesing's Publications, Ltd., weekly).

"Presidential Documents": Weekly Compilation of Presidential Documents (Washington: GPO, weekly). Most references are to vol. 12 (1978).

"Stat.": Statutes at Large of the United States (Washington: GPO, published irregularly).

"TIAS": U.S. Department of State, *United States Treaties and Other International Agreements* (Washington: GPO, published irregularly).

"UST": U.S. Department of State, *United States Treaties and Other International Agreements* (Washington: GPO, published irregularly).

"USUN Press Releases": Press releases of the U.S. Mission to the United Nations, as reprinted in the *Department of State Bulletin.*

PART I: INTRODUCING 1978

INTRODUCING 1978

NINETEEN SEVENTY-EIGHT will be remembered as a year of alternating lights and shadows—a year, in foreign policy, that brought the United States within sight of some important diplomatic objectives, yet failed to dispel a prevalent uneasiness about the trend of national and world affairs.

Legally and formally, the 219,000,000 Americans of 1978 continued to enjoy the state of peace that had officially prevailed since the conclusion of the Vietnam adventure five years earlier. At home, however, they remained caught in an inflationary treadmill in which consumer prices were increasing at a rate of 9 percent a year. Abroad, the nation was still enmeshed in a life-and-death political and military competition with the Soviet Union, a power whose challenge to American interests appeared if anything to be increasing as its earlier strategic inferiority gave place to an open quest for global military strength.

There was an inconclusive quality to even the most hopeful among the international events of 1978. American and Soviet negotiators made progress toward a new strategic arms limitation (SALT) treaty to replace the original SALT agreement that had been signed in 1972 and expired in 1977; yet 1978 concluded, as had earlier years, without a settlement of the myriad details to be included in such an arrangement.

American diplomacy registered a brilliant triumph when President Jimmy Carter persuaded Egypt's President Anwar al-Sadat and Israel's Prime Minister Menahem Begin to accept a "framework" for peace between their two countries—which, however, failed to resolve a number of central questions pertaining to the destiny of the Israeli-occupied West Bank, the Gaza Strip, and the Palestinian Arab populations.

A surprise agreement to normalize relations between the United States and the People's Republic of China provided means of correcting a diplomatic anomaly of nearly 30 years' standing, yet was flawed for many Americans because it required the severance of even older ties to the Republic of China on Taiwan.

1

A shattering blow to American interests occured in Asia when the imperial government of Iran, a keystone in the global security structure created by the United States since World War II, collapsed amid the revolutionary hysteria fanned by Muslim zealots and Marxist ideologues.

In economic affairs, the United States belatedly equipped itself with some of the elements of a national energy program and interrupted a precipitous decline of the dollar in the foreign exchange markets. The Tokyo Round of multilateral trade negotiations, designed to set a pattern for international commerce over the next several years, approached, but failed to reach, the conclusive stage which would ultimately be attained in the spring of 1979.

A similarly inconclusive quality was evident in still other areas of American concern. In southern Africa, what looked like progress toward peaceful independence for Namibia was balanced by deteriorating conditions in Rhodesia, the scene of a large-scale guerrilla conflict that extended into neighboring Zambia and Mozambique as well. Threats of direct attacks on U.S. interests in the Western Hemisphere receded with the Senate's approval, by the narrowest of margins, of new treaties governing the future of the Panama Canal and the Canal Zone; but discontent with the United States in Latin America persisted, and internal political conflict in some Latin American countries—notably Nicaragua—took on a new acuteness. Hopes for improved relations with Fidel Castro's Cuba were torpedoed by the latter's large-scale involvement in revolutionary activities in Africa.

The United States was not itself involved in all of the conflict situations that still abounded in a world where the United Nations, as the principal trustee of humanity's hopes for a better world, was fast approaching its goal of universal membership, yet remained comparatively ineffective in discharging its primary responsibility for the maintenance of international peace and security. Added to the perennial quarrels between the Soviet Union and China, between the Arabs and Israel, between North and South Korea and between Northern and Southern Yemen, new battles erupted in 1978 between Vietnam and Cambodia, between Vietnam and China, and between Uganda and Tanzania. The chronic civil war in Lebanon flared up anew, and Israeli military forces occupied the southern part of the country for several months before retiring in favor of a United Nations peacekeeping force. Even then, a strip of frontier territory was left in the control of Israeli-backed Lebanese Christian forces.

Nicaragua and Northern Ireland, Iran and Turkey, meanwhile, were prominent among the many countries in which political and social discontent found vent in large-scale violence. Afghanistan experienced a military coup that presaged a close alignment with the Soviet Union. The Cambodian regime headed by Pol Pot and Ieng Sary—"the worst violator of human rights in the world today," according to President Carter—added fresh atrocities to a record already replete with "mass killings, inhuman treatment of the supporters of the previous government, the forced deportation of urban dwellers, and the total suppression of recognized political and religious freedoms, as well as deprivation of food and health care for the general population."[1] Similar charges were regularly leveled against the regime of President Idi Amin Dada in Uganda.

There were also fresh examples of the warfare being waged by small, fanatical groups against the foundations of the social order if not of civilization itself. Among the more horrifying occurrences of a gruesome decade were the captivity and martyrdom of Aldo Moro, a former Italian Prime Minister and head of Italy's Christian Democratic Party, at the hands of members of the extreme leftist "Red Brigades." Dismaying in a different manner were the mass deaths at Jonestown, Guyana, of over 900 Americans whose alienation from American life had swelled the ranks of the self-exiled "People's Temple" cult led by the Reverend Jim Jones. A third offense to any notion of human dignity was the plight of the tens of thousands of refugees from the Indochinese countries, particularly the so-called "boat people" who had bought their way out of Vietnam and now wandered the oceans in leaky, overcrowded vessels with no assurance of acceptance in another country.

Not all of the year's developments were of such macabre quality, however. Millions who had mourned the death in August of Pope Paul VI were cheered by the friendly smile and outgoing deportment of his successor, John Paul I; nor was the sense of renewal diminished by the sudden death of the new pontiff and the election of Karol Cardinal Wojtyla, Archbishop of Cracow, to succeed him as John Paul II and the first non-Italian Pope in 455 years. Other deaths in 1978 provided a reminder of the power of political ideals. Jomo Kenyatta of Kenya, Golda Meir of Israel, and Houari Boumediene of Algeria had each inspired a constituency not limited by national frontiers. Senator Humbert H. Humphrey of the United States had radiated a comparable influence, despite his failure to attain his country's highest office.

Other hopeful tendencies could readily be discovered in the year's events. Aside from the progress toward a SALT agreement and a peace in the Middle East, the relationship among the great industrial democracies of Europe, North America, and the Pacific was closer perhaps than at any time in the past. Nineteen seventy-eight was also a good year for political rights and civil liberties, according to the annual Freedom House survey, which listed gains

[1] Carter statement, Apr. 21, in *Presidential Documents,* 14: 767.

in freedom for 563 million people in 24 countries and decreases in freedom for only 144 million people in eight countries.[2] But it was also the year when Yuri Orlov, Aleksandr Ginzburg, and Anatoly Shcharansky, among other Soviet citizens, were sentenced to prolonged imprisonment for their efforts to induce their government to live up to the liberal promises it had made in subscribing to the Helsinki Final Act of 1975.

As was to be expected, the negative manifestations of 1978 evoked abundant prophecies concerning the supposedly impending doom of a decrepit civilization. "The Western world has lost its civil courage," said Aleksandr I. Solzhenitsyn as he accepted an honorary Harvard doctorate on June 8. " . . . Political and intellectual bureaucrats show depression, passivity and perplexity in their actions and in their statements. . . . they get tongue-tied and paralyzed when they deal with powerful governments and threatening forces, with aggressors and international terrorists. Should one point out that from ancient times decline in courage has been considered the beginning of the end?"[3]

Less militant, but scarcely less pessimistic, were the views enunciated by Isaac Bashevis Singer on accepting the Nobel Prize for Literature six months later. "All the dismal prophecies of Oswald Spengler have become realities since World War II," he said. "No technological achievements can mitigate the disappointment of modern man, his loneliness, his feeling of inferiority, and his fear of war, revolution, and terror. Not only has our generation lost faith in Providence but also in man himself, in his institutions and often in those who are nearest to him. . . ."[4] To banker Felix G. Rohatyn, "despite our current prosperity, our economy is out of control, our currency is in danger, our institutions of government are unresponsive or inept. . . . We face the possible loss of our most precious asset, Western democracy, surely the most magnificent form of organized life, because we are lazy, cynical and unwilling to make the effort, unwilling to demand the kind of leadership democracy requires."[5]

Politicians naturally took a more optimistic view. Britain's Prime Minister James Callaghan, in a New York address interpreted by some as a reply to Solzhenitsyn, referred to Communism as a "burnt-out case: an idea whose time has been and gone," and urged his hearers to steer clear of zealotry as well as excessive complacency.[6] President Carter, too, drew strength and confidence

[2]Michael Goodwin in *New York Times,* Jan. 8, 1979.
[3]*Harvard University Gazette,* June 8, 1978.
[4]*New York Times,* Dec. 9, 1978.
[5]Same, Dec. 7, 1978.
[6]Same, June 26 and 30, 1978.

from what to him was "the innate greatness and strength of our country." "We're the strongest nation on Earth militarily, and we intend to stay that way," he declared at a White House dinner for newly elected members of Congress. "We're the strongest nation on Earth economically; God's blessed us beyond all reasonable expectation, compared to other people on Earth. And, of course, we have the best political system as well. And that blessing that's fallen upon us gives us a great responsibility not only to our own people to maintain a good life, yes, but to maintain the spirit and the ideals and the principles and the compassion and the love, the unselfishness that are the most important components of a person's life. But let our own influence be spread throughout the world in a beneficial way. . . . Not only in the Middle East but in Namibia, Rhodesia, Cyprus, Nicaragua, perhaps even in Iran, the beneficial effect of our government's influence can be a profound resolution of possible catastrophe for others."[7]

1. AMERICAN FOREIGN POLICY: THE SECOND YEAR

President Carter's tendency to stress the positive had been amply demonstrated during his initial year in office, and further illustrations had accumulated in the course of a seven-nation tour in Europe, Asia, and Africa to which the Chief Executive had devoted the New Year holidays of 1977–78. From Warsaw, where his observations pertaining to religious freedom and human rights had encouraged a belief that "the [Iron] Curtain is being parted,"[8] the President and his party had proceeded to Tehran for a New Year's Eve dinner with Muhammad Reza Shah and Empress Farah. "I think it is a good harbinger of things to come," the President had declared on this occasion, "that we could close this year and begin a new year with those in whom we have such great confidence and with whom we share such great responsibilities for the present and for the future. . . . Iran, because of the great leadership of the Shah, is an island of stability in one of the more troubled areas of the world. . . . "[9] Though such exuberance seemed more or less routine at the time, it was to echo strangely in subsequent months when the revolutionary fever that broke out in Iran soon after the

---

[7]Dec. 6 remarks, in *Presidential Documents,* 14: 2168-9.
[8]Warsaw news conference, Dec. 30, 1977, in *Presidential Documents,* 13: 1959-66; in-flight remarks, Jan. 6, 1978, in same, 14: 45.
[9]Same, 13: 1974-5.

presidential visit had not only convulsed that country but was threatening to spread to other Middle Eastern lands as well.

Hand of Friendship

A flying visit to India on January 1-3, 1978, provided the American leader with an opportunity for conferences with Prime Minister Moraji R. Desai and an address to the Indian Parliament that stressed the two nations' joint commitment to democracy, human rights, and the satisfaction of human needs (Document 35). From New Delhi, Mr. Carter went on to Riyadh, Saudi Arabia, for a meeting with King Khalid; to Aswan, Egypt, to reassure Sadat about his commitment to "the legitimate rights of the Palestinian people"; and to Paris, France, for an address on the challenges to democracy (Document 11) and meetings with President Valéry Giscard d'Estaing. Still glowing from the welcome extended him by the French populace, the President began his homeward flight on January 6 with a midday visit to Brussels and renewed assurances of American support for the European Communities and the North Atlantic Treaty Organization (NATO).[10]

Throughout the trip, Mr. Carter told reporters as Air Force One flew westward across the Atlantic, he had "tried to emphasize the concepts of morality and decency and goodness and friendship and human rights."[11] A welcoming crowd assembled on the White House lawn that evening was assured, in the President's words, that "We were received with open arms and friendship, even among nations who in the past have been kind of cool toward us, and I was able to see very clearly what the United States means to those people around the world. When we are clean and decent they are pleased. When we are honest they are relieved. When we are strong, they're protected, and when we extend the hand of friendship they respond with an open heart."[12]

Agenda for 1978

Such sentiments might or might not contribute to a solution of the concrete, intractable issues of international policy. Inevitably, the euphoria of the President's trip was succeeded by a period of concentration on the often difficult realities that faced the nation and the world as his administration moved into its second year.

An illuminating survey of the national foreign relations at this moment of transition was offered by Secretary of State Cyrus R. Vance in a January 13 address to the Los Angeles World Affairs

[10]For details see the following chapters.
[11]*Presidential Documents*, 14: 47.
[12]Same: 41.

Council (Document 1). "Our strength," Mr. Vance emphasized, "lies not only in our ideals but in the practical way we identify problems and work systematically toward their solution." In 1977, the Secretary of State recalled, the Carter administration had "made a conscious and deliberate effort to construct a foreign policy based upon American interests and upon American values and ideals." In 1978, there were "actions, decisions, and choices which we must make here in America—some of them difficult—which will help to determine how such a policy can be nourished and further evolve."

Six major issues were seen by Secretary Vance as central to the foreign policy process in the year ahead. Two treaties governing the future of the Panama Canal had been drawn up and signed in 1977, and now awaited the Senate's advice and consent to ratification. The Tokyo Round of multilateral trade negotiations, begun in 1973, was approaching its conclusion and would soon require an affirmative decision on the future of U.S. economic relations with the outside world. The whole relationship between the advanced industrial powers and the "third world" nations of Asia, Africa, and Latin America was increasingly in need of clarification. One aspect of that relationship, the problem of racial and political relations in southern Africa, had already assumed a character of urgency that spelled a critical test of American attitudes and intentions.

The problem of arms limitation and of U.S.-Soviet relations, with its special blend of competitive and cooperative elements, seemed also to be entering a decisive phase as negotiations for a new SALT agreement approached their culminating stage. Concerning the critical problem of the Middle East, finally, the Secretary of State noted that he himself was about to depart for Jerusalem in order to take a hand in the negotiating process so hopefully initiated by President Sadat's memorable visit to the Israeli capital in November 1977.

Reviewing all these issues at the end of his 51st week in office, Secretary Vance characteristically described himself as "basically optimistic about our foreign policy and the chances for future advances in the cause of peace." "We have great strength," he observed. "Properly channeled, our strength can be a catalytic and vital force in bringing peace, opportunity, and material well-being to millions of people—in America as well as abroad."

The State of the Union

An equally confident tone marked President Carter's first annual address on the State of the Union, delivered before a Joint Session of the Congress on January 19 (Document 2). "Militarily, politically, economically, and in spirit, the state of our Union is sound," the President affirmed. " . . . For the first time in a generation, we are not haunted by a major international crisis or by domestic turmoil, and we now have a rare and a priceless opportunity to address persistent problems and burdens which come to us as a nation—quietly and steadily getting worse over the years."

Like some of his Republican predecessors, the Democratic Chief Executive seemed anxious to point out that the problems facing the nation could not be solved by government alone. "We need patience and good will, but we really need to realize that there is a limit to the role and the function of government," he insisted. "Government cannot solve our problems, it can't set our goals, it cannot define our vision. Government cannot eliminate poverty or provide a bountiful economy or reduce inflation or save our cities or cure illiteracy or provide energy. And government cannot mandate goodness. Only a true partnership between government and the people can ever hope to reach these goals."

One of the most urgent tasks for such a partnership, the President intimated, would be the establishment of a national energy policy to help meet the problems that stemmed from the industrialized world's excessive dependence on high-priced imported petroleum. The continued absence of a comprehensive policy such as he had proposed the year before, Mr. Carter averred, was undermining the national interest at home and abroad—entailing, among other things, a current daily expenditure of over $120 million for foreign oil. Energy, said Mr. Carter, must be a central element in a national effort to continue the process of economic recovery, make further reductions in unemployment and inflation, improve the national trade balance, and protect the integrity of the dollar overseas.

On the political side, the President affirmed with obvious satisfaction that "We've restored a moral basis for our foreign policy." "The very heart of our identity as a nation," he added, "is our firm commitment to human rights"; and he reported "significant movement toward greater freedom and humanity in several parts of the world," notably in the release of "thousands of political prisoners." Even America's ideological adversaries, he said, "now see that their attitude toward fundamental human rights affects their standing in the international community, and it affects their relations with the United States."

Three major goals, the President suggested, provided a framework for the nation's foreign policy endeavors: "the security of our country," "a world at peace," and "world economic growth and stability". Reviewing highlights of the current agenda—details of which were to be put forward in a separate message to Congress[13]—

[13]Message of Jan. 19, in *Presidential Documents*, 14: 98–123.

Mr. Carter laid special emphasis on the importance of the forth-coming Senate votes on the two Panama Canal treaties. "We Americans have a great deal of work to do together," the President noted in conclusion. "In the end, how well we do that work will depend on the spirit in which we approach it. . . . It has been said that our best years are behind us. But I say again that America's best is still ahead. We have emerged from bitter experiences chastened but proud, confident once again, ready to face challenges once again, and united once again. . . . Our individual fates are linked, our futures intertwined. And if we act in that knowledge and in that spirit, together, as the Bible says, we can move mountains."

Defense and the Soviet Union

National security was the policy objective that invariably claimed the largest share of American effort and resources, involving, among other things, an active military force of over 2,000,000 and a growing annual budget that already exceeded $100 billion and represented some 5 percent of the entire gross national product (GNP). President Carter, who had come to office with a desire to reverse this trend and a promise to reduce defense expenditure by $5 to $7 billion, had already instituted a number of cutbacks in ongoing defense programs, among them the cancellation of the B-1 bomber and postponement of a decision regarding production of the so-called "enhanced radiation weapon" or "neutron bomb." But Mr. Carter had also agreed with other NATO leaders that the Western allied countries needed to increase their annual defense spending by as much as 3 percent in real terms—after allowing for inflation—in order to keep pace with the sustained expansion in the military power of the Soviet Union and its Warsaw Pact allies.

President Carter's $500.2 billion Federal budget for the fiscal year 1979, transmitted to Congress January 23, 1978, paid heed to the new NATO principle by setting the total figure for national defense expenditure at $117.8 billion—a 3 percent increase over the preceding year, although it also represented an $8 billion reduction from the estimate of the previous administration. "My request," the President wrote, " . . . provides for the steady modernization of our strategic forces, and for substantial improvements in the combat readiness of our tactical forces. To parallel commitments made by our European allies, I am proposing significant increases in our overall defense effort, with special emphasis on those forces and capabilities most directly related to our NATO commitments. The defense budget I recommend also emphasizes modernization and research and development to meet future challenges to our security. But at the same time, I am restraining defense expenditures by introducing important efficiencies and by placing careful priorities upon our defense needs. The 1979 defense budget is prudent and tight. . . . ''[14]

Inevitably, however, the budget and the military policy that underlay it would be subject to attack from at least two directions. On one side would be those who thought the contemplated outlays still too great. This group of critics would include not only the Russians, who were accustomed to accuse the United States of fomenting a continued arms race under cover of the SALT negotiations, but also those Americans who had been disappointed when military spending failed to subside after Vietnam and still believed such outlays should be drastically reduced.

An equally critical frame of mind prevailed, however, among another group of Americans, frequently though not invariably associated with the Republican Party, who thought defense expenditures already had been cut too much and that the nation's defenses were being undermined by the policies that had led, for example, to the cancellation of the B-1 and to severe restrictions of naval shipbuilding programs. Such critics tended to be skeptical about the SALT negotiations and were quick to call attention to any evidence of hostile behavior on the part of the Soviet Union or its allies. As will be noted in a later chapter, activities attributed to the Soviet Union during the early months of 1978, particularly in Africa, offered abundant ammunition to such critics and became a source of no little concern to the administration itself.

President Carter seemed to have both types of criticism in mind when he delivered his noted address on American defense policy at Wake Forest University, in Winston-Salem, North Carolina, on March 17 (**Document 3**). It was a fact that Soviet military preparations and international conduct presented a serious problem for the United States, Mr. Carter acknowledged. "Over the past 20 years," he said, "the military forces of the Soviets have grown substantially, both in absolute numbers and relative to our own. There has also been an obvious inclination on the part of the Soviet Union to use its military power—to intervene in local conflicts, with advisers, with equipment, and with full logistical support and encouragement for mercenaries from other Communist countries, as we can observe in Africa."

Faced with such challenges, the President asserted, the United States would continue to seek the cooperation of the U.S.S.R. and other nations for as long as support for such policy was not eroded by the U.S.S.R.'s own conduct. At the same time, he emphasized, the United States would continue to modernize its own strategic systems and to revitalize its conventional forces. "We shall imple-

---

[14]Budget message, dated Jan. 20, in *Presidential Documents,* 14: 187.

ment this policy . . . in three different ways," Mr. Carter explained: "by maintaining strategic nuclear balance; by working closely with our NATO allies to strengthen and modernize our defenses in Europe; and by maintaining and developing forces to counter any threats to our allies and friends in our vital interests in Asia, the Middle East, and other regions of the world."

The President presumably was well aware that some of his administration's conservative critics considered it incurably addicted to sentimentality and wishful thinking. "Too many in positions of importance," as former California Governor Ronald Reagan asserted on this same March 17, "believe that through generosity and self-effacement we can avoid trouble, whether it's with Panama and the Canal or the Soviet Union and SALT."[15] But President Carter himself, in winding up his Wake Forest address, appeared to be warning against precisely such self-deception.

"For most of human history," the President recalled, "people have wished vainly that freedom and the flowering of the human spirit, which freedom nourishes, did not finally have to depend upon the force of arms. We, like our forebears, live in a time when those who would destroy liberty are restrained less by their respect for freedom itself than by their knowledge that those of us who cherish freedom are strong. . . . No matter how peaceful and secure and easy the circumstances of our lives now seem, we have no guarantee that the blessings will endure. That is why we will always maintain the strength which, God willing, we shall never need to use."

Events in the ensuing weeks appeared increasingly to justify the somber tonalities of the Wake Forest speech. Relations with the Soviet Union continued to deteriorate through the spring and summer, in large part because of the disquieting Soviet involvement in disturbances in east and central Africa. "A competition without restraint and without shared rules will escalate into graver tensions, and our relationship as a whole with the Soviet Union will suffer," President Carter warned in a second speech, delivered at the U.S. Naval Academy at Annapolis on June 7 (**Document 8**). But far from amending its line of conduct, Moscow appeared increasingly to be going out of its way to flout American sensibilities, not only by its persecution of domestic dissidents but by its harassment of American citizens engaged on business and journalistic pursuits within its jurisdiction.

Congressional Tug of War

A counterpart to the Washington-Moscow tussle during this

---

[15] *Vital Speeches of the Day,* 14: 425 (May 1, 1978).

period was a similar back-and-forth contest in the American capital between the Carter administration and the Democratic-controlled 95th Congress, which had proved increasingly inhospitable to recent presidential initiatives in the international field. No fewer than four epic struggles were fought out between the Executive and Legislative branches during the spring and summer. Each of them was eventually won by the Executive, though only by narrow margins and after days of harrowing uncertainty.

The first of these administration victories—to be more fully considered, like others, in a later chapter—was won when the Senate, in two historic votes on March 16 and April 18, conferred a grudging and conditional assent to the two treaties on the Panama Canal. Approval in each case was granted by the narrow margin of 68 votes to 32 and hedged with numerous amendments, conditions, reservations, and understandings. In a second action of almost equal importance, the Senate on May 15 voted 54 to 44 to let the administration proceed with a highly controversial "package" sale of military aircraft to Egypt, Israel, and Saudi Arabia. A third crucial session on July 25 found the Senate concurring by 57 votes to 42 in the administration's plan to discontinue the embargo on military assistance to Turkey, imposed in 1975 in the wake of that country's 1974 intervention in Cyprus. The House, in a closer vote of 208 to 205, took parallel action on August 1 in passing its version of the International Security Assistance authorization bill.

These hard-won but critical victories were expected to be of some assistance to the President in combating a growing reputation for indecisiveness and slipshod administration, accentuated to some degree by recent developments in the area of military policy and East-West relations. Among the factors that had contributed to this deterioration of the presidential image had been the uncertainty and tergiversation that preceded Mr. Carter's decision of April 7 to defer production of the "neutron bomb" pending further observation of Soviet conduct.[16] Another had been a seeming disagreement on policy toward the Soviet Union between Secretary of State Vance, the advocate of a patient and conciliatory approach to East-West relations, and Zbigniew Brzezinski, the President's Assistant for National Security Affairs, who had emerged in recent months as a vigorous, even militant, critic of Soviet global conduct. Although the President several times insisted that he himself and not his subordinates determined American policy, the impression of unresolved conflicts and presidential wavering persisted and, by late June, had helped reduce the President's overall rating in the opinion polls to the unusually low figure of 38 percent.

This gradual decline of presidential prestige was, however, to be

[16]*Presidential Documents,* 14: 702; cf. below at note 39.

arrested, if not reversed, by the outcome of a fourth administration-congressional battle, the struggle over the $36.9 billion defense procurement authorization bill for the coming fiscal year 1979. The central focus of the dispute was the insistence of influential naval and congressional quarters on the alleged need for a new nuclear-powered aircraft carrier—the fifth—to be built at a cost that was variously estimated at $1.9 billion, $2 billion, or $2.1 billion. Although the President and Defense Secretary Harold Brown insisted that the project was militarily unsound as well as economically disastrous, provision for the fifth nuclear carrier was firmly included in the defense procurement bill that was passed by the House in May, passed the Senate by an 87 to 2 margin on July 11, and subsequently was again approved by both houses after the reconciliation of minor differences.

Responding with what many observers thought unusual boldness, President Carter announced on August 17 that he would refuse to sign a bill which, in his judgment, not only wasted "scarce defense dollars" but actually "would weaken our national security in certain critical areas." By skimping on "much more serious and immediate defense needs," the President argued, the bill as passed "actually would lead to less defense capability than I have requested."[17] Despite considerable grumbling, the House on September 7 voted to sustain the presidential veto, with 206 members—less than a two-thirds majority—voting to override while 191 stood by the President. A substitute bill without the nuclear carrier was later passed by both houses.

This reassertion of presidential strength preceded by only a few days the successful conclusion of the Camp David meetings on the Middle East, from which the President emerged with a renewed prestige that fundamentally altered the executive-legislative balance for the remainder of the congressional session. Among the legislative fruits that ripened—most belatedly—in this more benign climate were five bills signed November 9 that undertook to implement the national energy program proposed by President Carter more than eighteen months earlier.

Defense Policy and SALT

Some further insight into the problems of national defense in an age of superpowers had meanwhile been offered by Defense Secretary Brown in an address of August 22 to the annual convention of the American Legion at New Orleans (Document 4). Defending President Carter's veto of the defense procurement bill, the Secretary insisted that the objections to another nuclear carrier were rooted not in antipathy to the Navy but in concern for that service's

[17]Veto message, Aug. 17, in *Presidential Documents*, 14: 1447.

own best interests. "We want to keep ours the world's strongest navy—not to build the world's most expensive ship," he said.

Mr. Brown addressed himself to some other prevalent misconceptions in the defense area. Despite the long-term Soviet military buildup, he emphasized, the United States had not ceased to be "the most powerful country in the world." "Right now, even after a Soviet surprise attack, we could deliver literally thousands of thermonuclear weapons to targets in the Soviet Union," he said. That capability, he added, would not be weakened by a new SALT agreement, because no SALT agreement was going to be signed unless it was clear "that the security of the United States and its allies be at least as assured with a SALT agreement as without it." Nor, he warned, would a SALT agreement signify "a mutual end to competition in military strenth"—in other words an end to the arms race. It would, presumably, provide some increased measure of "security, stability, and predictability," said Secretary Brown. ". . . But with or without SALT, our defense programs will, in the main, have to continue."

Secretary Brown did not refer in this address to problems connected with the neutron bomb or the possibility of supplying cruise missiles to NATO allies, matters that were currently causing headaches in NATO defense circles. He did devote a few words to the discussion in U.S. defense quarters about the so-called MX mobile missile, which was being developed as a potential replacement for the United States' aging, increasingly vulnerable fixed-base intercontinental ballistic missiles (ICBMs). No decision had yet been reached, the Secretary stated, on whether or not to deploy mobile ICBM systems, and, if so, what "basing concepts" or methods of deployment to adopt. Among the possibilities under discussion was the so-called "alternate launch point" or "multiple aim point" system—less formally known as the "shell game"—which involved the shifting of some 200 missiles and launchers among perhaps 4,000 previously prepared sites.

There would be ample time to decide this issue, Secretary Brown observed, since the SALT agreement currently under consideration "explicitly permits deployment of mobile ICBM launchers during its term, after the expiration of an interim protocol period which would end well before mobile ICBM systems would be ready for deployment." The United States, he stated, would insist that any mobile system deployed by either side "be fully consistent with all provisions, including verification provisions, of a strategic arms limitation agreement."

Military judgments might vary with respect to what was actually needed to maintain and strengthen the U.S. strategic deterrent. Some movement to bolster the deterrent, however, seemed likely to prove necessary on purely political grounds in case a SALT II agreement was in fact concluded and submitted to the Senate for its advice and consent. Powerful interests in the Pentagon and in Congress had been observing the SALT negotiations with skepticism mingled with apprehension, and, as will be shown, the administration was already engaged in a full-scale effort to "sell" the prospective agreement even at a time when vital points remained to be negotiated with the Russians. The fight for ratification of SALT II, in fact, seemed likely to prove no less critical than the recent battle over the Panama Canal treaties.

Guns and/or Butter

With or without a SALT agreement, the claims of national defense would obviously continue to enjoy a high priority and to exert a commensurate influence on the development of the national life. Without a SALT agreement, the two powers would presumably revert to a virtually unchecked race for more, bigger, and more accurate strategic weapons. Even with an agreement, the United States would have to maintain a public posture of defense readiness sufficient to satisfy those Senators who would not otherwise agree to ratification of the pending treaty. In addition, it would be deeply concerned with preparations for the period after 1985, when SALT II would reach its expiration date.

The influence of these conditions was already apparent in the preliminary work on preparation of the Federal budget for the fiscal year 1980, which would be submitted to Congress at the beginning of 1979. Inflation, by the autumn of 1978, had become by all odds the dominant influence on government economic plans, explicitly supplanting unemployment as the number one economic priority; and the President was accordingly insisting on the most stringent economies in the new budget with a view to limiting the deficit to a maximum of $30 billion.

Inevitably, it was social expenditures that became the principal target of this budget-cutting endeavor. Defense outlays, in contrast, were exempted from the rule of retrenchment and were actually expected to increase, from the $117.8 billion level projected for the 1979 fiscal year to over $122 billion in fiscal 1980. Though consistent with the President's pledges to the NATO allies, this switch in priorities was not so easily reconciled with the socially progressive and antimilitarist emphasis that had helped secure his election two years earlier.

Like President Lyndon B. Johnson in a similar situation, however, President Carter insisted that there was no real conflict between "guns and butter," or between defense requirements and the needs of a healthy society. The social goals of his administration were not being shelved, Mr. Carter emphasized; at most, some necessary readjustments were being made in the interest of fighting an inflation whose most tragic victims were the poor and under-privileged themselves.

Even now, some critics maintained that the planning for America's defense fell short of the necessities created by the expansion of Soviet military power. But though many were prepared to join in the demand for a stronger national defense, virtually no one of any prominence (except for Robert S. McNamara, the American President of the International Bank for Reconstruction and Development) suggested that the United States should be doing more to help the people of other lands in their struggle for a more tolerable existence.

Political idealism was out of fashion in late 1978. Cynicism, mistrust of government, preoccupation with private advantage were the hallmarks of a national mood in which the lingering poison of the Vietnam and Watergate years had been reanimated by more recent scandals involving, for example, the wholesale bribery of American congressmen by persons acting on behalf of the Republic of Korea government.

One symptom of this mood of retrenchment was the enthusiasm engendered by California's "Proposition 13," the symbol of a middle-class tax revolt that seemed for a time to threaten the evisceration of governmental programs at every level. Another was the phenomenally high abstention rate in the congressional and gubernatorial elections of November 7, in which only 37.9 percent of eligible voters took part. On the whole, the members of the new 96th Congress selected on that day looked slightly more conservative than their predecessors. One notable absentee when Congress reconvened in 1979 would be Democratic Senator Dick Clark of Iowa, the Senate's most conspicuous spokesman for African nationalist aspirations, whose bid for reelection was unsuccessful.

The mood of national withdrawal conspicuous in these latter months of 1978 was obviously not well tailored to support the active foreign policy espoused by the Carter administration. Paradoxically, the American people were showing signs of retiring into their shell at the very moment when American involvement in world affairs was becoming more active and intense. The Arab-Israeli conflict was but one among a host of issues, in southern Africa, in Central America, in Cyprus, on which the Carter administration was attempting to provide constructive and innovative leadership. "In international affairs," the President observed in December, "our country has injected itself, I think wisely, into regional disputes where we have no control over the outcome. But we've added our good services, in some instances with almost no immediate prospect of success. My own reputation has been at stake and that of our country."[18]

That the country would approve such efforts, at least when they appeared fruitful, had been evidenced by the dramatic improvement in the President's standing in the opinion polls in the weeks that followed the Camp David meeting with Sadat and Begin. It seemed equally clear, however, that in putting itself forward as an active agent and would-be catalyst, the administration was acting in response to no compulsive tide of national opinion. If indeed there was a predominant trend in national opinion, it was one that sought withdrawal from, rather than more active engagement in, the world's affairs.

"The Soul of Our Foreign Policy"

One phase of foreign policy in which the President appeared unlikely to accept retrenchment was the international campaign for the promotion and defense of basic human rights. "As long as I am President," Mr. Carter told a White House gathering commemorating the adoption of the Universal Declaration of Human Rights by the U.N. General Assembly on December 10, 1948, "the Government of the United States will continue throughout the world to enhance human rights. No force on Earth can separate us from that commitment."

As already suggested, however, the results of American efforts in this vein were open to diverse evaluations, and 1978 had disappointed U.S. human rights advocates in more than one respect. Not only had the U.S.S.R. "cracked down" on human rights agitation within its jurisdiction with a severity unparalleled in recent years. Some critics suggested that American advocacy of human rights had actually played a part in unsettling Iran's topheavy political structure. In the United States itself, administration efforts appeared to have aroused no special enthusiasm. The Senate, for example, had shown no haste to act on President Carter's suggestion that it promptly approve four pending human rights treaties, three of them signed by him within the past year.[19]

President Carter seemed not the less convinced that his administration's endeavors in support of human rights were bearing fruit. The effectiveness of our human rights policy is now an established fact," he told the White House commemorative meeting (**Document 5**). "It has contributed to an atmosphere of change—sometimes disturbing—but which has encouraged progress in many ways

---

[18]News conference, Dec. 12, in *Presidential Documents,* 14: 2221.
[19]Message of Feb. 23, in *Presidential Documents,* 14: 395-6.

and in many places. In some countries, political prisoners have been released by the hundreds, even thousands. In others, the brutality of repression has been lessened. In still others there's a movement toward democratic institutions or the rule of law when these movements were not previously detectable."

"I want to stress again," the President added, "that human rights are not peripheral to the foreign policy of the United States. Our human rights policy is not a decoration. It is not something we've adopted to polish up our image abroad or to put a fresh coat of moral paint on the discredited policies of the past. Our pursuit of human rights is part of a broad effort to use our great power and our tremendous influence in the service of creating a better world, a world in which human beings can live in peace, in freedom, and with their basic needs adequately met.

"Human rights is the soul of our foreign policy. And I say this with assurance, because human rights is the soul of our sense of nationhood."

Difficult and sometimes equivocal problems would naturally confront the United States as it pursued its ideals both nationally and internationally. "We do live in a difficult and complicated world," the President conceded. " . . . Often, a choice that moves us toward one goal tends to move us further away from another goal. Seldom do circumstances permit me or you to take actions that are wholly satisfactory to everyone." Mr. Carter might almost have been thinking of the sensational actions he was to take, a mere nine days later, when he announced the decision to establish diplomatic relations with the People's Republic of China and break relations with Taiwan (Document 39). But while specific actions might be open to criticism, the essential thing, in Mr. Carter's view, was to "persevere by ensuring that this country of ours, leader in the world, which we love so much, is always in the forefront of those who are struggling for that great hope, the great dream of universal human rights."

2. ARMS LIMITATION AND THE SOVIET UNION

Among the ambiguities and paradoxes of foreign relations in the 1970s, the situation that existed between the United States and the Soviet Union was perhaps the most prominent. These were the powers on whose mutual forbearance depended, in a fundamental manner, not only the peace of the world but their own survival as organized nations; and, at the same time, they were the leading exponents of two antithetical forms of social and political organization and, possibly even more relevant, of political ethics. Deeply mistrustful of one another yet fearful of the consequences of their own antagonism, they habitually divided their attention between their preparation for mutual hostilities, should they become necessary, and the search for ways of rendering such hostilities less likely—or, at least, less suicidal.

Dr. Brzezinski on Soviet Conduct

Overlaying this central paradox was a whole series of lesser paradoxes, the natural product of a multilayered relationship in which military competition, geopolitical maneuver, SALT negotiations, multilteral arms control efforts, trade and cultural initiatives, and debates on human rights and moral principle went forward simultaneously, often at quite different levels of cooperation or competitiveness. Within the United States, there was a running debate as to whether the SALT negotiations, as the single most important venture in U.S.-Soviet relations, should be pursued so far as possible in isolation from other, more negative influences—the view most often attributed to Secretary Vance as well as to Ambassador Marshall D. Shulman, his Special Adviser on Soviet Affairs—or whether such a separation was impracticable, as Dr. Brzezinski was believed to argue. In practical terms, there seemed no doubt that the ultimate fate of a new SALT agreement— assuming that one was eventually completed—would be strongly influenced by congressional and popular reaction not only to its specific terms but to the totality of Soviet conduct.

The conduct of the Soviet government during 1978, however, seemed hardly calculated to enlist American approval at either the public or the official level. An impromptu comment by Dr. Brzezinski in the course of a "Meet the Press" television program on May 28 (**Document 25b**) reflected what was undoubtedly a widespread national attitude. "I am troubled," said the President's National Security Assistant, "by the fact that the Soviet Union has been engaged in a sustained and massive effort to build up its conventional forces, particularly in Europe, to strengthen the concentration of its forces on the frontiers of China, to maintain a vitriolic worldwide propaganda campaign against the United States, to encircle and penetrate the Middle East, to stir up racial difficulties in Africa, and to make more difficult a moderate solution of these difficulties, perhaps now to seek more direct access to the Indian Ocean.

"This pattern of behavior," Dr. Brzezinski asserted, "I do not believe is compatible with what was once called the code of detente, and my hope is, through patient negotiations with us but also through demonstrated resolve on our part, we can induce the Soviet leaders to conclude that the benefits of accommodation are greater than the shortsighted attempt to exploit global difficulties." Conceivably some of the Soviet leaders may themselves have had some notion of the superior benefits of accommodation. If so, however, they would seem to have been in no position to keep the policy of the Soviet government consistently pointed in that direction.

Mr. Vance on Arms Control

International competition in armaments was, of course, a phenomenon much wider than the U.S.-Soviet relationship. By 1976, it was estimated, world expenditure on armaments had already neared the staggering total of $400 billion. Secretary of State Vance, who was scheduled to visit Moscow late in April for another round of talks on SALT and other bilateral matters, reviewed the broader range of efforts to control the international arms race in an illuminating address to the American Society of Newspaper Editors in Washington on April 10 (Document 6).

Like Secretary Brown on the military side, the Secretary of State professed to see defense and arms control as complementary rather than opposed endeavors. "A strong defense and effective arms control are not separate paths to national security; both are essential steps along the same path," he said. Nor did Mr. Vance profess to look on arms control as a panacea that would allay all dangers to the United States or "dramatically reduce" the defense budget. "There are clear limits to what we should expect from arms control," he declared. "But it is equally clear that arms control, pursued in a deliberate and measured way, will contribute significantly to reducing the prospect of war."

Like other official spokesmen, the Secretary of State gave primary attention to the long-drawn-out negotiations for a SALT II agreement that could take the place of the original, now expired Interim Agreement on Strategic Offensive Arms that President Nixon had signed in Moscow in 1972. Noting that the agreement under negotiation would for the first time subject both sides to equal numerical limits on strategic delivery vehicles, and would actually require the Soviets—though not the United States—to destroy several hundred weapons, Mr. Vance expressed hope that an agreement could be reached in the near future. But even if that did not prove possible, he emphasized, the United States was resolved to continue negotiating as long as might be necessary to secure an agreement fair to both sides.

Since 1977, the American and Soviet governments had also been discussing a number of other arms control matters, and Secretary Vance revealed in his April 10 address that the two governments would soon be opening talks on suspending the testing of antisatellite weapons or "hunter-killer satellites," an undertaking spurred by evidence that the U.S.S.R. was already engaged in developing an antisatellite capability. Trilateral talks with the U.S.S.R. and Britain, aimed at banning nuclear testing below the ground and thus supplementing the existing ban on tests in other environments, had also been under way since the previous year, and, Secretary Vance reported, had "made some progress although problems remain." As for the Vienna talks between NATO and Warsaw Pact members about a "mutual and balanced" reduction of forces in Central Europe, Secretary Vance said only that they had "moved extremely slowly." Mentioned in passing was still another set of U.S.-Soviet exchanges initiated within the past few months with regard to a possible mutual limitation and/or reduction of military forces in the Indian Ocean.

Side by side with these East-West discussions, the quest for arms limitation on a wider, hopefully universal basis had gone forward under the auspices of the United Nations and the Geneva-based Conference of the Committee on Disarmament. Secretary Vance had less to say in his address about this range of endeavors, which would be coming up for more intensive scrutiny at a special session of the U.N. General Assembly later in the spring. He did, however, devote some cogent sentences to still another arms control area in which the United States had played a pioneering and, thus far, a somewhat lonely role. This was the attempt to check, by international agreement or by unilateral action, "the growth and spread of arms around the world"—both as a safety measure and in order to reduce an economic burden that weighed especially heavily on the developing countries.

Fighting Arms Proliferation

Since the advent of the Carter administration, the United States had in fact addressed itself with redoubled energy to the effort to inhibit the proliferation of nuclear weapons and to limit the dissemination of conventional arms as well. On the nuclear side, it had among other things launched a campaign to develop alternatives to the prevalent plutonium-based technology—widely regarded as a possible short cut to the acquisition of a nuclear weapons capability—and had recently armed itself, in the new Nuclear Non-Proliferation Act of 1978,[20] with detailed criteria to govern future international cooperation in developing the peaceful use of nuclear energy. "While I recognize that some of these provisions may

---

[20]Public Law 95-242, Mar. 10; Carter signature statement in *Presidential Documents,* 14: 500-502.

involve adjustments by our friends abroad," President Carter had said in signing this legislation, " . . . I believe that they will ultimately join us in our belief that improved world security justifies the steps which we all must take to bring it about."

On the conventional weapons front, President Carter early in his administration had enunciated a new policy principle whereby, in effect, transfers of conventional weapons by the United States to other countries—other than close allies—were to be the exception rather than the rule.[21] Under this policy, the President reported on February 1, 1978, the value of new arms sales by the United States had already been sharply cut, and new commitments for all countries other than NATO, Japan, Australia, and New Zealand would be reduced by a further 8 percent—from $9.3 billion to $8.6 billion—in the fiscal year ending September 30, 1978. Although still further reductions were said to be contemplated for the fiscal year 1979, the President warned that their extent "will depend upon the world political situation and upon the degree of cooperation and understanding of other nations."[22]

A hopeful augury in this regard was Secretary Vance's disclosure, in his April 10 speech, that the U.S.S.R.—America's chief competitor in the supply of arms to Middle Eastern and other third world countries—had lately accepted a U.S. proposal to hold bilateral talks on the problem of limiting international transfers of conventional arms. Although these consultations were to lead to no immediate result, President Carter would announce in November that new American commitments for the fiscal year 1979—with the exceptions already noted—would again be cut by 8 percent in real terms to a total (after allowing for inflation) of $8.43 billion.[23]

Secretary Vance, meanwhile, had brought his April 10 address to a typically balanced conclusion. "I hope that you will bear in mind my basic message," he said: "that while the benefits of arms control are not boundless, there are terribly important, practical advantages that only arms control measures can bring. . . ."

The General Assembly Session

A conviction that arms control was indeed a "terribly important" matter had inspired the decision of the U.N. General Assembly, acting on the initiative of the nonaligned nations, to hold a special session exclusively devoted to disarmament matters in the spring of 1978. The United States, familiar from long experience with the tendency of such large assemblages to degenerate into

---

[21]Statement of May 19, 1977, in *AFR, 1977:* 187–9.
[22]Feb. 1 statement, in *Presidential Documents,* 14: 256.
[23]Nov. 29 statement, in same: 2094–5. Although sales to developing countries declined, *total* military sales in fiscal 1978 reached an all-time high of $13.7 billion.

occasions for windy propaganda exchange, had viewed this plan without enthusiasm. Nevertheless, it had adopted a "positive approach," in the belief, according to Secretary Vance, that the special session "can give a new impetus to arms control negotiations in a variety of areas and can serve as an occasion to stimulate new ideas which could open opportunities for further progress in disarmament."[24] In the meantime, the Secretary of State conferred in Moscow with Soviet Foreign Minister Andrei A. Gromyko and President Leonid I. Brezhnev on April 20–22. Although there was no breakthrough toward a SALT agreement, both sides renewed their pledge to work intensively toward that end.[25]

Neither President Brezhnev nor President Carter was among the numerous heads of state or government who personally attended the General Assembly's Tenth Special Session, which convened at U.N. Headquarters in New York on May 23 and continued until June 30/July 1. In Mr. Carter's absence, it was left to Vice-President Walter F. Mondale to present the basic views of the United States in an address delivered on May 24 (**Document 7a**). "Arms control," the Vice-President declared, "must not be the agenda only of this session or this year alone. It must be the moral agenda of our time." To maintain the pressure of world opinion toward this end, he announced, the United States was proposing that still another special session be held as early as 1981.

Aside from a suggestion that a "peacekeeping reserve force" be established under the United Nations, the Mondale speech included no startling novelties. Already, the Vice-President pointed out, the United States together with its negotiating partners had "developed an agenda more extensive than any nation has ever attempted. We are taking concrete actions in 10 different areas—from nuclear weapons accords, to regional restraint, to limits on conventional and unconventional arms such as antisatellite and radiological weapons." What the eight-point agenda Mr. Mondale laid before the special session amounted to was a review of current efforts, a reaffirmation of ultimate goals, and a reminder that arms control would be meaningless if bought at the expense of genuine security needs. Deprecating national actions that might be inconsistent with the Assembly's purposes, the U.S. spokesman drew specially critical attention to the new Soviet SS-20 missiles currently being deployed against Western Europe.

As had been forseen, the nonaligned states that made up a majority among the Assembly's 149 members showed little patience with the security preoccupations of the United States or the other

[24]Vance report, Mar. 16, in *Bulletin,* May 1978: 31–2.
[25]Moscow communiqué, Apr. 22, and Vance statements, Apr. 23–24, in *Bulletin,* June 1978: 26–7.

big powers. Instead they seized on every opportunity of voicing their discontent at the slow pace of progress toward a comprehensive nuclear test ban and other disarmament objectives. Their views were prominently featured in the 129-paragraph "Final Document" that was adopted by consensus at the Assembly's concluding session.[26] Consisting of an Introduction, a Declaration, a Program of Action, and a section on Machinery, this diplomatic behemoth provided among other things for an expansion of the existing Committee on Disarmament on a basis that would permit the return of France, a long-time absentee, to the negotiations and might pave the way for the early inclusion of China as well.

"That we have been able to reach a consensus agreement on a Final Document is, in the view of many here, no small miracle," said Ambassador James F. Leonard, Jr., Deputy U.S. Representative to the United Nations, in a concluding summary of American views (Document 7b). "It is certainly an achievement that all delegations can be proud of." The United States, Mr. Leonard explained, was unable to agree with some of the specific points regarding nuclear-free zones, zones of peace, nonproliferation, nuclear testing, and reduction of military budgets. Nevertheless, he insisted, it had learned much from the exchange of ideas and proposals, and hoped that other participants had gained a better understanding of the complexities involved—and of the firm desire of the United States "to join in diverting from the present dangerous course." "We cannot act alone," said the Deputy U.S. Representative. "But we have committed ourselves to a new beginning, a more cooperative policy which we believe must fully involve all nations to be successful."

Admonition at Annapolis

Relations between two of the most important nations involved, the United States and the Soviet Union, had unfortunately deteriorated even further while the special session was in progress. Not only had discussions with Gromyko in New York and Washington failed to resolve the impediments to a SALT II agreement. If anything, the Soviet Foreign Minister appeared to have erected a new impediment with his suggestion that the testing and deployment of all new intercontinental missiles—such as the American MX—be barred through 1985.

A serious crisis had meanwhile developed in the African Republic of Zaire as the result of an invasion of that country's Shaba Province—the former Katanga—by dissident forces based in Soviet-oriented Angola. As will be recounted in a later chapter,

[26]General Assembly Resolution A/RES/S-10/2, June 30; unofficial text in *Bulletin*, Aug. 1978: 48–57.

emotion in Western countries had mounted rapidly as Europeans on the scene were massacred by rebels, French and Belgian paratroops were sent to the rescue, and the air resounded with charges of Cuban (and, inferentially, Soviet) complicity in mounting the invasion. "As I speak today, the activities of the Soviet Union and Cuba in Africa are preventing individual nations from determining their own future," President Carter told a NATO summit meeting in Washington on May 30 **(Document 13a)**. "As members of the world's greatest alliance, we cannot be indifferent to these events because of what they mean for Africa and because of their effect on the long-term interests of the alliance itself."

Developments in the Far East were also causing concern as the longstanding hostility between the U.S.S.R. and Communist China began to affect the international lineup. Communist Vietnam, which had increasingly emerged as a Soviet protégé, was by this time quarreling vehemently with Communist Cambodia, which looked to China as its international protector, and was also beginning to come into conflict with China itself. Some were already talking of a "proxy war" in which, it was suggested, the U.S.S.R. and China were in effect attacking one another through their respective Indochinese puppets. Dr. Brzezinski, a reputed advocate of the "China card" strategy—i.e., the exploitation of friendship with China in order to curb the Soviet Union—returned from a visit to the People's Republic with harsh words for the U.S.S.R. and an assurance that U.S. and Chinese interests did indeed run parallel in certain respects **(Document 25b)**.

The U.S.S.R. itself did not, or course, remain silent in this multinational discussion. It was the Western powers, rather than the Soviet Union, whose actions in Africa could threaten détente, Brezhnev declared in Prague on May 31. Denouncing what he called the talk of returning to a "lukewarm war," the Soviet President appeared to be deliberately invoking East-West tension as a means of consolidating Czechoslovakia's enforced membership in the Soviet camp.

A conspicuous element in this ongoing debate on Soviet behavior was what was known as the question of "linkage"—i.e., the question whether Soviet misconduct in one area should be requited by the withholding of possible advantages in other areas. President Carter addressed himself to this and other issues of U.S.-Soviet relations in his unusually forthright speech at the U.S. Naval Academy commencement exercises on June 7 **(Document 8)**. "I'm convinced that the people of the Soviet Union want peace," the President declared, in words that seemed to emphasize the gravity of the issue. "I cannot believe that they could possibly want war." But if détente was to be supported by the American people and to serve as a basis for widening cooperation, Mr. Carter warned, it "must be broadly defined and truly reciprocal. Both nations must exercise restraint in troubled areas and in troubled times. Both must honor meticulously those agreements which have already been reached to widen cooperation, . . . mutually limit nuclear arms production, permit the free movement of people and the expression of ideas, and . . . protect human rights.''

"We have no desire to link this negotiation for a SALT agreement with other competitive relationships nor to impose other special conditions on the process," the President declared. "In a democratic society, however, where public opinion is an integral factor in the shaping and implementation of foreign policy, we do recognize that tensions, sharp disputes, or threats to peace will complicate the quest for a successful agreement. This is not a matter of our preference but a simple recognition of fact." "The Soviet Union can choose either confrontation or cooperation," Mr. Carter added. "The United States is adequately prepared to meet either choice."

Bad to Worse

The Soviet response to these remonstrances was far from encouraging, however, and confrontation rather than cooperation seemed definitely to be in the ascendant as spring gave place to summer. To the recriminations over Africa and the Far East there now were added a number of bilateral matters that exacerbated the prevailing irritation. Cases of espionage were publicized by both parties. An American businessman, F. Jay Crawford, was arrested by Soviet authorities, charged with currency violations, and—eventually— given a five-year suspended sentence and permitted to leave the Soviet Union. Two American journalists, Craig R. Whitney of the *New York Times* and Harold D. Piper of the *Baltimore Sun,* were charged with libeling the U.S.S.R.'s state-operated television system and assessed heavy fines and court costs.

Not less dismaying was the culmination during these same weeks of the U.S.S.R.'s longstanding campaign of judicial harassment against such domestic dissidents as Yuri Orlov, Aleksandr Ginzburg, and, above all, Anatoly Shcharansky, a prominent Soviet Jewish spokesman who had been arrested the previous year and was now brought to trial on charges of high treason and espionage that carried a potential death penalty. Although Shcharansky's tormentors had made much of his American contacts—unofficially, he had even been called an agent of the Central Intelligence Agency—President Carter saw the trial as more than a mere attack on the American people or their government. "I think," he said, "it's an attack on every human being who lives in the world who believes in basic human freedom and who's willing to speak for these freedoms or to fight for them."[27] Despite the President's renewed rejection of the allegation that Shcharansky had spied for the United States, the defendant was found guilty of treason, espionage, and "anti-Soviet agitation" and sentenced on July 14 to three years in prison plus ten years in a Soviet labor camp. (Orlov and Ginzburg had been sentenced previously.) Unable to influence the course of Soviet "justice," the United States did initiate an exploration of the possibility of obtaining the release of imprisoned Soviet dissidents in exchange for convicted Soviet spies imprisoned in the United States. In addition, the American government began to reexamine some phases of the bilateral "cooperation" that had developed between the two countries in recent years. Two unmistakable signs of American displeasure were the halting, assertedly at the instance of Dr. Brzezinski, of a shipment of $144 millions' worth of oil drilling equipment and a Univac computer to the U.S.S.R., and the cancellation of two minor official missions to Moscow.

"I have not embarked on a vendetta against the Soviet Union," President Carter explained on July 20. "I know that we cannot interfere in the internal affairs of the Soviet Union. I would like to have better relationships with the Soviets. We have continued our discussions with the Soviet Union on SALT and other matters. We would like to even enhance trade with the Soviet Union. But we have to let our own foreign policy be carried out."[28]

Insulating SALT

Throughout these difficult months, the American administration—and, it would seem, the Soviets—had made a serious effort to protect the ongoing strategic arms discussions in Geneva from the negative influences that so clouded the political atmosphere. In July, Messrs. Vance and Gromyko held still another meeting in Geneva, asserting as usual that they had made progress in overcoming differences and announcing plans for a further discussion in September, when the Soviet Foreign Minister would be visiting the United States for the regular session of the U.N. Assembly.

There was no secret about the outlines of the pending agreement, established as long ago as September 1977 and widely publicized. One summary of this necessarily technical material was provided jointly by the State Department's Bureau of Public Affairs and the

---

[27]Interview, July 11, in *Presidential Documents,* 14: 1252.
[28]News conference, July 20, in same: 1323.

Arms Control and Disarmament Agency (ACDA) headed by Ambassador Paul C. Warnke:[29]

> SALT TWO will consist of a basic agreement which will remain in force through 1985, a Protocol which will expire well before that date, and a Statement of Principles which will establish general guidelines for subsequent negotiations, SALT THREE.
>
> Each country initially will be limited to an equal total number of 2400 strategic nuclear delivery vehicles, a ceiling which will be reduced to 2250 well before 1985. Under this overall ceiling, there will also be three important sublimits: a 1320 sublimit on launchers of land-based intercontinental ballistic missiles (ICBMs) equipped with multiple independently targetable warheads (MIRVs), launchers of MIRVed submarine-launched ballistic missiles (SLBMs), and airplanes equipped for long-range cruise missiles; within the 1320, a 1200 sublimit on launchers of MIRVed ballistic missiles (ICBMs and SLBMs); and within the 1200, an 820 sublimit on launchers of MIRVed ICBMs.

These restrictions, designed to give effect to the principle of "equal aggregates" agreed upon by President Gerald R. Ford and General Secretary Brezhnev at Vladivostok in 1974, would be included in the main SALT II treaty, which was to run until 1985 and—it was hoped—would be followed by a new, SALT III agreement providing for, still further limitations and reductions. Additional restrictions under SALT II would be included in the proposed Protocol, which, as noted, was to be effective only for a much shorter period, perhaps only through 1980. Highlights of the Protocol were conveniently summarized in another official publication:[30]

> The Protocol will place temporary limits on cruise missiles, mobile ICBMs, and new types of strategic ballistic missiles. We have proposed that the Protocol expire at the end of 1980. The Protocol will permit flight testing and deployment of cruise missiles with a range of up to 2,500 km, while banning the deployment of ground- and sea-launched cruise missiles with a range greater than 600 km. It will also ban deployment (but not development) of mobile ICBM launchers, and ban the testing and deployment of long-range, air-launched ballistic missiles. The sides are presently negotiating the restrictions which would be placed on the introduction of new types of ICBMs and SLBMs.

[29]U.S. Department of State, *SALT and American Security* (Washington: GPO, Nov. 1978): 5.
[30]U.S. Department of State, Bureau of Public Affairs, Office of Public Communication, *The Strategic Arms Limitation Talks (Special Report* No. 46, July 1978): 8.

As Defense Secretary Brown observed in the speech already quoted (**Document 4**), the Protocol would *not* limit the deployment of systems like the MX missile, since the latter would not be ready for deployment until after its expiration.

Among the issues still to be agreed upon in the SALT negotiations, there were two to which the United States attached particular importance. The first involved a proposed ban on new types of ICBMs and on extensive modification of existing ICBMs, one of the objects being to offset the superior throw-weight of the U.S.S.R.'s heavy missiles by limiting the number of warheads or reentry vehicles with which they could be fitted. A second issue had to do with the status of the Soviet "Backfire" bomber, to which the United States ascribed an intercontinental capability even though the U.S.S.R. insisted it was a medium bomber and, as such, excludable from SALT restrictions. The U.S. position was officially stated as follows:[31]

The United States has taken the position that Backfire can be excluded from the aggregate if the Soviets undertake commitments which will inhibit Backfire from assuming an intercontinental role in the future, as well as impose limits on its production rate. These commitments would have the same status as the agreement, binding the Soviets to the commitments contained therein . . . .

Successful resolution of these and a few minor issues would presumably remove the last remaining obstacles to completion of a SALT II package, a goal originally set for 1977 at latest. But though President Carter and other civilian authorities insisted that the success of the negotiations would represent a most significant contribution to the security of the United States and its allies, not all Americans were convinced that this was so. Important voices within the military profession, in Congress, and in unofficial bodies like the Committee on the Present Danger had already been raised in warning that far from enhancing American security, SALT II might actually undermine it.

Aware that such opposition could destroy the treaty even before it entered into force, the administration was making strenuous efforts to commend the package to American consumers even before its contents had been fully agreed upon. Ambassador Warnke, in addition to his responsibility for conducting the SALT negotiations under Secretary Vance's direction, was bearing the brunt of an intensive speechmaking campaign similar to that which had preceded approval of the Panama Canal treaties.

[31]Same: 11.

A typical contribution to this effort was Mr. Warnke's statement at Hartford on July 25 at a conference on U.S. Security and the Soviet Challenge (Document 9). Like other administration statements, it tended to emphasize the fact that SALT would in no way abridge American striking power. SALT's very purpose, the ACDA chief affirmed, was "to bring the strategic nuclear competition under control" and, at the same time, "to preserve our retaliatory capability." SALT, Mr. Warnke averred, "will protect and preserve the strategic stability which deters nuclear aggression. SALT will at the same time leave open to us all of the military options that will enable us to modernize our forces and insure that our retaliatory capability continues for the foreseeable future."

Specifically, Mr. Warnke pointed out, the agreed provisions would permit the United States to modernize its force of 420 operational B-52 bombers (out of a total of 574) by equipping them with long-range cruise missiles that could strike any worthwhile Soviet target; and it would also leave open the option of proceeding with the deployment of a mobile ICBM launcher (the MX) on expiration of the projected Protocol. In addition, he claimed, the proposed agreement would contribute to nuclear nonproliferation by convincing the nonnuclear-weapon countries that the two superpowers were serious about controlling their own nuclear armaments. In no sense would a SALT agreement set a seal of approval on Soviet political behavior, Mr. Warnke insisted; yet it would promote the security interests of the United States in a much more satisfactory manner than any other available course of action.

"Slogging It Out"

Mr. Warnke's enthusiasm for SALT was no great recommendation in the eyes of those Americans who had originally opposed his appointment out of fear that he would prove too lenient a negotiator, and who now maintained that the United States had already yielded too much in its attempt to reach agreement with the Russians. In October, it was learned that the ACDA Director was in fact about to resign, ostensibly for personal reasons, and would be succeeded by a military man, retired Lieutenant General George M. Seignious, 2nd, whose commitment to the SALT process had been much less apparent. Like the projected increases in the new defense budget, the change of U.S. leadership in the disarmament area appeared to be a part of a general "toughening-up" process as the administration prepared for the congressional battles ahead.

Happily from most points of view, however, the atmosphere of U.S.-Soviet relations had already improved to some extent as compared with the period of the Shcharansky trial. "In this short perspective, one can only speak of trends with fingers crossed,"

Ambassador Shulman told a congressional committee on September 26 **(Document 10);** "but it appears possible that the deterioration in Soviet-American relations might have bottomed out in midsummer. . . . A number of steps on the Soviet side in recent weeks suggests that the Soviet Union wishes to reverse the tide of events."

Despite continuing frictions and recriminations, this gentler trend appeared on the whole to have remained in effect as Moscow absorbed the impact of the Camp David agreement on the Middle East, worried about China's improving relations with both Japan and the United States, and watched the developing chaos on its southern frontier as Iran stumbled into anarchy. Two matters especially interesting to Americans in the U.S.-Soviet experience of 1978 were a near-doubling, from 17,000 to 30,300, in the annual rate of Jewish emigration from the U.S.S.R., and an increase in Soviet-American trade from 1977's $1.86 billion to a record $2.8 billion, largely because of heavy Soviet purchases of American grains.[32]

Renewed progress in the SALT talks contributed its share to a modest revival of optimism as the autumn advanced. After conferring in Washington on October 1 and again in Moscow on October 22–23, Messrs. Vance and Gromyko appeared convinced that one more meeting would be enough to clear away the last remaining obstacles to a treaty. By early December it had been arranged that the two Foreign Ministers would meet again in Geneva shortly before Christmas, and President Carter let it be known that he was looking forward to a visit from Brezhnev, perhaps as early as January 1979, to sign the completed treaty and discuss a wide range of other matters.

Then, on December 15, the President astounded the Russians as well as the rest of the world with his announcement that the United States and mainland China were about to "normalize" their relationship, and that Deputy Premier Teng Hsiao-ping (Deng Xiaoping) would be visiting Washington at the end of January **(Document 39).** According to President Carter's later statement, a personal message from President Brezhnev in response to this development showed "understanding" and was "very positive in tone," and Mr. Carter consequently hoped the Soviet leader might come to Washington in mid-January, even before the Chinese guest was due.[33]

This neat arrangement, however, would seem to have had little appeal to the Soviet leadership, whose antipathy toward the Peking regime appeared even more unwavering than their mistrust of the United States. Any possibility that Brezhnev might adopt the Carter timetable disappeared in the course of Secretary Vance's Geneva

---

[32]Moscow dispatch, *New York Times,* Mar. 7, 1979.
[33]Interview with Walter Cronkite, Dec. 19, in *Presidential Documents,* 14: 2276.

meeting with Foreign Minister Gromyko on December 21–23. Far from bringing the negotiators close to "the end of the road," as initially appeared to be the case, the Geneva discussions actually registered a fresh setback as the Soviets suddenly fell to reopening issues supposedly settled long before.

Opinions differed as to the seriousness of this reversal, which would defer the actual signature of SALT II to June 18, 1979. Secretary Vance, presumably, persisted in his familiar contention that the problems at issue were inherently complex and that the best approach was to "slog it out."[34] Dr. Brzezinski, who had been voicing his misgivings about hostile activities along an "arc of crisis" in the countries around the Indian Ocean,[35] may have found confirmation of some of his own theories. Both, undoubtedly, would have agreed with President Carter's definition of the twofold obligation of the American government: to protect the nation's security and "cover every eventuality if we don't make progress toward peace with the Soviet Union"; and, at the same time, "to explore every possibility to have a peaceful relationship with the Soviet Union, to alleviate tensions, and to find common grounds on which we can actually build friendships in the future."[36]

3. EUROPE AND THE ATLANTIC ALLIANCE

Deeply as he believed in the friendship of all countries and peoples, President Carter had never disguised his sense of personal identification with the Western democratic nations that had banded together a generation earlier to protect their threatened civilization through the commitments of the North Atlantic Treaty and its related institutions. It was, therefore, with a special sense of homecoming that the American leader arrived in Paris on the afternoon of January 4, 1978, toward the end of a New Year's journey that had carried him from the Communist "people's democracy" of Poland to the burgeoning "third world" democracy of India, with glimpses along the way of the monarchical institutions of Iran and Saudi Arabia as well as Egypt's nominally republican regime.

[34]Bernard Gwertzman, in New York Times Magazine, Mar. 18, 1979: 100.
[35]Address to the Foreign Policy Association, Washington, Dec. 20, in Atlantic Community Quarterly, 17: 13 (Spring 1979).
[36]Interview with Bill Moyers, Nov. 13, in Presidential Documents, 14: 2017.

New Agenda for Democracy

The virtues of Western-style democracy, and the need to rise to the challenges that confronted the democratic order, provided a theme for the philosophic address that President Carter delivered to a Franco-American audience that gathered at the Palais des Congrès on the evening of his arrival in Paris **(Document 11)**. "Democracy is not merely right and just," the President asserted. "It's also the system that is most consistent with human nature. It's the most effective way to organize society for the common good." "The burden that democratic society imposes on those like us who are part of it," he declared, "is to proclaim our unshaken faith in the values of our democratic nations and our belief that those values are still relevant—to the rich and the poor, the North and South, East and West, as constant now as they were when our forebears signed the Declaration of Independence and your forebears proclaimed the Declaration of the Rights of Man."

Mr. Carter brusquely rejected the contention that democratic institutions lacked the capacity to meet the challenges of the modern world. "It's precisely when democracy is up against difficult challenges," he said, "that its leaders must show firmness in resisting the temptation of finding solutions in nondemocratic forces." What was needed, according to the President, was "a new agenda for democracy"; and he proposed to enumerate five major areas where, in his view, the democracies faced common problems. Briefly, they were:

(1) Making government more responsive to human needs;
(2) Meeting the challenge of the contemporary world economy;
(3) Providing for the mutual security of the democracies;
(4) Reshaping the future of Europe; and
(5) Adapting to global change—and, in particular, reordering the relations between the industrialized nations of the North and the developing countries of the South.

In all of these endeavors, Mr. Carter emphasized, the United States was playing and would continue to play a full and constructive part. "The commitment of the American Government and the American people to the security of Europe is absolute," he said. "There should be no doubt that we will maintain in Europe whatever forces are needed to meet that commitment." Nor did he withhold the customary commendation of the nine-nation European Economic Community, with whose policies the United States had so often been at odds in recent years: "The United States will give its unqualified support to what you and your partners in the Nine are doing to strengthen European cooperation, for we see European strength and unity as a boon and not as a threat to us. The real threat to the interests of us all would be economic weakness and disunity.''

Similar but more detailed assurances were conveyed directly to the European Communities and the Atlantic alliance when the President visited their respective headquarters in Brussels on January 6, following a day spent visiting the Normandy beaches with President Giscard d'Estaing and attending a state dinner at Versailles. To the Commission of the European Communities, headed by Roy Jenkins of the United Kingdom, the President particularly stressed his hopes for an early windup of the multilateral trade negotiations in Geneva. At a meeting of the North Atlantic Council, presided over by Secretary-General Joseph M.A.H. Luns of the Netherlands, Mr. Carter emphasized the complementary role of military defense and arms control in ensuring security at regional as well as national levels.[37] "At the end," he reported, "I told our allies who were represented there that we have nothing to conceal from them; they are partners in every sense of the word . . . . I think any concerns have been alleviated, and I leave here with a great sense of trust and a great sense of appreciation for not only the strength of the Alliance in the past, the ties that have bound us together philosophically and politically and morally, but also with a sense of assurance about the future."[38]

Follow-Up at Belgrade

Scarcely mentioned in Mr. Carter's remarks in Paris and Brussels were the problems of Europe's "other side"—the side where Communist regimes had been established and were still maintained, primarily by Soviet compulsion rather than by the will of the inhabitants. That the United States was keenly interested in the fate of the Eastern European peoples, and eager to welcome any sign of an improvement in their lot, had nevertheless been amply demonstrated in the course of President Carter's year-end visit to Poland, and would be demonstrated afresh on many occasions during 1978. Even before the President's return to America, Secretary Vance detached himself from the presidential party to deliver Hungary's national treasure, the historic Crown of St. Stephen, into the hands of the Communist authorities at Budapest in recognition of their government's improving relations with the United States. Later in the year, the United States would be extending its hospitality to President Josip Broz Tito of Yugoslavia and, later still, to President Nicolae Ceausescu of Romania, another doughty champion of national independence in Communist Eastern Europe.

---

[37] *Presidential Documents*, 14: 34-8.
[38] Same: 39.

Such gestures could, however, be described as merely incidental to the major negotiations in progress on the issues of security and cooperation in Europe and of Mutual and Balanced Force Reduction (MBFR). From the beginning, the United States had been a full participant in both of these discussions, which had been initiated earlier in the 1970s but, thus far, had proved more successful in illuminating East-West differences than in resolving them.

The current phase of the protracted negotiations on Security and Cooperation in Europe had gotten under way at Belgrade in October 1977 in the guise of a "follow-up meeting" to the celebrated 35-nation Conference on Security and Cooperation in Europe (CSCE), which had itself begun in 1973 and concluded with the adoption of a lengthy Final Act at Helsinki in 1975. The object of the Belgrade meeting, at which the U.S. delegation was headed by former Supreme Court Justice Arthur J. Goldberg, had been to review progress and exchange views on the implementation of the Helsinki Final Act and on the future development of cooperation and détente. From their beginning, however, the proceedings had been impeded by fundamental differences between the Western participants, who had insisted on the need for thorough, detailed discussion of the situation regarding human rights in both the Eastern and Western camps, and the Soviet Union and its Warsaw Pact allies, who had made every effort to evade the human rights issue and concentrate on less sensitive matters having to do with military cooperation, East-West trade, and the like.

This basic difference, which had prevented the Belgrade meeting from meeting its original adjournment target in December 1977, continued to clog its operations during a further session which lasted from January 17 to March 9, 1978. Most of this period was consumed in efforts to draft some kind of face-saving final document that would preserve at least an appearance of mutuality and thus provide some basis for further efforts in the future. Since agreement on a genuinely substantive statement proved out of the question, the conferees eventually were forced to settle for a brief and factual "Concluding Document" (**Document 12a**) dealing mainly with procedural matters. Its most encouraging element was an affirmation that the participating states intended to hold further meetings and would next convene in Madrid on November 11, 1980.

"We cannot make our world a better one if we turn a blind eye to its faults," Ambassador Goldberg warned in a concluding statement (**Document 12b**). " . . . Efforts to squelch the truth at Belgrade or at home will not change the truth." Admitting "that some hopes may not be as high as they might have been when we came to Belgrade," the former Supreme Court Justice insisted none the less that the meeting had fulfilled its essential purpose, deepened the engagement of the participating states, and assured the continuity of the CSCE process. "We have always known that the road to peace and security and cooperation is a long and arduous one," he said. "The United States is determined to continue. Between now and Madrid and thereafter we will seek to further implementation of all the provisions of the Final Act. And we pledge to do all in our power to keep the hopes of Helsinki alive."

Politics in the West

Political processes in some of the Western countries were not without their problematic side, despite the feelings of superiority with which Western spokesmen were accustomed to contrast the virtues of Western democracy with the repressive practices prevailing in Eastern, Communist countries. In one or two important Western countries, indeed, the experience of recent years had raised a question as to whether Western-style democracy could survive at all.

Italy, with its burgeoning population and fragile social structures, had been a conspicuous instance, and there were many who had viewed with uneasiness the demands of the large Italian Communist Party led by Enrico Berlinguer for a share of responsibility in the government headed by Christian Democrat Giulio Andreotti. A protracted crisis during the early months of 1978 was ended only when the Communists dropped their insistence on direct participation, agreeing in mid-March to an arrangement whereby they would support the government in parliament but would themselves hold no portfolios. This matter had hardly been settled when there began the harrowing period of the kidnapping and murder of Aldo Moro by terrorists of the ultra-leftist "Red Brigades." Still another, lesser shock was in store in the resignation on June 15 of Christian Democratic President Giovanni Leone, who had been implicated in the Lockheed Aircraft bribery scandals and was eventually succeeded by Socialist Alessandro Pertini.

A potentially even more critical issue for the West was meanwhile being resolved in France, where two rounds of elections to the National Assembly on March 12 and 19 had produced a defeat for the leftist front of Socialists and Communists and given a comfortable majority to the supporters of the existing order, as symbolized by President Giscard d'Estaing. Actually, the probability of a leftist majority coming to power in France had been receding since the previous autumn, when Georges Marchais' Communists and François Mitterrand's Socialists had suddenly begun a violent quarrel about their future governmental program. With the evaporation of their joint bid for power, attention in France would refocus on the rift within the governing majority between the supporters of

President Giscard and those of the ambitious Mayor of Paris, the neo-Gaullist Jacques Chirac.

There were other Western governments whose tenure of office had become precarious. British Prime Minister Callaghan, whose Labour government depended on Liberal support in Parliament, showed just enough strength to postpone the next general election until late 1978 or 1979. In Canada, Prime Minister Pierre Elliott Trudeau was leaning toward a similar tactic in the hope that the twofold challenge of a depressed economy and of Quebec separatism might lose some of its disruptive potency over the coming months.

Conditions in the Federal Republic of Germany, in contrast, appeared remarkably stable, in spite of gruesome terrorist episodes and embarrassing incidents of Communist espionage. Another sort of notoriety had fallen to Social Democratic Chancellor Helmut Schmidt and his government, for it was they who had come to symbolize and lead the resistance to the policies of the United States which had become an important element in the life of the Western community. While the French-American tensions of the past dozen years had been abating under the emollient influence of President Giscard d'Estaing, tension between the United States and West Germany had been mounting ever since President Carter's arrival in the White House. A lack of personal rapport between the American and German leaders had exacerbated the differences between their governments over atomic policy, economic affairs, and defense arrangements.

Neutron Bomb and MBFR

Especially conspicuous had been Bonn's stubborn resistance to American pressure to expand or "reflate" the West German economy as a contribution to economic recovery in the industrialized world. A special visit from Secretary of the Treasury W. Michael Blumenthal in February had failed to shake the Chancellor's conviction that restraining inflation at home was more important than serving as a "locomotive" for other troubled economies.

A more notable display of acerbity followed President Carter's decision to defer production of the neutron bomb or advanced radiation warhead, a matter of primary importance to Europeans because it was in the European area that the neutron weapon was expected to find its primary application. Western ground and air forces in the European theater, as will be noted, were numerically inferior to those of the Warsaw Pact, and NATO military authorities like General Alexander M. Haig, Jr., the Supreme Allied Commander in Europe, had looked to the neutron weapon—which was understood to kill by radiation but to do little physical damage—as a convenient way of redressing the balance and offsetting the Eastern superiority in main battle tanks. To civilians in the potential combat zone, the idea had been unattractive at best, but political leaders like Chancellor Schmidt had reluctantly reached the conclusion that the weapon was necessary even though repellent.

President Carter, however, had been reluctant to take responsibility for approving production of the neutron weapon unless he was positively asked to do so by the NATO governments; and this his European colleagues had been exceedingly reluctant to do. A period of prolonged uncertainty and tergiversation preceded Mr. Carter's April 7 announcement that he was, in effect, going only half way—i.e., that production of enhanced radiation weapons as such would be deferred, but that the Department of Defense had been ordered "to proceed with the modernization of the Lance missile nuclear warhead and the 8-inch weapon system, leaving open the option of installing the enhanced radiation elements."[39] Though no one outside the White House appeared to think highly of this compromise, it was Chancellor Schmidt who led the chorus of recrimination over the next several days.

As with other aspects of Western military policy, the search for more effective means of military defense in Europe had its counterpart in a quest for regional arms limitation through agreement with potential adversaries. In Europe, this effort centered in the four-and-one-half-year-old Vienna talks on Mutual and Balanced Force Reduction (MBFR)—officially, the Conference on Mutual Reduction of Forces and Armaments and Associated Measures in Central Europe. Its object, as the name implied, was to find ways of reducing the burden of military preparedness on both sides, but without impairing the security of any of the parties.

The Western participants in these talks, which included all the principal NATO powers except France, had entered the discussions in a position of some inferiority. At that time, in 1973, the Warsaw Pact had been credited with some 925,000 in ground force personnel within the proposed reduction area, while Western ground force strength had been estimated at only 777,000. Under these circumstances, it had been the Western objective to persuade the U.S.S.R. and its Warsaw Pact allies to accept some common numerical level—preferably about 700,000 for ground forces, and 900,000 for ground plus air forces—as a target for the reductions to be made by both sides. The most recent version of the Western plan, put forward in December 1975, had called for a two-phased reduction in which, during the first phase, the United States would withdraw 29,000 ground troops and certain nuclear warheads and delivery

[39]Presidential statement, Apr. 7, in *Presidential Documents*, 14: 702.

vehicles, while the U.S.S.R. would withdraw an entire tank army of 68,000 plus 1,700 main battle tanks.[40]

But while they refused to provide reliable figures on the strength of their own forces in the European theater, the U.S.S.R. and the other Warsaw Pact states had consistently rejected the Western approach and had held out instead for a system of *proportionate* reductions that would—in the Western view at least—serve mainly to preserve the East bloc's numerical edge. In consequence, not only had no reductions actually taken place, but the existing disproportion in favor of the Warsaw Pact had been preserved and in some respects even strengthened. As of 1978, the Warsaw Pact superiority to the West was estimated at 925,000 to 780,000 in ground force personnel (including about 460,000 Soviet and 200,000 U.S. troops); 16,000 to 6,000 in operational main battle tanks; and 3,000 to 1,300 in tactical aircraft.[41]

In a renewed attempt to break the Vienna deadlock, the NATO participants introduced what was described as a new "major initiative" as the fourteenth round of MBFR talks was concluding on April 19, 1978. Designed "to meet some of the concerns expressed by the East without harming the basic security interests of the Allied participants," the new initiative addressed itself to "two major issues of the talks: commitments on the amount and timing of Phase II reductions by direct participants, and the composition of Soviet reductions in Phase I."[42] Its principal effect, according to one knowledgeable critic, would be to soften the Western stand by waiving the previous Western insistence on withdrawal of a complete Soviet tank army from East Germany and permitting the U.S.S.R. instead to withdraw 68,000 men from among any of its five divisions in the reduction area.[43]

No Soviet response was to be expected before the resumption of MBFR negotiations later in the year. In the meantime, this and other matters of Western concern would be coming up for further discussion at the highest level of Western leadership. Another so-called "NATO summit"—a follow-up to the meeting held in London in 1977—was scheduled to take place in Washington at the end of May, to be followed in July by an "economic summit" of the main industrial powers in Bonn.

In the background of these discussions would be a perceptible alteration in the psychological climate in Europe since the begin-

[40]*AFR, 1975:* 554–5; same, *1976:* 33–4.
[41]*Bulletin,* Feb. 1979: 43.
[42]Alexander Liebowitz, "MBFR Reaches Crucial Stage," *NATO Review* (Brussels: NATO Information Service), Aug. 1978: 14–15.
[43]Jeffrey Record, "MBFR: Little Progress but Disquieting Trends," *Strategic Review* (Washington: U.S. Strategic Institute), Summer 1978: 14.

ning of the year. A new if temporary surge of European—as distinct from Atlantic—enthusiasm had been occurring even while American prestige in Europe was slipping as a result of the neutron bomb and other matters. This trend had been particularly evident at a meeting of the nine European Community leaders which took place at Copenhagen on April 7-8, at the very time the President was announcing his neutron bomb decision. The most decisive action taken at Copenhagen was the establishment of specific dates—June 7-10, 1979—for the long-planned direct elections to the European Parliament. Other points of emphasis included a reassertion of European viewpoints on atomic energy issues and a call for a European economic recovery effort, independent of the United States, with a common growth target and closer monetary coordination. Implicit in such plans, in which most observers perceived the joint influence of Messrs. Schmidt and Giscard d'Estaing, was a feeling that the United States was not providing the kind of leadership the West required, and that Europe must supply the deficiency.

The NATO Summit

American leadership had not, it is true, been wholly lacking, especially in the defense area. The plan for an "across the board," 3 percent annual increase in real defense spending, by this time accepted by almost all alliance members, had stemmed from a suggestion advanced by President Carter at the previous summit conference of NATO leaders in London in May 1977. Also suggested by the President at that time had been the need for a thoroughgoing reexamination of the East-West relationship; improved cooperation in defense procurement; the drafting of a long-term NATO defense program; and the holding of another summit to review progress in the spring of 1978.

The fruits of this year-long effort were awaiting the allied leaders as they assembled in Washington at the end of May for what was technically billed as a meeting of the North Atlantic Council "with the participation of heads of state and government." A 150-page study of long-term trends in East-West relations confirmed—to no one's surprise—"the continuing validity of the two complementary aims of the Alliance, to maintain security and pursue detente." "Members of the alliance," said an official paraphrase, "must maintain their solidarity and their vigilance, and keep their defenses at the level rendered necessary by the Warsaw Pact's offensive capabilities, while, at the same time, striving to promote detente."[44]

---

[44]Document 13c, para. 4. A summary of the East-West study appears in *NATO Review*, Aug. 1978: 31.

The Long-Term Defense Program,[45] already approved by the NATO Defense Ministers in preparation for the summit, was designed to provide a more comprehensive framework for NATO defense planning over a fifteen- to twenty-year period—at a reported cost of $60 to $80 billion—and thus provide a better focus for national efforts. Specific recommendations included measures "to improve the readiness of NATO's forces and the mobilization of reserves, to strengthen NATO's air defenses, to counter the electronic warfare threat, to enhance NATO's maritime posture, to provide more effective logistic support for all NATO forces and to improve NATO's command, control and communications arrangements." Particularly welcomed by the other Defense Ministers had been Defense Secretary Brown's announcement that the United States intended to strengthen its readiness to meet a military emergency involving NATO by prepositioning heavy equipment for three additional divisions in Central Europe by 1982.[46]

"Our Alliance centers on Europe, but our vigilance cannot be limited just to that continent," President Carter observed in welcoming the other summit participants on May 30 (**Document 13a**). Denouncing "the activities of the Soviet Union and Cuba in Africa," he praised the efforts being made by individual NATO allies "to work for peace in Africa and to support nations and peoples in need, most recently in Zaire." The idea that NATO should make a practice of assuming responsibility in regional conflicts outside of Europe did not, however, hold great appeal for other Western leaders. Acknowledging that Soviet and allied exploitation of "situations of instability and regional conflict in the developing world" could "jeopardize the further improvement of East-West relations," they also cautioned that "these situations should not be viewed exclusively in an East-West context." In addition, they "reaffirmed the importance they attach to encouraging peaceful settlements through negotiation by the countries and regional organizations themselves."[47]

President Carter endeavored to allay some other allied anxieties in a special statement on defense policy made on May 31, the second day of the summit meeting (**Document 13b**). Observing that the defense of Western Europe continued to be heavily dependent on the deterrent role of American strategic forces, he reaffirmed that these forces would not be withheld in the event of need. In addition, he offered reassurance to those in Europe who had feared

---

[45]Summary in same: 29–31. The final communiqué of the Defense Planning Committee (London, May 19) is printed in *Atlantic Community Quarterly*, 16: 251–6 (Summer 1978).
[46]Document 13c, para. 23.
[47]Document 13c, para. 5.

a crippling of European defense through some American-Soviet bargain that might deny the cruise missile to allied defense forces. "We need to consider jointly the relation of long-range theater nuclear systems to arms control," the President said. "This will require considering the full scope of political and military issues, and being sure that we maintain the coupling of American strategic forces to the defense of Europe. As we examine this together, I assure you that the United States will protect the options before us as the SALT II negotiations move toward completion."

As was customary on such occasions, the full range of allied concerns was passed in review in a concluding communiqué (**Document 13c**) in which the allied leaders took the opportunity to renew their commitment to mutual consultation and to cooperation in political and economic as well as military affairs. "The most vivid impression that I have is one of a well-acknowledged common purpose," President Carter told reporters as the meeting ended (**Document 13d**). The "more experienced" leaders, he averred, had called it "the most comprehensive and candid and productive discussion of any NATO conference to date." "I feel much better about what NATO is, what it can be, and I think the potential frictions that arise among autonomous peoples, individualistic and proud, have been minimized," the President declared. " . . . It was a productive and constructive meeting, which will only result in an enhanced possibility for peace in the European theater, for our own country, and Canada, indeed for the entire world."

Ending the Turkish Embargo

One subject which, in President Carter's words,[48] produced "a very good . . . sometimes heated" discussion at the NATO summit had reference to the parlous condition of NATO's "southern flank," the congenitally strained relationship between Greece and Turkey, and the efforts being made by the American administration to secure repeal of the three-year-old congressional ban on U.S. military aid to the latter country. Section 620 (x) of the U.S. Foreign Assistance Act, as originally enacted in 1974[49] and continued in modified form in 1975,[50] reflected the sense of outrage felt by many in Congress at Turkey's military intervention in Cyprus in the summer of 1974 and its continued occupation of some 40 percent of that island country pending the adoption of satisfactory arrangements to protect the interests of the Turkish-speaking minority. Although the significance of the ban was more

[48]Document 13d.
[49]Public Law 93-559, Dec. 22, 1974; excerpt in *AFR, 1974:* 574-5.
[50]Public Law 94-104, Oct. 6, 1975; cf. *AFR, 1975:* 264.

symbolic than real—Turkey still could and did obtain its most urgent requirements via U.S.-financed military credit sales—the Turks had considered themselves deeply insulted, had closed down important U.S.-operated electronic monitoring posts and other joint military facilities, and, under the government now headed by Prime Minister Bülent Eçevit, seemed even to be toying with the idea of closer relations with the U.S.S.R.

The reasons the Carter administration considered it necessary to put an end to this situation had been outlined at some length by Secretary Vance, notably in an April 6 appearance before the House International Relations Committee. "The lifting of the embargo and the negotiation of new defense arrangements with Turkey," said the Secretary of State, "will provide a core of stability to our bilateral relations and enable us to establish a renewed sense of trust so that we may work together to resolve important problems . . . . Continued maintenance of the embargo would be harmful to U.S. security concerns, harmful to NATO, harmful to our bilateral relations with Turkey, and harmful to our role as a potential contributor to a Cyprus settlement." The removal of the embargo, Mr. Vance emphasized, would in no way signal any weakening of the United States' friendship for Greece, or of its commitment to a normalization of the relations between Greece and Turkey.

Though upheld by an 18-17 vote of the House International Relations Committee, the administration's recommendations were subsequently rejected by the Senate Foreign Relations Committee by a vote of 8 to 4. There followed a protracted, intricate legislative battle over what President Carter declared in July to be "the most important foreign affairs subject that the Congress will consider the rest of this session.[51] The log jam was not broken until July 25, when the Senate adopted by 57 to 42 a crucial amendment to the military aid bill that repealed the embargo but, at the same time, expressed continuing disapproval of Turkey's actions and laid down various limiting conditions. A similar amendment, in some respects even more severe, was soon afterward approved by a 208-205 vote of the House of Representatives; but it was September 26 before the two versions had been reconciled and President Carter was in a position to sign the completed legislation,[52] hail "the prudent decision of Congress," and initiate immediate action "to fully terminate the force and effect of the embargo on arms transfers to Turkey" (Document 14a).

[51]News conference, July 20, in *Presidential Documents,* 14: 1327.
[52]Sec. 13, International Security Assistance Act of 1978 (Public Law 95-384, Sept. 26, 1978).

In careful conformity to the terms of the act, the President proceeded to make a formal determination **(Document 14b)** to the effect "(1) that the resumption of full military cooperation with Turkey is in the national interest of the United States and in the interest of the North Atlantic Treaty Organization; and (2) that the Government of Turkey is acting in good faith to achieve a just and peaceful settlement of the Cyprus problem, the early peaceable return of refugees to their homes and properties, and continued removal of Turkish military troops from Cyprus in the context of a solution to the Cyprus problem, and the early serious resumption of inter-communal talks aimed at a just, negotiated settlement."

Although these actions led to a prompt, if still partial and provisional, resumption of U.S.-Turkish military cooperation, they failed to cure the deep malaise prevailing both in Turkey and throughout the Eastern Mediterranean. Already close to bankruptcy and plagued by political violence that had by autumn taken some 300 lives, Turkey remained a prey to internal instability that tended to grow worse amid the contagion of deteriorating conditions in neighboring Iran. Greece's government, still headed by the venerable Constantine Caramanlis, persisted meanwhile in its posture of quasi-alienation from the United States and NATO, as well as from Turkey. Concerning Cyprus, President Carter reported at the end of November that the United States not only had been encouraging the parties to work with the U.N. Secretary-General on an early reconvening of intercommunal talks between Greek and Turkish Cypriot representatives, but had "gone into some detail on how to bridge the gap between the parties, so as to arrive at a mutually acceptable basis for negotiations."[53] As with the Middle East problem, however, this immersion in the details of a regional conflict was destined not to bear fruit in 1978.

Diplomacy on the Move

The warmer months of 1978 were crowded with events that testified, if nothing else, to the rich variety of the European tapestry so many hands were weaving. Still another round of MBFR talks—the fifteenth—had begun in mid-May, and on June 8 the Eastern participants had put forward a new proposal that seemed to many observers to go some way toward meeting Western requirements. As described by President Brezhnev in a speech at Minsk on June 25, the plan included provision for Soviet withdrawal within a year of three divisions and 1,000 tanks, and for the establishment of "an identical overall ceiling . . . for each grouping in Central Europe."[54]

[53]Nov. 30 message, in *Presidential Documents,* 14: 2103–4.
[54]*Soviet News* (London: Press Department of the Soviet Embassy), June 27, 1978.

But though the West remained continuously on the alert for signs of "movement" in the opposing camp, it could not overlook the fact that there was no agreement as yet about even so elementary a matter as the numbers of men already under arms on both sides of the dividing line in Central Europe. "The East, in June 1978, accepted the principle of a common ceiling on ground and air force manpower," the State Department later commented. "However, the East denies that any significant manpower asymmetry now exists and thus rejects the asymmetrical manpower reductions needed to reach parity in manpower. Moreover, the East continues to seek to limit the flexibility of our European allies. The Eastern position has other significant deficiencies as well."[55]

This, of course, was also the period when Soviet internal repression was reaching a climax in the preparation for the trials of Orlov, Shcharansky, and other dissidents who had attempted to enlarge the area of freedom in the U.S.S.R. in conformity with the promises of the Helsinki Final Act. Shcharansky's condemnation on July 14 occurred at the very moment when President Carter was making a hasty visit to the Federal Republic of Germany in connection with the economic summit in Bonn, and trying to infuse some cordiality into relations with Chancellor Schmidt's government. The highlight of an otherwise unexciting trip was Mr. Carter's brief appearance in West Berlin on July 15 with the assurance that *"Was immer sei, Berlin bleibt frei"*[56] (Whate'er may be, Berlin stays free).

A missionary effort of a more unusual kind occurred a few weeks later on the other side of Europe, where China's Communist Party Chairman and Prime Minister, Hua Kuo-feng, made a highly public visit to Romania and Yugoslavia that impressed observers as all the more remarkable in view of the Chinese leaders' normal stay-at-home habits. Unabashedly dedicated to encouraging resistance to Soviet domination in Eastern Europe, the visit caused visible disquiet in Moscow and undoubtedly helped to animate the growing Soviet opposition to Chinese influence in Southeast Asia.

Chinese patronage must also have encouraged Romanian President Ceausescu in his perennial resistance to any Soviet or Warsaw Pact demands that ran counter to his conception of national sovereignty. This latent rift within the Soviet bloc was dramatically brought to public attention late in 1978 in the aftermath of a meeting of the Warsaw Pact's Political Consultative Committee—the Eastern counterpart of the North Atlantic Council—that took place in Moscow on November 22–23. Like the NATO powers, the Warsaw countries were following a "two-track" policy that called for

[55]*Bulletin,* Feb. 1979: 44.
[56]*Presidential Documents,* 14: 1295.

military preparedness as well as arms control negotiations; and the principal purpose of the top-level Moscow meeting—the first since 1976—would seem to have been the consummation of an agreement on an increase in military expenditures that would be comparable to the 3 percent increase recently adopted by NATO.

This plan, however, encountered stubborn resistance on the part of the Romanian President. In a series of public statements at the end of November and the beginning of December, Ceausescu insisted that there was no need for supplementary military expenditures such as Moscow was now demanding; nor, he said, could he accept the Warsaw Pact's condemnation of the U.S.-sponsored Mideast negotiations between Israel and Egypt.[57] A hastily arranged visit to Bucharest by Secretary of the Treasury Blumenthal enabled President Carter to send the Romanian leader a message of American admiration and of support for his steadfast championship of national independence. The gesture may, of course, have been less appreciated in Moscow at a moment when a Brezhnev visit to the United States was under consideration.

The annual December meeting of the North Atlantic Council, held at NATO's Brussels headquarters on December 7–8, afforded the Western governments another opportunity for a review in common of this and other aspects of current East-West relations. Secretary Vance, at the moment, was urgently involved with the Middle East problem, and it was Deputy-Secretary of State Warren M. Christopher who acted as principal spokesman for the United States on this occasion. Although British Foreign Secretary David Owen argued vigorously for the initiation of a dialogue with the Warsaw Pact countries at Foreign Ministers' level—a possibility already hinted at the Washington summit—most ministers took the view that such a move would be premature in the absence of further progress in the MBFR negotiations.

An interesting feature of the Brussels meeting and its communiqué (Document 15) was the renewed emphasis on human rights issues as defined in the Helsinki Final Act. Noting with regret that "certain negative developments" had occurred in this area during 1978—an obvious reference to the dissident trials in the U.S.S.R.—the participants "stressed the need for improvement in implementation to be shown between now and the Madrid meeting so that the participating states could take part on the political level." This, of course, was a diplomatic way of stating that the level at which the NATO countries were represented at the 1980 meeting would depend upon the performance of the Warsaw Pact and other CSCE participants during the interim.

---

[57]Details in *Europa-Archiv* (Bonn: Deutsche Gesellschaft für Auswärtige Politik), 1979: D12-14.

"We Have That Will"

Though prevented from attending the NATO meeting, Secretary Vance was able to keep an important speaking engagement at the Royal Institute of International Affairs in London on December 9. Disseminated over the facilities of the British Broadcasting Corporation, the Secretary's address on "The U.S.-European Partnership" **(Document 16)** was hailed by some of the press as the most important American pronouncement on Western policy to be made since the advent of the Carter administration. It was, at any rate, one of the more optimistic pronouncements of a year when Western spirits had risen and fallen in response to rapid alternations in the international outlook. "We have passed through a particularly difficult period during the 1970's," the Secretary of State declared. "But we have navigated these turbulent waters. Although the course ahead remains demanding, the progress we have made should give us great confidence in our future."

Certain recent developments within the Western family may have helped to buttress Mr. Vance's naturally positive outlook. Plans for the creation of a new European Monetary System, originally inspired by Messrs. Schmidt and Giscard d'Estaing, had just been approved at a meeting of Community leaders in Brussels and were expected to enter into force for most members—other than the United Kingdom—on January 1, 1979. "We welcome and support" the emerging role of the Community, said Secretary Vance, "for a strong European Community is in America's interest as well as in the interests of all European nations."

The Secretary of State voiced equal satisfaction with the progress of political affairs in the Atlantic world. "For the first time in its history," he pointed out, "all members of the NATO alliance are democracies." Spain, though not a member of NATO, likewise seemed more than ever committed to a democratic course with the approval of its new democratic constitution in a national referendum held three days earlier. All of the Western democracies, Mr. Vance observed, "share in support and concern for the democracies in southern Europe," and "should recognize a special responsibility to those democracies in the region threatened by a faltering economy." In countries like Portugal, where democratic government was of recent growth and and was already proving increasingly difficult, the Secretary felt that "supportive action before it is too late is an investment in the future of freedom."

Unlike some earlier American pronouncements on European and Atlantic policy, the Vance address was not so much an enumeration of things that Europe should do as a listing of areas demanding common action from both sides of the Atlantic. "No single nation, or group of nations, can dictate solutions to these complex problems," the Secretary of State averred. " . . . Increasingly, our leadership must therefore take the form of inspiring other nations to work with us toward goals we share and can best achieve in concert. And on each of these issues, we look to our European allies as a core around which we must build these cooperative efforts."

Mr. Vance's survey of specific issues, primarily in the economic and security fields, was less remarkable for its originality of content than for its resolute emphasis on the positive aspects of each situation and its almost willful disregard of those negative phenomena which, to observers like Solzhenitsyn, forbade so optimistic an assessment. "In each of the areas I have addressed today, whether economic, political, or military, one finds extraordinary challenges," he said. "But together, America and Europe have extraordinary resources with which to meet them. The physical, industrial, and technological resources of our alliance are unequaled. If we have the will to develop our economies with equity and maintain our defenses with determination, we can achieve a safer and more stable world. And we have that will . . . . "

4. NEW MOVEMENT IN THE MIDDLE EAST

The confident tone of Secretary Vance's London speech undoubtedly owed much to the recollection of foreign policy difficulties already overcome. Since the beginning of 1978, the Carter administration had, among other things, won Senate approval of the Panama Canal treaties, secured the lifting of the Turkish arms embargo, overcome the resistance to a "package sale" of military aircraft to Middle Eastern countries, and, perhaps most remarkable of all, persuaded Israel and Egypt to conclude an early peace treaty which, if all went well, could be the prelude to a general settlement in the explosive Mideast area.

Resuming the Peace Search

Among the international events of 1978, it would undoubtedly be the Camp David meeting on the Middle East that the world would most vividly remember. Despite its vast historical significance, however, even Camp David was but one scene in a lengthening drama that already began to rival the three parts of Shakespeare's *Henry VI*. "I have put hundreds of hours in both preparation and direct negotiation with the leaders in the Middle East, particularly Egypt and Israel," President Carter remarked on one occasion. "And Secretary Vance, even to the extent of abandoning some of his other responsibilities in foreign affairs, has tried to bring about a successful conclusion of the peace treaty negotiations."[58]

Even the President's New Year's tour at the beginning of 1978 had been heavy with Middle Eastern preoccupations. In addition to a scheduled stop in Saudi Arabia, devoted to cultivating the government that was considered America's most influential friend among the Arab states, the President made a special detour to Aswan to meet with Egypt's President Sadat and to assure him that the United States' endeavors to promote a peace betweeen Egypt and Israel would not be slanted in favor of the latter country, but would continue to be guided by fundamental principles acceptable to the Arab side as well.

The Egyptian-Israeli peace initiative that had begun with Sadat's November 1977 visit to Jerusalem *must* succeed, the American President insisted during his stopover in Aswan on the morning of January 4, 1978. At the same time, Mr. Carter emphasized, "We believe that there are certain principles, fundamentally, which must be observed before a just and a comprehensive peace can be achieved. First, true peace must be based on normal relations among the parties to the peace. Peace means more than just an end to belligerency. Second, there must be withdrawal by Israel from territories occupied in 1967 and agreement on secure and recognized borders for all parties in the context of normal and peaceful relations in accordance with United Nations Resolutions 242 and 338. And third, there must be a resolution of the Palestinian problem in all its aspects. The problem [sic] must recognize the legitimate rights of the Palestinian people and enable the Palestinians to participate in the determination of their own future."[59]

This formulation, obviously, would not have been accepted by the Israelis without substantial qualifications. To Israel, withdrawal from occupied territories and the Palestinians' "legitimate rights" were dangerous concepts which, if indiscriminately applied, might easily prove incompatible with Israel's physical safety, not to mention its sense of historic mission. It was primarily because of Israel's hesitation on these two points—both of them of fundamental importance to the Arabs as well as to Israel—that so many earlier peace endeavors had come to naught. It was essentially for the same reason that the new negotiating committees set up by Egypt and Israel at the end of 1977 were to prove unable to function effectively when they assembled early in 1978. A bilateral Military Committee which met in Cairo on January 11 ran into immediate difficulties that stemmed, for the most part, from Israel's desire to retain and even expand its settlements in the occupied

[58]Interview with Bill Moyers, Nov. 13, in *Presidential Documents,* 14: 2020.
[59]Same: 20.

Sinai Peninsula and West Bank territories. The parallel Political Committee, which was supposed to include an American member and which met in Jerusalem on January 17 with Secretary Vance on hand to represent the United States, broke up the very next day as Sadat recalled his delegation in what appeared to be a protest against Israel's general attitude.

Presenting the Arms Package

Despite these setbacks, the United States made clear that it would not allow itself to be deflected from its search for common ground between Israelis and Egyptians, a search maintained through constant dialogue and frequent high-level meetings with Sadat, Begin, and others. In the meantime, the United States had also to face demands that it assist a number of its Middle Eastern friends on both sides of the Arab-Israeli quarrel by selling them new military aircraft and other weapons, ostensibly for the purpose of improving their ability to defend themselves while, at the same time, maintaining a balance of military strength in the area. Despite its well-known desire to cut back on sales of conventional arms abroad, the Carter administration had inherited or assumed a series of commitments which, as of the beginning of 1978, involved the sale of a total of 200 warplanes to Egypt, Israel, and Saudi Arabia over a period of several years and at an aggregate price amounting to $4.8 billion.

Such a plan could not, however, be carried out by the administration on its own reponsibility. Under the terms of the Arms Export Control Act adopted in 1976, Congress must be notified in advance of any arms sale exceeding $7 million, and must be given 30 days to review and, if so minded, disapprove the sale by concurrent resolutions of both houses.[60] As a preliminary to the required notification, Secretary Vance provided an outline of the administration's plans in an announcement made public on February 14 **(Document 17a)**.[61] Israel, he said, was to buy 15 of the ultramodern F-15 interceptors (in addition to 25 previously sold) and 75 of the less advanced F-16s, at a cost respectively of $0.4 billion and $1.5 billion. Egypt would purchase 50 of the comparatively old-fashioned F-5s, costing $0.4 billion. The most controversial item was an allotment to Saudi Arabia of 60 F-15s, valued at $2.5 billion, in recognition of what was described as that country's moderating role in regional and world affairs as well as its legitimate air defense needs.

In the eyes of Israel and its American partisans, Saudi Arabia's

[60]Section 211(a), Public Law 94-329, June 30, 1976.
[61]Additional details from Department of State, Bureau of Public Affairs, "Middle East Aircraft Sales" (GIST Series, Mar. 1978).

INTRODUCTION 51

merits might possibly be open to discussion but were in no sense such as to justify the award of 60 of America's most sophisticated warplanes. How, they asked, could one be sure these F-15s would not some day be used directly against Israel, or transferred to some other Arab country that would not scruple to use them against Israel? Despite administration insistence that the whole arrangement had been carefully balanced and constituted an indivisible "package," even those legislators who were prepared to go along with the sales to Israel and Egypt promptly began to talk of eliminating the Saudi Arabian item.

New Crisis in Lebanon

Even while this debate was gathering momentum, new incidents of violence served to remind the world that the threat of war in the Middle East was not yet exorcised. On March 11, a group of eleven Al Fatah terrorists arriving from Lebanon seized an Israeli bus proceeding along the coastal highway near Tel Aviv. Thirty-four Israelis and an American lost their lives, together with nine of the terrorists, in what became the bloodiest such incident in Israeli history. Three days later, on March 14–15, Israeli military forces moved into southern Lebanon, occupying a so-called security zone that ultimately extended north as far as the Litani River,[62] and announcing their intention to remain until satisfied that the terrorists who had caused so much havoc in Israel would be permanently excluded from the area.

Although this action spelled new tragedy for many thousands of southern Lebanon's long-suffering inhabitants, the threat of a wider military conflagration—such as might have been touched off by a clash between the Israelis and the Syrian peace-keeping troops already in Lebanon—was averted. On March 19, the U.N. Security Council voted to establish a multinational U.N. Interim Force in Lebanon (UNIFIL) to confirm the withdrawal of Israeli forces and assist the Lebanese government in reestablishing its authority in the area. By June, UNIFIL had taken over all of the occupied zone except for a six-mile-wide strip along the border, which the Israelis preferred to turn over not to the United Nations but to Lebanese Christian militia units, whose hostility to the Palestinians and willingness to cooperate with the Israelis had already been amply demonstrated.

Victory on the Hill

These developments did nothing to lessen the acrimony that had been creeping into U.S.-Israeli relations as the result of differences

[62]See map in *AFR, 1974:* 159.

over Israel's settlements policy in occupied territories, its attitude on other peace questions, and, above all, its open lobbying against the proposed Mideast arms sales. By April 28, when a formal notification was transmitted to Congress, the White House was already beginning to moderate its "all-or-nothing" stand in recognition of the powerful domestic forces arrayed against the Saudi Arabian part of the package. The administration, said Secretary Vance **(Document 17b)**, was not "attempting to place conditions on the scope of the congressional review or the action by Congress. Indeed, we understand that the Congress will want to review these important transactions separately and with great care. . . . "

The decisive vote, it appeared, was going to take place in the Senate, where sentiments still appeared predominantly hostile to the plan in spite of further placatory gestures by the administration— among them, assurances that the Saudis would forego certain offensive armament on the F-15s, that they would not deploy them in a way that could threaten Israel, and that the administration would later ask for twenty additional F-15s for Israel itself.[63] An ominous development for the administration occurred on May 11 when the Senate Foreign Relations Committee, dividing 8 to 8 on the substance of the issue, decided to send the blocking motion to the Senate floor without a recommendation for or against. "The choice is stark and fundamental," President Carter declared next day in a letter to every member of the Senate **(Document 17c)**. "Shall we support and give confidence to those in the Middle East who work for moderation and peace? Or shall we turn them aside, shattering their confidence in us and serving the cause of radicalism?"

The independent stand of at least one normally pro-Israeli Senator, Abraham Ribicoff of Connecticut, was among the factors that ultimately brought about the defeat of the blocking motion on May 15 by the close vote of 44 in favor to 54 opposed. This deeply gratifying outcome, said President Carter **(Document 17d)**, "reaffirms our historic and unshakable commitment to the security of Israel" and, at the same time, "strengthens our ties with moderate Arab nations who share our goal of peace and stability in the region. . . . With this issue resolved, the sharp debate over the proposed sales can now be put behind us. . . . All of us can now concentrate our full attention on finding a sound and just basis for permanent peace."

"Time Is Running Out"

For some Americans, the Senate's failure to reject the arms package amounted to an historic act of national emancipation, equiva-

[63]*Congressional Record* (Daily Edition), May 15, 1978: S 7376-7.

lent, in effect, to "breaking the back of the Israeli lobby" and releasing the United States from what had been perceived as a far-reaching dependence on the pleasure of a foreign state. To Israelis, conversely, it seemed that their country had been repudiated by its one reliable friend. Betrayed and isolated as they now felt, they were in no mood to offer the kind of concessions that might have served to revive the stalled negotiations with Egypt. Yet President Sadat, who had staked his career if not his life on opening the dialogue with Israel six months previously, could hardly continue to brave the wrath of other Arab countries unless the Israelis would give him something to show for his efforts.

The "long hot summer" that followed the approval of the arms package was consequently filled with recrimination and discouragement as the United States attempted to probe Israeli intentions regarding the West Bank; Israel peremptorily rejected a Sadat peace plan that seemed to the Israelis to offer minimal room for compromise; and tension over Lebanon mounted once again amid renewed fighting between Lebanese Christian and Syrian peace-keeping units. On July 18–19, Secretary Vance held an inconclusive meeting with the Egyptian and Israeli Foreign Ministers— Muhammad Ibrahim Kamel and Moshe Dayan, respectively—at Leeds Castle, England, announcing at its close that he would visit the Middle East for further talks at the beginning of August. Time was running out, the Secretary told a congressional committee on August 4, and U.S. peace efforts had reached a "critical point." The next step, he implied, might be nothing less than a face-to-face meeting of the Israeli and Egyptian leaders with President Carter.[64] The scheduling of such a face-to-face meeting, to begin at Camp David on September 5, was in fact the principal result of the Secretary's talks in Jerusalem and Alexandria on August 6–8.

The meeting at Camp David would be the third encounter between Begin and Sadat, but the first in which the President of the United States would be a full participant. For domestic as well as international reasons, all three leaders would have an important stake in a successful outcome; yet how could the talks succeed if Egypt and Israel continued to stick to their announced positions? In itself, the Egyptian demand for the return of the Sinai Peninsula might present no insurmountable difficulty, provided it was treated as a separate, bilateral issue between the two neighboring states. The real difficulty lay in Egypt's insistence, in common with the other Arab states, that Israel must also withdraw from all the other Arab territories it had occupied since 1967—and, in addition, must accommodate itself to the political aspirations of the Palestinian Arabs. Reasonable as such a requirement might appear from an

Arab standpoint, in Israeli eyes its full acceptance would be practically tantamount to national suicide.

The Miracle of Camp David

These wider Arab demands relating to the occupied territories and the Palestinians were to become the central issue in the talks that began at Camp David on September 5, to the accompaniment of shrill denunciation from Soviet and Arab quarters and of sonic booms created by Israeli jets over strife-torn Beirut. For the first day or two, a superficial cordiality prevailed at the presidential retreat; thereafter, Sadat and Begin ceased to meet directly, and President Carter and his aides were left to carry the burden of communication and to lead the search for points of agreement.

By Friday, September 15, the meeting was already ten days old and its discouraged host, admitting the lack of positive results, was suggesting that it be terminated the following Sunday. Asked later whether Camp David had been the "high" of his administration so far, Mr. Carter replied: "Well, I'd say the first 12½ days were probably the lower of my administration; the last half day at Camp David was one of the highest." The framework that ultimately resulted, the President recalled, "was almost miraculous in its conclusion," and, indeed, "seems more miraculous in retrospect than it did at the time."[65]

The substance of this miracle—essentially, the promise of an Egyptian-Israeli peace treaty within three months—was revealed at a televised White House ceremony attended by the three conferees on Sunday evening, September 17 (**Document 18**). Prayers for the success of the negotiations, President Carter declared, had "been answered far beyond any expectations. We are privileged to witness tonight a significant achievement in the cause of peace, an achievement none thought possible a year ago, or even a month ago, an achievement that reflects the courage and wisdom of these two leaders. . . . All of us owe them our gratitude and respect. They know that they will always have my personal admiration."

President Sadat, in his public comments, was equally unstinting in his praise of President Carter's performance as "a full partner in the peace process." But it was left to Prime Minister Begin to bestow the ultimate accolade. "The Camp David conference should be renamed," he declared. "It was the Jimmy Carter conference." " . . . The President worked," Mr. Begin insisted. "As far as my historic experience is concerned, I think that he worked harder than our forefathers did in Egypt building the pyramids. . . . The President showed interest in every section, every paragraph, every sentence, every word, every letter—[*laughter*]—of the

⁶⁵Interview with Bill Moyers, Nov. 13, in *Presidential Documents,* 14: 2023, 2020.

framework agreements."

"We had some difficult moments," Mr. Begin continued: "—as usually there are some crises in negotiations, as usually somebody gives a hint that perhaps he would like to pick up and go home. [*Laughter*] It's all usual. But ultimately, ladies and gentlemen, the President of the United States won the day. And peace now celebrates a great victory for the nations of Egypt and Israel and for all mankind."

Parsing the Agreements

Even in the euphoria of that Sunday evening, no one pretended that all the problems had been solved. " . . . The long days at Camp David are over," said President Carter. "But many months of difficult negotiations still lie ahead." A clearer indication of what had been accomplished—and of what still remained to be accomplished—became available next day with the release of the Camp David documents and with President Carter's appearance at a special Joint Session of the Congress at which his Egyptian and Israeli guests were also present.

Two separate documents embodied the results of the Camp David discussions, as Mr. Carter explained in his address to Congress **(Document 19)**. Both were in the form of "framework agreements," a device employed in other recent negotiations in which agreement had been reached on general guidelines that would later be filled out in detail. The first of the Camp David documents, a "Framework for Peace in the Middle East" **(Document 20a)**, purported to establish "a basis for peace not only between Egypt and Israel, but also between Israel and each of its other neighbors which is prepared to negotiate peace with Israel on this basis." Within this comprehensive framework, the second document, entitled "Framework for the Conclusion of a Peace Treaty between Egypt and Israel" **(Document 20b)**, laid down more detailed specifications for a bilateral settlement of Egyptian-Israeli differences.

In terms of logic, the first or general Middle Eastern framework naturally took precedence over the Israeli-Egyptian document, which dealt with only a part of the subject matter included in the larger whole. In practical terms, however, it was the second, Egyptian-Israeli framework that constituted by far the more substantial of the two agreements. Its twenty paragraphs, containing the bulk of the specific points the two leaders had been able to agree upon, provided a comprehensive if sketchy basis for an actual, bilateral peace treaty. The general Middle Eastern framework, in contrast, consisted largely of points on which Sadat and Begin did not agree in any realistic sense but found it possible to put aside for later negotiations.

The most substantial commitment assumed by the two leaders at Camp David was their promise (**Document 20b**) to conclude within three months (i.e., by December 17, 1978) a bilateral peace treaty to be fully implemented between two and three years after its signature. Between three and nine months after the treaty was signed (i.e., not later than September 17, 1979), Israeli forces would withdraw from the western two-thirds of the occupied Sinai Peninsula, and normal relations would be established between the two countries. A system of security zones, with limited military forces, would be established in the Sinai with United Nations assistance, and Israeli vessels would be guaranteed free passage through the Gulf of Suez and the Suez Canal as well as the Strait of Tiran and the Gulf of Aqaba.

Additional relevant principles were set forth in the general Middle Eastern framework document (**Document 20a**). The primary function of that document, however, was to provide a separate methodology for dealing with the problems of the West Bank, the Gaza Strip, and the Palestinian interests that President Sadat took so much to heart. What the document said, in effect, was that these problems would be more or less put "on ice" for a five-year transitional period, an expedient that had previously figured in Prime Minister Begin's "peace plan" of December 1977.[66] During that period, the Camp David document specified, the inhabitants of the West Bank and Gaza would enjoy "full autonomy" under a "freely elected" "self-governing authority." Israeli military government would be terminated, and Israeli military forces would be in part withdrawn, in part redeployed into "specified security locations." The details of these arrangements, as well as the "final status" of the West Bank and Gaza, would—the document optimistically affirmed—be worked out in negotiations between Egypt, Israel, Jordan, and "the representatives of the Palestinian people."

Unsettled Issues

These last arrangements, to be effective, would naturally depend on the cooperation of the local Palestinian Arabs, of Jordan, and, in a larger sense, of at least the more moderate among the other Arab governments. In his address to Congress, President Carter announced that Secretary Vance would be leaving the very next day to explain the agreements and seek the support of King Hussein of Jordan, King Khalid of Saudi Arabia, and "perhaps other leaders later."

One important point, the President noted, had still to be worked out between Egypt and Israel. Egypt had insisted that there would

[66]Cf. *AFR, 1977*: 59–60.

be no peace negotiations unless Israel committed itself in advance to remove its settlements in the occupied Sinai; and Prime Minister Begin, although he thought the issue was one to be settled in the actual negotiations, had agreed to submit the matter to a free vote of the Israeli Knesset within two weeks of his return home. The positions of the respective leaders were formally set forth in correspondence later released by the White House (**Document 21a**). The pill—a bitter one for Israel—was swallowed on September 27 when the Knesset voted approval of the Camp David accords, including removal of the settlements, by a majority of 84 to 19 with 17 abstentions.

Another issue which Mr. Carter described as already agreed upon concerned a supposed Israeli pledge to establish no new settlements in the area of the West Bank and Gaza "during the negotiations concerning the establishment of the Palestinian self-government." This, however, was not correct, Mr. Begin asserted; his pledge was valid not for the period of the negotiations on Palestinian self-government (which might, presumably, take a long time), but only for the period of negotiations with Egypt concerning the Sinai. This "honest difference of opinion," President Carter said later, was not a source of personal animosity or an obstacle to peace.[67]

Certain other points were clarified in the explanatory letters exchanged among the Camp David conferees (**Document 21a**). Each of the three leaders reaffirmed his government's established position on the status of Jerusalem, a point of bitter contention that had been completely bypassed in drafting the Camp David "framework." President Sadat stated that Egypt was prepared to speak for the Arabs in the West Bank-Gaza negotiations in case Jordanian and Palestinian representatives were unavailable. Prime Minister Begin was assured by President Carter that "Palestinians" meant "Palestinian Arabs," and that the expression "West Bank" referred to the territories Israel called "Judea and Samaria." Defense Secretary Brown assured his Israeli opposite, Ezer Weizman (**Document 21b**), that the United States stood ready to assist in the creation of two new airbases in the Negev to replace the two that Israel would be losing in the Sinai.

A much larger question concerned the long-run practicability of the agreements and the true intentions of the Egyptian and Israeli leaders. That Israel and Egypt had, at long last, decided to make peace with one another no longer seemed open to doubt; but what significance was to be attached to the elaborate provisions relating to the West Bank, Gaza, and the rights of the Palestinians? Did

[67]News Conference, Sept. 28, in *Presidential Documents,* 14: 1654–5.

they offer serious guarantees of Arab interests, such as might ultimately prove acceptable at least to the more moderate sections of
Arab opinion? Or were they a mere smoke screen, thrown up to
conceal the reality of a separate deal between Israel and Egypt?
Had Sadat, after all, "sold out" the Palestinians in order to regain
the Sinai?

Sadat's own Foreign Minister, Muhammad Ibrahim Kamel,
appeared to suspect a sellout, and resigned in protest just as his
predecessor had resigned at the time of Sadat's visit to Jerusalem
the year before. Nor did there appear to be any doubt concerning
Egypt's perfidy among the leaders of Syria, Libya, Algeria, Southern Yemen, and the Palestine Liberation Organization, who immediately convened a "Steadfastness and Confrontation Summit" in
Damascus to devise a strategy for wrecking the Camp David
accords. Even in Jordan and Saudi Arabia, Secretary Vance
encountered grave misgivings and a marked unwillingness to
assume commitments within the Camp David framework. Prime
Minister Begin himself appeared to view the framework more as a
safeguard than as a threat to Israeli interests. Jerusalem would
remain in its present status, he claimed, and there was nothing to
prevent Israeli troops from remaining on the West Bank even after
the five-year transition period.[68]

Yet the Egyptian President obviously could not feel comfortable
in the traitor's role to which more bellicose Arabs were trying to
assign him. From Sadat's point of view, the Camp David exercise
would make sense only if the West Bank-Gaza portions really did
have meaning. He could have no desire to conclude a peace with
Israel that would merely free the latter to work its will in these
Arab-claimed territories. It was true that the Camp David agreements had weakened, if not broken, the link between the Egyptian
and the other elements of a Middle East peace settlement. Sadat's
attempt to reestablish that link would be the key to his attitude
throughout the ensuing negotiations. Israel's behavior, on the
other hand, would be dictated by an equally resolute determination
to keep the two issues separate, to gain a peace with Egypt and, so
far as possible, avoid commitments about the West Bank and
Gaza.

Down to Fundamentals

Still another crisis in Lebanon occupied the weeks before the
commencement of detailed Egyptian-Israeli peace negotiations.
American diplomacy played an active though little publicized role
in efforts to stem the destructive fighting between Christian milita

[68]Press reports, Sept. 19–20, 1978.

and Palestinian forces in Beirut. France, too, was now displaying increased initiative and was credited with helping to quiet the situation through its restraining influence on ex-President Camille Chamoun, currently the most intransigent of Lebanon's Christian leaders.

Provided an international conflagration over Lebanon was averted, the auguries for quick conclusion of an Israeli-Egyptian peace treaty seemed highly favorable as negotiations began in Washington on October 12. Egypt was represented by its Defense Minister, Kamal Hassan Ali, and its Acting Foreign Minister, Butros Ghali; the Israeli representatives were Foreign Minister Dayan and Defense Minister Weizman. Although the talks would naturally deal primarily with the Egyptian-Israeli part of the Camp David framework, President Carter pointed out in an opening ceremony **(Document 22a)** that the "peace between these two great nations must be the foundation and the first step toward the larger, even greater, more important result which we all seek—a comprehensive and a lasting settlement between Israel and all her neighbors."

Consistent with the active responsibility assumed by the United States, Secretary Vance presented a preliminary draft for an Egyptian-Israeli treaty, and agreement was reached within ten days on a modified draft for submission to the Egyptian and Israeli governments. Neither Jerusalem nor Cairo proved to be completely satisfied, however, and new tensions arose with the disclosure of a plan to "thicken" some of the existing Israeli settlements—as distinct from establishing new settlements—on the occupied West Bank. By October 27, when it was announced that Sadat and Begin were being awarded the Nobel Peace Prize in recognition of their past and future contributions to peace, the United States was already trying to dispel the familiar impression that the talks had entered a state of crisis.

As might have been foreseen, the principal issue at this stage had less to do with the details of an Egyptian-Israeli settlement than with the "linkage" to be established between a bilateral peace settlement and a settlement of the West Bank-Gaza-Palestinian issues. Sadat, throughout this period, was being subjected to tremendous pressure from the other Arab countries, which held a summit conference in Baghdad at the beginning of November and, despite the moderating efforts of Saudi Arabia, agreed to threaten Egypt with a formal Arab League boycott if the Camp David plan was implemented. Although Sadat showed only contempt for such threats, the Egyptian leader insisted none the less that Israel's obligations regarding the occupied territories and the Palestinians must be clearly spelled out in the Egyptian-Israeli treaty. "I wouldn't want to start saying who's being more stubborn," President Carter observed on November 13 (Document 22b). "I think there's adequate stubbornness to be allotted to both sides."

In another American treaty draft produced on November 11, an attempt was made to deal with the West Bank-Gaza problem by way of an accompanying "side letter" containing a timetable for the establishment of self-governing institutions by the end of 1979[69]—a concept soon to be specifically rejected by the Israeli cabinet. The December 17 deadline for completion of the treaty was now fast approaching, and, as already noted, it was decided in Washington that Secretary Vance would skip the NATO Council meeting in Brussels in order to hold still another round of talks with Sadat and Begin. "The decision is primarily in the hands now of the Israeli Cabinet," said President Carter on December 14. "But if we don't succeed in getting an agreement . . . we will continue tenaciously to pursue the peace prospects and to try to reach an agreement between Israel and Egypt at a later date."[70]

Other unagreed issues had meanwhile bubbled to the surface, among them the schedule for normalization of Egyptian-Israeli ties, provisions for review and amendment of the treaty, and the relationship between Egypt's peace commitment to Israel and its defense commitments to the Arab League countries. Israel's patience, it seemed, was the first to give out as the December 17 deadline passed without agreement; nor was Israeli irritation directed solely at the Egyptians. The attitude of the United States, the Knesset declared on December 19, was "one-sided and unjust and does not contribute to the advancement of peace."[71] "Autonomy," Prime Minister Begin asserted two days later, "will never, never lead to an independent Palestinian Arab state on the West Bank."[72]

Secretary Vance held still another inconclusive meeting, this one with Foreign Minister Dayan and Egyptian Prime Minister Mustafa Khalil, in Brussels on December 23-24. Although the participants agreed to remain in touch "to discuss views and next steps to be taken,"[73] it is doubtful whether any of them would have been willing to predict that a treaty of peace between Egypt and Israel would actually be signed in Washington as early as March 26, 1979. Before that event occurred, the balance of forces in the Middle East would have been fundamentally altered as the result of new developments attendant on the revolution in Iran.

---

[69]Details in New York Times, Nov. 25, 1978.
[70]Interview with Barbara Walters, in Presidential Documents, 14: 2253.
[71]New York Times, Dec. 20, 1978.
[72]Same, Dec. 22, 1978.
[73]Vance news conference, Dec. 24, in Bulletin, Feb. 1979: 10.

5. AFRICAN HOPES AND FEARS

A notable feature of the Camp David agreements was the exclusion of the Soviet Union from any responsibility in filling out the peace framework. The Geneva Conference on the Middle East, in which the U.S.S.R. had originally held coequal responsibility with the United States as one of the two prime sponsors of the peace process, appeared by this time to have all but dropped from sight. Whether by accident or design, the Soviets had now been wholly relegated to outer darkness, so far as the Middle East was concerned, and were reduced to "weeping and gnashing of teeth" in company with Syria, Iraq, and other irreconcilable foes of Israel.

Development of a Policy

This momentary check to Soviet ambitions was more than offset, however, by concurrent Soviet advances elsewhere in the third world. Not since the 1950s had Moscow appeared so openly embarked upon a course of overseas adventure, whether alone or, as seemed more and more frequently to be the case, in association with Fidel Castro's Cuba. Already firmly lodged in Southern Yemen at the tip of the Arabian Peninsula, the U.S.S.R. acquired a new if still unsteady Asian satrapy in 1978 with the overthrow of Afghanistan's royal government and the installation of the Marxist regime of Nur Muhammad Taraki. In Africa, the Soviets and Cubans had already installed themselves in force in Angola, gained lesser footholds in a number of other left-leaning African countries, and, in 1977, given up an established position in Somalia in order to stake out a still more promising field of influence in neighboring Ethiopia, Somalia's irreconcilable adversary.

This apparent upsurge of Soviet-Cuban imperialism had helped to spur an intensification of American interest in Africa that had become apparent in 1976, the final year of President Ford's administration, and had reached a still higher pitch in President Carter's opening year. It .was a basic tenet of both the Ford and Carter administrations that the "cold war" should in no circumstances be extended to Africa, but that African problems should be dealt with on their own merits, by Africans operating through African institutions and without regard to great-power rivalries. But since the Soviets appeared to recognize no such restraints upon their own conduct, the United States had found itself increasingly drawn into association with those African governments and movements that shared its mistrust of Soviet-Cuban intentions. By the same token, American relations with countries like Angola and Ethiopia, which had disregarded U.S. advice in opening their doors to Soviet-

Cuban influence, had been denuded of any semblance of cordiality. Matters had reached a critical stage in the summer of 1977, when open war had broken out between Somalia and Ethiopia. After a series of defeats in the Somali-populated Ogaden region, the Ethiopians had rallied with Soviet and Cuban support, beginning the preparation of a counteroffensive which actually got under way in February 1978 and, by late March of that year, had cleared the invaders from Ethiopian territory. Although the Ethiopians and their Cuban comrades in arms showed no intention of advancing into Somalia proper, the United States was seriously troubled by the steady growth of the Cuban military presence in Ethiopia, which by March had reached a level of 12,000 or more and was supplemented by perhaps 1,000 Soviet advisers as well as MIG aircraft and tanks. Among other U.S. worries was the fear that the Cubans might also join in an impending drive to regain control of the unruly Ethiopian province of Eritrea, scene of a longstanding movement for liberation from Ethiopian overlordship.

Misgivings about the Soviet-Cuban advance in Africa had also heightened the concern of American officials about the problems of race relations in southern Africa, where white resistance to the aspirations of the nonwhite majority populations had already led to expanding guerrilla conflict in both Southern Rhodesia (Zimbabwe) and South West Africa (Namibia). The intrusion of Soviet and Cuban influence into the area threatened to convert what had thus far remained essentially a regional issue into a problem of great-power politics. Believing that the time for peaceful settlement was already fast running out, the United States had joined in vigorous diplomatic efforts to promote a peaceful transition to majority rule in Rhodesia and Namibia, as well as urging the government of white-ruled South Africa to do away with that country's racially segregated apartheid system.

Concerning Rhodesia, a nominally British territory whose white authorities had unilaterally issued a proclamation of national independence in 1965, the United States and Britain had joined in 1977 in putting forward a detailed plan for the achievement of a legally valid form of independence based on free elections to be held in 1978, with full participation by the black majority population, under the auspices of a transitional regime to be established with United Nations assistance. This plan, however, had satisfied neither the white Rhodesian government of Prime Minister Ian D. Smith nor the exiled guerrilla leaders of the "Patriotic Front," Robert Mugabe in Mozambique and Joshua Nkomo in Zambia. While the embattled nationalist chieftains swore to prosecute the "war of liberation" to final victory, Prime Minister Smith had undertaken to negotiate an alternate arrangement—the so-called "internal settlement"—with less militant black leaders inside the country.

Such a compromise agreement, ostensibly directed toward majority rule and independence by December 31, 1978, was in fact concluded in Salisbury, the Rhodesian capital, on March 3, 1978. Despite the vehement disapproval of the U.N. Security Council[74] and of black African and most other governments, no time was lost in setting up a "transitional government" whose most conspicuous feature was a four-member Executive Council in which the three most prominent black leaders inside the country—Bishop Abel Muzorewa, the Reverend Ndabaninge Sithole, and Chief Jeremiah Chirau—were to share responsibility with Prime Minister Smith in organizing elections on a common voters' roll, the installation of a government with a black majority, and the achievement of formal independence by the end of the year. Beneath the Executive Council, a Ministerial Council was formed with equal numbers of black and white ministers, each portfolio being held jointly by a black and a white with shared responsibility.

To many observers in the United States and Britain, particularly those of conservative outlook, this seemed an eminently reasonable and satisfactory arrangement. But the American government, as U.S. Representative Andrew Young assured the Security Council on March 14, considered the plan entirely inadequate in view of the fact that it excluded the Patriotic Front leaders, enabled Prime Minister Smith to exercise veto powers during the transition period, and failed to provide adequately for outside supervision of the elections, for maintenance of law and order during the transition period, or for constitutional change.[75] An even more basic flaw, in the eyes of U.S. and British authorities, was the unlikelihood that such a plan could be successfully carried through at all in view of the passionate opposition of the guerrilla movements and most of the independent African countries. Rather than persisting with this unpromising experiment, the United States and Britain believed, the various interested parties should come together in an "all-party conference" for the purpose of trying to find a solution acceptable to all concerned.

Concerning Namibia, meanwhile, the United States had joined with Canada, France, West Germany, and the United Kingdom in forming a high-level "contact group," composed of the five Western members of the U.N. Security Council, to conduct negotiations looking toward a peaceful transition to independence. Since early in 1977, representatives of the five powers had been endeavoring to

---

[74]Resolution 423 (1978), Mar. 14, adopted by a vote of 10-0-5 (West).
[75]*Bulletin*, Apr. 1978: 57.

bring about a meeting of minds between the South African government of Prime Minister John Vorster, which exercised *de facto* authority in the territory, and the various South West African factions, especially the principal guerrilla group, the South West Africa People's Organization (SWAPO) led by Sam Nujoma.

The point of departure for the contact group's efforts had been provided by Security Council Resolution 385 of January 30, 1976, in which the U.N. body had unanimously insisted "that free elections under the supervision and control of the United Nations be held for the whole of Namibia as one political entity." South Africa itself had seemingly become reconciled to the idea of Namibian independence, provided its own interests in the territory were safeguarded, and by late 1977 the parties seemed to have reached general agreement on a procedure for bringing the territory to independence in the course of 1978. A number of important points had remained to be clarified, however, among them the division of responsibility between South Africa and the United Nations for maintaining law and order in the territory in the period prior to the contemplated elections.

A detailed Western proposal dealing with this and other pertinent matters was submitted to South Africa and to other interested parties in March 1978, not long before the opening of a special session of the U.N. General Assembly that was being convened especially to consider the problem. A discouraging event that occurred about the same time was the fatal shooting on March 26, by unidentified assailants near the territorial capital of Windhoek, of Chief Clemens Kapuuo, a leader of the Herrero tribe and President of the Democratic Turnhalle Alliance, SWAPO's principal competitor for primacy in an independent Namibia. This occurrence did not, however, appear to affect the prospects for independence in any fundamental way.

A Presidential Visit

That American concern for Africa ran deeper than the crises of the moment was a theme much emphasized by President Carter during a brief but significant visit he paid to the West African republics of Nigeria and Liberia at the beginning of April—actually, the first American presidential visit to the sub-Saharan part of Africa. Originally planned for the fall of 1977, the Carter visit was preceded by stops in Venezuela and Brazil and constituted, in effect, a second installment of the Polish-Indian-French itinerary the President had followed during the New Year holidays. Apart from Nigeria's high significance to the United States as its second largest supplier of imported crude oil, the visit enabled Mr. Carter to observe at first hand the progress of one of Africa's most richly endowed countries, now largely recovered from its civil war of 1967–70 and currently preparing to exchange its military government for a constitutional regime in 1979.

"We . . . share three basic commitments to the future of Africa," the President declared in the principal address of his African tour, delivered at Lagos under the auspices of the Nigerian Institute of International Affairs on April 1 **(Document 23)**. "We share with you a commitment to majority rule and individual human rights. In order to meet the basic needs of the people, we share with you a commitment of economic growth and to human development. We share with you a commitment to an Africa that is at peace, free from colonialism, free from racism, free from military interference by outside nations, and free from the inevitable conflicts that can come when the integrity of national boundaries are not respected. We share these things with you as well."

". . . This departure from past aloofness by the United States," Mr. Carter observed, "is not just a personal commitment of my own, but I represent the deep feelings and the deep interest of all the people of my country." Reviewing American plans and efforts in the various fields of African concern, the President laid special emphasis on the dangers of foreign intrusion into African disputes. "The military intervention of outside powers or their proxies," he observed, " . . . too often makes local conflicts even more complicated and dangerous and opens the door to a new form of domination or colonialism." Applauding Nigeria's efforts to moderate the Ethiopia-Somalia conflict under a mandate from the Organization of African Unity (OAU), Mr. Carter voiced lively concern at indications "that foreign [i.e., Cuban] troops are already planning for military action inside Ethiopia against the Eritreans, which will result in greatly increased bloodshed among those unfortunate peoples."

The cordiality of Nigeria's Head of State, Lieutenant General Olesegun Obasanjo, did not exclude the expression of some differences in the evaluation of current problems. "Obviously, we don't see everything from the same perspective," President Carter remarked as his plane flew on to a final stopover in Monrovia, Liberia, on April 3.[76] On the whole, the Nigerian leader appeared less worried than his American guest about the Russians and Cubans, and at the same time more insistent on the evils of South African apartheid, more resolute concerning the need for prompt solutions in Zimbabwe and Namibia, and more than a little skeptical about the United States' professed support for third world economic aspirations.[77]

[76]*Presidential Documents,* 14: 671.
[77]Toast, Apr. 2, in same: 654–8.

Apart from ceremonial observances, the two days spent in Lagos had afforded an opportunity for diplomatic consultations involving not only the Americans and Nigerians but also the foreign ministers of some of the "front-line" African countries bordering on Rhodesia and Namibia. Out of these discussions came plans for further meetings on Rhodesia, accelerated consultations on Namibia, and a continuance of Nigerian peacemaking efforts in the Horn of Africa.[78] The subsequent visit to Liberia, involving an airport reception and a working luncheon with President William R. Tolbert, Jr., could only confirm the depth of the African revulsion against the type of racial discrimination still practiced in southern Africa. "The ugly cranium of apartheid is intent on the course of dangerous self-perpetuation," President Tolbert warned, " . . . The heinous hammer of repression must be staid in all nations of the world, of whatever description."[79]

What had impressed him most about his tour, President Carter declared on returning to the White House that evening, had been the warmth with which his party had been received in every country both in South America and in Africa. "I think the day of the so-called ugly American is over," he said. "I never saw, among the hundreds of thousands of people who welcomed us, a single gesture or sign or poster or indication of anything except friendship. This is quite different from what it has been in the past. The friendly crowds that greeted us everywhere showed an affection for the United States, based not so much on our country's power or even our accomplishments but on what we stand for in the world."[80]

Mr. Vance Reports

Events moved rapidly, if inconclusively, in the weeks that followed the President's African sortie. Secretary Vance and Foreign Secretary Owen, visiting southern Africa in mid-April in an attempt to drum up support for an all-party conference on Rhodesia, met some encouragement from the Patriotic Front leaders but encountered a much more skeptical attitude on the part of Prime Minister Smith's new "transitional government" in Salisbury. As stipulated in the March 3 agreement, that government had already instituted a system of dual responsibility in which each white minister was flanked by a black associate with nominally equal status. But skeptics viewed the arrangement as a mere facade for the perpetuation of white control; and their theory gained a measure of support when the black co-Minister of Justice, Law and

[78]Carter and Vance remarks, Apr. 2–3, in same: 652–3 and 667–71.
[79]Toast, Apr. 3, in same: 675.
[80]Same: 680.

Order, Byron Hove, was dismissed on April 28 for failing to withdraw certain political statements to which his superiors objected.

Rhodesia's guerrilla struggle, meanwhile, continued to gain in intensity. "Whole tracts of the country," in Foreign Secretary Owen's words, were "answerable to the authority of whichever fighting forces happen to be operating in the area at any given moment." The danger, Dr. Owen told the House of Commons on May 4, was that the "liberation struggle" in Rhodesia would be converted into a genuine civil war between rival black liberation movements, one of them identified with the "white minority regime" and the other—the Patriotic Front—perhaps inclined to seek support "not just from countries sympathetic to its cause in Africa, but also from countries outside Africa." It was primarily in the hope of averting such developments, Dr. Owen explained, that Britain and the United States intended to continue their drive for an all-party conference and were sending a two-man team, consisting of John Graham, a Deputy Under-Secretary in the Foreign Office, and Stephen Low, U.S. Ambassador to Zambia, to undertake further negotiations to this end.[81]

The U.N. General Assembly, meanwhile, had held its special session on Namibia—formally, the Assembly's Ninth Special Session—at U.N. Headquarters on April 14–May 3. Spokesmen for the five-power contact group had given a full account of the Western plan for U.N.-supervised elections to a constituent assembly which, in turn, would draw up a constitution for an independent Namibia. Also envisaged in the Western plan were the appointment of a U.N. Special Representative and a U.N. Transition Assistance Group; a cessation of hostile acts, and the restriction of South African and SWAPO armed forces to established bases under U.N. monitoring; and a phased withdrawal of all South African troops except for a residual force of 1,500—which, moreover, would be restricted to one or two bases and would itself be withdrawn after the election.[82]

This plan turned out to be acceptable to South Africa, but not to SWAPO or its supporters at the United Nations. Prime Minister Vorster stated on April 25 that South Africa would accept the Western proposal, as he understood it in light of the clarifications provided him by its authors. Nujoma, in contrast, insisted on further modifications of the Western plan. Particularly objectionable, in his view, was the bypassing of Namibia's claim to Walvis Bay, an important harbor and political enclave that South Africa hoped to retain even after Namibia became independent.

[81]*Survey of Current Affairs* (New York: British Information Services), June 1978: 206–7.
[82]U.N. Document S/12636, Apr. 10, in *Bulletin,* June 1978: 53–4.

Taking its cue from SWAPO, the General Assembly likewise withheld its approval of the Western plan, adopting instead a "Declaration and a Programme of Action for Namibian Independence" that called, among other things, for "comprehensive economic sanctions" against South Africa,[83] an expedient long advocated by the anticolonial countries but never seriously considered by the Western powers. Next day, May 4, South African air and ground forces launched a major attack on SWAPO concentrations in Angola, exacting a heavy toll in killed and wounded and eliciting an immediate, unanimous condemnation by the U.N. Security Council.

Angola, in addition to providing bases for SWAPO, was still harboring large numbers of Cuban troops, whose principal function, presumably, was to support the Marxist government of President Agostinho Neto in its perennial struggle with the UNITA guerrillas led by Jonas Savimbi in the southern part of the country. This Cuban presence had been largely responsible for the bad relationship prevailing between the United States and Angola ever since the latter's achievement of independence in 1975. The United States, however, had been barred by Act of Congress from attempting to involve itself in Angolan internal conflicts.

A more immediate concern in Washington had to do with the intentions of the 16,000 to 17,000 Cubans now estimated to be in Ethiopia. That country's military strongman, Lieutenant Colonel Mengistu Haile Mariam, had recently paid a mysterious visit to the Cuban capital, and it was widely believed that Cuban forces were destined to take part in Ethiopia's impending campaign for the reconquest of Eritrea. Still another African conflict had meanwhile entered a critical phase as landlocked Chad's beleaguered government attempted, with the help of French troops and planes, to cope with a longstanding insurrectionary movement that was understood to have the support of Colonel Muammar al-Qaddafi, Libya's militant chief of state.

Secretary of State Vance reviewed these developments with measured optimism in an appearance on May 12 before the Senate Foreign Relations Subcommittee on African Affairs (Document 24). Ranging widely over the African scene, the Secretary reserved his most trenchant comments for the "serious problems" created by Soviet and Cuban activities in that continent. "Their increasing intervention," he warned, "escalates the level of conflict. It jeopardizes the independence of African states. It creates concern among moderates that Soviet weapons and Cuban troops can be used to determine the outcome of any dispute on the continent." The Soviets and Cubans had been "told . . . publicly and privately,"

[83]Resolution S-9/2, May 3, adopted by a vote of 119-0-21.

Secretary Vance pursued, "that we view their willingness to exacerbate armed conflict in Africa as a matter of serious concern." In addition, he said, he had personally directed the Soviets' attention to "the dangers which their activities in Africa pose for our overall relations."

At the same time, Mr. Vance came out firmly against the suggestion that Soviet misbehavior in Africa should be repaid by American obstruction in SALT. ". . . We do not believe," he said, "that it is in our national interest to make a negotiating linkage between reaching a good SALT agreement, which is clearly in our basic security interests, and the inevitable competition with the Soviets which will continue to take place in Africa and elsewhere in the Third World. A SALT agreement should not be a reward for good behavior. It should be signed if it maintains our national interest and that of our allies, and not otherwise." Good policy, rather than "linkage," Mr Vance implied, was the key to overcoming Soviet and Cuban maneuvers in Africa.

Crisis in Zaire

The doctrine of non-linkage was destined, however, to be severely tested by the crisis that broke out in central Africa only two days after Mr. Vance had spoken. The Republic of Zaire, a country long viewed with special favor by the United States, had already suffered one incursion by Angola-based exiles in 1977. On May 14, 1978, the government of President Mobutu Sese Seko reported that Zaire's southeastern province of Shaba again was being invaded by irregular forces associated with the secessionist Katanga government that had flourished there in the 1960s. Once again, it was asserted, the invading forces had been prepared and trained in Angola, although on this occasion they had entered Zaire by way of Zambian territory. In view of the large-scale Cuban military presence in Angola, Mobutu's assertion that the rebels enjoyed Cuban and Soviet backing did not lack plausibility and was widely accepted at face value, particularly in the United States.

The most urgent task for the Western countries was to try to assure the safety of the estimated 2,500 Europeans and Americans in the copper-mining areas around the southeastern town of Kolwezi, which was quickly occupied by the invaders. Some 1,500 Belgian and French troops, mainly parachutists, were rushed to the scene with logistical aid from Britain and from the United States, which provided eighteen C-141 transport aircraft in what was clearly intended as a dramatic demonstration of American readiness to respond to Soviet-Cuban moves. But Western intervention was not quick enough to save the lives of up to 200 whites who perished at the hands of the invaders, along with an equal or greater number of blacks, in what was undoubtedly the largest-scale massacre of whites to have occurred in Africa up to that time.

Although the rebels quickly faded back into the landscape, the world continued to resound with charges and countercharges about the origins and implications of the incident. The Cubans, naturally enough, categorically disclaimed any responsibility. "I can reaffirm before this Assembly," Vice-President Carlos Rafael Rodríguez told the United Nations, "that Cuba has not participated directly or indirectly in the events in Shaba; that not only were there no Cubans present in this action but that furthermore, Cuba did not supply the arms for that purpose nor did it train those who attacked."[84]

But President Carter, who seemed to some observers to have rather jumped to conclusions in this instance, made light of such disavowals. "We have never accused the Cuban troops of being part of the invading force," he said, "but there is no doubt about the fact that the Cubans have a heavy—even dominant—position in Angola, that they were involved in training the Katangans, who did invade Zaire." Furthermore, the President insisted, "there is no doubt that the Cubans knew about it, encouraged it and were responsible for their training," and that the weapons used were "the same the Cubans use and which are supplied by the Soviet Union."[85]

The U.S.S.R., for its part, appeared alternately pained and outraged by the American assertions. The United States was wrong on its facts, Foreign Minister Gromyko implied in an interval of his SALT discussions with the President and Secretary Vance. Soviet protestations of innocence did not, however, deter the American Chief Executive from voicing some unusually bitter complaints about Soviet and Cuban activities in Africa, both at the NATO summit at the end of May (Document 13a) and at the U.S. Naval Academy graduation ceremonies early in June (Document 8).

Apparently suffering an unwonted sense of frustration, Mr. Carter also let it be known that he was looking for more effective ways of responding to Cuban-Soviet provocations. There had already been some talk about the possibility of competing with the Cubans in Angola by resuming U.S. assistance to the UNITA insurgency in the south, whose only current external backer was believed to be South Africa. This course, however, appeared to be excluded by the so-called Clark amendment to the International Security Assistance and Arms Export Control Act of 1976,[86] named for Senator Dick Clark of Iowa, which had reaffirmed an earlier

[84]*New York Times,* May 31, 1978.
[85]Kathleen Teltsch, in same.
[86]Sec. 404, Public Law 94–329, June 30, 1976.

congressional ban on U.S. aid to any of the parties in Angola in the absence of congressional authorization. Addressing a news conference in Chicago on May 25 (**Document 25a**), the President stated that while he did not currently intend to seek repeal of the Clark amendment, he did believe the time had come for a review of various restrictions in the foreign aid legislation that limited the government's ability, "without becoming involved in combat, to act promptly and decisively to help countries whose security is threatened by external forces."

Mr. Carter also took this opportunity to utter one of his most emphatic disavowals of the "linkage" theory: ". . . I have never favored the establishment by me or Brezhnev of a linkage between the two; saying that if the Soviets and the Cubans stay in Ethiopia, for instance, we would cancel the SALT talks. I think that the SALT agreement is so important for our country, for the safety of the entire world, that we ought not to let any impediment come between us and the reaching of a successful agreement. But there is no doubt that if the Soviets continue to abuse human rights, to punish people who are monitoring the Soviets' compliance with the Helsinki agreement, which they signed on [*sic*] their own free will, and unless they show some constraints on their own involvement in Africa and on their sending Cuban troops to be involved in Africa, it will make it much more difficult to conclude a SALT agreement and to have it ratified once it is written."[87]

Dr. Brzezinski took a rather similar line on May 28 in the celebrated television interview (**Document 25b**) in which he accused the Russians of violating the "code of detente" and suggested that there were "a variety of ways in which concerned countries can convince the Soviets and the Cubans that their involvement, their intrusion [in Africa], is not only conducive to greater international instability but in fact carries with it consequences which may be inimical to them as well." Rather than inciting the United States to set out singlehanded to punish the intruders, however, the President's Assistant for National Security Affairs suggested that "the proper response to this problem is not by the United States alone, but . . . by the international community as a whole, with the United States taking a part in it, perhaps not even the leading part. . . ."

This in fact was the pattern followed in the early days of June as the local situation in Zaire was being stabilized once again and the debate continued as to whether or not the incident had been a part of some sinister global plot. The United States, in token of its continuing interest, provided a force of eleven C-141s to help remove the French troops and to fly in a force of 1,500 Moroccans who

[87]*Presidential Documents,* 14: 973.

were dispatched by King Hassan II to assist in reestablishing order under a new mandate from the OAU. The United States was also represented at meetings held in Paris and Brussels early in June to consider the possibilities of assisting Zaire's rickety economy.

A Change of Course?

Not everyone in the United States—or Africa—appeared to accept the Carter-Brzezinski interpretation of the Shaba affair. Ambassador Andrew Young was one of those who doubted the strategic significance of Soviet-Cuban incursions, deprecated "panic" and "responding emotionally," and urged a "quiet, steady approach" and "a rational, analytical response to the Russians and the Cubans in Africa."[88] Joshua Nkomo, the Rhodesian insurgent leader, who asserted that several dozen Cubans were helping to train his guerrilla army in Zambia,[89] was particularly critical of the American attitude. "All this worry about Soviets and Cubans is an insult to Africans," Nkomo fulminated. "It makes us look as if we are morons who need to be rescued from [sic] the Western world. The West is not prepared to work with the real forces in the country. You want to safeguard Africa for Africans. Who gave you that right? Please leave us alone. We can look after ourselves."[90]

Nor was Nkomo alone in this reaction. Even President Julius K. Nyerere of Tanzania was heard to defend the Soviet role in Africa, condemn "hysterical" voices in the United States, and assert that "the greater immediate danger to Africa's freedom comes from nations in the Western bloc."[91]

Secretary Vance presumably had these critical currents much in mind while preparing the important address on African policy which he was to deliver on June 20 before the 58th annual meeting of the United States Jaycees in Atlantic City (Document 26). "It will not be our policy to mirror Soviet and Cuban activities in Africa," the Secretary of State reiterated, "because such a course would not be effective in the long run and would only escalate military conflict with great human suffering. Our best course is to help resolve the problems which create the excuse for external intervention and to help strengthen the ability of Africans to defend themselves."

Reviewing what he described as the United States' "affirmative approach to African aspirations and problems," Secretary Vance

[88]*New York Times,* May 22, 1978; same, June 5, 1978, quoting *US News and World Report.*
[89]Same: June 7, 1978.
[90]Reuters dispatch, London, in same: June 2, 1978.
[91]Same: June 9, 1978.

offered an intriguing comment about the role that even much-criticized Angola might play in African stabilization efforts. " . . . if we are to avoid more Shaba incidents in the future," he said, "Zaire and Angola must reach agreement to respect their common border and not to interfere in each other's internal affairs. In this connection, we believe it could be helpful to increase our consultations with the Angolan Government and begin working with it in more normal ways in order to improve the prospects for reconciliation between Angola and Zaire, as well as for achieving a peaceful settlement in Namibia." Far from supporting guerrilla resistance in Angola, it appeared, the United States was now prepared to seek the aid of Angola's rulers in smoothing out existing trouble spots.

On the heels of Secretary Vance's speech came the news that Donald F. McHenry, Deputy U.S. Representative to the Security Council and principal U.S. participant in the Namibia "contact group," was already en route to Luanda for talks with Angolan officials. There was nothing particularly new in such a move, according to President Carter, who told his June 26 news conference that intermittent consultations with Angolan officials had been occurring ever since he took office. There were no present plans to "normalize" relations with Angola, the President added, although the United States did want to take advantage of President Neto's influence with SWAPO and, in addition, "to hold the Angolan leaders responsible for any future possible invasions into the Shaba Province in Zaire." To the wonderment of some journalists and members of Congress, Mr. Carter also stated that the United States had never contemplated sending "back-door weapons to the rebels" in Angola or "getting militarily involved . . . directly or indirectly."[92]

Whether or not as a result of this American olive branch, there were no further invasions of Zaire in 1978, and a partial reconciliation between Angola and Zaire was effected when President Neto visited the capital of the neighboring republic in August. In addition, SWAPO's uneasiness about the Western proposals for Namibia was sufficiently allayed to bring a U.N.-supervised election in that territory at least within the realm of possibility.

Namibian Shuttlecock

The still tenuous prospect of a peaceful outcome in Namibia gained added substance with the adoption on July 27 of a Security Council resolution that authorized the appointment of a U.N. Special Representative for Namibia and asked a detailed report on ways and means of implementing the Western plan for indepen-

[92]*Presidential Documents,* 14: 1185.

dence.[93] To South Africa's extreme annoyance, however, a second resolution unanimously adopted the same day declared that the disputed enclave of Walvis Bay must be "reintegrated" into Namibia,[94] an assertion whose legal validity would presumably become a matter for subsequent challenge.

South African misgivings about the trend of events concerning Namibia were redoubled by the report on election arrangements submitted by Secretary-General Kurt Waldheim a few weeks later, following a survey mission by his newly appointed Special Representative for Namibia, Martti Ahtisaari of Finland. Asserting that it was already too late to meet the December 31 deadline for Namibian independence, the report administered a shock to the South Africans by calling for a U.N. Transitional Assistance Group of quite unexpected size, with a military component of not less than 7,500 as well as a civilian component of 1,860. These recommendations were wholly unacceptable, Prime Minister Vorster declared on September 20. South Africa, he said, would consequently go ahead with its own electoral plans, leaving it up to the future Namibian assembly to decide what role, if any, should be allowed the United Nations. In spite of this rejection, however, the Secretary-General's plan was formally approved by the Security Council a few days later.[95]

On that same September 20, Prime Minister Vorster announced his own resignation as part of a realignment in South Africa's ruling National Party that was shortly to place him in the post of President while another reputed "hard-liner," Defense Minister Pieter W. Botha, succeeded him as Prime Minister of the embattled republic.

One of Prime Minister Botha's earliest obligations was to meet with Secretary Vance and other Foreign Ministers of the Western "contact group," who visited Pretoria in a body on October 15–18 to try to win South African agreement to a somewhat modified U.N. election plan. Though insistent on holding its own "internal" election in December in accordance with previous plans, South Africa indicated that it would be willing to resume contact with the United Nations and would advise the Namibian leaders elected in December to try to cooperate in a second round of elections that might be held later under international supervision.[96]

Unsatisfactory to the Western governments, this stand was even more radically unacceptable to the other members of the Security Council. A resolution adopted by that body on November 13, with

[93]Resolution 431 (1978), adopted by a vote of 13-0-2 (Czechoslavakia, U.S.S.R.).
[94]Resolution 432 (1978), adopted unanimously.
[95]Resolution 435 (1978), Sept. 29, adopted by a vote of 12-0-2 (Czechoslovakia, U.S.S.R.), with China not participating.
[96]Texts of statements in *Bulletin,* Dec. 1978: 24-5.

the five Western countries abstaining, condemned South Africa's "clear defiance" of the United Nations and threatened action under Article VII of the U.N. Charter, dealing with threats to the peace and other critical situations, unless South Africa amended its conduct.[97]

In spite of U.N. warnings and SWAPO threats, South Africa persisted in its plan, and elections without benefit of U.N. supervision were duly held throughout Namibia on December 4–8, with some reports of violence but with an asserted participation rate of 81 percent. To no one's surprise, the Democratic Turnhalle Alliance, SWAPO's principal rival within the territory, was credited with 82 percent of the vote and 41 of the 50 seats in the new constituent assembly.

That body's initial task was to decide whether or not to permit a second election to be held under U.N. sponsorship; and its decision, as reported December 22, did not lack Machiavellian traits. Avoiding an immediate confrontation by accepting the principle of a U.N.-supervised election, it nevertheless insisted that the United Nations must first withdraw its recognition from SWAPO and cease its financial aid to that body. Such a turnabout would obviously not be easy for an organization that had long ago decided that SWAPO was "the sole and authentic representative of the Namibian people."[98]

Rhodesian Postponements

In Rhodesia, meanwhile, violence had reached a much higher pitch and the chances for accommodation between internal and external forces appeared even more murky. The security situation had "sharply deteriorated," Foreign Secretary Owen told the House of Commons on November 7, with nearly 4,000 deaths inside and 3,000 outside the country thus far in 1978. In the most horrifying incident to date, a Rhodesian airliner with 56 persons on board had been shot down by Nkomo forces on September 3, and ten of the eighteen white survivors had subsequently been massacred by persons unknown. Modified martial law was imposed in parts of the country in the wake of this incident and subsequently extended to cover three-fourths of Rhodesia's entire area. Later in September, Rhodesian forces conducted a series of heavy raids against Mugabe bases in Mozambique; more raids, directed against alleged guerrilla concentrations in Mozambique and Zambia, followed a rocket and mortar attack on Umtali on the Mozambique border in mid-October, and still another series of raids on Mozambique occurred in late November and early December.

[97]Resolution 439 (1978), adopted by a vote of 10-0-5 (West).
[98]General Assembly Resolution 31/46, Dec. 20, 1976, quoted in *AFR, 1976:* 60.

The political atmosphere, meanwhile, showed signs of further degeneration and was not improved by the disclosure that a secret meeting between Smith and Nkomo had taken place in Zambia in mid-August. At the same time, the prospects for an all-party conference appeared to be receding from day to day, and Prime Minister Smith's "transitional government" was markedly stepping up its efforts to gather support abroad.

A prime objective of this campaign was to persuade the United States to discontinue observing the economic sanctions imposed by the Security Council on the heels of Rhodesia's unilateral declaration of independence in 1965. The sanctions had never been exactly popular with the American Congress, and had already been suspended for several years, without U.N. authorization, prior to the repeal of the so-called Byrd amendment in 1977. In 1978, a new amendment calling for the repeal of sanctions was put forward by Republican Senator Jesse H. Helms of North Carolina during consideration of the annual mutual security assistance legislation. Ultimately, however, Congress preferred to adopt a more flexible amendment devised by Republican Senators Clifford P. Case of New Jersey and Jacob K. Javits of New York. In its final form, the Case-Javits amendment made the discontinuance of sanctions after December 31, 1978 contingent on a presidential determination that (1) the Rhodesian government had demonstrated its willingness to negotiate in good faith at an all-parties conference, and (2) a government had been installed that had been chosen in free, impartially observed elections.[99] Should the President find that these conditions had been fulfilled, he would have no choice but to discontinue the sanctions.

Those who were disturbed by the willingness of Congress to set aside an order of the Security Council found cause for even greater dismay in the action of 27 American Senators who actually invited the members of Rhodesia's four-man Executive Council to come and tell their story in the United States. Approved with obvious reluctance by the Department of State, the invitation drew a formal expression of regret from the Security Council as still another American contravention of U.N. sanctions.[100] Arriving early in October, Smith and his three black colleagues barnstormed the country over a two-week period, endeavoring to dispel American "misunderstandings" and to claim the credit allegedly due them for having done away with racial discrimination and established majority rule in Rhodesia. Professing willingness to attend "a well-prepared all-parties conference without preconditions," the Rhodesian quadrumvirate also had occasion to listen to some tren-

---

[99]Sec. 27, Public Law 95-384, Sept. 26, 1978.
[100]Resolution 437 (1978), Oct. 10, adopted by a vote of 11-0-4 (U.S.).

chant criticism of the Rhodesian raids into Mozambique and Zambia that took place during their visit.[101]

Returning to Rhodesia late in October, Prime Minister Smith indicated that some postponement in the commencement of majority rule would probably be necessary for "purely mechanical reasons"; and the transitional government subsequently announced a new timetable that called for publication of the independence constitution on December 22, a referendum on the new constitution, limited to the white electorate, on January 30, 1979, and a general parliamentary election on April 30, 1979. Any hope of holding an all-party conference would likewise have to be put forward into 1979, Prime Minister Callaghan conceded on November 23, when he informed the House of Commons that he was sending a personal representative, Cledwyn Hughes, to assess the possibilities of convening such a conference in Britain in the new year. The Anglo-American proposals on Rhodesia had recently been updated, Mr. Callaghan noted, and President Carter had agreed that Ambassador Low should again accompany the British representative on his travels.

South African Conundrum

Both in Rhodesia and in Namibia, the developments of the coming months would obviously depend in a substantial degree upon the course of events within South Africa itself; and the United States was losing no opportunity of pointing out that it expected the South African government to initiate decisive improvements in its internal relations, as well as promoting a favorable outcome in the neighboring countries. Unlike Rhodesia and Namibia, however, South Africa was an independent, sovereign nation, economically and militarily powerful in its own right, and the opportunities available to the United States and to other governments for influencing its policy were correspondingly restricted.

The central issues of American-South African relations were examined in an address by Anthony Lake, Director of the State Department's Policy Planning Staff, before the Conference on U.S. Foreign Policy in Africa in San Francisco on October 31 (**Document 27**). The problem of racial polarization in South Africa, Mr. Lake asserted, was serious and growing; and, though change was bound to come, there remained a critical question whether or not it was going to come peacefully. American efforts to promote constructive and peaceful change in South Africa, the Policy Planning chief observed, had involved "both cooperation and strong differences" with the government of that country; and the differences, over the years, "have grown as the problems in South Africa have grown."

[101]*Bulletin,* Nov. 1978: 13–14; same, Dec. 1978: 25–6.

Two opposing concepts, according to Mr. Lake, had tended to dominate American approaches to the South African problem: "on the one hand pressure and isolation; on the other, communication and persuasion." In stressing its abhorrence of apartheid and striving to multiply its ties to the South African black community, the United States had thus endeavored to maintain its relationship to the white ruling class as well. This dual course, the Policy Planning chief indicated, "is the policy which we believe brings the best chance of encouraging the peaceful change so much in everyone's interest. It avoids, I believe, the dangers presented either by policies which would convince South Africa's whites that we are implacably hostile to them, and that they must therefore go it alone without regard for our concerns," or by "policies which falsely imply that we could ever be indifferent to the plight of the victims of institutionalized racial injustice."

Mr. Lake did not refer in his address to the recent political changes in South Africa, which, as noted, had elevated former Defense Minister Pieter W. Botha to the position of Prime Minister while ensconcing his predecessor, Mr. Vorster, in the less exhausting post of national President. Nor would the State Department representative have been in a position to evalute the political tempest that was to burst upon South Africa soon afterward with the disclosure of major abuses in the handling of pro-apartheid propaganda funds under the Vorster regime. Such developments would not, in any case, have affected the validity of the policy planner's basic contention: " . . . If significant peaceful progress does not begin soon, the gap between black and white could become irremediable. This would have tragic consequences for the people of South Africa and for the region . . . . Our influence is limited. We must therefore use it with all the skill we can find. We must continue to put our minds to the complexities of issues that our hearts—as well as our brains—tell us are terribly important. . . ."

Pluses and Minuses

The mixed impressions arising from the year's experience in southern Africa were not less characteristic of the rest of Africa in this year of mingled lights and shadows. Some major positive aspects of the African record were easily recognized. There was, for instance, the continued, dynamic progress of Nigeria, so warmly hailed by President Carter early in the year. There was the impeccable adherence to constitutional procedures that marked the installation of Vice-President Daniel arap Moi as Kenya's Chief Executive and successor to the patriarchal Jomo Kenyatta. But no contemporary could be certain whether these signs of growing African political maturity would strengthen and multiply in the coming years, or whether Africa as a whole was doomed to a future of chaos and internecine strife of the sort that currently raged in half a dozen other places.

In the northwest, throughout these months, Morocco had continued its exhausting fight against the Algerian-supported "Polisario" guerrillas in the Western Sahara—a fight in which King Hassan's government had found itself virtually friendless following a change of regime and policy in nearby Mauritania, where the government of President Moktar Ould Daddah had been deposed in a military coup in July. Elsewhere in the Sahara and its borderlands, there was continued struggle between Chad's French-supported, predominantly Christian government and the Libyan-supported Muslim rebellion in the north.

In Eritrea, meanwhile, increasing death and devastation attended the Ethiopian attempt, with Soviet and Cuban support, to win a decisive victory over two loosely united Eritrean liberation movements. It is true that Cuban military forces appeared not to be participating on any scale in the Ethiopian offensive that began in May; but even without their direct involvement, the Eritrean patriots suffered devastating setbacks as the Ethiopians gradually reconquered Asmara, Keren, and other major towns. Like Somalia's President Muhammad Siad Barre a few years earlier, Ethiopia's Mengistu Haile Mariam went to Moscow in November and concluded on November 20 a treaty of friendship and cooperation with the Soviet Union. Presumably the relationship thus sealed would enable the U.S.S.R. to develop port facilities in Eritrea, replacing those it had earlier lost in Somalia when the latter had come to realize the full extent of Soviet political cynicism.

Still another international conflict broke out in East Africa at the end of October when a section of northern Tanzania was occupied and later "annexed" by Ugandan forces responsible to President Idi Amin Dada, whose cruel and capricious rule had become a cause of shame and scandal even to those Africans who most resented the air of moral superiority occasionally assumed by Western spokesmen. The Amin dictatorship was among the home-grown evils that would surely have to be purged—as was to happen, at Tanzania's hands, in April 1979—before Africa could even begin to enter upon the happy future its friends and partisans desired for it.

6. NEW ERA FOR THE AMERICAS

Deplorable though it might seem in other respects, Cuba's African involvement had one exceedingly consoling feature from the standpoint of U.S. policy-makers. The mischief that Cuba was making in Africa was at least not being made in Cuba's own hemisphere. On the contrary, the vast resources the Castro government was committing to revolutionary activity in another continent bore vivid testimony to its inability to achieve a like effect in areas nearer home. Throughout the 1960s, the United States and other American governments had gone through recurrent spasms of apprehension about the campaign of subversion and sporadic "aggression" being waged by Castro's Cuba against the political and social order existing elsewhere in Latin America and the Caribbean. By the 1970s, however, such fears had largely subsided. As the Cuban threat increasingly lost its novelty and its appeal for Latin Americans, new problems had come to the forefront, and Cuba had been at least partially readmitted to inter-American respectability. Although the political temperature of the Americans had remained at fever pitch, the symptoms had altered with the times.

The Panama Treaties

The transcendent inter-American issue of the 1970s had to do not with Cuba but with the future of the U.S.-owned Panama Canal and the U.S.-administered Canal Zone, the ten-mile-wide strip of Panamian territory in which the United States had exercised quasi-sovereign powers for nearly three-quarters of a century in accordance with the bilateral treaty concluded between the two countries in 1903. Like the revolutionary challenge of Castro's Cuba, the Panamian drive for correction of the fundamentally unequal arrangement laid down by the 1903 treaty—and preserved in its subsequent revisions—was part of a much broader effort by Latin American countries, acting for the most part individually rather than as a group, to curb and limit the preponderant position the United States had acquired throughout the hemisphere in the nineteenth and early twentieth centuries. Over and above its intrinsic importance, therefore, the recent evolution of the U.S.-Panamanian relationship had been closely watched in Latin America— and in the United States—as an historic test whose outcome would decisively affect the hemisphere as a whole.

The protracted efforts of the United States and Panamaniam governments to effect a fundamental revision of their existing treaty relationship had been initiated as far back as 1964, and, after various ups and downs, had culminated in the signature in Washington, on September 7, 1977, of two separate treaties, each dealing with a different aspect of the overall problem. The first of the two, the so-called Panama Canal Treaty,[102] provided for a gradual substitution of Panamanian for U.S. authority over the Canal and the Canal Zone during a period ending December 31, 1999. The second, known

[102] AFR, 1977: 345–64.

informally as the Neutrality Treaty,[103] undertook to ensure the subsequent neutrality of the Canal, as an international waterway, in both peacetime and wartime. Certain controversial points relating to the two treaties had been further clarified in a Joint Statement of Understanding, made public by President Carter and General Omar Torrijos, the Panamanian Chief of State, on October 14, 1977.[104] In addition to confirming each country's right to act to defend the Canal in case of need, it explicitly debarred the United States from intervening in Panama's internal affairs, and assured the vessels of each country the right to "go to the head of the line" of ships awaiting transit through the Canal in case of need or emergency.

Approved by a 2 to 1 majority of Panamanian voters in a national plebiscite held October 23, 1977, the treaties still awaited the verdict of the U.S. Senate, where approval by a two-thirds majority of members present and voting would be required before either treaty could be ratified by the President. "The world is watching to see how we act on one of our most important and controversial pieces of business," Mr. Carter noted in his State of the Union address **(Document 2)**. " . . . Ratifying the Panama Canal treaties will demonstrate our good faith to the world, discourage the spread of hostile ideologies in this hemisphere, and directly contribute to the economic well-being and the security of the United States."

The reasons the administration considered the treaties so important to the United States had already been set forth on numerous occasions by Secretary Vance and other qualified official spokesmen such as Ambassador-at-Large Ellsworth Bunker, who had led the U.S. negotiating team under three successive administrations. President Carter rehearsed the arguments once again in a televised "fireside chat" on February 1 **(Document 28)**, two days after the Senate Foreign Relations Committee had voted qualified approval of the treaties by a 14 to 1 margin.

"The most important reason—the only reason—to ratify the treaties," Mr. Carter asserted, "is that they are in the highest national interest of the United States and will strengthen our position in the world. Our security interests will be stronger. Our trade opportunities will be improved. We will demonstrate that as a large and powerful country, we are able to deal fairly and honorably with a proud but smaller sovereign nation. We will honor our commitment to those engaged in world commerce that the Panama Canal will be open and available for use by their ships—at a reasonable and competitive cost—both now and in the future."

In addition, the President asserted, approval of the treaties would strongly benefit the standing of the United States in Latin America. "The treaties will increase our Nation's influence in this

[103]Same: 364–9.
[104]Same: 377–8.

hemisphere," he said, "will help to reduce any mistrust and disagreement, and . . . will remove a major source of anti-American feeling. The new agreement has already provided vivid proof to the people of this hemisphere that a new era of friendship and cooperation is beginning and that what they regard as the last remnant of alleged American colonialism is being removed." Acknowledging that the Panama Canal involved "very deep and elemental feelings about our own strength," Mr. Carter insisted none the less that the agreement with Panama must be regarded as "a strong, positive act of a people who are still confident, still creative, still great"—the kind of agreement, he said, that Theodore Roosevelt would surely have endorsed because it embodied what that statesman had called "the lift toward nobler things which marks a great and generous people."

Opposition to the treaties, which was known to be much wider in the Senate as a whole than in the Foreign Relations Committee, was clearly rooted not solely in rational calculations but also, to a considerable extent, in those complex emotional regions to which the President had briefly referred. In their attempts to mobilize a national spirit of rejection, conservative spokesmen like California's Ronald Reagan, North Carolina's Jesse Helms, and South Carolina's Strom Thurmond had skillfully exploited the ordinary man's instinctive fear of being "ripped off," perhaps even physically mutilated, by alien and malevolent forces. But the opponents of the treaties had also supplied themselves with an abundance of rational arguments that demanded careful consideration by any conscientious citizen or legislator. Contrary to administration assurances, the treaties' foes insisted, these ill-conceived documents were going to cost the American people stupendous sums of money; deprive America's defense forces of vitally needed positions and facilities; and place America's future at the mercy of a Panamanian government that was neither stable, nor friendly, nor democratic, nor free from criminal, Castroite, or Communist associations. With only 34 adverse votes required to deprive the administration of the two-thirds majority needed for ratification of each treaty, opponents planned a tenacious floor fight and prepared to submit a multitude of amendments which, if adopted, could provoke repudiation of the treaties by Panama itself.

Approving the Neutrality Treaty

The strategy devised for the administration by the Senate's Majority Leader, Robert F. Byrd of West Virginia, involved a procedural novelty entailing the consideration of the two treaties in reverse order—first the relatively less controversial Neutrality Treaty, then the Panama Canal Treaty itself. In its report commending the treaties to the full Senate, the Foreign Relations Committee had recommended that the Neutrality Treaty be amended in one respect by incorporating in its terms the text of the Carter-Torrijos Statement of Understanding of October 14, 1977, which, as already noted, spelled out the right of the United States to defend the Canal and to "go to the head of the line of vessels" in case of need.[105] Amendments to this effect, submitted jointly by Senator Byrd and the Republican Minority Leader, Senator Howard F. Baker of Tennessee, were adopted on March 10 and 13 by votes of 84 to 5 and 85 to 3 respectively.[106]

More controversial were some of the reservations and conditions submitted from the Senate floor, many though not all of them inspired by hostility to the treaty. On March 15, the Senate adopted by an 82 to 16 vote the so-called Nunn Condition, submitted by Democratic Senator Sam Nunn of Georgia, which stipulated that nothing in the treaty prevented Panama and the United States from making bilateral agreements or arrangements involving the stationing of U.S. forces or maintenance of defense sites in Panamanian territory even after 1999.[107] Also on March 15, the Senate approved by large majorities a series of reservations relating to American battle monuments and cemeteries[108] as well as an understanding relating to the criteria for adjustment of Canal tolls.[109]

These stipulations, it was hoped, would prove palatable—if hardly welcome—to Panama as the treaty's other signatory. Decidedly more risky from the standpoint of possible Panamanian reaction was the surprise condition put forward on March 16 by Democratic Senator Dennis DeConcini of Arizona, and promptly approved by a vote of 75 to 23. Ostensibly directed against the possibility of the Canal's being closed by a strike, the Deconcini Condition provided that if the Canal was closed or its operation interfered with, the United States and Panama would each independently be entitled "to take such steps as it deems necessary, in accordance with its constitutional processes, including the use of military force in Panama, to reopen the Canal or restore the operations of the Canal, as the case may be."[110] Also on March 16, the Senate approved by voice vote a number of "understandings" asserting, among other things, that either signatory "may, in accordance with its constitutional processes, take unilateral action

---

[105]Text of committee amendments in *Congressional Record* (Daily Edition), Feb. 8, 1978: S 1517.
[106]Document 29a, paras. (a)(1) and (2).
[107]Document 29a, para. (b)(2).
[108]Document 29a, para. (c)(1)–(3).
[109]Document 29a, para. (d)(1).
[110]Document 29a, para. (b)(1).

to defend the Panama Canal against any threat, as determined by the Party taking such action."[111]

All of these matters were set forth at length in the omnibus Resolution of Ratification **(Document 29a)** that now, on March 16, awaited the Senate's final vote. With all 100 Senators present and voting, 68 Senators—one more than a two-thirds majority—voted for advice and consent to ratification, while 32 voted in the negative. "The people of our Nation owe a debt of thanks to the Members of the United States Senate for their courageous action taken today in voting for the Panama Canal neutrality treaty," said President Carter later that afternoon **(Document 29b)**. " . . . This vote today is, of course, only the first step in the process of ratification, but I am confident that the Senate will show the same courage and foresight when it considers the second treaty . . . . Perhaps the most encouraging lesson of all in these last long months is that in a full and open debate, even in a very controversial and difficult issue, in our foreign policy objectives, we can still reach the decisions that are in our Nation's long-term, best interests."

. . . and the Panama Canal Treaty

In a sense, the Senate debate and vote on the Panama Canal Treaty, which took place more than a month later, amounted to a replay of the drama completed on March 16. Opponents of the two treaties, among whom Republican Senator Paul D. Laxalt of Nevada was particularly conspicuous, spared no effort to win over the two additional votes which were all that would be needed to produce a negative outcome on the second treaty and thus to nullify the whole arrangement. Senators of various persuasions outdid themselves in devising reservations and understandings aimed at clarifying the meaning of the treaty's language and erecting new barriers against its being interpreted to the disadvantage of the United States. In the end, on April 18, the Senate voted its advice and consent to ratification by the identical margin of 68 in favor and 32 opposed—one more than the necessary two-thirds.

In another sense, however, the Senate's action on the Panama Canal Treaty was largely concerned with remedying the mischief done in the course of its previous work on the Neutrality Treaty. The DeConcini Condition to the Neutrality Treaty, with its reference to the possible use of U.S. military force to reopen or restore the operation of the Canal in case of its closure or of interference with its operations, had been received in Panama as a bitter affront and one that, unless repaired, must inevitably wreck the entire settlement. Much more than General Torrijos' personal vanity was at stake, since the political opposition in Panama had become increas-

[111]Document 29a, para. (d)(2).

ingly active and the stability of the Torrijos regime itself, as well as the viability of the treaties, could easily be called in question if nationalistic sentiment were further outraged.

In an attempt to forestall these dangerous possibilities, intricate three-cornered negotiations were instituted among (1) the White House and the Senate leadership, (2) Senator DeConcini and other treaty skeptics, and (3) the Panamanian government and head of state. Again, it was Senate Majority Leader Byrd who at length succeeded in evolving a formula that could be taken as superseding the DeConcini Condition without actually saying so. Adopted April 18 by a vote of 73 to 27 and included as Reservation No. 1 in the Senate's Resolution of Ratification, it stated that any action by the United States in the exercise of its treaty rights "shall be only for the purpose of assuring that the canal shall remain open, neutral, secure, and accessible, and shall not have as its purpose or be interpreted as a right of intervention in the internal affairs of the Republic of Panama or interference with its political independence or sovereign integrity."

Most of the other five reservations and six understandings incorporated in the Resolution of Ratification to the Panama Canal Treaty (**Document 30a**) had to do with financial matters. An important exception was Reservation No. 4, adopted April 17 by a vote of 84 to 3, which delayed the entry into force of both treaties while Congress addressed itself to the enactment of necessary implementing legislation. Specifically, this reservation provided that the exchange of instruments of ratification should not be effective before March 31, 1979, and that the treaties should not enter into force before October 1, 1979, unless Congress had (most improbably) enacted the necessary implementing legislation before March 31, 1979. The discussion of implementing legislation would, of course, provide new opportunities for the opponents of the settlement, not only in the Senate but also in the House of Representatives, many of whose members had resented their exclusion from the debate on ratification.

"This is a day of which Americans can feel proud," President Carter told a national radio and television audience on learning of the Senate's final, 68 to 32 vote on the afternoon of April 18 (**Document 30b**). ". . . These treaties can mark the beginning of a new era in our relations not only with Panama but with all the rest of the world. They symbolize our determination to deal with the developing nations of the world, the small nations of the world, on the basis of mutual respect and partnership." In addition, Mr. Carter emphasized, "the treaties . . . reaffirm a spirit that is very strong, constant, and old in the American character . . . . Today we've proven that what is best and noblest in our national spirit will prevail. Today we've shown that we are still builders, with our face still turned confidently to the future. That is why I believe all Americans should share the pride I feel in the accomplishments which we registered today.''

Political Miscellany

Although the Senate had stipulated that the Panama treaties should not enter into force until certain additional conditions had been fulfilled, nothing prevented the scheduling of a ceremonial exhange of ratifications that could be made legally effective at a later date. General Torrijos, who had come to regard the friendship of President Carter as an important prop to his regime, accordingly proposed that the U.S. Chief Executive come to Panama for a ratification ceremony in the middle of June, and Mr. Carter's acceptance was announced within ten days of the Senate's final votes.

The wheels of inter-American relations had not, of course, stood still while the world awaited the Senate's verdict. President Carter himself had made brief visits to two South American countries, Venezuela and Brazil, at the end of March as part of the delayed itinerary that subsequently took him to Nigeria and Liberia. The lukewarm, somewhat ambivalent tone of his discussions in Caracas, in Brasilia, and in Rio de Janeiro was echoed in Mr. Carter's observations on his return to Washington:

In Venezuela we strengthened our good relationship which has existed for a long time with that country. And we worked with Venezuela to develop a more cooperative approach for the future between the industrialized, developed nations like our own and the poor nations of the world.

In Brazil, one of our close allies over the years, we reestablished the understanding of the long term common interests and friendship between our people. And we stressed, perhaps in different ways, our mutual concern about nuclear nonproliferation and human rights.[112]

This was another way of saying that Brazil and the United States continued to differ sharply on both of these crucial issues, as Mr. Carter himself had frankly conceded at a news conference in the Brazilian capital.[113]

Back in Washington on April 17, the President had signed the instrument of ratification of the Protocol of Amendment to the Inter-American Treaty of Reciprocal Assistance (Rio Treaty), which had been signed at San José in 1975[114] and approved by a

[112]Homecoming remarks, Apr. 3, in *Presidential Documents*, 14: 679.
[113]News conference, Brasilia, Mar. 30, in same: 627–34.
[114]*AFR, 1975:* 269–77.

Senate vote of 95–0 in 1977. Additional ratifications by other signatories would, however, be needed before the amendments could enter into force. In the meantime, Mr. Carter transmitted to the Senate on May 24 the text of Additional Protocol I to the Treaty for the Prohibition of Nuclear Weapons in Latin America (Treaty of Tlatelolco), signed on behalf of the United States in 1977.[115] Should the Senate approve, the protocol would obligate the United States to establish and maintain a nuclear-weapon-free status in such territories as Puerto Rico, the Virgin Islands, the Canal Zone (pending the entry into force of the new treaties), and the Guantanamo military base in Cuba. The Senate, however, was to take no action on the matter during 1978.

Political developments in the individual American republics were a constant preoccupation for the United States in a year when numerous countries had scheduled presidential elections and, in at least one or two cases, there seemed to be good hope of a return to democratic processes after years of military rule. In contrast to the ambiguity of U.S. policy in the years when zeal for Latin American democracy had been limited by concern for U.S. investment and general economic progress, the present U.S. administration appeared to have few qualms about championing the cause of democracy and human rights wherever it was in eclipse or under challenge. As President Carter observed in Brazil, however, the opportunities for action in support of U.S. beliefs remained strictly limited.

In Argentina and Chile, for instance, there currently seemed no likelihood of major amendment in the military regimes headed respectively by Generals Jorge Rafael Videla and Augusto Pinochet Ugarte. The chances for a widening of the area of freedom in Brazil, where President Ernesto Geisel was due to be succeeded in another year by General João Baptista Figueiredo, appeared hardly less problematical. Uruguay and Paraguay were groaning under notoriously repressive regimes, with no alleviation in prospect. Bolivia, on the other hand, was looking forward to a presidential election and a restoration of civilian government later in 1978; a similar process was under way in Ecuador; Peru was about to elect a constituent assembly as a step toward superseding its ten-year-old military regime; and Colombia and Venezuela, where democratic practices were thoroughly at home, were similarly immersed in preparations for the election of new presidents.

Among the Central American countries, Costa Rica had already held a democratic election in February, and Guatemala had also managed to adhere to constitutional norms in choosing a new chief

---

[115] Text in same, *1977*: 334–5; message of transmittal in *Presidential Documents*, 14: 961–2.

executive in March. Nicaragua, on the other hand, had been severely shaken by the assasination in January of Pedro Joaquín Chamorro Cardenal, a prominent editor and opponent of the quasi-dictatorial regime of President Anastasio Somoza Debayle, and revolutionary feeling still smoldered in spite of Washington's assumption that Somoza would complete his term expiring in 1981. Panama, as already noted, was in a state of nationalistic excitation over the treaty question. Although opposition activity had revived strongly in recent months, General Torrijos and the nominal President, Demetrio Basilio Lakas Bahas, clearly hoped that the outcome of the negotiations with the United States would help to prolong the life of their regime.

The United States was also much concerned with political problems centering in the Caribbean, particularly in Cuba and the Dominican Republic. This was the period when President Carter and other Washingtonians were so intensely disturbed by Cuban activities in Africa and the seeming collusion of the Soviet and Cuban governments. Hopeful as he had been for improved relations with Cuba during his early months in office, the American President no longer concealed his exasperation at the conduct of the Castro regime. "It's a joke to call Cuba nonaligned," he remarked on one occasion. Cuba, he said, was "probably one of the most intensely aligned countries in the world."[116]

Anxieties of a different kind arose in connection with the May 16 presidential election in the Dominican Republic, where the twelve-year rule of conservative President Joaquín Balaguer and his Reformist Party was being challenged by a reinvigorated Dominican Revolutionary Party under Antonio Guzmán. Conducted under observation by representatives of the Organization of American States (OAS), the elections eventually produced a tally of 832,319 votes for Guzmán to only 669,112 for the 70-year-old incumbent. Before this result could be announced, however, the army suspended the counting of votes for a period of 30 hours and the United States gave strong expression to its dismay at any deviation from democratic procedures. "I am seriously concerned . . . and have been in touch with the Presidents of several neighboring countries in Latin America and with the Secretary General of the [OAS]," said President Carter on May 19. " . . . We share a common concern for the integrity of the democratic process . . . . The degree of our country's support for the Dominican government will depend upon the integrity of the election process."[117] Military interference, in other words, might mean the forfeiture of U.S. aid.

[116]Chicago news conference, May 25, in *Presidential Documents*, 14: 978.
[117]*Presidential Documents*, 14: 931-2.

Panama Pageant

Some of the American presidents whom Mr. Carter contacted on this occasion were probably among the selected heads of state and government who joined with him and General Torrijos for the formal exhange of ratifications in Panama City on Friday, June 16. Present on that occasion, in addition to the U.S. and Panamanian heads of state, were the Presidents of Colombia (Alfonso López Michelsen), Costa Rica (Rodrigo Carazo Odio), Mexico (José López Portillo), and Venezuela (Carlos Andrés Pérez), together with Prime Minister Michael N. Manley of Jamaica. "We are honored," said President Carter in his formal remarks at the signature ceremony **(Document 31a)**, "by the presence of the leaders of the five democratic countries who gave encouragement to us and advice to both nations during the final treaty negotiations. I'm grateful to them not only for the serious and helpful role they played in those final days and weeks but also for their continuing leadership in dealing with such crucial matters as world peace, nuclear nonproliferation, the status of human rights and democratic governments, and better relationships between the developed nations and the developing countries of the world."

The essential business at Panama City consisted in the signature by President Carter and General Torrijos of a nine-paragraph document entitled "Protocol of Exchange of Instruments of Ratification Regarding the Treaty Concerning the Permanent Neutrality and Operation of the Panama Canal and the Panama Canal Treaty" **(Document 31b)**. This document stated, among other things, that the respective instruments of ratification had been "delivered" on that day, although the effective date of the exchange would be April 1, 1979, as stipulated in the resolution of the U.S. Senate.

Appended to the Protocol were the two countries' formal Instruments of Ratification to the Panama Canal Treaty **(Document 31c)** and to the Neutrality Treaty **(Document 31d)**. As the Senate had directed, the U.S. Instruments of Ratification included, with minor editorial variations, the texts of all the amendments, conditions, reservations, and understandings that had been written into the two resolutions of advice and consent. Panama's Instruments of Ratification repeated these same texts and referred, in addition, to the parties' overriding obligations under international law, the principles of mutual respect and cooperation on which their relationship was based, and Panama's rejection of "any attempt by any country to intervene in its internal or external affairs."

There were other matters to engage the attention of President Carter during his two-day visit to Panama. On Friday evening and again on Saturday morning, June 17, he took part in multilateral discussions with the leaders from Colombia, Costa Rica, Jamaica, Panama, and Venezuela, who joined with him in issuing a joint statement embodying the fruit of their deliberations (**Document 32**). Hailing the Panama Canal treaties as harbingers of a new spirit of cooperation and peaceful settlement, the six leaders pledged "to work actively and in cooperation with each other and with other states" to conclude a number of items of unfinished inter-American business in the promotion of "peace, human rights, participatory government, and a just and equitable international economic system."

Before returning to Washington, Mr. Carter also addressed the group of Americans who, of all others, possessed least reason to hail the settlement with Panama. These were the American military and civilian personnel who had hitherto exercised exclusive responsibility for the operation and defense of the Panama Canal. Complimenting them on their past performance and expressing sympathy in the difficult adjustments they now faced, Mr. Carter promised full protection of their rights and said he was confident of their cooperation in easing the transition to Panamanian control.[118]

The OAS Assembly

The ceremonies in Panama preceded by just five days the opening in Washington of the Eighth General Assembly of the Organization of American States, which met at the inter-American organization's headquarters in the Pan American Union from June 21 to July 1. The preceding OAS Assembly, held in St. George's, Grenada, in June 1977, had received a very general report from Secretary of State Vance on the status of the then pending Panama Canal negotiations. This year, it fell to President Carter to greet the delegates in an opening-day speech (**Document 33**) in which he was able to report the full success of this bilateral venture—and, once again, to hail "the beginning of a new era of inter-American understanding, reflecting a new spirit of commitment and cooperation."

Once more the President chose "peace, human rights and dignity, and economic development" as the themes of his address. "The resolution of the Panama Canal issue," he said, "should be a good omen that other disputes in our hemisphere can also be settled peacefully. Let us approach other problems, such as Bolivian access to the sea, the Honduras-El Salvador border dispute, the future of Belize, in the same spirit of accommodation and friendship." He did not mention the longstanding Beagle Channel dispute between Argentina and Chile, which late in the year was to occasion real fears of war before being defused by a papal envoy sent by Pope John Paul II.

[118]*Presidential Documents*, 14: 1125-7.

Concerning human rights, Mr. Carter did not confine himself to endorsing the multilateral endeavors undertaken through the OAS, but offered strong, specific assurance that the influence of the United States would always be exerted on the side of human freedom. "My government will not be deterred from our open and enthusiastic policy of promoting human rights, including economic and social rights, in whatever ways we can," he promised. "We prefer to take actions that are positive, but where nations persist in serious violations of human rights, we will continue to demonstrate that there are costs to the flagrant disregard of international standards." In countries undergoing a transition from authoritarian to democratic rule, the President added, "my Government pledges not to intervene nor to show favoritism toward particular individuals or particular parties. But we will continually support and encourage political systems that allow their people to participate freely and democratically in the decisions that affect their lives."

Economic issues, President Carter continued, in many ways would be "our most important foreign policy concerns in the coming year"; and, he promised, the United States intended to give greatly increased emphasis to "those economic issues which most directly affect the developing countries, particularly trade and aid." The United States, he admitted, had "not moved far enough or fast enough" in this area in the past, but the fault was not all on one side. "Many of you," said Mr. Carter, "have not been aggressive enough in alleviating economic disparities and abuses in the system which we help to control." He urged the other OAS members to engage in constructive collaboration, rather than "public confrontation, through the news media," in such fields as the reduction of tariff and nontariff barriers, the creation of jobs, and the promotion of regional and subregional cooperation and integration.

President Carter's insistence that human rights were gradually gaining wider recognition received a measure of confirmation when the OAS Assembly approved three important resolutions in this area on the closing day of the session. The first, adopted by a vote of 22 in favor with 3 abstentions, took note of the annual report of the Inter-American Commission on Human Rights and specifically called on Chile to cooperate with the Commission in improving its human rights performance. The other two resolutions, both adopted by votes of 16 to 1 with 8 abstentions, urged Paraguay and Uruguay to accept the same Commission's help in remedying the grave deficiencies it had reported with respect to the human rights situation in those two countries.[119]

---

[119]OAS Documents AG/RES. 368–370 (VIII–0/78), in *Bulletin,* Sept. 1978: 57–8.

Latin American Chiaroscuro

President Carter's remarks on human rights before the OAS Assembly included a passage that could have served as a hopeful epigraph to the political history of the Americas in 1978. "This past year has seen a measure of progress," he said. "In many countries, political prisoners have been released, states of siege have been lifted, or constraints on freedom of the press have been loosened. In the coming year, we hope for more progress. For many in Latin America, the struggle has just begun. But the direction of history toward the expansion of human rights is clear. Where basic human rights are concerned, all of our governments must be accountable not only to our own citizens but to the conscience of the world."

The second half of 1978, though it produced few documents of significance in the inter-American field, was marked by an abundance of incident illustrative of Mr. Carter's remark that "For many . . . the struggle has just begun." A rough chronology sufficiently suggests the inconsistencies of Latin American political development, the precariousness as well as the vitality of democratic institutions at this period.

Colombia's scheduled presidential election, for example, had been held without major incident on June 5, and the successful Liberal candidate, Julio César Turbay Ayala, was inaugurated on schedule on August 7. Peru's constituent assembly was also duly elected, after one postponement, on June 19, although the prospect of a return to civilian government failed to assuage the widespread social unrest and economic discontent that had developed under the military regime installed a decade earlier.

In Bolivia, presidential and congressional elections were held on July 9, for the first time in a dozen years—but only to be superseded on July 21 when the government candidate, Air Force General Juan Pereda Asbún, elected to take power in a military coup rather than await the results of a somewhat uncertain ballot. Pereda, in turn, was toppled on November 24 in a second coup which brought the Army commander, General David Padilla Arancibia, to power as head of a three-man junta which promised new elections on July 1, 1979.

In Ecuador, the return to civilian government encountered parallel difficulties. Here the incumbent military chiefs, who had begun by debarring the controversial populist leader, Assad Bucaram, from becoming a candidate in the July 16 presidential election, subsequently took exception to the strong showing of Bucaram's nephew-in-law and substitute, Jaime Roldós Aguilera. The threatened cancellation of a runoff election between the two leading candidates was averted in September when the U.S. State Department publicly deprecated such an idea and the junta made haste to promise a runoff in April 1979.

General Pinochet of Chile had already declared that no elections would be held in his country before 1986, and this determination seemed not to have been altered by a shakeup in the military junta during July that removed the principal reform advocate and left Pinochet more firmly in control than ever. A minor embarassment to the Chilean dictator was the indictment by the United States of Chile's former intelligence director, General Juan Manuel Contreras Sepúlveda, and two other Chileans in the 1976 assassination of former Defense Minister Orlando Letelier in Washington.

Argentina's military government underwent what seemed to be primarily a cosmetic change as General Videla contrived to eliminate the military junta that had hitherto sustained his power and, on August 1, assumed the title of President with promises to promote a "civil-military convergence"'leading to a restoration of democratic government at some unspecified future date.

More solicitous for constitutional forms, the military-backed Brazilian government went through the motions of a presidential election on October 15 when an electoral college, as had been universally foreseen, officially delegated General Figueiredo to a six-year term beginning in March 1979. Of possibly greater import was the strong opposition showing in Brazil's congressional elections just a month later.

Last among the South American countries, Venezuela held a thoroughly up-to-date, U.S.-style election on December 4 which resulted in the choice of Luis Herrera Campins of the Social Christian party to succeed the incumbent Democratic Action leader, Carlos Andrés Pérez, in March 1979.

Once again, it was in Central America and the Caribbean—specifically, in Nicaragua and in Cuba—that there arose the most immediate challenges to democratic principle and diplomatic ingenuity. Nicaragua was the single Western Hemisphere country during 1978 in which the pent-up deprivations of the masses combined with the frustrations of the middle class to push a long-established politico-economic hegemony to the brink of collapse. From August 22 onward, when leftist guerillas associated with the "Sandinist National Liberation Front" temporarily took over the National Palace in the capital city of Managua, Nicaragua found itself in a state of brutal civil war from which, months later, it was reprieved less by the efforts of outside well-wishers than by the temporary exhaustion of the combatants. In the course of these months, the whole of Central America was subjected to a measure of political polarization in which the liberal or leftist governments of Costa Rica and Panama tended to side with the revolutionaries while the more conservative authorities in Guatemala, Honduras, and El Salvador stood firmly with the Nicaraguan regime and the Somoza family.

The United States, for its part, was torn between its dislike of the

Somoza government's repressive policies, its sympathy for the reform demands of Nicaragua's business and professional classes, and its abhorrence of the violent tactics, if not the revolutionary aims, of the Sandinist guerrillas. Whether acting as an independent mediator or as a member of the OAS, the United States appeared primarily concerned to get the fighting stopped and to work out a political compromise that would forestall its resumption at a later date. Ambassador William J. Jorden devoted weeks to this effort under a special mandate from the President and the State Department, while Ambassador William G. Bowdler later served as U.S. member of a special mediating group that also included Guatemala and the Dominican Republic.

Although Somoza eventually agreed to accept the "friendly cooperation" of outsiders in seeking a solution, no amount of argument could persuade him to relinquish his office before the expiration of his term in 1981. "The prospects for resolution of all these very difficult questions are sometimes quite undetectable or remote," President Carter conceded in December. Nevertheless, he added, he was encouraged by the fact that massive bloodshed and violence in Nicaragua had by that time given way—temporarily, as it turned out—to negotiations about a possible plebiscite to determine the country's future.[120]

The situation regarding Cuba, meanwhile, had seemed to ease somewhat as excitement over the Shaba invasion subsided and the Cuban forces in Africa refrained from provocative maneuvers elsewhere. U.S. authorities were further encouraged by Premier Castro's apparent determination to resolve the longstanding issue of the political prisoners held, in some instances, since the early days of his regime. In November, the Cuban chieftain was quoted as telling exile representatives that he was prepared to release some 3,000 persons in this category, provided the United States would accept those desiring to go there.[121]

Offsetting this positive gesture was a recurrence of old anxieties concerning Cuba's function as a possible base for the projection of Soviet military power in the Western Hemisphere. Late in October came reports that Cuba had received up to twenty MIG-23 fighter planes, the first examples of this advanced Soviet aircraft to appear in the Western Hemisphere. Soon afterward the United States resumed its aerial reconnaissance flights over Cuba, which had been suspended early in the Carter administration. The accompanying apprehensions were only partially relieved by President Carter's public statements following discussion of this development with the Soviets. It was true, the President said, that there had been

[120]News conference, Dec. 7, in *Presidential Documents,* 14: 2177-8.
[121]*New York Times,* Nov. 23, 1978.

MIG-23s in Cuba since the late spring; but while such planes undoubtedly could be outfitted and their crews trained to carry atomic weapons, there was no indication that this had been done, nor was there any evidence or allegation that atomic weapons were present in Cuba. Furthermore, said Mr. Carter, the U.S.S.R. had given assurances that no shipments of weapons to the Cubans had or would violate the 1962 agreements barring the reintroduction of offensive weapons into that country. A Soviet violation of that agreement, said the President, would be considered a very serious development, and the United States would continue to monitor compliance very carefully "to be sure that there is no offensive threat to the United States possible from Cuba."[122]

Relations between the United States and Mexico had seldom reached the top of the U.S. foreign policy agenda during 1978, despite the multiplicity of bilateral problems between those two adjacent nations. But a visit by President Carter to Mexico, proposed by President López Portillo and planned for February 1979, would undoubtedly serve as a reminder that relations with even the closest neighbors required constant cultivation if mutual harmony was to be preserved.

7. ASIAN "ARC OF CRISIS"

No single concept is elastic enough to encompass a year's experience in Asia and the Pacific. Events within the various geographic subdivisions of this enormous area customarily go forward with every appearance of mutual unrelatedness, so that the United States, for example, could gain an important diplomatic success in China in December 1978 at the very moment when it was losing a critical foothold in Iran. The student in search of a cohesive principle may find a helpful point of departure in Dr. Brzezinski's geopolitical notion of an "arc of crisis," a phrase that was limited by the Presidential Assistant to the lands around the Indian Ocean[123] but could, in a wider sense, be taken to apply to the entire perimeter of eastern and southern Asia, thus comprehending the totality of the countries situated within the ambit of Soviet-Marxist imperialism. At some point, however, one is compelled to abandon general views and direct attention to the individual regions of Asia,

[122]News conference, Nov. 30, in *Presidential Documents,* 14: 2100-1; see also news conference, Dec. 7, in same: 2176-7.
[123]Cf. note 35 above.

whether the analysis proceeds from east to west or rather, as in the present instance, from west to east.

Farewell the "Northern Tier"

Like capitalist society as conceived by Karl Marx, the geopolitical barriers to Soviet expansion that had been erected in the 1950s by Secretary of State John Foster Dulles may be said to have borne within themselves the seeds of their own destruction. Such a contraption as the Baghdad Pact of 1955, known later as the Central Treaty Organization (CENTO), owed far more to Western anti-Communist thinking than it did to the deeper preoccupations of the constituent Asian countries. Iraq, on the heels of a nationalist revolution, had defected from the Baghdad Pact as early as 1958. Turkey and Pakistan had been progressively alienated by the lack of Western support in their respective regional conflicts, Turkey's with Greece and Pakistan's with India. Afghanistan, never a CENTO member, had remained a gaping breach through which some measure of Soviet influence had never ceased to flow.

Of all the countries making up what Mr. Dulles had called the "Northern Tier," it was Iran that had appeared most firmly committed, if not to CENTO as such, at least to close association with the United States and to the global security system with which the latter was identified. Not only was the United States the principal guarantor of Iranian independence. It was also the country whose liberal arms export policies had in recent years enabled the government of Muhammad Reza Shah Pahlevi to devote an important share of Iran's growing petroleum revenues to the large-scale purchase of sophisticated armaments. By 1977, such purchases had reached the impressive annual total of $5.8 billion, the largest such allocation attributable to any single purchaser, though later figures showed Saudi Arabi to be ahead of Iran in the fiscal year 1978.[124] The notion that these astronomical expenditures might not be healthy from Iran's own point of view had been outweighed, from an American standpoint, by the desire to cultivate a ruler whose country held so important a place in the global structure of free world defense, and whose oil production seemed vital to the prosperity of both industrial and developing nations.

The value of the Iranian connection, accentuated by the turmoil in South Arabia and the Horn of Africa, had been enthusiastically attested by President Carter on his year-end visit to Tehran,[125] and was emphasized once again by Secretary Vance in his address at the annual ministerial meeting of the CENTO Council, held in London on April 19–20, 1978 (**Document 34**). Iran's importance as a pillar

[124]*City News* (New York), Aug. 25; *Christian Science Monitor,* Oct. 4, 1978.
[125]Cf. above at note 9.

of regional stability was to be thrown into still higher relief when President Muhammad Daud of Afghanistan was overthrown and killed in a military coup on April 27—just a week after the CENTO meeting—that paved the way for the installation of an overtly pro-Soviet regime led by Nur Muhammad Taraki. As in Ethiopia, this internal turnover became the prelude to an accelerated influx of Soviet "advisers" and to the conclusion later in the year of a twenty-year treaty of friendship and cooperation between Afghanistan and the U.S.S.R., signed in Moscow December 5, 1978.

Even at the time of the CENTO meeting, moreover, there had been disconcerting signs of instability within Iran itself. As the year advanced, these mounting fever symptoms were to reach a point at which even the most basic American assumptions about Iran were ceasing to be tenable and Iran's own future as a nation appeared very much in doubt. For years Americans had put their faith in the stern but, presumably, enlightened rule of the Shah and in the efficacy of his "White Revolution," which combined forced-draft modernization with vigorous repression of dissenting elements and with opportunities for large-scale corruption in quarters close to the throne. Now, suddenly, it became apparent that the Shah's rule was detested by the population at large and that its enemies ranged across the political spectrum, from the reactionary Shiite Muslim clergy led by the exiled Ayatollah Ruhallah Khomeini to the leftist National Front headed by Karim Sanjabi.

Encouraged, some said, by the new U.S. emphasis on human rights, these dissident factions mounted an increasingly formidable campaign of street agitation and strikes which continued through the spring and summer and, by September, had inspired the Shah to issue a promise of free parliamentary elections, to install a somewhat more conciliatory government under Jaafer Sharif-Imani, and to remove his relatives from high positions. These concessions, however, seemed only to increase the prevalent hysteria. While Ayotallah Khomeini, now domiciled outside Paris, clamored for the Shah's outright removal, labor agitation in the oil fields led to a virtual shutdown of the petroleum industry, the backbone of Iran's economy as well as a vital resource for many consuming nations.

In a show of firmness that was outspokenly approved (and perhaps inspired) by the United States, the Shah on November 6 imposed military rule throughout the country and installed a new cabinet, led by General Golam Riza Azhari, Chief of Staff of the Armed Forces, which began an immediate crackdown not only against the Shah's critics but also against some of his intimate collaborators, notably Court Minister and former Premier Amir Abbas Hoveida. The United States, though warm in its support of the Shah's cause, had disclaimed any intention of interfering in Iran's internal affairs, and President Carter had publicly expressed his confidence that the U.S.S.R. would exercise a like restraint.[126] All the greater was the President's indignation, therefore, when Brezhnev undertook on November 18 to issue a peremptory warning against U.S. involvement. A sharp rejoinder to this "highly inappropriate" statement was promptly issued by the United States,[127] and there was little public emphasis thereafter on the East-West aspect of the Iranian crisis.

Even in the White House and the State Department, however, support for the Shah began to weaken in the following days as the disorders in Iran acquired an increasingly anti-foreign and anti-American edge and a special task force headed by former Under-Secretary of State George W. Ball undertook a "new look" at the available policy options. By mid-December, large numbers of Americans had been evacuated by the U.S. Air Force, and the American government, reversing its position of a few weeks earlier, was urging the Shah to compromise with his foes and set up a civilian regime—possibly even a regency which could take charge if he was obliged to leave the country temporarily.

But even if the Shah were willing to compromise, his enemies were not. What they wanted was not a compromise within the existing governmental framework, but the Shah's definitive abdication. The National Front, whose tactics were closely coordinated with those of the Khomeini forces despite the two movements' radically different philosophies, officially refused to entertain the idea of a coalition. Eventually, however, a less militant National Front figure, Shahpur Bakhtiar, was persuaded to come forward and entrusted on December 29 with the task of forming a civilian government. Left in abeyance for the moment was the question whether the Shah would be required to relinquish some of his powers or even to leave the country, as was actually to happen as early as January 16, 1979. In the meantime, the U.S. Embassy in Tehran suggested on December 31 that the dependents of the 30,000 Americans still in Iran would do well to depart at least temporarily, even though no formal "evacuation" was thought necessary for the moment.

The events in Iran were scarcely calculated to encourage a feeling of security on the part of other governments, in Asia or elsewhere, which had allowed themselves to become dependent on the support of the United States. First Vietnam, now Iran; and who would be next? they asked. Saudi Arabia, another country in the throes of rapid modernization, was particularly susceptible to the nervous malady that had become increasingly prevalent throughout the Red Sea-Persian Gulf-Indian Ocean area. Could any of these countries be certain that the Soviet Union, after its recent successes in Afghan-

[126]Interview with Bill Moyers, Nov. 13, in Presidential Documents, 14: 2018–20.
[127]New York Times, Nov. 20 and 21, 1978.

istan, Ethiopia, and Southern Yemen, would refrain from further mischief-making amid the ruins of the "Northern Tier"?

It was presumably with a view to calming such anxieties and, at the same time, conveying a discreet warning to the U.S.S.R. that the United States revealed on December 29 that a carrier task force from the Seventh Fleet, including the nuclear-powered U.S.S. *Constellation,* had been ordered to proceed from the Philippines to the South China Sea as a precaution against future eventualities. At a later stage, the United States would perhaps endeavor to compensate for the "loss" of Iran by intensifying its support of such friendly if politically disparate Asian states as Israel, Turkey, Pakistan, and Yemen, as well as Egypt, Somalia, and the Sudan in Africa. But no such *ersatz* arrangements would be able to mask the collapse of one of the major bastions of the U.S.-supported global security system.

Friends Once More: The United States and India

Stepped-up military activity in the Indian Ocean was the last thing sought by most of the nonaligned states of the region, as President Carter had been sharply reminded on his visit to India at the beginning of the year. "We believe this is no time for increasing but, rather, arresting and eliminating great power deployment in the hitherto tension-free areas such as the Indian Ocean," Indian President N. Sanjiva Reddy had pointed out at a state dinner on January 2.[128] President Carter, in his address to the Indian Parliament earlier that day (**Document 35**), had himself affirmed that "we are taking steps to forestall, along with the Soviets, great power rivalry and the escalation of military presence in your own Indian Ocean."

Although the U.S.-Soviet negotiations on Indian Ocean arms limitation were destined to remain in suspense through most of 1978, President Carter's visit to India undoubtedly set the seal upon a marked improvement in the relationship between the countries which he described in his New Delhi address as, respectively, "the second largest democracy on earth, the United States of America," and "the largest democracy, the Republic of India."

The relations of these two leading democracies had not always run smoothly in the past. American policy, at most times, had tended to lean more heavily on Pakistan, a military ally, than on nonaligned India, Pakistan's rival and frequent adversary and an uninhibited critic of American policies. Of late, however, a shift in the political kaleidoscope had placed new governments in office in all three countries. A military coup in Pakistan had brought to power a sternly dictatorial government, led by General Mohammad Zia al Haq, which was now engaged in pressing capital charges against the

[128]*Presidential Documents,* 14: 13.

country's leading civilian statesman and the head of the preceding government, Zulfikar Ali Bhutto. In India, in March 1977, the voters had rejected the emergency regime of Mrs. Indira Gandhi and espoused the loosely democratic rule of the Janata Party led by Prime Minister Morarji R. Desai. It was also in 1977 that the United States itself had acquired a new administration that made a point of its attachment to democratic principle as distinguished from strategic expediency.

President Carter made much of the affinities between the United States and India, both in his address to Parliament and on other occasions during his two-day stay. Its culminating event was the issuance with Prime Minister Desai of a "Delhi Declaration" enunciating a number of elevated politico-moral principles.[129] "You know, I'm not an objective analyst," the President later remarked. "But I felt that the progress we made with India was extraordinary. . . . Under Mrs. Ghandi, there is no doubt that the orientation of India, which has been an historic friend of ours, had been away from us, perhaps toward the Soviets. I felt like Desai and his government has at least come back to a completely neutral or nonaligned position. And there was a genuine feeling of compatibility and friendship, based on deep religious convictions, a commitment to democracy, the principle of human rights, that was very encouraging to me. It was more than I had anticipated.[130]

President Carter did not ignore the fact that there remained important areas of disagreement between the two governments. "I know that there will be times when we will disagree on specific issues and even on general approaches to larger problems," he told the Indian Parliament. The most conspicuous disagreement at the moment had to do with the U.S. role in India's plans for nuclear development, plans that collided in some respects with the American approach to nuclear nonproliferation. India, as a matter of national dignity, was disinclined to submit to international inspection of its nuclear activities; whereas the United States, under the new Nuclear Non-proliferation Act, intended to strengthen its reliance on such inspections as a condition of U.S. assistance with nuclear fuel and equipment.

"This is a cold, technological subject," Mr. Carter observed in his parliamentary address. "But Prime Minister Desai and I had warm and productive discussions about this field." Their discussions, admittedly, were complicated to some degree by the accidental amplification of the President's oral instruction to Secretary Vance to set forth the U.S. position in "a blunt and cold letter"—by which, Mr. Carter later explained, he had actually meant no

[129]*Presidential Documents,* 14: 17–18.
[130]Airborne question-and-answer session, Jan. 6, in same: 44.

more than "a very frank and factual letter."[131] Despite this contretemps, the President was able to announce agreement on shipments of low-enriched uranium for the Indian power plant at Tarapur, near Bombay, as well as supplies from U.S. reserves of heavy water.

The issue of fuel for the Tarapur reactor nevertheless continued to vex relations between the two countries. In April, President Carter was obliged to intervene in order to release a shipment that had been blocked by a split vote in the Nuclear Regulatory Commission.[132] Further discussions of the whole problem took place in June, when Prime Minister Desai came to the United States for an official visit that coincided with the U.N. General Assembly session on disarmament. The upshot was a renewal of President Carter's pledge "to make every effort consistent with American law to maintain fuel supplies for Tarapur and continue nuclear cooperation with India."[133] Even then, another nine months were to elapse before the Nuclear Regulatory Commission decided, this time by a vote of 3 to 2, to approve a much larger shipment of nuclear fuel for Tarapur.[134] In the meantime, both countries could at least take satisfaction in the knowledge that their relations were no longer in need of repair but henceforth needed only to be cultivated.

East Asian Partnership: The United States and Japan

One factor that had helped assure the restoration of American-Indian friendship was the termination of the American involvement in Vietnam, which Indians had perceived—and vigorously condemned—as an imperialistic assault on the liberties of an Asian people. To an extent, the U.S. withdrawal from Vietnam had also helped relieve the anxieties of other countries in Southeast and East Asia, from Burma and Thailand all the way around to Japan and Korea. None of these countries had been especially happy about the United States' Vietnam adventure; yet, paradoxically, its conclusion had exposed them to another kind of anxiety—the fear, namely, that the reduction of U.S. commitments in Asia might be carried so far as to undermine the regional balance of power and leave the smaller Asian countries at the mercy of other, perhaps less benign forces. These misgivings, already apparent in the later years of the Nixon and Ford administrations, had been kept alive by the Carter administration's decision to give priority to relations with the U.S.S.R. and NATO, by its announced determination to reduce the defense budget, and, most particularly, by its proclaimed intention of withdrawing the U.S. ground forces which had been helping in

---

[131]Same: 42-3.
[132]Message to Congress, Apr. 27, in same: 790-91.
[133]Communiqué, June 15, in same: 1108.
[134]*New York Times,* Mar. 24, 1979.

the defense of the Republic of Korea ever since the Korean armistice of 1953.

The soothing of these apprehensions about the future course of the United States had itself become a primary concern of U.S. policy in Asia, reflected since around 1975 in a series of authoritative pronouncements to the effect that the United States emphatically intended to remain a Pacific power and had no intention of abandoning its friends in the area. Typical of the assurances which still seemed necessary in 1978 was the statement of Presidential Assistant Brzezinski in an April 27 address to the Japan Society in New York (Document 36): "There have been recurrent suggestions that the United States is withdrawing from Asia. These suggestions are untrue. The United States will maintain a strong and diversified military presence and an active diplomacy in the Asian-Pacific region to support our growing economic and political stakes in the area."

The weeks ahead, Mr. Brzezinski promised, would offer "visible evidence of our resolve to intensify America's diplomatic efforts in Asia." Vice-President Mondale, he pointed out, would be departing April 29 on an exploratory visit to Southeast Asia and the Southwest Pacific. On May 3, Japanese Prime Minister Takeo Fukuda would be in Washington for consultations with President Carter. Dr. Brzezinski himself would be leaving on May 19 on a trip to Northeast Asia featuring consultations with the leaders of the People's Republic of China, Japan, and the Republic of Korea.

Of special importance in an Asian context, Dr. Brzezinski observed, were "a widening of our cooperation with Japan and an expansion of our relationship with China." Close partnership between the United States and Japan, he declared, "is a vital foundation for successful pursuit of America's wider objectives in the world. If relations between America and Japan are strong, we benefit and the world benefits; when we run into difficulties, we suffer and others suffer with us. . . . In short, we are mutually dependent. No relationship in our foreign policy is more important. None demands more careful nourishment."

Indispensable though it was, Japanese-American cooperation was "not automatically assured," the Presidential Assistant pointed out. Particularly in the economic field, he recalled, the relationship had been "marked over the past year by a growing Japanese current-account surplus, sharp imbalance in our bilateral trade, a huge U.S. balance-of-payments deficit, and currency disorders." These common problems of the two nations, Dr. Brzezinski asserted, could be effectively dealt with only within a framework of "concerted action by all the advanced industrial democracies"; but certain areas could also be singled out in which there was a need for decisive action by both Japan and the United States. While Japanese and U.S. views on major international issues were generally consonant, Dr. Brzezinski added, "We look for Japan to play a more active political role" in regard to such matters as "our approaches toward the major Communist powers, toward Asian issues, toward the North-South dialogue, and toward major international negotiations"—undoubtedly a comprehensive list.

"The relationship that has developed between the United States and Japan is uniquely significant," Dr. Brzezinski stated in conclusion. "Despite differences in our national situation and national styles, we have fashioned ties that are rooted in shared interests and common values—our commitment to democratic procedures, civil rights, the market system, a free press, and open societies. . . . Looking back at what we have created over the past 30 years, we can assert with confidence that we have established a permanent partnership of value not only to ourselves but to the entire world community. We shall work to assure its durability."

Report on Southeast Asia

The message carried by Vice-President Mondale on his twelve-day visit to the Philippines, Thailand, Indonesia, Australia, and New Zealand was predictably similar. "In each capital I visited," the Vice-President reported in a May 10 address at Honolulu's East-West Center **(Document 37)**, "I reaffirmed one central proposition: America is unalterably a Pacific power. . . . Our ties with Asian nations are central to the success of our global policy." The basic question, Mr. Mondale intimated, was whether America's "new foreign policy concerns—such as human rights and arms transfer restraints"—could be successfully engrafted upon a Pacific policy traditionally dominated by security interests. "We will not cling to past patterns of involvement in the Pacific," he promised. "We will shape our future involvement to assure a balance between preserving security and promoting constructive change, between government actions and private enterprise. We will meet necessities of power and fulfill the claims of principle."

Mr. Mondale entered into some detail in enumerating American concerns on both the traditional and the more novel sides of the foreign policy ledger. Among security preoccupations, he listed the ongoing negotiations with the Philippines over the future of the key American bases at Subic Bay and Clark Field, and with Indonesia and Thailand over the supply of defensive aircraft; the ANZUS commitment to Australia and New Zealand; and the difficulties placed by the Communist government of Vietnam in the way of the establishment of diplomatic relations with the United States. In reviewing the "new agenda" and its objectives of "national resilience, economic growth, social justice, and regional cooperation," Mr. Mondale particularly stressed the United States' desire to cooperate with the Association of South East Asian Nations (ASEAN) as well as with its individual members, Indonesia, Malaysia, the Philippines, Singapore, and Thailand.

The Vice-President also spoke briefly concerning two of the more tragic legacies of the war in Indochina, the rapidly increasing outflow of refugees from the Indochinese countries and the brutal repression being carried on by the Pol Pot regime in Cambodia. Concerning the refugee problem, which had imposed a particularly heavy burden on Thailand and Malaysia as the nations of first arrival, he mentioned a U.S. plan to admit a further 25,000 refugees—half of them land refugees from Laos and Cambodia, and the remainder "boat people" from Vietnam—in addition to nearly 165,000 already resettled in the United States since the end of the war in 1975.[135] Regarding Cambodia, Mr. Mondale admitted that there was little the United States could do except to "continue to try to focus the world's attention on the horror of what is happening there."

In spite of these sinister exceptions, Mr. Mondale appeared convinced that the Pacific basin had begun "an unprecedented and exciting era of change and growth," with a future that promised "rapid economic advance and relative political stability, nationalism accompanied by regional cooperation, security without huge defense budgets, effective governmental authority combined with a growing respect for the rights of individuals." Admittedly, this roseate prospect hinged upon "the wisdom, vision, and determination of the Asian-Pacific countries themselves, including the United States." The American role, the Vice-President emphasized, "is crucial. . . . But it is not a burden to be borne, it is a challenge that we welcome."

Pacific Shop Talk

Consultation, with both friends and one-time adversaries, continued to be the keynote of U.S. Pacific policy over the next few months. Japan's Premier Fukuda arrived in Washington at the beginning of May, accompanied by Foreign Minister Sunao Sonoda and External Economic Affairs Minister Nobuhiko Ushiba, primarily for a review of economic questions in advance of the Bonn economic "summit" in June. Overshadowing the Washington discussions was the continued explosive growth of Japan's exports, which had saddled the Japanese with a record $2.45 billion trade surplus in the single month of March and had helped to bring about a 30 percent appreciation of the yen against the dollar in the brief period since the beginning of 1978. No major decisions resulted

---

[135]Figures adapted from U.S. Department of State, Bureau of Public Affairs, "Indochinese Refugees" (GIST Series, July 1978).

from Mr. Fukuda's meeting with the President, although Japan announced an increased contribution in support of Indochinese refugees and the two leaders agreed to expand cooperation in science and technology.[136]

Dr. Brzezinski's trip to China on May 20–23 was a more spectacular event, extensively dramatized by television and spiced by Brzezinskian quips that left no doubt about the Presidential Assistant's preferences in the Sino-Soviet quarrel. The major purposes of his visit, as Dr. Brzezinski later explained **(Document 25b)**, had been to review the two countries' positions on international affairs, see whether their bilateral relationship could be further developed "within the present context," and, finally, "to reaffirm our commitment to normalization and perhaps to make a modest contribution of an indirect sort to it."

"Both myself and the Chinese leaders agreed that the visit was beneficial," Dr. Brzezinski stated; "we agreed that it could be described as useful, important, and constructive." But though both sides emphasized the existence of "certain common basic interests" shared by the two powers, there was no visible lessening of the Chinese insistence that full normalization of relations would be impossible while the United States maintained its existing close relationship with the Republic of China on Taiwan. It was during this visit, however, that the United States made known that Ambassador Leonard Woodcock, the Chief of the U.S. Liaison Office in Peking, was ready to begin serious discussions with Foreign Minister Huang Hua "to see whether normalization could be achieved on mutually acceptable terms."[137]

Dr. Brzezinski's subsequent stops in Tokyo and Seoul had not been expected to yield major, concrete results. Japan, he found, was already immersed in the negotiations that were to lead on August 12 to the signature of a treaty of peace and friendship with the People's Republic of China, an event that would cause more irritation in Moscow than it did rejoicing in Tokyo. In South Korea, Dr. Brzezinski found the government of President Park Chung Hee resentful of U.S. pressures on human rights, annoyed by the negative American reaction to past Korean bribery attempts, persistently unhappy about the pending withdrawal of U.S. ground forces, and troubled about a recent visit to North Korea by Chinese Communist leader Hua Kuo-feng.

The presidential envoy undoubtedly found opportunities to remind the South Koreans that plans for withdrawal of U.S. ground forces had already been substantially modified in the face of South

---

[136]*Bulletin,* June 1978: 2.
[137]U.S. Department of State, Bureau of Public Affairs, Office of Public Communication, *News Release: Diplomatic Relations With the People's Republic of China and Future Relations With Taiwan* (Dec. 1978): 2.

Korean and U.S. military and congressional apprehensions. President Carter, indeed, had only recently announced that there would be a further slowdown as the result of congressional delays in approving his proposal that $800 million worth of military equipment be transferred to South Korea by the departing ground forces. Instead of the 6,000-man brigade that had beeen scheduled for withdrawal in 1978, Mr. Carter stated, a single combat battalion from that brigade would be withdrawn in December, together with 2,600 noncombat personnel, while the other two battalions of the brigade would remain until 1979.[138] In approving the transfer program later in the session, Congress would append to the International Security Assistance Act a caveat to the effect "that further withdrawal of ground forces of the United States from the Republic of Korea may seriously risk upsetting the military balance in that region and requires full advance consultation with the Congress."[139]

Korea was not too remote to engage the interest of the ANZUS Council, the trilateral organ comprising the Foreign Ministers of Australia, New Zealand, and the United States, which held its 27th meeting in Washington on June 7-8. As always, the formal communiqué that concluded the meeting (Document 38) extolled the ANZUS connection and offered unexceptionable sentiments on various aspects of Pacific and global affairs. Regarding Korea, for example, the three ministers "expressed the conviction that the important progress made by the Republic of Korea's armed forces would allow them to assume a greater role in the defense of that country with continuing support to be provided by the United States." They also expressed support for a South Korean invitation to North Korea to resume their interrupted dialogue "as a first step toward peaceful solution of the Korea question."

Also noted by the ANZUS representatives was the progress of U.S. efforts to reach a permanent accommodation with the people of the Trust Territory of the Pacific Islands (Micronesia), a former mandated territory administered by the United States under the authority of the U.N. Security Council. Arrangements to protect the principal U.S. strategic interest in the territory, involving the establishment of a separate, U.S.-oriented Commonwealth of the Northern Marianas, were already far advanced; and negotiations with other Micronesian representatives had recently produced agreement on certain "Principles of Free Association" which might, it was hoped, provide a basis for termination of the entire trusteeship arrangement as early as 1981. In expressing support for this objective, the ANZUS ministers noted that the citizens of the territory would have an opportunity to express their views in a U.N.-observed referendum on July 12, 1978. They could not know, however, that

[138]Apr. 21 statement, in *Presidential Documents* 14: 768.
[139]Sec. 23(e)(1), Public Law 95-384, Sept. 26, 1978.

voters from two of Micronesia's six districts would seize the opportunity to reject the plan, thus creating a likelihood that this poor and widely scattered ocean territory would ultimately be divided into at least four separate, self-governing national units under some form of U.S. protection.

Still another consultative session of some importance took place in Washington on August 2–4 when ministerial delegates from the five ASEAN countries, led by Philippine Foreign Minister Carlos P. Romulo, joined Secretaries Vance, Blumenthal, and others for the second meeting of an "ASEAN-United States Dialogue" initiated the previous year. Exchanging views on a wide range of economic issues of interest to Southeast Asian developing countries, the participants agreed that they had taken "an important step in strengthening further the friendship and close ties between the ASEAN and the United States." They therefore promised to "continue their efforts toward the consolidation of a durable, long-range, mutually beneficial relationship," and to "take measures to facilitate more active economic cooperation to that end."[140]

Breakthrough to China

The tempo of Far Eastern affairs accelerated markedly in the later months of 1978. The Sino-Soviet quarrel intensified, and the United States and China moved closer to a resolution of their differing perspectives on "normalization." China's new, more open style of diplomacy, reflected in the treaty with Japan and in Hua Kuo-feng's visits to North Korea and, later, to Romania, Yugoslavia, and Iran, caused obvious misgivings in Moscow and seemingly encouraged the U.S.S.R. to strengthen its own ties to Vietnam, a country that was already quarreling with China and could conceivably provide the Soviet Union with a base for operations directed toward China's southern flank.

By the beginning of November, matters in this area appeared to be approaching a crisis as the U.S.S.R. and Vietnam concluded a treaty of friendship and cooperation in Moscow (November 3) even while Chinese First Deputy Premier Teng Hsiao-ping, whom many were coming to regard as the real "boss" of the People's Republic, was setting out on a tour of non-Communist Southeast Asia that obviously aimed at countering Soviet diplomatic efforts in the area. Vietnam, meanwhile, was stepping up its military pressure on Cambodia—China's ally—and, on December 3, announced the formation under its sponsorship of a full-fledged Cambodian national liberation front, the "Kampuchean United Front for National Salvation" under Heng Samrin. With the support of a Vietnamese invasion force, this organization was actually to supplant Cambo-

[140]Joint press statement, Aug. 4, in *Bulletin,* Sept. 1978: 25.

dia's Pol Pot regime in nominal control of the country during the first days of 1979.

Paradoxically, these quarrels created a favoring atmosphere for the "normalization" of bilateral relations which had become a leading objective of both the American and the mainland Chinese governments. Encouraged by what seemed an increasingly liberal attitude in Peking in regard to economic and even political matters, American businessmen did not disguise their eagerness for large-scale trade expansion and for opportunities to invest in China's economic modernization. Concurrently, the U.S. Government intensified its efforts toward an understanding on the ways and means of "normalizing" the official relationship between the two powers. On President Carter's instructions, U.S. views in this regard were conveyed to the Chinese by Ambassador Woodcock in a series of five meetings that began early in the summer and concluded on November 4, by which time the Ambassador was able to suggest the possibility of a January 1, 1979 target date for consummation of the normalization process.[141]

President Carter himself received the new Chinese liaison representative in Washington, Ambassador Ch'ai Tse-min, on September 19 and, according to the official accounts, made clear that U.S. concerns about the future well-being of the people of Taiwan would have to be met if normalization efforts were to succeed. Specifically, the United States throughout the negotiations took the position that (1) it would not abrogate its 1954 mutual defense treaty with the Republic of China in advance of normalization, as Peking demanded, but *would* give the required one-year notice of its intent to terminate the treaty in such a way that it would formally expire, under its own terms, on December 31, 1979; (2) Peking should offer reliable assurances that it would not attempt to take Taiwan by force; and (3) the United States must be able to maintain a wide range of nongovernmental relations with the people on Taiwan, including the continued sale, "on a restrained basis," of defensive weapons.

Unwilling to accept these conditions as they stood, the Chinese Communists nevertheless proved helpful in finding a way around them. "After further negotiations," says an official U.S. account, "Ambassador Woodcock was invited to meet with Vice Premier Teng Hsiao-ping on December 13. This was the crucial meeting. The Vice Premier indicated that the P.R.C. was prepared to normalize on the basis of a position acceptable to the United States.

---

[141]U.S. Department of State, Bureau of Public Affairs, Office of Public Communication, *News Release,* cited in note 137; same, *China: Special Briefing on Normalization of Relations with the People's Republic of China (Current Policy,* No. 52, Jan. 1979): 4. Fuller documentation appears in same, *U.S. Policy Toward China, July 15, 1971–January 15, 1979 (Selected Documents,* No. 9, Jan. 1979).

After further discussion, the two sides agreed on the December 15 announcement."[142]

The joint communiqué of December 15—which stated that the two governments had agreed to recognize each other, to establish diplomatic relations as of January 1, 1979, and to exchange ambassadors and establish embassies on March 1, 1979—was presented to the American public by President Carter in a television address **(Document 39a)** in which he also revealed that Vice-Premier Teng had accepted an invitation to visit Washington at the end of January 1979, thus affording the two governments an opportunity to consult on global issues and "begin working together to enhance the cause of world peace."

" . . . We will continue to have an interest in the peaceful resolution of the Taiwan issue," the President emphasized. "I have paid special attention to ensuring that normalization of relations between our country and the People's Repubic will not jeopardize the well-being of the people of Taiwan. The people of our country will maintain our current commercial, cultural, trade, and other relations with Taiwan through nongovernmental means. Many other countries in the world are already successfully doing this."

Additional details were provided in a special U.S. Government statement **(Document 39b)** which noted, among other things, that the remaining U.S. military personnel in Taiwan would be withdrawn within a period of four months. Conversing with reporters after his speech **(Document 39c)**, the President appeared confident that the actions taken would have the understanding both of the Soviet Union and of U.S. congressional leaders—whose initial response had, he admitted, been "mixed"—and that everything possible would be done to assure the people of Taiwan of the United States' continued concern for their "well-being."

The nature of the understandings reached with regard to Taiwan was further clarified by an official Chinese government statement **(Document 39d)** and by subsequent official comment in both countries.[143] Peking, admittedly, had refused to go along with the United States' declared opposition to the use of force against Taiwan, which was embodied in a unilateral declaration that the United States "continues to have an interest in the peaceful resolution of the Taiwan issue and expects that the Taiwan issue will be settled peacefully by the Chinese themselves." China's reunification—i.e., the reunification of Taiwan with the mainland—was, Peking insisted, "entirely China's internal affair." Nevertheless, the fact that the Communist Chinese government refrained from explicitly contradicting the U.S. statement was interpreted by the United States as tacit acquiescence in its position.

[142]*News Release*, cited in note 137: 2.
[143]Department of State sources as previously cited.

With regard to the continued sale of defensive weapons to Taiwan, Premier Hua Kuo-feng asserted on December 16 that China definitely did *not* agree with the American stand, although it had not allowed the matter to prevent the issuance of the joint communiqué. Later it was revealed that the United States had actually promised that it would conclude no new arms deals with Taiwan until the mutual defense treaty expired at the end of 1979.[144]

"I doubt if there will be massive applause in Taiwan," President Carter conceded after his December 15 announcement **(Document 39c).** In fact, he may well have been taken aback by the scathing character of the Republic of China's official comment **(Document 39e).** The U.S. decision, Taiwan declared, "has not only damaged the rights and interests of the Government and the people of the Republic of China, but has also had a tremendously adverse impact upon the entire free world. . . . the United States Government cannot be expected to have the confidence of any free nation in the future." Not dissimilar was the reaction of such conservative U.S. legislators as Senator Barry Goldwater of Arizona, who joined with other members of Congress in seeking judicial intervention to bar termination of the mutual defense treaty without congressional consent. Soviet reaction, as already recounted,[145] also appeared less understanding than the President had hoped, though Moscow showed no disposition to resort to the kind of threats it had sometimes used on past occasions involving China.

It fell to Deputy Secretary of State Christopher to visit a distinctly hostile Taiwan at the end of December in a not very successful attempt to lay foundations for the projected new era of intense (but unofficial) friendly intercourse between the people of Taiwan and those of the United States. As one step in this direction, the President on December 30 addressed a memorandum to all U.S. Government departments and agencies **(Document 40).** Citing a contemplated request for legislation relative to "non-governmental relationships between the American people and the people on Taiwan," he indicated that U.S. interests in this respect would be represented, as appropriate, by "an unofficial instrumentality in corporate form, to be identified shortly." This was the American Institute in Taiwan which was to be set up under legislation enacted early in 1979.

*   *   *

Elsewhere in East and Southeast Asia, the year-end situation remained mixed and, in part, distinctly volatile. Thanks to the *rapprochement* between Japan and China, however, the United States could currently enjoy the unusual luxury of good relations with

[144]Washington dispatch, Jan. 12, in *New York Times,* Jan. 13, 1979.
[145]Cf. above at note 33.

both of those countries. In addition, Tokyo's efforts to reduce the Japanese export surplus, in conjunction with Washington's moves to support the dollar, had drawn at least a part of the tension from the Japanese-American economic relationship. Masayoshi Ohira, who succeeded Mr. Fukuda as Prime Minister early in December, might consequently face a situation slightly easier than that with which his predecessor had grappled.

Americans would have been more than human if they had not felt some measure of satisfaction in contrasting the relatively peaceful and progressive condition of Southeast Asia's non-Communist states—"the dominoes that did not fall," as they were sometimes called—with the internecine quarreling of their country's former Communist adversaries in Indochina. Aside from the serious dangers inseparable from further hostilities in that area, however, no one could fail to be dismayed by the plight of the ever-growing masses of refugees, whose swelling number had recently prompted a U.S. decision to admit another 17,500 of the Vietnamese "boat people," together with a total of 4,375 Cambodians.[146] Such numbers, alas, bore little relation to the real dimensions of the problem.

A more cheerful year-end note was the announcement that the United States and the Philippines, after more than two years' negotiations, had reached an agreement that would assure the United States unhampered use of Clark Air Base and the Subic Bay naval complex, in return for up to $500 million in U.S. aid over a five-year period—substantially less than had reportedly been offered by the previous administration.[147]

8. AMERICA AND THE WORLD ECONOMY

It was a truism of the 1970s that while military and security issues were tending to lose their former preeminence in world affairs, economic questions were coming to exert an ever more decisive influence on the relations among nations. This view might seem a trifle exaggerated to those who noted Washington's intense preoccupation with the nuclear arms race, the European military balance, the Soviet-Cuban penetration in Africa, and the military budget for the coming fiscal year. It was a fact, however, that economic considerations played a highly significant, if not a decisive, role in the United

[146]U.S. Department of State, Bureau of Public Affairs, "Indochina Refugees" (GIST Series, Feb. 1979).
[147]*New York Times*, Jan. 1, 1979.

States' relations with its friends and allies of the industrial world, with the U.S.S.R. and Eastern Europe, with the newly receptive People's Republic of China, and, possibly most of all, with the predominantly "have-not," "less developed" countries óf the so-called third world.

Two major purposes had visibly dominated America's foreign economic policy throughout the period since World War II. The first and fundamental one had been to promote the economic welfare and prosperity of the United States in its interaction with the rest of the world; the second, to alleviate hardship and, so far as possible, promote prosperity abroad, in part for humanitarian reasons but primarily as a means of fostering a world political and economic climate favorable to U.S. interests. In the early postwar years, these two concerns had seemed to reinforce each other, since economic recovery abroad had demonstrably redounded to the economic benefit of the United States as well. More recently, such factors as the recovery and consolidation of Western Europe, industrial development in third world countries, the economic distortions associated with the war in Indochina, and the major increase in world petroleum prices had led to a more complicated situation in which short-term and long-term, domestic and foreign economic considerations did not invariably appear to point in the same direction.

A Forward Look

The opening year of President Carter's administration had been, for the United States, a time of somewhat uneven recovery from the 1974–75 recession. Among its features had been a 4.9 percent increase in real gross national product, a reduction in unemployment from 7.9 to 6.4 percent of the civilian labor force, a 6.8 percent increase in consumer prices, and a 17.2 percent decline in the stock market values registered by the Dow Jones Industrial Average. It was in foreign economic policy that the United States had made its least effective showing. Largely because of its continuing and even increased reliance on high-priced foreign oil, the nation's chronic trade deficit had widened to a record $26.7 billion, while the overall balance of payments on current account had been in deficit by $15.3 billion and the dollar had undergone a precipitous decline, particularly in the latter part of the year, that had evoked expressions of alarm from many parts of the world.

Admitting that there was need for prompt and vigorous action to reverse these trends, President Carter late in 1977 had promised to submit to Congress a comprehensive economic program which, in conjunction with the energy legislation he had recommended as far back as April 1977, would "underscore our commitment to a strong and sound U.S. economy."[148] A $25 billion tax cut, coupled with modest tax reforms, voluntary wage and price restraints, and enactment of the energy legislation, was the principal recommendation presented in Mr. Carter's State of the Union address of January 19, 1978.[149] "Economic success at home," the President said, "is also the key to success in our international economic policy. An effective energy program, strong investment and productivity, and controlled inflation will provide [improve] our trade balance and balance it, and it will help to protect the integrity of the dollar overseas."

A more detailed account of Washington's preoccupations in the international economic arena was provided in the President's annual message on the Economic Report, submitted to Congress on January 20 (Document 41). Although the United States' recovery from the recession was by this time virtually complete, the President pointed out, recovery had lagged severely in most other countries, and low growth rates, high and even rising unemployment, and severe inflation still prevailed among America's major trading partners.[150] In addition, he noted, the world economy continued to be strained by imbalances in the international economic system, in part because the surpluses accumulated by oil-exporting countries had led to sizable deficits in many other countries, including the United States. Some of the industrial nations, the President observed, in what seemed an obvious reference to West Germany and Japan, were also running large and persistent surpluses; and the resultant imbalances had been "a major factor contributing to disorder in exchange markets in recent months."

"The condition of the international economy requires above all that nations work together to develop mutually beneficial solutions to global problems," Mr. Carter emphasized. " . . . It is important that other strong nations join with us to take direct actions to spur demand within their own economies. World recovery cannot proceed if nations rely upon exports as the principal source of economic expansion." Here again, West Germany and Japan were the obvious targets. "At the same time," the President added, "all countries must continue the battle against inflation. . . . "

Several parallel steps were needed to reduce the existing imbalances in international payments, according to President Carter. The United States could take "a most constructive step . . . by moving quickly to enact the National Energy Plan." Surplus countries—again, he seemed to be thinking primarily of West Germany and Japan—could appropriately stimulate the growth of domestic

[148]Statement of Dec. 21, 1977, in *AFR, 1977:* 453.
[149]*Presidential Documents,* 14: 91-4; partial text in Document 2.
[150]*Presidential Documents,* 14: 129.

demand and, in Japan's case at least, lift restraints on imports and reduce "excessive government efforts to promote exports." In addition, Mr. Carter promised, the United States intended to do its part in promoting the success of the system of flexible exchange rates introduced in recent years. Washington, he said, remained ready "to step in when conditions become disorderly and to work in close cooperation with our friends abroad in this effort." The United States, he noted, also stood behind the pending proposal to strengthen the capabilities of the International Monetary Fund (IMF) through the establishment of a new multibillion-dollar Supplementary Financing Facility—the so-called Witteveen Facility—to assist countries with special balance-of-payments problems.

Referring briefly to the United States' determination to contribute to the economic growth of developing countries, the President passed on to what was to be in many ways the central international economic preoccupation of 1978, the projected windup of the Multilateral Trade Negotiations at Geneva, initiated as far back as 1973 under the auspices of the General Agreement on Tariffs and Trade (GATT). Working with our trading partners to protect a free and open trading system was "a keystone of our international economic policy," Mr. Carter averred, and the United States would be firm in its resistance to demands for protection as well as to unfair trade practices. "The importance of these discussions [at Geneva] can hardly be overemphasized," the President declared. "The trading system that emerges . . . will set the tone for international commerce well into the 1980s. Our commitment to a successful conclusion to these talks underscores our long-term emphasis on the retention and expansion of open and fair trade among nations."

Plea for Foreign Aid

Though mentioned only in passing in the President's economic message, the Carter administration was also well aware of the important position occupied by the 120 or so developing countries in the economic life of the contemporary world. Secretary Vance touched on some of the relevant statistics in an address on "Foreign Assistance and U.S. Policy," delivered before the national convention of the League of Women Voters in Cincinnati on May 1 (**Document 42**). In the preceding year, Mr. Vance pointed out, non-oil-producing developing countries had actually absorbed one-fourth of all U.S. exports, and products from developing countries had accounted for nearly one-fourth of U.S. imports. The proceeds of direct American private investment in the developing world had amounted to over $7 billion in 1975, and such investment had continued at a rate of nearly $11 billion in 1976. Developing countries, moreover, were purchasing 50 to 70 percent of U.S. exports of cotton, wheat, and rice, as well as substantially benefiting the U.S. economy through the spending of aid dollars on U.S. commodities and services. In summary, Secretary Vance asserted, the economic health and the security of the United States were "more closely tied than ever before" to the economic well-being of the developing world.

The converse, moreover, seemed equally true. For many developing countries, Mr. Vance pointed out, "the most critical international factors in their growth and development are our policies toward trade, investment, commodities, and technology. Our economic aid, as well as that provided by other developed nations, also makes a crucial contribution to their well-being. For some countries—particularly the low-income nations—it is the principal source of foreign exchange and technical assistance. But for many others, it serves as an essential complement to other components of their development strategy."

Convinced in advance of the vital importance of helping to maintain the rhythm of development in less privileged parts of the world, the Carter administration had come to office with plans for dramatically stepped-up American participation in this effort. But here as elsewhere, its ambitions had had to be curtailed as it encountered the facts of economic life, accentuated in this instance by what amounted to a tradition of national indifference to foreign aid questions. Far from expanding in response to perceived needs, the scale of American participation in international development financing had actually been contracting year after year. "Clearly, we are not shouldering a disproportionate burden of global aid flows," Secretary Vance told the League of Women Voters. "While in absolute terms the U.S. aid program is larger than that of any other nation, as a percentage of GNP we rank in the bottom 25% of all non-Communist country donors. . . . And as a percentage of the Federal budget for 1979, our economic assistance is only 1.4%. Adding our security assistance programs does not increase this figure substantially."

President Carter's budget request for the 1979 fiscal year, the first to fully reflect the policies and priorities of the new administration, had done little to alter this situation. Although the $8.4 billion he was requesting for foreign assistance substantially exceeded the $6.8 billion appropriated the previous year, the new figure included, in addition to straight economic assistance, a total of $2.7 billion in military and security supporting assistance, largely in the Middle East; $835 million in overdue contributions to the International Development Association and other international financial institutions; and some $1.4 billion in government guarantees or "callable capital" that would not result in actual spending. Not included in the $8.4 billion total was a proposed $1.4 billion in Food for Peace aid to be allocated in the coming year.

Within these overall limitations, Secretary Vance could point to a number of pending innovations in the management and direction of the aid program. A sweeping reorganization, proposed by the late Senator Humphrey shortly before his death in January, was already pending before the Congress, where its basic purposes, if not its details, had been assured the support of the Carter administration. In the meantime, Secretary Vance noted, the administration had taken steps to improve coordination among existing aid agencies and bureaus; had begun to focus its assistance efforts more directly on meeting the necessities of the poorest countries, and on responding so far as possible to such "basic human needs" as nutrition, shelter, education, and health care; and had endeavored to grapple with the admittedly complex problem of linking foreign aid allocations to the human rights performance of recipient countries.

Secretary Vance did not address himself on this occasion to the broader aspects of the "North-South dialogue" between developed and developing countries, evolved in recent years in such forums as the U.N. Conference on Trade and Development (UNCTAD) and the Conference on International Economic Cooperation (CIEC). From an American standpoint, the developing countries' ideologically charged insistence on a "new international economic order," their emotional demands for a commodity stabilization fund, blanket debt relief, and permanent trade preferences, represented more of an impediment than an aid to fruitful cooperation in the development process. Some of these problems would, however, undoubtedly surface at the United Nations and elsewhere as the year continued.

Nor could the Secretary of State anticipate in detail the changes that Congress would introduce when it came to act upon the President's foreign aid recommendations. As matters turned out, the total appropriation for foreign assistance and related programs in fiscal 1979, as voted by Congress and signed by the President on October 18,[151] amounted to $9.2 billion, more than the President's original request. This figure, however, included $1.8 billion for the new IMF Supplementary Financing (Witteveen) Facility, while other presidential recommendations were actually cut by some $1.25 billion. A separate and potentially most damaging congressional action, to be explained in the next chapter, was the passage of other legislation that blocked all U.S. funding for U.N. technical assistance programs and, potentially, for other U.N. programs as well.[152]

[151]Foreign Assistance and Related Programs Appropriations, 1979 (Public Law 95–481).
[152]Cf. Chapter 9 at note 190.

Meeting of the OECD

That the management of the world economy required close and constant collaboration among the leading industrial nations had come to be generally acknowledged by the middle of the 1970s. Within the 24-nation Organization for Economic Cooperation and Development (OECD), the Bank for International Settlements (BIS), and other multilateral bodies, these nations were by now engaged in virtually continuous economic dialogue, punctuated at intervals by special meetings at the ministerial or heads of government level. Important among the recurring occasions of this kind was the annual meeting at ministerial level of the OECD Council, which took place as usual in Paris on June 14–15, 1978, with Secretaries Vance and Blumenthal speaking for the United States. Like the preceding Council session in 1977, the meeting could also be regarded as a "warmup" for the seven-nation "economic summit" scheduled for later in the same season.

The condition of the international economy as 1978 approached its midpoint afforded few grounds for rejoicing, as Secretary Vance acknowledged frankly in his statement to the OECD meeting (**Document 43a**). "We meet in a time when unemployment remains high, when inflation recedes too slowly, when payment imbalances remain large, and the development problems of poorer countries persist," he said. " . . . The challenge before us now is to go beyond keeping our heads above water, to develop a coordinated program that will return our economies to a pattern of sustained economic growth."

The United States itself had experienced renewed misgivings in recent weeks as the pace of economic recovery began to slacken, trade deficits accumulated, and inflation quickened to a point where it overshadowed even the unemployment problem as a source of official concern. With President Carter's energy program still bottled up in Congress and the thirteen-member Organization of Petroleum Exporting Countries (OPEC) debating still another price increase (but eventually postponing it, at the insistence of Saudi Arabia and Iran, until at least the beginning of 1979), the dollar had continued its sickening slide against the Japanese yen and other major world currencies, reaching a record low of 216.20 yen to the dollar on the very eve of the OECD meeting.

Concern about inflation and the trade deficit had already prompted the United States to turn thumbs down on an OECD Secretariat plan for concerted economic expansion by OECD member nations during the coming year. "Our situations are different," Secretary Vance pointed out in his Paris statement. Each country, he said, must act "in a way compatible with our national circumstances but consistent with our shared objectives." The major task for the United States, according to Mr. Vance, was "to reduce its dependence on imported oil and to control inflation.'' Promotion of faster growth, on the other hand, was a matter for "countries which have trade surpluses and relatively low inflation.'' All member countries, the Secretary of State insisted, should "support positive steps to expand trade and strengthen the trading systems"; and they should also join in strengthening relations with the developing countries and fashioning policies "in our mutual interest.''

Having listened to this and other statements, the participating ministers agreed that the most suitable objective for their countries was still the one enunciated in 1976: "a moderate but sustained rate of expansion, sufficient to achieve a progressive return to full employment over a number of years, but not so fast as to risk the re-emergence of bottlenecks and an upsurge of inflationary expectations.'' Basic to the "programme of concerted action" developed to this end—and set forth in the final communiqué of the meeting (**Document 43b**)—was a recognition of the need for "differentiated action on various fronts" by individual member states. Germany, Japan, and several others (Belgium, Canada, France, Italy, Switzerland, and the United Kingdom) were urged to ensure that the expansion of domestic demand in their countries was "significantly greater than in 1977.'' Most other member states, in contrast, were advised to "concentrate primarily on reducing inflation and improving their balance-of-payments position.'' "It is particularly important,'' said the communiqué, "that the recent acceleration of inflation in the *United States* should be reversed"—a sentiment with which few Americans would have disagreed.

Convinced that "firm commitments to maintain an open market-oriented economic system" were essential to the success of their program, the OECD ministers also renewed their countries' 1974 pledge to avoid restrictive trade measures, at the same time affirming their determination to bring the Multilateral Trade Negotiations to a successful outcome in the near future. Stressing the role of strengthened energy policies in the concerted action program, they also pointed to the "decisive importance that the United States should complete the adoption of a comprehensive energy policy . . . as soon as possible.'' Other points of agreement had to do with the continuance of close cooperation in the international monetary field and with "increased and more effective support" of accelerated economic and social development in the developing countries.

The Bonn Summit

Detailed elaboration of the strategic concept offered by the OECD Council would necessarily await the meeting of the heads of state and government of the principal industrial nations at the "economic summit" to be held in Bonn on July 16–17. Meeting in the West German capital at the invitation of Chancellor Schmidt, this would be the fourth in the series of encounters initiated in 1975, and, in this instance, was to coincide with a visit by the American President to the Federal Republic of Germany and West Berlin. Participating, in addition to Chancellor Schmidt and President Carter, would be Prime Minister Trudeau of Canada, President Giscard d'Estaing of France, Prime Minister Andreotti of Italy, Prime Minister Fukuda of Japan, Prime Minister Callaghan of the United Kingdom, and another Britisher, Roy Jenkins, in his capacity as President of the Commission of the European Communities.

The economic outlook had not improved significantly in the weeks preceding the Bonn discussions. With inflation now at an average rate of 8.8 percent in the OECD area as a whole, that organization's economists were already predicting slower growth and higher unemployment, together with higher prices, in 1979. In the United States, the President's $25 billion tax cut and tax reform plan had already been whittled down in consequence of the inflationary upsurge, and expectations now centered around a $15 billion tax cut with little or no reform. Although U.S. officials had lately found indications of what looked like a slight decrease in U.S. oil consumption and imports, the President's energy package was still tied up in Congress, and foreign criticism of U.S. dilatoriness in this respect was mounting steadily.

Two major developments on the international economic front also occurred during this pre-summit period. At Bremen on July 6–7, the leaders of the nine-nation European Communities agreed—with reservations on the part of Messrs. Callaghan and Andreotti—to set up by the end of the year a new European Monetary System (EMS) that would feature a joint currency "float" in relation to the dollar and a $50 billion European Monetary Fund to serve as a hedge against speculative attacks. At Geneva, on July 13, the twenty developed countries among the 98 participants in the Multilateral Trade Negotiations announced their agreement on a "framework of understanding" which reflected a resolution of many of the outstanding issues and would, it was hoped, permit the windup of the negotiations by December 15 so that the resultant agreements could be presented to the U.S. Congress early in 1979.

This development, in turn, reduced the area of possible discord at the Bonn summit, whose participants had in any case decided to adopt a low-keyed approach in the hope of avoiding too obvious an airing of their disagreements. The elements of a possible compromise between the United States and Germany, as leading protagonists of more or less opposing economic viewpoints, had in fact been visible for several months. Germany, so the theory ran, could be persuaded to accept a modest amount of domestic expansion if the United States would move effectively to curb inflation and reduce its oil imports. An understanding along these lines at Bonn in fact unlocked the doors to what was eventually hailed as an unexpectedly successful meeting.

The principal results of the discussions at Bonn were embodied in a concluding Declaration (**Document 44**) purporting, once again, to set forth "a comprehensive strategy covering growth, employment and inflation, international monetary policy, energy, trade and other issues of particular interest to developing countries." Unlike the concluding statements promulgated at earlier summits, this one reported in precise and quantitative detail the commitments undertaken by the various national participants. West Germany, for instance, promised to recommend additional stimulative measures up to 1 percent of its gross national product, or roughly $6 billion, while other surplus countries reported or promised similar actions of varying magnitude.

President Carter, for his part, described in detail the actions being taken by the United States to curb inflation. Possibly even more important, he promised to have in place by the end of the year both a "comprehensive policy framework" on energy and a set of specific measures that would lead, by 1985, to a reduction of 2.5 million barrels in daily oil imports. In addition, he agreed that the U.S. domestic price of petroleum would rise to the world level by the end of 1980. Responding to European apprehensions about the United States' new Nuclear Non-proliferation Act, the President also expressed his intention to "use the full powers of his office to prevent any interruption of enriched uranium supply and to ensure that existing agreements will be respected."

Japan, too, responded to the demand for specific pledges. Not only was his country trying hard to meet its existing 7 percent growth target, said Prime Minister Fukuda; the Japanese government was also anxious to facilitate imports, was urging "moderation" in Japanese exports, and would "strive to double Japan's official development assistance in three years."

Renewing their commitment to "the open international trading system," the summit conferees called in addition for successful completion of the Geneva negotiations by December 15; promised an increased flow of financial assistance and other resources to developing countries, "particularly those most in need"; pledged continued intervention in foreign exchange markets "to the extent necessary to counter disorderly conditions"; instructed their representatives to convene by the end of 1978 in order to review the Declaration; and indicated that there would be another summit meeting at an appropriate time in 1979.

"I can tell you in complete candor," said President Carter on his return to the White House, "that our allies in other nations were willing to make economic sacrifices for the good of us all, so that we might sell out own products more successfully, that we might have in that way more jobs for the people of this country. We made promises also that I intend to keep: to hold down inflation and to meet the greatest single concern of others, . . . the excessive waste of energy in this country and the excessive imports of foreign oil. . . . We have some problems that we've addressed very thoroughly. But overall our feeling was one of confidence, of mutual purpose, of the willingness to address the difficult issues without timidity and without fear."[153]

Reassuring the Bank and Fund

Next on America's economic and financial calendar was the annual meeting of the Boards of Governors of the International Bank for Reconstruction and Development (IBRD) and the International Monetary Fund (IMF), two U.N.-related institutions that continued to play a central and indispensable role amid the proliferation of new financial and economic instrumentalities. Having successfully come through the international monetary storms of the early 1970s, the IMF under its Dutch Managing Director, H. Johannes Witteveen, had lately been strengthened by a one-third increase in the resources contributed by member governments[154] and was now preparing to expand its services to financially hard-pressed countries through the new, $10 billion "Witteveen Facility" or Supplementary Financing Facility, which currently awaited governmental approval. In the meantime, the IMF Interim Committee, meeting in Mexico City on April 29–30, had decided to recommend a further, 50 percent increase in IMF quotas, an allocation of some $15 billion in IMF special drawing rights (SDRs) over a three-year period, and the appointment of France's Jacques de Larosière to succeed Dr. Witteveen as Managing Director on the latter's retirement later in the year.[155]

In addition, the Interim Committee had agreed in principle on the desirability of an increase of roughly $30 billion, or nearly 100 percent, in the capital resources of the World Bank, whose American President, Robert S. McNamara, was perhaps the world's most indefatigable advocate of massive aid to third world economic development. Surveying the record of the past quarter-century, Mr. McNamara had lately pointed to some highly significant gains. At the same time, he had predicted little reduction during the rest of the century in the incidence of what he described as "absolute poverty"—i.e., "a condition of life so characterized by malnutrition, illiteracy, disease, squalid surroundings, high infant mortality, and

[153]*Presidential Documents* 14: 1316.
[154]"The increase in IMF quotas and the Second Amendment to the IMF Articles of Agreement entered into force Apr. 1, 1978 (*IMF Survey*, 7: 97–106, Apr. 3, 1978).
[155]Same: 134–6 (May 8, 1978).

low life expectancy as to be beneath any reasonable definition of human decency."[156]

As previously noted, the task of the IBRD and of its affiliated institutions, particularly the International Development Association (IDA), had been complicated of late by the failure of the U.S. Congress to authorize and appropriate funds already pledged by the executive branch. But President Carter had some good news to offer the assembled Governors, representing some 135 nations, as they began their proceedings in Washington on September 25. "I might report to you," he said in his address of welcome (**Document 45**), "that this year, the attitude of the United States Congress is better than it has been in my own memory toward supporting international financial institutions and toward foreign aid as well. . . . Last week, the United States Senate, as the House of Representatives had already done, met our Nation's obligations for both multilateral and bilateral aid beyond, I must admit, my own expectations."[157]

The President's other references to current congressional business suggested the degree to which the policy of the United States and, indeed, the world's financial outlook had become dependent on the judgment of American legislators. "I'm pleased that legislative consideration of U.S. participation in the supplementary financing facility is nearing completion," Mr. Carter said. "I expect final action to be taken shortly." (This authorization, and the necessary appropriation, were in fact accorded within the next few days[158] in what was to be a major step toward the activation of the new facility in February 1979.)

Of even more critical importance, both to the United States and to the world at large, was the status of the long-pending energy legislation, the prompt enactment of which was clearly necessary if the President's commitments at Bonn were to be implemented. While Congress continued its backing and filling in the weeks that followed the Bonn summit, the dollar had entered upon a further precipitous decline, apparently unaffected by new reports that U.S. oil imports in the first half of 1978 had actually declined by as much as 12.8 percent—and that consumption had increased by only 2.4 percent—as compared with the corresponding period of 1977.[159] Although the dollar's fall had been temporarily arrested by use of the technical expedients available to the Treasury and the Federal

---

[156]Quoted in *Christian Science Monitor*, Aug. 16, 1978.
[157]The President referred to the passage of the Foreign Assistance and Related Programs Appropriations Act, 1979 (Public Law 95–481, Oct. 18, 1978).
[158]Authorization provided by Public Law 95–435, Oct. 10, 1978; for the appropriation cf. above at note 151.
[159]*New York Times*, July 19, 1978.

Reserve Board, enactment of the energy program had by this time come to be everywhere regarded as an acid test of the United States' ability to retrieve its position in the world.

"I've also intensified my efforts, which were already great," President Carter told the IBRD-IMF meeting, "to obtain legislation that will curtail United States imports of oil, imports which are entirely too high. The United States Senate is scheduled to vote this week . . . on the key bill, natural gas regulation and pricing. This is one of the most complicated and difficult and challenging assignments that the United States Congress has ever faced. . . . I hope to have other bills comprising a strong package of energy legislation enacted before the Congress adjourns, probably, hopefully, less than a month from now."

The President made still other points in his attempt to prove United States determination to carry out the pledges made at Bonn, "on my own word of honor and on behalf of the people of the United States." Mr. Carter would, he said, announce in the near future "the first phase of a long-term program to expand American exports." He also intended "very shortly to announce a further series of important and specific and tough measures to strengthen our fight against inflation." Determined as he was "to maintain a sound dollar," he further promised support for a new increase in IMF quotas, a new allocation of special drawing rights, and "a growing international effort to eliminate the worst aspects of human poverty." "I reiterate my Nation's commitment to the common effort that is required," the President declared. "I am confident that this joint effort will succeed."

Secretary Blumenthal continued the reassurance exercise on the following day. Lower inflation, reduced oil imports, and increased exports, he said, should combine to decrease the U.S. balance-of-payments deficit in 1979 by as much as 30 to 40 percent as compared with the admittedly large deficit in prospect for 1978. As on other occasions, Secretary Blumenthal also sought to dispel the notion that the United States might be heading for an economic recession.

Such assurances were heard with respectful attention by the other finance ministers, whose sense of the need for a concerted, worldwide economic strategy appeared to be intensified by the Washington deliberations. The principal concrete results of the meeting were agreements (subject to governmental approval) on a 50 percent increase in IMF quotas, which would increase general Fund resources to SDR 58.6 billion or about $73.0 billion and would increase the U.S. quota to $14.66 billion; new allocations of SDRs to a total of 21.3 billion, more than doubling the number in existence; and "widespread affirmation" that the coordinated economic strategy adopted in April would yield improvements in the world economy in 1979 and 1980.[160]

Exports, Oil, and Dollars

The first among the actions promised by President Carter in his IBRD-IMF address occurred the very next day, September 26, with the issuance of a formal presidential statement on "United States Export Policy" **(Document 46)**. Drawn up by a special task force headed by Secretary of Commerce Juanita Kreps, this somewhat controversial document set forth a number of innovations designed to gain a larger slice of the world market for U.S. exports through increased direct assistance to U.S. exporters, reduction of domestic barriers to exports, and reduction of foreign barriers to U.S. exports within a fairer international trading system. In addition to increased export financing, a more vigorous promotional effort, and a renewed assault on other countries' unfair trade practices, it called for clarification and lenient interpretation by the United States of regulatory standards, foreign policy criteria, and antibribery, antitrust, and environmental provisions which might "unnecessarily inhibit our firms from selling abroad."

Another accomplishment of this eventful week was the Senate's passage of a compromise natural gas bill resolving, at long last, the most controversial of the issues holding up adoption of the energy program. Although the leading feature of the bill—the gradual lifting of price controls on newly produced gas over a period ending in 1985—was not what President Carter had wanted, almost anything now seemed preferable to further uncertainty and delay. In the House, the natural gas bill was considered in conjunction with a cluster of other bills relating to conservation, utility rates, taxes, and conversion to coal, all of which were cleared by the two houses before the adjournment of Congress on October 15 and were signed by the President on November 9.[161]

Admittedly, essential features of the President's original energy program were lacking from the legislative package thus enacted. Particularly conspicuous was the absence of the so-called "wellhead" tax on domestically produced crude oil, which was supposed to help in raising the domestic price to the world price level. Without this feature, it was difficult to see how the President's Bonn commitment "that the prices paid for oil in the U.S. shall be raised to the world level by the end of 1980"[162] was to be implemented.

[160]*IMF Survey,* 7: 305 ff. (Oct. 2, 1978).

[161]Public Utility Regulatory Policies Act of 1978; Energy Tax Act of 1978; National Energy Conservation Policy Act; Powerplant and Industrial Fuel Use Act of 1978; Natural Gas Policy Act of 1978 (Public Laws 95–617 to 95–621 inclusive, Nov. 9, 1978).

[162]Document 44, para. 7.

Although there seemed good hope of achieving the Bonn target of "oil import savings of approximately 2.5 million barrels per day by 1985,"[163] that target itself fell short of the original plan to reduce consumption by 4.6 million barrels per day and slash imports to less than 6 million barrels per day.[164] "This is not the end of the road, but it is a beginning, and an important one," said President Carter. "We have declared to ourselves and the world our intent to control our use of energy and thereby to control our own destiny as a nation."[165]

Another necessary step in regaining control over the national destiny was the adoption of an effective anti-inflation program such as the President had promised at the IBRD-IMF meeting. The somewhat meager results of another four weeks' deliberation were laid before the nation and the world in a presidential "fireside chat" on October 24.[166] Acknowledging that neither he nor anyone else had "all the answers," Mr. Carter offered a conglomerate of measures that featured governmental economy, deferment of further tax cuts, and voluntary wage and price restraints designed to limit wage increases to a maximum of 7 percent a year and hold price increases to an average of 5¾ percent. "This approach I've outlined will not end inflation," the President admitted. "It simply improves our chances of making it better rather than worse."

This modest claim, and the modest measures that accompanied it, proved quite inadequate to stem the adverse tides that had been mounting as the world awaited the President's declaration. "Fear and confusion have struck the world's financial markets," wrote Ron Scherer in *The Christian Science Monitor* a few days later. "The dollar, the stock market, and the credit markets have all shuddered in the last few weeks as if trying to take in an outlook that is as unfriendly as a cold winter sky. . . . The US dollar, long the major reserve currency of the world, in recent days has plunged sharply in alarmed foreign exchange markets despite massive efforts by the European central banks to keep the markets orderly. . . ." [167] From early August to the end of October, the dollar in fact fell by 18 percent against the West German mark, 17 percent against the Swiss franc, 10 percent against the French franc, 8 percent against the British pound, and 7 percent against the Japanese yen.[168]

Appreciating the dangers of letting this decline continue, U.S. authorities made contact with their counterparts abroad and, by

---

[163]Same.
[164]White House fact sheet, Apr. 20, 1977, in *Presidential Documents*, 13: 574 (1977).
[165]Oct. 15 statement, in same, 14: 1784.
[166]Same: 1839–45.
[167]*Christian Science Monitor,* Nov. 1.
[168]Interim report by the Federal Reserve Bank of New York, in *Federal Reserve Bulletin,* Dec. 1978: 940.

the end of October, had worked out with the latter "the essential elements of a coordinated approach to correct the situation."[169] "The continuing decline in the exchange value of the dollar is clearly not warranted by the fundamental economic situation," said President Carter as he and Secretary Blumenthal disclosed the new decisions to reporters on the morning of November 1 (**Document 47**). "That decline threatens economic progress at home and abroad and the success of our anti-inflation program. As a major step in the anti-inflation program, it is now necessary to act to correct the excessive decline in the dollar which has recently occurred."

Conspicuous among the specific measures listed by Secretary Blumenthal, many of them highly technical in character, were (1) a further tightening of monetary policy, including a one-point increase in the Federal Reserve discount rate to an historic high of 9½ percent; and (2) the assembling of a $30 billion package of German, Japanese, and Swiss currencies, put together with the cooperation of the central banks of those countries and the IMF, to finance the U.S. contribution to coordinated intervention in exchange markets by the four countries.

This show of determination, backed by vigorous action by authorities of the four countries over the next few days, produced conspicuous effects. "The dollar rebounded sharply," says an official report, "and there were similar favorable responses in U.S. financial markets generally." By November 30, the dollar had advanced 11¾ percent against the German mark, 15½ percent against the Swiss franc, and 11½ percent against the Japanese yen.[170] Not all of this improvement was permanent, however. "Although the dollar more than recovered its October decline in November," said a later report, " . . . more than one-third of the gain was lost in December." For the year as a whole, it was calculated, the dollar declined 10 percent on a trade-weighted basis against the currencies of ten industrial countries, and 8 percent on a similar basis against the currencies of 22 OECD countries."[171]

Year-End Uncertainties

One factor in this renewed reversal was a prevalent fear that the high interest rates imposed by the United States as an anti-inflationary measure might prove so effective as to precipitate an economic recession. Another decidedly negative influence was the chaotic condition to which the world's oil markets had been reduced in consequence of the revolutionary events in Iran and the cessation

[169]Same.
[170]Same: 941,
[171]Christopher L. Bach, in *Survey of Current Business* (Washington: U.S. Department of Commerce), Mar. 1979: 39, 41.

of Iranian oil production and exports. Moving to exploit the resultant scarcity, the thirteen OPEC countries at a meeting in Abu Dhabi on December 16–17 decided to impose a phased, 14.5 percent increase in the price being charged for "marker crude" petroleum—from $12.70 to $14.54 per barrel—over the period ending October 1, 1979. Such an increase, the White House immediately commented, was unwarranted by market conditions and would "impede programs to maintain world economic recovery and to reduce inflation."[172] By the middle of 1979, however, the increases authorized at that time were to seem almost moderate in comparison with the further price gouging carried out by OPEC nations in the following months.

Other Western expectations were suffering mutilation amid the crush of year-end events. Activation of the new European Monetary System, which had been planned for January 1, 1979 despite a British decision to remain aloof for the time being, was delayed by a last-minute dispute on agricultural policy between France and West Germany and consequently did not take place until March 13, 1979.

Of more immediate concern to the United States was the inability of the President's Special Representative for Trade Negotiations, Robert S. Strauss, and his European and Japanese colleagues to meet the December 15 deadline for completion of the Multilateral Trade Negotiations in Geneva. Although the United States voiced general satisfaction with the shape of the emerging agreements, it still remained exceedingly unhappy about limitations on its agricultural exports to the European Common Market area. The Europeans, in turn, were deeply upset by the failure of Congress to renew the President's authority to waive the application of countervailing duties on subsidized exports. Such problems, in conjunction with the chronic dissatisfaction of the 78 developing-country participants in the GATT negotiations, would delay completion of the final, 99-nation agreement until April 12, 1979—after which, of course, it would still face minute scrutiny by the U.S. Congress and by similar bodies in other countries.

In the meantime, preliminary analysis of America's economic experience in 1978 invited still more of the mixed and carefully shaded appraisals so appropriate in the political field. Inflation had obviously been the key phenomenon, and the official gross national product of $2,107.6 billion—a gain of 11.7 percent over the preceding year—would shrink to only $1,385.7 billion—a gain of only 4 percent—when measured in constant (1972) dollars. Consumer prices, as already noted, increased by a full 9 percent, a rise exceeded only twice in the entire postwar period, while corporate

---

[172]Dec. 17 statement, in *Presidential Documents,* 14: 2271.

profits increased by 26 percent. Employment swelled by more than 3 million, to 95,906,000 while unemployment by December had declined to 6,012,000 or 5.9 percent of the labor force. The Dow Jones Industrial Average experienced a further decline, from 831.17 at the end of 1977 to 805.01 at the end of 1978.

On the international front, imports at $172.046 billion again exceeded exports at $143.575 billion, and the resultant merchandise trade deficit was charted by the Department of Commerce at a record $28.451 billion—almost $2 billion more than in 1977. The deficit on petroleum account, however, was reduced to $39.5 billion, from $42.4 billion the previous year.[173] Oil imports, which had reached a peak of nearly 8.7 barrels per day in 1977, were down to 8.1 million barrels per day in 1978. Although the balance-of-payments deficit for the year remained at a record level of $15.961 billion, it declined significantly from quarter to quarter as merchandise exports increased in response to improving economic conditions abroad and other factors.[174]

"Nineteen hundred and seventy-eight was a year of significant progress in the world economy," President Carter would insist in another message on the Economic Report, sent to Congress on January 25, 1979. " . . . We have made great progress at home in recovering from the recession, and we have strengthened the stature of the United States in the world economy. In the year ahead, we can secure and extend those gains by working together to moderate inflation. I am confident that we will rise to the challenge."[175]

9. LIFE IN THE HUMAN COMMUNITY

Though seldom cataloged in official documents, the emotional presuppositions of American foreign policy in the later 1970s were readily recognizable in the words of statesmen and the actions of government. Among them, most observers would have agreed, were a compassionate yet basically optimistic response to the manifestations of the human condition; a marked, if sometimes fitful, sensitivity to suffering and injustice in other lands; a vigorous, though possibly rather spasmodic, concern with the protection of threatened U.S. national interests; and a seemingly unshakable conviction that the interests of the United States were ultimately

[173]*New York Times,* Jan. 31, 1979.
[174]*Survey of Current Business,* Mar. 1979: 39–40; *Federal Reserve Bulletin,* Apr. 1979: A54, A56.
[175]*Presidentйal Documents,* 15: 118–19 (1979).

compatible, not to say identical, with those of the larger world community of which it formed a part.

The effects of this outlook could be observed not only in the strategic, political, and economic areas already discussed but also in the myriad legal, social, technical, and cultural matters that make up so much of the substance of contemporary international life. Each year increased the range, as well as the intensity, of international interest in a host of questions that had formerly been dealt with, if at all, at national and provincial levels. No longer was it possible even to delimit the broadening concerns of the "global village," as some now called it. Even the far-flung network of United Nations agencies did not encompass the totality of the international agenda, important segments of which were handled by other organizations or *ad hoc* instrumentalities operating partially or wholly outside the U.N. framework.

No comprehensive, systematic survey of the United States' participation in this broader realm of international endeavor had been made public since the discontinuance of the annual "State of the World" reports issued by the Nixon administration. Many of the problems touched upon in those reports, however, continued to occupy the foreground of world attention even in 1978. Among matters of special international concern in that year were the means of defending organized society against the depredations of international terrorists and the evils of the drug traffic; the perennial quest for a modernized regime to govern the use and exploitation of the oceans; the responsibilities of the family of nations in the safeguarding and promotion of human rights; and the role of the communications media in an age of global ideological discord.

Combating International Terrorism

Since the middle of the 1960s, the gruesome phenomena of political terrorism had become an increasingly characteristic feature of a global civilization whose technological complexity provided discontented persons with unprecedented opportunities for threatening or destroying other people's lives in the attempt to advance their own particular aims. Though some important terrorist activity took place entirely within a national context, a considerable part of it affected the citizens and governments of more than one nation at a time. Between January 1968 and December 1977, the State Department calculated, there had been some 2,690 international terrorist incidents, of which 1,148 had involved U.S. citizens and property.

Some of these incidents had achieved a permanent place in the world's memory, in one or two instances because of the successful rescue operations organized by the victims' home governments. Such had been the Israeli rescue of the passengers and crew of a hijacked French airliner at Entebbe, Uganda, in 1976, and the West

German commando raid that saved the occupants of a Lufthansa jetliner hijacked to Mogadishu, Somalia, in the fall of 1977.

Attempts to organize the community of nations for concerted resistance to hijacking and other forms of terrorism had been less successful, mainly because a good many governments either sympathized with the Palestinian groups who were responsible for much of the terrorism, or, at any rate, feared to oppose them publicly. Such international safeguards as existed against terrorist interference with the safety of air travel were mainly limited to the three conventions negotiated under the auspices of the International Civil Aviation Organization (ICAO) at Tokyo in 1963, at The Hague in 1970, and at Montreal in 1971.[176] Up to January 1978, however, only 62 countries had ratified all three of these conventions, and 55 countries had ratified none of them. The U.N. General Assembly, in a resolution adopted in November 1977, had voiced its own condemnation of aerial hijacking, called on states to adhere to the ICAO conventions, and admonished them to take the necessary security steps to deter terrorist attacks.[177] Like other General Assembly resolutions, however, this one had only advisory status.

Secretary Vance reviewed some salient aspects of the terrorist problem in a January 23 appearance before the Senate Committee on Governmental Affairs, which was considering legislation aimed at strengthening the government's hand in dealing "rapidly, decisively, and effectively" with terrorist acts. The United States, Mr. Vance pointed out (**Document 48a**), had already taken strong action on a number of fronts, making "clear to all that we will reject terrorist blackmail" and "reject demands for ransom and for the release of prisoners." In addition, said the Secretary of State, the administration would support "the concept of a public list of countries which aid or abet terrorist action," together with the imposition of "appropriate sanctions" against such countries. He seemed lukewarm, however, to the idea of suspending airline service to countries abetting terrorism, a proposal that had won little international support when advanced by the Nixon administration a few years earlier.[178]

Congress, as matters turned out, was too occupied with other business to adopt specific antiterrorist legislation in 1978, although the early months of the year brought few if any signs of abatement in the rhythm of new terrorist incidents. The kidnapping and subsequent murder of Aldo Moro, which would surely stand out among the more horrendous crimes of the century, could be regarded as at least technically an internal Italian matter. But there were other ter-

---

[176]For full listing see Appendix.
[177]Resolution 32/8, Nov. 3, 1977.
[178]*AFR, 1972:* 488, 516.

rorist outrages of a more cosmopolitan kind, such as the murder in February of two prominent Egyptians by Palestinians in Cyprus, followed by a hijacking and a bloody, unplanned encounter at Larnaca airport between arriving Egyptian commandos and the Cypriot National Guard. In March occurred the Al Fatah coastal raid on Israel that provoked the latter's military intervention in southern Lebanon; in May, three Palestinians attacked Israeli airline passengers in the lounge at Orly Airport near Paris; in August came still another Palestinian attack on an Israeli airline crew lying over at London's Heathrow Airport.

International terrorism, particularly aircraft hijacking, was the single topic outside the economic area that engaged the attention of the heads of state and government at the "economic summit" in Bonn on July 16–17. In a joint statement expressing their concern about terrorism and the taking of hostages **(Document 48b)**, the seven leaders declared that their governments would intensify joint efforts to combat international terrorism, and, specifically, would jointly take "immediate action" to suspend air traffic to and from any country that refused extradition or prosecution of aircraft hijackers or failed to return a hijacked aircraft. Other governments were urged to join in this commitment. A subsequent seven-nation meeting of experts, convened in Bonn on August 1–2, agreed on a specific procedure to be followed in a future hijacking incident, and on the diplomatic initiatives to be undertaken in seeking wider international support.[179] Such a show of resolve by the seven countries whose airlines carried two-thirds of the free world's airline passenger traffic may help to explain the fact that the remainder of 1978 saw no occurrences of a nature to trigger the contemplated action.

International Narcotics Control

Comparable to international terrorism in its devastating effects, though even broader in its international incidence, was another typical scourge of late twentieth-century society, the abuse of narcotic drugs with its accompaniments of criminality, sickness, and death. That drug abuse was an international as well as a national problem had long been evident to the American government, and President Carter's drug abuse message of August 2, 1977[180] had marked a shift from what had been primarily a domestic focus to what administration aides now described as "a truly global concept."

Over and above the human suffering involved in drug addiction, the President had noted, the illicit drug traffic with its enormous profits was having a devastating economic impact on many of the smaller countries involved, and was engendering corruption and

[179]*Bulletin,* Sept. 1978: 5.
[180]*Presidential Documents,* 13: 1154–60 (1977).

eroding political stability and democracy. Victim countries, in this view, included not only "those which suffer the devastating health and social consequences of drug abuse," but also "those whose political, economic, and social integrity was threatened by the illicit drug traffic."[181] "To implement this broadened perspective," the Department of State reported in the summer of 1978, "the Administration is encouraging all relevant US agencies to work together to curtail illicit drug production and traffic through diplomatic efforts and program assistance in key countries. Our basic objectives are to reduce the flow of illicit drugs from foreign countries into the US and to assist other nations to strengthen their drug control capabilities."[182]

A detailed survey of these efforts was offered by K. Mathea Falco, the State Department's Senior Adviser and Director for International Narcotics Control Matters, in a statement before the Senate subcommittee considering the $40 million budget of the international narcotics control program for 1979 (Document 49). This figure, Ms. Falco pointed out, amounted to less than 5 percent of the total of more than $800 million expended annually by the Federal Government for drug control efforts in law enforcement, treatment and rehabilitation. Outlining the major cooperative efforts undertaken with the nine countries that were considered the principal sources of illicit drugs coming into the United States, Ms. Falco also stressed the increased emphasis being placed on working with multilateral and regional organizations like the U.N. Fund for Drug Abuse Control, the Colombo Plan, and ASEAN. Through these organizations, the State Department representative observed, "approaches can be made to countries unresponsive to bilateral overtures by the United States to insure that they do not themselves become victims of the ever-changing patterns of the illicit drug traffic."

Heroin and cocaine were the primary targets of the United States' campaign, Ms. Falco explained, with heroin far in the lead because of "its devastating impact on the health and welfare of our society." Since Mexico was known to be the principal source of illicit heroin entering the United States, at least one-third of the total funds available was being concentrated on assistance to the Mexican government in eradicating illicit poppy cultivation and breaking up major trafficking networks. The success of these efforts in recent years, Ms. Falco asserted, was reflected in the reduced amounts of heroin reaching the United States, an upward movement of wholesale prices, a decrease in purity levels of street her-

[181]U.S. Department of State, Bureau of Public Affairs, "International Narcotics Control" (GIST Series, Aug. 1978).
[182]Same.

oin, and a decline in heroin overdose deaths to the lowest point since 1973.

Southeast Asian heroin, originating in the "Golden Triangle" area of Burma, Thailand, and Laos, was also moving into the United States in increasing quantities, Ms. Falco observed; but she had been encouraged during a recent visit to the area by what appeared to be unusually favorable prospects for curtailing this illicit traffic. Burma, in particular, had been pursuing an "aggressive" narcotics eradication and interdiction program, aided by U.S. cooperation in providing helicopters, communications equipment, and maintenance services. Of less immediate concern, Ms. Falco added, was the large-scale opium production taking place in Afghanistan and Pakistan. Though currently consumed mainly within the region, she said, South Asian opium nevertheless created a potential for a massive influx of illegal heroin into the United States.

Cocaine production, which centered in Bolivia and Peru and depended on processing and transshipment facilities in Ecuador and Colombia, was not at present regarded as a "significant public health threat" in the United States, Ms. Falco stated, despite the annual arrival of 15 to 17 tons of the drug from South America. Nevertheless, she said, it was recognized that increased use could lead to a dramatic increase in fatalities, overdoses, and other adverse health and social consequences, and the United States was working intensively with the four governments in trying "to restrict the usage of cocaine through curtailing its availability." In addition, Ms. Falco reported, the State Department was stepping up its support of regional cooperation in narcotics control by encouraging Latin American countries to coordinate their narcotics efforts more closely.

Implicit in these activities was a multilateral dimension which was more fully brought out in the Department of State report already referred to: "The State Department is actively involved in planning international narcotics control activities. We are placing increased emphasis on comprehensive and integrated rural development, alternative crop identification for primary drug producing areas, and implementation of a poppy/heroin forecasting system. These activities support our overall diplomatic efforts to contain the threat that drug addiction and illicit trafficking pose to the health and welfare of mankind."[183]

Progress on the Law of the Sea

In working to curb the illegal flow of narcotics, the United States considered its interests to be broadly identical to those of the coun-

[183]Same as note 181.

tries where the drugs originated. Drug abuse was one of the common enemies of mankind, as damaging in the long run to the supplier as to the consumer.

Such a coincidence of interest had been much less apparent in the long-drawn-out negotiations on the law of the sea, which had been going forward under U.N. auspices since the late 1960s. Here, as in the global economic discussions known as the "North-South dialogue," there had been a definite clash of ideology and interest between the United States and other industrial powers on the one hand and the 119 or so developing countries that made up the misnamed "Group of 77" on the other. It was primarily because of this division that the Third United Nations Conference on the Law of the Sea, officially convened toward the end of 1973, had by this time reached its fifth year of substantive discussions, had held no fewer than six full-dress negotiating sessions, yet still had not completed its assignment to produce a comprehensive treaty resolving the many disputed points about the management and use of the oceans. Still a Seventh Session was held in Geneva from March 28 to May 19, 1978, continuing in New York from August 21 to Sep-. tember 15 of the same year. Again, however, the more than 150 nations involved were unable to complete their task and made tentative plans for still another session, the eighth, to begin in Geneva in the spring of 1979.

Both the positive and the negative aspects of this record had been reviewed from time to time by Ambassador at Large Elliot L. Richardson, President Carter's Special Representative for the Law of the Sea Conference. "Although some observers have disparaged it as a tedious talkathon," the Special Representative observed early in 1978,[184] "the conference has in fact made remarkable progress on a vast range of issues of vital importance to the United States and the world community. Provisions have been negotiated which safeguard traditional high seas freedoms within the 200-mile economic zone except for specific resource-related rights accorded coastal states by the convention. The generally satisfactory texts on transit passage of straits have survived. There have been improvements over previous texts in respect of environmental control and settlement of disputes." And yet, the Ambassador warned, there remained a very real possibility that the conference might fail, that there would be no treaty, and that the United States would have to fall back on other means of protecting its interests.

The reason for this disturbing prospect lay in the differences of opinion that still prevailed with reference to the single most difficult issue before the conference, the nature of the future interna-

[184]Jan. 18 address, in *Bulletin,* Feb. 1978: 39–41.

tional regime that was to supervise the exploitation of the mineral resources of the deep seabed. Briefly, U.S. mining interests, with considerable congressional and executive branch support, were eager to begin exploiting the wealth of the seabed with as little international interference as possible. Members of the Group of 77, on the other hand, were determined to subject this activity to various conditions and restrictions reflecting their insistence that the resources in question were part of the "common heritage" of mankind and should be treated as such. A compromise arrangement, suggested by the United States in 1976 and providing for a system of parallel exploitation by private companies and by an international "Enterprise," had failed to win the Group of 77's approval, and the Carter administration had decided in 1977 that it could not wait longer for a treaty but would support the enactment of domestic legislation to govern U.S. seabed activity until such time as an international regime might be established.[185]

Ambassador Richardson went over these matters once again in a statement to the press on March 16, 1978, a few days before the conference began its Seventh Session—and just one day before the world's attention was drawn to oceanic problems by the breakup of the American-owned tanker *Amoco Cadiz* off the Breton coast in what soon became the worst oil spill in history.

Detailed review of U.S. positions since the previous session of the conference, Mr. Richardson stated on this occasion (**Document 50**), had reinforced the American conviction "that a comprehensive treaty is the clearly preferable means to promote orderly use of the oceans and to insure responsible and fruitful development of their resources." The United States, he said, "shares with the world community as a whole the aim of avoiding chaos and conflict in the utilization of the world's oceans." Nevertheless, the Special Representative warned, "the United States must be prepared to protect its interests by other means than a comprehensive treaty if an acceptable treaty proves unattainable. Indeed, it would be irresponsible not to begin consideration of viable alternatives." Among alternative solutions for the seabed, Mr. Richardson referred to the possibility of "reciprocal legislation," or, perhaps better, "a multilateral arrangement in which all countries could join and which provided for revenue-sharing with developing countries."

Most of the 158 countries participating in the Seventh Session undoubtedly shared the American preference for a comprehensive treaty that would do justice to their particular interests, and the year's negotiations, which were once again presided over by Ambassador H.S. Amerasinghe of Sri Lanka, brought definite movement

[185]*AFR, 1977:* 470–72.

in that direction. In another situation report early in 1979,[186] Ambassador Richardson was to state that the delegates to the conference had reached agreement on not less than 90 percent of the more than 400 articles in the current negotiating text, with only a few hard-core issues still to be resolved before the world community found itself at "the very threshold of a global treaty covering all of mankind's uses of the oceans."

The American concept of parallel exploitation of seabed resources had by now gained general acceptance, Mr. Richardson reported in his review of the Seventh Session, and the most difficult of the remaining issues pertaining to the seabed had to do with the decision-making structure of the proposed International Seabed Authority. This, too, he emphasized, was a matter of real importance to the United States, which would insist on "retaining the legal means to prevent our legitimate interests from being overridden by arbitrary action authorized through a nosecount of Third World nations." Other important issues relating to the delimitation of the continental shelf, the conduct of marine scientific research, and compulsory settlement of disputes would, the President's Special Representative suggested, "fall into place rather quickly if we can solve the seabeds problem."

Ambassador Richardson also referred in this connection to the still pending U.S. legislation "designed to create a legal framework for American companies to go forward on their own pending Conference agreement on a treaty." An administration-supported bill, designed to "promote the orderly development of hard mineral resources in the deep seabed, pending adoption of an international regime relating thereto" (H.R. 3350), had passed the House of Representatives on July 26, 1978, by a vote of 312 to 80—but, in Mr. Richardson's words, had "failed on the last day of the 95th Congress because one Senator refused to let it go to the floor for a vote."

Though drafted with considerable regard for third world interests, this bill had been sharply criticized by the Group of 77 representatives at the conference on the ground that unilateral exploitation was basically incompatible with the "common heritage" principle enshrined in U.N. resolutions. The United States, however, had totally rejected the view that there was anything illegal or improper about the contemplated activities. "We are convinced," Ambassador Richardson emphasized, "that nations retain their rights to mine the deep oceans as one of the freedoms of the seas." Furthermore, he pointed out, "Potential seabed miners want [the legislation] badly. With their heavy investment in the development of technology, they need positive signals now in order to make the

[186]Address of Mar. 14, 1979, in U.S. Department of State, Bureau of Public Affairs, Office of Public Communication, *Current Policy*, No. 60 (Mar. 1979).

costly, long lead-time decisions that will enable them to initiate mining operations six or seven years from now."

"Even after two years as Special Representative," Mr. Richardson observed in concluding his March 1979 address, " . . . I am hesitant to predict the outcome [of the negotiations]. I believe success is possible. I know that success is in our national interest. . . . I have said before, we need a treaty, and we want a treaty, but for a treaty to be acceptable to the United States, it cannot leave us with any of our essential interests impaired. That remains our criterion."

The U.N. on Trial

Elsewhere in the same address, Ambassador Richardson touched on one of the larger matters at stake in the law of the sea negotiations. "We should realize," he declared, "that the United Nations itself is on trial at the Law of the Sea Conference. Its effectiveness as an institution is being subjected to a harsh test. It has to prove at this Conference that it can successfully mediate the burgeoning problems of global interdependence. . . . "

Both as an idea and as an institution, the United Nations and the U.N. system were in fact on trial in a number of different tribunals in 1978. The advent of the Carter administration, for all its humanistic bias and its commitments to world cooperation, had not sufficed to resolve the practical and emotional issues that had, over the years, caused a degree of estrangement between the United States and the global institution it had done so much to foster. Officials of the Carter administration conceded frankly that there was a problem of "declining U.S. support—particularly congressional support—for the United Nations." The "sources of our discontent," according to C. William Maynes, the Assistant Secretary of State for International Organization Affairs, boiled down to four specific accusations about the world organization:

* That it is anti-Israeli.
* That it is antiwhite.
* That it is antidemocratic.
* That it is anti-American.

Though Mr. Maynes was able to offer elaborate refutation of each of these contentions,[187] there were identifiable reasons for the state of mind in which they had taken root. It was a fact that the United States and its associates of the industrial world were heavily outnumbered by newer, less developed, third world, predominantly nonwhite countries, which, not less than the Communist states, insisted on their own solutions for the world's ills. Actions imposed

[187]Nov. 20 address, in *Bulletin,* Jan. 1979: 46–50.

by this non-Western majority had, in fact, already led to some curtailment of U.S. participation in U.N. activities. In 1974, a series of anti-Israel actions by the U.N. Educational, Scientific and Cultural Organization (UNESCO) had precipitated a temporary congressional cutoff of U.S. financial support for that agency. In 1975, a General Assembly resolution equating Zionism with "racism and racial discrimination" had prompted a U.S. boycott that still applied to all activities under the U.N. Decade for Action to Combat Racism and Racial Discrimination, including a World Conference to Combat Racism and Racial Discrimination which met at Geneva in the summer of 1978.[188] In 1977, the United States had actually withdrawn from membership in the International Labour Organisation (ILO), the oldest of the U.N. specialized agencies, in protest against its increasing "politicization" and pro-Communist and anti-Israeli tendencies.

Despite its manifest shortcomings, however, the United States continued to express its interest in preserving and strengthening the United Nations as an "essential instrument of world peace and U.S. diplomacy." "If we are to develop adequate machinery for management of the world's common problems," President Carter told the Congress early in 1978, "a central concern of our foreign policy in the remaining years of this century must be the building of a more effective U.N. system. To this end, this Administration is committed to working for a stronger and more effective United Nations." In line with this intention (and as requested by the Congress itself), the President submitted a detailed report on U.N. reform, one that stressed the possibilities for improving U.N. performance—e.g., through increased use of the consensus procedure—without embarking on a controversial and time-consuming attempt to amend the organization's basic Charter.[189]

Congress, it is true, had little patience with such diplomatic subtleties, and, as already noted, had more than once attempted to impose its will on the United Nations by direct if undiplomatic means. In a particularly striking manifestation of this proclivity during the summer of 1978, it followed the lead of Senator Helms and others by amending the annual State Department appropriation bill[190] in such a way as to deny a presidential request for $27.7 million in U.N. technical assistance funds—and, in addition, to prohibit the use of other appropriated funds "for the funding of technical assistance by the United Nations or any of its specialized

[188]Same, Nov. 1978: 48.
[189]U.S. Department of State, Bureau of Public Affairs, Office of Public Communication, Selected Documents, No. 8 (June 1978).
[190]Department of State Appropriation Act, 1979 (Title I, Public Law 95-431, Oct. 10, 1978).

agencies." The ostensible reason for this action was a belief that U.N. technical assistance should be financed entirely by voluntary contributions, rather than by assessment on the member states. Its effect, however, was to contravene a well-established legal principle which forbade the United Nations or its component agencies to accept conditional contributions from member governments.[191]

"As a result," Assistant Secretary Maynes commented, " . . . as of January 1, 1979, for the first time in its history the United States probably will be unable to make any of its assessed contributions to the United Nations and many of the specialized agencies. . . . The Congress of the United States has not simply followed the example of the Soviet Union—as bad as that example is—and refused to pay for a portion of the U.N. budget with which it disagreed. It has gone beyond this by insisting on attaching conditions to the rest of the U.S. contributions—a step no other member state has ever taken. It is potentially the most damaging blow any member state has directed against the United Nations."[192]

Address to the General Assembly

Promising to seek a reversal at the earliest opportunity, President Carter reluctantly signed this legislation on October 10.[193] In the meantime, the General Assembly of the United Nations had commenced its 33rd Regular Session in New York on September 19, electing Colombian Foreign Minister Indalecio Liévano as its President and admitting the former British protectorate of the Solomon Islands as the United Nations' 150th member state. (The admission of the newly independent West Indian state of Dominica would later raise total U.N. membership to 151.) Unlike the Assembly's Ninth and Tenth Special Sessions, held earlier in 1978 and devoted respectively to the single topics of Namibia and Disarmament, the 33rd Regular Session faced a varied agenda of 129 items and began its work with a three-week "General Debate" in which statements were offered by no fewer than 131 member countries.

President Carter, who had twice addressed the United Nations in 1977, did not appear at the Assembly's 1978 session, and it was Secretary Vance who delivered a thoughtful exposition of American views at the plenary session of September 29 (**Document 51**). "Our challenge today," the Secretary of State declared, "is to summon the political will to act in concert toward the goals we share—to go beyond the rhetoric of interdependence and to begin to recognize its inescapable implications for the national interests of each of us. We must build a new consensus on this proposition: that in this new

[191]Details in *Bulletin,* Jan. 1979: 46–8.
[192]Same: 46.
[193]Signature statement in *Presidential Documents,* 14: 1735–6.

era, each nation must weigh more carefully than ever before its long term interest in a healthy global community when making decisions about its immediate concerns. For only through cooperation and compromise in the short run can we assure our longer term future.''

Reversing the usual emphasis of such speeches, Secretary Vance gave only limited attention to international political problems and devoted more than half of his remarks to ''those issues that so centrally touch people's lives around the globe—economic security, equitable development of the Earth's resources, and individual freedom.'' ''The resolution of dangerous regional disputes and progress in limiting weaponry must always be at the top of the immediate international agenda,'' he conceded. ''But we cannot so concentrate our energies on the political diplomacy of international peace, essential as it is, that we discover too late that international inequities, and poverty and injustice within nations, make peace among nations impossible.''

Both in his detailed review of international economic problems and in his briefer survey of current political issues, Mr. Vance's message was essentially the same: ''that no nation, acting alone, can assure its people peace and economic security; that the future of each of our nations depends upon the future of all of our nations.'' ''Let me emphasize,'' he said in his peroration, ''that on all the issues I have addressed today, what we share is greater than how we differ. We share the same small planet. We share human aspirations—for better lives, for greater opportunity, for freedom and security. And because we share a common destiny, we are compelled to resolve our differences. . . . ''

In the course of his address, Mr. Vance referred also to the human rights issues that had so long preoccupied both the world organization and his own government. ''The ultimate purpose of all our policies,'' the Secretary of State averred, ''is the enhancement of human dignity. The rights to food, to shelter, to a decent education, to adequate health—the rights which lie at the heart of our approach to economic issues—are hollow without political and civil freedoms—freedom from torture and government mistreatment; freedom to worship, to travel, and to speak without fear; freedom to participate in the affairs of one's government.'' This was an issue that members of the Carter administration seemed never to tire of stressing, whether in a United Nations or in some other context.

Andrew Young on Human Rights

Another American with a longstanding interest in human rights was Ambassador Andrew Young, the outspoken U.S. Permanent Representative to the United Nations, and, as such, the leader of the U.S. Delegation to the 33rd General Assembly. It is true that Ambassador Young's opinions on this and other issues occasionally differed from those of the President and the Secretary of State, both of whom had been visibly dismayed by his assertion earlier in the year, at the time of the Shcharansky trial in the U.S.S.R., that "there are hundreds, perhaps thousands, of political prisoners in the United States."[194] As U.S. spokesman in the United Nations, however, the former Georgia civil rights leader had become known for his eloquent articulation of standard—or nearly standard—U.S. positions.

A typical example was Ambassador Young's statement in a plenary session on Deeember 14 (**Document 52**) in connection with the 30th anniversary of the Assembly's adoption of the Universal Declaration of Human Rights. "The sad fact is," said the American spokesman, "that most of the people in [the poorest] countries who were born in the year we adopted the Universal Declaration of Human Rights are not around anymore to celebrate this occasion. And most of those who are still here have very little to celebrate." Poverty, in the Ambassador's view, was actually "the basic obstacle to the realization of human rights for most people in the world today." "We are faced," he said, "with the necessity of promoting worldwide rapid, peaceful social change if we are to move toward the goals of the Universal Declaration of Human Rights."

There was nothing to fear in such a prospect, the Ambassador insisted. "We need not fear change if we build into it more equity and more participation. . . . I believe that cooperation for the common good of humankind can be as powerful an incentive to our imaginations as fear for our survival. Indeed, I submit that cooperation for the common good, for the protection and promotion of human rights, is the way to survival. . . . There are many forms of tyranny, and none of us are exempt from the temptation to conspire with tyranny against freedom by remaining indifferent to the struggle of others to be free. But our very humanity rests in our capacity to identify with the other and to join in the struggle to make all persons free. . . . "

Aside from some emotional rhetoric with regard to Namibia and Rhodesia, few traces of this messianic spirit were to be found in the official records of the 33rd Assembly, which failed to complete its work on schedule and, before recessing on December 21, decided to reconvene on January 15, 1979, for a week or ten days devoted to finishing its agenda. (It was also decided to reconvene at a later date to give further consideration to the situation in Namibia.) "Dull, uninspiring, and repetitious" was the comment of British Representative Sir Ivor Richard[195] on a session whose distinctive quality may have lain precisely in the absence of the acuter forms of

[194]*New York Times,* July 13, 14, 16, 1978.
[195]Quoted in *Political Handbook of the World: 1979* (New York: McGraw-Hill, 1979): 10.

ideological or institutional conflict. "We have the potential of a new pragmatism in these halls," Andrew Young had observed in the statement already quoted, "and I hope it grows. Behind this new pragmatism is, I think, the growing realization that if we stop fearing and fighting each other we might find some practical solutions."

UNESCO and the Media

A more dramatic confrontation had meanwhile been threatened, but ultimately averted, at the Twentieth Session of the UNESCO General Conference in Paris, where another U.S. delegation, headed by another black American, Director John E. Reinhardt of the International Communication Agency—successor to the U.S. Information Agency (USIA)—had defended the Western concept of intellectual freedom against a concerted assault by third world and Communist delegations. Although the earlier difficulties between UNESCO and the United States had by this time been largely ironed out, the threat of a new clash between developing and developed countries, particularly the United States, had overhung the 146-nation Twentieth Conference from the moment of its opening on October 24.

The issue, in this instance, was primarily an ideological one: how might the mass communications media best contribute to such generally accepted goals as "strengthening peace and understanding, the promotion of human rights and . . . countering racialism, apartheid and incitement to war"? To countries like the United States, it seemed self-evident that these ends would be best served by an enlightened public opinion, formed through maximum freedom in the dissemination of information and by an uninhibited interplay of ideas. The developing countries, however—backed strongly by the Soviet Union, which regarded the Western mass media with perhaps even more suspicion and hostility—tended to embrace an opposite view and to advocate the submission of the media to strict government control in order to ensure that they maintained a proper ideological stand. Such, in fact, had been the philosophy behind a draft declaration on the mass media that had been prepared for consideration and, its sponsors hoped, adoption at this UNESCO conference.

Aware, however that the United States would never agree to the kind of declaration the conference was being asked to adopt, Ambassador Reinhardt argued eloquently for the more liberal, Western viewpoint. In doing so, he stressed the fact that the American government and communications media, though basically opposed to governmental restriction, stood ready to provide important assistance in building up the communications networks of developing countries.[196] Though other Western governments took a largely similar line, the advocates of government regulation stood firm. Attempts to devise a compromise that might stand a chance of winning the unanimous consent required by UNESCO rules initially met with little success.

In the end, however, UNESCO's Director-General, Amadou Mahtar M'Bow of Senegal, succeeded in concocting an eleven-article text that buried the essential issue under a shower of pious affirmations about the sanctity of "freedom of opinion, expression and information" and about the contribution of the mass media to "promoting human rights, in particular by giving expression to oppressed peoples who struggle against colonialism, neocolonialism, foreign occupation and all forms of racial discrimination and oppression and who are unable to make their voices heard within their own territories."

Though scorned by the *New York Times* as a "triumph of obfuscation" and "an affront to the very idea of communication,"[197] the M'Bow draft was strongly defended by the State Department, which pointed out that it "not only is stripped of all language implying state authority over the mass media but also includes positive language on freedom of information."[198] Nothing better, in any case, could be hoped for by either side, and the declaration **(Document 53)** was accordingly approved by consensus in the appropriate commission on November 22 and by the full conference on its closing day, November 28.

Among its other actions, UNESCO's Twentieth Conference also adopted a Declaration on Race and Racial Prejudice—this one heartily approved by the United States—that defined basic principles of equality and condemned all forms of racial discrimination. In addition, it approved an international charter on physical education and sports, and, to the disgust of the United States, reaffirmed its earlier actions penalizing Israel for the latter's archeological activities affecting Islamic sites in Jerusalem.

The main significance of the session, in the judgement of Director-General M'Bow, lay in the demonstrated desire of the member states "not to limit the concept of a new world order to the economic level but to widen and deepen it in its social and cultural dimensions." Such a trend, though unlikely to ease the task of U.S. policy makers, would not be inconsistent with the underlying emphasis of American foreign policy as the American people and their government approached the end of the turbulent 1970s.

[196]Nov. 3 statement, in *Bulletin,* Feb. 1979: 50–54.
[197]*New York Times,* Nov. 27, 1978.
[198]Nov. 22 statement, in *Bulletin,* Feb. 1979: 55.

PART TWO: DOCUMENTS

1. AMERICAN FOREIGN POLICY: THE SECOND YEAR

*(1)   Foreign Policy Decisions for 1978: Address by Secretary of
State Cyrus R. Vance before the Los Angeles World Affairs
Council, January 13, 1978.*[1]

Our country, within sight and memory of some Americans still
living, has been transformed from a largely agrarian society to the
world's greatest industrial power—one in which economic, political,
and social mobility are the accepted order of the day. The fantastic
stories of Horatio Alger, as well as those of H.G. Wells, have come
true. Of course, there is still poverty in America. There is still lack
of sufficient opportunity for many. There is still discrimination.

But, day by day, and despite a few deplorable detours, we have
held remarkably to the journey begun by our Founding Fathers—
toward a new nation in a new world in which each citizen might
stand free and equal beside his neighbor, able to make the most of
his or her human potential.

When I am asked about the American people—as I often am by
leaders of other countries—I say that as a people we have today a
renewed faith in our old dreams, and this is something President
Carter and I believe in very deeply. Because of who and what we
are, both the basic interests and the ideals of our people must be
present in our foreign policy, or it will not be long sustained.

- We must maintain a defense establishment modern and strong
  enough to protect ourselves and our allies.
- We must protect American investment overseas and insure
  continuing access to vital raw materials.
- We must be strongly competitive economically so that American families can continue to enjoy their standard of living.
- We must maintain our close relations with our allies, while we
  seek at the same time improved contacts with our main competitor, the Soviet Union, and with the nonaligned nations.

[1]Department of State Press Release 18; text from *Bulletin,* Feb. 1978: 23-6.

All of this, and more, can be pursued—as we pursue our national interest—while still expressing the deeper ideals and aspirations that have led us to our remarkable economic and social progress here at home.

Our strength lies not only in our ideals but in the practical way we identify problems and work systematically toward their solution. We do the best when we are true to ourselves.

That is why America was at her best in the Marshall plan, why we have felt at home with Food for Peace and the Peace Corps. That is why I find such broad public support for President Carter's emphasis upon human rights—including not only rights to the integrity of the person and political rights but the rights to food, clothing, shelter, housing, health, and education.

That is why, with all its difficulties, we have embarked on a course of diplomacy in the Middle East which may help bring peace to the people of that region.

That is why we are trying to help bring solutions—not our solutions but solutions through free elections—in Rhodesia and in Namibia so that people there will have their chance for human emancipation and development.

That is why we seek arms control arrangements through negotiations and have adopted a conscious policy of restraint on conventional arms transfers.

That is why we took tangible first steps in 1977 toward other goals, as well: to stop further nuclear proliferation; to reach agreements on the control of strategic weapons, agreements that will enhance the security of our nation and all the world; to reach agreement with our Western industrial partners on policies leading to economic revival and growth; to reaffirm our commitment to normalization of relations with the People's Republic of China; to reduce military competition in the Indian Ocean; to emphasize our support for racial equality and full political participation of all the people of South Africa.

The Carter Administration in 1977 made a conscious and deliberate effort to construct a foreign policy based upon American interests and upon American values and ideals.

In 1978, there are actions, decisions, and choices which we must make here in America—some of them difficult—which will help determine how such a policy can be nourished and further evolve.

Panama Canal Treaties

One involves the decision of the U.S. Senate on the Panama Canal treaties—treaties which are the culmination of 14 years' work by four American Presidents of both major political parties and their Secretaries of State. This is a decision which is being watched not only by all the nations of Latin America—all of which favor the treaties—but by other nations around the world.

Through these treaties, we can secure—definitively and permanently—our right to use the canal and to protect it. It is a place for us to put the lie, once and for all, to the wornout charge that we Americans are interested only in making the Southern Hemisphere safe for our own economic interests.

Imagine, if you will, that a foreign country controlled and administered a 10-mile-wide strip of land running the length of the Mississippi River. How long do you think the people of this country would willingly accept such a situation? This is an issue requiring understanding and foresight.

If we ratify the treaties, we can make clear to the world that disputes can and should be settled peaceably—through the rule of law and negotiation. And, most importantly, we can insure and safeguard the long-term usefulness and viability of the canal itself to all who use it, including ourselves.

Economic Relations

Another decision we must make is one regarding our economic relations with the rest of the world.

In 1978 we shall be moving toward a conclusion of the Tokyo Round of trade negotiations with other importing and exporting countries.

In 1962, when President Kennedy argued for the passage of the historic Trade Expansion Act, which led to 10 years of worldwide economic expansion, he rightly pointed out that "a rising tide lifts all boats."

Today the world is badly in need of economic recovery. Other major nations are suffering rates of inflation and unemployment which rival or are even higher than ours. The Tokyo Round, of and by itself, will not instantly restore worldwide economic prosperity. It will, however, encourage new investment and profitable exchange. If it fails and falls victim to a new wave of international protectionism, we can be sure that many of the "boats" will founder and some may sink.

I know that this is not an abstract, theoretical matter for the American worker or businessman or farmer who depends for his family's living on production of steel, CB radios, color television sets, microwave ovens, textiles, footwear, automobiles, computers, sugar, and many other items. The changing world economy has made other nations competitive in production of these products, and we are feeling the result of it.

The Carter Administration knows this and is doing its best to help the American industries and people affected. The new steel program, announced in December,[2] is a part of that. So are our present discussions with Japan on reducing its import barriers and increasing its rate of growth.

But we and others must help ourselves in ways that do not throw the world back into the kind of disastrous protectionist spiral that we all experienced in the Great Depression.

Under economic pressure, one country, and then another, in the 1930's closed its borders to foreign goods. High tariffs increased the price of everything to everyone, everywhere. Then we closed our banks and our businesses and farms as we fell into worldwide depression. The great ports of our country were, as you well know, empty and forlorn places.

A new wave of protectionism would imperil the American profits and 10 million jobs which depend on those exports. The hardest hit of all would be the American farmer, who is having a hard time staying in the black right now. California is an agricultural state.

I have just learned that there is more acreage under cultivation in the United States to produce food which we sell to Japan than there is total acreage under cultivation in Japan. If Japan, for instance, were to close its borders to our food and fiber as part of a trade war, farms and rural communities in this State and elsewhere in America would be severely harmed.

So we must make the necessary decision to keep our commitment to both domestic and world economies which are open to competition and which reward productivity. That will involve knocking down barriers to our products elsewhere in the world. But it will also involve our acceptance of the fact that to buy from us, other countries must able to sell to us.

Third World

We also have decisions to make—beyond those surrounding the Panama Canal treaties and the Tokyo Round—about a whole range of relations with the so-called Third World. These countries, most of them gaining their independence after World War II, are increasingly involved in our daily lives.

You know how the amount and cost of oil from these countries affect this country.

We also get more than 50% of the tin, aluminum, and manganese we need from less developed countries and substantial amounts of our lead, tungsten, and copper.

In addition, we depend on the emerging countries for an important share of our exports. Recent figures show, for instance, we exported $29 billion in goods to the non-oil-producing developing

[2]Cf. *AFR, 1977:* 117.

countries. This was three times the 1970 figure, three times our exports to Japan, and $3 billion more than our exports to all of industrialized Europe. These exports, of course, mean American jobs.

At the same time, it is in the developing world that many of the so-called global problems are most evident and threatening.

Inefficient and wasteful use of the Earth's resources, pollution of the oceans and atmosphere, nuclear proliferation, unchecked arms competitions—all of these problems which involve not only these countries but also the safety of the human race.

Most countries of the Third World have too little food; many lack the means to produce enough of their own. Almost all have exploding populations.

Even the most optimistic projections for the future point to population increases in the Third World of some 75% by the year 2000. Perhaps even more troubling, this growth seems certain to be concentrated in already hard-pressed urban centers. Imagine, if you will, as the projections indicate, a Mexico City with 32 million people; Sao Paulo with 26 million; and Calcutta, Bombay, Rio de Janeiro, Seoul, Peking, and Shanghai each with some 19 million in 22 years.

In the years immediately ahead, many of the key nations of the Third World will be even more a part of our daily dialogue than they are today. We must decide how we shall relate to them.

These countries believe that they should no longer be the "hewers of wood and drawers of water" for the rich Western nations, and we understand this. In the past year, we have reduced their suspicion of the United States and, thereby, lessened the likelihood that we could be faced with attempts at new cartels, built around raw materials and commodities other than oil, and unending political and economic hostility.

The countries of the Third World now feel that we regard them as important and sovereign nations and that we identify with their human aspirations. The emerging nations of the world can be constructive partners of the United States.

Make no mistake about it. These countries are not early-day miniatures of the United States. Many will choose paths of political and economic development which we will not approve. But a majority, at least, will be looking to us for understanding and assistance as they seek to build modern societies.

Will we be willing to share our technology with these countries? Will we be ready to help stabilize the basic commodity prices on which many of their economies are based? Will we treat their products fairly in the international marketplace? Will we be willing to support their national economic development plans when they do not always suit our own tastes? All these questions are complex and some pose difficult problems. But this Administration fully realizes that we shall harm our own interests and we shall not be true to our own values if we fail to address these issues sympathetically.

Southern Africa

An immediate and tangible test of our intentions toward the Third World lies in southern Africa. I speak of the three principal problems of Rhodesia, Namibia, and the situation within South Africa itself. We cannot impose solutions in southern Africa. We cannot dictate terms to any of the parties; our leverage is limited.

But we are among the few governments in the world that can talk to both white and black Africans frankly and yet with a measure of trust. We would lose our ability to be helpful if we lost that trust. It is, therefore, essential that our policies of encouraging justice for people of all races in southern Africa be clear to all.

After careful consideration, this Administration is actively pursuing solutions to all three southern African problems. These problems must be addressed together, for they are intertwined.

Some have argued that apartheid in South Africa should be ignored for the time being in order to concentrate on achieving progress on Rhodesia and Namibia. Such a policy would be wrong and would not work. It would be blind to the reality that the beginning of progress must be made soon within South Africa if there is to be a possibility of peaceful solutions in the longer run. It could mislead the South Africans about our real concerns. It would prejudice our relations with our African friends. It would do a disservice to our own beliefs. And it would discourage those of all races who are working for peaceful progress within South Africa.

We believe that we can effectively influence South Africa on Rhodesia and Namibia while expressing our concerns about apartheid.

We believe that whites as well as blacks must have a future in Namibia, Zimbabwe, and South Africa. We also believe that their security lies in progress. Intransigence will only lead to greater insecurity.

We will welcome and recognize positive action by South Africa on each of these three issues. But the need is real for progress on all of them, and we shall need the continued support of the American people for a policy which can encourage and press for that progress.

Arms Limitation

Another decision facing us, as a people, is one which is now reflected in our discussions on strategic arms limitation with the Soviet Union. Security is the issue here. We pursue our security in two ways:

- By maintaining a military establishment which will see to the safety of ourselves and our allies and
- By arms control.

What we cannot achieve by mutual, equal limitations, we insure by our own strength.

Thus, we have to think of the Strategic Arms Limitation Talks (SALT) as a process. It is a process of discovering whether we can work out some of our security problems with the Soviet Union. It is a process also in the sense that we try to solve what strategic problems we can at each stage; then, we move on to the next stage and the next level of problems.

We do not seek reductions in arms for their own sake but only when reductions promote security. But there can be an important result from arms reductions alongside an increase in our security: the potential for us and for others, including those in the developing world, to cut spending on armaments and to reorder priorities.

If we have the courage and patience to see it through, I believe we can both lower the threshold of international danger and release new resources for the works of peace through SALT and other such negotiations. But we must summon the will to do it. For it is in our relations with the Soviet Union that war and peace issues and decisions are most involved.

Our policies toward the Soviet Union are based upon a realistic appreciation that this is a serious competitive relationship and that Soviet objectives in the world are very different from ours. It is also important to recognize, however, that there are specific matters on which our interests are not in conflict—not least, in the avoidance of nuclear war.

In the cause of peace and of our own interest, we have engaged the Soviet Union on a wide range of concrete matters intended in the first instance to stabilize the military competition and to regulate the political competition. These are our first objectives, because they go to the heart of the issue of war and peace.

Beyond these objectives, we seek to enlarge areas of common understanding and common action on a range of international issues, including human rights; cooperation on matters affecting the lives of people everywhere, such as disease, food supply, pollution of the environment, and the application of science and technology.

Progress in these fields is uneven and may take a long time, but we draw patience and a long-term perspective from our realization of how far we have come from the intense and dangerous cold war spirit that prevailed only a few decades ago.

The alternative to this active dialogue with the Soviets implies a return to the tensions and mutual isolation of the cold war. Many of you and the leadership of this Administration remember what that period was like. In good conscience, we cannot recommend that we lead the country back to the troubles and fear of that era.

Middle East

Tomorrow I leave for Jerusalem to assist at an event that we all would have regarded as impossible just a few short months ago. The Foreign Ministers of Egypt and Israel will sit down together, around a conference table, to start the detailed negotiations of peace between Israel and the Arab states. After three decades of estrangement and hostility, the process of reconciliation has begun.

I am sure that you, as all Americans and peoples the world over, have been as moved as I was by the dramatic events of the weeks just past. President Sadat's sudden and spectacular visit to Jerusalem captured the imagination of all of us; it was an act of vision and statesmanship. The warmth of his reception by Prime Minister Begin and the people of Israel, surmounting the bitter memories of four wars which had brought tragedy to every family, gave clear testimony to the desire for peace.

President Sadat's initiative and Prime Minister Begin's response have set in motion a negotiating process which began with the Cairo preparatory conference in December and will continue at ministerial level in a Military Committee in Cairo and a Political Committee in Jerusalem. Both Egypt and Israel have emphasized that they view the negotiations now underway as laying the groundwork for negotiations among all parties to the Arab-Israeli conflict, looking toward a comprehensive peace in the Middle East.

After his discussion with President Sadat last week, President Carter made clear the task facing the Middle Eastern Political Committee meeting in Jerusalem.[3]

- First, true peace must be based on normal relations among the parties to the peace. Peace means more than just an end to belligerency.
- Second, there must be withdrawal by Israel from territories occupied in 1967 and agreement on secure and recognized borders for all parties in the context of normal and peaceful relations in accordance with U.N. Resolutions 242 and 338.
- Third, there must be a resolution of the Palestinian problem in all its aspects; it must recognize the legitimate rights of the Palestinian people and enable the Palestinians to participate in the determination of their own future.

[3] Cf. Introduction at note 59.

I believe that these principles, as stated by the President, should be acceptable to the governments and peoples on both sides of the Arab-Israeli conflict.

To move from principles to concrete achievement will require flexibility and courage, qualities of statesmanship of which the leaders of Egypt and Israel have already given full display.

For our part, we stand ready to help Arabs and Israelis achieve their peace. It is important to our national interests that we do so; our values and character as a people demand no less than our greatest effort to help resolve this tragic conflict.

We will participate actively in the work of the Jerusalem meeting, as the parties have asked us to do. When difficulties in the negotiations arise, we may be able to make some helpful suggestions to bridge the gaps between the parties; however, we will not impose a blueprint for resolution of issues which ultimately only the peoples of the area can resolve.

There can be no turning back from Jerusalem. Arab and Israeli peoples would bitterly resent a diplomatic failure now that these long-hostile nations have found the will and the capacity to approach each other in mutual respect.

From what I have said today, I believe that you can tell that I am basically optimistic about our foreign policy and the chances for future advances in the cause of peace.

Despite our problems, this is a strong and free country and one which is filled with hope and vitality.

Some 33 years into the nuclear age, the world has not blown itself up. Indeed, we have in those years, through diplomacy and international leadership, lessened the chances of that ever happening.

We have, since World War II, seen more than 100 new countries enter nationhood. They are becoming productive, self-sustaining members of the international community.

The task ahead, as I see it, will be to persevere on the course we have charted. This is a time when political and economic change is taking place so rapidly—Peter Drucker has aptly called this "an age of discontinuity"—that it might tempt some to retreat to our old, inward fortress America habitudes.

However, we are now being true to ourselves, and faithful to what one 200-year-old document called "a decent respect for the opinions of mankind." In the past year, President Carter has led us to make the hard decisions that have shown again that our country has not lost its faith in man's perfectibility.

We have great strength. Properly channeled, our strength can be a catalytic and vital force in bringing peace, opportunity, and material well-being to millions of people—in America as well as abroad.

(2)   The State of the Union: Address by President Jimmy Carter before a Joint Session of the Congress, January 20, 1978.[4]

(Excerpts)

Mr. President, Mr. Speaker,[5] *Members of the 95th Congress, ladies and gentlemen:*

* * *

I return tonight to fulfill one of those duties of the Constitution: to give to the Congress—and to the Nation—information on the state of the Union.

Militarily, politically, economically, and in spirit, the state of our Union is sound.

We are a great country, a strong country, a vital and dynamic country—and so we will remain.

We are a confident people and a hard-working people, a decent and a compassionate people—and so we will remain.

I want to speak to you tonight about where we are and where we must go, about what we have done and what we must do. And I want to pledge to you my best efforts and ask you to pledge yours.

Each generation of Americans has to face circumstances not of its own choosing, but by which its character is measured and its spirit is tested.

There are times of emergency, when a nation and its leaders must bring their energies to bear on a single urgent task. That was the duty Abraham Lincoln faced when our land was torn apart by conflict in the War Between the States. That was the duty faced by Franklin Roosevelt when he led America out of an economic depression and again when he led America to victory in war.

There are other times when there is no single overwhelming crisis, yet profound national interests are at stake.

At such times the risk of inaction can be equally great. It becomes the task of leaders to call forth the vast and restless energies of our people to build for the future.

That is what Harry Truman did in the years after the Second World War, when we helped Europe and Japan rebuild themselves and secured an international order that has protected freedom from aggression.

We live in such times now, and we face such duties.

We've come through a long period of turmoil and doubt, but

⁴Text from *Presidential Documents,* 14: 90–98.
⁵Vice-President Walter F. Mondale and Representative Thomas P. (Tip) O'Neill.

we've once again found our moral course, and with a new spirit, we are striving to express our best instincts to the rest of the world.

There is all across our land a growing sense of peace and a sense of common purpose. This sense of unity cannot be expressed in programs or in legislation or in dollars. It's an achievement that belongs to every individual American. This unity ties together, and it towers over all our efforts here in Washington, and it serves as an inspiring beacon for all of us who are elected to serve.

This new atmosphere demands a new spirit, a partnership between those of us who lead and those who elect. The foundations of this partnership are truth, the courage to face hard decisions, concern for one another and the common good over special interests, as a basic faith and trust in the wisdom and strength and judgment of the American people.

For the first time in a generation, we are not haunted by a major international crisis or by domestic turmoil, and we now have a rare and a priceless opportunity to address persistent problems and burdens which come to us as a nation—quietly and steadily getting worse over the years.

As President, I've had to ask you, the Members of Congress, and you, the American people, to come to grips with some of the most difficult and hard questions facing our society.

We must make a maximum effort, because if we do not aim for the best, we are very likely to achieve little. I see no benefit to the country if we delay because the problems will only get worse.

We need patience and good will, but we really need to realize that there is a limit to the role and the function of government. Government cannot solve our problems, it can't set our goals, it cannot define our vision. Government cannot eliminate poverty or provide a bountiful economy or reduce inflation or save our cities or cure illiteracy or provide energy. And government cannot mandate goodness. Only a true partnership between government and the people can ever hope to reach these goals.

Those of us who govern can sometimes inspire, and we can identify needs and marshal resources, but we simply cannot be the managers of everything and everybody.

We here in Washington must move away from crisis management, and we must establish clear goals for the future—immediate and the distant future—which will let us work together and not in conflict. Never again should we neglect a growing crisis like the shortage of energy, where further delay will only lead to more harsh and painful solutions.

Every day we spend more than $120 million for foreign oil. This slows our economic growth, it lowers the value of the dollar overseas, and it aggravates unemployment and inflation here at home.

Now we know what we must do—increase production. We must

cut down on waste. And we must be fair to people, and we must not disrupt our Nation's economy and our budget.

Now, that sounds simple, But I recognize the difficulties involved. I know that it is not easy for the Congress to act. But the fact remains that on the energy legislation, we have failed the American people. Almost 5 years after the oil embargo dramatized the problem for us all, we still do not have a national energy program. Not much longer can we tolerate this stalemate. It undermines our national interest both at home and abroad. We must succeed, and I believe we will.

Our main task at home this year, with energy a central element, is the Nation's economy. We must continue the recovery and further cut unemployment and inflation.

Last year was a good one for the United States. We reached all of our major economic goals for 1977. Four million new jobs were created—an alltime record—and the number of unemployed dropped by more than a million. Unemployment right now is the lowest it has been since 1974, and not since World War II has such a high percentage of American people been employed.

The rate of inflation went down. There was a good growth in business profits and investments, the source of more jobs for our workers, and a higher standard of living for all our people. After taxes and inflation, there was a healthy increase in workers' wages.

And this year, our country will have the first $2 trillion economy in the history of the world.

Now, we are proud of this progress the first year, but we must do even better in the future.

We still have serious problems on which all of us must work together. Our trade deficit is too large. Inflation is still too high, and too many Americans still do not have a job.

Now, I didn't have any simple answers for all these problems. But we have developed an economic policy that is working, because it's simple, balanced, and fair. It's based on four principles:

First, the economy must keep on expanding to produce new jobs and better income, which our people need. The fruits of growth must be widely shared. More jobs must be made available to those who have been bypassed until now. And the tax system must be made fairer and simpler.

Secondly, private business and not the Government must lead the expansion in the future.

Third, we must lower the rate of inflation and keep it down. Inflation slows down economic growth, and it's the most cruel to the poor and also to the elderly and others who live on fixed incomes.

And fourth, we must contribute to the strength of the world economy.

*   *   *

Economic success at home is also the key to success in our international economic policy. An effective energy program, strong investment and productivity, and controlled inflation will provide [improve] our trade balance and balance it, and it will help to protect the integrity of the dollar overseas.

By working closely with our friends abroad, we can promote the economic health of the whole world and with fair and balanced agreements lowering the barriers to trade.

Despite the inevitable pressures that build up when the world economy suffers from high unemployment, we must firmly resist the demands for self-defeating protectionism. But free trade must also be fair trade. And I am determined to protect American industry and American workers against foreign trade practices which are unfair or illegal.

*   *   *

During these past years, Americans have seen our Government grow far from us.

For some citizens, the Government has almost become like a foreign country, so strange and distant that we've often had to deal with it through trained ambassadors who have sometimes become too powerful and too influential—lawyers, accountants, and lobbyists. This cannot go on.

We must have what Abraham Lincoln wanted—a government for the people.

*   *   *

In our foreign policy, the separation of people from government has been in the past a source of weakness and error. In a democratic system like ours, foreign policy decisions must be able to stand the test of public examination and public debate. If we make a mistake in this administration, it will be on the side of frankness and openness with the American people.

In our modern world, when the deaths of literally millions of people can result from a few terrifying seconds of destruction, the path of national strength and security is identical to the path of peace.

Tonight, I am happy to report that because we are strong, our Nation is at peace with the world.

We are a confident nation. We've restored a moral basis for our foreign policy. The very heart of our identity as a nation is our firm commitment to human rights.

We stand for human rights because we believe that government has as a purpose to promote the well-being of its citizens. This is true in our domestic policy; it's also true in our foreign policy. The world must know that in support of human rights, the United States will stand firm.

We expect no quick or easy results, but there has been significant movement toward greater freedom and humanity in several parts of the world.

Thousands of political prisoners have been freed. The leaders of the world—even our ideological adversaries—now see that their attitude toward fundamental human rights affects their standing in the international community, and it affects their relations with the United States.

To serve the interests of every American, our foreign policy has three major goals.

The first and prime concern is and will remain the security of our country.

Security is based on our national will, and security is based on the strength of our Armed Forces. We have the will, and militarily we are very strong.

Security also comes through the strength of our alliances. We have reconfirmed our commitment to the defense of Europe, and this year we will demonstrate that commitment by further modernizing and strengthening our military capabilities there.

Security can also be enhanced by agreements with potential adversaries which reduce the threat of nuclear disaster while maintaining our own relative strategic capability.

In areas of peaceful competition with the Soviet Union, we will continue to more than hold our own.

At the same time, we are negotiating with quiet confidence, without haste, with careful determination, to ease the tensions between us and to ensure greater stability and security.

The strategic arms limitation talks have been long and difficult. We want a mutual limit on both the quality and the quantity of the giant nuclear arsenals of both nations, and then we want actual reductions in strategic arms as a major step toward the ultimate elimination of nuclear weapons from the face of the Earth.

If these talks result in an agreement this year—and I trust they will—I pledge to you that the agreement will maintain and enhance the stability of the world's strategic balance and the security of the United States.

For 30 years, concerted but unsuccessful efforts have been made to ban the testing of atomic explosives—both military weapons and peaceful nuclear devices.

We are hard at work with Great Britain and the Soviet Union on an agreement which will stop testing and will protect our national security and provide for adequate verification of compliance. We are now making, I believe, good progress toward this comprehensive ban on nuclear explosions.

We are also working vigorously to halt the proliferation of nuclear weapons among the nations of the world which do not now have them and to reduce the deadly global traffic in conventional arms sales. Our stand for peace is suspect if we are also the principal arms merchant of the world. So, we've decided to cut down our arms transfer to abroad on a year-by-year basis and to work with other major arms exporters to encourage their similar constraint.

Every American has a stake in our second major goal—a world at peace. In a nuclear age, each of us is threatened when peace is not secured everywhere. We are trying to promote harmony in those parts of the world where major differences exist among other nations and threaten international peace.

In the Middle East, we are contributing our good offices to maintain the momentum of the current negotiations and to keep open the lines of communication among the Middle Eastern leaders. The whole world has a great stake in the success of these efforts. This is a precious opportunity for a historic settlement of a long-standing conflict—an opportunity which may never come again in our lifetime.

Our role has been difficult and sometimes thankless and controversial. But it has been constructive and it has been necessary, and it will continue.

Our third major foreign policy goal is one that touches the life of every American citizen everyday—world economic growth and stability.

This requires strong economic performance by the industrialized democracies like ourselves and progress in resolving the global energy crisis. Last fall, with the help of others, we succeeded in our vigorous efforts to maintain the stability of the price of oil. But as many foreign leaders have emphasized to me personally and, I am sure, to you, the greatest future contribution that America can make to the world economy would be an effective energy conservation program here at home. We will not hesitate to take the actions needed to protect the integrity of the American dollar.

We are trying to develop a more just international system. And in this spirit, we are supporting the struggle for human development in Africa, in Asia, and in Latin America.

Finally, the world is watching to see how we act on one of our most important and controversial items of business—approval of the Panama Canal treaties. The treaties now before the Senate are the result of the work of four administrations—two Democratic, two Republican.

They guarantee that the canal will be open always for unrestricted use by the ships of the world. Our ships have the right to go to the head of the line for priority of passage in times of emergency or need. We retain the permanent right to defend the canal with our own military forces, if necessary, to guarantee its openness and its neutrality.

The treaties are to the clear advantage of ourselves, the Panamanians, and the other users of the canal. Ratifying the Panama Canal treaties will demonstrate our good faith to the world, discourage the spread of hostile ideologies in this hemisphere, and directly contribute to the economic well-being and the security of the United States.

I have to say that that's very welcome applause. [*Laughter*]

There were two moments on my recent journey which, for me, confirmed the final aims of our foreign policy and what it always must be.

One was in a little village in India, where I met a people as passionately attached to their rights and liberties as we are, but whose children have a far smaller chance for good health or food or education or human fulfillment than a child born in this country.

The other moment was in Warsaw, capital of a nation twice devastated by war in this century. There, people have rebuilt the city which war's destruction took from them. But what was new only emphasized clearly what was lost.

What I saw in those two places crystallized for me the purposes of our own Nation's policy: to ensure economic justice, to advance human rights, to resolve conflicts without violence, and to proclaim in our great democracy our constant faith in the liberty and dignity of human beings everywhere.

We Americans have a great deal of work to do together. In the end, how well we do that work will depend on the spirit in which we approach it. We must seek fresh answers, unhindered by the stale prescriptions of the past.

It has been said that our best years are behind us. But I say again that America's best is still ahead. We have emerged from bitter experiences chastened but proud, confident once again, ready to face challenges once again, and united once again.

We come together tonight at a solemn time. Last week the Senate lost a good and honest man—Lee Metcalf of Montana.[6]

And today, the flag of the United States flew at half-mast from this Capitol and from American installations and ships all over the world, in mourning for Senator Hubert Humphrey.[7]

Because he exemplified so well the joy and the zest of living, his death reminds us not so much of our own mortality, but of the possibilities offered to us by life. He always looked to the future with a special American kind of confidence, of hope and enthusiasm. And the best way that we can honor him is by following his example.

[6]The Democratic Senator died on Jan. 12.
[7]Sen. Hubert H. Humphrey (Democrat, Minnesota) died on Jan. 13.

Our task—to use the words of Senator Humphrey—is "reconciliation, rebuilding, and rebirth."

Reconciliation of private needs and interests into a higher purpose.

Rebuilding the old dreams of justice and liberty, and country and community.

Rebirth of our faith in the common good.

Each of us here tonight—and all who are listening in your homes —must rededicate ourselves to serving the common good. We are a community, a beloved community, all of us. Our individual fates are linked, our futures intertwined. And if we act in that knowledge and in that spirit, together, as the Bible says, we can move mountains.

Thank you very much.

(3) *National Security in the Nuclear Age: Address by President Carter at Wake Forest University, Winston-Salem, North Carolina, March 17, 1978.*[8]

(Excerpt)

* * *

A hundred and ninety-eight years ago, in the southern part of your State, 400 North Carolina militiamen took up arms in our own War of Independence. Against a force of 1,300 British soldiers, the North Carolinians prevailed—and their battle at Ramsour's Mill became a step on the road to victory at Yorktown 1 year later.

Your ancestors in North Carolina and mine in Georgia and their neighbors throughout the Thirteen Colonies earned our freedom in combat. That is a sacrifice which Americans have had to make time and time again in our Nation's history. We've learned that strength is the final protector of liberty.

This is a commitment and a sacrifice that I understand well, for the tradition of military service has been running deep for generations in my own family. My first ancestor to live in Georgia, James Carter, who moved there from North Carolina, fought in the Revolution. My father was a first lieutenant in World War I. My oldest son volunteered to go to Vietnam. And I spent 11 years of my life as a professional military officer in the United States Navy. This is typical of American families.

Down throughout the generations, the purposes of our Armed Forces have always been the same, no matter what generation it was: to defend our security when it's threatened and, through dem-

[8]Text from *Presidential Documents,* 14: 530–35.

onstrated strength, to reduce the chances that we will have to fight again.

These words of John Kennedy will still guide our actions, and I quote him, "The purpose of our arms is peace, not war—to make certain that they will never have to be used."[9]

That purpose is unchanged. But the world has been changing, and our responses as a nation must change with it.

This morning I would like to talk to you about our national security—where we now stand, what new circumstances we face, and what we are going to do in the future.

Let me deal at the beginning with some myths. One myth is that this country somehow is pulling back from protecting its interests and its friends around the world. That is not the case, as will be explained in this speech and demonstrated in our actions as a nation.

Another myth is that our defense budget is too burdensome and consumes an undue part of our Federal revenues. National defense is, of course, a large and important item of expenditures, but it represents only about 5 percent of our gross national product and about a quarter of our current Federal budget.

It also is a mistake to believe that our country's defense spending is mainly for intercontinental missiles or nuclear weapons. Only about 10 percent of our defense budget goes for strategic forces or for nuclear deterrence. More than 50 percent is simply to pay for and support the services of the men and women in our Armed Forces.

Finally, some believe that because we do possess nuclear weapons of great destructive power, that we need do nothing more to guarantee our Nation's security. Unfortunately, it's not that simple.

Our potential adversaries have now built up massive forces armed with conventional weapons—tanks, aircraft, infantry, mechanized units. These forces could be used for political blackmail, and they could threaten our vital interests unless we and our allies and friends have our own military strength and conventional forces as a counterbalance.

Of course, our national security rests on more than just military power. It depends partly on the productive capacity of our factories and our farms, on an adequate supply of natural resources with which God has blessed us, on an economic system which values human freedom above centralized control, on the creative ideas of our best minds, on the hard work, cohesion, moral strength and determination of the American people, and on the friendship of our neighbors to the north and south.

Our security depends on strong bonds with our allies and on whether other nations seek to live in peace and refrain from trying to dominate those who live around them.

[9]From Kennedy message, Mar. 28, 1961, in *Documents, 1961:* 52. The quote reads "The primary purpose . . . "

But adequate and capable military forces are still an essential element of our national security. We, like our ancestors, have the obligation to maintain strength equal to the challenges of the world in which we live, and we Americans will continue to do so.

Let us review briefly how national security issues have changed over the past decade or two.

The world has grown both more complex and more interdependent. There is now a division among the Communist powers; the old colonial empires have fallen, and many new nations have risen in their place; old ideological labels have lost some of their meaning.

There have also been changes in the military balance among nations. Over the past 20 years, the military forces of the Soviets have grown substantially, both in absolute numbers and relative to our own. There also has been an ominous inclination on the part of the Soviet Union to use its military power—to intervene in local conflicts, with advisers, with equipment, and with full logistical support and encouragement for mercenaries from other Communist countries, as we can observe today in Africa.

This increase in Soviet military power has been going on for a long time. Discounting inflation, since 1960 Soviet military spending has doubled, rising steadily in real terms by 3 or 4 percent a year, while our own military budget is actually lower now than it was in 1960.

The Soviets, who traditionally were not a significant naval power, now rank number two in world naval forces.

In its balanced strategic nuclear capability, the United States retains important advantages. But over the past decade, the steady Soviet buildup has achieved functional equivalence in strategic forces with the United States.

These changes demand that we maintain adequate responses—diplomatic, military, and economic—and we will.

As President and as Commander-in-Chief, I am responsible, along with the Congress, for modernizing, expanding, and improving our Armed Forces whenever our security requires it. We've recently completed a major reassessment of our national defense strategy. And out of this process have come some overall principles designed to preserve our national security during the years ahead.

We will match, together with our allies and friends, any threatening power through a combination of military forces, political efforts, and economic programs. We will not allow any other nation to gain military superiority over us.

We shall seek the cooperation of the Soviet Union and other nations in reducing areas of tension. We do not desire to intervene militarily in the internal domestic affairs of other countries, nor to aggravate regional conflicts. And we shall oppose intervention by others.

While assuring our own military capabilities, we shall seek security through dependable, verifiable arms control agreements wherever possible.

We shall use our great economic, technological, and diplomatic advantages to defend our interests and to promote American values. We are prepared, for instance, to cooperate with the Soviet Union toward common social, scientific, and economic goals. But if they fail to demonstrate restraint in missile programs and other force levels or in the projection of Soviet or proxy forces into other lands and continents, then popular support in the United States for such cooperation with the Soviets will certainly erode.

These principles mean that, even as we search for agreement in arms control, we will continue to modernize our strategic systems and to revitalize our conventional forces. And I have no doubt that the Congress shares my commitment in this respect.

We shall implement this policy that I've outlined so briefly in three different ways: by maintaining strategic nuclear balance; by working closely with our NATO allies to strengthen and modernize our defenses in Europe; and by maintaining and developing forces to counter any threats to our allies and friends in our vital interests in Asia, the Middle East, and other regions of the world.

Let me take up each of these three in turn.

Our first and most fundamental concern is to prevent nuclear war. The horrors of nuclear conflict, and our desire to reduce the world's arsenals of fearsome nuclear weapons, do not free us from the need to analyze the situation objectively and to make sensible choices about our purposes and means.

Our strategic forces must be—and must be known to be—a match for the capabilities of the Soviets. They will never be able to use their nuclear forces to threaten, to coerce, or to blackmail us or our friends.

Our continuing major effort in the SALT talks taking place every day in Geneva are one means toward a goal of strategic nuclear stability.

We and the Soviets have already reached agreement on some basic points, although still others remain to be resolved. We are making good progress. We are not looking for a one-sided advantage. But before I sign any SALT agreement on behalf of the United States, I will make sure that it preserves the strategic balance, that we can independently verify Soviet compliance, and that we will be at least as strong, relative to the Soviet Union, as we would be without any agreement.

But in addition to the limits and reductions of a SALT II agreement, we must take other steps to protect the strategic balance. During the next decade, improvements in Soviet missiles can make our land-based missile forces in silos increasingly vulnerable to a Soviet first strike. Such an attack would amount to national suicide for the Soviet Union. But however remote, it is a threat against which we must constantly be on guard.

We have a superb submarine fleet, which is relatively invulnerable to attack when it's at sea, and we have under construction new Trident submarines and missiles which give our submarine ballistic missile force even greater range and security.

I have ordered rapid development and deployment of cruise missiles to reinforce the strategic value of our bombers. We are working on the M-X intercontinental ballistic missile and a Trident II submarine-launched ballistic missile to give us more options to respond to Soviet strategic deployments. If it becomes necessary to guarantee the clear invulnerability of our strategic deterrent, I shall not hesitate to take actions for full-scale deployment and development of these systems.

Our strategic defense forces, our nuclear forces, are a triad—land-based missiles, sea-based missiles, and air-breathing missiles, such as bombers and cruise missiles. Through the plans I've described, all three legs of this triad will be modernized and improved. Each will retain the ability, on its own, to impose devastating retaliation upon an aggressor.

For 30 years and more we've been committed to the defense of Europe, bound by the knowledge that Western Europe's security is vital to our own. We continue to cooperate with our NATO allies in a strategy for flexible response, combining conventional forces and nuclear forces so that no aggressor can threaten the territory of Europe or its freedom, which in the past we have fought together to defend.

For several years we and our allies have been trying to negotiate mutual and balanced reduction in military forces in Europe with the Soviets and with the Warsaw Pact nations who are their allies. But in the meantime, the Soviets have continued to modernize their forces beyond a level necessary for defense. In the face of this excessive Soviet buildup, we and our NATO allies have had to take important steps to cope with short-term vulnerabilities and to respond to long-term threats. We are significantly strengthening U.S. forces stationed in Western Europe and improving our ability to speed additional ground and air forces to the defense of Europe in a time of crisis.

Our European allies, who supply the major portion of NATO's conventional combat strength, are also improving their readiness and their reinforcement capabilities and their antitank defenses. The heads of the NATO governments will be here in our country attending a summit meeting in May, where we will address our long-term defense program which will expand and integrate more closely allied defense plans.

For many years, the United States has been a major world

power. Our long-standing concerns encompass our own security interests and those of our allies and friends far beyond our own shores and Europe.

We have important historical responsibilities to enhance peace in East Asia, in the Middle East, in the Persian Gulf, and throughout our own hemisphere. Our preference in all these areas is to turn first to international agreements that reduce the overall level of arms and minimize the threat of conflict. But we have the will, and we will also maintain the capacity, to honor our commitments and to protect our interests in those critical areas.

In the Pacific, our effective security is enhanced by mutual defense treaties with our allies and by our friendship and cooperation with other Pacific nations.

Japan and South Korea, closely linked with the United States, are located geographically where vital interests of great powers converge. It is imperative that Northeast Asia remain stable. We will maintain and even enhance our military strength in this area, improving our air strength and reducing our ground forces, as the South Korean army continues to modernize and to increase its own capabilities.

In the Middle East and the region of the Indian Ocean, we seek permanent peace and stability. The economic health and well-being of the United States, Western Europe, Japan, depend upon continued access to the oil from the Persian Gulf area.

In all these situations, the primary responsibility for preserving peace and military stability rests with the countries of the region. But we shall continue to work with our friends and allies to strengthen their ability to prevent threats to their interests and to ours.

In addition, however, we will maintain forces of our own which can be called upon, if necessary, to support mutual defense efforts. The Secretary of Defense at my direction is improving and will maintain quickly deployable forces—air, land, and sea—to defend our interests throughout the world.

Arms control agreements are a major goal as instruments of our national security, but this will be possible only if we maintain appropriate military force levels. Reaching balanced, verifiable agreements with our adversaries can limit the cost of security and reduce the risk of war. But even then, we must—and we will—proceed efficiently with whatever arms programs our own security requires.

When I leave this auditorium, I shall be going to visit with the crew aboard one of our most modern nuclear-powered aircraft carriers in the Atlantic Ocean. The men and women of our Armed Forces remain committed, as able professionals and as patriotic Americans, to our common defense. They must stand constantly ready to fight, in the hope that through strength, combat will be prevented. We as Americans will always support them in their courageous vigil.

This has been a serious and a sober talk, but there is no cause for pessimism. We face a challenge, and we will do whatever is necessary to meet it. We will preserve and protect our country and continue to promote and to maintain peace around the world. This means that we shall have to continue to support strong and efficient military forces.

For most of human history, people have wished vainly that freedom and the flowering of the human spirit, which freedom nourishes, did not finally have to depend upon the force of arms. We, like our forebears, live in a time when those who would destroy liberty are restrained less by their respect for freedom itself than by their knowledge that those of us who cherish freedom are strong.

We are a great Nation made up of talented people. We can readily afford the necessary costs of our military forces, as well as an increased level, if needed, to prevent any adversary from destabilizing the peace of the world. The money we spend on defense is not wasted any more than is the cost of maintaining a police force in a local community to keep the peace. This investment purchases our freedom to fulfill the worthy goals of our Nation.

Southerners, whose ancestors a hundred years ago knew the horrors of a homeland devastated by war, are particularly determined that war shall never come to us again. All Americans understand the basic lesson of history: that we need to be resolute and able to protect ourselves, to prevent threats and domination by others.

No matter how peaceful and secure and easy the circumstances of our lives now seem, we have no guarantee that the blessings will endure. That is why we will always maintain the strength which, God willing, we shall never need to use.

Thank you very much.

(4) Approaches to Military Security: Address by Secretary of Defense Harold Brown before the National Convention of the American Legion, New Orleans, August 22, 1978.[10]

I want to talk today about how we are working to assure our military security—both by building balanced and fully adequate armed forces of the kind we most need and by seeking arms control agreements consistent with the interests of this country.

Last week President Carter sent back to Congress, without his approval, a defense procurement bill[11] which would have weakened our defense by taking $2 billion from high priority defense needs in order to pay for one nuclear-powered aircraft carrier. The President and I support the full amount of the Defense budget of $126

[10]Text from *Bulletin*, Nov. 1978: 14–17.
[11]Cf. Introduction at note 17.

billion which he requested. We want no congressional cut to be made from it. But we do want that money spent wisely and spent where it is most needed.

The nuclear aircraft carrier costs nearly a billion dollars more than would a future non-nuclear carrier. We plan to build carriers in the future, but we do not need to build this one now at the expense of more urgent needs. And we do not need to add $1 billion to the price tag.

The President is asking the Congress that in the coming year, instead of building a $2 billion carrier with a nuclear power plant, that great amount of money be applied to more urgent needs like the following:

- $800 million for helicopters, combat vehicles, and ammunition for the Army;
- $200 million for airlift, electronic warfare equipment, and modern electronically guided ordnance for all the services;
- Half a billion dollars to upgrade the readiness of all our Armed Forces by providing spare parts, ship overhauls, training, communications, and logistical support;
- Several hundred million dollars more for research and development; and
- More construction of modern general purpose naval ships. For instance, we could build next year two new guided missile frigates, three antisubmarine warfare ships, and a fleet oiler—all for less than one-third the cost of a nuclear-powered carrier.

The President's action is one to enhance our defense, and it certainly is not anti-Navy. We have the strongest navy in the world, and we intend to keep it that way. We need to have balanced forces to meet all our defense needs, including particularly the need for our forces that are in Europe or are oriented for combat there to combine with the forces of our NATO allies to counter the steady Soviet buildup. The Navy itself needs to bring the ship construction program into balance. It must stop the drift of the past 10 years toward a navy of fewer and fewer ships, each of which costs more and more to build. No ship, no matter how costly and capable, can be in more than one place at a time. We want to keep ours the world's strongest navy—not to build the world's most expensive ship.

The Military Balance

Let me turn now to a broader look at where we stand in the world and how it shapes our defense decisions. I should note first, of course, that the overall relative strength of the United States and the Soviet Union depends on more than military force alone, although those forces are a necessary and crucial element. The total balance includes many parts—economic strength and productivity, political stability and cohesion, our technological skill, the appeal of our way of life and our international policies, and our national will. In these overall terms, there is no doubt in my mind that the United States is the most powerful country in the world. We outstrip the Soviets in nearly every category I have mentioned. It is only on the military side that their society has been able to rival us. But the fact that they have turned so much of their effort to military activities is serious and has to be troubling us. We need to do what is necessary to keep a military balance as well as a favorable overall budget of national power.

I noted a moment ago that we are urging the Congress to keep our Defense budget for next year at the full amount the President requested in January.[12] We have also pledged, along with our NATO allies, to increase our defense effort in real terms, after allowing for inflation, with a goal of about 3% increase per year.

Why are we making this effort to increase our defense? In deciding just how many defense dollars we need, we have to start by looking at the military efforts and capabilities of the Soviet Union. I have examined those Soviet capabilities carefully with the help and advice of the Joint Chiefs of Staff. They and I meet at least once a week, and I meet daily with Gen. Jones, the Chairman of the Joint Chiefs of Staff. We consider frequently what responses the United States should make to growth in Soviet military power. We find that the Soviets have been engaged in a substantial military buildup for nearly 20 years. Over that period they have increased their military expenditures by about 4% each year in real terms, compounded, year in and year out. And their buildup is continuing.

But that does not mean that we and our allies have been sitting on our hands or that we have suddenly become inferior to the Warsaw Pact. We are not. And it does not mean that, as we continue to improve our forces, we should make them a carbon copy of the Soviet posture or that we should plan forces simply to match certain Soviet capabilities.

The Soviets must wrestle with a number of problems that we do not now have, especially with respect to China. Their planning has to take into account a difficult geography and a harsh climate—though they do have the advantage of internal lines of communication. They lack willing and effective allies. Our planning should neither forget their burdens nor assume we have the same problems; we have problems, but ours are different.

The Nuclear Deterrent

Thus, simple comparison of Soviet and American forces is only the beginning of understanding our military needs. In planning our forces, we need to be careful not to be misled by such comparisons.

Take the case of our strategic nuclear posture. With the warheads we already deploy, we can target all significant military objectives in the Soviet Union, even after undergoing a first strike by the Soviets. Our basic offensive strength, in other words, is adequate today. But as strategic forces have grown more sophisticated in both the Soviet Union and the United States, the requirements of deterrence have become more demanding, not necessarily in terms of missile throw-weight or megatonnage or warheads—the sorts of measures one often hears about—but rather in other dimensions.

For example, control and ability to withhold some offensive forces—to be able to attack some targets and spare others at a particular phase of combat—may be as important as rapid reaction against the entire enemy target system. As a consequence, our offense needs improved communications, command, and control, even though such capability tends to be ignored in most simple comparisons of Soviet and American strategic capabilities.

Age also often is ignored in simple comparisons, and some of our offensive forces are growing old. Also, some, particularly the ICBM component, are becoming more vulnerable than is desirable from the standpoint of flexibility, even though we might decide to use those forces under attack before they were destroyed.

We have not been idle in the face of these needs. Aging of the force is being brought under control. The modernization of the submarine and bomber forces—with the Trident missile and with cruise missiles—is well under way. We are moving toward development of a new and more sophisticated ICBM. And we are continuing to examine possible replacements for our B-52 bombers.

We are giving equal priority to our other strategic force needs, even though they are less visible and do not lend themselves to simple, numerical comparisons with Soviet capabilities.

- Our warning systems are being improved.
- We are developing increased accuracy for all our missiles— ballistic and cruise.
- We are upgrading our communications and ability to use those communications selectively.
- New warheads soon will be deployed, and advanced avionics systems for our bombers are being tested.

Right now, even after a Soviet surprise attack, we could deliver literally thousands of thermonuclear weapons to targets in the Soviet Union. Despite the improving Soviet offensive and defensive forces, that capability of ours is not going to decline in the future. It is going to increase.

In response to the potential threat new Soviet ICBM's pose to our ICBM's, I have asked the military services and the Joint Chiefs of Staff to consider a number of options to enhance the survivability of that leg of our nuclear deterrence triad, a triad which is composed of bombers and cruise missiles, submarine-launched ballistic missiles, and intercontinental land-based missiles. A number of mobile ICBM-basing concepts are being evaluated, including some involving alternate launch points for each missile. This concept envisions moving missiles and their launchers among multiple sites which might themselves be hardened, thus substantially complicating Soviet targeting of our deterrent.

No decision has been made whether or not to deploy mobile ICBM systems, like the alternate launch point system (or multiple aim point system, as it is sometimes called) that I just mentioned. Nor have we decided which particular concept we would implement, if we were to elect to deploy a mobile ICBM system. The current and projected capabilities of our strategic forces give us time to study thoroughly questions of technical feasibility, military effectiveness, and cost prior to making decisions about deploying mobile ICBM's.

Any mobile ICBM-basing system would, of course, have to be fully consistent with all provisions, including verification provisions, of a strategic arms limitation agreement. The United States will not deploy a mobile ICBM system that would not permit adequate verification of the number of launchers deployed and other provisions of the agreement. You may be confident that we will insist that any Soviet system meet the same verification standards.

The parts of the joint draft text of the SALT II agreement that have already been agreed allow deployment of mobile ICBM systems of the types we are considering. The draft agreement explicitly permits deployment of mobile ICBM launchers during its term, after the expiration of an interim protocol period which would end well before mobile ICBM systems would be ready for deployment.

I know that some of you are concerned about SALT. I want to assure you that no SALT agreement will be signed unless it is in the interests of the United States to sign it. That means particularly that it must not undermine our military security. An acceptable strategic arms limitation agreement is not going to weaken the U.S. second-strike capability that I have described. We will retain our assurance, and the Soviets will know, that we can deliver such a devastating second-strike blow. And that will remain true despite the current Soviet civil defense program.

Conventional Forces

Let me turn finally to conventional forces. Here detailed comparisons count even more than in strategic forces. Despite the growth in Soviet theater capabilities, we and our allies already have bought and are paying for the land, naval, and air forces needed to protect our interests in the world. Despite our global responsibilities, we already are well equipped to deal with contingencies that allow ample time for readying and deploying our forces. If NATO could be sure of a month or more to set up its defenses, for example, I doubt that any Soviet marshal would recommend an attack on Western Europe.

Unfortunately, however, we and our allies no longer can count on having that kind of time. The Soviet theater forces have changed most significantly not in numbers but in their ability to wage short, intense, non-nuclear campaigns using large, modernized forces with relatively little advance preparation. In consequence, as Gen. Haig, the Supreme Allied Commander in Europe, recently observed, surprise attack has become more feasible. Our needs have changed accordingly, not toward larger forces but toward higher combat readiness, greater shortrun sustainability, improved interoperability with allies, and more long-range mobility for the forces we already have.

Don't misunderstand me; I recognize the need for modern weapons. We need improved equipment. But our modern weapons must be fully effective. Therefore, the members of our Armed Forces must be able to maintain them, adequately train on them, and get them into a combat theater before our defenses are overrun.

Combat effectiveness depends on many factors. We must keep the size of our forces, their modernization, their readiness (including their mobility), and their sustainability in balance, especially when the incentives for surprise attack and short, intense campaigns have gone up. Spending money on spare parts, unit training, and field exercises may not grab the headlines. But considering the investment we already are making in hardware, that is the right way at the right time to neutralize the Soviet buildup. That is what the President had in mind, as I said earlier, when he sent the Defense authorization bill back to the Congress last week with a request to put our dollars where they will provide us the greatest protection from the Soviet military effort.

Security and Arms Control

An adequately and properly balanced Defense budget, then, is one way we assure our security against the Soviet military threat. It is a necessary way, but it is not the only one.

Although some may still be skeptical about arms control agreements—and it is a particular responsibility of mine not to be gullible about them—such agreements are another and complementary way of dealing with Soviet military efforts. The interests of the Soviet Union and the United States clearly diverge in many respects.

But the Soviets understand that, as long as we remain strong—and I intend that we will—direct conflict with the United States and its friends could quickly lead to disaster. At a minimum, they share our interest in avoiding such a conflict. And there are other problems of mutual concern on which communication remains necessary and cooperation should be possible. We cannot afford to ignore those possibilities.

I say that because the interests of the United States are best advanced under conditions of peace and orderly change. We need as much stability and predictability as we can manage in our internal relations, consistent with national security. U.S. and allied arms buildups offer one way of obtaining security, stability, and predictability; arms control provides another. What mix of the two works best depends on the circumstances.

As matters now stand, we are well positioned for further competition and an arms buildup. But that is not our preferred path, if we can obtain security, stability, and predictability through precise, equitable, and verifiable arms control. In that case we prefer agreed restraints and reductions to competition and buildups. As a nation, we have no vested interest in arms races.

Our preference for restraint is bound to be especially strong where nuclear forces are concerned. I say this for several reasons. Nuclear weapons represent the only real threat to the survival of the United States and, for that matter, to that of the Soviet Union. Those weapons could destroy in hours all that the two nations have built over centuries.

Both the United States and the Soviet Union already deploy nuclear forces capable of this kind of destruction. As a consequence, it is increasingly unlikely that further buildups by one side will yield a meaningful advantage, providing that the other side takes prudent countermeasures. This is so even though civil defense or exotic technologies may continue to create the illusion of potential advantage.

This is not say that agreements to limit strategic or other armaments can solve all problems, remove all grounds for fear and suspicion, or bring all competition to a complete halt. But carefully drawn agreements, backed by verification of compliance with them, can accomplish a great deal.

- They can make the achievement of future advantage even more unlikely while allowing current vulnerability to be removed.
- They can make future structures more predictable and lower the need for extreme conservatism in our defense planning.
- They can contribute to a healthier political environment, an environment in which still further restraints can be imposed on both sides according to the principle of equivalence.

I do not see any immediate prospect of achieving a mutual end to competition in military strength. A reasonable objective today is to maintain the modest momentum toward arms control. But arms control as such, I can assure you, is not our sole or even principal objective in SALT. What we want, what we insist on, is that the security of the United States and its allies be at least as assured with a SALT agreement as without it. If an agreement does not meet that test, it will not be signed. If it does, it will be.

But with or without SALT, our defense programs will, in the main, have to continue. As we proceed with them, the issue is not whether to have as much defense as we need to protect our domestic and foreign interests. Nobody should doubt the absolute priority of that requirement. To the extent that there is an issue, it is over what, in detail, constitutes the necessary defense.

Experts can argue for hours—my own time is heavily involved in such considerations—about how important, absolutely or relatively, it is to add a 17th Army Division, a 27th fighter-attack wing, or a 13th attack carrier. The fact of the matter is that, with the force structure we already have, individual changes of that order are not going to make much difference to our overall military effectiveness. But changes in our ability to maintain, move, supply, and operate professionally the weapons already in our inventories can make all the difference in the world in our effectiveness and in our deterrent power. You can recall your own military experiences. You probably remember the difficulties of performing your mission when weapons and equipment were not in adequate supply or not functioning properly or down for lack of spare parts.

The President and I want fully effective forces. The competition from the Soviet Union demands it. Real readiness to fight is the most effective counter to the Soviet military threat. Our resources must be spent to assure effectiveness for the kinds of conflicts that are the most likely now and in the foreseeable future. We must not drift back toward the old strategy of sacrificing immediate readiness but counting on a long time for mobilization—a strategy that was barely feasible in the 1930's.

Today we do not have the luxury of time, and combat readiness and quick response are what we need. As Secretary of Defense, I, with the concurrence of the President, intend to shape and provide for our forces to meet those very real requirements. You are a group who, because of those very real requirements, can understand this. I hope I will have your support.

In closing, let me add that there is another and more fundamental reason why priority should go to combat readiness, assuring the immediate fighting capability of our people in uniform. It is that only people—professionally trained people with high morale—can make our weapons work. Even pushbuttons have to be pushed.

As the Legion knows better than most, people are the greatest asset we have in defense. Technologically, we have a comparative advantage over the Soviet Union. But it is not nearly as great as the advantage we obtain from being a free people. The Soviets may be able to close the gap in weapons production and to narrow the gap in military technology. They will never come close to the spirit, the dedication, and the initiative of the men and women in the Armed Forces of the United States.

You, our veterans, gave us the margin necessary to win victory in the past. The men and women of our Armed Forces today offer us the opportunity for the same decisive margin. As long as I am Secretary of Defense, I intend to make the most of it. I hope to have your support in doing so.

(5)   Human Rights and Foreign Policy: Remarks by President Carter at a White House Meeting Commemorating the 30th Anniversary of the Signature of the Universal Declaration of Human Rights, December 6, 1978. [13]

What I have to say today is fundamentally very simple. It's something I've said many times, including my acceptance speech when I was nominated as President and my inaugural speech [14] when I became President. But it cannot be said too often or too firmly nor too strongly.

As long as I am President, the Government of the United States will continue throughout the world to enhance human rights. No force on Earth can separate us from that commitment.

This week we commemorate the 30th anniversary of the Universal Declaration of Human Rights. We rededicate ourselves—in the words of Eleanor Roosevelt, who was the chairperson of the Human Rights Commission—to the Universal Declaration as, and I quote from her, "a common standard of achievement for all peoples of all nations."

The Universal Declaration and the human rights conventions that derive from it do not describe the world as it is. But these documents are very important, nonetheless. They are a beacon, a guide to a future of personal security, political freedom, and social justice.

For millions of people around the globe that beacon is still quite distant, a glimmer of light on a dark horizon of deprivation and repression. The reports of Amnesty International, the International Commission of Jurists, the International League for Human Rights, and many other nongovernmental human rights organizations amply document the practices and conditions that destroy the lives and the spirit of countless human beings.

[13] Text from *Presidential Documents,* 14: 2161–5.
[14] Address, Jan. 20, 1977, in *AFR, 1977:* 154–6.

Political killings, tortures, arbitrary and prolonged detention without trial or without a charge, these are the cruellest and the ugliest of human rights violations. Of all human rights, the most basic is to be free of arbitrary violence, whether that violence comes from government, from terrorists, from criminals, or from self-appointed messiahs operating under the cover of politics or religion.

But governments—because of their power, which is so much greater than that of an individual—have a special responsibility. The first duty of a government is to protect its own citizens, and when government itself becomes the perpetrator of arbitrary violence against its citizens, it undermines its own legitimacy.

There are other violations of the body and the spirit which are especially destructive of human life. Hunger, disease, poverty, are enemies of human potential which are as relentless as any repressive government.

The American people want the actions of their government, our government, both to reduce human suffering and to increase human freedom. That's why—with the help and encouragement of many of you in this room—I have sought to rekindle the beacon of human rights in American foreign policy. Over the last 2 years we've tried to express these human concerns as our diplomats practice their craft and as our Nation fulfills its own international obligations.

We will speak out when individual rights are violated in other lands. The Universal Declaration means that no nation can draw the cloak of sovereignty over torture, disappearances, officially sanctioned bigotry, or the destruction of freedom within its own borders. The message that is being delivered by all our representatives abroad—whether they are from the Department of State or Commerce or Agriculture or Defense or whatever—is that the policies regarding human rights count very much in the character of our own relations with other individual countries.

In distributing the scarce resources of our foreign assistance programs, we will demonstrate that our deepest affinities are with nations which commit themselves to a democratic path to development. Toward regimes which persist in wholesale violations of human rights, we will not hesitate to convey our outrage, nor will we pretend that our relations are unaffected.

In the coming year, I hope that Congress will take a step that has long been overdue for a generation, the ratification of the Convention on the Prevention and Punishment of the Crime of Genocide. As you know, the genocide convention was also adopted by the United Nations General Assembly 30 years ago this week, 1 day before the adoption of the Universal Declaration. It was the world's affirmation that the lesson of the Holocaust would never be forgotten, but unhappily, genocide is not peculiar to any one historical era.

Eighty-three other nations have ratified the genocide convention. The United States, despite the support of every President since 1948, has not. In international meetings at the United Nations and elsewhere, when I meet with foreign leaders, we are often asked why. We do not have an acceptable answer.

I urge the United States Senate to observe this anniversary in the only appropriate way, by ratifying the genocide convention at the earliest possible date.

This action must be the first step toward the ratification of other human rights instruments, including those I signed a year ago.[15] Many of the religious and human rights groups represented here have undertaken a campaign of public education on behalf of these covenants. I commend and appreciate your efforts.

Refugees are the living, homeless casualties of one very important failure on the part of the world to live by the principles of peace and human rights. To help these refugees is a simple human duty. As Americans, as a people made up largely of the descendants of refugees, we feel that duty with special keenness.

Our country will do its utmost to ease the plight of stranded refugees from Indochina and from Lebanon and of released political prisoners from Cuba and from elsewhere. I hope that we will always stand ready to welcome more than our fair share of those who flee their homelands because of racial, religious, or political oppression.

The effectiveness of our human rights policy is now an established fact. It has contributed to an atmosphere of change—sometimes disturbing—but which has encouraged progress in many ways and in many places. In some countries, political prisoners have been released by the hundreds, even thousands. In others, the brutality of repression has been lessened. In still others there's a movement toward democratic institutions or the rule of law when these movements were not previously detectable.

To those who doubt the wisdom of our dedication, I say this: Ask the victims. Ask the exiles. Ask the governments which continue to practice repression. Whether in Cambodia or Chile, in Uganda or South Africa, in Nicaragua or Ethiopia or the Soviet Union, governments know that we in the United States care. And not a single one of those who is actually taking risks or suffering for human rights has ever asked me to desist in our support of basic human rights. From the prisons, from the camps, from the enforced exiles, we receive one message: Speak up, persevere, let the voice of freedom be heard.

I'm very proud that our Nation stands for more than military

15Cf. *AFR, 1977:* 73 and 136-7.

might or political might. It stands for ideals that have their reflection in the aspirations of peasants in Latin America, workers in Eastern Europe, students in Africa, and farmers in Asia.

We do live in a difficult and complicated world, a world in which peace is literally a matter of survival. Our foreign policy must take this into account. Often, a choice that moves us toward one goal tends to move us further away from another goal. Seldom do circumstances permit me or you to take actions that are wholly satisfactory to everyone.

But I want to stress again that human rights are not peripheral to the foreign policy of the United States. Our human rights policy is not a decoration. It is not something we've adopted to polish up our image abroad or to put a fresh coat of moral paint on the discredited policies of the past. Our pursuit of human rights is part of a broad effort to use our great power and our tremendous influence in the service of creating a better world, a world in which human beings can live in peace, in freedom, and with their basic needs adequately met.

Human rights is the soul of our foreign policy. And I say this with assurance, because human rights is the soul of our sense of nationhood.

For the most part, other nations are held together by common racial or ethnic ancestry, or by a common creed or religion, or by ancient attachments to the land that go back for centuries of time. Some nations are held together by the forces, implied forces of a tyrannical government. We are different from all of those, and I believe that we in our country are more fortunate.

As a people we come from every country and every corner of the Earth. We are of many religions and many creeds. We are of every race, every color, every ethnic and cultural background. We are right to be proud of these things and of the richness that lend to the texture of our national life. But they are not the things which unite us as a single people.

What unites us—what makes us Americans—is a common belief in peace, in a free society, and a common devotion to the liberties enshrined in our Constitution. That belief and that devotion are the sources of our sense of national community. Uniquely, ours is a nation founded on an idea of human rights. From our own history we know how powerful that idea can be.

Next week marks another human rights anniversary—Bill of Rights Day. Our Nation was "conceived in liberty," in Lincoln's words, but it has taken nearly two centuries for that liberty to approach maturity.

For most of the first half of our history, black Americans were denied even the most basic human rights. For most of the first two-thirds of our history, women were excluded from the political process. Their rights and those of Native Americans are still not constitutionally guaranteed and enforced. Even freedom of speech has been threatened periodically throughout our history. Only in the last 10 to 12 years have we achieved what Father Hesburgh has called "the legal abandonment of more than three centuries of apartheid." And the struggle for full human rights for all Americans—black, brown, and white; male and female; rich and poor—is far from over.

To me, as to many of you, these are not abstract matters or ideas. In the rural Georgia country where I grew up, the majority of my own fellow citizens were denied many basic rights—the right to vote, the right to speak freely without fear, the right to equal treatment under the law. I saw at first hand the effects of a system of deprivation of rights. I saw the courage of those who resisted that system. And finally, I saw the cleansing energies that were released when my own region of this country walked out of darkness and into what Hubert Humphrey, in the year of the adoption of the Universal Declaration, called "the bright sunshine of human rights."

The American Bill of Rights is 187 years old, and the struggle to make it a reality has occupied every one of those 187 years. The Universal Declaration of Human Rights is only 30 years old. In the perspective of history, the idea of human rights has only just been touched.

I do not draw this comparison because I want to counsel patience. I draw it because I want to emphasize, in spite of difficulties, steadfastness and commitment.

A hundred and eighty-seven years ago, as far as most Americans were concerned, the Bill of Rights was a bill of promises. There was no guarantee that those promises would ever be fulfilled. We did not realize those promises by waiting for history to take its in evitable course. We realized them because we struggled. We realized them because many sacrificed. We realized them because we persevered.

For millions of people around the world today the Universal Declaration of Human Rights is still only a declaration of hope. Like all of you, I want that hope to be fulfilled. The struggle to fulfill it will last longer than the lifetimes of any of us. Indeed, it will last as long as the lifetime of humanity itself. But we must persevere.

And we must persevere by ensuring that this country of ours, leader in the world, which we love so much, is always in the forefront of those who are struggling for that great hope, the great dream of universal human rights.

Thank you very much.

2. ARMS LIMITATION AND THE SOVIET UNION

(6)   Arms Control and National Security: Address by Secretary of State Vance before the American Society of Newspaper Editors, April 10, 1978. [1]

I am delighted to have this opportunity to discuss with you an issue that is vital to this nation's security—the effort to slow down the dangerous and burdensome arms race through effective arms control.

This is an effort in which I deeply believe. My years in the Defense Department, my activities as a private citizen in studies of military issues, and my experience as Secretary of State have made one fact increasingly clear to me: A strong defense and effective arms control are not separate paths to national security; both are essential steps along the same path.

Our nation's safety continues to depend upon a strong, modern military defense capable of meeting the full spectrum of our military needs. We have had that strength in the past. We have it now. And we will maintain it.

Yet we cannot assure our security by military strength alone. New weapons systems acquired by one side stimulate the other side to develop more sophisticated countermeasures. The net effect is the expansion of weapons systems on both sides without real increase in the security of either.

As I have met with leaders around the world over the past year, I have found that many share this perception. They too cannot and will not allow their nations to become vulnerable to military threat. But they also recognize that the heavy burden of military competition diverts limited resources and energies from social and economic development on which peace also rests.

The effort to slow arms competition through mutual and balanced restraints has been a central element of this nation's security

[1]Department of State Press Release 154; text from *Bulletin*, May 1978: 20–22.

policy under the past seven American Presidents—Democratic and Republican.

- President Kennedy, building on the efforts of Presidents Truman and Eisenhower, concluded the first arms control agreement with the Soviet Union in 1963—halting nuclear weapons testing in the atmosphere and the contamination that entailed. Subsequently, we concluded agreements prohibiting nuclear and other weapons of mass destruction from the ocean floor and from outer space.
- The Nuclear Nonproliferation Treaty, concluded in 1968, is binding today on more than 100 nations. Clearly, it has not ended the specter of nuclear proliferation, but it has significantly advanced that objective.
- Since first proposed by President Johnson, we have been engaged in broader Strategic Arms Limitation Talks (SALT). These negotiations succeeded, during the Nixon Administration, in severely restricting the deployment of antiballistic missile systems by either the United States or the Soviet Union. Such systems would have been costly to build and would have added new uncertainties into the strategic balance. SALT I also placed the first limits on the number of offensive weapons.

We are engaged today in a broader range of arms control negotiations than ever before in our history, because the opportunities we can grasp and the challenges we face are greater than ever before.

As we pursue these negotiations, we must be realistic about what effective arms control can—and cannot—do for our security. For if we judge arms control measures against unrealistic standards, we may lose the possibility of making any practical progress.

- No single arms control agreement will eliminate all, or even most, of the potential challenges against U.S. and allied forces. But by controlling the size, nature, and direction of arms programs on both sides, we can reduce the uncertainties that fuel the arms race.
- For the foreseeable future, arms control will not dramatically reduce our defense budget. The cost of an adequate defense will remain high. But the drain on our resources from an unrestricted arms race would be much greater.
- Arms control cannot by itself guarantee stability in the U.S.-Soviet relationship. We continue to compete, because in many areas we have different interests and values. We need not be sanguine about Soviet power or intentions, however, to recognize that as inhabitants of the same planet who share awe-

some power, we have a common interest in reducing the most serious risks to our survival.

• Arms control will not by itself resolve the regional tensions that threaten peace. But by lessening the level of military confrontation and regulating the diffusion of new weapon technologies, we can enhance regional stability and free resources for the task of improving the human condition.

There are clear limits to what we should expect from arms control. But it is equally clear that arms control, pursued in a deliberate and measured way, will contribute significantly to reducing the prospect of war. This is why I believe so strongly that our security is best protected by policies of strength in our national defense and by practical arms control agreements that limit the dangers to which we must, and always will, respond.

As President Carter said in his Wake Forest speech: "Arms control agreements are a major goal as instruments of our national security, but this will be possible only if we maintain appropriate military force levels."[2]

SALT

Let me turn first to the Strategic Arms Limitation Talks with the Soviet Union.

Any SALT agreement must be measured against the yardstick of our national safety. It must clearly maintain or improve our overall security as compared to the likely situation without an agreement. It must take full account of the interests of our allies as well as ourselves. And we must have confidence in our independent ability to verify adequately Soviet compliance with an agreement and to detect any effort, contrary to the agreement, that could leave us at a strategic disadvantage. We should not and we will not accept any agreement that does not meet these essential requirements.

We have made substantial progress over the past year toward such an agreement. Important differences still remain. I will be meeting with the Soviet leaders later this month in an effort to narrow those remaining differences. I hope that we can reach an agreement in the near future. But we will continue to negotiate for as long as it takes to achieve a SALT agreement which enhances our security and that of our allies.

Let me explain what the agreement that we are seeking to negotiate would accomplish and how it would strengthen our security.

First, it would establish equal limits for both sides on the overall number of strategic missile launchers and strategic bombers. As you know, under the first SALT agreement the Soviets maintained greater numbers than the United States. Following that agreement, Congress called for any new agreement to be based on equal numbers. This agreement would firmly establish that principle.

Second, the agreement would reduce the number of strategic weapons below the level that the Soviets now have—and very much below what they could have without an agreement. It would require the Soviets to destroy several hundred weapons. We would not be required to destroy any weapons currently operational.

Third, the agreement would establish sublimits on those systems we see as most threatening and destabilizing, such as intercontinental ballistic missiles (ICBM's) equipped with MIRV'd [multiple independently-targetable reentry vehicles] warheads and on MIRV'd ballistic missiles more generally.

Fourth, we are trying to impose restraints on the improvement of existing weapons and the development of new and more sophisticated systems.

Fifth, the agreement we are negotiating would permit the United States to preserve essential options for modernizing our forces. Specifically, it would allow us to continue our major development programs, such as the cruise and MX missiles and Trident program.

Sixth, it would protect the interests of our allies. Mindful of the relationship between strategic arms negotiations and our security commitments in NATO, we have consulted closely with our allies at each step of the negotiations, and we will continue to do so.

Finally, we are insisting on an agreement which is independently and satisfactorily verifiable. Our ability to verify must have sufficient reliability to deter and to deal with possible violations before they have a significant effect on the strategic balance. We must be able to assure ourselves that the Soviets are living up to their commitments.

We and the Soviets both know the kind of terrible destruction that would result from a nuclear war. We both know that each will ultimately match the other if the race continues.

Therefore, despite the fact that we are both intently pursuing our own self-interests—despite fundamental differences that exist between us—we hope to be able to find common ground for limiting our most destructive weapons. The essence of this negotiation is mutuality of benefits. An arrangement which benefits one side at the expense of the other cannot be agreed on.

Failure to achieve an equitable agreement could result in new weapons programs on both sides, with a corresponding increase in costs of several billion dollars a year but with no more, and probably less, security. This Administration is prepared to pay the extra price of maintaining our security. I am convinced that the Congress and the American people are prepared to pay that price. But an effective SALT agreement can assist us in maintaining the strategic balance at reduced levels of cost and risk.

Antisatellite Arms Control

Along with SALT, there are numerous other aspects to the military competition which must be addressed. An expansion of the arms race to space would undermine our security as well as that of other nations. Evidence that the Soviet Union is developing an antisatellite capability is disturbing. We are prepared to protect ourselves against such a threat and to match the Soviets if necessary. But a far preferable course is to prevent an antisatellite race from occurring.

While there are many problems in devising effective and verifiable limits, there is an area for arms control here too. We have proposed talks with the Soviets aimed at suspending antisatellite testing and keeping space open for free and peaceful use by all. I can confirm today that the Soviet Union has recently accepted our proposal, and talks will begin next month.

Comprehensive Test Ban

We are also engaged with the British and Soviet Governments in negotiations for a comprehensive ban on nuclear testing. These talks have made some progress, although problems remain. Achievement of such a ban would reduce the likelihood of further nuclear proliferation by demonstrating the seriousness of the nuclear weapons powers in accepting restraints on their own activities.

We are committed to seeking such a treaty. It must be adequately verifiable. And we will assure that we maintain confidence in the reliability of our nuclear warheads.

Arms Control in Europe

Just as we are negotiating for agreements that can further allied security in the area of strategic weapons, so too the mutual and balanced force reduction talks in Vienna are intended to enhance our mutual security in the European theater. In recent years, the Soviets and other Warsaw Pact countries have built up their forces and materiel to the point where the regional balance has become of increasing concern to ourselves and our allies.

Our central goal in the Vienna talks is to codify the principles of parity and collectivity of forces in central Europe. We and the NATO allies have made clear to the Soviet Union that we will only accept an agreement which enhances the security of the region.

These talks have moved extremely slowly. It is important that we work toward an agreement in this area, however, even as we negotiate on SALT. We and our allies will soon be making a new effort to get the talks moving more productively. It is time for the Warsaw Pact nations, through meaningful actions, to help move these talks forward.

While seeking progress in these talks, we have also made a firm commitment to the modernization and strengthening of NATO forces, and we are taking concrete steps to that end. The United States has sharply increased the emphasis on NATO defense in our current budget. Along with our allies, we are introducing new tactical aircraft, new generations of armored vehicles, and new precision-guided munitions. NATO leaders will be meeting in Washington in May, and one of the principal topics will be a long-term program to improve alliance defense.

As you know, the President, after having consulted our allies and with their full backing, has deferred production of weapons with enhanced radiation effects. He has ordered the modernization of the Lance missile nuclear warhead and the 8-inch weapons system, keeping open the option of later deciding to install the enhanced radiation elements. His ultimate decision will be influenced, as he has said, ". . . by the degree to which the Soviet Union shows restraint in its conventional and nuclear arms programs and force deployments affecting the security of the United States and Western Europe."[3]

The Global Dimension

Another threat to the peace lies in the growth and spread of arms around the world.

In the long run, the peaceful settlement of regional disputes is the surest way to reduce the demand for arms. We will continue our efforts to help find lasting solutions to such disputes. And we will continue to press for restraint on the part of the great powers so that local conflicts are not exacerbated. But we must also seek restraint in the growth of arms.

First, in addition to our efforts to halt further nuclear proliferation through a comprehensive test ban, we have begun to investigate new technologies and examine new institutional arrangements that will enable the nations of the world to harness nuclear energy without spreading the most deadly instruments of war.

Second, we are giving new emphasis to controlling the international traffic in conventional arms. We will continue to make arms transfers to advance our own security and that of our friends, but at the same time, we are beginning to check the flow of our own arms exports.

Because we recognize that slowing down conventional arms races

[3]Cf. Introduction at note 39.

cannot be achieved by the United States alone, we are discussing possible multilateral measures with other arms suppliers, and we are encouraging the purchasing nations to adopt regional agreements that limit arms competition.

I am pleased to be able to state today that the Soviet Union has agreed to proceed with our talks on restraint of conventional sales. This is an important step in our efforts to bring about a serious international discussion on multilateral restraint.

Third, we are seeking to limit and control the spread and the use of new weapons systems whose impact on civilian populations is particularly deadly. Biological, chemical, and environmental weapons treaties have been or are being negotiated. The indiscriminate and random character of many weapons in these categories is so great that virtually all nations agree they should be forsworn forever as instruments of war.

Fourth, we are seeking to prevent arms competition and major power rivalry from spreading to areas largely free of them in the past. We have launched new negotiations with the Soviet Union to avert an arms race in the Indian Ocean. Our objective is first to stabilize the military presence of both sides at the levels which prevailed until recent months and then to consider possible reductions. The buildup in Soviet naval forces in the area, however, is of deep concern, and we will not accept an increased Soviet naval presence as part of such an agreement.

Conclusion

Each of the arms control efforts I have discussed is devoted to increasing the safety and well-being of Americans and individuals everywhere.

Military competition today is carried out in highly technical terms, and military judgments must often be made based on complex calculations. But we cannot let technical debates cloud the simple truths and common sense which must lie behind these calculations.

- We must maintain military defense that is second to none. We have the human and physical resources, the knowledge, and the will to do so.
- We must also recognize that no nation gains, none is more secure when all continue to expend their resources on ever more devastating weapons. We all gain, we are all more secure when practical, equitable agreements can be reached to limit the arms race.

This is a long-term process. We will work with others to further this effort—in the talks between East and West, at the U.N. Special

Session on Disarmament opening in New York next month, and in other forums.

I have spoken to you today about arms control because you will play a crucial role in the coming months and years. Your opinions and explanations will help decide whether we maintain our sensible and historic policies of seeking security through both arms control and a stable military equilibrium.

There are people in our country who have come to doubt this course—some because they expect too much of arms control measures; others because they believe too little can be achieved. Those who expect too much will be disillusioned when such agreements do not put an end to military competition. Those who believe such agreements are not worth pursuing seriously undervalue their returns.

I hope that you will bear in mind my basic message: that while the benefits of arms control are not boundless, there are terribly important, practical advantages that only arms control measures can bring.

I ask each of you to consider the difference between a world with a SALT agreement of the kind I have described and a world without such a limitation on strategic weaponry; a world in which we have begun to stabilize in an acceptable balance the military relationship in Central Europe and one in which we have not; a world in which we are starting to head off a military competition in space—or to put some limits on the international flow of conventional arms—or to reduce the prospects for nuclear proliferation; and a world in which we fail to achieve such steps.

In the long run, the security of every American depends on our devoting the same determination, the same careful planning and sustained energy to the challenge of bringing military competition under sensible control as we do to devising new weapons for our protection. Our challenge—the challenge to all nations—is to make sure that man's technical ingenuity is guided by wisdom.

(7)   Special Session on Disarmament of the United Nations General Assembly, New York, May 23–June 30, 1978.

  (a)   The Position of the United States: Address by Vice-President Walter F. Mondale to the Assembly, May 24, 1978. [4]

I am honored to represent the President of the United States at this Special Session on Disarmament of the U.N. General Assem-

[4]Text from *Bulletin,* June 1978: 31-5.

bly. The nations of the world are gathered here today to pursue the most vital and solemn obligation of the U.N. Charter—"to save succeeding generations from the scourge of war."

We meet today at the initiative of the nonaligned states. These nations, comprising the bulk of the world's people, are particularly aware of the helplessness and hopelessness spawned by the arms race. I salute them for calling us together to confront this challenge.

And we applaud, as well, the dedication and contribution of the many nongovernmental organizations represented here. The arms race touches the lives of every man, woman, and child in the world. The control of arms is too crucial to leave to a few governments or even all governments alone. You are our conscience and inspiration.

My beloved friend, Hubert Humphrey, was one of the earliest voices calling for arms control and disarmament. He spoke of the challenge we face today. He said:

> Ours is a new era, one which calls for a new kind of courage. For the first time in the history of mankind, one generation literally has the power to destroy the past, the present, and the future; the power to bring time to an end.

And if we do not curb the arms race, we not only threaten the future, we impoverish the present.

While the people of the world cry for food and shelter, for medicine and education, the vast resources of our planet are being devoted more and more to the means of destroying, instead of enriching, human life. The global cost of arms has reached $400 billion a year. The world is spending almost $1 million a minute for weapons. Over 20 million men and women are in military service around the world.

No world leader, no parent, and no individual on this Earth can live securely in the shadow of the growing world arsenal. But in the face of that mounting danger, this conference is a symbol of hope. This Special Session on Disarmament of the U.N. General Assembly offers hope of greater progress toward disarmament and a world in which the threat of war is vastly diminished and the security of each nation more fully insured.

U.S. Commitment

The United States attaches major importance to the work of this conference. Last October, President Carter made a special trip to the United Nations to emphasize America's strong commitment to arms control and disarmament.[5] He stressed our willingness to work toward a world truly free of nuclear weapons. He pledged our

⁵AFR, 1977: 201-8.

total commitment to reversing the buildup of armaments and reducing their trade.

Since that time, the United States has been engaged in the broadest set of arms control negotiations in our history. Together with our negotiating partners, the United States has developed an agenda more extensive than any nation has ever attempted. We are taking concrete actions in 10 different areas—from nuclear weapons accords, to regional restraint, to limits on conventional and unconventional arms such as antisatellite and radiological weapons. Before too long, the United States expects to take part in two historic achievements.

- For the first time since the dawn of the atomic era, we will reach an agreement to reduce the combined total of strategic nuclear weapons delivery vehicles of the Soviet Union and the United States.
- After two decades of negotiations, we will produce a comprehensive test ban controlling nuclear explosions by the United States, the United Kingdom, and the Soviet Union.

The United States welcomes this opportunity to review what is being accomplished, to chart our course for the years ahead, and to rededicate ourselves to further success.

Assuring Security Needs

We are here to listen to the voices of other nations, as well as to raise our own in behalf of arms control and disarmament. For this session is a part of a process in which all of us must work together, in a spirit of openness and mutual respect. As President Kennedy once said: "Genuine peace must be the product of many nations, the sum of many acts."

To avoid a world a decade hence in which three-quarters of a trillion dollars is spent on arms, in which there are more nuclear-weapons states, we must have a program that is visionary in concept and realistic in action.

Realism requires that we face squarely the central issue of the arms race—the concern of each nation and government for the security of its people. If the arms race were driven by madmen, there would be no hope. Controls would be beyond the reach of rational discourse. Irrational forces no doubt play a part, but the arms race is driven by other considerations as well—technology, international tensions, legitimate security concerns.

The prudent policy of any nation must include both sufficient military preparedness and arms control efforts—if its security is to be assured. In the short run, no nation can be asked to reduce its defenses to levels below the threat it faces. But without arms control among nations, in the long run weapon will be piled on weapon with a loss in security for all.

These meetings at the United Nations and the NATO summit next week in Washington dramatize the determination of the United States to take every step possible toward greater arms control while at the same time assuring essential security needs.

Today, our defense budget is no larger in real terms than in the late 1950's and less than it was a decade ago. But other nations have increased their military budgets in real terms by more than one-third over the past decade.

We and our NATO allies are strong, and we will remain strong to provide for the defense of our peoples. But we face a continuing buildup of unprecedented proportions in Europe. The Warsaw Pact has developed an almost three to one advantage in tanks. The SS-20 nuclear missile now being deployed against Western Europe is a new departure in destructive power and represents a substantial increase in the nuclear threat of the Soviet Union.

The NATO summit meeting next week in Washington will recommit the Western democracies to a military posture capable of deterring and defending against attacks. We will remain prepared to resist attack across the spectrum of conventional, tactical nuclear, and strategic forces. In the face of the continuing buildup of Warsaw Pact forces, we will moderately increase the defense budgets of our nations. We do so not from preference but necessity.

At the same time, the NATO summit will reaffirm and re-emphasize the commitment of the West to the other dimension of our common security policy—the pursuit of arms control. We will address the arms control initiatives the West has recently taken and will continue to take. We will offer our continued strong support for the success of the special session.

In his Day of Peace message this January, His Holiness, Pope Paul, in effect, spoke of the work of this special session. He said:

. . . the conscience of the world is horrified by the hypothesis that our peace is nothing but a truce and that an uncontrollable conflagration can be suddenly unleashed.

We would like to be able to dispel this threatening and terrible nightmare by proclaiming at the top of our voice the absurdity of modern war and the absolute necessity of peace—peace not founded on the power of arms that today are endowed with an infernal destructive capacity . . . nor founded on the structural violence of some political regimes, but founded on the patient, rational and loyal method of justice and freedom, such as the great international institutions of today are promoting and defending.

Program of Action

Today, I want to speak to that message. I want to set forth bold objectives and realistic steps—a vision that should guide our arms control efforts, and that can help us develop the centerpiece of our work over the next few weeks—the program of action.

First, we should substantially cut the number of strategic nuclear arms and place increasingly stringent qualitative limitations on their further development.

The United States recognizes that it bears, together with the Soviet Union and other nuclear-weapons powers, a very special responsibility. The SALT II agreement which is rapidly taking shape will:

- Reduce the number of strategic delivery vehicles now in existence and put a ceiling on the remainder;
- Establish sublimits on those systems which are most threatening and destabilizing; and
- Impose restraints on the improvement of existing weapons and the development of new and more sophisticated systems.

Equally important, the SALT II agreement must and will be adequately verifiable. Neither side can be permitted to emerge suddenly superior through undetected cheating, thus upsetting the strategic balance upon which deterrence of nuclear war depends.

Successful SALT negotiations will make a major contribution to peace. SALT II serves all nations' interests. It deserves universal support. But SALT II is only a step in a very difficult long-term process. We hope soon to begin SALT III. The United States is committed—and I emphasize this point—to a further substantial reduction in nuclear weapons and to still stricter limitations on modernization and new types of delivery vehicles.

A commitment by others will also be required if SALT, and other negotiations, are to succeed.

Yet, Soviet theater nuclear forces have increased. The most significant development has been the deployment of the SS-20—a new, mobile intermediate-range ballistic missile. Each one of these missiles, which may number in the hundreds when deployment is complete, carries three nuclear warheads, each with an estimated yield of 500 kilotons. This high yield, coupled with the SS-20's accuracy, has significantly increased the Soviets' military capability against both military and civilian targets. But the high yield also means that damage to innocent civilians would be extensive, with effects extending 12 kilometers from an explosion.

The SS-20 missile, while not targeted at the United States, is capable of striking targets not only in Western Europe but in Asia,

Africa, and the Middle East. Its deployment runs totally contrary to all that this special session seeks to achieve. What can justify this escalation in nuclear arms?

Second on our agenda, there should be an end to explosions of nuclear devices.

Soon after his inauguration, President Carter announced his intention to proceed quickly and aggressively with a comprehensive test ban treaty, eliminating the testing of all nuclear devices whether for peaceful or military puposes. Subsequently, the United States, the United Kingdom, and the Soviet Union entered into trilateral negotiations aimed at accomplishing this historic objective. If successful, this will represent the culmination of a process which began in the late 1950's. It will build on the interim results of the Limited Test Ban Treaty of 1963 and the U.S.-U.S.S.R. Threshold Test Ban and Peaceful Nuclear Explosions Treaties signed in 1974 and 1976.

A comprehensive test ban would make a major contribution to curbing the nuclear competition between the superpowers. It would lessen incentives for the development of nuclear weapons by states which do not now possess them and thus re-enforce the Nonproliferation Treaty.

Trilateral negotiations are underway in Geneva. Important progress toward an adequately verifiable agreement has been made. Once agreement is reached, we will move vigorously to seek a multilateral comprehensive test ban treaty accepted by all states. All nations must be persuaded to forswear testing. The continued explosion of nuclear devices has been the major symbol of man's unwillingness to put aside the further development of the world's most devastating weapon. It can, must, and will be stopped.

Third, as we limit and reduce the weapons of existing nuclear states, we must work in concert to insure that no additional nuclear-weapons states emerge over the next decade and beyond.

The spread of nuclear weapons to an ever-increasing number of countries and regions is a chilling prospect. It brings ever closer the probability of their use. Such proliferation would seriously heighten regional and global tensions. It would impede peaceful commerce in the field of nuclear energy. And it would make the achievement of nuclear disarmament vastly more difficult.

The United States understands the concerns of some non-nuclear-weapons states that they are being discriminated against. To help meet these concerns and to prevent the proliferation of nuclear weapons:

- I reiterate today the solemn declaration which President Carter made from this podium in 1977. The United States will not use nuclear weapons except in self-defense—that is, in circumstances of an actual nuclear or conventional attack on the United States, our territories, or armed forces, or such an attack on our allies. I call on other nations to make this pledge;

- The President will propose new and expanded contributions by the United States to the peaceful nuclear programs of states which support nonproliferation;

- As President Eisenhower said as long ago as 1956, we must ultimately work out, with other nations, suitable, verifiable, and safeguarded arrangements so that the future production of fissionable materials anywhere in the world would no longer be used to increase the stockpiles of explosive weapons; and

- We will pursue the International Nuclear Fuel Cycle Evaluation to explore further how to insure the benefits of nuclear energy to all without its proliferation risks.

We must redouble our efforts to increase still further the distance between the military and peaceful uses of nuclear energy. Nuclear power stations should produce energy for people—not plutonium for bombs.

Let us learn from the example set by Latin America. Let us expand the regions of the Earth where nuclear weapons will be banned. At the initiative of several Latin American nations, the treaty of Tlatelolco, which bans nuclear weapons from the area, was signed in Mexico City in 1967. Since then, almost all potential parties to the treaty, including the United States, have signed. The United States congratulates the Soviet Union for its recent signing of Protocol II of the treaty. There is now only one country in this region which has yet to indicate its interest in signing.[6] That should be remedied now.

It is our hope that the treaty will come fully into force as soon as possible, thereby creating the first major nuclear-weapons-free zone in the world. We hope that Latin America's bold initiative will be a model for other regions to follow.

Fourth, as we move to gain control over the nuclear threat, we must seek mutual agreement to ban other weapons of mass destruction.

The horror of gas warfare during World War I is etched in the memory of mankind. We have made some progress in recent years by prohibiting biological weapons. The United States and the Soviet Union are moving closer to an agreement on banning radiological weapons, which we would then put before the Conference of the

[6]Cuba.

Committee on Disarmament (CCD). Our discussions on chemical weapons are proving more difficult. Any agreement on chemical or new and exotic weapons must be adequately verifiable. The United States is committed to finding a solution, assuming there is a fair-minded approach on the other side.

Fifth, we must immediately slow down and then reverse the sharp growth in conventional arms.
The vast bulk of the $400 billion spent for military purposes in 1976 was spent on conventional weapons. We recognize the legitimate concern of nations that they not be denied arbitrarily access to arms needed for their legitimate defense. Such needs must and will be met. At the same time, our common interests demand a vast reduction in the flow of conventional arms.

Fresh thought is required to come to grips with this neglected, increasingly important dimension of arms control. But we can and we must take action now. Fueling the conventional arms race is the rapidly expanding international trade in these arms. The value of arms imports by the developing nations has increased 75% from 1967 to 1976. A limited, but growing, number of suppliers and recipients accounts for most of this $20 billion trade.

The United States has on its own initiative begun to reduce the volume of the arms it sells. Under President Carter's conventional arms policy:

- We have placed a ceiling—a reduction of 8% in FY 1978—on weapons and weapons-related items to countries other than NATO, Australia, New Zealand, and Japan;
- The United States will not be the first to introduce into a region a newly developed advanced weapons system which would create a new or significantly higher combat capability;
- We will not sell any such weapons systems until they are operationally deployed with U.S. forces;
- We will not permit development or modification of advanced systems solely for export; and
- We have placed strict controls on coproduction and retransfers.

Recognizing that this problem requires action by all suppliers, we have initiated discussions with other major suppliers and consumers. The results have so far been modest. Much more needs to be done. It will be increasingly difficult for us to sustain our policy unilaterally unless there is more rapid movement toward a meaningful multilateral effort at restraint.

Sixth, regional arms control arrangements and capabilities should be expanded and strengthened.

Regional arms control is at a very primitive stage. Few negotiations are underway. Only a few nations have the technical competence required to verify agreements. Many of the techniques, like confidence-building measures which increase predictability and lessen the fear of sudden attack, are largely untried.

For our part, in Europe, the United States and our allies have recently taken an initiative to get the 5-year-old MBFR talks moving.[7] And we are considering additional measures to increase stability and security in central Europe. In still another region, while we have proposed and commenced talks with the Soviet Union on arms limitations in the Indian Ocean, increases in the Soviet naval presence there have hampered those talks.

Beyond our own negotiations, the United States would like to stimulate regional arms control efforts by offering others assistance with verification and stabilizing measures.

- Our experience in the Middle East has demonstrated that technical assistance with monitoring systems, such as aerial photography and ground detection devices, can help create the confidence necessary to make disengagement and stabilizing agreements work.
- Building on that experience, we are prepared to consider joint requests for these "eyes and ears of peace" from countries that want such monitoring services. Such requests should come preferably via regional organizations or the United Nations.
- The United States is prepared to provide specialists who can help other nations find ways to use confidence-building and stabilizing measures, including notification of maneuvers, invitation of observers to maneuvers, and U.N. machinery to promote such measures.

Seventh, we should fully develop the institutions and expertise required for arms control.

We must continue to strengthen U.N. arms control institutions without undercutting those institutions we have developed. While we are prepared to consider changes in the CCD, our major concern is to insure the continued, productive activity of a serious negotiating body operating by consensus.

The peacekeeping and peacemaking capabilities of the United Nations and of regional organizations like the Organization of

[7]Cf. Introduction at notes 42–43.

American States and the Organization of African Unity should be an integral part of arms reduction efforts. The role of such regional organizations is critical to minimize intrusion by outsiders. We encourage a strong and prominent role for these organizations.

The United Nations plays an essential role. At this moment U.N. forces in Lebanon, Cyprus, the Golan Heights, and Sinai are making it possible for negotiations to move toward lasting peaceful settlements.

To make these U.N. efforts even more effective, we propose the establishment of a U.N. peacekeeping reserve force. Such a force would comprise national contingents trained in U.N. peacekeeping methods and earmarked by their governments for U.N. duty. This peacekeeping reserve would be drawn upon by the Secretary General whenever the Security Council decided to establish a U.N. force to maintain international peace and security.

There is also a critical national dimension. Every government must strengthen the institutions and expertise needed for arms control. Let each of us resolve at this session that our nations will examine the priority which we now give disarmament in organization, budgets, and personnel.

Eighth, progress in arms control agreements should release additional resources for economic and social development.

Collectively, we have the capacity to eliminate the worst vestiges of poverty from the world by the end of the century. The tremendous expenditure of resources devoted to building military strength stands in the path of development today. The developing countries share of world military expenditures has grown from 15% to 23% in the last decade. The developing nations are now spending a greater portion of their GNP for military purposes than the developed countries.

Just 1% of the world's annual military budget would be enough to provide food and a healthy development of 200 million malnourished children today. Let us, through the work of this conference, begin to turn the world's resources from ever-growing stockpiles of destruction to ever-growing opportunities for life.

Arms control agreements can help free the economies of industrial as well as developing nations to solve pressing social problems. We realize the vast potential of the American economy. The American people have no more fervent wish than to turn more of that potential from the manufacture of arms to the fulfillment of human needs.

As nations conclude arms control agreements and show restraint in arms expenditures, the United States favors reallocating funds to development projects which previously were earmarked for military assistance.

Our ability to redirect funds for development hinges on the willingness of other nations to limit their current arming of developing nations. If the United Nations is to deal effectively with the problems of development, we cannot have countries pouring arms into the developing world while at the same time devoting minimal funding to development assistance. We cannot have nations using their military power to exploit differences between nations and to exacerbate serious conflicts.

My country for years sought to limit military shipments to Africa. Our economic development assistance far outstrips the amount of military assistance we have provided. In 1977, the United States contributed $327 million in economic assistance to African nations, compared to only $59 million in military aid. This record, with its special emphasis on funding for food, stands in marked contrast to the predominant military assistance extended by others. Our orientation represents, I believe, a far better contribution to the long-term future of the people of Africa. The choice here is one of encouraging the constructive and creative capabilities of the developing world or of encouraging those tendencies which generate conflict. Let us place our hopes in development.

Our recognition of the relationship between disarmament and development should inform and give urgency to all our arms control objectives. In addition:

* We strongly support the U.N. study of disarmament and development. This study should include consideration of the economic problems which may result from disarmament;
* We favor efforts to reduce military expenditures and have volunteered to provide our own accurate information on national military expenditures to a U.N. pilot project testing a method to measure such expenditures; and
* We encourage others to be equally open. Greater openness about military expenditures is a necessary companion to arms restraint. Over time, openness can gradually replace fear with trust, promote confidence, encourage self-restraint, and eliminate needless sources of conflict.

The Challenge

Thirty-three years ago, President Harry Truman addressed the first delegates to the United Nations at their meeting in San Francisco. And he said: "By your labors at this Conference, we shall know if suffering humanity is to achieve a just and lasting peace."[8]

That is our challenge at this special session. The world watches what we do here, and mankind's deepest hopes are with us today.

[8]*Documents, 1944–1945:* 423.

The success or failure of our efforts will determine, more than any other endeavor, the shape of the world our children will inherit, or whether they will inherit a habitable world at all. And it is their interests which unite us today.

No matter what nation we are from, no matter what our political philosophy, our children are 100% of our future. We owe them 100% of our efforts to halt the arms race today.

Arms control must not be the agenda only of this session or this year alone. It must be the moral agenda of our time. Our work must be kept in full view of the world community. We need the pressure of world opinion to give urgency to our task. And that is why the United States calls on this conference to follow up our efforts with another special session of the General Assembly in 1981. Let our next meeting monitor the progress we have made. And let it press upon us the agenda of issues which we must still resolve.

The challenge of controlling the arms race is awesome. But Emerson said we measure a man's wisdom by his hope. Let us proceed with hope today. I am confident that if each of our nations can look beyond its own ambitions; if, in the work of this conference, we can bridge the distances of geography and history and fear; and if all of us can bring to our efforts the deepest yearnings of the peoples we represent, then we shall serve all the world's children with our labors and, in the words of Isaiah, the work of righteousness shall be peace.

(b) *Accomplishments of the Session: Statement by Ambassador James F. Leonard, Jr., Deputy Representative of the United States to the United Nations, in Plenary Session, June 30, 1978.* [9]

(Excerpts)

This is an historic occasion. We are meeting today in the final session of the largest meeting of states to discuss and deliberate on disarmament in the history of our small planet. We came together with many differing viewpoints, reflecting the inevitable but healthy variety that results when 149 states attempt to address a subject as complicated and important as disarmament, which touches almost all aspects of international affairs. Our meeting together in this session has itself been an important event. That we have been able to reach a consensus agreement on a Final Document[10] is, in the view of many here, no small miracle. It is certainly an achievement that all delegations can be proud of. This is in a

[9] USUN Press Release 66; text from *Bulletin*, Aug. 1978: 46-8.
[10] Cf. Introduction at note 26.

very real sense the first consensus document on disarmament in a very long time. That the effort to achieve a consensus document was successful—an objective regarded by many as too ambitious—is due to goodwill displayed by all delegations. It also reflects the fact that the world community today takes the subject of disarmament seriously.

As must be the case in any consensus document, the text, in some cases, does not have wording that individual states would have preferred. Like other delegations who have spoken, that applies to the U.S. delegation. On this occasion, I will limit my remarks to a few comments on instances of this nature.

The United States supports the creation of nuclear-weapon-free zones under appropriate circumstances and, at this very time, is proceeding to ratification of Protocol I to the treaty of Tlatelolco. In this connection, the Program of Action calls upon the nuclear-weapon states to give undertakings with respect to such zones, the modalities of which are to be negotiated with the competent authorities of the respective zones. I wish to note our understanding that the term "modalities" refers to both substantive provisions and procedures to be included in such undertakings.

The United States also supports the general proposition that an appropriately defined zone of peace, freely determined by all states concerned wherever situated, can be a way to promote and maintain international peace and security in conformity with the U.N. Charter. The United States considers that zones of peace must be consistent with, and cannot abridge, the inherent right of individual or collective self-defense guaranteed in the charter or other rights recognized under international law, including the right of innocent passage, historic high seas freedoms, and other relevant rights. The U.S. position on the creation of any particular zone of peace will depend on its characteristics.

In addition, I would like to address myself to an aspect of the vital question of nonproliferation which is of concern to many states.

We recognize the right of any state to peaceful nuclear development, and the United States will continue to strongly support international cooperation in this area. This was further evidenced during this special session by the announcement of a program designed to strengthen our peaceful nuclear assistance programs, particularly through the IAEA. However, any such cooperation must be carried out with the realization that we all share in the responsibility for its safe use. It is essential that each nation plan its peaceful nuclear programs with full consideration for nonproliferation concerns. In the long run, this is the best insurance; that all nations will be able to realize the substantial benefits of nuclear energy without increasing the risk of catastrophic nuclear conflict and with assurance that the prospects for nuclear disarmament will not be endangered.

Regarding nuclear testing, the U.S. Government fully shares the desire, expressed by an overwhelming majority of the participants in this special session, for an early suspension of all nuclear tests. This objective has occupied a central place in our approach to arms control and disarmament and has guided our efforts in the trilateral negotiations currently underway in Geneva. President Carter has repeatedly emphasized his commitment to this goal.

We would like, however, to explain the reasons why an immediate moratorium on nuclear testing, which we recognize is strongly desired by many nations, does not seem to us to be a good idea. We have strongly and consistently held the view that a comprehensive test ban, in order to promote stability and mutual confidence among its participants, must be based on adequate measures of verification.

At this moment, we are engaged in the detailed and technically complex process of elaborating such measures. We have made steady progress in these efforts and are confident that effective and mutually agreeable solutions can be achieved before too long. But an immediate cessation of nuclear testing could seriously complicate efforts to finalize satisfactory arrangements. It could even have the effect of lengthening the negotiating process.

Therefore, while we understand the motivations of those who have called for a moratorium and, indeed, sympathize with them, we believe that the surest way of arriving at our common goal— that is, the earliest possible achievement of a comprehensive test ban that can truly promote mutual confidence among its parties—is through the negotiations in Geneva. And we can assure you that the U.S. Government will make every effort to bring those negotiations to a prompt and satisfactory conclusion.

I would also wish to say a word about the question of reduction of military budgets. This session has correctly noted the excessive amount of resources devoted to national military capabilities. The limitation or reduction of military budgets hold promise of benefits for all. Therefore, we regret that it was not possible to reach consensus on language identifying the essential first steps—standardized measurement and reporting, development of techniques for international comparison that would be an important step, and verification—which must be taken if we are to advance toward negotiated reductions. My government continues to attach importance to this subject, and it is our hope that the General Assembly, at its 33rd Session will be able to return to it in a constructive manner.

* * *

These few comments I have made are in no way intended to reflect on the high significance my delegation attaches to the document we have just adopted, or on the importance of the fact that it has been adopted by consensus.

In this document, we have prepared not only a Declaration on Disarmament, but in the Program of Action, a guide for future efforts. That guide is broad in scope. It also reflects the effort to bridge the differences that have existed. If in some cases it lacks the precision we might wish, we must remember it is our first effort in a forum like this to chart our future course of action. In the period ahead we, together, seek to sharpen our focus and narrow our differences, in both the deliberative and negotiating bodies.

In this regard it is proper to note the significance of the agreements reached regarding disarmament machinery.[11]

For example, the reactivation of the Disarmament Commission will enable us to bring the insights of many nations into our common effort to halt and reverse the arms race.

With regard to the negotiating body, we have achieved a significant breakthrough in having agreed on a negotiating body open to all nuclear-weapon states. The United States welcomes the return to active participation in negotiations of our old friend and ally, France. We look forward to participation, at an early date, of the People's Republic of China.

We have begun a process. We hope that process will be aided by a second special session on disarmament in 1981.

Vice President Mondale stated at the beginning of this extraordinary meeting that the United States was here not only to act, but also to listen. I want to assure the delegates here present that my government has not only listened but heard the call for more rapid progress in halting and reversing the arms race. We wish to commend the leaders of our fellow nations for the bounty of ideas and the sincerity of the challenges they have laid before the family of nations in this forum.

We have heard the nations of the world give expression to the urgent need for disarmament and have learned much from this exchange of ideas and proposals. We hope that others can come away from this session with a better understanding of our own firm desire to join in diverting from the present dangerous course. At the same time, we hope they have also gained a new appreciation for the enormous complexities involved in charting a new course, a course fundamentally different from that of any other period in

[11]Paras. 118–120 of the Final Document provided for (1) the establishment of a new Disarmament Commission composed of all U.N. member states; (2) the holding of a second special session on disarmament at a date to be decided; and (3) the replacement of the existing Conference of the Committee on Disarmament (CCD) by a new negotiating body, the Committee on Disarmament, which would be open to the nuclear-weapon states and 32 to 35 other states.

history, necessitated by the destructive capacity available to a small number of governments. We cannot act alone. But we have committed ourselves to a new beginning, a more cooperative policy which we believe must fully involve all nations to be successful.

One of the significant results of this session has been the stimulation it has given to public interest and participation in our common efforts. The work of the nongovernmental organizations in connection with this session should be an inspiration to us all. We hope it will continue and grow. Governments do not have a monopoly on wisdom, nor can they act boldly without public support. Thus, however important our final document is, it may be that much of the significance of this session in the long run will lie in the public area.

(8)   The United States and the Soviet Union: Address by President Carter at the United States Naval Academy, Annapolis, June 7, 1978. [12]

(Excerpt)

* * *

As officers in the modern Navy, you will be actors in a world-wide political and military drama. You will be called upon not only to master the technicalities of military science and military leadership but also to have a sensitive understanding of the international community within which the Navy operates.

Today I want to discuss one of the most important aspects of that international context—the relationship between the world's two greatest powers, the United States of America and the Soviet Union.

We must realize that for a very long time our relationship with the Soviet Union will be competitive. That competition is to be constructive if we are successful. Instead it could be dangerous and politically disastrous. Then our relationship must be cooperative as well.

We must avoid excessive swings in the public mood in our country—from euphoria when things are going well, to despair when they are not; from an exaggerated sense of compatability with the Soviet Union, to open expressions of hostility.

Détente between our two countries is central to world peace. It's important for the world, for the American public, and for you as future leaders of the Navy to understand the complex and sensitive nature.

The word "détente" can be simplistically defined as "the easing of tension between nations." The word is, in practice, however further defined by experience, as those nations evolve new means by which they can live with each other in peace.

[12]Text from *Presidential Documents,* 14: 1052–7 (introductory pleasantries omitted).

To be stable, to be supported by the American people, and to be a basis for widening the scope of cooperation, then détente must be broadly defined and truly reciprocal. Both nations must exercise restraint in troubled areas and in troubled times. Both must honor meticulously those agreements which have already been reached to widen cooperation, naturally and mutually limit nuclear arms production, permit the free movement of people and the expression of ideas, and to protect human rights.

Neither of us should entertain the notion that military supremacy can be attained, or that transient military advantage can be politically exploited.

Our principal goal is to help shape a world which is more responsive to the desire of people everywhere for economic well-being, social justice, political self-determination, and basic human rights.

We seek a world of peace. But such a world must accommodate diversity—social, political, and ideological. Only then can there be a genuine cooperation among nations and among cultures.

We desire to dominate no one. We will continue to widen our cooperation with the positive new forces in the world.

We want to increase our collaboration with the Soviet Union, but also with the emerging nations, with the nations of Eastern Europe, and with the People's Republic of China. We are particularly dedicated to genuine self-determination and majority rule in those areas of the world where these goals have not yet been attained.

Our long-term objective must be to convince the Soviet Union of the advantages of cooperation and of the costs of disruptive behavior.

We remember that the United States and the Soviet Union were allies in the Second World War. One of the great historical accomplishments of the U.S. Navy was to guide and protect the tremendous shipments of armaments and supplies from our country to Murmansk and to other Soviet ports in support of a joint effort to meet the Nazi threat.

In the agony of that massive conflict, 20 million Soviet lives were lost. Millions more who live in the Soviet Union still recall the horror and the hunger of that time.

I'm convinced that the people of the Soviet Union want peace. I cannot believe that they could possibly want war.

Through the years, our Nation has sought accommodation with the Soviet Union, as demonstrated by the Austrian Peace Treaty, the Quadripartite Agreement concerning Berlin, the termination of nuclear testing in the atmosphere, joint scientific explorations in space, trade agreements, the antiballistic missile treaty, the interim agreement on strategic offensive armaments, and the limited test ban agreement.

Efforts still continue with negotiations toward a SALT II agreement, a comprehensive test ban against nuclear explosives, reductions in conventional arms transfers to other countries, the prohibition against attacks on satellites in space, an agreement to stabilize the level of force deployment in the Indian Ocean, and increased trade and scientific and cultural exchange. We must be willing to explore such avenues of cooperation despite the basic issues which divide us. The risks of nuclear war alone propel us in this direction.

The numbers and destructive potential of nuclear weapons has been increasing at an alarming rate. That is why a SALT agreement which enhances the security of both nations is of fundamental importance. We and the Soviet Union are negotiating in good faith almost every day, because we both know that a failure to succeed would precipitate a resumption of a massive nuclear arms race.

I'm glad to report to you today that the prospects for a SALT II agreement are good.

Beyond this major effort, improved trade and technological and cultural exchange are among the immediate benefits of cooperation between our two countries. However, these efforts to cooperate do not erase the significant differences between us.

What are these differences?

To the Soviet Union, détente seems to mean a continuing aggressive struggle for political advantage and increased influence in a variety of ways. The Soviet Union apparently sees military power and military assistance as the best means of expanding their influence abroad. Obviously areas of instability in the world provide a tempting target for this effort, and all too often they seem ready to exploit any such opportunity.

As became apparent in Korea, in Angola, and also, as you know, in Ethiopia more recently, the Soviets prefer to use proxy forces to achieve their purposes.

To other nations throughout the world, the Soviet military buildup appears to be excessive, far beyond any legitimate requirement to defend themselves or to defend their allies. For more than 15 years, they have maintained this program of military growth, investing almost 15 percent of their total gross national product in armaments, and this sustained growth continues.

The abuse of basic human rights in their own country, in violation of the agreement which was reached at Helsinki, has earned them the condemnation of people everywhere who love freedom. By their actions, they've demonstrated that the Soviet system cannot tolerate freely expressed ideas or notions of loyal opposition and the free movement of peoples.

The Soviet Union attempts to export a totalitarian and repressive form of government, resulting in a closed society. Some of these characteristics and goals create problems for the Soviet Union.

Outside a tightly controlled bloc, the Soviet Union has difficult political relations with other nations. Their cultural bonds with others are few and frayed. Their form of government is becoming increasingly unattractive to other nations, so that even Marxist-Leninist groups no longer look on the Soviet Union as a model to be imitated.

Many countries are becoming very concerned that the nonaligned movement is being subverted by Cuba, which is obviously closely aligned with the Soviet Union and dependent upon the Soviets for economic sustenance and for military and political guidance and direction.

Although the Soviet Union has the second largest economic system in the world, its growth is slowing greatly, and its standard of living does not compare favorably with that of other nations at the same equivalent stage of economic development.

Agricultural production still remains a serious problem for the Soviet Union, so that in times of average or certainly adverse conditions for crop production, they must turn to us or turn to other nations for food supplies.

We in our country are in a much more favorable position. Our industrial base and our productivity are unmatched. Our scientific and technological capability is superior to all others. Our alliances with other free nations are strong and growing stronger, and our military capability is now and will be second to none.

In contrast to the Soviet Union, we are surrounded by friendly neighbors and wide seas. Our societal structure is stable and cohesive, and our foreign policy enjoys bipartisan public support which gives it continuity.

We are also strong because of what we stand for as a nation: the realistic chance for every person to build a better life; protection by both law and custom from arbitrary exercise of government power; the right of every individual to speak out, to participate fully in government, and to share political power. Our philosophy is based on personal freedom, the most powerful of all ideas, and our democratic way of life warrants the admiration and emulation by other people throughout the world.

Our work for human rights makes us part of an international tide, growing in force. We are strengthened by being part of it.

Our growing economic strength is also a major political factor, potential influence for the benefit of others. Our gross national product exceeds that of all nine nations combined in the European Economic Community and is twice as great as that of the Soviet Union. Additionally, we are now learning how to use our resources more wisely, creating a new harmony between our people and our environment.

Our analysis of American military strength also furnishes a basis for confidence. We know that neither the United States nor the Soviet Union can launch a nuclear assault on the other without suffering a devastating counterattack which could destroy the aggressor nation. Although the Soviet Union has more missile launchers, greater throw-weight, and more continental air defense capabilities, the United States has more warheads, generally greater accuracy, more heavy bombers, a more balanced nuclear force, better missile submarines, and superior antisubmarine warfare capability.

A successful SALT II agreement will give both nations equal but lower ceilings on missile launchers and also on missiles with multiple warheads. We envision in SALT III an even greater mutual reduction in nuclear weapons.

With essential nuclear equivalence, relative conventional force strength has now become more important. The fact is that the military capability of the United States and its allies is adequate to meet any foreseeable threat.

It is possible that each side tends to exaggerate the military capability of the other. Accurate analyses are important as a basis for making decisions for the future. False or excessive estimates of Soviet strength or American weakness contributes to the effectiveness of the Soviet propaganda effort.

For example, recently alarming news reports of the military budget proposals for the U.S. Navy ignored the fact that we have the highest defense budget in history and that the largest portion of this will go to the Navy.

You men are joining a long tradition of superior leadership, seamanship, tactics, and ship design. And I'm confident that the U.S. Navy has no peer, no equal, on the high seas today, and that you, I, and others will always keep the Navy strong.

Let there be no doubt about our present and future strength. This brief assessment which I've just made shows that we need not be overly concerned about our ability to compete and to compete successfully. Certainly there is no cause for alarm. The healthy self-criticism and the free debate which are essential in a democracy should never be confused with weakness or despair or lack of purpose.

What are the principal elements of American foreign policy to the Soviet Union? Let me outline them very briefly.

We will continue to maintain equivalent nuclear strength, because we believe that in the absence of worldwide nuclear disarmament, such equivalency is the least threatening and the most stable situation for the world.

We will maintain a prudent and sustained level of military spending, keyed to a stronger NATO, more mobile forces, and undiminished presence in the Pacific. We and our allies must and will be able to meet any foreseeable challenge to our security from either strategic nuclear forces or from conventional forces. America has the capability to honor this commitment without excessive sacrifice on the part of our citizens, and that commitment to military strength will be honored.

Looking beyond our alliances, we will support worldwide and regional organizations which are dedicated to enhancing international peace, like the United Nations, the Organization of American States, and the Organization for [of] African Unity.

In Africa we and our African friends want to see a continent that is free of the dominance of outside powers, free of the bitterness of racial injustice, free of conflict, and free of the burdens of poverty and hunger and disease. We are convinced that the best way to work toward these objectives is through affirmative policies that recognize African realities and that recognize aspirations.

The persistent and increasing military involvement of the Soviet Union and Cuba in Africa could deny this hopeful vision. We are deeply concerned about the threat to regional peace and to the autonomy of countries within which these foreign troops seem permanently to be stationed. That is why I've spoken up on this subject today. And this is why I and the American people will support African efforts to contain such intrusion, as we have done recently in Zaire.[13]

I urge again that all other powers join us in emphasizing works of peace rather than the weapons of war. In their assistance to Africa, let the Soviet Union now join us in seeking a peaceful and a speedy transition to majority rule in Rhodesia and in Namibia. Let us see efforts to resolve peacefully the disputes in Eritrea and in Angola. Let us all work, not to divide and to seek domination in Africa, but to help those nations to fulfill their great potential.

We will seek peace, better communication and understanding, cultural and scientific exchange, and increased trade with the Soviet Union and with other nations.

We will attempt to prevent the proliferation of nuclear weapons among those nations not now having this capability.

We will continue to negotiate constructively and persistently for a fair strategic arms limitation agreement. We know that no ideological victories can be won by either side by the use of nuclear weapons.

We have no desire to link this negotiation for a SALT agreement with other competitive relationships nor to impose other special conditions on the process. In a democratic society, however, where public opinion is an integral factor in the shaping and implementation of foreign policy, we do recognize that tensions, sharp disputes, or threats to peace will complicate the quest for a successful agreement. This is not a matter of our preference but a simple recognition of fact.

The Soviet Union can choose either confrontation or cooperation. The United States is adequately prepared to meet either choice.

We would prefer cooperation through a détente that increasingly involves similar restraint for both sides; similar readiness to resolve

[13]Cf. Introduction at pp. 69–72.

disputes by negotiations, and not by violence; similar willingness to compete peacefully, and not militarily. Anything less than that is likely to undermine détente. And this is why I hope that no one will underestimate the concerns which I have expressed today.

A competition without restraint and without shared rules will escalate into graver tensions, and our relationship as a whole with the Soviet Union will suffer. I do not wish this to happen, and I do not believe that Mr. Brezhnev desires it. And this is why it is time for us to speak frankly and to face the problems squarely.

By a combination of adequate American strength, of quiet self-restraint in the use of it, of a refusal to believe in the inevitability of war, and of a patient and persistent development of all the peaceful alternatives, we hope eventually to lead international society into a more stable, more peaceful, and a more hopeful future.

You and I leave here today to do our common duty—protecting our Nation's vital interests by peaceful means if possible, by resolute action if necessary. We go forth sobered by these responsibilities, but confident of our strength. We go forth knowing that our Nation's goals—peace, security, liberty for ourselves and for others—will determine our future and that we together can prevail.

To attain these goals, our Nation will require exactly those qualities of courage, self-sacrifice, idealism, and self-discipline which you as midshipmen have learned here at Annapolis so well. That is why your Nation expects so much of you, and that is why you have so much to give.

I leave you now with my congratulations and with a prayer to God that both you and I will prove worthy of the task that is before us and the Nation which we have sworn to serve.

Thank you very much.

(9)   In Defense of SALT: Address by Ambassador Paul C. Warnke, Director, U.S. Arms Control and Disarmament Agency, before the Conference on U.S. Security and the Soviet Challenge, Hartford, July 25, 1978.[14]

For almost six years, in three administrations, two Republican and one Democratic, the United States has been negotiating a new strategic arms limitation agreement. That agreement is now reaching completion and I'm happy to say that it will meet the goals that have been sought since the fall of 1972.

So it's a little ironic that, with success imminent, we now hear voices that question the wisdom of even trying to negotiate strategic arms control with the Soviet Union. What I would like to do today

[14]Text from Department of State, Bureau of Public Affairs, Office of Public Communication, *Current Policy,* No. 27, Aug. 1978.

in my brief remarks is to speak to these questions and to discuss with you the reasons why I am convinced that our new SALT agreement will contribute in a major way to the security of the United States.

Because this is the simple, paramount objective of arms control. It's not an exercise in international idealism. It's not a smoke screen for unilateral disarmament. It is a way to see that we are safer and the world is further removed from the unimaginable catastrophe of nuclear war.

The Importance of a New SALT Agreement

The new SALT agreement which is taking final shape will establish the principle of equal ceilings on strategic nuclear weapons systems, it will require reductions in the number of such Soviet weapons systems targeted against the United States and it will impose restrictions on new and even more threatening Soviet nuclear weapons. But despite these facts, there are those who I think quite sincerely propose that we should suspend our SALT talks because of concern about Soviet and Cuban activities in Africa or because of revulsion toward Soviet internal policies that stifle any independent voices of protest. And there are some that maintain that these activities, which contrast sharply with our demonstrated willingness to work with the Soviet Union for a more stable and more productive world, indicate that any agreement we reach would not in fact be observed by the Soviets.

Then, in the last few weeks and months we have seen the trials of Orlov, Ginzburg, Shcharansky; we've noted the forcible arrest of an American businessman and the slander trials of two journalists who committed the crime of reporting in American papers news of which the Soviet authorities did not approve.[15] Now all of us abhor and resent these episodes. They reflect, I believe, weakness, not strength; they are the product of fear, and not confidence.

But this isn't anything new to us. We've always recognized that the Soviet system is very different from our own. They have no Bill of Rights. The Soviet system finds no room for freedom of speech as guaranteed by our Constitution. And the Soviet leadership has never made any secret of its intention to support what they describe as friendly socialist governments anywhere in the world.

And I think it's clear that these Soviet policies and activities necessarily affect our own attitudes toward the Soviet Union. But they don't cancel out the underlying reasons for seeking an effective and verifiable SALT agreement, because our purpose in SALT is to bring the strategic nuclear competition under control, to preserve our retaliatory capability that deters any possibility of Soviet use of

---

[15]Cf. Introduction at notes 27–28.

its nuclear war [*sic*]. And this, as I say, is our primary aim—not just to save money, not just to meet the demands of other nations that we try and bring nuclear arms under control, and certainly not just to improve U.S.-Soviet relations. All of these are potential and maybe even likely benefits of SALT. But they are of decidedly secondary importance when compared with the contribution that SALT can make to the security of the United States.

Now in emphasizing this fact, I don't mean to suggest that we ought to trim or contort our policies toward the Soviet Union in order to pursue SALT. We have instead pursued and will continue to pursue our aims in the field of human rights and we've already taken specific measures to that end. We have pursued and will continue to pursue our goal that the emerging countries of the world must be free to set their own course without outside influence. But it's essential, when we hear suggestions that our arms control negotiations should be linked to Soviet behavior in other respects, that we remember one main principle. Effective and verifiable control over strategic arms is not a reward for Soviet good behavior. It's a benefit that we want to achieve for ourselves.

And I think you can see the inherent fallacy of an attempted link between arms control negotiations and our reaction to Soviet foreign and domestic policy if you turn the linkage argument upside down. What, for example, if all of the Soviet personnel were to leave Africa tomorrow and to bring every Cuban with them, and what if the Soviet leadership were to free all political prisoners and extol the American Bill of Rights? Should we then change any negotiating position in Geneva? Should we then look with favor on Soviet arguments for further limits on our forces and the lessening of restrictions on their own? I think it's clear that strategic arms control has to stand on its own feet and that a SALT agreement has to be judged on its own merits. We couldn't accept the reduction of one ballistic missile submarine in order to get the Soviets out of the Horn of Africa. Our ballistic missile submarines are too important to our strategic position and thus to our national security.

But those who point to Soviet behavior as a reason for cancelling or slowing down our SALT negotiations sometimes claim that such behavior indicates that no agreement would be worthwhile because we couldn't trust the Soviets to comply. And the answer to this criticism is that the SALT agreement we are working out will not depend on trusting the Soviet Union.

Verification and Compliance

Instead, the SALT agreement will depend on limits and rules that we can verify ourselves by our own national technical means. Without adequate assurance of compliance with arms control provisions, these provisions would be a source of suspicion and friction rather than any source of comfort. But our highly sophisticated national technical means give us the ability to determine that the SALT limits, both quantitative and qualitative, are in fact being met by the Soviet Union. They'll enable us to tell what new strategic nuclear delivery systems the Soviets have, what new systems they are testing and what existing systems are being destroyed in order to bring them down to the reduced SALT ceilings which are being negotiated.

The first SALT agreements, signed in May of 1972, prohibited any interference with our national technical means of verification. They also prohibited any measures of deliberate concealment which would interfere with our ability to verify compliance. The new SALT agreement will continue and expand on these prohibitions and, in fact, it will contain additional detailed provisions to improve verification. For example, one of the complaints during SALT ONE was that the Soviet Union would never furnish figures on its own forces and as a consequence we were compelled to rely on our own figures—our own estimates as to what the Soviet forces were.

For many months, beginning in May of 1977, we argued with the Soviet negotiators and maintained that we had to have an agreed data base, that they had to furnish figures on their own forces that would be controlled by SALT and we would no longer rely exclusively on American figures. That became very important because of the fact that SALT TWO will not only set ceilings but will also bring about reductions. So you have to have an agreed base from which you can determine that those reductions have in fact taken place. After protracted discussions, the Soviet negotiators accepted this principle.

Also during the negotiations, we've developed precise counting rules under which we can verify particular types of launchers as a result of their physically observable features. With our national technical means—which still are highly classified, but I'm sure that most of you know the general nature of these means—we can tell what launchers look like. We can't tell what's inside a launcher. There's no way, even with a permanent inspection team, that you can be sure whether a particular silo launcher is empty or full or what kind of missile it contains. So that in order to implement the ceilings under SALT TWO, you have to have arbitrary rules that are susceptible to being determined by national technical means. The rules we have developed are that, first of all, if a particular missile has ever been tested with MIRVs—that's the multiple independently targetable reentry vehicles—then all missiles of that type are counted as MIRVed missiles, whether they have a single warhead or whether they have multiple reentry vehicles. But even that isn't enough. You have to have a further rule under which if a particular launcher has ever launched or contained a missile of a type which has ever been tested with MIRVs, then all launchers of that type are counted as launchers of MIRVs. Now this again was a very bitter pill for the Soviets to swallow. They did swallow it; and, as a matter of fact, since our delegations went back to Geneva in May of 1977, the Soviet Union has agreed to each of the basic elements of the American position on verification.

Now, the first SALT agreements also set up a formal body to consider and resolve questions of compliance—that's the Standing Consultative Commission made up of U.S. and Soviet experts.[16] And after five years of experience with that Commission, it's very clear to the Soviets that we will raise there any issues on which there is any question of compliance.

This morning Professor Eugene Rostow referred to the fact that the Soviets did not abide by certain unilateral declarations made by the U.S. I can assure you there will be no such unilateral declarations in SALT TWO. The very fact that you are compelled to make a unilateral statement as to what the other side will do and the other side refuses to join you in that statement is sufficient ground for suspicion. And I would agree with Professor Rostow that this is not a sound course. It will not be followed in SALT TWO. Professor Rostow also referred to the fact that the SALT ONE agreement has continued in effect despite its formal expiration in October of 1977. I hate to disagree with an old colleague, but the fact is that there is no SALT agreement in effect now. We have indicated that, while negotiations continue, we do not plan to breach the terms of SALT ONE. The Soviet Union has done the same.[17] It's been suggested that this is a precedent indicating that the protocol in SALT TWO might be extended.

I'd like to explain that in SALT TWO we will have three parts. There will be the basic agreement lasting through 1985 that contains the restrictions on Soviet forces. There is also a protocol that will contain some short-term restrictions on some American forces. There will also be a third part which is the Joint Statement of Principles which will govern the negotiations of SALT THREE.

Now, I would submit that the example of SALT ONE is not a precedent for any extension of the protocol. The fact is that the Soviets in agreeing to abide by the restraints of SALT ONE after the expiration have in fact restrained their forces. We couldn't violate SALT ONE in the next two years even if we tried, because we don't have a single program that would push us over those limits. So it's a unilateral restriction on the Soviet Union and hence no precedent for any acceptance of the protocol restrictions on our forces past the expiration date of that protocol.

[16]Cf. *AFR, 1972:* 110–12.
[17]Same, *1977:* 198–200.

So I would suggest that our continued pursuit of a SALT agreement does not constitute any implied endorsement of Soviet misbehavior. Nor will assured compliance with the terms of the agreement depend upon our trust in Soviet motives and Soviet actions. Under these circumstances I submit that there is no reason why any one of us should willingly forego the benefits to the security of the United States that can be brought to us by SALT TWO. And I believe that these benefits are clear and considerable. SALT will protect and preserve the strategic stability which deters nuclear aggression. SALT will at the same time leave open to us all of the military options that will enable us to modernize our forces and insure that our retaliatory capability continues for the foreseeable future. And in addition and entirely apart from the question of the U.S.-Soviet relationship, a SALT TWO agreement will advance our objective of preventing the further proliferation of nuclear arms.

Strategic Stability

Turning first to the question of strategic stability, we have today a situation that fully meets that criterion. No Soviet military planner could possibly contemplate launching a nuclear strike against the United States because of the certainty that our retaliatory strike could devastate the Soviet Union and end its existence as a modern society. As a matter of fact, we could do more damage in response than they could do by striking first. Now that, I submit, is a situation of assured deterrence and of strategic stability. And the SALT agreement will protect and improve a stable strategic balance.

Because of the major breakthrough that was achieved by President Ford in his meeting with General Secretary Brezhnev in Vladivostok in 1974, SALT TWO will establish the principle of equal aggregates in intercontinental nuclear delivery vehicles. Each side will be entitled initially to a total of 2,400 and within that total there will be equal entitlement in the number of launchers of MIRVed missiles—the multiple warheads that can strike separate targets widely dispersed. President Ford was able to achieve this understanding without giving the Soviet side any compensation for the fact that we have located in Europe the so-called forward based systems that can strike Soviet targets. We have, for example, over 160 F-111s in the United Kingdom that can deliver nuclear bombs and nuclear missiles on Soviet targets. These have not been constrained by SALT TWO and will not be. Strategic stability will be further improved by agreed upon reductions. As a consequence of these reductions, the Soviets will have to dismantle and destroy about 300 nuclear delivery systems. In the absence of SALT, our intelligence sources indicate that they would increase their present total by more than 600 nuclear delivery systems. So what SALT means is that there will be some 1,000 fewer strategic nuclear weapons directed against the territory of the United States.

And on the other hand, because our present total is below the new ceiling, we will not have to make any cuts, but can actually add another 250 ballistic missile launchers or heavy bombers. Reference has been made to the decision to cancel the B-1 bomber. I want to make it very clear that that was not an arms control decision. There is nothing in SALT that would prevent the United States from building B-1s. The halt in that program was decided by the Pentagon and by the President on the basis of cost effectiveness, the conclusion being reached that the cruise missiles on our existing B-52 bombers provided a more effective and surer way of penetrating Soviet defenses. But if we sign SALT TWO next month, we could begin immediately to build the full program of B-1s. It would not be stopped by SALT in any sense whatsoever. We have the slack of something like 250 additional systems, so that we could build a full program of 244 B-1s. I doubt that we'll do it, but that's not because of SALT.

Now, also contributing to a stable, even strategic balance are certain sub-ceilings that we have been able to work out with the Soviet Union during the SALT talks. For many years, it's been recognized that the most destabilizing of the weapons systems is the MIRVed ICBM. That's because the particular combination of accuracy and yield that can be given to a MIRVed ICBM could threaten at least in theory the survivability of the intercontinental ballistic missiles of the other side. Now what that means, unfortunately, is that as the technological competition continues, the intercontinental ballistic missiles of each side are becoming at one and the same time both more deadly and more vulnerable, and that of course increases the risk that at a time of extreme international tension, one side might be tempted to use its intercontinental ballistic missiles first because of the fear that they wouldn't be there to be used in a second retaliatory strike. This tends to promote the adoption of such strategic doctrines as that of launch-on-warning which would mean, of course, a greatly increased risk of nuclear war at a time of international tension. But as I say, we have been able to work out certain sub-ceilings and one of the sub-ceilings related to intercontinental ballistic missiles with MIRVs. The Soviets have now agreed to set a ceiling which would mean 100 fewer launchers of this type of missiles than they would otherwise have. Now, that's not enough of a cut in itself to eliminate all future risks to the survivability of our own ICBM forces. But it's a very desirable first step for bringing about a more durable situation of assured stability.

And then finally, as an attempt to strengthen strategic stability, we have been trying since March 1977 to negotiate a ban on new types of intercontinental ballistic missiles. The kind of ban we have in mind would also prevent extensive modification of existing missiles. For example, one key objective is to prevent further fractionation of these missile warheads, to prevent the addition of additional reentry vehicles to the large Soviet missiles. It is well known that their missiles are bigger than ours. The decision not to build bigger missiles was made consciously by the United States. Nonetheless, the result is a difference in the throw-weight of the missiles of the two sides. As a consequence, the very large Soviet missiles could be given at least twice as many reentry vehicles as those with which they are presently equipped. What we are negotiating is a freeze that would prevent that further fractionation of reentry vehicles and thus would reduce the number of nuclear weapons with which they could strike the United States. The Soviets have agreed in principle to that kind of a prohibition, depending on the resolutions of other issues. This would for the first time begin to restrain the qualitative aspect of the nuclear arms competition. It will mean not just quantitative limits and reductions, but also actual qualitative controls.

The exact nature and scope of this limitation is one of the most important problems and remains fully to be resolved. When Secretary Vance and I met with Foreign Minister Gromyko, just about two weeks ago, this was discussed at length and both sides have made new proposals. I think that the distance between us is beginning to narrow, but nonetheless it does remain on the negotiating agenda. It's not hard to see why it remains. It's a particularly tough negotiating problem because of the asymmetry in the forces. The Soviet Union is more dependent upon ICBMs than we are. We've divided our forces about equally among the three parts of our deterrent triad. We have something slightly in excess of 30 percent in manned bombers, the same in ballistic missile submarines and the same in the intercontinental ballistic missiles. The Soviet Union, on the other hand, has something like 70 percent of its strategic nuclear resources in the land-based ballistic missiles. Thus a restraint on ICBMs will affect them more than it will us.

This brings me to a couple of remarks about recurrent comments as to the vulnerability of our land-based ICBMs. This is the issue of so-called Minuteman vulnerability—Minuteman being the name of our ICBMs.

The Maintenance of U.S. Nuclear Strength

A theoretical risk, at least, will exist as the Soviet forces gain more accuracy in their own ICBM reentry vehicles. But that's the very reason why we developed the ballistic missile submarines. It's why we've gone ahead with an extensive program of MIRVing our submarine launched ballistic missiles. We're developing two new missiles which can go on the new Trident submarines. At least the first one can be retrofitted into the present Poseidon fleet. These ballistic missiles launched from submarines will have the kind of range that would mean that you could operate just off the coast of the United States and still blow up the Soviet Union. It's going to be a very powerful addition to our retaliatory capability. The Soviet Union, on the other hand, because of its greater reliance on ICBMs, is more subject to this vulnerability problem. They have been far less successful than we have in developing the MIRV technology for submarine launched ballistic missiles. They are still basically in the testing phase of their first MIRVed submarine launched ballistic missiles.

Our objective has to be to insure that we retain the retaliatory capability that would deter the use or the threatened use of Soviet nuclear arms against us or against our allies. The nuclear umbrella has to be protected in order that it can continue to protect not only us but our friends. The SALT agreement that is being negotiated will enable us to go ahead with the military options that we have been told by the Pentagon are necessary in order to update and modernize our strategic nuclear forces. Under the agreed upon provisions, heavy bombers are a part of the overall total, and we will have the right to modernize our B-52 force by equipping the B-52s with long-range cruise missiles. These will allow our bombers to stay outside of Soviet air defense and strike every Soviet target that's worth striking. It will insure the viability of the manned bomber part of our deterrent, not only through 1985, but on any projections well beyond that point.

It's interesting that, beginning immediately after the Vladivostok understanding in 1974, the Soviet Union tried to put constraints on our modernization of our heavy bomber force. What they wanted to do was to count a heavy bomber with long-range cruise missiles as if it were a MIRVed ballistic missile. Now at Vladivostok, as I mentioned, the overall total of strategic nuclear delivery vehicles was set at 2,400. There was a subtotal of 1,320 set for MIRVed ballistic missile launchers. What the Soviets had been insisting was that we should also count against that 1,320 any heavy bomber that was armed with long-range cruise missiles. It would have meant in effect a reduction in the number of MIRVed ballistic missile launchers that we could have as compared to the Soviet Union. We refused to accept that argument and proposed instead an approach whereby each side would have the same entitlement for MIRVed ballistic missiles and then each could have, in addition, over 100 heavy bombers equipped with long-range cruise missiles. This formula is now agreed upon, and it fully accommodates the cruise missile program that the Pentagon has in mind. I might note that the Soviet Union is unlikely to have this kind of long-range cruise missile until many years after ours are deployed.

Then, in addition, the Soviets have accepted our proposal that limits on the deployment of ground launched cruise missiles and sea launched cruise missiles will only be contained in the three-year protocol. This will permit us to decide during the duration of the protocol whether to trade off continuing restrictions on some of these systems for certain additional limitations on Soviet forces or whether instead we should go ahead and deploy them. The same is true of mobile ICBM launchers. The only restriction on a mobile ICBM launcher will be a deployment restriction for the duration of the protocol. We will be free at the end of that time to go ahead with a mobile ICBM launcher. Now we would have to recognize that if we did so the Soviets would also be able to go ahead with a mobile ICBM launcher system. Because I don't mean to suggest by my remarks today that in SALT or in any other arms control negotiation you can get something for nothing. That's just not possible. If we are to get meaningful restrictions on Soviet systems that we regard as particularly threatening, we have to recognize that some of our freedom to develop and deploy new weapon systems will necessarily have to be restricted.

But in developing our negotiating positions—and this I might point out is done through the National Security Council system on an exhaustive interagency basis—we have made sure to preserve all the options that we might need for our strategic nuclear strength.

SALT and Nonproliferation

Then there's one final point I want to make with regard to the benefits of a SALT agreement. I've suggested earlier that it would greatly lessen the risk that some indefinite number of countries might be motivated to develop nuclear weapons with the consequent wide proliferation of such weapons. This interest in nonproliferation is one that we have in common with the Soviet Union. In the Non-Proliferation Treaty, which came into effect in 1970, the United States and the Soviet Union undertook in Article VI to take prompt steps to bring nuclear armaments under control. We haven't really done enough about that yet. The other countries that signed the treaty in reliance on that promise are reminding us of this fact. At the recently completed United Nations Special Session on Disarmament there was a great deal of complaint about the fact that the two nuclear superpowers had not as yet given meaningful content to that pledge. I think we would be kidding ourselves if we thought that we could wait indefinitely to bring about meaningful measures of nuclear arms control and still expect the rest of the world to continue to forego the acquisition of nuclear weapons capability of their own. They won't indefinitely listen to lectures about nonproliferation without seeing hard evidence that we ourselves and the Soviet Union are prepared to accept nuclear restraint.

I think, too, that the Soviet Union fully recognizes that connection between SALT and nonproliferation. I think it is one principal reason why they are interested in pursuing the SALT talks. When they look at the other nuclear powers today—China, France, Britain—they know that all these countries view the Soviet Union as the threat, not the United States. Fortunately, our world situation is such, and our world relationships are such, that as other countries acquire nuclear weapons, they again would, for the most part, be targeted principally against the Soviet Union rather than us. That doesn't mean that we can be calm and indifferent to the prospect of proliferation because we know that as nuclear weapons become more available they could not only fall into the hands of unstable governments, but also could come into the hands of subnational terrorist groups.

In conclusion, I think it's clear that there would be little disagreement among any of us here as to how we feel about certain features of Soviet conduct, both within the Soviet Union and in its dealing with other countries. We hold views that are very different from those of the Soviet leaders with regard to a desirable world order, the way in which other countries should shape their destinies, the tolerance of independent thought and free speech. I think there's no disagreement among us on these differences. I believe there should also be little disagreement among us on benefits that can be achieved by agreeing with the Soviet Union to restrain further increases in strategic arms, and actually to begin the process of reducing such arms.

SALT will, in fact, advance the security interest of the United States. In no sense would it put us in a position of actual or potential strategic inferiority. As Secretary Brown said in a recent interview: "It is very important that we do not underrate our strategic capability in our own planning or in what we say. If we keep saying that we are much weaker than the Russians strategically', they may begin to believe it; and since I am so convinced that it is not so, I think that is the worst thing that could happen."

There are, in fact, no circumstances under which we would allow the Soviet Union to become superior overall in strategic nuclear strength. We're not dealing from fear, but from economic, political, and military power. If there has to be an unrestrained nuclear arms race, the Soviet Union won't win it. I'm certainly not one of those who believes that you've got to grab SALT because otherwise you're going to be outpaced by the Soviet Union. I think our history is such as to indicate that that would not occur, and I'm conscious of no erosion of American will. We could not, of course, hope to regain the dominant strategic superiority we once had. There's no substitute for a monopoly, but it's awfully hard to get one back once it's gone. No matter how much we are willing to spend, any increment in our nuclear might could be offset by the other side just as we can offset any increment that they acquire. The SALT agreement that is now being negotiated provides, in my view, a better way of preventing any erosion of the strategic balance, surer ways of protecting the retaliatory capability which enables us to deter nuclear attack, and greater confidence in a secure future in which we have brought the world further away from the unexampled horror of nuclear war.

(10)   An Overview of U.S.-Soviet Relations: Statement by Ambassador Marshall D. Shulman, Special Adviser to the Secretary of State on Soviet Affairs, before the Subcommittee on Europe and the Middle East of the Committee on International Relations, House of Representatives, September 26, 1978. [18]

(Excerpts)

Last year when I had the privilege of testifying before your subcommittee, I presented an overview of U.S.-Soviet relations as of that time—October 1977.[19] Today, I propose to discuss the developments that have occurred in U.S.-Soviet relations since that time, to analyze the reasons for those developments, and to discuss present prospects for the relationship.

It has been characteristic of U.S.-Soviet relations since World War II that they have fluctuated between periods of high and low tension. During the past year, relations have moved toward relatively higher tension, continuing an uneven trend from the latter part of 1975.

From the point of view of the United States, the causes of this deterioration were to be found mainly in the following Soviet actions.

- In exploiting opportunities for the expansion of its influence in Africa, the Soviet Union exceeded a reasonable level of restraint in the transport of weapons and Cuban combat personnel onto the continent, thereby exacerbating local conflict situations.
- The deployment of new strategic weapons systems and the continued upgrading of Soviet armaments in the European theatre raised uncertainties about Soviet intentions.
- The heightening of Soviet police actions against Soviet dissidents, American correspondents, and an American businessman, and the continued harassment of Soviet citizens who

[18] Text from *Bulletin,* Nov. 1978: 28–33.
[19] Same, Jan. 1978: 1–8.

apply for emigration, reflected a lack of regard for commitments under the Helsinki agreement.

While we cannot accept the Soviet view, it is important for us to engage in a serious analytical effort to identify key elements of the present Soviet world view. As we understand Soviet perceptions, the following charges which they have levied against the United States loom largest for them.

* Moscow complains of dilatory conduct of negotiations on SALT, mutual and balanced force reductions, a comprehensive test ban, and the Indian Ocean.
* In the global political arena, the Soviet Union is suspicious of Western steps to strengthen China against the Soviet Union, resents exclusion from the Middle East negotiations, and believes the reaction to its competition for influence in Africa is disproportionate and unreasonable.
* The Soviet regime sees a U.S. effort to use human rights issues to undermine its political authority.
* It is disturbed by what it sees as efforts to rekindle the cold war by economic pinpricks.

One of the difficulties of the situation is that the Soviet leadership sees the deterioration in relations as largely stemming from cold war pressures within the United States and does not perceive how actions of the Soviet Union—its security apparatus, its military, its propagandists—have contributed to a hardening of American attitudes toward the Soviet Union. It is, of course, a natural tendency not "to see oursels as ithers see us," as the poet Bobby Burns put it, and we are not immune from this tendency. But the problem is compounded in the Soviet case by the fact that these are the actions of institutions deeply rooted in the Soviet system, and the world view of the leadership is circumscribed by its limited experience of the outside world.

Analysis of Recent Developments

In seeking to understand why relations have deteriorated, we can sort out some objective factors in the situation. The relationship between the United States and the Soviet Union has always been subject to changes in the external international situation, which is the terrain on which the two countries meet.

In the present period, a principal factor is that the continent of Africa, culminating several decades of post colonial change, has entered upon a period of extraordinary fluidity, in which many sources of conflict have come to a head. This creates situations in which the Soviet Union sees opportunities for the expansion of its influence, and this in turn inevitably heightens the competitive tension in the U.S.-Soviet relationship. The Soviet Union has not interpreted "detente" or "peaceful coexistence" as precluding such actions.

There are also factors within the Soviet Union that contribute to heightened tension in the relationship. The powerful entrenched police bureaucracy inevitably presses for tighter control and punitive actions against the expression of dissident opinion during periods of reduced international tension, thus precipitating international reactions which cut across the foreign policy interests of the Soviet Union. Moreover, the considerable strength of the military bureaucracies tends to perpetuate support for military programs without regard for their impact on the other international policies of the government.

In addition, there are factors in the American situation which affect the relationship.

- The blurring of popular understanding of the limitations of "detente" contributed to a sense of disillusionment and anger when the competitive aspects of the relationship became more evident.
- A measured and effective reaction to the military and political competition from the Soviet Union has been made more difficult by the persisting post-Vietnam apprehension that the United States may be seen as lacking sufficient will and resolution.
- The implementation of a unified and coordinated foreign policy by the United States has become more complex, both because the issues themselves have become more complex and also as a result of the shifting balance of responsibility for the conduct of foreign policy between the executive and legislative branches of government.

Given the existence of these factors in the external international situation and within the Soviet Union and the United States, it should not be surprising that the course of U.S.-Soviet relations does not follow a straight line. Nevertheless, it lies within our power to magnify or moderate the effect of these factors. It should be evident that it is in our national interest to moderate them, as much as possible, since a high level of tension in the U.S.-Soviet relationship inevitably makes all other problems facing us in our foreign relations more difficult and more dangerous.

Present State of U.S.-Soviet Relations

In this short perspective, one can only speak of trends with fingers crossed, but it appears possible that the deterioration in Soviet-

American relations may have bottomed out in midsummer. During the August holidays, a lull in the chain of actions and reactions gave both sides an opportunity to reflect on the consequences of the momentum that had been developing in the downward spiral.

A number of steps on the Soviet side in recent weeks suggests that the Soviet Union wishes to reverse the tide of events.

- The court action against two American correspondents, who had been charged with slander as part of an effort to limit Western news reporting on Soviet dissidents, was terminated.
- An American businessman who had been charged with currency violations, apparently in retaliation for the arrest of two Soviet citizens for espionage, was allowed to leave the country after a transparently contrived trial.
- The inhumane severity of sentences in human rights cases has been relatively reduced in the most recent series of trials, following the conviction of Shcharanskiy, and the Soviet leadership has agreed to allow a number of families to leave the country who had previously been denied permission to do so. The level of Jewish emigration from the Soviet Union has continued to rise and is now higher than at any time since 1973.
- Although further serious problems may lie ahead in southern Africa, there are some grounds for a tentative judgment that the Soviet Union has observed certain limitations in Ethiopia and has not sought to prevent Angola from playing a constructive role in composing its relations with Zaire and in the Namibian problem.

The logic of the Soviet situation suggests that the same reasons that prompted the Brezhnev regime about a decade ago to commit itself decisively to a foreign policy of "peaceful coexistence" (that is, a continuation of the competition without war and at reduced levels of tension) are, if anything, more compelling today than they were then. Domestically, the Soviet system still faces the need for structural changes to raise both agricultural and industrial productivity and to encourage the growth of the advanced technological sector of its economy.

In its foreign relations, the Soviet Union is concerned about delicate instabilities in Eastern Europe, a mounting challenge from China, and relatively unpromising prospects elsewhere in the world, with the partial and still uncertain exception of parts of Africa. In the military balance, the continued high level of resources devoted by the Soviet Union to its strategic and conventional forces has stimulated a higher level of military effort by the United States and its NATO allies.

Each of these problems would be compounded by a foreign policy that would result in higher tensions. Miscalculation, irrationality, and bureaucratic free wheeling are always possible, but if prudence and logic prevail, and if present and future Soviet leaders perceive that the United States is equally willing to conduct the relationship at reduced levels of tension, it should be possible to put matters onto a more sensible footing.

For its part, the United States has been taking measured steps to encourage further movement by the Soviet Union toward the resolution of fundamental problems still unresolved.

The strains of the recent past may create an opportunity for us to put the U.S.-Soviet relationship on a more realistic and steady course, in place of the alternations between extreme hostility and shallow optimism which have dominated our attitudes in the past.

The President has made it clear that it is an integral element in U.S. foreign policy to recognize that the Soviet-American relationship in the present period, while fundamentally competitive in nature as a result of our different views of the world and our conflicting long term aims, at the same time also includes some important overlapping interests. Preeminent among these common interests is the necessity of navigating the mine fields of conflict in the world today so that they do not precipitate a world nuclear war.

From this it follows that the priority governing our relations with the Soviet Union in the present period is to strengthen our security by seeking to stabilize the military competition between the two superpowers and by working toward a regulation of the political competition so that it does not increase the danger of war. Viewing the relationship with the Soviet Union as a process extending over many decades, it is part of our longer term purpose to encourage a widening of the sphere of cooperative actions to effect a moderating influence on the fundamental character of the relationship to the extent that this may become possible.

* * *

Conclusion

It is evident that the difficulties in the U.S.-Soviet relationship in recent months have astringently washed away the remnants of any euphoric expectations from the period of detente as it appeared to exist 6 years ago.

What remains, however, is an opportunity to build upon a realistic assessment of the fundamental nature of the relationship and in particular to realize in concrete steps the interests that both countries should have in stabilizing the strategic military competition and in setting recognized constraints on the conduct of the political competition. This is the most urgent aspect of the relationship.

For the future, one cannot escape the impression that the Soviet Union may be approaching some fundamental choices—whether to allow the elements of conflict in the relationship to deepen or to follow the course of restraint and responsibility, leading to a widening of measures of cooperation.

The United States has the means and the will to protect its interests in either case. But by our actions and by what we say, we should make it clear beyond any doubt that if the Soviet leadership chooses the wiser course of restraint and responsibility, they will find the United States fully responsive.

3. EUROPE AND THE ATLANTIC ALLIANCE

(11)   A New Agenda for Democracy: Address by President Carter at the Palais des Congrès, Paris, January 4, 1978.[1]

Mr. Foreign Minister,[2] *presidents of the organizations who daily work to ensure friendship between our two countries, ladies and gentlemen of France and the United States who have come this evening:*

This afternoon I laid a wreath, along with the President of France, on the grave of the soldier who commemorated the bravery of the French people. And standing on my left was a group of men in the same regiment who fought with George Washington at Yorktown 200 years ago.

When our democracy was born, France was there. And for more than 200 years, our two nations have shared the same ideals and the same culture.

There is one belief above all others that has made us what we are. This is the belief that the rights of the individual inherently stand higher than the claims or demands of the state. This is a message that the American and French peoples, each in turn, carried forward to the world two centuries ago, and these are the values which the world still depends upon us to affirm.

Democracy was then a new and an untried concept. Now it is a standard for our Western civilization. The American Declaration of Independence inspired so greatly by French philosophy, spoke of the "unalienable rights" of persons, of life and liberty and the pursuit of happiness. These rights were controversial then, and now they are the measure by which the faithfulness of governments is tested. Democracy is indeed a compelling idea, an idea so attractive that even its enemies now attempt to cloak repression with false democratic labels.

[1] Text from *Presidential Documents,* 14: 21-7.
[2] Louis de Guiringaud.

But our democratic order has come under challenge. There are those who question whether democratic values are appropriate for contemporary circumstances. Voices in the developing world ask whether notions of free speech, personal liberty, freely chosen governments should not be pushed aside in the struggle to overcome poverty. Voices in the industrialized world ask whether democracy equips us for the frenzied pace of change in our own modern lives.

We've heard warnings that a democratic society cannot impose on itself the restraint and self-discipline which is necessary to cope with persistent economic problems. We've heard that the disparate elements of our societies cannot cohere in a democratic system. Governments everywhere have begun to seem remote and impersonal, incompetent. Many people question whether any government can hear their distant and solitary voices.

These problems are real, and we must admit their existence. But we must also bear the burden that democratic society imposes on those like us who are part of it. That is to proclaim our unshaken faith in the values of our democratic nations and our belief that those values are still relevant—to the rich and the poor, the North and South, East and West, as constant now as they were when our forebears signed the Declaration of Independence and your forebears proclaimed the Declaration of the Rights of Man.

We defend these values because they are right, because there is no higher purpose for the state than to preserve these rights for its citizens. But we defend them also in the faith that there is no contradiction between preserving our democratic values on the one hand and meeting challenges which face our modern societies.

It's precisely when democracy is up against difficult challenges that its leaders must show firmness in resisting the temptation of finding solutions in nondemocratic forces.

This week, in India, I discussed our belief that only through respect for individual liberties can developing nations achieve their full economic and political potential. That is our faith. And India, the world's largest democracy—they are proving that it is still true.

Here in France we meet as industrialized powers to affirm that our confidence in a democratic future for these developed societies is equally strong.

Democracy is not merely right and just. It's also the system that is the most consistent with human nature. It's the most effective way to organize society for the common good.

Where the state dominates everything, only the narrow talents of the bureaucrat are free to flower. But the pluralistic society that exists within a democracy allows for a broad range to succeed—in government, in the arts, in labor, in technology, in the sciences, and in the marketplace as well.

Democracy unleashes the innate creative energy of each of us.

We need to look no further back than the last three decades to see unparalleled success. These years have been extraordinary in the time for France, for Western Europe, the United States, and other democratic nations.

France and its partners in Western Europe rose from the destruction and the turmoil of World War II to build economies and societies more thriving and productive than ever before and to regain positions of world leadership very rapidly.

Never have so many new jobs and so much new wealth been created or so much change in people's lives been managed so effectively and yet with so much freedom.

All of this is no accident. Nations with other political systems, in spite of their great human and natural resources, have not done as well.

And democracy protects us also against the excesses of modernization. It helps us constantly to reduce the rising complexity of modern life to human terms. At a time when the computer makes total state control more possible than ever—processing people like numbers—democracy stands guard, protecting the uniqueness of the individual.

This is why the great trend of emigration is from those states which deny basic rights to their people and toward the free nations of the West. That's why India, under the greatest trial and tension, has reaffirmed its commitment to rule by the people, and that's why Portugal and Spain and Greece have rejoined the ranks of Europe's democratic nations.

We do not fear the challenges which test our chosen form of government. But today we need a new agenda for democracy. The first task on this agenda is to devise ways in which government and social institutions can better and more quickly respond to the higher standards of leadership and service which are now being demanded by our people.

It's a time of testing. Already the varied experiments are underway, according to the unique traditions and needs of each individual country. In Western Europe successful sharing of the fruits of economic growth at all levels has provided a way to help in society [sic] overcoming mounting social problems.

In France you are making a young constitution work in balancing authority between the executive and the legislature.

In some countries, like Germany and Scandinavia, there are continuing experiments in new forms of interrelationship between labor and management.

The member nations of the European Community are planning to hold direct elections among the nations for the European Parliament.

In my own Nation, we are trying to reduce government regulation in areas better left to private enterprise or to the individuals.

And in several nations, including some of our own; there is emphasis on strengthening the role of local government, on decentralizing power, and on working through voluntary associations to meet particular problems and needs.

In these and other ways we can make government more responsive, accountable, and also closer to the people, fostering a renewed sense of confidence in our national and in our local communities.

We can also find new answers to the old problems of combining freedom with responsibility. As President Giscard d'Estaing wrote in his book, "Towards a New Democracy," "The pluralism of power guarantees freedom. . . . Democratic progress does not result in disorder, but in a better balance of order within freedom and responsibility."

The second item on the new agenda for democracy is the economic challenge. We must not only restore growth, control inflation, and reduce unemployment; we must also demonstrate that our democratic economic system can adapt to the demands that are constantly changing and placed upon it. This means proving again that we have the self-discipline to pursue our future, no less than our current interests, so that contending domestic groups will not produce chaos and discord, but a new harmony of effort for the common good.

It means increasing efforts to ensure that the fruits of economic growth reach all parts of society, so that each individual will share in the benefits of economic progress. And it means using our resources to promote human development—not just growth for its own sake.

Our democratic economies now have unprecedented strength to meet this challenge. We have skilled work forces. We have productive plants and equipment, effective management, and the will and the means to cooperate closely with one another—both within nations and also among nations.

And in the free market we have a means of matching production to human needs that is swifter and more subtle than any computer, more sensitive to society's requirements than any state committee.

My country is able and willing to join with its partners in building on that strength, to put the global economy on the path to growth and to rising prosperity.

America's efforts will be directed toward maintaining the strength of the dollar, continuing steady progress against unemployment and inflation, and stimulating private investment.

This year we will cut taxes substantially for both business and consumers, and we'll take these steps primarily because they are in our own interests, but also because we recognize the importance of continued noninflationary recovery in the United States to the economies of the rest of the world.

We are working with our economic partners also in the Geneva trade negotiations to reach rapid agreement that will improve the open trading system, expand commerce, and create new jobs.

And following the French example, we are hard at work on a comprehensive energy program which will lessen our imports of foreign oil, reduce undue dependence, and cut the deficit in our balance of trade.

France and America and the other industrial democracies are emerging from the economic recession of recent years. Some of us can turn our attention at once to noninflationary growth, like the United States. Others must first take painful measures simply to reduce inflation. As more nations are able to pursue higher growth, our economies will create more jobs, and unemployment will go down.

Confidence in steady growth will reduce pressures for trade restrictions, protectionism, make it easier for us to adapt to changes within our societies, help us to make more efficient use of energy, and make it easier for countries with payments surpluses to open their markets to developed and developing nations alike.

But there are also many other economic needs today. The economic institutions that served us well in the past need to be strengthened. We must reach a better understanding of basic economic forces so that we can solve the problems simultaneously of inflation and unemployment. We've not yet been able to do this.

We must devote much greater effort to further advances in high technology to help all our nations compete effectively in tomorrow's markets.

We must develop new and productive industries and services so that we can moderate the impact on our peoples of change imposed by increased global competition for jobs and markets that's sure to come. And we must solve the problem of youth unemployment. Unless we do, an entire generation could be estranged from our democratic societies.

We must take steps to avoid exporting our economic difficulties to other nations, whether rich or poor. And we must use the tools of shared freedom to increase the choices and opportunities of our economic system. We can share our experience in social development, in education, health care, social services, and the organization and management of farms and factories.

At the heart of all these efforts is continued cooperation along with our other economic partners in such ways as the economic summits, which were first proposed by France. This cooperation should recognize the individuality of each nation, while acknowledging that our economic well-being will rise or fall together.

The third task on the new agenda for democracy is to provide for our mutual security.

I come to France today recognizing that our two nations share a basic commitment to preserve our hard-won freedom. We are able, with our allies, to keep our freedom precisely because we are militarily strong.

Our central security system today and our central problem is maintaining our will to keep the military strength we need, while seeking at the same time every opportunity to build a better peace. Military power without détente may lead to conflict, but détente would be impossible without the NATO alliance and popular support for a strong defense.

Both France and America prove that the peoples of a democracy can and will support these joint goals of constant strength and also a commitment to peace. The commitment of the American Government and the American people to the security of Europe is absolute. There should be no doubt that we will maintain in Europe whatever forces are needed to meet that commitment. We are also grateful that France maintains and improves its forces that are essential for defense.

But we also see the need to move beyond confrontation, to resolve the differences between East and West, and to progress toward arms control and disarmament.

We are determined to seek balanced and mutual limits on both qualitative and quantitative deployment of nuclear weapons, and then substantial reductions, leading to the eventual elimination of nuclear weapons as a potential destructive force among the nations of the world.

We are determined to seek early agreement on a comprehensive ban of the testing of all nuclear explosives, both military weapons and also the so-called peaceful nuclear devices. And we are determined to seek a substantial reduction of the international commerce in conventional weapons.

We'll work with other nations to achieve the advantages which such agreements can bring. While the approaches of France and the United States to these issues may sometimes differ, our desire to build a more stable peace is one and the same. And in all these efforts, we will consult and cooperate closely with you and with our other allies, recognizing the independence of each nation but also our mutual interests and our mutual commitments.

The fourth task on democracy's new agenda is the effort of Europeans to shape your future. For the goal that you've set for yourselves, with your partners in the European Community, is nothing less than to transform—in an unprecedented fashion in history—and to improve relations among states with ancient traditions, unique histories, and legitimate pride in national achievement.

The United States will give its unqualified support to what you and your partners in the Nine are doing to strengthen European cooperation, for we see European strength and unity as a boon and not as a threat to us. The real threat to the interests of us all would be economic weakness and disunity.

The fifth and the final item on the new agenda for democracy is to cooperate among ourselves in adapting to global change. The same factors which led to our economic successes over the past two generations—science, technology, education, health, will and wisdom of our people—have also altered the interrelationship between the industrial democracies on the one hand and the developing world on the other.

European nations, individually or together, also have an increasing role to play beyond this continent, particularly in reordering relations between North and South.

It was less than 100 years ago that the European powers met and divided the continent of Africa among you, and yet today colonialism has nearly ended. Before World War II, 80 percent of the world's land mass and 75 percent of its people were under Western authority, but today there are more than 100 new nations, each with insistent needs and insistent demands. A few years ago, the West made virtually all the decisions about the global economy, but now important resources are also under the control of the developing countries—as the energy crisis has made very clear. The councils of economic action can no longer be limited just to a few.

During this trip, I've seen how the developing nations are creating a new role for themselves in the world's economic system, redistributing global power, posing new global problems, and assuming new rights and new responsibilities.

We've long understood that greater individual equality can bring forth greater prosperity in our domestic societies. But now we also see how greater equality among nations can promote the health of the global economy, including our own. No nation, nor any small group of nations, can any longer shape its destiny alone.

In proposing the North-South conference, President Giscard spoke of creating new forms of international cooperation.[3] What he said then stands as a watchword of all our efforts together, and I quote him again: "(This) should not constitute a victory for some countries over others, achieved by taking advantage of temporary power relationships. Rather it must be a victory of mankind over itself. . . ."

If we move in that spirit and direct our efforts together to solving the problems that face the nations of the world, then we shall surely gain that victory of which he spoke. We will vindicate our deep and abiding faith in the strength of democracy to grow and to develop with the times.

Six days ago, I left the United States on a tour whose constant

[3]Cf. *AFR, 1974:* 453 and 558.

theme has been the universal vitality of democracy. In Poland, Iran, Saudi Arabia, Egypt, India, and now in France, I've emphasized that our modern struggle is not only to establish peace but also to protect the individual from abuse by the state.

Tomorrow, with President Giscard d'Estaing, I will leave Paris and visit the beaches at Normandy. If the names Omaha, Utah, Juno, Gold, and Sword will always live in the memories of both our peoples, it's because they remind us at what cost our liberties have been purchased and what a precious heritage has been left for us to attend and to defend. These names remind us that liberty is not secured with just one defense but must be struggled for again and again and again.

Our ancestors made their defense with principles and with revolution. People of my parents' generation, and of my own, bore arms in the name of freedom. Many of them were left at Normandy Beach and at the thousands of other shrines to liberty across the world.

Though we will always be prepared, we pray that their sacrifice in battle need never be repeated. And we know that war need not come again so long as we transmit our devotion to those values of free people, strengthened and renewed, to each succeeding generation that comes after us.

Thank you very much.

(12) Follow-up Meeting to the Conference on Security and Cooperation in Europe, Belgrade, October 4, 1977–March 9, 1978.

(a) Concluding Document of the Belgrade Meeting, March 8, 1978.[4]

CONCLUDING DOCUMENT OF THE BELGRADE MEETING 1977 OF
REPRESENTATIVES OF THE PARTICIPATING STATES OF
THE CONFERENCE ON SECURITY AND CO-OPERATION IN EUROPE,
HELD ON THE BASIS OF THE PROVISIONS OF
THE FINAL ACT RELATING TO
THE FOLLOW-UP TO THE CONFERENCE

The representatives of the participating States of the Conference on Security and Co-operation in Europe, appointed by the Ministers of Foreign Affairs of these states, met at Belgrade from 4 Octo-

[4]Text from Department of State.

ber 1977 to 8 March 1978 in accordance with the provisions of the Final Act relating to the follow-up to the Conference.

The participants received a message from the President of the Socialist Federal Republic of Yugoslavia, Josip Broz Tito and were addressed by Mr. Milos Minic, Vice-President of the Federal Executive Council and Federal Secretary for Foreign Affairs of the Socialist Federal Republic of Yugoslavia.

Contributions were made by the following non-participating Mediterranean States: Algeria, Egypt, Israel, Lebanon, Morocco, Syria and Tunisia.

The representatives of the participating States stressed the importance they attach to detente, which has continued since the adoption of the Final Act in spite of difficulties and obstacles encountered. In this context they underlined the role of the CSCE, the implementation of the provisions of the Final Act being essential for the development of this process.

The representatives of the participating States held a thorough exchange of views both on the implementation of the provisions of the Final Act and of the tasks defined by the Conference, as well as, in the context of the questions dealt with by the latter, on the deepening of their mutual relations, the improvement of security and the development of cooperation in Europe, and the development of the process of detente in the future.

The representatives of the participating States stressed the political importance of the Conference on Security and Cooperation in Europe and reaffirmed the resolve of their governments, to implement fully, unilaterally, bilaterally and multilaterally, all the provisions of the Final Act.

It was recognized that the exchange of views constitutes in itself a valuable contribution towards the achievement of the aims set by the CSCE, although different views were expressed as to the degree of implementation of the Final Act reached so far.

They also examined proposals concerning the above questions and the definition of the appropriate modalities for the holding of other meetings in conformity with the provisions of the chapter of the Final Act concerning the follow-up to the conference.

Consensus was not reached on a number of proposals submitted to the meeting.

In conformity with the relevant provisions of the Final Act and with their resolve to continue the multilateral process initiated by the CSCE, the participating States will hold further meetings among their representatives. The second of these meetings will be held in Madrid commencing Tuesday 11 November 1980.

A preparatory meeting will be held in Madrid commencing Tuesday 9 September 1980 to decide on appropriate modalities for the main Madrid meeting. This will be done on the basis of the Final Act as well as of the other relevant documents adopted during the process of the CSCE.[5]

It was also agreed to hold, within the framework of the follow-up to the CSCE, the meetings of experts of the participating States indicated below.

In conformity with the mandate contained in the Final Act and according to the proposal made to this effect by the Government of Switzerland a meeting of experts will be convened at Montreux on October 31, 1978 charged with pursuing the examination and elaboration of a generally acceptable method for peaceful settlement of disputes aimed at complementing existing methods.

Upon the invitation of the Government of the Federal Republic of Germany, the Meeting of Experts envisaged in the Final Act in order to prepare a "Scientific Forum" will take place in Bonn starting on June 20, 1978. Representatives of UNESCO and the United Nations Economic Commission for Europe shall be invited to state their views.

Upon the invitation of the Government of Malta, a meeting of experts on the Mediterranean will be within the framework of the Mediterranean Chapter of the Final Act, convened on February 13, 1979 in La Valletta. Its mandate will be to consider the possibilities and means of promoting concrete initiatives for mutually beneficial cooperation concerning various economic, scientific and cultural fields, in addition to other initiatives relating to the above subjects already under way. The non-participating Mediterranean States will be invited to contribute to the work of this meeting. Questions relating to security will be discussed at the Madrid meeting.

The duration of the meetings of experts should not exceed 4–6 weeks. They will draw up conclusions and recommendations and send their reports to the governments of the participating States. The results of these meetings will be taken into account, as appropriate, at the Madrid Meeting.

All the above-mentioned meetings will be held in conformity with paragraph 4 of the Chapter on "Follow-up to the Conference" of the Final Act.

The government of the Socialist Federal Republic of Yugoslavia is requested to transmit the present document to the Secretary-General of the United Nations, to the Director-General of UNESCO and to the Executive Secretary of the United Nations Economic Commission for Europe. The government of the Socialist Federal Republic of Yugoslavia is also requested to transmit the present

[5]The other relevant documents adopted during the process of the CSCE are: The Final Recommendations of the Helsinki Consultations; The Decisions of the Preparatory Meeting to Organize the Belgrade Meeting 1977; this Concluding Document. [Footnote in the original.]

document to the governments of the Mediterranean non-participating States.

The representatives of the participating States expressed their profound gratitude to the people and government of the Socialist Federal Republic of Yugoslavia for the excellent organization of the Belgrade Meeting and the warm hospitality extended to the delegations which participated in the meeting.

(b) Statement by Ambassador Arthur J. Goldberg, Chairman of the United States Delegation, at the Final Plenary Meeting, March 8, 1978.[6]

I wish to thank our Yugoslav hosts for the manner in which they have provided for us at this conference. The Secretariat—under the able direction of Ambassador Bozinovic, the Yugoslav delegation, and the Government and people of Yugoslavia—expended every effort to make our conference a success. I wish particularly to express appreciation to His Excellency, Ambassador Pesic. His constant steadfastness and determination, even when our work was in its most difficult hours, was an inspiration to all of us. It is a source of gratification to the American delegation that President Tito is this very week in the United States where President Carter is conveying to him his personal appreciation for the uniquely constructive role that Yugoslavia has played not only in the Belgrade meeting but in the entire process of building security and cooperation in Europe.[7]

I consider it appropriate in this final statement to express frankly the views of the U.S. Government on the Belgrade meeting and on the Conference on Security and Cooperation in Europe (CSCE) process that was begun in Helsinki and will continue in Madrid and thereafter.

The Belgrade meeting of the Conference on Security and Cooperation in Europe—the first formal sequel to the Helsinki summit—is now at its end. In the judgment of the delegation of the United States, the meeting has fulfilled its basic mandate and although it has been difficult, it has also been successful.

In these past months—with the support of our gracious, patient Yugoslav hosts and through the conscientious efforts of the delegates—our meeting has confirmed the vitality of the Helsinki concept. Belgrade has tested the validity and flexibility of the CSCE process. It has not been an easy passage, but we have delineated the scope of that process and added to its depth. Most important of all,

[6]Text from *Bulletin*, Apr. 1978: 40–43.
[7]Mar. 6–9; text of Carter-Tito joint statement, Mar. 9, in *Presidential Documents*, 14: 485–8.

we have given our commitment to preserving the process and to making its growth our common enterprise.

We have had the exchange of views of which the Final Act mandates on the implementation of its provisions and on the prospects for improved mutual relations. We have spoken our own minds and have heard out the opinions of those who differ from us. In doing so, we have been able to make a sober assessment of past accomplishments, continuing shortcomings, and future challenges. We have agreed to continue this discourse bilaterally and in Madrid in 1980.

The United States has always viewed the fulfillment of Final Act commitments as part of a gradual but steadily advancing process of bridging the East-West divide, of extending the benefits of security and cooperation throughout Europe—including of course Berlin. The contribution of CSCE has been to engage 35 states—different in size and system, history and outlook—in that vital effort. The role of the Belgrade meeting has been to deepen that engagement and to make specific the conduct which it entails.

From our talks has emerged a clearer sense of the tasks before us. No country can be allowed to single out particular sections of the Final Act for their attention while ignoring others. Progress in the area of human rights and human contacts as well as disarmament and economic, scientific, and cultural cooperation are inextricably linked together in the Final Act. The significance of Final Act implementation—and of the Belgrade review of its progress—lies precisely in combining the various elements of detente in a coherent, related whole.

Last October I also spoke of giving detente a humanitarian face and a human measure.[8] That has, indeed, been the theme of this conference. For though we are here to represent governments, we have managed to address the problems of people as well as of power. We have weighed the claims of individuals, not just the interests of states.

Thus we explored the promises made at Helsinki to respect the role of the individual and groups in monitoring the implementation of the Final Act; to heal the wounds of divided families; to facilitate the right of free emigration; and to better the conditions in which scientists, journalists, scholars, and businessmen work. There has been some progress in some of these areas but not nearly enough and regrettably there have been retrogressions.

The favorable resolution of such questions in the days to come will do much to create the climate of openness in which detente itself will flourish. A detente relationship which betters the lot of individuals and smooths contact between them is also certain to improve the ties between the states.

[8]Text in *AFR, 1977:* 239-46.

Human Rights

Crucially, of course, our meeting dealt at length with the question of human rights and fundamental freedoms. Our citizens' freedom of thought, conscience, religion, or belief; their ability to exercise their civil rights effectively—individually or in groups—raised sensitive issues at Belgrade. Their sensitivity was part of their significance. Our meeting was the first to put those questions prominently and legitimately into the framework of multilateral East-West diplomacy.

That idea is a powerful one, and at Belgrade it has won powerful support. It has also aroused strong opposition. We have heard the contention that human rights are purely internal affairs, that to discuss their observance in another nation is to violate that nation's sovereignty, to interfere in matters that are no outsider's concern.

The Final Act refutes that reasoning. The Belgrade meeting has made it untenable. By virtue of Principle VII, human rights are direct concerns of all Final Act signatories. Under the terms of the U.N. Charter, the Universal Declaration of Human Rights and the international covenants—as well as the Final Act—they are the subject of international undertakings. They are then, without question, the proper subject of the diplomatic examination and debate we have had in Belgrade. And they will remain, after Belgrade, the proper focus of continuing comment and efforts.

For the pursuit of liberty is an unending enterprise for man, the surest guarantee of this security and of peace. What the Final Act obliged us all to pursue is what Aleksandr Pushkin defined long ago as a better kind of freedom. That, he wrote, is the freedom not to bow your conscience, thought, or neck to rank or power. That concept of individual dignity is still the vision offered us by the Final Act, the vision all of us pledged to respect and promote.

We know, however, that not all of us have fulfilled that pledge in full or in good faith. The American delegation has spoken forthrightly at Belgrade of the broken and unfulfilled promises of Principle VII and basket 3. We have expressed our concern and our regret and—at times—our outrage at the incidents which have occurred in direct contravention of the Final Act and in profound disregard of its provisions in the area of human rights and fundamental freedoms.

Our meeting could not overlook such episodes, especially when unwarranted repression is directed against men and women whose only offense seems to be that they have merely sought to monitor or enforce or implement the provisions and the promises of the Helsinki Final Act. Their activity is encouraged by the Final Act. It needs to be protected, not punished.

Similarly, in our review of implementation, we could not gloss over—and cannot now—the plight of men and women persecuted for their religious beliefs and for trying to pass those beliefs on to their children. Nor can we be silent now—or in the future—when numbers of ethnic minorities are denied their equality, particularly in their efforts to preserve the language and culture which are essential to their special identity.

We cannot pretend that such questions are irrelevant to the implementation of the Final Act, intrusive at this meeting and injurious—if discussed—to the development of detente. We live in the real world, not one of make-believe. We cannot make our world a better one if we turn a blind eye to its faults.

Those faults—just as much as our accomplishments and opportunities—were the legitimate subject of the Belgrade review. That review dealt productively with real shortcomings in Final Act implementation so that from our examination we could each and all move to remedial action.

That action is still required of us. Unfortunately, it is not detailed in the meeting's concluding document. The reason is plain. Consensus was denied and this I profoundly deplore.

Efforts to squelch the truth at Belgrade or at home will not change the truth. And they will not deflect the United States from insisting that candor is as important to the healthy development of international confidence as is respect for sovereign equality and individuality.

Candor and respect must be companion elements in the pursuit of security and cooperation. The foundation laid down in the Final Act—augmented by the record made at Belgrade—enables us to build an ever firmer structure of detente. Our first priority—always our overriding challenge—remains simply to implement the Final Act in all of its parts, to do so in good faith and with appropriate speed. The initial pace is not as important as the fact of continuing, forward movement.

From Belgrade, the United States intends to move forward. My country has had its performance questioned here and some of the questioning has been constructive. It will aid my country to improve its record. I wish others were of equal mind.

My delegation has also taken careful note of the thoughtful ideas advanced by many delegations for action consonant with the thrust and spirit of the Final Act. Some such proposals can be set in motion by unilateral action; many can be refined and readied for decisions in Madrid. The United States is prepared to participate constructively in such enterprises.

Political Cooperation

We especially value CSCE as a framework for increasing political intercourse among all participating states. The many and varied specific provisions of the Final Act provide a rich content for this commerce. The United States, in its efforts to deepen political relations with all CSCE states, will continue to work to translate that potential into reality.

In the area of confidence-building measures, for example, we have already seen in practice how states can build from the language of the Final Act to implement its spirit. In notifying smaller scale maneuvers, in making notifications amply informative, and in affording observers good overall views of maneuvers, some states have set an example others can productively emulate. Such experience has been constructive; it remains to be applied to major troop movements. In general, moreover, we can all think afresh about ways of "developing and enlarging measures aimed at strengthening confidence," a possibility the Final Act explicitly sets before us. Although CSCE was not conceived as a forum for negotiating disarmament, we have all recognized the impetus it can give to that vital process.

Economic Cooperation

Further, in the field of economic and commercial cooperation, our frank discussions have reinforced the awareness of the need to reduce—indeed, through mutual action, to eliminate—existing impediments to trade. The potential for cooperation in this field is great, and the United States is fully prepared to explore the many possibilities for productive unilateral and reciprocal action. In such an endeavor, of course, other states must also engage in expanding the flow of timely and accurate economic information on which close, broadened contacts among traders and investors so heavily depend.

If the Belgrade meeting has aided the flow of people, it has yet to make a similar impact on the transmission of information. Too many Eastern states continue to impede access to what many of their citizens want to read and see and hear.

Finally there is much we can do in bilateral and multilateral cooperation to widen the range and improve the quality of contacts among scientists and scholars, men and women of letters and of the arts.

The United States will continue to be especially attentive to the question of human rights. We are greatly concerned about those individuals and organizations which my delegation has mentioned— by name and by country—in the course of our discussions who are being denied their elementary human rights. And they are by no means the only ones. The list of those suffering repression is far too long. And their fate arouses the greatest anxiety. Our concern is not limited to one country or one set of individuals. "Injustice anywhere," said Martin Luther King, Jr., "is a threat to justice everywhere."

The Final Act enshrines the concept of justice—not privilege or power—ruling the affairs of men and the relations between states. The Belgrade meeting has reaffirmed that central tenet in the context of detente in Europe. Peace, we have seen, depends on the just conduct of nations to each other and to their own citizens.

Helsinki aroused great hopes. In some quarters it also appears to have aroused great fear. In Belgrade we, on our part, have attempted forthrightly to discuss both the hopes and the fears of governments and peoples. We recognize that some hopes may not be as high as they might have been when we came to Belgrade. But we have always known that the road to peace and security and cooperation is a long and arduous one.

The United States is determined to continue. Between now and at[9] Madrid and thereafter we will seek to further implementation of all of the provisions of the Final Act. And we pledge to do all in our power to keep the hopes of Helsinki alive.

(13) Meeting of the North Atlantic Council with the Participation of Heads of State and Government, Washington, May 30–31, 1978.

(a) Remarks by President Carter at the Opening Ceremonies, May 30, 1978.[10]

Mr. President, Mr. Secretary General,[11] *Excellencies, members of the Council, and distinguished guests:*

On behalf of the people of the United States, I welcome here today our closest friends and allies, the leaders of the North Atlantic Alliance.

Twenty-nine years ago, at an uncertain time for world peace, President Truman spoke these words on signing the North Atlantic Treaty, and I quote from him: "In this pact, we hope to create a shield against aggression . . . —a bulwark which will permit us to get on with the real business of government and society, the business of achieving a fuller and a happier life for all our citizens."[12]

The alliance born that day in April 1949 has helped preserve our mutual security for nearly 30 years, almost a decade longer than the

[9]Other official texts omit "at."
[10]Text from *Presidential Documents,* 14: 1012–14.
[11]Prime Minister Bülent Eçevit (Turkey) and Secretary-General Joseph M.A.H. Luns (Netherlands).
[12]*Documents, 1949:* 611.

time between the two great wars of this century. History records no other alliance that has successfully brought together so many different nations for so long without the firing of a single shot in anger.

Ours is a defensive alliance. No nation need fear aggression from us, but neither should any nation ever doubt our will to deter and to defeat aggression against us. The North Atlantic Alliance is a union of peoples moved by a desire to secure a safe future for our children in liberty and freedom. Our Alliance is unique because each of us 15 democratic nations shares a common heritage of human values, the rule of law, and faith in the courage and spirit of free men and women.

The military strength and the common political purpose of the North Atlantic Alliance has led us to cooperate in a thousand individual efforts, rightly conferring upon us the name of "community." And it has given us the self-confidence and strength of will to seek improved relations with our potential adversaries.

As an American I am proud that the commitment of the United States to the security, independence, and prosperity of Europe is as strong as ever. We are part of you, and you are part of us. The mutual pledges of trust we exchanged here in 1949 still hold firm and true.

During the next 2 days we will reaffirm our commitment to the Alliance, to its strategy and doctrine, and to each other. We will review a year-long effort to assess East-West relations as they exist now and as they may develop in the future. We will review our cooperation in defense procurement. And through a broad program of defense cooperation, we will seek to reinforce our individual efforts to guarantee our security against aggression for many years ahead.

We must be aware of the new challenges that we face individually and collectively, which require new efforts of us all.

The Soviet Union and other Warsaw Pact countries pose a military threat to our Alliance which far exceeds their legitimate security needs. For more than a decade the military power of the Soviet Union has steadily expanded, and it has grown consistently more sophisticated. In significant areas the military lead we once enjoyed has been reduced.

Today we can meet that military challenge, but we cannot be sure of countering the future military threat unless our Alliance modernizes its forces and adds additional military power. In this effort the United States will play its part across the spectrum of conventional, theater nuclear, and strategic nuclear forces. I'm gratified that America's allies are joining with us in building up their military might.

In the past year the United States has increased substantially its conventional combat strength in Europe and is enhancing its capability for rapid deployment of additional forces to that continent. United States theater nuclear forces are being modernized, and the United States will maintain strategic nuclear equivalence with the Soviet Union.

Our Alliance centers on Europe, but our vigilance cannot be limited just to that continent. In recent years expanding Soviet power has increasingly penetrated beyond the North Atlantic area.

As I speak today, the activities of the Soviet Union and Cuba in Africa are preventing individual nations from determining their own future. As members of the world's greatest alliance, we cannot be indifferent to these events because of what they mean for Africa and because of their effect on the long-term interests of the Alliance itself.

I welcome the efforts of individual NATO Allies to work for peace in Africa and to support nations and people in need, most recently in Zaire.[13]

Our Alliance has never been an end in itself. It is a way to promote stability and peace in Europe and, indeed, peace in the world at large.

Our strength has made possible the pursuit of détente and agreements to limit arms, while increasing the security of the Alliance. Defense in Europe, East-West détente, and global diplomacy all go hand in hand. Never before has a defensive alliance devoted so much effort to negotiate limitations and reductions in armaments with its potential adversaries. Our record has no equal in the search for effective arms control agreements.

The United States continues to move forward in its negotiations with the Soviet Union on a new agreement to limit and reduce strategic nuclear weapons. Our objective is to preserve and advance the security of all the members of our Alliance. We will continue to consult and to work closely with our allies to ensure that arms control efforts serve our common needs.

NATO Allies are also working for the mutual and balanced reduction of forces in Europe to provide greater security for all European peoples at lower levels of armaments, lower tensions, and at lower costs. The Allies have recently made a new proposal to the Warsaw Pact, and we call upon those nations to respond in the positive spirit in which our offer was made.

Our efforts to reduce weapons and forces in both these negotiations are guided by the need for equivalence and balance in the military capabilities of the East and West. That is the only enduring basis for promoting security and peace.

The challenges we face as allies do not end here. Economic changes within our countries and throughout the world have increased our dependence upon one another and complicated our efforts to promote economic and social welfare for our people.

Social changes generated partly by economic and political progress will require creative thought and effort by each of our nations. Our Alliance derives additional strength through our shared goals and experiences.

Finally, we face the challenge of promoting the human values and human rights that are the final purpose and meaning of our Alliance. The task is not easy—the way to liberty has never been—but our nations preeminently comprise the region of the world where freedom finds its most hospitable environment.

As we seek to build détente, therefore, we must continue to seek full implementation by Warsaw Pact countries as well as our own of the Helsinki accords on security and cooperation in Europe that was signed 3 years ago.

If we continue to build on the fundamental strength of the North Atlantic Alliance, I am confident that we can meet any challenge in the years ahead. In the future, as in the past, the Government and people of the United States will remain steadfast to our commitment to peace and freedom that all of us as allies share together.

Thank you very much.

(b) Remarks by President Carter on NATO Defense Policy, May 31, 1978. [14]

Thank you, Mr. Secretary General.

These briefings illustrate the magnitude of the challenges we face. They do not justify alarm, but they should strengthen our resolve.

When I took office 16 months ago, I reviewed the condition of U.S. defenses. I found them strong, although needing improvement. In particular, I concluded that the United States should give top priority to Europe, especially the conventional defenses needed in the initial stages of a conflict.

I reached this conclusion for two reasons. First, the Warsaw Pact countries, especially the Soviet Union, have steadily expanded and modernized their conventional forces beyond any legitimate requirements for defense. They are now able to attack with large armored forces more rapidly than we previously believed. Second, although U.S. nuclear forces remain strong and are fundamental to deterrence, the long-recognized role of conventional forces in deterrence of war is increasingly important.

As a result, I directed the Secretary of Defense to strengthen initial conventional defense capacity in Europe. Of course, such ef-

[14]Text from Presidential Documents, 14: 1020–22.

forts would amount to little unless accompanied by improvements in the conventional capacity of our NATO Allies. European NATO countries, not the United States, provide the bulk of our military forces in Europe. Also, the competing demands of our free societies limit the portion of our resources we can use for defense. Therefore, we must coordinate our defense planning to make the best use of these limited resources.

From our discussions in London last year,[15] I know that you share my view of the challenges we face. The answers we have developed together are impressive. We are all making significant, real increases in our defense budgets. We are strengthening our national forces—and we will do more. Finally, we have designed a bold Long-Term Defense Program to pull together a more effective collective defense during the years ahead.

As we improve our conventional defenses, we must remember that the strength of our strategic and theater nuclear forces is also necessary for deterrence and defense. These forces are—and will be—fully adequate. Arms control can make deterrence more stable and perhaps less burdensome—but it will not, in the foreseeable future, eliminate the need for nuclear forces.

For years, the Alliance has relied principally on American strategic forces for deterring nuclear attack on Europe. This coupling of American strategic forces to Europe is critical, for it means that an attack on Europe would have the full consequences of an attack on the United States. Let there be no misunderstanding. The United States is prepared to use *all* the forces necessary for the defense of the NATO area.

As an alliance, we must continue to review our nuclear deterrence needs in light of developments in Soviet nuclear and conventional forces. As one result of the Long-Term Defense Program, the Nuclear Planning Group is examining in detail the modernizing of our theater nuclear forces, including the question of long-range nuclear systems. We need also to consider jointly the relation of long-range theater nuclear systems to arms control.

This will require considering the full scope of political and military issues, and being sure that we maintain the coupling of American strategic forces to the defense of Europe. As we examine this together, I assure you that the United States will protect the options before us as the SALT II negotiations move toward completion.

Let me now turn to conventional forces—the bulk of the Long-Term Defense Program. After all, our largest expenditures are for conventional, not nuclear, forces.

[15]Cf. *AFR, 1977:* 213-21.

We must prepare to fight more effectively together as an alliance. We must markedly improve our ability to work together on the battlefield. We should overcome unnecessary duplication in our national programs, thus buying more security for the same money.

That is what the Long-Term Defense Program is all about. It is an unprecedented attempt by NATO to look across a longer span of years than ever before. It seeks a more cooperative course, as the only sensible way to improve our defenses without unnecessary increases in defense spending. It lays out specific measures of Alliance cooperation. It is the blueprint we need, and we must carry it out vigorously.

Of course, each of us depends on legislative approval for particular programs and projects within the Long-Term Defense Program. Because we lead democracies, we cannot bind our people by fiat. We can, however, pledge to do what is necessary to secure this approval and make this program work.

The United States is already responding to many Long-Term Defense Program recommendations, particularly in the field of reinforcement. And the recommendations will receive the highest priority in our own national defense programming. In short, we will do our part in adapting or modifying U.S. programs to support the NATO Long-Term Defense Program. I am confident that you will take similar action.

Finally, I want to mention the one remaining unresolved aspect of the Long-Term Defense Program. Although the program calls for new and unprecedented Alliance cooperation, no procedures have yet been devised for ensuring that it is carried out. We must avoid bold programs heartily endorsed—then largely ignored. The report before us directs the Secretary General to present for national review what changes are essential for vigorous followthrough.

Both the NATO Task Forces and we Americans have made several specific proposals to this end. For example, we favor explicitly recognizing NATO's new focus on logistics. One way is to create a new Assistant Secretary General for Logistics. We also favor clear assignment of responsibility for each program to one NATO body. Where appropriate, we would prefer a major NATO command. But I do not ask that you discuss our proposals today. Instead, I ask that all Alliance leaders here today to join me in calling for vigorous followthrough of the program.

In conclusion, let me state that we confront a unique opportunity to bring our national defense programs closer together. The result will be a more effective defense. The consequences will be greater security for our people. It is our responsibility not to let this opportunity pass.

(c) Final Communiqué of the North Atlantic Council, May 31, 1978.[16]

I. 1. The North Atlantic Council met with the participation of Heads of State and Government in Washington on 30th and 31st May, 1978.

2. Since its inception the Alliance has served to guarantee security, enhance cooperation and cohesion and promote peace. Its fundamental vitality lies in the fact that all Allied countries enjoy democratic systems of government. The Allies remain convinced that these systems provide the most humane and effective means of organizing society to deal with the challenges of the modern world. They reaffirmed the central role of the Alliance as the guardian of their collective security and renewed their pledge to consult with one another about the common goals and purposes of the Alliance for the years ahead.

3. The Allied leaders noted that their meeting follows a year of intense activity, analysis and reassessment, aimed at ensuring that the Alliance can meet future tasks. In particular, the Allies have successfully undertaken the study and implementation of the decisions and initiatives taken in common at the Council's meeting in London last May.[17]

4. The fresh study of long-term trends in East-West relations, decided upon in London, has confirmed the continuing validity of the two complementary aims of the Alliance, to maintain security and pursue detente. Based on an examination of the situation and trends in the USSR and the other Warsaw Pact countries, the Council's study concludes that members of the Alliance must maintain their solidarity and their vigilance, and keep their defenses at the level rendered necessary by the Warsaw Pact's offensive capabilities, while, at the same time, striving to promote detente. The study has also confirmed that relations between the allies and the Warsaw Pact countries have become more extensive, but that serious causes of tension still persist.

5. The Allied leaders noted with concern the repeated instances in which the Soviet Union and some of its allies have exploited situations of instability and regional conflict in the developing world. Disregard for the indivisibility of detente cannot but jeopardise the further improvement of East-West relations. They also emphasized, however, that these situations should not be viewed exclusively in an East-West context and reaffirmed the importance they attach to encouraging peaceful settlements through negotiations by the countries and regional organizations themselves.

[16]NATO Press Release; text from *Bulletin,* July 1978: 8–10.
[17]*AFR, 1977:* 218–21.

6. The Allies reviewed the developments concerning Berlin and Germany as a whole. They noted that since the Ministerial Meeting in December 1977,[18] the situation in and around Berlin had been generally without serious disturbance, but that the difficulties had persisted in certain important fields. ·They reaffirmed the previously stated positions of the Alliance, particularly the conviction that the strict observance and full implementation of all provisions of the Quadripartite Agreement of 3rd September, 1971 are essential for the promotion of detente, the maintenance of security and the development of co-operation throughout Europe.

7. The Allies remain determined to pursue as constructive and positive a relationship as possible with the Soviet Union and the other East European countries, which they see as being essential to international peace. They reaffirmed their view that closer contact and understanding should be further encouraged, with a view to enlarging the basis for a more genuine and lasting detente.

8. The Allies remain convinced that full implementation of the CSCE Final Act is of essential importance to the improvement of East-West relations. The Allies welcomed the thorough review of implementation which took place in Belgrade,[19] and noted that human rights and humanitarian questions have been confirmed as legitimate areas of concern to the international community. They recalled that all participating states reaffirmed their resolve to implement the Helsinki Final Act in full and their will to continue the multilateral process initiated by the CSCE. They regretted, however, that the Belgrade meeting did not have a more substantial outcome; they stressed the importance of better implementation of all the provisions of the Final Act so that, by the time of the Madrid meeting in 1980, the review of implementation will show that significant improvement has been made not only in relations between states, but also in the lives of individuals. In this respect, they found it incompatible with the Final Act and with detente that the Soviet Union and some other Eastern European countries fail to recognise the right of their citizens to act upon the provisions of the Helsinki document without being subjected to repressive measures.

9. The Allied leaders reiterated their determination to work vigorously for a more effective and equitable world economic system. The governments of the Allied countries, by their long-standing efforts in extending aid to the developing countries, have demonstrated the importance they attach to this objective. They call upon the Warsaw Pact countries to participate fully in this endeavour.

10. International co-operation in the fields of science and technology and of the environment can likewise contribute to a better world. In this respect, Allied leaders noted with satisfaction the

[18]Same: 247–50.
[19]Document 12.

achievements of the NATO Science Committee, which recently celebrated its 20th Anniversary, and of the Committee on the Challenges of Modern Society.

11. Having in mind the provisions of Article 2 of the North Atlantic Treaty, the Allied leaders recognise the great importance of securing a sound basis for the further improvement of the economic and social conditions of their peoples. Difficulties in maintaining a sufficient and sustained economic growth are affecting the ability of some members of the Alliance to maintain an effective defence effort. In addition to Allied assistance and co-operation in the defence field, those countries also need economic assistance and co-operation aimed at helping them in their development programmes and in the improvement of the living standards of their peoples. To this end, the Secretary General was invited to conduct a study, taking into account existing efforts by Allied members bilaterally and in other international fora, and to report to the Council on the way in which this problem could be addressed.

12. The Allies noted with satisfaction the meeting of the Prime Ministers of Greece and Turkey.[20] They expressed the hope that this dialogue on bilateral questions will contribute to the solution of the differences between the two countries.

13. The Allies reaffirmed the importance they attach to the strengthening of cohesion and solidarity especially in the South Eastern flank. They expressed the hope that existing problems will be resolved, and that full co-operation among members of the Alliance in all aspects of the defence field would be resumed.

14. Having considered the situation in the Middle East, the Allied leaders expressed the hope that efforts aiming at a comprehensive settlement in the area would continue. They urged all parties concerned to redouble their efforts to reach a just and lasting peace.

15. The efforts by the Allies to reduce tensions between East and West and to discourage attempts to use military power for political ends, can only be successfully pursued in the context of a stable military balance. Such a balance would ensure that they can pursue their detente policies in safety and with confidence.

16. The Allied leaders expressed their concern at the continual expansion of Warsaw Pact offensive capabilities. Faced with this situation, and notwithstanding Soviet statements that these massive military resources are not designed to threaten the security of the Allied countries, the latter have no option but to continue two complementary approaches: on the one hand, strengthen their defensive capabilities and on the other, seek to promote negotiations on arms control and disarmament agreements. The Allies will continue to follow the latter approach whenever possible, but progress in

[20]Constantine Caramanlis and Bülent Eçevit.

this direction necessarily depends on a positive attitude on the part of the Warsaw Pact countries.

17. The Allied leaders recognised that effective and verifiable limitation of arms, aimed in particular at correcting the existing imbalances in Europe in the conventional field, is an indispensable condition for a durable improvement in East-West relations and for the consolidation of peace.

18. The Allied leaders discussed the US-USSR Strategic Arms Limitation Talks. They welcomed progress made in the negotiations and expressed support for US efforts to conclude an agreement which is responsive to the security interests and concerns of the Alliance and which enhances strategic stability and maintains deterrence.

19. With respect to Mutual and Balanced Force Reductions, the Allies who participate in the negotiations in Vienna reaffirmed their commitment to these negotiations which they first proposed at the Ministerial Meeting in Reykjavik ten years ago,[21] and their determination to bring them to a successful conclusion. They confirmed their endorsement of the agreed objective of the negotiations to contribute to a more stable relationship and the strengthening of peace and security in Europe. This objective would be achieved by their proposal to create approximate parity in ground forces in the area of reductions through the establishment of a common collective ceiling on ground force manpower and the reduction of the disparity in tanks.

They called attention to the important new initiative which they introduced into the negotiations on 19th April,[22] to which they now look for a serious and constructive response from the Warsaw Pact participants. These Allies consider that the data discussion in Vienna is an essential element in the efforts towards a satisfactory outcome and that the clarification of the data base is therefore decisive for substantial progress in the negotiations.

These Allies state that they will propose that a meeting of the negotiations at Foreign Minister level should be convened at an appropriate date once substantial progress has been made in the negotiations and it is clear that a meeting at this level could contribute effectively to the early conclusion of a mutually satisfactory agreement.

20. The Allies welcomed the United Nations Special Session on Disarmament.[23] They expressed their resolve to participate in it constructively and their hope that this important conference would produce substantial results. Allied leaders agreed that the destructiveness of modern weaponry, the danger of the proliferation of

[21]*Documents, 1968–69:* 133–4.
[22]Cf. Introduction at notes 42–43.
[23]Document 7.

nuclear weapons, the needs of the developing countries and the requirements of their own societies make co-operation on a wide range of disarmament and arms control issues an urgent task for all countries. Progress in this direction cannot but contribute to international prosperity and make easier the necessary growth in financial resources devoted to development. The Allies reaffirmed their determination to persevere, through negotiation, in the pursuit of realistic and verifiable disarmament and arms control measures that enhance stability, reduce force levels and promote security. To these ends, they agreed to make fuller use of the Alliance machinery for thorough consultation on arms control and disarmament issues.

21. Until such time as it proves possible to achieve a satisfactory military balance at lower levels of forces through realistic and verifiable force reduction agreements, the Allies will continue to devote all the resources necessary to modernize and strengthen their own forces to the extent required for deterrence and defence. They will continue the efforts they have undertaken to preserve and promote the strong industrial and technical capability which is essential to the defence of the Alliance as a whole. The provision of new and existing generations of weaponry will require the most effective use of defence resources and deepened co-operation in armaments. In this connection, the Allies welcomed the steps that had been taken pursuant to the initiative agreed in London on the intensification of the Transatlantic Dialogue. The Allies are convinced that the effectiveness of their forces can be increased through enhanced interoperability and standardization of equipment and defence equipment planning procedures.

II. 22. Against the background of the study of long-term trends in East-West relations and other matters affecting Western security, leaders of states taking part in the integrated defence structure of the Alliance considered on 31st May a report on the Long-Term Defence Programme prepared by their Defence Ministers, which had been commissioned at the London Summit Meeting in May 1977.

23. They noted with approval that emphasis was placed in the Long-Term Defence Programme on greater co-operative efforts and on the need for NATO co-ordinated defence planning to be projected into the longer term. The leaders of these states endorsed specific programmes approved by Defence Ministers to improve the readiness of NATO's forces and the mobilization of reserves, to strengthen NATO's air defences, to counter the electronic warfare threat, to enhance NATO's maritime posture, to provide more effective logistic support for all NATO forces and to improve NATO's command, control and communications arrangements. They approved programmes designed to accelerate the movement of significant reinforcements to the forward areas in a time of crisis, envis-

aging the commitment of civil air, sea, land and national infrastructure resources; and they welcomed in particular the United States intention to preposition heavy equipment for three additional ,United States divisions in the Central Region of Allied Command Europe by 1982, recognising the need for European Allies to provide the necessary support and other facilities. They also noted with interest the work underway in the Nuclear Planning Group towards meeting needs for the modernization of theatre nuclear forces.

24. These Allied leaders noted with satisfaction that almost all countries had indicated their intention to adjust their financial plans for defence in accordance with the aim, established in the 1977 Ministerial Guidance, of an annual increase in defence expenditure in the region of 3% in real terms. They also stressed the importance of achieving the most effective return from resources made available or planned for defence by the achievement of a greater degree of co-operation and rationalization; they welcomed the emphasis placed in the Long-Term Defence Programme on this objective.

25. They expressed their support for the Long-Term Defence Programme forwarded by their Defence Ministers, as a major contribution towards adapting NATO's forces to the changing needs of the 1980s. They called for vigorous follow-through action to be taken by national authorities and at NATO and international military headquarters. In this connection, Turkey pointed out the importance to her participation of sufficient support from her Allies as well as of the complete removal of existing restrictions on the procurement of defence equipment.

26. In taking these decisions, these Allied leaders concluded that, in the absence of equitable arms control and disarmament agreements, a satisfactory balance in strategic, theatre nuclear and conventional terms could only be assured by greater efforts to modernize and strengthen the military capacity of the Alliance. They stressed that the maintenance of security is indispensable for the continued freedom, individual liberty and welfare of their societies and for the furthering of detente.

(d) Remarks by President Carter to Reporters Following the Conclusion of the Final Session, May 31, 1978. [24]

I would like to say as the leader of the host government that it's been a gratifying experience to us to have the meeting of the NATO Alliance countries here in Washington. We've spent 2 days in what the more experienced leaders have said is the most comprehensive

[24]Text from *Presidential Documents*, 14: 1025–6.

and candid and productive discussion of any NATO conference to date.

The most vivid impression that I have is one of a well-acknowledged common purpose. The Alliance is obviously one of unity. It's one of complete dedication, and it is an alliance also that recognizes that 30 years of peace have been derived among 15 or so countries because we are mutually strong and mutually committed in a partnership based on common beliefs and ideals, common heritage, a common commitment to democracy, to freedom, and to the rule of law.

In addition to the maintenance of strength for common defense, we've also reconfirmed the fact that we want to have general peace with the Warsaw Pact countries, our potential adversaries, and that there is no incompatibility between the Special Session on Disarmament in New York, its purposes, and the purposes of the North Atlantic Alliance.

We believe that the most fruitful step toward general disarmament is an acknowledged strength among the NATO Allies. We considered three basic propositions. One was cooperation in the development and production of weapons, which can lead to a more balanced responsibility for this very important purpose, and also result in standardization of weapon components and systems, a much higher level of defense capability for a given expenditure of public funds.

Secondly, we completed the analysis of a year-long study of East-West relationships, political, economic, and military, which was an enlightening experience in its preparation, and I think it cemented a common understanding of the present and possible future interrelationships between the Warsaw Pact countries, their friends and other allies, and also the NATO community, friends and allies.

The most important subject, possibly, was to define and to commit ourselves to a Long-Term Defense Program. This, again, was proposed after a year-long study by our defense ministers and their subordinates. There was a unanimous endorsement of this commitment extending over the next 15 years and acknowledgement that incremental improvements in our defense capability was not needed as the result of fear or trepidation or crisis or deep concern, but just was a reconfirmation of the necessity for a strong alliance to be mirrored in a common revitalization of the Alliance because of our mutual commitment to sustain its military strength.

We also resolved to follow through on these recommendations. Additionally, we discussed matters that are of concern to us all, the SALT negotiations, present and future prospects; the mutual and balanced force reduction talks, which are gaining momentum, we believe; general questions concerning the Mideast, Africa, the economy of our countries. We had a very good discussion, I believe, sometimes heated, concerning the southern flank of NATO, involving the United States, Greece, Turkey. I reconfirmed to the entire group the purpose of our own administration to remove the legal barriers to the supply of military equipment and weapons to Turkey, an action still to be considered by the Congress.[25]

There was a strong statement to this effect by the entire Alliance. Greece expressed some predictable reservations, but there was a meeting of minds about the need to have harmony between Greece and Turkey and a strengthening of our southeastern flank of NATO.

And lastly, there was a sense of friendship, of shared history. We reconfirmed our commitment to an alliance that's strong. And I think all of us see the future much more clearly than we did when this long, tedious, but productive study was initiated.

I feel much better about what NATO is, what it can be, and I think the potential frictions that arise among autonomous peoples, individualistic and proud, have been minimized. And I think every participating leader in diplomacy and defense and as executive leaders would share the assessment that I have just made.

It was a productive and constructive meeting, which will only result in an enhanced possibility for peace in the European theater, for our own country, and Canada, indeed for the entire world.

Thank you very much.

(14) Ending the Turkish Arms Embargo.

(a) The International Security Assistance Act of 1978 (Public Law 95–384): Statement by President Carter on Signing the Act, September 26, 1978.[26]

I am pleased to be able to take the action authorized by the International Security Assistance Act to fully terminate the force and effect of the embargo on arms transfers to Turkey.

The Nation is well served by the prudent decision of Congress which makes this action possible. With the removal of these restrictions, the United States will be better able to accomplish its goals in the vital Eastern Mediterranean region: to improve our bilateral relationships with Greece, Turkey, and Cyprus; to strengthen NATO's southern flank; and to help promote a just and lasting settlement of the Cyprus problem. In this effort to encourage the restoration of a stable and peaceful atmosphere in the Eastern Mediterranean, we will be fully guided by the principles set forth in the act.

[25]Cf. Document 14.
[26]Text from *Presidential Documents,* 14: 1636.

This action will enable us to resume full military cooperation with Turkey and begin a new chapter in our relationship with Turkey. This relationship is important not only because of our mutual security concerns but also because of our shared commitment to democracy.

(b) Resumption of Full Military Cooperation with. Turkey: Memorandum from President Carter, September 26, 1978.[27]

Memorandum for the Secretary of State

Subject: Determination and Certification Under the International Security Assistance Act of 1978 Regarding Resumption of Full Military Cooperation with Turkey.

Pursuant to the authority vested in me by Section 13(a) of the International Security Assistance Act of 1978, I hereby determine and certify:

(1) that the resumption of full military cooperation with Turkey is in the national interest of the United States and in the interest of the North Atlantic Treaty Organization; and

(2) that the Government of Turkey is acting in good faith to achieve a just and peaceful settlement of the Cyprus problem, the early peaceable return of refugees to their homes and properties, and continued removal of Turkish military troops from Cyprus in the context of a solution to the Cyprus problem, and the early serious resumption of inter-communal talks aimed at a just, negotiated settlement.

You are requested on my behalf to report this determination and certification to the Congress.

This determination and certification shall be published in the FEDERAL REGISTER.

JIMMY CARTER

(15) Ministerial Session of the North Atlantic Council, Brussels, December 7–8, 1978: Final Communiqué.[28]

The North Atlantic Council met in Ministerial session in Brussels on 7th and 8th December, 1978.

[27]Text from *Presidential Documents,* 14: 1636.
[28]Department of State Press Release 451, Dec. 12, 1978; text from *Bulletin,* Jan. 1979: 36–7.

Ministers reaffirmed their resolve to preserve and strengthen the solidarity of the North Atlantic Alliance as the indispensable guarantor of their security, freedom and well-being, and as an important contribution to international peace and stability. They underlined their faith in the principles and purposes of the Alliance which have their foundation in the values of democracy, human rights, justice and social progress.

Ministers examined the Secretary General's study on economic cooperation and assistance within the Alliance which was undertaken at the request of the Council meeting in Washington in May, in view of the economic difficulties of some member countries.

Bearing in mind the close relationship between defense and the economy, as well as the fundamental importance of economic and social improvement for a stable democracy, they emphasized once again the need to secure a sound basis for the economies of these countries and to assist them in their economic growth.

As an expression of their solidarity and in the light of Article 2 of the North Atlantic Treaty, Ministers agreed on the urgent necessity of increasing financial assistance and economic cooperation by member governments which are in a position to do so through bilateral and multilateral channels. They requested the Council in permanent session to continue its consultations on this important question and to report to them.

Ministers discussed the current state of East-West relations in all its aspects and recalled especially the East-West Study adopted by Allied leaders at the meeting in Washington last May. They reaffirmed their resolve to seek further improvement in East-West relations and their continued commitment to a policy of detente as the best means of promoting stable and mutually beneficial relations between governments and better and more frequent contacts between individuals. In doing so they emphasized once again the indivisibility of detente, pointing out that disregard for this would inevitably jeopardize improvement in East-West relations. They stressed the need for peaceful solutions in all problem areas.

Ministers expressed again their firm conviction that full implementation of all sections of the CSCE Final Act is an essential element for promoting detente. They noted with regret certain negative developments in its implementation during 1978 especially in the field of human rights and fundamental freedoms, and in that of information. They stressed the need for improvement in implementation to be shown between now and and the Madrid meeting so that the participating states could take part on the political level. They emphasized that this meeting would provide a valuable opportunity for undertaking a further review of the implementation of the Final Act and for considering future progress. They agreed on the importance of careful preparation of the Madrid meeting and, to that end, expressed their intention to consult closely both among the Allies and with other CSCE participating states. They noted the positive outcome of the recent Bonn meeting on the preparation of a scientific forum.

Ministers reviewed the developments concerning Berlin and Germany as a whole. They noted with satisfaction the improvement of the economic situation in Berlin and welcomed the efforts undertaken in the last few months to strengthen the economic basis for the viability of the city. The continuation of an undisturbed climate in Berlin and on the access routes remains an essential element of detente in Europe. Ministers noted with satisfaction the conclusion of agreements and arrangements with the German Democratic Republic on 16th November, 1978[29] which are an important contribution to the stability of the Berlin situation and to detente in Europe in general.

Ministers noted with concern the continuing buildup of Warsaw Pact forces and armaments, both conventional and nuclear, notwithstanding repeated Eastern assurances that their aim is not to seek military superiority. In the face of these developments, and while seeking concrete and verifiable measures of arms control, Ministers stressed the need to continue to devote the resources necessary to modernize and strengthen Allied capabilities to the extent required for deterrence and defense. They reviewed with satisfaction the actions to this end taken by the Allies since the Washington meeting.

Ministers welcomed the increasing emphasis being placed on cooperative equipment programs aimed at achieving a more effective use of available resources. They also welcomed the efforts being made to achieve a more balanced relationship among the North American and the European members of the Alliance in sharing in the development and production of new defense equipment, and to enhance the quantity and quality of standardized or interoperable systems. They instructed national armaments directors to pursue this approach, bearing in mind the special concerns of the less industrialized countries of the Alliance.

Ministers welcome the agreement reached by the governments now participating in the NATO Airborne Early Warning Program, the largest cooperative equipment project so far launched within the Alliance.

Ministers reaffirmed their conviction that concrete and verifiable arms control and disarmament measures would contribute significantly to security, stability and peace. They therefore welcomed the increasing world-wide attention being paid to arms control and disarmament, as exemplified by important current negotiations, as

---

[29]The reference is to an agreement signed in Berlin providing for the construction of a Hamburg-Berlin highway.

well as the United Nations Special Session on Disarmament and the forthcoming first meeting in Geneva of the Committee on Disarmament in which Alliance members will actively participate. Ministers recalled their agreement to make fuller use of the Alliance machinery for thorough consultation on arms control and disarmament issues and noted with satisfaction that such consultations have been intensified. In this connection, they had a useful exchange of views on the French proposal for a conference on disarmament in Europe and on the prospects that this proposal might offer for confidence-building and security in the area.

The Ministers discussed the U.S.-U.S.S.R. Strategic Arms Limitation Talks. They welcomed the progress made in the negotiations and expressed support for U.S. efforts to bring them to a successful conclusion. Ministers continue to believe that a SALT Agreement, which enhances strategic stability, maintains deterrence and responds to the security interests and concerns of the Alliance, will be in the common interest.

The Ministers of countries which participate in the negotiations on Mutual Balanced Force Reductions reaffirmed their commitment to these negotiations and reemphasized their determination to bring them to a successful conclusion. They confirmed as the goal of these negotiations the establishment of approximate parity in ground forces in the form of a common collective ceiling on the manpower of each side and the reduction of the disparity in main battle tanks. The achievement of this aim would contribute to a more stable relationship and to the strengthening of peace and security in Europe. These Ministers recall that to this end an important Western initiative had been introduced in April of this year.[30] The Eastern response to these proposals, while containing some welcome movement in matters of structure and concept, leaves important differences of substance unresolved. Both sides should now address these open issues progressively and constructively.

These Ministers welcomed the Eastern movement towards agreement on the concept of approximate parity. They stressed, however, that this has made the clarification of the data base, which they always regarded as essential for substantial progress, even more urgent. They called on the Eastern side to respond positively to recent Western efforts relating to the data discussion designed to identify the reasons for the discrepancy between Western figures and Eastern data regarding existing manpower levels in the area of reductions.

These Ministers also recalled the announcement made by Allied leaders in Washington in May on a meeting of the negotiations at the foreign minister level. It was their view that, despite the move-

---

[30]Cf. note 22 to Document 13c.

ment, the requirements stated at that time for such a meeting had not yet been met but they agreed to keep this matter under review.

These Ministers continue to attach importance to the inclusion in an MBFR Agreement of associated measures which should also ensure undiminished security for the flank participants.

The Ministers welcomed the continuation of the dialogue started as a result of the Montreux Summit Meeting between the Prime Ministers of Greece and Turkey.[31] They expressed their hope that this constructive step taken by the two governments will produce positive and early results through further joint efforts, and the reaffirmation, where necessary, of their political will to attain this goal.

Ministers took note of the report on the situation in the Mediterranean and underlined again the necessity of maintaining the balance of forces in the whole Mediterranean region. They requested the Council in permanent session to pursue its consultations on this question and to report again at their next meeting.

Ministers reviewed developments in the Middle East and expressed the hope that all parties concerned would take the fullest advantage of the opportunities for a just and lasting peace offered by the current negotiations. They expressed hope for an early successful conclusion of these negotiations as a major step towards a comprehensive peace in the Middle East and expressed support for United States efforts for such a comprehensive settlement.

Ministers took note of the progress made by the Committee on the Challenges of Modern Society (CCMS) and in particular its efforts to strengthen international cooperation aimed at enhancing the environment and improving the quality of life. Ministers further noted with satisfaction that the Science Committee continued to serve as an effective mechanism and forum for international cooperation in areas of major scientific and technological concern to Allied countries.

In viewing world economic conditions Ministers noted that they remained unsettled, with all countries still adjusting to the recent adverse trends in the economic climate. They observed that vigorous efforts have been made by Allied countries in support of a more equitable world economic system, including strengthened world trade and payment arrangements, within the context of renewed growth. These efforts are continuing.

Ministers agreed that the next ministerial session of the North Atlantic Council will be held in the Hague on 30th and 31st May, 1979. They noted that 1979 will mark the 30th Anniversary of the Foundation of the North Atlantic Alliance and that since its creation it has enabled Europe to live in peace.

[31]On Mar. 10–11.

(16) The U.S.-European Partnership: Address by Secretary of State Vance before the Royal Institute of International Affairs, London, December 9, 1978. [32]

More than three decades ago the United States and the nations of Western Europe joined together to rebuild a devastated continent and to create a military alliance to protect freedom.

On both sides of the Atlantic, those who fashioned the Marshall Plan and worked to create NATO possessed a vision of a strong America and a strong Europe bound by common interests. From this vision, they created a self-renewing partnership that derives continuing vitality from the values and hopes that we share.

We have passed through a particularly difficult period during the 1970's. But we have navigated these turbulent waters. Although the course ahead remains demanding, the progress we have made should give us great confidence in our future.

- For the first time in its history, all members of the NATO alliance are democracies.
- NATO is strong and growing stronger.
- We have not only resisted the worst protectionist pressures in a generation; we are working together to shape a healthier and more open world trading system.
- We have established a pattern of closer consultation on economic and security matters than at any point in recent history.
- European integration is proceeding, confirming our belief that a strong Europe is good for a strong America.
- And we are moving toward more normal relations with the nations of Eastern Europe. Progress toward this goal has reflected our support for full implementation of the Helsinki Final Act and recognition of the sovereignty and independence of the nations of this area.

Today, I want to discuss with you how, building on this solid foundation, we can continue to assure our mutual security and foster a healthy resurgence of our economies. These are the most pressing items on our common agenda.

But even as we concentrate on these vital concerns, which have been the constant threads of our partnership, our common interests compel us to address together a broadened international agenda. For there are longer term challenges to our security and well-being that also demand serious and sustained attention.

[32]Department of State Press Release 446; text from *Bulletin,* Jan. 1979: 12–16.

- How will the international economic system, as well as our own economies, adapt to changing patterns of international trade and commerce?
- How can we meet increasing energy needs without heightening the risk of nuclear proliferation?
- How can we help meet the legitimate security needs of nations while seeking agreed limitations on the growth of conventional arms sales?
- And how can we find the political will to act now on issues which will have a profound impact on the world we leave our children, issues such as population growth and environmental protection?

These issues will tax our creativity and persistence to the fullest. For we approach all of these issues in a changing and pluralistic international system, with over 150 independent nations and emerging new power centers. No single nation, or group of nations, can dictate solutions to these complex problems. They are truly international in their origins and in the necessary scope of their solutions. Increasingly, our leadership must therefore take the form of inspiring other nations to work with us toward goals we share and can best achieve in concert. And on each of these issues, we look to our European allies as a core around which we must build these cooperative efforts.

Our ability to address this broader agenda will depend on the essential vitality of our partnership—and specifically on our economic and military strength.

Economic Security for Our Peoples

For most of our countries, the most pressing demand today is to revitalize our economies and to restore a sense of confidence in our economic system.

When the economic history of the last 5 years is written, two important trends will stand out. The United States and Europe, and indeed the industrialized democracies as a whole, have experienced the most severe economic problems of the last quarter century. These included sharp increases in world oil prices and inflation followed by a serious recession and high unemployment.

Yet despite these serious problems, we have been successful in strengthening our economic and political cooperation. Instead of sliding back into the beggar-thy-neighbor psychology that destroyed the global economy in the 1930's, we have created new and more effective mechanisms for serious, concerted actions. The institution of periodic summit meetings on economic matters, closer collaboration among monetary authorities, the creation of the International

Energy Agency and a more active Organization for Economic Co-operation and Development (OECD)—all these efforts reflect confidence in our capacities not despair in the face of difficulties.

We are increasing our economic coordination with one another for a simple reason: Because we all now understand that the economic health of each of us is important to the economic health of us all. This is especially true in times of economic difficulty. Pressures increase to protect domestic markets, competition sharpens, and we are all tempted to resolve our individual problems at the expense of our neighbors. But it is precisely then that we must be particularly sensitive to the impact our decisions at home will have on others abroad. If we make those decisions without sufficient regard for the problems of others, we only invite retaliation and a spiral of compensating actions. All of us will lose ground; all of us will be worse off.

As a result, we all have clearly recognized that only through the development of a common strategy, to which each country contributes, can we enhance the well-being of every nation.

Cooperating in this way can be difficult and frustrating. Domestic political support for tough economic decisions often comes slowly in democracies. In some cases, results fall short of our expectations and we must redouble our efforts. But actions by each of us, together with greater transatlantic cooperation, have placed the United States and the other industrialized nations on the path to sustained, noninflationary growth. Success will enhance our ability to expand individual opportunity and social justice, which are the greatest strengths of our democracies.

The U.S. Economy

The United States fully recognizes the importance of a strong and vital American economy to building greater economic security for Europe, Japan and other nations of the world. What we do in Washington can affect the lives of citizens of London or Rome, just as the decisions of other governments affect the well-being of Americans.

Accordingly, the domestic economic policies of the United States are fashioned with a view toward the economic interests of the Atlantic community as a whole. Fundamental to this effort are the commitments made by President Carter at the Bonn summit last July.[33] He pledged the United States to a major effort to reduce inflation and to an energy policy which significantly reduces U.S. oil imports.

We are taking specific actions to fulfill these commitments. On

---

[33]Document 44.

October 24, President Carter announced a broad-based program to fight inflation.[34] It includes monetary restraint, sharp reductions in governmental spending, and explicit standards for wage and price increases. The President's new budget will put a very tight lid on public expenditures and reduce our federal deficit to less than half that of 1976.

The President has stressed that controlling inflation is our overriding domestic priority. We will persist until we have achieved that objective. On November 1, we undertook further far-reaching actions to reinforce the anti-inflation effort and strengthen the dollar.[35] We have tightened monetary conditions significantly. The United States also joined with the three major surplus countries—Germany, Japan, and Switzerland—in coordinating direct intervention in the foreign exchange market to correct the excessive decline of the dollar. We will continue to cooperate in a forceful and coordinated way to assure stability in exchange markets. To finance its share, the United States is mobilizing an unprecedented $30 billion which will be used, together with resources of the other countries, to intervene massively if necessary to achieve our objectives. The United States has also expanded its gold sales program.

We expect that with the fundamental improvements in the U.S. economic position now underway, these actions will exert a continuing positive effect on the dollar. On November 9, the President signed legislation which lays the basis for a sounder U.S. energy policy.[36] This legislation should result in oil import savings of roughly 2.5 million barrels per day by 1985. We are already improving our energy situation. U.S. energy prices have risen significantly closer to world levels. And growth in energy consumption is now running well below growth in our GNP. We are also working to reduce our balance-of-payments deficit through a more vigorous export promotion program.[37]

President Carter is determined to build political support for serious actions to deal with our economic problems. That support is growing. Neither the President, Congress, nor the American people will be satisfied until we show marked progress in fighting inflation, strengthening the dollar, and creating a sound energy economy.

U.S.-European Economic Cooperation

While the first task for each of us is to put our domestic house in order, we must at the same time undertake those joint efforts that are needed to sustain our economic growth. There is no more immediate or more crucial test of our ability to join together for our

[34]Cf. Introduction at note 166.
[35]Document 47.
[36]Cf. Introduction at note 161.
[37]Document 46.

common gain than the successful completion, this month, of the multilateral trade negotiations.

During the last three decades, we have worked together to build a more open and better functioning world trading system. Now we have an opportunity to consolidate the progress we have made and further improve the structure of our trading relationships. In so doing, we can construct for the future a trading environment with greater certainty and confidence—one which will foster the continued expansion of world commerce. If we succeed, there will be economic gains for us all. If we fail, we will jeopardize the economic progress we have made. Failure would fuel our inflation, slow our growth, and make it more difficult for developing nations to play a full part in the world trading system. And if we fail, we will have also jeopardized the political cooperation that we have painstakingly achieved.

A major objective of the trade negotiations is to provide for an agreed framework to govern subsidies and countervailing duties. When our Congress convenes next month, the President will seek legislation to extend the authority to waive countervailing duties[38] to cover the period needed to implement the Tokyo Round agreements. And we will take measures to minimize the disruptive effects that could flow from expiration of the waivers on January 3.

Our negotiators in Geneva will strive to conclude their talks this month. But even as we gain ground toward a more open and better operating trading system, we must avoid piecemeal retreats toward protectionism which could undermine that progress. In each country, various groups will continue to ask governments to intervene in the trading system for economic, political, and social reasons. Our countries have recognized the importance of resisting demands which impede effective economic adjustment to change. Our response to such demands must be within the context of the trading framework we have designed together. Our policies must facilitate positive adjustment of our economies to changing economic conditions, rather than hindering such adjustment or shifting the burden onto others.

Beyond the immediate need to strengthen the world trading system, we all have a basic interest in promoting the emerging role of the European Community in international economic affairs. In the United States, we admire the vision of men and women who are working to broaden and deepen cooperation among the nations of Europe. We welcome and support this development, for a strong European Community is in America's interest as well as in the interests of all European nations; it provides a dynamic new force in international economic and political relations.

The new European monetary arrangements for closer monetary

[38]Congress temporarily extended such authority in Public Law 96–6, Apr. 3, 1979.

cooperation within the European Community, announced on December 5, represent an important step toward the economic integration of Europe we have long supported. We believe that the new arrangements will be implemented in a way which will contribute to sustainable growth in the world economy and a stable international monetary system. The United States looks forward to continued close consultations with its European trading partners as these arrangements evolve.

In general, the next few years will be critical ones for Europe, as the Community works toward closer economic integration, expands its membership, holds its first direct elections to the European parliament, and assumes a growing responsibility for the political and economic well-being of Europe as a whole.

All the Western democracies share in support and concern for the democracies in southern Europe. We in the United States respect the political commitment of Community leaders to open its membership to these states and to deal with the economic problems that will come with such a step.

As prospering Western democracies, we should recognize a special responsibility to those democracies in the region threatened by a faltering economy—where the short-term prospects are bleak but where, with a helping hand, economies can be put on a sound footing and the long-term prospects can be bright. There are established mechanisms to provide needed assistance—the International Monetary Fund and the World Bank. Some situations may also call for complementary informal or ad hoc arrangements. The consortium for Portugal is an example. Those nations in a position to help should concert their energies and resources. Supportive action before it is too late is an investment in the future of freedom.

Relations With the Developing World

As we consider means to strengthen the economic bonds among the developed countries, we must recognize that our interests—and our responsibilities—do not end there. Meeting the desire of our citizens for economic security and a rising standard of living requires us to respond more fully to the aspirations of peoples in developing nations. Increasingly, their economic well-being is indispensable to our own.

Together, the world's developing countries account for roughly one-third of total trade for the OECD nations. These countries provide the most rapidly expanding markets for exports of the industrial world—markets on which millions of jobs in our nations depend. Developing countries provide us with critical raw materials. And we need their cooperation to solve such critical global problems as energy and food.

In short, we cannot build a strong international economic system without steady economic progress by the developing nations. Together, we must attempt to push aside the ideological debates which often have characterized the relationship between the developing and industrial nations. We must seek practical and concrete measures to address the basic needs of roughly 800 million people who live in absolute poverty.

There is no more important challenge to the world's long-term well-being, to our political security, and to our essential values as free peoples than working together with the developing nations to foster their economic progress.

Security Issues

The cornerstone of our prospertiy is the confidence we have in our security. This security depends essentially on maintaining strong military forces; on managing effectively the West's relations with the Soviet Union; on seeking to limit and reduce arms in both East and West; and on the strength of the Atlantic partnership.

We can find cause for concern in the continuing increases in Soviet military programs and deployments. But we can also find cause for confidence in the steps we in the alliance are taking to preserve the military balance.

For some years now, the central fact of world security has been strategic nuclear parity between the United States and the Soviet Union. We and our partners have managed this situation without allowing either our deterrent or our will to be eroded.

The fact of strategic parity remains. Just as we will match Soviet increases, so we must assume that the Soviets are resolved to match us. Thus, the pursuit of superiority by either side would result in frustration, waste, increased tension, and in the end reduced security for all.

Our common security rests on three underlying principles.

First, just as we must remain alert and resolute about Soviet actions, so we must also be ready to explore and expand areas of mutual interest. To allow our fears to obscure our need to seek common ground is to condemn ourselves to unrelenting tension. But neither can we let our desire for better relations lead us into arrangements that will not adequately protect our national interests.

Second, we must be prepared to do what is necessary to assure our security, while preferring to maintain a balance at lower levels of armaments. Both the military and arms control paths have figured centrally in the history of NATO's pursuit of security.

Arms control is complicated and frustrating. Our goals and our efforts will inevitably be criticized by some who believe there is too little disarmament and by others who believe the Soviets are taking advantage of arms control agreements. Let us be clear and realistic about what we are seeking to accomplish. Arms control cannot put an end to military competition. But we can, and do, use arms control to cap arms buildups, to begin the difficult process of reductions and qualitative restraints, and to sustain a needed dialogue.

Arms control, correctly understood and wisely applied, is yet another way—a complementary way—to pursue security. We should not let our inability to accomplish everything immediately discourage us from significant steps we can achieve.

Third, while the United States will remain unsurpassed in military strength, we all must remain constantly aware that our security requires collective allied effort, and that our defense is indivisible. As an alliance, we share in decisions on security questions, just as we share in the burdens and risks of a common defense. Western strength—in a military sense and also in a larger sense—depends upon the health of our partnership and in our self-confidence about the future.

These fundamental principles guide our security decisions. A look at the actual military situation and trends and at how the United States and its allies manage the condition of strategic parity, shows that we face great challenges and we are meeting them through cooperative actions.

U.S. strategic modernization plans span the land, sea, and air components of our forces. We are developing a new intercontinental ballistic missile (ICBM), and options for new ICBM basing are under intensive review to allow us to choose the best among the various alternatives. We will begin deploying a new submarine-based missile next year, and we are building a new strategic submarine. We have a vigorous long-range cruise missile program underway, including not only the air-launched version but sea- and ground-launched versions as well. These programs will insure that the alliance's strength will continue to be sufficient to deter attack and protect our common interests.

SALT is another instrument for bolstering security. SALT I and the ABM treaty began the important process of limiting strategic arms. Without these agreements, we would have been launched into a defensive arms race on top of an unlimited race in offensive arms.

SALT II will be a major brake on the momentum of strategic arms competition. Facing a more regulated and predictable future, we will be able to devote more of our attention, talent, and resources to improving conventional and theater nuclear forces for NATO. SALT II will establish the principle of equality in the number of strategic delivery vehicles. And it will put a limit on the number of MIRV'd ICBM's, which are potentially most harmful to stability.

At the same time, SALT II will not rule out the force programs we have underway to meet the challenges that will remain even with an agreement. We have preserved all our major strategic force options. Other programs that can strengthen deterrence in NATO can go forward. Allied interests have been protected because allied interests are our interests.

Let me emphasize that in both our defense efforts and our arms control negotiations, our basic aim is to strengthen the security of the United States and that of our allies. This has been and will always be the fundamental touchstone of our policy.

That is why we are involved in SALT—because a sound agreement will improve Western and global security. Without an agreement our technological and economic strength would enable us to match any Soviet strategic buildup. But a good agreement can provide more security with lower risk and cost. And we recognize that without SALT the strategic competition could infect the entire East-West political relationship, damaging the effort to create a less dangerous world which is at the heart of Western foreign policies.

The emerging SALT II agreement will not solve all our problems. It will not, for example, reverse the trend toward increased vulnerability of fixed, land-based missiles, a problem in the long run for both sides. Necessary strategic force modernization must and will move forward, just as the SALT process must and will move forward. In SALT III we will work for further reductions and qualitative limits.

We cannot discuss the management of strategic parity without coming to grips with the issue of how NATO should respond to Soviet improvements in their nuclear forces targeted against Europe. Though the linkage to American strategic forces remain[s] NATO's ultimate deterrent, the Soviets must understand that we will not let a weakness develop at any point along the continuum of our deterrent, including theater nuclear forces. We have several theater nuclear modernization programs in process. We are exploring whether arms control efforts could be of benefit. Although no decisions have been reached regarding force requirements or arms control, we are consulting intensively within the alliance to fashion a common plan.

At the conventional level, improvements in Soviet forces continue. Here too the West is responding effectively. The May 1978 summit meeting in Washington agreed to a Long-Term Defense Program designed to improve the ability of NATO to function as a defense coalition. NATO is placing top priority on improving conventional forces. In the last few years, the United States has increased its forces in Europe by roughly 10,000. NATO is broadly engaged in a determined effort to increase readiness and capabilities for sustained defense. Wisely, we are emphasizing improvements which draw upon our collective technological strengths, and which will result in greater effectiveness rather than simply larger forces. Many of these steps are not glamorous; they do not attract headlines. But they are serious steps taken by a serious alliance, resolved to muster the resources and will to build a better common defense.

Here, too, we are striving to negotiate restraints based on parity—1978 has brought movement by both sides in the 5-year-old MBFR negotiations. Difficult problems remain. But gaining Soviet agreement to reduce forces to equal collective levels is worth a further sustained effort. Let us hope that the achievement of a strategic arms limitations agreement can impart a new momentum to the MBFR negotiations.

Of course, Western security concerns and interests are wider than NATO. We must also ask whether, in an age of strategic parity, we are at a disadvantage in competing with the Soviet Union in the Third World. The answer is no. While Soviet capabilities for projecting military power have improved, the United States retains not only unequalled naval forces and other forms of military power but also enjoys economic and political advantages.

We also welcome the growing spirit of national independence in the developing nations. They have demonstrated, time and again, their determination and ability to avoid domination by any outside powers.

Since 1960, the decolonization process, now nearly complete, has produced some 65 new nations, with widely differing political, economic and social systems. During these years, outside influence has waxed and waned in different countries and at different times. There have not been the permanent Communist advances many once feared.

This diversity and the irrepressible thirst for national freedom among the Third World nations are the surest barriers to foreign domination. We can best promote our own interests in these areas of the world by welcoming this diversity and respecting this spirit.

The economic, political, cultural, and security ties between the West and the Third World have supported this spirit of independence. We must strengthen those ties by continuing to support the economic development and, when necessary, the military security of these nations through our assistance; by pressing the Soviets and their allies to exercise restraint in troubled areas; and by working to resolve diplomatically those disputes which offer opportunities for foreign interference.

In the long run, it is the ability of the West to offer practical support to Third World nationalism, self-determination, and economic growth that should make us very confident about our future relations.

Conclusion

In each of the areas I have addressed today, whether economic, political, or military, one finds extraordinary challenges. But together, America and Europe have extraordinary resources with which to meet them.

The physical, industrial, and technological resources of our alliance are unequaled. If we have the will to develop our economies with equity and maintain our defenses with determination, we can achieve a safer and more stable world. And we have that will.

In the end, our alliance is held together not simply by what we are against, but by what we are for. Our greatest strengths are the ties that bind us together. These ties are founded on a vision of the rights and dignity of the individual, on political justice, and freedom for all people. The negotiations in which we are engaged, and the policies we pursue, lack meaning unless our foreign policies are in accord with these basic values of our peoples.

Winston Churchill spoke once of the need to pull together and firmly grasp the larger hopes of humanity. His charge remains, today, our challenge.

4. NEW MOVEMENT IN THE MIDDLE EAST

(17) The Middle East Arms Package, February 14–May 15, 1978.

(a) Planes for Israel, Egypt, and Saudi Arabia: Announcement by Secretary of State Vance, February 14, 1978.[1]

Consistent with our policy that arms transfers will be used to promote our national security and that of our close friends, I have recommended to the President and he has approved sales of certain aircraft to Israel, Egypt, and Saudi Arabia, subject to the usual congressional review. Next week we will begin the official process of informing and consulting with the Congress. The formal notifications will not be submitted until after the Easter recess in order to give Congress an opportunity to review fully the proposed sales.

These sales will be undertaken over a period of several years. Deciding to make the sales was a very complex decision, and I want to share our views on this matter with the American people.

Any new aircraft sales to this region must be seen in the context of both the negotiating process and our objective of a peace settlement. We have considered carefully this aspect of the matter and concluded that our interests in Middle East peace and security will be best served if we go forward with some part of the aircraft sales requested by these countries.

Our commitment to Israel's security has been and remains firm. Israel must have full confidence in its ability to assure its own defense. In particular, this means Israel must be able to plan for the continued modernization of its air force. The President's decision gives particular emphasis to these points.

Egypt, too, must have reasonable assurance of its ability to defend itself if it is to continue the peace negotiations with confidence. When President Sadat made his decision several years ago to follow a course in foreign affairs that involved a change in his

[1]Department of State Press Release 75; text from *Bulletin,* Mar. 1978: 37.

country's relations with the Soviet Union, he lost his major source of military equipment. This was particularly the case in Egyptian defensive aircraft capability. We believe we have a basic interest in responding to Egypt's legitimate needs.

Saudi Arabia is of immense importance in promoting a course of moderation in the Middle East—with respect to peacemaking and other regional initiatives—and more broadly in world affairs, as in petroleum and financial policy. The Saudi Government has a legitimate requirement to modernize its very limited air defenses. For several years, we and they have recognized the need to modernize their air force with an advanced interceptor. They have asked for a limited number of F-15's, the first of which would not be delivered for several years. We believe their request is reasonable and in our interest to fulfill.

We have concluded, therefore, that the sales of these aircraft to the countries in question will help to meet their legitimate security requirements, will not alter the basic military balance in the region, and will be consistent with the overriding objective of a just and lasting peace.

Accordingly, the Administration plans to notify Congress of our intent to make the following sales:

- For Israel, 15 F-15's, in addition to the 25 previously sold, and 75 F-16's;
- For Egypt, 50 F-5's; and
- For Saudi Arabia, 60 F-15's.

We will be signing contracts for these aircraft over the next several years. These sales will be consistent with the President's global arms transfer policy and will be within the dollar volume ceiling that he has established. The details will be reported to Congress when the statutory notifications are provided.

All of these sales are directly supportive of our overall objectives in the Middle East. Members of the Administration will be testifying before a number of congressional committees in support of this package so that Congress will have full opportunity to make its judgment during the period of its review.

(b) Notification to Congress: Remarks by Secretary of State Vance, April 28, 1978.[2]

The administration is today transmitting to Congress formal no-

---

[2]Text from Presidential Documents, 14: 801.

tification of proposals to sell aircraft to Israel, Egypt, and Saudi Arabia. As indicated in our informal notification last February, the proposed sales involve 75 F-16's and 15 F-15's to Israel, 50 F-5's to Egypt, and 60 F-15's to Saudi Arabia.

These proposals are an important part of our search for peace in the Middle East. They maintain and enhance our close relationship with three key governments in the Middle East. Each of the three countries has a unique contribution to make to the objective of achieving a lasting peace.

As a nation, we have a strong and unshakable commitment to the security of Israel. The proposed sales to Israel will help preserve Israel's ability to defend itself.

The proposed sales to Egypt and Saudi Arabia have been based upon careful analysis of how best to meet their defense needs while maintaining the military balance in the region. These transactions will enhance the confidence in and friendship toward the United States on the part of each of these two countries with which we share vital mutual interests.

The proposed sales make it possible for the United States to maintain our historic commitment to the security of Israel while at the same time developing closer ties with moderate Arab nations which strongly support the peace process. They reflect our best judgment as to the national interest of the United States.

In submitting these proposed sales to Congress on the same day, the administration is not attempting to place conditions on the scope of the congressional review or the action by Congress. Indeed, we understand that the Congress will want to review these important transactions separately and with great care. We stand ready to facilitate that process.

At the same time, the responsibility of the President for the conduct of foreign affairs requires that he reserve judgment on the ultimate action to be taken until he has had an opportunity to review the action taken by the Congress on the proposals announced today.

(c) A Test of National Purpose: Letter from President Carter to Members of Congress, May 12, 1978.[3]

The motion in the Senate next Monday to block all of the proposed aircraft sales to Israel, Egypt, and Saudi Arabia presents a vital test of our national purpose. In the hours before the Senate votes, it is my duty as President to draw attention to the powerful

[3]Text from *Presidential Documents,* 14: 896–7. The letter was addressed to all members of the Senate and to key leaders of the House of Representatives.

reasons supporting each of the sales and the dire consequences of rejecting them.

Our basic goal is to secure peace, stability, and harmonious relations among the nations of the Middle East. Since becoming President, I and my chief foreign policy advisers have spent more of our time and effort on this subject than any other foreign policy issue.

The number of aircraft proposed for each of the countries has been carefully considered to insure a regional balance, but the decision before the Senate transcends the particular transactions.

The choice is stark and fundamental. Shall we support and give confidence to those in the Middle East who work for moderation and peace? Or shall we turn them aside, shattering their confidence in us and serving the cause of radicalism?

It is my considered judgment that the aircraft sales to Egypt are essential to enable President Sadat to continue his efforts for peace. At great personal and political risk, President Sadat has taken an initiative which has created the best prospects for peace in the Middle East in three decades. With similar risks, he has turned away from a relationship with the Soviet Union and placed his trust in the United States.

To reject the proposed aircraft sale to Egypt would be a breach of that trust. Such a rejection would be a devastating blow to President Sadat, to the military forces of Egypt, to the people of Egypt, and to the forces of moderation in the Middle East.

Saudi Arabia has become a firm friend of the United States. As its influence dramatically expands in the world, Saudi Arabia has been not only a firm supporter of the peace process but a moderating and conciliatory force on a wide range of global issues.

It is beyond challenge that the Saudi air defense system must be modernized and augmented. The United States has an opportunity through these proposed sales to enhance its relationship with the Saudis as they take these vital steps to defend themselves against their radical neighbors armed by the Soviet Union. But I must tell you with great gravity that it is an opportunity that we will quickly lose if we do not grasp it immediately.

If the Saudis are forced to turn elsewhere to meet their defense needs, it will unquestionably impair the peace process. Moreover, the erosion of confidence will inevitably have a far broader—and adverse—impact on the wide range of issues on which we have been working in close harmony.

The aircraft sales to Israel are a reflection of our strong and unshakable commitment to the security of Israel. The American people fully understand that our commitment to Israel's survival and security is total, unequivocal, and firmly fixed in our national policy.

The long-term interests of Israel are served by the proposed sales to Egypt and Saudi Arabia. It is in Israel's interest to encourage the forces of moderation in the Middle East, and to promote their close relationship with the United States. It would not serve Israel's interest if we were to fail to keep bi-partisan commitments, made by the prior Administration as well as by mine, to provide aircraft for the defense of Saudi Arabia. It would be against Israel's interest if moderate nations are brushed aside by the United States, opening vast possibilities for the intrusion of hostile influences.

In the end, the national interest of the United States is the issue. On the basis of the most careful and serious analysis of all factors, I am convinced that the proposed sales will enhance U.S. national objectives, contribute to our national security, and promote peace in the Middle East.

JIMMY CARTER

(d) Approval by the Senate: Statement by President Carter, May 15, 1978.[4]

I am deeply gratified by the Senate's decision today which will permit the proposed arms sales to Israel, Egypt and Saudi Arabia. That action reaffirms our historic and unshakable commitment to the security of Israel—a commitment which will continue to have the unwavering support of this administration and the American people.

At the same time, the Senate vote strengthens our ties with moderate Arab nations who share our goal of peace and stability in the region. We also honor bi-partisan pledges made by the previous administration as well as my own to help our friends in the Middle East meet their legitimate needs for self-defense.

The approval of these sales will not violate the arms limitation policy of this administration, which I announced last May.[5] That pledge to limit arms sales will be met. If and when other nations are willing to join with us in mutual restraint on the sale of conventional weapons, even greater reductions will be possible.

In the meantime, the Senate's action makes it clear that the United States stands ready to provide needed assistance when unrestrained arms sales by other nations pose a threat to the security of our friends and allies.

With this issue resolved, the sharp debate over the proposed sales can now be put behind us. That debate has been among friends who share the same goals. All of us can now concentrate our full attention on finding a sound and just basis for permanent peace.

The United States will continue to play a responsible and active

[4]Text from Presidential Documents, 14: 915.
[5]Cf. Carter statement, May 19, 1977, in AFR, 1977: 187–9.

role in the search for peace in the Middle East. We will intensify our effort to help the parties narrow their differences. Our own national interest and moral values permit us to do no less.

(18) Camp David Meeting on the Middle East, Thurmont, Maryland, September 5–17, 1978: Remarks at the White House by President Carter, President Anwar al-Sadat of Egypt, and Prime Minister Menahem Begin of Israel, September 17, 1978.[6]

PRESIDENT CARTER. When we first arrived at Camp David, the first thing upon which we agreed was to ask the people of the world to pray that our negotiations would be successful. Those prayers have been answered far beyond any expectations. We are privileged to witness tonight a significant achievement in the cause of peace, an achievement none thought possible a year ago, or even a month ago, an achievement that reflects the courage and wisdom of these two leaders.

Through 13 long days at Camp David, we have seen them display determination and vision and flexibility which was needed to make this agreement come to pass. All of us owe them our gratitude and respect. They know that they will always have my personal admiration.

There are still great difficulties that remain and many hard issues to be settled. The questions that have brought warfare and bitterness to the Middle East for the last 30 years will not be settled overnight. But we should all recognize the substantial achievements that have been made.

One of the agreements that President Sadat and Prime Minister Begin are signing tonight is entitled "A Framework For Peace in the Middle East."[7]

This framework concerns the principles and some specifics, in the most substantive way, which will govern a comprehensive peace settlement. It deals specifically with the future of the West Bank and Gaza and the need to resolve the Palestinian problem in all its aspects. The framework document proposes a 5-year transitional period in the West Bank and Gaza during which the Israeli military government will be withdrawn and a self-governing authority will be elected with full autonomy. It also provides for Israeli forces to remain in specified locations during this period to protect Israel's security.

The Palestinians will have the right to participate in the determi-

[6]Text from *Presidential Documents,* 14: 1519–23.
[7]Document 20a.

nation of their own future, in negotiations which will resolve the final status of the West Bank and Gaza, and then to produce an Is- raeli-Jordanian peace treaty.

These negotiations will be based on all the provisions and all the principles of United Nations Security Council Resolution 242. And it provides that Israel may live in peace, within secure and recog- nized borders. And this great aspiration of Israel has been certified without constraint, with the greatest degree of enthusiasm, by Pres- ident Sadat, the leader of one of the greatest nations on Earth.

The other document is entitled, "Framework For the Conclusion of a Peace Treaty Between Egypt and Israel."[8]

It provides for the full exercise of Egyptian sovereignty over the Sinai. It calls for the full withdrawal of Israeli forces from the Sinai and, after an interim withdrawal which will be accomplished very quickly, the establishment of normal, peaceful relations between the two countries, including diplomatic relations.

Together with accompanying letters,[9] which we will make public tomorrow, these two Camp David agreements provide the basis for progress and peace throughout the Middle East.

There is one issue on which agreement has not been reached. Egypt states that the agreement to remove Israeli settlements from Egyptian territory is a prerequisite to a peace treaty. Israel states that the issue of the Israeli settlements should be resolved during the peace negotiations. That's a substantial difference. Within the next 2 weeks, the Knesset will decide on the issue of these settlements.

Tomorrow night, I will go before the Congress to explain these agreements more fully and to talk about their implications for the United States and for the world.[10] For the moment, and in closing, I want to speak more personally about my admiration for all of those who have taken part in this process and my hope that the pro- mise of this moment will be fulfilled.

During the last 2 weeks, the members of all three delegations have spent endless hours, day and night, talking, negotiating, grap- pling with problems that have divided their people for 30 years. Whenever there was a danger that human energy would fail, or pa- tience would be exhausted or good will would run out—and there were many such moments—these two leaders and the able advisers in all delegations found the resources within them to keep the chances for peace alive.

Well, the long days at Camp David are over. But many months of difficult negotiations still lie ahead. I hope that the foresight and

[8]Document 20b.
[9]Document 21a.
[10]Document 19.

the wisdom that have made this session a success will guide these
leaders and the leaders of all nations as they continue the progress
toward peace.

Thank you very much.

PRESIDENT SADAT. Dear President Carter, in this historic moment,
I would like to express to you my heartfelt congratulations and
appreciation. For long days and nights, you devoted your time and
energy to the pursuit of peace. You have been most courageous
when you took the gigantic step of convening this meeting. The
challenge was great and the risks were high, but so was your determination. You made a commitment to be a full partner in the peace
process. I'm happy to say that you have honored your commitment.

The signing of the framework for the comprehensive peace settlement has a significance far beyond the event. It signals the emergence of a new peace initiative, with the American nation in the
heart of the entire process.

In the weeks ahead, important decisions have to be made if we
are to proceed on the road to peace. We have to reaffirm the faith
of the Palestinian people in the ideal of peace.

The continuation of your active role is indispensable. We need
your help and the support of the American people. Let me seize this
opportunity to thank each and every American for his genuine interest in the cause of people in the Middle East.

Dear friend, we came to Camp David with all the good will and
faith we possessed, and we left Camp David a few minutes ago with
a renewed sense of hope and inspiration. We are looking forward
to the days ahead with an added determination to pursue the noble
goal of peace.

Your able assistants spared no effort to bring out this happy conclusion. We appreciate their spirit and dedication. Our hosts at
Camp David and the State of Maryland were most generous and
hospitable. To each one of them and to all those who are watching
this great event, I say thank you.

Let us join in a prayer to God Almighty to guide our path. Let us
pledge to make the spirit of Camp David a new chapter in the history of our nations.

Thank you, Mr. President.

PRIME MINISTER BEGIN. *Mr. President of the United States, Mr.
President of the Arab Republic of Egypt, ladies and gentlemen:*

The Camp David conference should be renamed. It was the Jimmy Carter conference. [*Laughter*]

The President undertook an initiative most imaginative in our
time and brought President Sadat and myself and our colleagues

and friends and advisers together under one roof. In itself, it was a great achievement. But the President took a great risk for himself and did it with great civil courage. And it was a famous French field commander who said that it is much more difficult to show civil courage than military courage.

And the President worked. As far as my historic experience is concerned, I think that he worked harder than our forefathers did in Egypt building the pyramids. [*Laughter*]

Yes, indeed, he worked day and night, and so did we— [*laughter*]—

PRESIDENT CARTER. Amen.

PRIME MINISTER BEGIN. Day and night. We used to go to bed at Camp David between 3 and 4 o'clock in the morning, arise, as we are used to since our boyhood, between 5 and 6, and continue working, working.

The President showed interest in every section, every paragraph, every sentence, every word, every letter—[*laughter*]—of the framework agreements.

We had some difficult moments—as usually there are some crises in negotiations, as usually somebody gives a hint that perhaps he would like to pick up and go home. [*Laughter*] It's all usual. But ultimately, ladies and gentlemen, the President of the United States won the day. And peace now celebrates a great victory for the nations of Egypt and Israel and for all mankind.

Mr. President, we, the Israelis, thank you from the bottom of our hearts for all you have done for the sake of peace, for which we prayed and yearned more than 30 years. The Jewish people suffered much, too much. And, therefore, peace to us is a striving, coming innermost from our heart and soul.

Now, when I came here to the Camp David conference, I said, perhaps as a result of our work, one day people will, in every corner of the world, be able to say, *Habemus pacem,* in the spirit of these days. Can we say so tonight? Not yet. We still have to go a road until my friend President Sadat and I sign the peace treaties.

We promised each other that we shall do so within 3 months. Mr. President [*referring to President Sadat*], tonight, at this celebration of the great historic event, let us promise each other that we shall do it earlier than within 3 months.

Mr. President, you inscribed your name forever in the history of two ancient civilized peoples, the people of Egypt and the people of Israel. Thank you, Mr. President.

PRESIDENT CARTER. Thank you very much.

PRIME MINISTER BEGIN. Oh, no, no, no. I would like to say a few words about my friend, President Sadat. We met for the first time in our lives last November in Jerusalem. He came to us as a guest, a former enemy, and during our first meeting we became friends.

In the Jewish teachings, there is a tradition that the greatest achievement of a human being is to turn his enemy into a friend, and this we do in reciprocity. Since then, we had some difficult days. [*Laughter*] I'm not going now to tell you the saga of those days. Everything belongs to the past. Today, I visited President Sadat in his cabin, because in Camp David you don't have houses, you only have cabins. [*Laughter*] And he then came to visit me. We shook hands. And, thank God, we again could have said to each other, "You are my friend."

And, indeed, we shall go on working in understanding, and in friendship, and with good will. We will still have problems to solve. Camp David proved that any problem can be solved if there is good will and understanding and some, *some* wisdom.

May I thank my own colleagues and friends, the Foreign Minister, the Defense Minister, Professor Barak, who was the Attorney General—and now he is going to be His Honor, the Justice of the Supreme Court, the Israeli Brandeis—and Dr. Rosenne,[11] and our wonderful Ambassador to the United States, Mr. Simcha Dinitz, and all our friends, because without them that achievement wouldn't have been possible.

I express my thanks to all the members of the American delegation, headed by the Secretary of State, a man whom we love and respect. And so, I express my thanks to all the members of the Egyptian delegation who worked so hard together with us, headed by Deputy Prime Minister, Mr. Touhamy, for all they have done to achieve this moment. It is a great moment in the history of our nations and, indeed, of mankind.

I looked for a precedent; I didn't find it. It was a unique conference, perhaps one of the most important since the Vienna Conference in the 19th century; perhaps.

And now, ladies and gentlemen, allow me to turn to my own people from the White House in my own native tongue.

[*At this point, the Prime Minister spoke briefly in Hebrew.*]

Thank you, ladies and gentlemen.

PRESIDENT CARTER. The first document that we will sign is entitled,

[11]Moshe Dayan, Ezer Weizmann, Aharon Barak, and Meir Rosenne (Legal Adviser).

"A Framework For Peace in the Middle East Agreed at Camp David," and the texts of these two documents will be released tomorrow. The documents will be signed by President Sadat and Prime Minister Begin, and it will be witnessed by me. We have to exchange three documents, so we'll all sign three times for this one.

[*At this point, President Sadat, Prime Minister Begin, and President Carter signed the first document.*]

I might say that the first document is quite comprehensive in nature, encompassing a framework by which Israel can later negotiate peace treaties between herself and Lebanon, Syria, Jordan, as well as the outline of this document that we will now sign.

And as you will later see, in studying the documents, it also provides for the realization of the hopes and dreams of the people who live in the West Bank and Gaza Strip and will assure Israel peace in the generations ahead.

This second document is the one relating to a framework for a peace treaty between Egypt and Israel. This is the document that calls for the completion of the peace treaty negotiations within 3 months. And I have noticed the challenge extended by these two gentlemen to each other. They will complete within 3 months—I might say that this document encompasses almost all of the issues between the two countries and resolves those issues. A few lines remain to be drawn on maps, and the question of the settlements is to be resolved. Other than that, most of the major issues are resolved already in this document.

We will now sign this document as well.

[*At this point, President Sadat, Prime Minister Begin, and President Carter signed the second document.*]

PRESIDENT CARTER. Thank you very much.

(19) Accomplishments of the Camp David Meeting: Address by President Carter before a Joint Session of the Congress, September 18, 1978. [12]

Vice President Mondale, Speaker O'Neill, distinguished Members of the United States Congress, Justices of the Supreme Court, other leaders of our great Nation, ladies and gentlemen:

It's been more than 2,000 years since there was peace between

[12]Text from *Presidential Documents*, 14: 1533-7.

Egypt and a free Jewish nation. If our present expectations are realized, this year we shall see such peace again.

The first thing I would like to do is to give tribute to the two men who made this impossible dream now become a real possibility, the two great leaders with whom I have met for the last 2 weeks at Camp David: first, President Anwar Sadat of Egypt and the other, of course, is Prime Minister Menahem Begin of the nation of Israel.

I know that all of you would agree that these are two men of great personal courage, representing nations of peoples who are deeply grateful to them for the achievement which they have realized. And I am personally grateful to them for what they have done.

At Camp David, we sought a peace that is not only of vital importance to their own two nations but to all the people of the Middle East, to all the people of the United States, and, indeed, to all the world as well.

The world prayed for the success of our efforts, and I am glad to announce to you that these prayers have been answered.

I've come to discuss with you tonight what these two leaders have accomplished and what this means to all of us.

The United States has had no choice but to be deeply concerned about the Middle East and to try to use our influence and our efforts to advance the cause of peace. For the last 30 years, through four wars, the people of this troubled region have paid a terrible price in suffering and division and hatred and bloodshed. No two nations have suffered more than Egypt and Israel. But the dangers and the costs of conflicts in this region for our own Nation have been great as well. We have longstanding friendships among the nations there and the peoples of the region, and we have profound moral commitments which are deeply rooted in our values as a people.

The strategic location of these countries and the resources that they possess mean that events in the Middle East directly affect people everywhere. We and our friends could not be indifferent if a hostile power were to establish domination there. In few areas of the world is there a greater risk that a local conflict could spread among other nations adjacent to them and then, perhaps, erupt into a tragic confrontation between us superpowers, ourselves.

Our people have come to understand that unfamiliar names like Sinai, Aqaba, Sharm el Sheikh, Ras en Naqb, Gaza, the West Bank of Jordan, can have a direct and immediate bearing on our own well-being as a nation and our hope for a peaceful world. That is why we in the United States cannot afford to be idle bystanders and why we have been full partners in the search for peace and why it is so vital to our Nation that these meetings at Camp David have been a success.

Through the long years of conflict, four main issues have divided the parties involved. One is the nature of peace—whether peace will simply mean that the guns are silenced, that the bombs no longer fall, that the tanks cease to roll, or whether it will mean that the nations of the Middle East can deal with each other as neighbors and as equals and as friends, with a full range of diplomatic and cultural and economic and human relations between them. That's been the basic question. The Camp David agreement has defined such relationships, I'm glad to announce to you, between Israel and Egypt.

The second main issue is providing for the security of all parties involved, including, of course, our friends, the Israelis, so that none of then need fear attack or military threats from one another. When implemented, the Camp David agreement, I'm glad to announce to you, will provide for such mutual security.

Third is the question of agreement on secure and recognized boundaries, the end of military occupation, and the granting of self-government or else the return to other nations of territories which have been occupied by Israel since the 1967 conflict. The Camp David agreement, I'm glad to announce to you, provides for the realization of all these goals.

And finally, there is the painful human question of the fate of the Palestinians who live or who have lived in these disputed regions. The Camp David agreement guarantees that the Palestinian people may participate in the resolution of the Palestinian problem in all its aspects, a commitment that Israel has made in writing and which is supported and appreciated, I'm sure, by all the world.

Over the last 18 months, there has been, of course, some progress on these issues. Egypt and Israel came close to agreeing about the first issue, the nature of peace. They then saw that the second and third issues, that is withdrawal and security, were intimately connected, closely entwined. But fundamental divisions still remained in other areas—about the fate of the Palestinians, the future of the West Bank and Gaza, and the future of Israeli settlements in occupied Arab territories.

We all remember the hopes for peace that were inspired by President Sadat's initiative, that great and historic visit to Jerusalem last November that thrilled the world, and by the warm and genuine personal response of Prime Minister Begin and the Israeli people, and by the mutual promise between them, publicly made, that there would be no more war. These hopes were sustained when Prime Minister Begin reciprocated by visiting Ismailia on Christmas Day. That progress continued, but at a slower and slower pace through the early part of the year. And by early summer, the negotiations had come to a standstill once again.

It was this stalemate and the prospect for an even worse future that prompted me to invite both President Sadat and Prime Minister Begin to join me at Camp David. They accepted, as you know, instantly, without delay, without preconditions, without consultation even between them.

It's impossible to overstate the courage of these two men or the foresight they have shown. Only through high ideals, through compromises of words and not principle, and through a willingness to look deep into the human heart and to understand the problems and hopes and dreams of one another can progress in a difficult situation like this ever be made. That's what these men and their wise and diligent advisers who are here with us tonight have done during the last 13 days.

When this conference began, I said that the prospects for success were remote. Enormous barriers of ancient history and nationalism and suspicion would have to be overcome if we were to meet our objectives. But President Sadat and Prime Minister Begin have overcome these barriers, exceeded our fondest expectations, and have signed two agreements that hold out the possibility of resolving issues that history had taught us could not be resolved.

The first of these documents is entitled, "A Framework for Peace in the Middle East Agreed at Camp David."[13] It deals with a comprehensive settlement, comprehensive agreement, between Israel and all her neighbors, as well as the difficult question of the Palestinian people and the future of the West Bank and the Gaza area.

The agreement provides a basis for the resolution of issues involving the West Bank and Gaza during the next 5 years. It outlines a process of change which is in keeping with Arab hopes, while also carefully respecting Israel's vital security.

The Israeli military government over these areas will be withdrawn and will be replaced with a self-government of the Palestinians who live there. And Israel has committed that this government will have full autonomy. Prime Minister Begin said to me several times, not partial autonomy, but full autonomy.

Israeli forces will be withdrawn and redeployed into specified locations to protect Israel's security. The Palestinians will further participate in determining their own future through talks in which their own elected representatives, the inhabitants of the West bank and Gaza, will negotiate with Egypt and Israel and Jordan to determine the final status of the West Bank and Gaza.

Israel has agreed, has committed themselves, that the legitimate rights of the Palestinian people will be recognized. After the signing of this framework last night, and during the negotiations concerning the establishment of the Palestinian self-government, no new Israeli settlements will be established in this area. The future settlements issue will be decided among the negotiating parties.

The final status of the West Bank and Gaza will be decided before the end of the 5-year transitional period during which the Palestinian Arabs will have their own government, as part of a negoti-

---

[13]Document 20a.

ation which will produce a peace treaty between Israel and Jordan specifying borders, withdrawal, all those very crucial issues.

These negotiations will be based on all the provisions and the principles of Security Council Resolution 242, with which you all are so familiar. The agreement on the final status of these areas will then be submitted to a vote by the representatives of the inhabitants of the West Bank and Gaza, and they will have the right for the first time in their history, the Palestinian people, to decide how they will govern themselves permanently.

We also believe, of course, all of us, that there should be a just settlement of the problems of displaced persons and refugees, which takes into account appropriate United Nations resolutions.

Finally, this document also outlines a variety of security arrangements to reinforce peace between Israel and her neighbors. This is, indeed, a comprehensive and fair framework for peace in the Middle East, and I'm glad to report this to you.

The second agreement is entitled, "A Framework for the Conclusion of a Peace Treaty Between Egypt and Israel."[14] It returns to Egypt its full exercise of sovereignty over the Sinai Peninsula and establishes several security zones, recognizing carefully that sovereignty right for the protection of all parties. It also provides that Egypt will extend full diplomatic recognition to Israel at the time the Israelis complete an interim withdrawal from most of the Sinai, which will take place between 3 months and 9 months after the conclusion of the peace treaty. And the peace treaty is to be fully negotiated and signed no later than 3 months from last night.

I think I should also report that Prime Minister Begin and President Sadat have already challenged each other to conclude the treaty even earlier. And I hope they—[applause]. This final conclusion of a peace treaty will be completed late in December, and it would be a wonderful Christmas present for the world.

Final and complete withdrawal of all Israeli forces will take place between 2 and 3 years following the conclusion of the peace treaty.

While both parties are in total agreement on all the goals that I have just described to you, there is one issue on which agreement has not yet been reached. Egypt states that agreement to remove the Israeli settlements from Egyptian territory is a prerequisite to a peace treaty. Israel says that the issue of the Isreali settlements should be resolved during the peace negotiations themselves.

Now, within 2 weeks, with each member of the Knesset or the Israeli Parliament acting as individuals, not constrained by party loyalty, the Knesset will decide on the issue of the settlements. Our own Government's position, my own personal position is well known on this issue and has been consistent. It is my strong hope, my prayer, that the question of Israeli settlements on Egyptian territory will not be the final obstacle to peace.

None of us should underestimate the historic importance of what has already been done. This is the first time that an Arab and Israeli leader have signed a comprehensive framework for peace. It contains the seeds of a time when the Middle East, with all its vast potential, may be a land of human richness and fulfillment, rather than a land of bitterness and continued conflict. No region in the world has greater natural and human resources than this one, and nowhere have they been more heavily weighed down by intense hatred and frequent war. These agreements hold out the real possibility that this burden might finally be lifted.

But we must also not forget the magnitude of the obstacles that still remain. The summit exceeded our highest expectations, but we know that it left many difficult issues which are still to be resolved. These issues will require careful negotiations in the months to come. The Egyptian and Israeli people must recognize the tangible benefits that peace will bring and support the decisions their leaders have made, so that a secure and a peaceful future can be achieved for them. The American public, you and I, must also offer our full support to those who have made decisions that are difficult and those who have very difficult decisions still to make.

What lies ahead for all of us is to recognize the statesmanship that President Sadat and Prime Minister Begin have shown and to invite others in that region to follow their example. I have already, last night, invited the other leaders of the Arab world to help sustain progress toward a comprehensive peace.

We must also join in an effort to bring an end to the conflict and the terrible suffering in Lebanon. This is a subject that President Sadat discussed with me many times while I was in Camp David with him. And the first time that the three of us met together, this was a subject of heated discussion. On the way to Washington last night in the helicopter, we mutually committed ourselves to join with other nations, with the Lebanese people themselves, all factions, with President Sarkis,[15] with Syria and Saudi Arabia, perhaps the European countries like France, to try to move toward a solution of the problem in Lebanon which is so vital to us and to the poor people in Lebanon who have suffered so much.

We will want to consult on this matter and on these documents and their meaning with all of the leaders. And I'm pleased to say to you tonight that just a few minutes ago, King Hussein of Jordan and King Khalid of Saudi Arabia, perhaps other leaders later, but these two have already agreed to receive Secretary Vance, who will be leaving tomorrow to explain to them the terms of the Camp David

<hr>

[15]Elias Sarkis.

agreement. And we hope to secure their support for the realization of the new hopes and dreams of the people of the Middle East.

This is an important mission, and this responsibility, I can tell you, based on my last 2 weeks with him, could not possibly rest on the shoulders of a more able and dedicated and competent man than Secretary Cyrus Vance.

Finally, let me say that for many years the Middle East has been a textbook for pessimism, a demonstration that diplomatic ingenuity was no match for intractable human conflicts. Today we are privileged to see the chance for one of the sometimes rare, bright moments in human history—a chance that may offer the way to peace. We have a chance for peace because these two brave leaders found within themselves the willingness to work together to seek these lasting prospects for peace, which we all want so badly. And for that, I hope that you will share my prayer of thanks and my hope that the promise of this moment shall be fully realized.

The prayers at Camp David were the same as those of the shepherd King David, who prayed in the 85th Psalm, "Wilt thou not revive us again: that thy people may rejoice in thee? I will hear what God the Lord will speak: for he will speak peace unto his people, and unto his saints: but let them not return again unto folly."

And I would like to say, as a Christian, to these two friends of mine, the words of Jesus, "Blessed are the peacemakers, for they shall be the children of God."

(20) Documents Agreed to at Camp David and Signed at Washington, September 17, 1978.

(a) A Framework for Peace in the Middle East. [16]

A FRAMEWORK FOR PEACE IN THE MIDDLE'
EAST AGREED AT CAMP DAVID

Muhammad Anwar al-Sadat, President of the Arab Republic of Egypt, and Menachem Begin, Prime Minister of Israel, met with Jimmy Carter, President of the United States of America, at Camp David from September 5 to September 17, 1978, and have agreed on the following framework for peace in the Middle East. They invite other parties to the Arab-Israeli conflict, to adhere to it.

PREAMBLE

The search for peace in the Middle East must be guided by the following:

[16]Text from *Presidential Documents,* 14: 1523-7.

—The agreed basis for a peaceful settlement of the conflict between Israel and its neighbors is United Nations Security Council Resolution 242, in all its parts.[17]

—After four wars during thirty years, despite intensive human efforts, the Middle East, which is the cradle of civilization and the birthplace of three great religions, does not yet enjoy the blessings of peace. The people of the Middle East yearn for peace so that the vast human and natural resources of the region can be turned to the pursuits of peace and so that this area can become a model for coexistence and cooperation among nations.

—The historic initiative of President Sadat in visiting Jerusalem and the reception accorded to him by the Parliament, government and people of Israel, and the reciprocal visit of Prime Minister Begin to Ismailia, the peace proposals made by both leaders, as well as the warm reception of these missions by the peoples of both countries, have created an unprecedented opportunity for peace which must not be lost if this generation and future generations are to be spared the tragedies of war.

—The provisions of the Charter of the United Nations and the other accepted norms of international law and legitimacy now provide accepted standards for the conduct of relations among all states.

—To achieve a relationship of peace, in the spirit of Article 2 of the United Nations Charter,[18] future negotiations between Israel and any neighbor prepared to negotiate peace and security with it, are necessary for the purpose of carrying out all the provisions and principles of Resolutions 242 and 338.

—Peace requires respect for the sovereignty, territorial integrity and political independence of every state in the area and their right to live in peace within secure and recognized boundaries free from threats or acts of force. Progress toward that goal can accelerate movement toward a new era of reconciliation in the Middle East marked by cooperation in promoting economic development, in maintaining stability, and in assuring security.

—Security is enhanced by a relationship of peace and by cooperation between nations which enjoy normal relations. In addition, under the terms of peace treaties, the parties can, on the basis of reciprocity, agree to special security arrangements such as demilitarized zones, limited armaments areas, early warning stations, the presence of international forces, liaison, agreed measures for monitoring, and other arrangements that they agree are useful.

---

[17]Texts of Resolutions 242 and 238, annexed to this document, not printed here. Full citation in Appendix under 1967 and 1973 respectively.

[18]Obligating all members to settle disputes by peaceful means, refrain from the threat or use of force, etc.

FRAMEWORK

Taking these factors into account, the parties are determined to reach a just, comprehensive, and durable settlement of the Middle East conflict through the conclusion of peace treaties based on Security Council Resolutions 242 and 338 in all their parts. Their purpose is to achieve peace and good neighborly relations. They recognize that, for peace to endure, it must involve all those who have been most deeply affected by the conflict. They therefore agree that this framework as appropriate is intended by them to constitute a basis for peace not only between Egypt and Israel, but also between Israel and each of its other neighbors which is prepared to negotiate peace with Israel on this basis. With that objective in mind, they have agreed to proceed as follows:

A. West Bank and Gaza

1. Egypt, Israel, Jordan and the representatives of the Palestinian people should participate in negotiations on the resolution of the Palestinian problem in all its aspects. To achieve that objective, negotiations relating to the West Bank and Gaza should proceed in three stages:

(a) Egypt and Israel agree that, in order to ensure a peaceful and orderly transfer of authority, and taking into account the security concerns of all the parties, there should be transitional arrangements for the West Bank and Gaza for a period not exceeding five years. In order to provide full autonomy to the inhabitants, under these arrangements the Israeli military government and its civilian administration will be withdrawn as soon as a self-governing authority has been freely elected by the inhabitants of these areas to replace the existing military government. To negotiate the details of a transitional arrangement, the Government of Jordan will be invited to join the negotiations on the basis of this framework. These new arrangements should give due consideration both to the principle of self-government by the inhabitants of these territories and to the legitimate security concerns of the parties involved.

(b) Egypt, Israel, and Jordan will agree on the modalities for establishing the elected self-governing authority in the West Bank and Gaza. The delegations of Egypt and Jordan may include Palestinians from the West Bank and Gaza or other Palestinians as mutually agreed. The parties will negotiate an agreement which will define the powers and responsibilities of the self-governing authority to be exercised in the West Bank and Gaza. A withdrawal of Israeli armed forces will take place and there will be a redeployment of the remaining Israeli forces into specified security locations. The agreement will also include arrangements for assuring internal and external security and public order. A strong local police force will be established, which may include Jordanian citizens. In addition, Israeli and Jordanian forces will participate in joint patrols and in the manning of control posts to assure the security of the borders.

(c) When the self-governing authority (administrative council) in the West Bank and Gaza is established and inaugurated, the transitional period of five years will begin. As soon as possible, but not later than the third year after the beginning of the transitional period, negotiations will take place to determine the final status of the West Bank and Gaza and its relationship with its neighbors, and to conclude a peace treaty between Israel and Jordan by the end of the transitional period. These negotiations will be conducted among Egypt, Israel, Jordan, and the elected representatives of the inhabitants of the West Bank and Gaza. Two separate but related committees will be convened, one committee, consisting of representatives of the four parties which will negotiate and agree on the final status of the West Bank and Gaza, and its relationship with its neighbors, and the second committee, consisting of representatives of Israel and representatives of Jordan to be joined by the elected representatives of the inhabitants of the West Bank and Gaza, to negotiate the peace treaty between Israel and Jordan, taking into account the agreement reached on the final status of the West Bank and Gaza. The negotiations shall be based on all the provisions and principles of UN Security Council Resolution 242. The negotiations will resolve, among other matters, the location of the boundaries and the nature of the security arrangements. The solution from the negotiations must also recognize the legitimate rights of the Palestinian people and their just requirements. In this way, the Palestinians will participate in the determination of their own future through:

1) The negotiations among Egypt, Israel, Jordan and the representatives of the inhabitants of the West Bank and Gaza to agree on the final status of the West Bank and Gaza and other outstanding issues by the end of the transitional period.

2) Submitting their agreement to a vote by the elected representatives of the inhabitants of the West Bank and Gaza.

3) Providing for the elected representatives of the inhabitants of the West Bank and Gaza to decide how they shall govern themselves consistent with the provisions of their agreement.

4) Participating as stated above in the work of the committee negotiating the peace treaty between Israel and Jordan.

2. All necessary measures will be taken and provisions made to assure the security of Israel and its neighbors during the transitional

period and beyond. To assist in providing such security, a strong local police force will be constituted by the self-governing authority. It will be composed of inhabitants of the West Bank and Gaza. The police will maintain continuing liaison on internal security matters with the designated Israeli, Jordanian, and Egyptian officers.

3. During the transitional period, representatives of Egypt, Israel, Jordan, and the self-governing authority will constitute a continuing committee to decide by agreement on the modalities of admission of persons displaced from the West Bank and Gaza in 1967, together with necessary measures to prevent disruption and disorder. Other matters of common concern may also be dealt with by this committee.

4. Egypt and Israel will work with each other and with other interested parties to establish agreed procedures for a prompt, just and permanent implementation of the resolution of the refugee problem.

B. Egypt-Israel

1. Egypt and Israel undertake not to resort to the threat or the use of force to settle disputes. Any disputes shall be settled by peaceful means in accordance with the provisions of Article 33 of the Charter of the United Nations.

2. In order to achieve peace between them, the parties agree to negotiate in good faith with a goal of concluding within three months from the signing of this Framework a peace treaty between them, while inviting the other parties to the conflict to proceed simultaneously to negotiate and conclude similar peace treaties with a view to achieving a comprehensive peace in the area. The Framework for the Conclusion of a Peace Treaty between Egypt and Israel will govern the peace negotiations between them. The parties will agree on the modalities and the timetable for the implementation of their obligations under the treaty.

C. Associated Principles

1. Egypt and Israel state that the principles and provisions described below should apply to peace treaties between Israel and each of its neighbors—Egypt, Jordan, Syria and Lebanon.

2. Signatories shall establish among themselves relationships normal to states at peace with one another. To this end, they should undertake to abide by all the provisions of the Charter of the United Nations. Steps to be taken in this respect include:

(a) full recognition;
(b) abolishing economic boycotts;
(c) guaranteeing that under their jurisdiction the citizens of the other parties shall enjoy the protection of the due process of law.

3. Signatories should explore possibilities for economic development in the context of final peace treaties, with the objective of
contributing to the atmosphere of peace, cooperation and friendship which is their common goal.

4. Claims Commissions may be established for the mutual settlement of all financial claims.

5. The United States shall be invited to participate in the talks on
matters related to the modalities of the implementation of the agreements and working out the timetable for the carrying out of the obligations of the parties.

6. The United Nations Security Council shall be requested to endorse the peace treaties and ensure that their provisions shall not be
violated. The permanent members of the Security Council shall be
requested to underwrite the peace treaties and ensure respect for
their provisions. They shall also be requested to conform their policies and actions with the undertakings contained in this Framework.

For the Government of the Arab Republic of Egypt:

AL-SADAT

For the Government of Israel:

M. BEGIN

Witnessed by:

JIMMY CARTER
*Jimmy Carter, President
of the United States of
America*

*(b) Framework for the Conclusion of a Peace Treaty Between
Egypt and Israel.*[19]

FRAMEWORK FOR THE CONCLUSION OF A PEACE TREATY BETWEEN
EGYPT AND ISRAEL

In order to achieve peace between them, Israel and Egypt agree
to negotiate in good faith with a goal of concluding within three
months of the signing of this framework a peace treaty between
them.

It is agreed that:

The site of the negotiations will be under a United Nations flag at
a location or locations to be mutually agreed.

[19]Text from *Presidential Documents*, 14: 1527–8.

All of the principles of U.N. Resolution 242 will apply in this resolution of the dispute between Israel and Egypt.

Unless otherwise mutually agreed, terms of the peace treaty will be implemented between two and three years after the peace treaty is signed.

The following matters are agreed between the parties:

(a) the full exercise of Egyptian sovereignty up to the internationally recognized border between Egypt and mandated Palestine;

(b) the withdrawal of Israeli armed forces from the Sinai;

(c) the use of airfields left by the Israelis near El Arish, Rafah, Ras en Naqb, and Sharm el Sheikh for civilian purposes only, including possible commercial use by all nations;

(d) the right of free passage by ships of Israel through the Gulf of Suez and the Suez Canal on the basis of the Constantinople Convention of 1888 applying to all nations; the Strait of Tiran and the Gulf of Aqaba are international waterways to be open to all nations for unimpeded and nonsuspendable freedom of navigation and overflight;

(e) the construction of a highway between the Sinai and Jordan near Elat with guaranteed free and peaceful passage by Egypt and Jordan; and

(f) the stationing of military forces listed below.

STATIONING OF FORCES[20]

A. No more than one division (mechanized or infantry) of Egyptian armed forces will be stationed within an area lying approximately 50 kilometers (km) east of the Gulf of Suez and the Suez Canal.

B. Only United Nations forces and civil police equipped with light weapons to perform normal police functions will be stationed within an area lying west of the international border and the Gulf of Aqaba, varying in width from 20 km to 40 km.

C. In the area within 3 km east of the international border there will be Israeli limited military forces not to exceed four infantry battalions and United Nations observers.

D. Border patrol units, not to exceed three battalions, will sup-

[20]Maps showing the agreed disposition of military forces were included in the Egyptian-Israeli Peace Treaty signed Mar. 26, 1979, and are reproduced in Department of State, Bureau of Public Affairs, Office of Public Communication, *The Egyptian-Israeli Peace Treaty, March 26, 1979 (Selected Documents,* No. 11, Apr. 1979): 13–16.

plement the civil police in maintaining order in the area not included above.

The exact demarcation of the above areas will be as decided during the peace negotiations.

Early warning stations may exist to insure compliance with the terms of the agreement.

United Nations forces will be stationed: (a) in part of the area in the Sinai lying within about 20 km of the Mediterranean Sea and adjacent to the international border, and (b) in the Sharm el Sheikh area to ensure freedom of passage through the Strait of Tiran; and these forces will not be removed unless such removal is approved by the Security Council of the United Nations with a unanimous vote of the five permanent members.

After a peace treaty is signed, and after the interim withdrawal is complete, normal relations will be established between Egypt and Israel, including: full recognition, including diplomatic, economic and cultural relations; termination of economic boycotts and barriers to the free movement of goods and people; and mutual protection of citizens by the due process of law.

INTERIM WITHDRAWAL

Between three months and nine months after the signing of the peace treaty, all Israeli forces will withdraw east of a line extending from a point east of El Arish to Ras Muhammad, the exact location of this line to be determined by mutual agreement.

For the Government of the Arab Republic of Egypt:

AL-SADAT

For the Government of Israel:

M. BEGIN

Witnessed by:

JIMMY CARTER
*Jimmy Carter, President
of the United States of
America*

(21) Letters to Accompany the Camp David Documents.

*(a) Letters Released by the White House, September 22,
1978.*[21]

[21]Text from *Presidential Documents,* 14: 1566–8.

(A

September 17, 1978

Dear Mr. President:

I have the honor to inform you that during two weeks after my return home I will submit a motion before Israel's Parliament (the Knesset) to decide on the following question:

If during the negotiations to conclude a peace treaty between Israel and Egypt all outstanding issues are agreed upon, "are you in favor of the removal of the Israeli settlers from the northern and southern Sinai areas or are you in favor of keeping the aforementioned settlers in those areas?"

The vote, Mr. President, on this issue will be completely free from the usual Parliamentary Party discipline to the effect that although the coalition is being now supported by 70 members out of 120, every member of the Knesset, as I believe, both on the Government and the Opposition benches will be enabled to vote in accordance with his own conscience.

Sincerely yours,

(signed)

Menachem Begin

[The President, Camp David, Thurmont, Maryland]

———

(B

September 22, 1978

Dear Mr. President:

I transmit herewith a copy of a letter to me from Prime Minister Begin setting forth how he proposes to present the issue of the Sinai settlements to the Knesset for the latter's decision.

In this connection, I understand from your letter that Knesset approval to withdraw all Israeli settlers from Sinai according to a timetable within the period specified for the implementation of the peace treaty is a prerequisite to any negotiations on a peace treaty between Egypt and Israel.

Sincerely,

(signed)

JIMMY CARTER

Enclosure: Letter from Prime Minister Begin (Letter at Tab A)

[His Excellency Anwar el-Sadat, President of the Arab Republic of Egypt, Cairo]

———

(C

September 17, 1978

Dear Mr. President:

In connection with the "Framework for a Settlement in Sinai" to be signed tonight, I would like to reaffirm the position of the Arab Republic of Egypt with respect to the settlements:

1. All Israeli settlers must be withdrawn from Sinai according to a timetable within the period specified for the implementation of the peace treaty.
2. Agreement by the Israeli Government and its constitutional institutions to this basic principle is therefore a prerequisite to starting peace negotiations for concluding a peace treaty.
3. If Israel fails to meet this commitment, the "Framework" shall be void and invalid.

Sincerely,
(signed)
MOHAMED ANWAR EL SADAT

[His Excellency Jimmy Carter, President of the United States]

———

(D

September 22, 1978

Dear Mr. Prime Minister:

I have received your letter of September 17, 1978, describing how you intend to place the question of the future of Israeli settlements in Sinai before the Knesset for its decision.

Enclosed is a copy of President Sadat's letter to me on this subject.

Sincerely,
(signed)
JIMMY CARTER

Enclosure: Letter from President Sadat (Letter at Tab C)

[His Excellency Menachem Begin, Prime Minister of Israel]

(E

September 17, 1978

Dear Mr. President.

I am writing you to reaffirm the position of the Arab Republic of Egypt with respect to Jerusalem:

1. Arab Jerusalem is an integral part of the West Bank. Legal and historical Arab rights in the City must be respected and restored.
2. Arab Jerusalem should be under Arab sovereignty.
3. The Palestinian inhabitants of Arab Jerusalem are entitled to exercise their legitimate national rights, being part of the Palestinian People in the West Bank.
4. Relevant Security Council Resolutions, particularly Resolutions 242 and 267,[22] must be applied with regard to Jerusalem. All the measures taken by Israel to alter the status of the City are null and void and should be rescinded.
5. All peoples must have free access to the City and enjoy the free exercise of worship and the right to visit and transit to the holy places without distinction or discrimination.
6. The holy places of each faith may be placed under the administration and control of their representatives.
7. Essential functions in the City should be undivided and a joint municipal council composed of an equal number of Arab and Israeli members can supervise the carrying out of these functions. In this way, the City shall be undivided.

Sincerely,

(signed)
MOHAMED ANWAR EL SADAT

[His Excellency Jimmy Carter, President of the United States]

(F

17 September 1978

Dear Mr. President,

I have the honor to inform you, Mr. President, that on 28 June

---

[22] Resolution 267, censuring Israeli measures to change the status of Jerusalem, was adopted unanimously July 3, 1969.

1967—Israel's Parliament (The Knesset) promulgated and adopted a law to the effect: "the Government is empowered by a decree to apply the law, the jurisdiction and administration of the State to any part of Eretz Israel (land of Israel—Palestine), as stated in that decree."

On the basis of this law, the Government of Israel decreed in July 1967 that Jerusalem is one city indivisible, the Capital of the State of Israel.

Sincerely,

(signed)

MENACHEM BEGIN

[The President, Camp David, Thurmont, Maryland]

———

(G

September 22, 1978

Dear Mr. President:

I have received your letter of September 17, 1978, setting forth the Egyptian position on Jerusalem. I am transmitting a copy of that letter to Prime Minister Begin for his information.

The position of the United States on Jerusalem remains as stated by Ambassador Goldberg in the United Nations General Assembly on July 14, 1967, and subsequently by Ambassador Yost in the United Nations Security Council on July 1, 1969.[23]

Sincerely,

(signed)

JIMMY CARTER

[His Excellency Anwar al-Sadat, President of the Arab Republic of Egypt, Cairo]

———

(H

September 17, 1978

Dear Mr. President:

In connection with the "Framework for Peace in the Middle East", I am writing you this letter to inform you of the position of the Arab Republic of Egypt, with respect to the implementation of the comprehensive settlement.

[23]Goldberg statement in *Bulletin,* 57: 148–51 (July 31, 1967); Yost statement in same, 61: 76–7 (July 28, 1969).

To ensure the implementation of the provisions related to the West Bank and Gaza and in order to safeguard the legitimate rights of the Palestinian people, Egypt will be prepared to assume the Arab role emanating from these provisions, following consultations with Jordan and the representatives of the Palestinian people.

Sincerely,

(signed)

MOHAMED ANWAR EL SADAT

[His Excellency Jimmy Carter, President of the United States, The White House, Washington, D.C.]

(I

September 22, 1978

Dear Mr. Prime Minister:

I hereby acknowledge that you have informed me as follows:

A) In each paragraph of the agreed framework document the expressions "Palestinians" or "Palestinian People" are being and will be construed and understood by you as "Palestinian Arabs."

B) In each paragraph in which the expression "West Bank" appears, it is being, and will be, understood by the Government of Israel as Judea and Samaria.

Sincerely,

(signed)

JIMMY CARTER

[His Excellency Menachem Begin, Prime Minister of Israel]

(b) Letter Released by the Department of Defense, September 29, 1978.[24]

September 28, 1978

Dear Mr. Minister:

The U.S. understands that, in connection with carrying out the agreements reached at Camp David, Israel intends to build two military airbases at appropriate sites in the Negev to replace the air-

[24]Department of Defense Press Release, Sept. 28; text from *Bulletin,* Oct. 1978: 11.

bases at Eitam and Etzion which will be evacuated by Israel in accordance with the peace treaty to be concluded between Egypt and Israel. We also understand the special urgency and priority which Israel attaches to preparing the new bases in light of its conviction that it cannot safely leave the Sinai airbases until the new ones are operational.

I suggest that our two governments consult on the scope and costs of the two new airbases as well as on related forms of assistance which the United States might appropriately provide in light of the special problems which may be presented by carrying out such a project on an urgent basis. The President is prepared to seek the necessary Congressional approvals for such assistance as may be agreed upon by the U.S. side as a result of such consultations.

(signed)
HAROLD BROWN
Secretary of Defense

The Honorable
Ezer Weizman
Minister of Defense
Government of Israel

(22) . The Quest for an Egyptian-Israeli Peace Treaty: Remarks by President Carter, October–December 1978.

    (a) Remarks at the Opening of Peace Negotiations in Washington, October 12, 1978. [25]

THE PRESIDENT. *Distinguished Ministers,* [26] *Mr. Vice President, Mr. Secretary,* [27] *friends:*

For 2,000 years in the Middle East, people have cried, "Peace, peace," when there was no peace. The burden of war has lain heavily on this troubled ground. But less than 1 month ago, President Sadat of Egypt and Prime Minister Begin of Israel created a chance for true peace. In their negotiations at Camp David, they displayed the wisdom and the courage necessary to forge a framework for peace in the Middle East.

Everyone who shares their dream of bringing divisions and bit-

---

[25]Text from *Presidential Documents,* 14: 1757–9.
[26]Israeli and Egyptian participants are listed in the text.
[27]Vice-President Mondale and Secretary of State Vance.

terness to an end in the Middle East will join me in welcoming their representatives to Washington as they take their next vital steps toward turning that framework into a lasting structure of peace.

No one who is aware of the history of our own generation or of this century or, indeed, of the last 20 or more centuries can over-look the historic importance of this event—the moment when Egyptians and Israelis meet to begin negotiating the terms of a treaty which will define in a practical and concrete way relations of peace between them.

Our meeting today gives us a measure of what has been accomplished and what remains to be done to make peace and dignity a reality for all the people of the Middle East. We have certainly not resolved all the issues, nor removed all the risks. We have established, however, principles and procedures for resolving the negotiations ahead.

Again, we invite Jordan, the inhabitants of the West Bank and Gaza, and others who are ready to seize this opportunity to join with us in our search for peace. The alternative is drift, stalemate, continued enmity, and perhaps even another war.

The talks that begin today deal primarily with that part of the Camp David framework related to a peace between Egypt and Israel, to establish the specific terms by which Egypt will assume its full exercise of authority and sovereignty over the Sinai, under which security will be assured to both nations, both peoples, and under which the two countries will live and work together as peaceful neighbors.

This peace between these two great nations must be the foundation and the first step toward the larger, even greater, more important result which we all seek—a comprehensive and a lasting settlement between Israel and all her neighbors. A peace treaty between Egypt and Israel should be complemented by progress toward fulfillment of the provisions of the general framework agreement which was concluded at Camp David dealing with the West Bank and Gaza and the just solution of the Palestinian question in all its aspects.

In the days since Camp David, we've seen difficult but important decisions made in both Egypt and Israel, decisions which demonstrate the firm commitment of the leaders, the government, and the peoples to this great effort, decisions which demonstrate their willingness and their ability to turn the existing commitment to peace into an early reality.

With President Sadat's striking vision of the future, he's made even more clear his nation's determination to achieve peace, not only for Egyptians but for all those involved in or affected by recent conflict, a peace that answers their yearning for an end to bloodshed, an end to destruction, and assures the legitimate rights of all who have suffered or who might suffer in the future through never-ending war.

In these recent days Prime Minister Begin has displayed once again his courage and his statesmanship, his determination in dealing with the very difficult decisions which are necessary and must be taken for peace. I appreciate how hard, how difficult it has been for him to make some of the decisions and for the members of his government to join in with him. They touch the very heart of every citizen of Israel. The Knesset's decisions confirm what we in this country have always known and believed, that Israel's greatest wish is to live at peace and in good neighborly relationships with all the countries around Israel.

The United States is committed without reservation to seeing this great process through until each party to the Arab-Israeli conflict is at peace with all the others. Our own national interests are deeply involved.

The question of peace or war in the Middle East affects the well-being of every American. But beyond this, the generations-old cycle of tragedy and suffering speaks to America's moral conscience and to our deep and lasting concern for human rights and the expansion of human potential for peoples everywhere.

We will work hand in hand with all involved parties until the job is done, and peace is assured.

Minister Moshe Dayan, Minister Kamal Hassan Ali, Minister Ezer Weizman, Minister Butrus Ghali, the Egyptian, Israeli, and American peoples and people throughout the world are depending on you now. Our assistance is available.

My own personal involvement is assured to you. Our hopes are with you, and our prayers.

Thank you very much.

(b) Remarks in a Televised Interview with Bill Moyers of the Public Broadcasting Service, November 13, 1978.[28]

(Excerpt)

* * *

EGYPTIAN-ISRAELI NEGOTIATIONS

MR. MOYERS. What about the Middle East, Mr. President?

THE PRESIDENT. I have put hundreds of hours in both preparation and direct negotiations with the leaders in the Middle East, particularly Egypt and Israel. And Secretary Vance, even to the extent of abandoning some of his other responsibilities in foreign affairs, has tried to bring about a successful conclusion of the peace treaty negotiations. There, again, we don't have any authority over anyone else. We can't use pressure to make the Israelis and Egyptians come to a peaceful settlement of the disputes that have divided them.

The Camp David framework, which was almost miraculous in its conclusion—it seems more miraculous in retrospect than it did at the time—is a sound basis for peace between Egypt and Israel. There's no doubt that both nations would be highly benefited by peace.

MR. MOYERS. But yet the talks seem to be at an impasse as of tonight.

THE PRESIDENT. The present disagreements, compared to the benefits to be derived, are relatively insignificant. The benefits are so overwhelming, in comparison with the differences, that I hope that the Egyptians and Israelis will move toward peace.

MR. MOYERS. What's holding it up tonight?

THE PRESIDENT. At Camp David it was a framework, it was an outline that had a lot of substance to it, but it required negotiation of details and specifics. And there is no way that you could have a peace treaty with all of the ends tied down and all of the detailed agreements reached, the maps drawn, the lines delineated, time schedules agreed, without going far beyond what the Camp David outline required.

And so, both sides have demanded from the others additional assurances far above and beyond what Camp David said specifically. This is inherent in the process. And I think in some cases, in many cases, the two governments have reached agreement fairly well.

Now I don't know what's going to happen. We hope that they will continue to work in reaching agreement, to understand one another, to balance the consequences of failure against the benefits to be derived from the success, and be flexible on both sides.

These are ancient arguments, historical distrust not easy to overcome. And the frustrating part about it is that we are involved in the negotiations, but we can't make Israel accept the Egyptians' demands, nor vice versa. We have to try to tone down those demands and use our influence. I don't know what will happen about it. We just pray that agreements will be reached.

MR. MOYERS. Are you asking both sides to make further concessions?

THE PRESIDENT. Oh, yes—every day and night. We ask both sides to please be constructive, to please not freeze your position, to please to continue to negotiate, to please yield on this proposal, to adopt this compromise. These have been and are our efforts on a constant basis.

It would be horrible, I think, if we failed to reach a peaceful agreement between Israel and Egypt—

MR. MOYERS. What would happen?

THE PRESIDENT.—and then see our children, our grandchildren, future generations look back and say these little tiny technicalities, phrases, phrasing of ideas, legalisms, which at that time seemed to be paramount in the eyes of the Egyptian and the Israeli agreements, have absolutely no historical significance. And that's basically what the problems are.

MR. MOYERS. Are you saying that the impasse as of today is because of technicalities and not major principles?

THE PRESIDENT. Yes, compared, to the principles that have already been resolved and the overall scope of things, the disagreements, now, relatively, are insignificant.

MR. MOYERS. Egypt wants to tie the present negotiations, I understand, to some future resolution of the Gaza Strip and the West Bank. Israel is resisting that. Who's being more stubborn?

THE PRESIDENT. Well, I wouldn't want to start saying who's being more stubborn. I think there's adequate stubbornness to be allotted to both sides.

MR. MOYERS. You mentioned grandchildren, and I heard you say after Camp David that at one critical moment that was resolved because of somebody thinking about grandchildren. Would you tell me about that?

THE PRESIDENT. It might be a mistake to attach too much importance to it, but during the last few hours of negotiations at Camp David, when it looked like everything was going to break down then, Prime Minister Begin sent me over some photographs of me and him and President Sadat and wanted me to autograph them. And the issue at that time was Jerusalem, which was an almost insurmountable obstacle that we later resolved by not including it at all in the framework. And instead of just putting my signature on it, which President Sadat had done, I sent my secretary, Susan Clough, over and got the names from one of his aides of all his grandchildren.

So, I personally autographed it to his granddaughters and grandsons and signed my name, and I carried it over to him in one of the most tense moments and I handed it to him. And he started to talk to me about the breakdown of the negotiations and he looked down and saw that I had written all of his grandchildren's names on the individual pictures and signed them, and he started telling me about his favorite grandchild and the characteristics of different ones.

And he and I had quite an emotional discussion about the benefits to my two grandchildren and to his if we could reach peace. And I think it broke the tension that existed there, that could have been an obstacle to any sort of resolution at that time.

MR. MOYERS. What does that say to you about the nature of these problems and their resolution?

THE PRESIDENT. Well, you know, when you put the problems in the focus of how they affect people, little children, families, the loss of life, the agreements and the need for agreement becomes paramount. When you put the focus in the hands of international lawyers and get it down to technicalities—is a certain event going to take place in 9 months or 8½ months or 10 months; is this going to happen before that; is this demarcation line going to go around this hill or through the hill, on the other side of the hill; can the observation towers be 150 feet high, 200 feet high, 125 feet high—the human dimension of it becomes obviously paramount. But when the negotiators sit around a table and start talking, the human dimension tends to fade away, and you get bogged down in the legalisms and the language and the exact time schedule, when from a historic perspective they have no significance.

Another problem has been—and this has been one of the most serious problems—at Camp David we didn't have daily press briefings, and this was the agreement when we started here in Washington, that neither side would make a direct statement to the press. As you know, this has not been honored at all, and it's created enormous additional and unnecessary problems for us.

MR. MOYERS. You mean leaks from both governments are—

THE PRESIDENT. Not just leaks. I mean, almost every day I see interviews in the national television of at least one of the sides in the dispute.

And also at Camp David I was working directly with the heads of state. Here we work with the negotiators, and the negotiators then refer their decision back to the head of state or the cabinet. The cabinet reverses themselves, reverses the negotiators on a language change or one word, and in effect you get the most radical members of the governments who have a major input into the negotiating process, rather than having the heads of state there 100 yards away so that they can resolve those issues once and for all.

So, I think the followup to Camp David has been much more time-consuming and much more frustrating than it was when the three of us were primarily leading the discussions.

*   *   *

5. AFRICAN HOPES AND FEARS

(23) Reaffirming U.S. Policy: Address by President Carter at Lagos, Nigeria, April 1, 1978.[1]

THE PRESIDENT. *Director Akinyemi, Commissioner Garba,*[2] *distinguished officials of the Government of Nigeria and of the United States, distinguished guests from other countries, and my friends, the Nigerian people:*

I come from a great nation to visit a great nation. When my voice speaks words, they are not the words of a personal person but the words of a country.

It's no coincidence that I come here to this institute, where free and open discussions and debate contribute to the comprehension and understanding and the reaching of agreements that solve problems that have separated people one from another.

It is no coincidence that I come to Nigeria to talk about our bilateral relationships and the problems of Africa. And it is no coincidence that our Nation has now turned in an unprecedented way toward Africa—not to give you our services but to share with you a common future, combining our strengths and yours, correcting our weaknesses and correcting yours. And this departure from past aloofness by the United States is not just a personal commitment of my own, but I represent the deep feelings and the deep interest of all the people of my country.

I'm proud and deeply moved to be the first American President to make an official visit to your country. And I'm especially grateful for the warmth and the generosity of my reception by the Government and by the people of Nigeria.

[1]Text from *Presidential Documents,* 14: 645–51.
[2]Bolaji Akinyemi, Director, Nigeria Institute of International Affairs, and Joseph Nanven Garba, Commissioner for External Affairs.

I don't know who's doing the work, but many Nigerians are standing beside the roadway to make me and my family feel welcome, and I thank you for it.

During my first year as President of the United States, I've been pleased to work closely with General Obasanjo, learning from him and from other African leaders. Our cooperation has had a special meaning for me, since Africa has been so much in my thoughts during the past 15 months.

Our countries have much in common. Nigeria and the United States are vast and diverse nations seeking to use our great resources for the benefit of all our people. That's the way it is now; that's the way it will continue to be in the future.

Americans admire the energy, the wisdom, the hard work, the sense of optimism of the Nigerian people, for these are exactly the same qualities which we admire in my country.

The Nigerian Government has shown these qualities in your own national accomplishments and in your efforts for worldwide peace and economic progress—in the Organization for [of] African Unity, in the United Nations, and in other councils where nations seek common ground so as to resolve differences and to work together.

We admire also the humane and the creative way which Nigeria has come through a divisive time in your own history. Through public debate and far-reaching planning, you are designing a democratic future for a new "One Nigeria," and we're grateful and excited about this prospect.

Our bonds of friendship go back many years. Nigerian students first came to the United States in the 19th century. Your first President, Nnamdi Azikiwe, studied in our country. In applying to Lincoln University, he wrote that he believed in education for service and service for humanity.

Tens of thousands of young Nigerians have followed him to America to prepare themselves for service here in their homeland. Many are present or future teachers, who will help you achieve your goal of universal primary education.

We in the United States are learning from you as well, for we are enriched by our ties and heritage in Africa, just as we hope to contribute to the realization of African hopes and African expectations.

Our nations and our continents are bound together by strong ties that we inherit from our histories. We also share three basic commitments to the future of Africa.

We share with you a commitment to majority rule and individual human rights. In order to meet the basic needs of the people, we share with you a commitment to economic growth and to human development. We share with you a commitment to an Africa that is at peace, free from colonialism, free from racism, free from military interference by outside nations, and free from the inevitable conflicts that can come when the integrity of national boundaries are not respected. We share these things with you as well.

These three common commitments shape our attitude toward your continent. You have been among the leaders of international efforts to bring the principles of majority rule and individual rights into reality in southern Africa.

During the past year, we've worked closely with your Government and the other frontline states in the quest to achieve these goals in Namibia and in Zimbabwe.

Our efforts have now reached a critical stage. On Namibia, there has been some progress, with the parties showing some degree of flexibility. It is important that accommodation be now reached. This past week, we and the other Western members of the United Nations Security Council have presented to the disputing parties our proposals for an internationally acceptable agreement based on free elections.

These proposals provide the best hope for a fair and peaceful solution that will bring independence to Namibia in a manner consistent with Security Council Resolution 385. No group is favored at the expense of another. They protect the rights of all. They should be accepted without further delay.

The tragic assassination of Chief Kapuuo should not lead to an era of violence and recrimination, but to an internationally supervised choice by the people of Namibia to elect leadership that will unite their country in peace and not divide it in war.

On Rhodesia, or Zimbabwe, Great Britain and the United States have put forward a plan for the solution, based on three fundamental principles: first, fair and free elections; secondly, an irreversible transition to genuine majority rule and independence; and third, respect for the individual rights of all the citizens of an independent Zimbabwe.

This plan provides the best basis for agreement. It is widely supported within the international community and by the Presidents of the frontline nations who surround Zimbabwe itself. Its principles must be honored. Let there be no question of the commitment of the United States to these principles or our determination to pursue a just settlement which brings a cease-fire and an internationally recognized legal government.

The present challenge to our diplomacy and to yours is to help all the parties get together, based on the Anglo-American plan, and build on areas of agreement. Only a fair arrangement with broad support among the parties can endure.

The transition to independence of a new Zimbabwe must ensure an opportunity for all parties to compete in the democratic process on an equal footing. The past must lead irrevocably to majority rule and a future in which the rights of each citizen of Zimbabwe are protected, regardless of tribal or ethnic origin or race. That is our Nation's position. We will not depart from it.

The hour is late with regard both to Zimbabwe and to Namibia. The parties must choose. They can choose a path of agreement and be remembered as men of vision and courage who created new nations, born in peace, or they can insist on rigid postures that will produce new political complications, generating new conflicts, growing additional bloodshed, and delay the fulfillment of their hopes.

We in the United States remain committed, as do the people of Nigeria, to the path of genuine progress and fairness, for the sake of all the nations of the region and for the sake of international peace.

In the name of justice, we also believe that South African society should and can be transformed progressively and peacefully, with assured respect for the rights of all. We've made it clear to South Africa that the nature of our relations will depend on whether there is progress towards full participation for all her people, in every respect of the social and economic life of her nation, and an end to discrimination, an end to apartheid, based on race or ethnic origin. We stand firm in that message as well.

I grew up in a society struggling to find racial harmony through racial justice. Though our problems were different, I know that progress can best be found if the determination to see wrongs righted is matched by an understanding that the prisoners of injustice include the privileged as well as the powerless.

I believe we should therefore combine our determination to support the rights of the oppressed people in South Africa with a willingness to hold out our hands to the white minority if they decide to transform their society and to do away with apartheid and the crippling burdens of past injustices.

I also believe that progress can be made. As Andrew Young said here in Lagos last August,[3] a belief in dreams for the future is not naive if we are ready to work to realize those dreams.

Our concern for human rights extends throughout this continent and throughout the world. Whatever the ideology or the power or the race of a government that abuses the rights of its people, we oppose those abuses.

We in America welcome the real progress in human rights that is being made in many countries, in Africa as well as in other regions.

Americans were particularly encouraged that the African group at the United Nations Human Rights Commission moved this year to consider the oppressive policies of two of its own member nations.

We are encouraged, too, by the movement towards democracy being made by many nations. Nigeria is an outstanding example.

[3]Statement, Aug. 25, 1977, in *Bulletin,* 77: 448.

The free and fair elections that you held in the past year leave no doubt that your Government is determined to pursue its decision to establish civilian rule in 1979. This action will be an inspiration to all those in the world who love democracy and who love freedom. And we congratulate you on this.

Each country must, of course, adapt the instruments of democracy to fit its own particular needs, a process now being completed by your constituent assembly. The basic elements are participation by individuals in the decisions that affect their lives, respect for civil liberties through the rule of law, and thus, protection of the dignity of all men and women.

Wherever these fundamental principles exist, a government can accommodate to necessary change without breaking, and its people can demand such change without being broken.

These principles are necessary for democracy, and they sustain development as well. For in a democracy, the people themselves can best ensure that their government will promote their economic rights, as well as their political and civil liberties.

I believe, as I know you do as well, that every person also has a right to education, to health care, to nutrition, to shelter, to food, and to employment. These are the foundations on which men and women can build better lives.

This is our second great, common goal between the United States and Nigeria—human development made possible by fair and equitable economic progress.

My country is ready to do its fair share in support of African development, both because it's in our own interest and also because it's right. More and more, the economic well-being of Americans depends on the growth of the developing nations here in Africa and in other parts of the world. A good example is our relationship with Nigeria, which is marked by respect for each other's independence and a growing recognition of our interdependence.

Nigeria, for instance, is the United States' second largest supplier of imported crude oil. The United States is the largest market for Nigeria's dynamic, economic development program.

But the scope of our commerce is much broader than in petroleum alone. Our growing trade serves the interests of both countries. When we purchase Nigerian products, we contribute to Nigerian development. But unless we can also share our technology and share our productive capacity with you, our own economy slows down, American workers lose their jobs, and the resulting economic sluggishness means that we can buy less from you.

Financial encouragement to developing nations is therefore in our interest, because a world of prosperous, developing economies is a world in which America's economy can prosper.

We are increasing our bilateral development assistance to Africa, and on my return to Washington, I will recommend to the Congress that the United States contribute $125 million to the second replenishment of the African Development Fund.

I'm happy to announce, also, that just before leaving Washington, I authorized our Corps of Engineers to offer to participate, as requested by you, in the comprehensive development of the Niger River System.

We are giving new priority to cooperating in international efforts to improve health around the world. We would like to study with you how we can best work with Nigeria and other nations of Africa to deal with the killing and the crippling diseases that still afflict this continent.

Three days ago I spoke in Caracas, Venezuela, about our commitment to international economic growth and equity.[4] All of us can gain if we act fairly toward one another.

Nigeria acted on this principle in helping to negotiate the Lomé Convention and the birth of the Economic Community of West African States.

All nations can act on this principle by making world trade increasingly free and fair. Private investment can help, under arrangements benefiting both the investors and also the host countries like your own. And sharing technology can make a crucial difference. We are especially pleased that Nigeria is sending so many of your young people to the United States for training in the middle-level technical skills.

There must be fair international agreements on such issues as stabilizing commodity prices, the creation of a Common Fund, and relieving the debt burden of the poorest nations.

Every government has the obligation to promote economic justice within its own nation, as well as among nations. American development assistance will go increasingly to those areas where it can make the greatest contribution to the economic rights of the poor.

Progress towards economic development requires the pursuit of our third goal as well—again which we share with you—a peaceful Africa, free of military intervention, for economic progress is best pursued in times of peace.

Africans themselves can best find peaceful answers to African disputes through the Organization of African Unity and, when needed, with the help of the United Nations.

We support your efforts to strengthen the peacemaking role of the Organization of African Unity, and we share Nigeria's belief in the practical contributions the United Nations can make.

U.N. peacekeeping forces are already, today, playing a crucial role in the Middle East. They can help bring independence and majority rule, in peace, to Namibia and to Zimbabwe.

[4]Remarks to Venezuelan Congress, Mar. 29, in *Presidential Documents,* 14: 619–23.

The military intervention of outside powers or their proxies in such disputes too often makes local conflicts even more complicated and dangerous and opens the door to a new form of domination or colonialism. We oppose such intervention by outside military forces. We must not allow great power rivalries to destroy our hopes for an Africa at peace.

This is one reason we applaud the leading role of Nigeria in seeking to find peaceful solutions to such tragedies as the recent struggle between Ethiopia and Somalia in the Horn of Africa.

We are concerned that foreign troops are already planning for military action inside Ethiopia against the Eritreans, which will result in greatly increased bloodshed among those unfortunate peoples. Although I will remain careful to see that our friends are not put at a disadvantage, I am working to curb our own role as a supplier of arms, and we urge others to show similar restraint.

We prefer to seek good relations with African and other nations through the works of peace, not war. America's contributions will be to life and development and not to death or destruction.

Plainly, military restraint by outsiders can best be brought about if all nations, including those who buy weapons, actively seek that constraint. We would welcome and support voluntary regional agreements among African leaders to reduce the purchase of weapons as a major step towards peace and away from the economic deprivation of the poor, when badly needed money that could give them a better life goes to purchase weapons to take lives.

I've talked about many subjects this afternoon, very briefly, but in one way or another, I've been talking about change in the world that we all share. Sometimes we grow impatient or cynical about that change, thinking that it's too slow, that it may not come at all.

I know something about social change. In my own lifetime, I've seen the region of my birth, the southern part of the United States, changed from a place of poverty and despair and racial division to a land of bright promise and opportunity and increasing racial harmony.

I've seen the towering wall between the races taken down, piece by piece, until the whites and the blacks of my country could reach across it to each other.

I know that our own society is different from any other, and I know that we still have much to do in the United States. But nothing can shake my faith that in every part of the world, peaceful change can come and bless the lives of human beings. Nothing can make me doubt that this continent will win its struggle for freedom—freedom from racism and the denial of human rights, freedom from want and suffering, and freedom from the destruction of war and foreign intervention.

Nigeria is a great and influential nation, a regional and an international leader. We stand by you in your work. We know that Africans will always take the lead in shaping the destiny of your own people. And we know that this continent will enjoy the liberation that can come to those who put racial division and injustice behind them.

I believe that this day is coming for Africa. And on that day, blacks and whites alike will be able to say, in the words of a great man from my own State, Dr. Martin Luther King, Jr., "Free at last, free at last, great God Almighty, we are free at last."

Thank you very much.

(24) Current African Issues: Statement by Secretary of State Vance before the Subcommittee on African Affairs of the Committee on Foreign Relations, United States Senate, May 12, 1978. [5]

I am pleased to have this opportunity to appear before the African Affairs Subcommittee. I look forward to discussing with you the many critical issues which we now face in Africa.

Over the past 2 years, under the previous Administration as well as this, we have made significant strides in our relations with Africa. I believe that these improved relations have resulted from a number of factors:

- Our willingness to work with African nations in a spirit of cooperation and understanding;
- Our active support for majority rule and racial equality in southern Africa;
- Our serious efforts to deal with the many economic issues which are part of the North-South dialogue and which directly affect the lives of Africans; and
- Our genuine interest in African problems in their own terms and not only in the context of East-West relations.

The progress we have made is of fundamental importance to the United States. Our economy is increasingly tied to the resources and markets of Africa. Our ability to deal with global issues depends on African cooperation. And the policies of African nations are the key to the peaceful resolution of African disputes which otherwise invite outside intervention.

The recent trip to Nigeria by President Carter is a concrete example of what improved relations can mean to the United States. President Carter and Lt. Gen. Obasanjo were able to develop joint

⁵Text from *Bulletin,* July 1978: 29–31.

strategies on strengthening economic ties between our two nations and on the problems of Rhodesia and Namibia.

As a result of this new atmosphere in our relations with Africa, we are now able to work with Africans on issues which previously could have been difficult even to discuss. This has been evident, for example, in the field of human rights. We have told African nations that we are concerned about human rights not only in southern Africa but throughout the continent. And Africans now accept our emphasis on minority rights because they believe we care about majority rule. We cannot claim primary credit, but there have been some real improvements in the human rights situations in a number of African nations during the past year. In the case of Uganda, we are encouraged by the increased attention being given to the human rights question there by African nations.

In talking about the gains we have made in our relations with black African governments, I do not mean to imply that we have no interest in our relations with South Africa as well. At the start of this Administration we asked ourselves whether we could express our opposition to apartheid and at the same time elicit South Africa's cooperation in working for peaceful change and transition to majority rule in Namibia and Rhodesia. I believe that the experience of the first year shows we can.

The Challenges Ahead

Our progress should not obscure the problems we face in the coming months. Four important questions define the challenges which lie ahead.

- Can we maintain and strengthen the gains made in our relations with African nations, and particularly with Nigeria and others where there has been a dramatic turnaround during the past year or two?
- How can we make it clear to African nations which have traditionally been our friends that we maintain a strong interest in our relations with them?
- How can we most effectively work for peaceful change in southern Africa?
- How can we avoid Africa's becoming an East-West battleground and head off growing Soviet and Cuban intervention?

The answers to these questions depend on our policies in two important areas.

First, our ability to provide economic and military assistance will be a critical yardstick by which African states measure our willingness to respond to their problems and needs. In FY 1979, the Carter

Administration is asking Congress for $294 million in bilateral development aid for Africa, $25 million for the African Development Fund, and $45 million for security supporting assistance for nations caught in political crisis and turmoil. I cannot emphasize enough that it is our economic and social ties which lie at the heart of our relations with African countries. Our failure to respond to their economic needs would gravely damage the progress we have recently made.

At the same time we must recognize that countries threatened by the build-up of Cuban troops and Soviet arms on their borders have justifiable concern over their legitimate defense needs. Other governments are making their own efforts to help. We are anxious to do so without exacerbating regional military competition. As I said last July in a speech on Africa policy in St. Louis,[6] we will only transfer arms to Africa in exceptional circumstances. This is still the policy of the Carter Administration. But it is very important that we help threatened African states to meet their legitimate security needs. Military as well as economic assistance is a vital element in our efforts to reassure the African moderates.

In Sudan we have, therefore, agreed to sell 12 F–5 fighter aircraft and six C-130's which will provide that nation with an air defense and troop transport capability against potential threats.

Chad, which is faced with a serious Libyan-backed insurgency, has been made eligible to buy U.S. arms and receive third-country transfers. The problem is that Chad's economic situation is such that it cannot afford to purchase arms, and we cannot engage in a grant program. France is now providing the bulk of military assistance.

With Kenya we are evaluating that country's security requirements and will shortly provide Congress with a recommendation for increased assistance.

In Zaire we are cooperating with European nations in providing training and basic military equipment to improve that nation's defense capabilities.

Beyond economic and military assistance, the second major concern of our policy is our commitment to help resolve disputes peacefully, whether in the Horn or in southern Africa, or elsewhere. Only through the active pursuit of such a policy can we remove the opportunity for outside intervention.

Horn of Africa

Recent developments in the Horn are an example of the complexity and difficulties we face.

As you know, we have wanted to improve our relations with

[6]*AFR, 1977:* 310–19.

Somalia. However, we were unwilling to do so as long as Somali forces were invading Ethiopia.

Following the withdrawal of the Somali army from the Ogaden, President Carter sent Assistant Secretary Moose[7] to Mogadiscio for discussions with President Siad Barre. During this trip we began our discussions to obtain assurances from Siad that he would respect the internationally recognized borders of his neighbors as a precondition for any U.S. military assistance. Mr. Moose also informed the Somali leader that any U.S. aid would be limited in scope and confined to defensive items only. This matter is under active and continuing review. We will, of course, keep the committee informed of our deliberations.

Our relations with **Ethiopia,** though not good, have not deteriorated completely, and we would not like to see them broken off. Continued dialogue with that government is in our interest and in the interest of peace and stability in the region. We expect to announce the naming of a new Ambassador to Ethiopia in the near future.[8]

The Cuban presence in Ethiopia which now is at the 16-17,000 level is of serious concern to us. I will discuss the Soviet and Cuban role in Africa later. But let me say now that it is still not clear whether the Cubans will play a major combat role in Eritrea similar to their operations in the Ogaden.

We will continue to urge all of the parties concerned to make every effort toward a peaceful resolution of the dispute and withdrawal of Cuban forces. We face no less a challenge in dealing with issues of transition to majority rule and racial equality in South Africa, Namibia, and Rhodesia.

South Africa

In South Africa the basic problem we face is simply stated, yet terribly complex: How best can we encourage peaceful change?

We cannot ignore apartheid and the growing crisis within South Africa. We have to make it clear that a deterioration in our bilateral relations is inevitable if progress is not made. Recent actions by the Congress clearly indicate that it shares this concern.

At the same time, we have to maintain our ability to work with the South African Government for peaceful change in Rhodesia, Namibia, and South Africa itself. We have made it clear to South Africa that progress on each of the three will be recognized and have done so with regard to Namibia.

We understand the difficulties involved in change within South

[7]Assistant Secretary of State for African Affairs Richard M. Moose visited Somalia Mar. 18-23.
[8]On May 31, President Carter named Frederic L. Chapin as Ambassador.

Africa. We are not seeking to impose a simplistic formula for South Africa's future. Rather, we have urged the South African Government to begin to take truly significant steps—such as talking with acknowledged representative black leaders—away from apartheid and toward a system in which the full range of rights would be accorded to all inhabitants of South Africa, black and white alike.

South Africa's potential for nuclear weapons developments is another reason why it is important that we try to maintain an effective working relationship with that government. South Africa has the technical capability to produce a nuclear weapon. In recent months we have actively sought South Africa's agreement to sign the Non-proliferation Treaty (NPT). We have held talks with them on this question and will again.[9]

Some have urged that we cease all nuclear cooperation with South Africa because of apartheid. We believe that this question must be addressed in the context of the strong desirability of South Africa's adherence to the NPT and the application of safeguards with respect to the operation of all nuclear facilities in South Africa.

Namibia

Substantial progress has been made toward resolution of the Namibia problem as a result of a year-long effort by ourselves and the other four Western Security Council members, operating as the so-called contact group. Recent South African acceptance of the contact group proposal for a Namibian settlement was a significant breakthrough.[10] We are now making approaches to the front-line states,[11] Nigeria, and the South West Africa People's Organization (SWAPO), urging SWAPO's prompt acceptance of the settlement proposal.

Time is critical. If we do not obtain SWAPO's acceptance of the proposal in the near future, South Africa may go ahead with Namibian independence on its own terms.

The May 4 South African raid into Angola has set back our efforts to obtain SWAPO's agreement to the contact group proposal. Mistrust has been intensified.

A major substantive issue which remains unresolved is the status of Walvis Bay. While we consider that Walvis Bay is geographically, ethnically, culturally, and economically tied to Namibia, we have taken the position that this issue should be resolved through negotiations between postindependence Namibia and South Africa.

[9]Ambassador Gerard C. Smith discussed nuclear issues in Pretoria on June 25–29.
[10]Cf. Introduction at note 96.
[11]Angola, Botswana, Mozambique, Tanzania, and Zambia.

Rhodesia

This is also a crucial time in the effort to achieve a peaceful resolution of the Rhodesian problem.

The front-line Presidents are now working with us to try to secure a negotiated settlement in Rhodesia that will include all parties and end the conflict.

South African leaders have acknowledged the need for an internationally acceptable settlement that can bring peace.

Ian Smith has made some concessions in the Salisbury agreement, but they do not provide for an irreversible transfer of power to majority rule. In our own judgment, without broader agreement among the parties, or international acceptance, there will be neither a cease-fire nor a lifting of sanctions.

The Hove incident demonstrates the inevitable strains within the Salisbury group, as African leaders seek the sharing of real power.

The major question remaining is whether the internal and external nationalist parties can agree either to some formula for power-sharing during the transition, or to a neutral transition administration. The nub of the problem is that each side now seeks to dominate the transition government in a way that is unacceptable to the other and would make fair elections impossible.

But it is also clear that it is in the interest of both sides to keep the door open to a negotiated settlement including all the parties. The patriotic front had said it would attend a meeting with all parties and is willing to discuss all issues further; the Salisbury parties have not totally rejected a meeting of all parties but say they are skeptical of its success.

We believe the Anglo-American proposals provide the best elements for a settlement that will be acceptable to both sides: a cease-fire; a U.N. peacekeeping force; U.N. observers to monitor elections and activities of the police; a neutral transition administration with powers over defense, law and order, and electoral arrangements in the hands of an impartial administrator; integration of existing forces into one army that would be loyal to the elected government; and a democratic constitution with guarantees of individual rights for all, white as well as black.

It is our job to work to keep the door open to an inclusive settlement that will bring peace. If we and the British do not do so, the door may swing shut, with appalling consequences. That is why Secretary Owen and I went to meet with the parties in Salisbury and Dar es Salaam.[12] I believe some progress was made in these meetings. We will be sending Ambassador Low and British representa-

[12]Apr. 13–17.

tive John Graham for talks with the parties to attempt to move forward a meeting of all the parties.

I do not know whether or not we will succeed. But I can tell you that if we either accept the patriotic front proposals—giving them predominance—or endorse the Salisbury agreements—which would give the internal parties a dominant position—we will lose our ability to work with all sides toward a settlement that can bring peace. We must maintain our neutrality among all the parties and continue to stand for a fair solution in which ballots rather than bullets will decide fairly who gets power. I cannot emphasize this point too strongly, for the stakes are very high.

If an agreement cannot be achieved, there is bound to be escalating conflict. This will have a devastating effect on surrounding countries. And increased involvement by the Soviet Union and Cuba on one side and South Africa on the other would be likely.

Soviets and Cubans

A discussion of the issues and problems we face in Africa would not be complete without mention of Soviet and Cuban activities. Their increasing intervention raises serious problems. It escalates the level of conflict. It jeopardizes the independence of African states. It creates concern among moderates that Soviet weapons and Cuban troops can be used to determine the outcome of any dispute on the continent.

We are making a strenuous effort to counter Cuban and Soviet intervention in the disputes of African nations.

First, we have told the Soviets and the Cubans, publicly and privately, that we view their willingness to exacerbate armed conflict in Africa as a matter of serious concern.

Second, we have pointed out to the Soviets the dangers which their activities in Africa pose for our overall relations. I conveyed this view most recently when I was in Moscow.

At the same time, we do not believe that it is in our national interest to make a negotiating linkage between reaching a good SALT agreement, which is clearly in our basic security interests, and the inevitable competition with the Soviets which will continue to take place in Africa and elsewhere in the Third World. A SALT agreement should not be a reward for good behavior. It should be signed if it maintains our national interest and that of our allies, and not otherwise.

Third, we will continue to take advantage of our long-term strengths in relations with Africa. These are found primarily in our substantial aid, trade, and investment ties. During the period from

1970 to 1976 the United States provided over $2 billion in direct economic assistance to sub-Saharan Africa. In that same period the Soviets only provided $200 million. It is clear that the Soviet Union relies almost exclusively on arms transfers and its ability to take advantage of short-run military conflicts as the basis of its African policy. This is not, I believe, a viable long-term political strategy, as the history of Soviet involvement in Africa over the past decade demonstrates.

The fact that the West alone is able and willing to help resolve the long-term economic problems of African nations through the transfer of capital and technology gives us a fundamental advantage that we must continue to maintain.

Fourth, our continued support for peaceful resolution of disputes and building closer diplomatic ties is in itself a barrier to Soviet and Cuban designs. African trust in the sincerity of our commitment to peaceful but meaningful change in southern Africa has been critical to minimizing Soviet and Cuban involvement. If we should abandon our efforts in support of peaceful change, the front-line states would conclude that change can only come militarily.

If we abandon our current efforts, increasing conflict will thus tend not only to radicalize southern Africa itself but to alter the policies of nations elsewhere in Africa that are now becoming increasingly friendly to us.

Conclusion

Major challenges lie ahead, in implementing our policy and in countering Soviet and Cuban intervention.

It will be necessary for us to work closely with the Congress if we are to achieve our goals. We will need your support in a variety of ways:

• In providing long-term development assistance and humanitarian relief;
• In giving sympathetic consideration to military assistance for countries threatened by Soviet arms and Cuban troops; and
• In achieving and implementing negotiated settlements in southern Africa.

The involvement of the Foreign Relations Committee and the Congress as a whole in our Africa policy is key to the greater public understanding we seek. We need your counsel and your advice. We also need your help in explaining to the American people the great stakes our country has in a positive approach to Africa.

(25)   The Crisis in Zaire, May 1978.

(a)   Limitations on U.S. Action: News Conference Statement by President Carter, Chicago, May 25, 1978.[13]

U.S FOREIGN ASSISTANCE PROGRAMS

Our action to help rescue those who have been threatened in Zaire has virtually come to an end. Our transport aircraft, having completed their mission, will be returning to their bases within the next few days. I know that I speak for all Americans in expressing my abhorrence and distress over the violence and the killing that resulted from the Katangan invasion from Angola into Zaire. As great as the human tragedy was, it could have been much worse for the European nationals and for the Zairians, and the consequences much more severe for that country, if we had not joined in with our allies in a common effort.

Our action in Zaire was an appropriate and measured response to the situation. In this endeavor, we demonstrated both our ability to cooperate with our allies and our willingness to consult fully with the Congress before taking any actions. I imposed strict limits on the scope of our involvement and they were rigorously observed. I'm gratified that we had the full support of congressional leaders before and during the rescue efforts in Zaire.

The Government of Angola must bear a heavy responsibility for the deadly attack which was launched from its territory, and it's a burden and a responsibility shared by Cuba. We believe that Cuba had known of the Katangan plans to invade and obviously did nothing to restrain them from crossing the border. We also know that the Cubans have played a key role in training and equipping the Katangans who attacked.

Our action to support the rescue efforts in Zaire was taken pursuant to present law and under my constitutional powers and duties as Commander in Chief. However, the tragedy in Zaire as well as other recent developments has caused me to reflect on the ability of our Government, without becoming involved in combat, to act promptly and decisively to help countries whose security is threatened by external forces.

Our military and economic assistance programs are one of the most important means of assisting our friends. Some of the legislation governing these foreign aid programs has the effect of placing very narrow limits on where and when they can be used. Some of these limitations, though they were enacted many years ago and un-

[13]Text from *Presidential Documents,* 14: 971-2.

der special circumstances, continue to be entirely appropriate and advisable today. Others may be outmoded. For that reason, I have concluded that we should review the full range of legislation which now governs the operation of these programs. I've asked the Secretary of State to conduct this review and to consult with Congress constantly in preparing the study for me. We want to take a careful look at whether our legislation and procedures are fully responsive to the challenges that we face today.

I will meet with the congressional leadership myself in the near future, so that we can reach a joint decision on the appropriate steps to be taken.

As for the Clark amendment,[14] which prohibits action in regard to Angola, I have no present intention of seeking its modification, nor that of any other special piece of legislation. Any proposal for modifications will await our review of all restrictions and consultations with the appropriate committees of the Congress.

In the meantime, the existing provisions of law will, of course, be faithfully observed by me. But also in the meantime, we must resist further restrictions being attached to legislation now before the Congress.

As we consider new legislation, it is vital that we recognize our need to be able to adapt to rapidly changing circumstances. The foreign assistance legislation now pending in Congress contains several proposed restrictions on Presidential authority in economic and military aid programs. While I am prepared to report to Congress and to remain fully accountable to the American people, I will oppose further restrictions. I do so not necessarily because I intend to exercise my authority in the areas of question, but to preserve Presidential capacity to act in the national interests at a time of rapidly changing circumstances.

I believe that the congressional leadership and the American people will support this position.

Thank you very much.[15]

(b) *Implications of the Zaire Crisis:. Televised Interview with Zbigniew Brzezinski, Assistant to the President for National Security Affairs, on the "Meet the Press" Program of the National Broadcasting Company, May 28, 1978.*[16]

[14]Cf. Introduction at note 86.
[15]For the remainder of the news conference, see *Presidential Documents*, 14: 972-9.
[16]Text from *Bulletin,* July 1978: 26-8. Dr. Brzezinski was interviewed by Bob Abernathy (NBC News), Elizabeth Drew *(The New Yorker),* Bill Monroe (NBC News), and Carl T. Rowan (Field Syndicate).

Q. Castro says the Cubans were not involved in the invasion of Zaire. President Carter says they were. Foreign Minister Gromyko says that the President had bad information about Soviet and Cuban involvement in Africa. The Senate Foreign Relations Committee would like to know what the evidence is of Cuban involvement in the Zaire invasion. What can you tell us about the evidence?

A. First of all, I can assure you that what the President said was right. The invasion of Katanga or Shaba from Angola could not have taken place without the full knowledge of the Angolan Government.

It could not have taken place without the invading parties having been armed and trained by the Cubans and, indeed, perhaps also the East Germans, and we have sufficient evidence to be quite confident in our conclusion that Cuba shares the political and the moral responsibility for the invasion; indeed, even for the outrages that were associated with it.

If the Senate desires more information, I am certain that we can provide it, and I am quite confident that the judgment expressed by the President will stand up.

Q. Is this evidence from the Central Intelligence Agency, and, if so, will you be able to lay it out in the open for all to examine?

A. The information comes from a variety of sources, and we will provide it, if it is requested, to the legislative branch in an appropriate forum and in an appropriate way, depending on the nature of the information.

Q. Is the evidence clear and specific that the Cubans were directly involved in the invasion of Zaire or is it, as some U.S. officials have suggested, ambiguous, open to several interpretations?

A. I think there is a difference between direct involvement and responsibility. Direct involvement would mean direct participation, direct participation in the fighting, in command and control, presence on the ground, and all of that.

We are talking about responsibility, responsibility for something which should not have taken place, which is a violation of territorial integrity, which in fact is a belligerent act. We believe that the evidence we have sustains the proposition—more than that, sustains the conclusion that the Cuban Government and in some measure the Soviet Government bear the responsibility for this transgression, and this is a serious matter. This is a matter which is not conducive to international stability nor to international accommodation.

Q. While you were in China;[17] *did you encourage the Chinese to*

[17]May 20–23.

act any more openly to oppose Soviet ventures in the developing world?

A. The foreign policy of the People's Republic of China I don't think is based on encouragement from abroad. It reflects a comprehensive Chinese view of the international situation. I did note the fact that in the public statements, the Chinese have been very critical of the Soviet-Cuban intrusion into internal African affairs, and in my very comprehensive consultations with the Chinese leaders I did have the opportunity to discuss this issue.

Q. Last week the President, in talking about Angola, said that he did not have any interest in getting militarily involved in Angola and he was not interested in repeal of the Clark amendment[18] which sharply circumscribes our overt and covert activities in Angola.

You had expressed for some time interest in involving ourselves in Angola. Do you now see that that is a closed matter?

A. I am not quite sure on what you base your assertion that I have expressed an interest in becoming involved in Angola. I have held the view, and I do hold the view, that the Soviet-Cuban intrusion into African matters not only has the unfortunate effect of transforming difficult racial conflicts, of transforming the struggle for majority rule into also a very complicated and dangerous international conflict, as well as an ideological conflict.

I do not believe that this kind of Soviet-Cuban involvement ought to be cost-free, and there are a variety of ways in which concerned countries can convince the Soviets and the Cubans that their involvement, their intrusion, is not only conducive to greater international instability but in fact carries with it consequences which may be inimical to them as well.

I believe this is the responsible and the right course of action to contemplate because, otherwise, we will be faced in the longer run with an increasingly difficult situation, and I think we know from history that it is wiser to contain a conflict at a time when it is still subject to containment through discussion, responsible negotiation, limited counter moves than at the point at which it has already become a major conflagration.

Q. In talking about the lifting of congressional restrictions on our government's foreign policy actions, the President really pretty much confined himself last week to talking about economic restrictions. Are there other restrictions that you would like to see lifted so that you can oppose these Soviet and Cuban moves in Africa?

A. It really isn't a matter of me wanting this or that restriction lifted. What is involved is a serious discussion between the execu-

[18]Same as note 14 to Document 25a.

tive and the legislative branches about the best way to conduct our foreign policy at this time in history in response to the existing problems. I think it is useful for all of us to reflect on the historical origins of some of these restrictions. They were imposed at a time of very intense suspicion as to the intentions and conduct of the executive branch. They were imposed at the time of the Vietnamese war and the Watergate affair.

These conditions have changed. It seems to me that in the light of this change and given the nature of the problems that we now confront in some parts of the world, a serious constructive joint discussion between the executive and the legislative branches about the relevance, the scope of the existing restrictions, is timely and that is all that is involved.

I think the whole issue has been somewhat sensationalized and it is not being looked at in the proper political, as well as historical, perspective.

Q. You just put part of the blame for what you call the transgression in Zaire on East Germany and the Soviet Union. Our Vice President was just at the United Nations criticizing the Russians for deploying the SS-20 missile against Western Europe.[19] *You have been quoted as ridiculing Soviet actions in Ethiopia as you stood on the Great Wall in China. Are we to read from all this that detente is dead?*

A. First of all, I really wasn't ridiculing Soviet actions as I stood on the Great Wall of China. I did make some reference to it in the course of a casual conversation with a very charming Deputy Foreign Minister of the People's Republic of China.

As far as detente is concerned, I think it is terribly important for all of us to understand what it is and what it is not. There is a tendency to assume that detente is the equivalent of a comprehensive, indeed, total accommodation between the United States and the Soviet Union. That has never been the case.

Detente really is a process of trying to contain some of the competitive aspects in the relationship, competitive aspects which I believe still are predominant, and to widen the cooperative aspects. In that process at one time or another either the cooperative or the competitive aspects tend to be more predominant.

I would say that today the competitive aspects have somewhat surfaced and I would say categorically that this is due to the shortsighted Soviet conduct in the course of the last 2 or so years.

Q. Do you have any reason whatsoever to believe that Soviet conduct will cease to be shortsighted?

A. I think that if the Soviet Union realizes that there are genuine

[19]Cf. Document 7a.

rewards in accommodation and genuine costs in unilateral exploitation of the world's troubles, then the cooperative aspects will expand.

I am troubled by the fact that the Soviet Union has been engaged in a sustained and massive effort to build up its conventional forces, particularly in Europe, to strengthen the concentration of its forces on the frontiers of China, to maintain a vitriolic worldwide propaganda campaign against the United States, to encircle and penetrate the Middle East, to stir up racial difficulties in Africa, and to make more difficult a moderate solution of these difficulties, perhaps now to seek more direct access to the Indian Ocean.

This pattern of behavior I do not believe is compatible with what was once called the code of detente, and my hope is, through patient negotiations with us but also through demonstrated resolve on our part, we can induce the Soviet leaders to conclude that the benefits of accommodation are greater than the shortsighted attempt to exploit global difficulties.

Q. The President and the Secretary of State, you and Soviet Foreign Minister Gromyko, and others, have been talking about strategic arms limitations agreements. How close are we to some kind of agreement?

A. We are close, very close, and in some ways quite far away. That is to say, it is within grasp, if reason prevails. We have made, it seems to me, very proper, balanced proposals. If they are accepted, we could have agreement within days. If they are not accepted, we will wait until they are accepted.

Q. What, specifically, would you like this country to be able to do in Africa that Congress in some way prevents us from doing?

A. It seems to me that any course of action the United States undertakes in Africa ought to be a course of action which is undertaken in close consultation and conjunction with concerned African countries, with concerned European countries, and on the basis of mutual understanding between the executive and legislative branches.

Q. Do you have some specific thing that you would like us to do that we cannot now do?

A. Yes. I think from time to time there have been some things which perhaps it might have been desirable for the United States to do which, in the light of the legislation developed because of the events of the last few years, it has been difficult to undertake.

Q. What, Dr. Brzezinski?

A. But I wouldn't say these are major things. What is really needed, I think, is a broad discussion, a wider understanding, of the longer term strategic significance of this problem and on that basis a national policy which aims at consolidating and stabilizing the situation.

Q. Here is the United States with enormous power; there is Cuba, a small country. You and others denounce the presence in Africa of what, 40,000 Cuban troops? The other day you called them international marauders. But we don't seem to be able to do anything about it. Does that embarrass you?

A. It doesn't embarrass me; it concerns me. But it concerns me only in the sense that it seems to me that the proper response to this problem is not by the United States alone, but it is by the international community as a whole, with the United States taking a part in it, perhaps not even the leading part, but to be able to do that we first have to have an adequate national understanding of what the stakes are and then on that basis an international response which can take a variety of forms. In the first instance, diplomatic forms.

It seems to me essential for everyone to understand that in this day and age the intrusion of foreign military power to determine the outcome of specific and particular African conflicts is intolerable to international peace and is an insult to the Africans themselves.

The Africans are intelligent and mature people. They have international organizations of their own. It seems to me that African problems ought to be solved by the Africans themselves and not by 40,000 Cuban troops armed and delivered by the Soviet Union.

Q. Reports from China indicate that you pleased Chinese leaders by making a number of anti-Soviet remarks but that your visit did not result in any change in our relationship with China, any particular progress in that area. Is that roughly accurate?

A. No, I would say that is roughly inaccurate. The purpose of my visit to China was threefold. The first was to engage in a comprehensive consultative review of our respective positions on international affairs.

The second was to see whether, within the present context, our bilateral relationship can in some respects be further developed.

The third was to reaffirm our commitment to normalization and perhaps to make a modest contribution of an indirect sort to it. Both myself and the Chinese leaders agreed that the visit was beneficial; we agreed that it could be described as useful, important, and constructive. It focused largely on the long-term strategic nature of our relationship; the fact that we have certain common basic interests. And it stressed particularly the importance of mutual understanding of some of the key issues that confront respectively China and the United States.

Q. Those phrases you have been using fit into the category of diplomatic language that many people can't make heads nor tails of. Was there any specific change in our policy, any progress that resulted that you can put your finger on?
A. If two major countries engage in detailed reviews of their respective policies regarding major issues—and in the course of my visit to China I spent some 14 hours in sustained discussions not only with the Foreign Minister,[20] who plays an important role in his own right, but with Vice Premier Ch'en Hsi-lien and Chairman Hua Kuo-feng, and this as of itself entails certain longer range consequences.

The United States and the People's Republic of China do have parallel interests. In the pursuit of these parallel interests, we do undertake certain actions. If we understand each other better, this as of itself is of great significance.

Q. You have made several references to the strategic importance in Africa. Last week Ambassador Andrew Young said it is ridiculous to assign strategic importance to countries in Africa simply because the Cubans go in there. Do you think that is clear geopolitical thinking?
A. I think the question whether individual African countries are strategically important is not determined by whether the Cubans go into them, but by the nature of location or resources of these countries.

The African Horn is important because of its location, because of the size of the population of Ethiopia, because of its strategic consequences for access to Suez, because of its political impact on Saudi Arabia, if Saudi Arabia feels encircled.

Zaire is an important country because of its natural resources and size. These are the strategic concerns that have to be taken into account. The nature of these strategic concerns can be given an altogether new dimension. If a proxy power acting on behalf of our major rival in the world intrudes itself militarily, this does entail political consequences which one cannot afford to ignore.

The proper response to it is not panic or hysteria, but serious discussion of what this might mean in the longer run and on that basis a proper international response. I do not believe that sticking one's head into the sand is the best solution to difficult problems in the world.

Q. A few minutes ago you laid out a long list of horrible things done by the Soviet Union. Yet the Administration seems to do nothing but wring its hands. Would you be in favor of linkage to the extent of saying, "We will cease trade with you. You don't get

[20]Huang Hua.

our wheat. We will not transfer our technology if you continue to do the things you are doing."

A. First of all, I don't think it was a string of horrible things. It was a list of actions undertaken apparently in a combative or competitive spirit in order to gain political advantage in relationship to us. This is the kind of a conduct we wish to transform, to moderate.

Our response to it does operate on many levels. On the one hand we try to negotiate with the Soviets where it is mutually useful to negotiate—for example, the Strategic Arms Limitation Talks. On the other hand, we are trying to strengthen ourselves where it is necessary, and we have done a great deal, for example, in regard to NATO.

Beyond that we are trying to develop stronger relationships with various regional powers which do feel threatened by the Soviet Union and which, if encouraged and supported, can themselves help to provide overall global stability. Last but not least, we are enhancing our long-term relationship with the People's Republic of China as a contribution to global stability.

I don't believe we are wringing our hands. I think we are trying to respond responsibly to a complicated and difficult challenge.

Q. You talked several times on this program about the need for an international response to the Soviet and Cuban actions in Africa. Again, specifically what do you have in mind?

A. It seems to me that, in the first instance, the African countries themselves have to seriously review the question whether they wish to become the battlefield for foreign purposes, and therefore response by the African countries either through the Organization of African Unity or in some other form ought to be the first step. Secondly, the future of Africa does have a bearing on the situation in the Middle East to some extent and in Europe and hence these countries are concerned.

Q. Would you like to see an international peacekeeping force in Africa?

A. I don't think I want to be that specific at this moment and through this medium. What I am saying is there has to be an international response to an international problem.

(26) "An Affirmative Approach": Address by Secretary of State Vance before the 58th Annual Meeting of the U.S. Jaycees, Atlantic City, June 20, 1978. [21]

[21]Department of State Press Release 257; text from *Bulletin,* Aug. 1978: 10-13.

I want to speak today about an area of the world that has been much in the news recently: Africa. The headlines of today are about the so-called "trouble spots"—southern Africa, Ethiopia, Zaire, and elsewhere. The deeper reality of Africa, however, includes much more than the conflicts, crises, and foreign involvement that seize our immediate attention. Africa is a huge continent with great natural and human resources. Most of its people now live in peace and are making steady progress in building the economic and political strength of their nations. We are working to help the nations and people of Africa in this task.

African nations play a key role in the United Nations and in other international arenas. They can help make the difference between success and failure in our efforts to stop the spread of nuclear weapons, to control the accumulation of conventional armaments, to stop hunger and malnutrition, and to help manage the world's resources for the future.

Africa is increasingly important to us in even more immediate ways. Some of you buy and sell goods that require copper, manganese, cobalt, or potash. You have coffee and cocoa in your kitchens. Africa supplies us with between a quarter and one-half of our imports of these and many other raw materials, including 40% of our petroleum imports.

Similarly, our exports to Africa are increasing rapidly. Many of you come from farm States. You have a direct interest in the fact that Africa provided a market last year for well over $1 billion worth of U.S. agricultural produce.

I want to describe today our policy toward Africa and how it is based on American interests and African realities.

U.S. Approach

Last July in a speech on the future of U.S.-Africa policy,[22] I said that we can be neither right nor effective if we treat Africa simply as an arena for East-West competition. Our Africa policy has not changed. Its objectives remain forward looking and positive.

President Carter restated our commitment to a positive strategy in his recent speech at Annapolis.[23] He said that our Africa policy is based on an affirmative approach—an approach that emphasizes working with the nations of Africa to help resolve African problems and meet African aspirations. The President went on to say that our goal is an Africa that is free: ". . . free of the dominance of outside powers, free of the bitterness of racial injustice, free of conflict, and free of the burdens of poverty and hunger and disease."

[22]*AFR, 1977:* 310–19.
[23]Document 8.

This is our vision of Africa's future—a vision we share with the people of Africa. But its realization has been complicated in recent months by conflict and outside interference.

The continued presence of large quantities of Soviet arms and thousands of Cuban troops in certain parts of Africa raises serious concerns. The size and duration of their military presence jeopardizes the independence of African states. It creates concern on the part of African nations that outside weapons and troops will be used to determine the outcome of any conflict on the continent. And it renders more difficult the efforts of Africans to resolve these disputes through peaceful means.

It will not be our policy to mirror Soviet and Cuban activities in Africa because such a course would not be effective in the long run and would only escalate military conflict with great human suffering. Our best course is to help resolve the problems which create the excuse for external intervention and to help strengthen the ability of Africans to defend themselves.

What are the ingredients of a positive African policy? Simply stated they are:

- A strong U.S. commitment to social justice and economic development in Africa;
- Efforts to help resolve African disputes peacefully;
- Respect for African nationalism;
- Support for legitimate African defense needs; and
- Finally, helping to foster respect for human rights which strengthens the political fabric of African nations.

We are ready to work with all African nations toward these common goals. We now have good relations with almost every nation there. We have not been preoccupied with labels or categories for these are particularly misleading in the African context. We do not want to see Africa divided along ideological or other lines.

Application of Policy

Let me describe briefly how we are applying this policy to the African issues of greatest concern.

For a generation, the anguish of southern Africa has posed a special challenge to American foreign policy. Our own society has struggled with racial discrimination, and we have made great progress. But our struggle remains profoundly difficult, as individuals of all races look into their own souls and find answers that shape the soul of our nation. We thus feel a particular sympathy for those in South Africa, Namibia, and Rhodesia who are going through a similar struggle—both blacks and whites.

Our policy toward the region of southern Africa proceeds from the unmistakable fact that change is coming. The great question is whether peace or violence will be the instrument of change. For the sake of the peoples in the region and for the sake of our own interests there, we are working for peaceful change. Violence in southern Africa bears many costs—in human terms, in a legacy of political polarization, in damage to economic progress and our own economic interests, in the harm done to other nations in the area, and in the excuse it presents for outside interference.

Rhodesia. With respect to Rhodesia, we have developed a proposal, in partnership with the British Government and with the encouragement of African governments in the region, that would facilitate a rapid and peaceful transition to majority rule.

The plan provides for bringing together the external nationalists who have formed the patriotic front with Ian Smith and the black leaders who have joined him in an "internal settlement." It also calls for free elections, an impartial administration during the election period, and a constitution protecting the rights of all citizens— white and black.

Concessions toward peace have been made by all parties in this gathering conflict. However, neither side can create a new nation with a decent chance for a peaceful and prosperous future without the participation of the other. And each now rejects the other's claim to predominance during the critical election period.

It is our hope to bring them together, either to work out power-sharing arrangements among themselves or to agree on a neutral solution such as the one we have proposed.

In the course of these long and difficult negotiations, we have often been asked to favor one side or the other. Why, some ask, do we not support the "internal settlement"? Why, others suggest, do we not throw our weight behind the patriotic front?

The answer is simple but important. If we were to choose one side or the other, the chance for a peaceful solution would be greatly diminished. We would become a party to the conflict rather than a party to the effort to prevent it. We want to help find a way for all groups to participate so the people of Rhodesia can fairly decide how they will govern themselves.

I do not know whether we will succeed. But I can tell you that if we and the governments with which we are cooperating should give up on our efforts, the door to peace will slam shut with tragic consequences. We must maintain our impartiality among all the parties and continue to stand for a fair solution—to be reached, not by spilling blood but by casting ballots.

Namibia. In Namibia we are also at a critical stage. For over a year, the United States has joined with Britain, France, Germany, and Canada—what is called the contact group—to assure that the people of this territory achieve independence fairly and peacefully and in a fashion which will bring international recognition and support.

Significant progress has been made. South Africa has accepted the proposal which the contact group put forward. Both they and the black nationalists of the South West Africa People's Organization (SWAPO) agree on a number of important ingredients for a settlement:

* Free and fair elections for the people to determine their own government;
* A substantial U.N. military and civilian presence to insure that the agreement is fully and fairly implemented; and
* The phased withdrawal of the majority of the South African forces pending independence.

Important issues remain to be resolved however. Mistrust between SWAPO and South Africa is great, and our representatives are continuing their efforts to reach a final agreement.

South Africa. Regarding South Africa itself, we and others are using what influence we have to try to persuade its leaders that a future of peaceful progress best serves their interests, the interests of all the people of South Africa, and the interests of the world community.

We have made it clear to the South African Government that a failure to begin to make genuine progress toward an end to racial discrimination and full political participation for all South African citizens can only have an increasingly adverse impact on our relations.

Our policy toward South Africa should not be misunderstood. We have no wish to see the whites driven from the home of their forbears. We suggest only that they seek a way to live in peace and justice with the majority of their fellow citizens. South Africans of all races, and not just its white citizens, should decide their country's future. We do not seek to impose either a timetable or a blueprint for this progress. But I hope, as do all who have sympathy for the problems any society encounters in facing fundamental change, that the beginning of basic progress will soon be seen.

Horn of Africa. Elsewhere in Africa, as well, we are seeking to dampen the flames of conflict. In the Horn of Africa this year, decades of bitter rivalry among ethnic groups and nations culminated in a war between the Ethiopian Government and the separatist movements in the Province of Eritrea. These problems have been complicated further by substantial quantities of Soviet arms and the continued presence of large numbers of Cuban troops. We have vigorously supported African efforts to mediate the border dispute between Somalia and Ethiopia.

Peace and stability will not come to the region as long as Ethiopia and Somalia believe they can solve their problems through military means. Any encouragement by Somalia of insurgent forces in the Ogaden can only increase tensions in the region. We believe that a lasting settlement to the Eritrean problem can only come from political reconciliation, not from recourse to arms.

Conflicts in the Horn have diverted material and human resources from the serious economic and social problems which affect millions of people in the region. A grave famine now threatens over a million Ethiopian people with starvation. The food situation throughout the region—and as far away as Tanzania and Pakistan—could be worsened by large swarms of locusts which are not being adequately controlled. The United States has already contributed $1.5 million for relief operations in the famine area. We are also proceeding to provide assistance to the regional organization which is conducting the fight to curb the spread of locusts and save croplands.

Zaire. In Zaire, as in the Horn, historical disputes and ethnic differences have fueled a serious conflict. When Zaire's Shaba Province was invaded last month from Angola, we cooperated with other nations to rescue those trapped in the fighting, to help preserve Zaire's territorial integrity, and to help prevent its economic collapse. We demonstrated that we can act immediately, firmly, and sensibly in response to African requests.

Even if stability is restored in Shaba, however, it would not finally solve Zaire's problems. That nation is still threatened by severe economic problems and the prospect of territorial fragmentation. The future depends primarily on what Zaire itself is willing to do, with the help of others, to meet the serious problems it faces.

We are prepared, along with others, to help Zaire get back on its feet. But the economic and security assistance we provide must be accompanied by a genuine effort on Zaire's part to solve its long-term problems. Increased economic aid to Zaire without internal economic reforms would be fruitless. Western security assistance must be accompanied by the cooperation of Zaire in strengthening the management and organization of its armed forces. And until there is broader participation in the political life of Zaire, it will be difficult to achieve real stability.

In addition, if we are to avoid more Shaba incidents in the future, Zaire and Angola must reach agreement to respect their common border and not to interfere in each other's internal affairs.

In this connection, we believe it could be helpful to increase our consultations with the Angolan Government and begin working with it in more normal ways in order to improve the prospects for reconciliation between Angola and Zaire, as well as for achieving a peaceful settlement in Namibia.

In these areas of conflict, and in the peaceful development of the continent, we are pursuing a firm and sensible strategy to promote our long-term interests and strengthen our ties with African nations. It combines efforts to avoid East-West confrontation and positive regional policies that respond to local realities.

Essential Elements of Approach

Let me return to the essential elements of our approach.

* We will rely on our strengths—our trade, aid, economic, and cultural ties—which have developed over the years. To these we have added our common commitment to social justice and human development. These are the most enduring elements in the relationship between Africa and America. They bind us to nations throughout the continent.

  It is essential to the success of our policies that Africans know that we share their goal of economic development. This means increasing trade and investment in ways that benefit both Africa and the United States. And it means continuing to increase our aid to African nations. We will do so because there is genuine need, because it is important to our own economic well-being, and because it will strengthen the independence of African nations.

* Our strategy is to work with others in Africa and beyond for the peaceful resolution of disputes. We can help African nations avoid human suffering and prevent the diversion of resources from human development. Moreover, a potential conflict resolved is a conflict of which others cannot take advantage. We will help to strengthen the effectiveness of the United Nations and regional organizations such as the Organization of African Unity which can play a vital role in working for peace. Ultimately, it is Africans themselves who will bring peace to their continent.

* We will continue to respect the growing spirit of African national independence because it is important to economic and political progress and because Africans will firmly resist yielding their hard-won independence to outside powers. The history of the last 20 years demonstrates this fact.

* It has been our policy since the beginning of the Administra-

tion to consider security requests from African nations with legitimate defense needs. Our friends in Africa must know that we can and will help them to strengthen their ability to defend themselves. Any increase in American military assistance will be done prudently and will be consistent with this Administration's policy of seeking arms restraint and concentrating our assistance on economic development.

• In private and public, we have emphasized our concern about the nature of Soviet activities in Africa and we have been in contact with European, Arab, and African countries and members of the nonaligned movement who share our concern. We have pointed out to the Soviets the problems which their activities pose for Africa and for our overall relations. Our actions will continue to be consistent with our commitment to the peaceful resolution of disputes and with due regard for the concerns of those African countries affected.

• In Africa as elsewhere, we will work along with others of all races to foster respect for individual human rights. We believe that civil and political liberties and the right of each individual to basic necessities, such as decent health care, education, and food, should be respected throughout the continent.

The strategy we are pursuing is a realistic approach that emphasizes our strengths and encourages an evolution of events that is in both Africa's interests and our own. It is a strategy that has earned the support of African leaders throughout the continent.

We do not ignore that there is a residue of suspicion among some Africans who have fought against colonialism that our policy is simply a tactic and not a reflection of a genuine commitment to African needs. Only time and our continued demonstration that we mean what we say will meet this problem.

We are convinced that an affirmative approach to African aspirations and problems is also the most effective response to Soviet and Cuban activities there. Any other strategy would weaken Africa by dividing it. And it would weaken us by letting others set our policies for us.

(27)   Policy. Toward South Africa: Address by Anthony Lake, Director of the Policy Planning Staff of the Department of State, before the Conference on U.S. Foreign Policy in Africa, San Francisco, October 31, 1978. [24]

[24]Text from *Bulletin,* Jan. 1979: 18-20.

As we consider U.S. policy toward South Africa, it is important that we keep in mind three basic facts.

* The problem of racial polarization in South Africa is serious and is growing.
* Change will come in South Africa. The welfare of the people there, and American interests, will be profoundly affected by the way in which it comes. The question is whether it will be peaceful or not.
* Our efforts to promote constructive and peaceful change have involved both cooperation and strong differences with South Africa. Over the years, the differences have grown as the problems in South Africa have grown.

I would like to discuss each of these briefly.

Increased Racial Polarization

Over the years, a system has been built in South Africa which mandates racial separation and perpetuates inequality; the problems within South Africa are therefore growing.

* In distribution of the land, 13% is reserved for the 71% of the population who are black; 87% is reserved for the 17% who are white.
* Over 60% of the black population lives in areas reserved for whites. Think for a moment what this means for those people: All of them must carry passes; most would be forced to overcrowded so-called "homelands" if they lost their jobs; their families are often not allowed to live with them.
* The average black income is less than one-eighth of average white earnings.
* Education is compulsory and free for white students. It is neither compulsory nor free for blacks; and spending per child in white schools is over 15 times that in black schools.
* Basic facilities—housing, electricity, plumbing, health care— are woefully inadequate for blacks, far inferior to those for whites.
* South African blacks who live and work in white areas have no say in making the laws which so dominate every area of their lives. They are defined by the South African Government as citizens of small and fragmented homelands which they may never have seen; they have no citizenship rights where they live and work and form an essential part of economic life.

The white Afrikaners who dominate the politics of South Africa have their own historic roots and their own fears for the future. Their forebears came to South Africa in the 16th century; they have developed their own language, culture, and religion. If their security were jeopardized in South Africa, they would have nowhere else to go. They, too, are Africans.

Our hope must be that they can be convinced, while there is still time, that racial progress will do more to secure their future than to threaten it. There has been, and there may continue to be, some relaxation in the practice of apartheid in South Africa. Some hotels, restaurants, bars, and theaters have been integrated. "Whites Only" barriers in some public facilities have been removed. It has been made easier for blacks to own homes in white areas.

We should welcome these changes. But most black South Africans see little sign that fundamental change is being achieved. For generations, most black South African leaders have tried to engage white leaders in constructive dialogue on the future of the country; they have sought to reason and persuade; they have attempted to find a way to work together with whites toward greater political and economic equality. Yet many of these leaders have been detained. Their organizations have been banned.

With each failure to achieve progress, blacks have become more doubtful about a strategy of dialogue and peaceful demonstrations. Events in recent months have added greatly to this bitterness and may have convinced many, particularly of the younger generation, that efforts to achieve peaceful change are futile. The killing of students during the Soweto uprisings, the deaths in detention of Steven Biko and other young leaders, and finally the bannings and detentions of numerous black leaders and organizations on October 19 of last year have left a deep legacy of bitterness.[25]

Promoting Peaceful Change

Recognizing that our influence is limited, it is deeply in our interest to do what we can to halt this trend toward racial polarization and violence and to promote serious, peaceful change.

It is clear that change will come in South Africa. But if significant peaceful progress does not begin soon, the gap between black and white could become irremediable. This would have tragic consequences for the people of South Africa and for the region. If an organic, irreversible crisis developed, we would have fewer and fewer policy choices. And it would have serious impact on our own national interests.

• Such a crisis could produce strains in our relations with other

[25]Cf. *AFR, 1977:* 325-7.

African nations. Our ties—economic and political—to these countries are increasingly important.

- A growing racial confrontation in South Africa could have serious domestic repercussions for the United States.
- South Africa has great natural wealth and is an important source of key raw materials. We and the rest of the world have an interest in economic stability in South Africa and in the development of all her human as well as natural resources.
- Growing racial conflict in South Africa would provide an opportunity for intervention by outside powers and could bring ideological as well as racial polarization.

I think most Americans agree that we should do what we can to promote peaceful change in South Africa, although some are more concerned that it be peaceful, others that it be change. The major arguments come with regard to how best we can use our influence—recognizing its limits—to promote peaceful change. I look forward to exploring those arguments with you this morning.

Broadly speaking, there have been, I believe, two poles in approaches to this question: on the one hand pressure and isolation; on the other, communication and persuasion.

Over the past three decades, some have argued that through closer ties with South Africa, we can help the whites find a way to liberalize South African society. Our economic ties, they would argue, help provide opportunities for blacks; and higher positions for blacks in the economy, particularly in skilled jobs and management, will eventually lead to political rights. They would also point to the positive example which American companies can set by following fair employment practices, as in the code developed by the Reverend Leon Sullivan and endorsed by a number of American companies.

A second school rejects this theory, primarily on the grounds that three decades of economic growth have not produced fundamental change in South Africa; that foreign economic investment has helped strengthen a repressive system; and that the only course which can bring the whites to allow real change is to use economic leverage against them. They would argue that the South African Government must be isolated from the international community if it persists in a system which all regard as unjust; and that strong, clear opposition by the world community to apartheid will provide encouragement to the majority within South Africa who have been denied their freedom.

The primary charges leveled against this approach have been that cutting off our economic and other relations with South Africa could not force change, since the South Africans could survive such measures; and that we would therefore only be damaging our own economic interests while driving the white South Africans further behind a defensive and rigid shell.

Our own approach has been to try to make the following points clear to the South African Government.

We hope that a deterioration in American relations with South Africa can be avoided—this would not be in our interest or South Africa's.

We wish to work together with the South African Government toward resolution of all three of the region's critical problems: Rhodesia, Namibia, and apartheid in South Africa itself. There must be progress on all of these issues. We will welcome and recognize South African efforts to achieve progress on any of them.

We will do whatever we can to support meaningful change in South Africa; but we recognize that we cannot dictate the precise nature of change. It is for the people of South Africa themselves— all the people—to determine the future of their society. We have urged that leaders in the South African Government soon begin a serious dialogue with representative leaders of all the people to explore ways to resolve the country's growing problems.

But if there is not significant progress in South Africa, relations between our two countries will inevitably deteriorate. This is a fact, not a preference. Our own values, the fundamental national commitment of the American people to the political, civil, and economic rights of every individual born on this Earth, as well as our standing in the international community and our long-term interests in the region, require our disassociation from racial discrimination and a denial of basic human rights. We would prefer, of course, a future in which progress within South Africa allowed us to strengthen our ties to that country. Such a future would be better for the people of South Africa, for the region, and for us. It depends, as I have said, on the decisions of the South African Government.

Basic U.S. Efforts

Over the years, we have sought to encourage this peaceful change in four basic ways.

First, we have sought to demonstrate in constructive ways our strong commitment to racial equality.

- We have brought South African representatives of all races to the United States to obtain a first-hand understanding of our outlook and our commitment to racial equality.
- Through investment guidelines, we have encouraged American firms in South Africa to follow fair employment practices. And we have supported the Sullivan code.

- Our diplomatic representatives as a matter of policy have integrated their social functions.

Second, we have expressed our concern about the impact of apartheid on the lives of black South Africans and have sought to maintain ties with the black South African community.

- Our Embassy has been in the forefront among diplomatic missions in demonstrating opposition to political repression and support for black leadership.
- Ours was the only foreign ambassador to attend the funerals of Robert Sobukwe and Steve Biko.
- We have consistently protested detentions and bannings of political leaders.
- We have tried to keep in contact with students, labor and political leaders, religious leaders, and other representatives of the black community.
- We maintain a library in Soweto.
- We have provided refugee assistance for the students who have fled South Africa to Botswana and Lesotho.

Third, in encouraging the South African Government to work toward peaceful resolution of the Namibian and Rhodesian conflicts, we could have some impact on the nature of change in South Africa itself.

- These efforts demonstrate clearly the value of peaceful change as opposed to mounting racial conflict. They also demonstrate our willingness to work cooperatively with the South African Government in implementing change.
- These negotiations show that there will be broad international support for efforts to bring peace and justice in southern Africa; and that the international community will work to find reasonable compromises in resolving these difficult problems.
- If change can be brought peacefully in Rhodesia and Namibia—in ways that protect the rights of all individuals, black and white—it could have a significant impact on how South Africans regard internal change.

Fourth, we have indicated to South Africa the fact that if it does not make significant progress toward racial equality, its relations with the international community, including the United States, are bound to deteriorate.

- Over the years, we have tried through a series of progressive steps to demonstrate that the United States cannot and will not be associated with the continued practice of apartheid.

* In 1962 the United States imposed a voluntary arms embargo against South Africa, strengthened in 1963.
* In 1964 we restricted Export-Import Bank (Eximbank) financing to South Africa to exclude any support for trade with the government and ended direct loans.
* In 1967 we terminated all U.S. naval ship visits to South African ports.
* In November of last year we supported the U.N. mandatory arms embargo on South Africa.[26] This February regulations were issued implementing our own decision to prohibit all sales of any kind to the South African military or police.
* We have recently tightened procedures on the sale of civilian aircraft to South Africa, to help assure that they will not be used for paramilitary purposes.
* Recently, Congress passed legislation further restricting Eximbank facilities for South Africa, stating that they could only be made available to firms which are proceeding toward implementation of fair employment practices.
* And we have refused to recognize the "homelands" which the South African government has declared to be "independent."

There are limits to our ability to encourage change in South Africa. We cannot dictate a blueprint or a timetable for progress, nor should we. It is for the people of South Africa—both black and white—to determine their own future.

We have tried in such policies both to make it clear that we cannot support apartheid and to demonstrate that we are concerned about the rights of all South Africans. It is not white South Africans as human beings that we oppose but a system of racial separation and inequality. We believe that the best way to assure the future rights and security of all South Africans is for them to begin a progressive transformation of that system.

In 1962 ex-Chief Albert Luthuli, an extraordinary leader and winner of the 1960 Nobel peace prize, wrote that a future of anguish and suffering for people of all races in South Africa could be avoided. "We seek no vengeance," he wrote. "More than other continents, perhaps, and as much as any other nation on this continent, we need the ways of peace, the ways of industry, the ways of concord." "Will," he asked, "the outstretched hand be taken?"

Sixteen years have passed. Divisions run deeper. It is fundamen-

[26]U.N. Security Council Resolution 418 (1977), unanimously adopted Nov. 4, 1977; cf. *AFR, 1977:* 77–8.

tally in our interest to work all the more for the grasping of that hand, while it still may be offered.

The course I have described is the policy which we believe brings the best chance of encouraging the peaceful change so much in everyone's interest. It avoids, I believe, the dangers presented either by policies which would convince South Africa's whites that we are implacably hostile to them, and that they must therefore go it alone without regard for our concerns or policies which falsely imply that we could ever be indifferent to the plight of the victims of institutionalized racial injustice.

These are the best policies we have found. I do not pretend that they are the only possible policies, or that they will necessarily succeed. Our influence is limited. We must therefore use it with all the skill we can find. We must continue to put our minds to the complexities of issues that our hearts—as well as our brains—tell us are terribly important. That is why I look forward so much to hearing and learning from your comments today.

6. NEW ERA FOR THE AMERICAS

(28) *The Treaties with Panama: Radio-Television Address by President Carter, February 1, 1978.* [1]

Good evening.

Seventy-five years ago, our Nation signed a treaty which gave us rights to build a canal across Panama, to take the historic step of joining the Atlantic and Pacific Oceans. The results of the agreement have been of great benefit to ourselves and to other nations throughout the world who navigate the high seas.

feats of history. Although massive in concept and construction, it's relatively simple in design and has been reliable and efficient in operation. We Americans are justly and deeply proud of this great achievement.

The canal has also been a source of pride and benefit to the people of Panama—but a cause of some continuing discontent. Because we have controlled a 10-mile-wide strip of land across the heart of their country and because they considered the original terms of the agreement to be unfair, the people of Panama have been dissatisfied with the treaty. It was drafted here in our country and was not signed by any Panamanian. Our own Secretary of State who did sign the original treaty said it was "vastly advantageous to the United States and . . . not so advantageous to Panama."

In 1964, after consulting with former Presidents Truman and Eisenhower, President Johnson committed our Nation to work towards a new treaty with the Republic of Panama. [2] And last summer, after 14 years of negotiations under two Democratic Presidents and two Republican Presidents, we reached and signed an agreement that is fair and beneficial to both countries. [3] The United States Senate will soon be debating whether these treaties should be ratified.

[1]Text from *Presidential Documents,* 14: 258–63.
[2]Cf. Johnson statement, Dec. 18, 1964, in *Documents, 1964:* 312–14.
[3]Summary of the two treaties, signed in Washington Sept. 7, 1977, in *AFR, 1977:* 343–5; Carter-Torrijos Statement of Understanding, Oct. 14, 1977, in same: 377–8.

Throughout the negotiations, we were determined that our national security interests would be protected; that the canal would always be open and neutral and available to ships of all nations; that in time of need or emergency our warships would have the right to go to the head of the line for priority passage through the canal; and that our military forces would have the permanent right to defend the canal if it should ever be in danger. The new treaties meet all of these requirements.

Let me outline the terms of agreement. There are two treaties—one covering the rest of this century,[4] and the other guaranteeing the safety, openness, and neutrality of the canal after the year 1999, when Panama will be in charge of its operation.[5]

For the rest of this century, we will operate the canal through a nine-person board of directors. Five members will be from the United States and four will be from Panama. Within the area of the present Canal Zone, we have the right to select whatever lands and waters our military and civilian forces need to maintain, to operate, and to defend the canal.

About 75 percent of those who now maintain and operate the canal are Panamanians; over the next 22 years, as we manage the canal together, this percentage will increase. The Americans who work on the canal will continue to have their rights of employment, promotion, and retirement carefully protected.

We will share with Panama some of the fees paid by shippers who use the canal. As in the past, the canal should continue to be self-supporting.

This is not a partisan issue. The treaties are strongly backed by President Gerald Ford and by former Secretaries of State Dean Rusk and Henry Kissinger. They are endorsed by our business and professional leaders, especially those who recognize the benefits of good will and trade with other nations in this hemisphere. And they were endorsed overwhelmingly by the Senate Foreign Relations Committee which, this week, moved closer to ratification by approving the treaties, although with some recommended changes which we do not feel are needed.

And the treaties are supported enthusiastically by every member of the Joint Chiefs of Staff—General George Brown, the Chairman, General Bernard Rogers, Chief of Staff of the Army, Admiral James Holloway, Chief of Naval Operations, General David Jones, Chief of Staff of the Air Force, and General Lewis Wilson, Commandant of the Marine Corps—responsible men whose profession is the defense of this Nation and the preservation of our security.

The treaties also have been overwhelmingly supported through-

[4]Text of the Panama Canal Treaty in same: 345–64.
[5]Text of the Neutrality Treaty in same: 364–9.

out Latin America, but predictably, they are opposed abroad by some who are unfriendly to the United States and who would like to see disorder in Panama and a disruption of our political, economic, and military ties with our friends in Central and South America and in the Caribbean.

I know that the treaties also have been opposed by many Americans. Much of that opposition is based on misunderstanding and misinformation. I've found that when the full terms of the agreement are known, most people are convinced that the national interests of our country will be served best by ratifying the treaties.

Tonight, I want you to hear the facts. I want to answer the most serious questions and tell you why I feel the Panama Canal treaties should be approved.

The most important reason—the only reason—to ratify the treaties is that they are in the highest national interest of the United States and will strengthen our position in the world. Our security interests will be stronger. Our trade opportunities will be improved. We will demonstrate that as a large and powerful country, we are able to deal fairly and honorably with a proud but smaller sovereign nation. We will honor our commitment to those engaged in world commerce that the Panama Canal will be open and available for use by their ships—at a reasonable and competitive cost—both now and in the future.

Let me answer specifically the most common questions about the treaties.

Will our Nation have the right to protect and defend the canal against any armed attack or threat to the security of the canal or of ships going through it?

The answer is yes, and is contained in both treaties and also in the statement of understanding between the leaders of our two nations.

The first treaty says, and I quote: "The United States of America and the Republic of Panama commit themselves to protect and defend the Panama Canal. Each Party shall act, in accordance with its constitutional processes, to meet the danger resulting from an armed attack or other actions which threaten the security of the Panama Canal or [of] ships transiting it."

The neutrality treaty says, and I quote again: "The United States of America and the Republic of Panama agree to maintain the regime of neutrality established in this Treaty, which shall be maintained in order that the Canal shall remain permanently neutral. . . ."

And to explain exactly what that means, the statement of understanding says, and I quote again: "Under (the Neutrality Treaty), Panama and the United States have the responsibility to assure that the Panama Canal will remain open and secure to ships of all nations. The correct interpretation of this principle is that each of

AMERICAN FOREIGN RELATIONS 1978

the two countries shall, in accordance with their respective constitutional processes, defend the Canal against any threat to the regime of neutrality, and consequently [shall] have the right to act against the Canal or against the peaceful transit of vessels through the Canal.''

It is obvious that we can take whatever military action is necessary to make sure that the canal always remains open and safe.

Of course, this does not give the United States any right to intervene in the internal affairs of Panama, nor would our military action ever be directed against the territorial integrity or the political independence of Panama.

Military experts agree that even with the Panamanian Armed Forces joined with us as brothers against a common enemy, it would take a large number of American troops to ward off a heavy attack. I, as President, would not hesitate to deploy whatever armed forces are necessary to defend the canal, and I have no doubt that even in a sustained combat, that we would be successful. But there is a much better way than sending our sons and grandsons to fight in the jungles of Panama.

We would serve our interests better by implementing the new treaties, an action that will help to avoid any attack on the Panama Canal.

What we want is the permanent right to use the canal—and we can defend this right through the treaties—through real cooperation with Panama. The citizens of Panama and their government have already shown their support of the new partnership, and a protocol to the neutrality treaty will be signed by many other nations, thereby showing their strong approval.

The new treaties will naturally change Panama from a passive and sometimes deeply resentful bystander into an active and interested partner, whose vital interests will be served by a well-operated canal. This agreement leads to cooperation and not confrontation between our country and Panama.

Another question is: Why should we give away the Panama Canal Zone? As many people say, "We bought it; we paid for it; it's ours."

I must repeat a very important point: We do not own the Panama Canal Zone. We have never had sovereignty over it. We have only had the right to use it.

The Canal Zone cannot be compared with United States territory. We bought Alaska from the Russians, and no one has ever doubted that we own it. We bought the Louisiana Purchases—Territories from France, and that's an integral part of the United States.

From the beginning, we have made an annual payment to Panama to use their land. You do not pay rent on your own land. The Panama Canal Zone has always been Panamanian territory. The U.S.

Supreme Court and previous American Presidents have repeatedly acknowledged the sovereignty of Panama over the Canal Zone.

We've never needed to own the Panama Canal Zone, any more than we need to own a 10-mile-wide strip of land all the way through Canada from Alaska when we build an intérnational gas pipeline.

The new treaties give us what we do need—not ownership of the canal but the right to use it and to protect it. As the Chairman of the Joint Chiefs of Staff has said, "The strategic value of the canal lies in its use."

There's another question: Can our naval ships, our warships, in time of need or emergency, get through the canal immediately instead of waiting in line?

The treaties answer that clearly by guaranteeing that our ships will always have expeditious transit through the canal. To make sure that there could be no possible disagreement about what these words mean, the joint statement says that expeditious transit, and I quote, "is extended . . . to assure the transit of such vessels through the Canal as quickly as possible, without any impediment, with expedited treatment, and in case of need or emergency, to go to the head of the line of vessels in order to transit the Canal rapidly."

Will the treaties affect our standing in Latin America? Will they create a so-called power vacuum, which our enemies might move in to fill? They will do just the opposite. The treaties will increase our Nation's influence in this hemisphere, will help to reduce any mistrust and disagreement, and they will remove a major source of anti-American feeling.

The new agreement has already provided vivid proof to the people of this hemisphere that a new era of friendship and cooperation is beginning and that what they regard as the last remnant of alleged American colonialism is being removed.

Last fall, I met individually with the leaders of 18 countries in this hemisphere. Between the United States and Latin America there is already a new sense of equality, a new sense of trust and mutual respect that exists because of the Panama Canal treaties. This opens up a fine opportunity for us in good will, trade, jobs, exports, and political cooperation.

If the treaties should be rejected, this would be lost, and disappointment and despair among our good neighbors and traditional friends would be severe.

In the peaceful struggle against alien ideologies like communism, these treaties are a step in the right direction. Nothing could strengthen our competitors and adversaries in this hemisphere more than for us to reject this agreement.

What if a new sea-level canal should be needed in the future? This question has been studied over and over throughout this century, from before the time the canal was built up through the last few years. Every study has reached the same conclusion—that the best place to build a sea-level canal is in Panama.

The treaties say that if we want to build such a canal, we will build it in Panama, and if any canal is to be built in Panama, that we, the United States, will have the right to participate in the project.

This is a clear benefit to us, for it ensures that, say 10 or 20 years from now, no unfriendly but wealthy power will be able to purchase the right to build a sea-level canal, to bypass the existing canal, perhaps leaving that other nation in control of the only usable waterway across the isthmus.

Are we paying Panama to take the canal? We are not. Under the new treaty, any payments to Panama will come from tolls paid by ships which use the canal.

What about the present and the future stability and the capability of the Panamanian Government? Do the people of Panama themselves support the agreement?

Well, as you know, Panama and her people have been our historical allies and friends. The present leader of Panama has been in office for more than 9 years, and he heads a stable government which has encouraged the development of free enterprise in Panama. Democratic elections will be held this August to choose the members of the Panamanian Assembly, who will in turn elect a President and a Vice President by majority vote.[6] In the past, regimes have changed in Panama, but for 75 years, no Panamanian government has ever wanted to close the canal.

Panama wants the canal open and neutral—perhaps even more than we do. The canal's continued operation is very important to us, but it is much more than that to Panama. To Panama, it's crucial. Much of her economy flows directly or indirectly from the canal. Panama would be no more likely to neglect or to close the canal than we would be to close the Interstate Highway System here in the United States.

In an open and free referendum last October,[7] which was monitored very carefully by the United Nations, the people of Panama gave the new treaties their support.

The major threat to the canal comes not from any government of Panama, but from misguided persons who may try to fan the flames of dissatisfaction with the terms of the old treaty.

There's a final question—about the deeper meaning of the treaties themselves, to us and to Panama.

Recently, I discussed the treaties with David McCullough, author

[6]Following the Aug. 6 elections for a National Assembly, the latter at its inaugural session elected Aristide Royó as President and Ricardo de la Espriella as Vice-President for a six-year term beginning Oct. 11, 1978.
[7]On Oct. 23, 1977.

of "The Path Between the Seas," the great history of the Panama Canal. He believes that the canal is something that we built-and have looked after these many years; it is "ours" in that sense, which is very different from just ownership.

So, when we talk of the canal, whether we are old, young, for or against the treaties, we are talking about very deep and elemental feelings about our own strength.

Still, we Americans want a more humane and stable world. We believe in good will and fairness, as well as strength. This agreement with Panama is something we want because we know it is right. This is not merely the surest way to protect and save the canal; it's a strong, positive act of a people who are still confident, still creative, still great.

This new partnership can become a source of national pride and self-respect in much the same way that building the canal was 75 years ago. It's the spirit in which we act that is so very important.

Theodore Roosevelt, who was President when America built the canal, saw history itself as a force, and the history of our own time and the changes it has brought would not be lost on him. He knew that change was inevitable and necessary. Change is growth. The true conservative, he once remarked, keeps his face to the future.

But if Theodore Roosevelt were to endorse the treaties, as I'm quite sure he would, it would be mainly because he could see the decision as one by which we are demonstrating the kind of great power we wish to be.

"We cannot avoid meeting great issues," Roosevelt said. "All that we can determine for ourselves is whether we shall meet them well or ill."

The Panama Canal is a vast, heroic expression of that age-old desire to bridge the divide and to bring people closer together. This is what the treaties are all about.

We can sense what Roosevelt called "the lift toward nobler things which marks a great and generous people."

In this historic decision, he would join us in our pride for being a great and generous people, with the national strength and wisdom to do what is right for us and what is fair to others.

Thank you very much.

(29)   Approval of the Neutrality Treaty, March 16, 1978.

   *(a)   Resolution of Ratification, Agreed to by the Senate by a
          Vote of 68 to 32.* [8]

The resolution of ratification as agreed to is as follows:

[8]Text from *Congressional Record* (Daily Edition), Mar. 16, 1978: S3857–8.

Resolved, (two-thirds of the Senators present concurring therein), That the Senate advise and consent to the ratification of the Treaty Concerning the Permanent Neutrality and Operation of the Panama Canal, together with the Annexes and Protocol relating thereto, done at Washington on September 7, 1977, (Executive N, Ninety-fifth Congress, first session),[9] subject to the following—

(a) AMENDMENTS:

(1) At the end of Article IV, insert the following:
"A correct and authoritative statement of certain rights and duties of the Parties under the foregoing is contained in the Statement of Understanding issued by the Government of the United States of America on October 14, 1977,[10] and by the Government of the Republic of Panama on October 18, 1977, which is hereby incorporated as an integral part of this Treaty, as follows:
" 'Under the Treaty Concerning the permanent Neutrality and Operation of the Panama Canal (the Neutrality Treaty), Panama and the United States have the responsibility to assure that the Panama Canal will remain open and secure to ships of all nations. The correct interpretation of this principle is that each of the two countries shall, in accordance with their respective constitutional processes, defend the Canal against any threat to the regime of neutrality, and consequently shall have the right to act against any aggression or threat directed against the Canal or against the peaceful transit of vessels through the Canal.
" 'This does not mean, nor shall it be interpreted as, a right of intervention of the United States in the internal affairs of Panama. Any United States action will be directed at insuring that the Canal will remain open, secure, and accessible, and it shall never be directed against the territorial integrity or political independence of Panama.' "
(2) At the end of the first paragraph of Article VI, insert the following:
"In accordance with the Statement of Understanding mentioned in Article IV above: 'The Neutrality Treaty provides that the vessels of war and auxiliary vessels of the United States and Panama will be entitled to transit the Canal expeditiously. This is intended, and it shall so be interpreted, to assure the transit of such vessels through the Canal as quickly as possible, without any impediment, with expedited treatment, and in the case of need or emergency, to go to the head of the line of vessels in order to transit the Canal rapidly.' "

[9] *AFR, 1977:* 364-9.
[10] Same: 377-8.

(b) Conditions:

(1) Notwithstanding the provisions of Article V or any other provision of the Treaty, if the Canal is closed, or its operations are interfered with, the United States of America shall have the right to take such steps as it deems necessary, in accordance with its constitutional processes, including the use of military force in Panama, to reopen the Canal or restore the operations of the Canal, as the case may be.

(2) The instruments of ratification of the Treaty shall be· exchanged only upon the conclusion of a Protocol of Exchange, to be signed by authorized representatives of both Governments, which shall constitute an integral part of the Treaty documents and which shall include the following:

"Nothing in this Treaty shall preclude Panama and the United States from making, in accordance with their respective constitutional processes, any agreement or arrangement between the two countries to facilitate performance at any time after December 31, 1999, of their responsibilities to maintain the regime of neutrality established in the Treaty, including agreements or arrangements for the stationing of any United States military forces or maintenance of defense sites after that date in the Republic of Panama that Panama and the United States may deem necessary or appropriate."

(c) Reservations:

(1) Before the date of entry into force of the Treaty, the two Parties shall begin to negotiate for an agreement under which the American Battle Monuments Commission would, upon the date of entry into force of such agreement and thereafter, administer, free of all taxes and other charges and without compensation to the Republic of Panama and in accordance with the practices, privileges, and immunities associated with the administration of cemeteries outside the United States by the American Battle Monuments Commission, including the display of the flag of the United States, such part of Corozal Cemetery in the former Canal Zone as encompasses the remains of citizens of the United States.

(2) The flag of the United States may be displayed, pursuant to the provisions of paragraph 3 of Article VII of the Panama Canal Treaty, at such part of Corozal Cemetery in the former Canal Zone as encompasses the remains of citizens of the United States.

(3) The President—

(A) shall have announced, before the date of entry into force of the Treaty, his intention to transfer, consistent with an agreement with the Republic of Panama, and before the date of termination of the Panama Canal Treaty, to the American Battle Monuments Commission the administration of such part of Corozal Cemetery as encompasses the remains of citizens of the United States; and

(B) shall have announced, immediately after the date of exchange of the instruments of ratification, plans, to be carried out at the expense of the United States Government, for—

(i) removing, before the date of entry into force of the Treaty, the remains of citizens of the United States from Mount Hope Cemetery to such part of Corozal Cemetery as encompasses such remains, except that the remains of any citizen whose next of kin objects in writing to the Secretary of the Army not later than three months after the date of exchange of the instruments of ratification of the Treaty shall not be removed; and

(ii) transporting to the United States for reinterment, if the next of kin so requests, not later than thirty months after the date of entry into force of the Treaty, any such remains encompassed by Corozal Cemetery and, before the date of entry into force of the Treaty, any remains removed from Mount Hope Cemetery pursuant to subclause (i); and

(C) shall have fully advised, before the date of entry into force of the Treaty, the next of kin objecting under clause (B) (i) of all available options and their implications.

(4) To carry out the purposes of Article III of the Treaty of assuring the security, efficiency, and proper maintenance of the Panama Canal, the United States of America and the Republic of Panama, during their respective periods of responsibility for Canal operation and maintenance, shall, unless the amount of the operating revenues of the Canal exceeds the amount needed to carry out the purposes of such article, use such revenues of the Canal only for purposes consistent with the purposes of Article III.

(d) UNDERSTANDINGS:

(1) Paragraph 1(c) of Article III of the Treaty shall be construed as requiring, before any adjustment in tolls for use of the Canal, that the effects of any such toll adjustment on the trade patterns of the two Parties shall be given full consideration, including consideration of the following factors in a manner consistent with the regime of neutrality:

(1) the costs of operating and maintaining the Panama Canal;

(2) the competitive position of the use of the Canal in relation to other means of transportation;

(3) the interests of both Parties in maintaining their domestic fleets;

(4) the impact of such an adjustment on'the various geographical areas of each of the two Parties; and

(5) the interest of both Parties in maximizing their international commerce. The United States and the Republic of Panama shall cooperate in exchanging information necessary for the consideration of such factors.

(2) The agreement 'to maintain the regime of neutrality established in this Treaty' in Article IV of the Treaty means that either of the two Parties to the Treaty may, in accordance with its constitutional processes, take unilateral action to defend the Panama Canal against any threat, as determined by the Party taking such action.

(3) The determination of 'need or emergency' for the purpose of any vessel of war or auxiliary vessel of the United States or Panama going to the head of the line of vessels in order to transit the Panama Canal rapidly shall be made by the nation operating such vessel.

(4) Nothing in the Treaty, in the annexes or the Protocol relating to the Treaty, or in any other agreement relating to the Treaty obligates the United States to provide any economic assistance, military grant assistance, security supporting assistance, foreign military sales credits or international military education and training to the Republic of Panama.

(5) The President shall include all amendments, reservations, understandings, declarations, and other statements incorporated by the Senate in its resolution of ratification respecting this Treaty in the instrument of ratification exchanged with the Government of the Republic of Panama.

(b) Statement by President Carter.[11]

I have a brief statement to make.

The people of our Nation owe a debt of thanks to the Members of the United States Senate for their courageous action taken today in voting for the Panama Canal neutrality treaty.

I add my sincere personal congratulations to the entire Senate, and especially to the three men who have led their colleagues with bipartisan statesmanship and wisdom through this long debate— Senator Robert Byrd, the majority leader, Senator Howard Baker, the minority leader, and Senator John Sparkman, chairman of the Senate Foreign Relations Committee.

As a nation, we also owe our gratitude and admiration to former

[11]Text from Presidential Documents, 14: 516-17.

President Ford and to Democratic and Republican leaders who have served in previous administrations who, by giving the treaties their support, gave us the opportunity to judge the treaties on their merits and not on a partisan, political basis.

This vote today is, of course, only the first step in the process of ratification, but I am confident that the Senate will show the same courage and foresight when it considers the second treaty. This is a promising step toward a new era in our relationships with Panama and with all of Latin America.

General Torrijos and the Panamanian people have been patient and forbearing during the negotiations and during the Senate debate. They've earned the confidence and respect of the American people. Their actions during the last few months is proof of their willingness to form a partnership with us, to join in cooperation rather than confrontation.

It's been more than 14 years since negotiations began with Panama, and we've been through many months of discussion and debate about the two treaties that the Senate has considered. This has been a long debate, but all of us have learned from it.

The basic purpose and the underlying principles of the treaty have been affirmed and strengthened by the actions of the Senate. Under the treaty as approved, the United States and Panama will have joint responsibility to assure that the canal after the year 2000 will remain neutral and secure, open and accessible.

The United States can take whatever actions are necessary to make sure the canal remains open and safe. The vessels of war and auxiliary vessels of the United States and Panama are assured of transit through the canal as quickly as possible and can go to the head of the line in time of emergency or need.

While the right of the United States and Panama to act against any threat to the regime of neutrality is assured by this treaty, it does not mean that there is a right of intervention, nor do we want a right of intervention by the United States in the internal affairs of Panama.

But perhaps the most encouraging lesson of all in these last long months is that in a full and open debate, even in a very controversial and difficult issue, in our foreign policy objectives, we can still reach the decisions that are in our Nation's long-term, best interests.

I congratulate again the Senators for their decision and give them, on behalf of the Nation, my sincere thanks.

(30) Approval of the Panama Canal Treaty, April 18, 1978.

(a) Resolution of Ratification, Agreed to by the Senate by a Vote of 68 to 32.[12]

[12]Text from *Congressional Record* (Daily Edition), Apr. 18, 1978: S5796–7.

Resolved (two-thirds of the Senators present concurring therein), That the Senate advise and consent to the ratification of the Panama Canal Treaty, together with the Annex and Agreed Minute relating thereto, done at Washington on September 7, 1977 (Executive N, Ninety-Fifth Congress, first session),[13] subject to the following—

(a) RESERVATIONS:

(1) Pursuant to its adherence to the principle of nonintervention, any action taken by the United States of America in the exercise of its rights to assure that the Panama Canal shall remain open, neutral, secure, and accessible, pursuant to the provisions of this Treaty and the Neutrality Treaty and the resolutions of advice and consent thereto, shall be only for the purpose of assuring that the canal shall remain open, neutral, secure, and accessible, and shall not have as its purpose or be interpreted as a right of intervention in the internal affairs of the Republic of Panama or interference with its political independence or sovereign integrity.

(2) Notwithstanding any other provisions of this Treaty, no funds may be drawn from the United States Treasury for payments under Article XIII, paragraph 4, without statutory authorization.

(3) Any accumulated unpaid balance under paragraph 4(c) of Article XIII at the termination of the Treaty shall be payable only to the extent of any operating surplus in the last year of the Treaty's duration, and that nothing in that paragraph may be construed as obligating the United States of America to pay after the date of the termination of the Treaty any such unpaid balance which shall have accrued before such date.

(4) Exchange of the instruments of ratification shall not be effective earlier than March 31, 1979, and the treaties shall not enter into force prior to October 1, 1979, unless legislation necessary to implement the provisions of the Panama Canal Treaty shall have been enacted by the Congress of the United States of America before March 31, 1979.

(5) The instruments of ratification to be exchanged by the United States and the Republic of Panama shall each include provisions whereby each Party agrees to waive its rights and release the other Party from its obligations under paragraph 2 of Article XII.

(6) After the date of entry into force of the Treaty, the Panama Canal Commission shall, unless it is otherwise provided by legislation enacted by the Congress, be obligated to reimburse the Treasury of the United States of America, as nearly as possible, for the interest cost of the funds or other assets directly invested in the Commission by the Government of the United States of America and for the interest cost of the funds or other assets directly in-

[13]The text of the treaty is printed in *AFR, 1977:* 345–64.

vested in the predecessor Panama Canal Company by the Government and not reimbursed before the date of entry into force of the Treaty. Such reimbursement of such interest costs shall be made at a rate determined by the Secretary of the Treasury of the United States of America and at annual intervals to the extent earned, and if not earned, shall be made from subsequent earnings. For purposes of this reservation, the phrase "funds or other assets directly invested" shall have the same meaning as the phrase "net direct investment" has under section 62 of title 2 of the Canal Zone Code.

(b) UNDERSTANDINGS:

(1) Nothing in paragraphs 3, 4, and 5 of Article IV may be construed to limit either the provisions of paragraph 1 of Article IV providing that each party shall act, in accordance with its constitutional processes, to meet danger threatening the security of the Panama Canal, or the provisions of paragraph 2 of Article IV providing that the United States of America shall have primary responsibility to protect and defend the Canal for the duration of this Treaty.

(2) Before the first date of the three-year period beginning on the date of entry into force of this Treaty and before each three-year period following thereafter, the two parties shall agree upon the specific levels and quality of services, as are referred to in Article III, paragraph 5 of the Treaty, to be provided during the following three-year period and, except for the first three-year period, on the reimbursement to be made for the costs of such services, such services to be limited to such as are essential to the effective functioning of such canal operating areas and such housing areas referred to in Article III, paragraph 5 of the Treaty. If payments made under Article III, paragraph 5 of the Treaty for the preceding three-year period, including the initial three-year period, exceed or are less than the actual costs to the Republic of Panama for supplying, during such period, the specific levels and quality of services agreed upon, then the Commission shall deduct from or add to the payment required to be made to the Republic of Panama for each of the following three years one-third of such excess or deficit, as the case may be. There shall be an independent and binding audit, conducted by an auditor mutually selected by both parties, of any costs of services disputed by the two parties pursuant to the reexamination of such costs provided for in this Understanding.

(3) Nothing in paragraph 4(c) of Article XIII shall be construed to limit the authority of the United States of America through the United States Government agency called the Panama Canal Commission to make such financial decisions and incur such expenses as are reasonable and necessary for the management, operation, and maintenance of the Panama Canal. In addition, toll rates established

pursuant to paragraph 2(d) of Article III need not be set at levels designed to produce revenues to cover the payment to Panama described in paragraph 4(c) of Article XIII.

(4) Any agreement concluded pursuant to Article IX, paragraph 11 with respect to the transfer of prisoners shall be concluded in accordance with the constitutional processes of both parties.

(5) Nothing in the Treaty, in the Annex or Agreed Minute relating to the Treaty, or in any other agreement relating to the Treaty obligates the United States to provide any economic assistance, military grant assistance, security supporting assistance, foreign military sales credits, or international military education and training to the Republic of Panama.

(6) The President shall include all reservations and understandings incorporated by the Senate in this resolution of ratification in the instrument of ratification exchanged with the government of the Republic of Panama.

(b) Statement by President Carter.[14]

THE PRESIDENT. This is a day of which Americans can always feel proud, for now we have reminded the world and ourselves of the things that we stand for as a nation. The negotiations that led to these treaties began 14 years ago, and they continued under four administrations, four Presidents. I'm proud that they reached their conclusion while I was President. But I'm far prouder that we, as a people, have shown that in a full and open debate about difficult foreign policy objectives, that we will reach the decisions that are in the best interest of our Nation.

The debate has been long and hard. But in the end, it's given our decision a firm base in the will of the American people. Over the last 8 months, millions of Americans have studied the treaties, have registered their views and, in some cases, have changed their minds. No matter which side they took in this debate, most Americans have acted out of sincere concern about our Nation's interest.

I would like to express my thanks to a few for the job they've done. Under the leadership of Senators Byrd and Baker and Sparkman and others, the Senate has carried out its responsibility of advice and consent with great care. All of us owe them our thanks. I feel a special gratitude and admiration for those Senators who have done what was right, because it was right, despite tremendous pressure and, in some cases, political threats.

The loyal employees of the Panama Canal Zone and the Canal Zone Government also deserve our gratitude and our admiration for their performance during these months of great uncertainty.

[14]Text from Presidential Documents, 14: 758-9.

And General Torrijos and the people of Panama, who have followed this debate closely and through every stage, have been willing partners and cooperative and patient friends. There is no better indication of the prospect for friendly relations between us in the future than their conduct during the last few months.

We now have a partnership with Panama to maintain and to operate and to defend the canal. We have the clear right to take whatever action is necessary to defend the canal and to keep it open and neutral and accessible. We do not have the right to interfere in Panama's internal affairs. That is a right we neither possess nor desire.

These treaties can mark the beginning of a new era in our relations not only with Panama but with all the rest of the world. They symbolize our determination to deal with the developing nations of the world, the small nations of the world, on the basis of mutual respect and partnership. But the treaties also reaffirm a spirit that is very stong, constant, and old in the American character.

Sixty-four years ago when the first ship traveled through the canal, our people took legitimate pride in what our ingenuity, our perseverance, and our vision had brought about. We were a nation of builders, and the canal was one of our greatest glories.

And today we have shown that we remain true to that determination, that ingenuity, and most of all, that vision. Today we've proven that what is best and noblest in our national spirit will prevail. Today we've shown that we are still builders, with our face still turned confidently to the future. That is why I believe all Americans should share the pride I feel in the accomplishments which we registered today.

When I was coming in to make this announcement, the Ambassador of Panama, Gabriel Lewis, informed me that General Torrijos has accepted the terms of the treaty that passed the Senate this afternoon. And I want to reaffirm my thanks and my commitment to a true partnership with General Torrijos and the people of a great nation, Panama.

Thank you.

REPORTER. Mr. President, are you going down to Panama now?

THE PRESIDENT. Now?

Q. With these treaties in a few weeks, for formal ceremonies?

THE PRESIDENT. I have been invited by General Torrijos to come to Panama. I would like very much to accept his invitation.

Q. Thank you.

THE PRESIDENT. Thank you.

(31)   Exchange of Instruments of Ratification, Panama City, June 16, 1978.

(a) Remarks by President Carter on Signing the Protocol of Exchange of Instruments of Ratification, June 16, 1978. [15]

General Torrijos, President Lakas, President Pérez, President López Michelsen, President López Portillo, President Carazo, Prime Minister Manley, [16] *distinguished guests and friends:*

First of all, I want to thank General Torrijos and President Lakas for their invitation to participate in this great ceremony.

I came to Panama and accepted this invitation, because I want to dramatize my appreciation for this great achievement—a firmer, more productive friendship between the United States of America and the Republic of Panama and, more broadly, a gain for the cause of peace and cooperation among all nations.

We are honored by the presence of the leaders of the five democratic countries who gave encouragement to us and advice to both nations during the final treaty negotiations. I'm grateful to them not only for the serious and helpful role they played in those final days and weeks but also for their continuing leadership in dealing with such crucial matters as world peace, nuclear nonproliferation, the status of human rights and democratic governments, and better relationships between the developed nations and the developing countries of the world.

It is now three quarters of a century since the first spade of earth was turned in the building of the Panama Canal. This path between two seas remains one of the greatest and most benevolent creations ever wrought by human labor and by human ingenuity.

As a neutral artery for the ships of all nations, the canal has contributed immensely to the peaceful work of the world. The treaties we solemnize today will help perpetuate that peaceful work for many generations to come.

Under the treaties, our two governments agree to maintain the neutrality and security of the canal. At the same time, we reaffirm our commitment to honor national sovereignty and the principle of nonintervention. These principles are enshrined in the charters of the Organization of American States and the United Nations.

During the long and difficult negotiations, both sides held to a vision of friendship and good will. Both sides were determined to build a new relationship of mutual respect, fairness, and equity.

[15]Text from *Presidential Documents,* 14: 1118-19.
[16]Brigadier General Omar Torrijos Herrera (Panama), President Demetrio B. Lakas (Panama), Presidents Carlos Andrés Pérez (Venezuela), Alfonso López Michelsen (Colombia), José López Portillo (Mexico), Rodrigo Carazo Odio (Costa Rica), and Prime Minister Michael N. Manley (Jamaica).

Because of that vision, because of that determination, we were finally able to reach agreement.

Now, after 14 years on opposite sides of the bargaining table, we sit together as partners. We are equally committed to putting into practice the agreements we have forged. During the period of transition which lies ahead, the United States and Panama will be working closely together. Both our countries want that transition to be smooth and effective.

Under the treaties, both nations are committed to safeguarding the interests of those Americans and Panamanians who have operated the canal so efficiently and so expertly during its period of American stewardship.

Together, our two countries have set an example for peaceful and successful negotiation that has few parallels in history. We have demonstrated our mutual sincerity and good will. In the face of disagreements not only between the two nations but within the nations themselves, disagreements that were initially very deep, in the face of our vast disparity in size and power, we dealt with each other in good faith as equals and with equal determination to overcome all differences.

During the years ahead we will work as partners to make the promise of the treaties a reality. We, the people of the United States, and you, the people of Panama, still have history to make together.

Thank you very much.

(b) Protocol of Exchange of Instruments of Ratification, Done at Panama, June 16, 1978.[17]

PROTOCOL OF EXCHANGE OF INSTRUMENTS OF RATIFICATION
REGARDING THE TREATY CONCERNING THE PERMANENT
NEUTRALITY AND OPERATION OF THE PANAMA CANAL AND THE
PANAMA CANAL TREATY

The undersigned, Jimmy Carter, President of the United States of America, and Omar Torrijos Herrera, Head of Government of the Republic of Panama, in the exercise of their respective constitutional authorities, have met for the purpose of delivering to each other the instruments of ratification of their respective governments of the Treaty Concerning the Permanent Neutrality and Operation of the Panama Canal and of the Panama Canal Treaty (the "Treaties").

The respective instruments of ratification of the Treaties have been carefully compared and found to be in due form. Delivery of

---

[17]Official text as communicated by the Department of State.

the respective instruments took place this day, it being understood and agreed by the United States of America and the Republic of Panama that, unless the Parties otherwise agree through an exchange of Notes in conformity with the resolution of the Senate of the United States of America of April 18, 1978,[18] the exchange of the instruments of ratification shall be effective on April 1, 1979, and the date of the exchange of the instruments of ratification for the purposes of Article VIII of the Treaty Concerning the Permanent Neutrality and Operation of the Panama Canal and Article II of the Panama Canal Treaty shall therefore be April 1, 1979.

The ratifications by the Government of the United States of America of the Treaties recite in their entirety the amendments, conditions, reservations and understandings contained in the resolution of March 16, 1978,[19] of the Senate of the United States of America advising and consenting to ratification of the Treaty Concerning the Permanent Neutrality and Operation of the Panama Canal, and the reservations and understandings contained in the resolution of April 18, 1978, of the Senate of the United States of America advising and consenting to ratification of the Panama Canal Treaty.

Said amendments, conditions, reservations and understandings have been communicated by the Government of the United States of America to the Government of the Republic of Panama. Both governments agree that the Treaties, upon entry into force in accordance with their provisions, will be applied in accordance with the above-mentioned amendments, conditions, reservations and understandings.

Pursuant to the resolution of the Senate of the United States of America of March 16, 1978, the following text contained in the instrument of ratification of the United States of America of the Treaty Concerning the Permanent Neutrality and Operation of the Panama Canal and agreed upon by both governments is repeated herewith:

"Nothing in the Treaty shall preclude the Republic of Panama and the United States of America from making, in accordance with their respective constitutional processes, any agreement or arrangement between the two countries to facilitate performance at any time after December 31, 1999, of their responsibilities to maintain the regime of neutrality established in the Treaty, including agreements or arrangements for the stationing of any United States military forces or the maintenance of defense sites after that date in the Republic of Panama that the Republic of Panama and the United States of America may deem necessary or appropriate."

[18]Document 30a.
[19]Document 29a.

The Republic of Panama agrees to the exchange of the instruments of ratification of the Panama Canal Treaty and of the Treaty Concerning the Permanent Neutrality and Operation of the Panama Canal on the understanding that there are positive rules of public international law contained in multilateral treaties to which both the Republic of Panama and the United States of America are Parties and which consequently both States are bound to implement in good faith, such as Article 1, paragraph 2 and Article 2, paragraph 4 of the Charter of the United Nations, and Articles 18 and 20 of the Charter of the Organization of American States.

It is also the understanding of the Republic of Panama that the actions which either Party may take in the exercise of its rights and the fulfillment of its duties in accordance with the aforesaid Panama Canal Treaty and the Treaty Concerning the Permanent Neutrality and Operation of the Panama Canal, including measures to reopen the Canal or to restore its normal operation, if it should be interrupted or obstructed, will be effected in a manner consistent with the principles of mutual respect and cooperation on which the new relationship established by those Treaties is based.

IN WITNESS THEREOF, the respective Plenipotentiaries have signed this Protocol of Exchange at Panama, in duplicate, in the English and Spanish languages on this sixteenth day of June, 1978, both texts being equally authentic.

FOR THE UNITED STATES
OF AMERICA:

(Signed): Jimmy Carter

FOR THE REPUBLIC
OF PANAMA:

(Signed): Omar Torrijos Herrera

(c) Instruments of Ratification to the Panama Canal Treaty.

(i) United States Instrument, Done at Washington, June 15, 1978.[20]

United States Instrument of Ratification with Reservations and Understandings to the Panama Canal Treaty

JIMMY CARTER
President of the United States of America

[20]Official text communicated by the Department of State.

TO ALL TO WHOM THESE PRESENTS SHALL COME, GREETING:

CONSIDERING THAT:

The Panama Canal Treaty was signed at Washington on September 7, 1977; and
The Senate of the United States of America by its resolution of April 18, 1978, two-thirds of the Senators present concurring therein, gave its advice and consent to ratification of the Treaty, subject to the following:

(a) RESERVATIONS:

(1) Pursuant to its adherence to the principle of non-intervention, any action taken by the United States of America in the exercise of its rights to assure that the Panama Canal shall remain open, neutral, secure, and accessible, pursuant to the provisions of the Panama Canal Treaty, the Treaty Concerning the Permanent Neutrality and Operation of the Panama Canal, and the resolutions of ratification thereto, shall be only for the purpose of assuring that the Canal shall remain open, neutral, secure, and accessible, and shall not have as its purpose or be interpreted as a right of intervention in the internal affairs of the Republic of Panama or interference with its political independence or sovereign integrity.

(2) The instruments of ratification of the Panama Canal Treaty to be exchanged by the United States of America and the Republic of Panama shall each include provisions whereby each Party agrees to waive its rights and release the other Party from its obligations under paragraph 2 of Article XII of the Treaty.

(3) Notwithstanding any provision of the Treaty, no funds may be drawn from the Treasury of the United States of America for payments under paragraph 4 of Article XIII without statutory authorization.

(4) Any accumulated unpaid balance under paragraph 4(c) of Article XIII of the Treaty at the date of termination of the Treaty shall be payable only to the extent of any operating surplus in the last year of the duration of the Treaty, and nothing in such paragraph may be construed as obligating the United States of America to pay, after the date of the termination of the Treaty, any such unpaid balance which shall have accrued before such date.

(5) Exchange of the instruments of ratification of the Panama Canal Treaty and of the Treaty Concerning the Permanent Neutrality and Operation of the Panama Canal shall not be effective earlier than March 31, 1979, and such Treaties shall not enter into force prior to October 1, 1979, unless legislation necessary to implement the provisions of the Panama Canal Treaty shall have been enacted by the Congress of the United States of America before March 31, 1979.

(6) After the date of entry into force of the Treaty, the Panama

Canal Commission shall, unless otherwise provided by legislation enacted by the Congress of the United States of America, be obligated to reimburse the Treasury of the United States of America, as nearly as possible, for the interest cost of the funds or other assets directly invested in the Commission by the Government of the United States of America and for the interest cost of the funds or other assets directly invested in the predecessor Panama Canal Company by the Government of the United States of America and not reimbursed before the date of entry into force of the Treaty. Such reimbursement for such interest costs shall be made at a rate determined by the Secretary of the Treasury of the United States of America and at annual intervals to the extent earned, and if not earned, shall be made from subsequent earnings. For purposes of this reservation, the phrase "funds or other assets directly invested" shall have the same meaning as the phrase "net direct investment" has under section 62 of title 2 of the Canal Zone Code.

(b) UNDERSTANDINGS:

(1) Before the first day of the three-year period beginning on the date of entry into force of the Treaty and before each three-year period following thereafter, the two Parties shall agree upon the specific levels and quality of services, as are referred to in paragraph 5 of Article III of the Treaty, to be provided during the following three-year period, and except for the first three-year period, on the reimbursement to be made for the costs of such services, such services to be limited to such as are essential to the effective functioning of the Canal operating areas and the housing areas referred to in paragraph 5 of Article III. If payments made under paragraph 5 of Article III for the preceding three-year period, including the initial three-year period, exceed or are less than the actual costs to the Republic of Panama for supplying, during such period, the specific levels and quality of services agreed upon, then the Panama Canal Commission shall deduct from or add to the payment required to be made to the Republic of Panama for each of the following three years one-third of such excess or deficit, as the case may be. There shall be an independent and binding audit, conducted by an auditor mutually selected by both Parties, of any costs of services disputed by the two Parties pursuant to the reexamination of such costs provided for in this understanding.

(2) Nothing in paragraph 3, 4, or 5 of Article IV of the Treaty may be construed to limit either the provisions of the first paragraph of Article IV providing that each Party shall act, in accordance with its constitutional processes, to meet danger threatening the security of the Panama Canal, or the provisions of paragraph 2 of Article IV providing that the United States of America shall have

primary responsibility to protect and defend the Canal for the duration of the Treaty.

(3) Nothing in paragraph 4(c) of Article XIII of the Treaty shall be construed to limit the authority of the United States of America, through the United States Government agency called the Panama Canal Commission, to make such financial decisions and incur such expenses as are reasonable and necessary for the management, operation, and maintenance of the Panama Canal. In addition, toll rates established pursuant to paragraph 2(d) of Article III need not be set at levels designed to produce revenues to cover the payment to the Republic of Panama described in paragraph 4(c) of Article XIII.

(4) Any agreement concluded pursuant to paragraph 11 of Article IX of the Treaty with respect to the transfer of prisoners shall be concluded in accordance with the constitutional processes of both Parties.

(5) Nothing in the Treaty, in the Annex or Agreed Minute relating to the Treaty, or in any other agreement relating to the Treaty obligates the United States of America to provide any economic assistance, military grant assistance, security supporting assistance, foreign military sales credits, or international military education and training to the Republic of Panama.

(6) The President shall include all reservations and understandings incorporated by the Senate in this resolution of ratification in the instrument of ratification to be exchanged with the Government of the Republic of Panama.

NOW, THEREFORE, I, Jimmy Carter, President of the United States of America, ratify and confirm the Panama Canal Treaty, subject to the aforementioned reservations and understandings, and on behalf of the United States of America undertake to fulfill it faithfully. I further hereby waive, in the name of the United States of America, the rights of the United States of America under paragraph 2 of Article XII of the Panama Canal Treaty and release the Republic of Panama from its obligations under paragraph 2 of Article XII of the Panama Canal Treaty.

IN TESTIMONY WHEREOF, I have signed this instrument of ratification and caused the Seal of the United States of America to be affixed.

DONE at the city of Washington,
this 15th day of June in
the year of our Lord
one thousand nine hundred
seventy-eight and of the
independence of the
United States of

America the two
hundred second.

By the President *(Signed):* Jimmy Carter
Acting Secretary of State: *(Signed):* Warren Christopher

*(ii) Panamanian Instrument, Done at Panama City,
June 16, 1978.*[21]

*Panamanian Instrument of Ratification with Understanding and
Declaration to the Panama Canal Treaty*

Whereas the Panama Canal Treaty was signed in Washington on
September 7, 1977, by the authorized representatives of the Gov-
ernment of the Republic of Panama and of the Government of the
United States of America;

Whereas the Republic of Panama, by means of the plebiscite
stipulated by Article 274 of its Political Constitution, ratified the
aforementioned Panama Canal Treaty;

Whereas the Senate of the United States of America gave its advice and consent to the ratification of the Panama Canal Treaty
with the following understandings and reservations:

[see the preceding document]

The Republic of Panama agrees to the exchange of the instruments of ratification of the Panama Canal Treaty on the understanding that there are positive rules of public international law
contained in multilateral treaties to which both the Republic of
Panama and the United States of America are Parties and which
consequently both States are bound to implement in good faith,
such as Article 1, paragraph 2 and Article 2, paragraph 4 of the
Charter of the United Nations and Articles 18 and 20 of the Charter
of the Organization of American States.

It is also the understanding of the Republic of Panama that the
actions which either Party may take in the exercise of its rights and
the fulfillment of its duties in accordance with the aforesaid Panama Canal Treaty, including measures to reopen the Canal or to restore its normal operation, if it should be interrupted or obstructed,
will be effected in a manner consistent with the principles of mutual
respect and cooperation on which the new relationship established
by that Treaty is based.

[21]Official text communicated by the Department of State.

The Republic of Panama declares that its political independence, territorial integrity, and self-determination are guaranteed by the unshakeable will of the Panamanian people. Therefore, the Republic of Panama will reject, in unity and with decisiveness and firmness, any attempt by any country to intervene in its internal or external affairs.

The Head of Government of the Republic of Panama, availing himself of the powers granted by Article 277 of the Constitution, after having considered the aforementioned Panama Canal Treaty, hereby ratifies it and, in the name of the Republic of Panama, undertakes to comply with it faithfully. The Head of Government further hereby waives, in the name of the Republic of Panama, the rights of the Republic of Panama under paragraph 2 of Article XII of the Panama Canal Treaty and releases the United States of America from its obligations under paragraph 2 of Article XII of the Panama Canal Treaty.

IN WITNESS THEREOF, this instrument of ratification is signed by the Head of Government of the Republic of Panama.

DONE at Panama City, Republic of Panama, this sixteenth day of June 1978.

Omar Torrijos Herrera

(d) *Instruments of Ratification to the Neutrality Treaty.*

(i) *United States Instrument, Done at Washington, June 15, 1978.*[22]

United States Instrument of Ratification with Amendments, Conditions and Reservations to the Treaty Concerning the Permanent Neutrality and Operation of the Panama Canal

JIMMY CARTER
President of the United States of America

TO ALL TO WHOM THESE PRESENTS SHALL COME, GREETING:

CONSIDERING THAT:

The Treaty Concerning the Permanent Neutrality and Operation of the Panama Canal (Neutrality Treaty) was signed at Washington on September 7, 1977; and

The Senate of the United States of America by its resolution of March 16, 1978, two-thirds of the Senators present concurring therein, gave its advice and consent to ratification of the Neutrality Treaty, subject to the following:

[22]Official text communicated by the Department of State.

(a) AMENDMENTS:

(1) At the end of Article IV, insert the following:
"A correct and authoritative statement of certain rights and duties of the Parties under the foregoing is contained in the Statement of Understanding issued by the Government of the United States of America on October 14, 1977,[23] and by the Government of the Republic of Panama on October 18, 1977, which is hereby incorporated as an integral part of this Treaty, as follows:

" 'Under the Treaty Concerning the Permanent Neutrality and Operation of the Panama Canal (the Neutrality Treaty), Panama and the United States have the responsibility to assure that the Panama Canal will remain open and secure to ships of all nations. The correct interpretation of this principle is that each of the two countries shall, in accordance with their respective constitutional processes, defend the Canal against any threat to the regime of neutrality, and consequently shall have the right to act against any aggression or threat directed against the Canal or against the peaceful transit of vessels throught the Canal.

" 'This does not mean, nor shall it be interpreted as, a right of intervention of the United States in the internal affairs of Panama. Any United States action will be directed at insuring that the Canal will remain open, secure, and accessible, and it shall never be directed against the territorial integrity or political independence of Panama.'."

(2) At the end of the first paragraph of Article VI, insert the following:
"In accordance with the Statement of Understanding mentioned in Article IV above: 'The Neutrality Treaty provides that the vessels of war and auxiliary vessels of the United States and Panama will be entitled to transit the Canal expeditiously. This is intended, and it shall so be interpreted, to assure the transit of such vessels through the Canal as quickly as possible, without any impediment, with expedited treatment, and in case of need or emergency, to go to the head of the line of vessels in order to transit the Canal rapidly.'."

(b) CONDITIONS:

(1) Notwithstanding the provisions of Article V or any other provision of the Treaty, if the Canal is closed, or its operations are interfered with, the United States of America and the Republic of Panama shall each independently have the right to take such steps as each deems necessary, in accordance with its constitutional processes, including the use of military force in the Republic of Pan-

²³*AFR, 1977:* 377-8.

ama, to reopen the Canal or restore the operations of the Canal, as the case may be.

(2) The instruments of ratification of the Treaty shall be exchanged only upon the conclusion of a Protocol of Exchange, to be signed by authorized representatives of both Governments, which shall constitute an integral part of the Treaty documents and which shall include the following:

"Nothing in the Treaty shall preclude the Republic of Panama and the United States of America from making, in accordance with their respective constitutional processes, any agreement or arrangement between the two countries to facilitate performance at any time after December 31, 1999, of their responsibilities to maintain the regime of neutrality established in the Treaty, including agreements or arrangements for the stationing of any United States military forces or the maintenance of defense sites after that date in the Republic of Panama that the Republic of Panama and the United States of America may deem necessary or appropriate.'."

(c) RESERVATIONS:

(1) Before the date of entry into force of the Treaty, the two Parties shall begin to negotiate for an agreement under which the American Battle Monuments Commission would, upon the date of entry into force of such agreement and thereafter, administer, free of all taxes and other charges and without compensation to the Republic of Panama and in accordance with the practices, privileges, and immunities associated with the administration of cemeteries outside the United States of America by the American Battle Monuments Commission, including the display of the flag of the United States of America, such part of Corozal Cemetery in the former Canal Zone as encompasses the remains of citizens of the United States of America.

(2) The flag of the United States of America may be displayed, pursuant to the provisions of paragraph 3 of Article VII of the Panama Canal Treaty, at such part of Corozal Cemetery in the former Canal Zone as encompasses the remains of citizens of the United States of America.

(3) The President—

(A) shall have announced, before the date of entry into force of the Treaty, his intention to transfer, consistent with an agreement with the Republic of Panama, and before the date of termination of the Panama Canal Treaty, to the American Battle Monuments Commission the administration of such part of Corozal Cemetery as encompasses the remains of citizens of the United States of America; and

(B) shall have announced, immediately after the date of exchange of instruments of ratification, plans, to be carried out at the expense of the Government of the United States of America, for—

(i) removing, before the date of entry into force of the Treaty, the remains of citizens of the United States of America from Mount Hope Cemetery to such part of Corozal Cemetery as encompasses such remains, except that the remains of any citizen whose next of kin objects in writing to the Secretary of the Army not later than three months after the date of exchange of the instruments of ratification of the Treaty shall not be removed; and

(ii) transporting to the United States of America for reinterment, if the next of kin so requests, not later than thirty months after the date of entry into force of the Treaty, any such remains encompassed by Corozal Cemetery and, before the date of entry into force of the Treaty, any remains removed from Mount Hope Cemetery pursuant to subclause (i); and

(C) shall have fully advised, before the date of entry into force of the Treaty, the next of kin objecting under clause (B) (i) of all available options and their implications.

(4) To carry out the purposes of Article III of the Treaty of assuring the security, efficiency, and proper maintenance of the Panama Canal, the United States of America and the Republic of Panama, during their respective periods of responsibility for Canal operation and maintenance, shall, unless the amount of the operating revenues of the Canal exceeds the amount needed to carry out the purposes of such Article, use such revenues of the Canal only for purposes consistent with the purposes of Article III.

(d) UNDERSTANDINGS:

(1) Paragraph 1(c) of Article III of the Treaty shall be construed as requiring, before any adjustment in tolls for use of the Canal, that the effects of any such toll adjustment on the trade patterns of the two Parties shall be given full consideration, including consideration of the following factors in a manner consistent with the regime of neutrality:

(A) the costs of operating and maintaining the Panama Canal;
(B) the competitive position of the use of the Canal in relation to other means of transportation;
(C) the interests of both Parties in maintaining their domestic fleets;

(D) the impact of such an adjustment on the various geographical areas of each of the two Parties; and

(E) the interests of both Parties in maximizing their international commerce.

The United States of America and the Republic of Panama shall cooperate in exchanging information necessary for the consideration of such factors.

(2) The agreement 'to maintain the regime of neutrality established in this Treaty' in Article IV of the Treaty means that either of the two Parties to the Treaty may, in accordance with its constitutional processes, take unilateral action to defend the Panama Canal against any threat, as determined by the Party taking such action.

(3) The determination of 'need or emergency' for the purpose of any vessel of war or auxiliary vessel of the United States of America or the Republic of Panama going to the head of the line of vessels in order to transit the Panama Canal rapidly shall be made by the nation operating such vessel.

(4) Nothing in the Treaty, in Annex A or B thereto, in the Protocol relating to the Treaty, or in any other agreement relating to the Treaty, obligates the United States of America to provide any economic assistance, military grant assistance, security supporting assistance, foreign military sales credits, or international military education and training to the Republic of Panama.

(5) The President shall include all amendments, conditions, reservations, and understandings incorporated by the Senate in this resolution of ratification in the instrument of ratification to be exchanged with the Government of the Republic of Panama.

NOW, THEREFORE, I, Jimmy Carter, President of the United States of America, ratify and confirm the Neutrality Treaty, subject to the aforementioned amendments, conditions, reservations and understandings, and on behalf of the United States of America undertake to fulfill it faithfully.

IN TESTIMONY WHEREOF, I have signed this instrument of ratification and caused the Seal of the United States of America to be affixed.

DONE at the city of Washington,
this 15th day of June in
the year of our Lord
one thousand nine hundred
seventy-eight and of the
independence of the
United States of

America the two
hundred second.

By the President. (*Signed*): JIMMY CARTER

Acting Secretary of State (*Signed*): WARREN CHRISTOPHER

(ii) Panamanian Instrument, Done at Panama City, June 16, 1978.[24]

Panamanian Instrument of Ratification with Understanding and Declaration to the Treaty Concerning the Permanent Neutrality and Operation of the Panama Canal

Whereas the Treaty Concerning the Permanent Neutrality and Operation of the Panama Canal was signed in Washington on September 7, 1977, by the authorized representatives of the Government of the Republic of Panama and of the Government of the United States of America;

Whereas the Republic of Panama, by means of the plebiscite stipulated by Article 274 of its Political Constitution, ratified the aforementioned Neutrality Treaty;

Whereas the Senate of the United States of America gave its advice and consent to the ratification of the aforementioned Neutrality Treaty with the following understandings, reservations, conditions, and amendments:

[see the preceding document]

The Republic of Panama agrees to the exchange of the instruments of ratification of the aforementioned Neutrality Treaty on the understanding that there are positive rules of public international law contained in multilateral treaties to which both the Republic of Panama and the United States of America are Parties and which consequently both States are bound to implement in good faith, such as Article 1, paragraph 2 and Article 2, paragraph 4 of the Charter of the United Nations, and Articles 18 and 20 of the Charter of the Organization of American States.

It is also the understanding of the Republic of Panama that the actions which either Party may take in the exercise of its rights and the fulfillment of its duties in accordance with the aforesaid Neutrality Treaty, including measures to reopen the Canal or to restore its normal operation, if it should be interrupted or obstructed, will be effected in a manner consistent with the principles of mutual respect and cooperation on which the new relationship established by that Treaty is based.

[24]Official text communicated by the Department of State.

The Republic of Panama declares that its political independence, territorial integrity, and self-determination are guaranteed by the unshakeable will of the Panamanian people. Therefore, the Republic of Panama will reject, in unity and with decisiveness and firmness, any attempt by any country to intervene in its internal or external affairs.

The Head of Government of the Republic of Panama, availing himself of the powers granted by Article 277 of the Constitution, after having considered the aforementioned Neutrality Treaty, hereby ratifies it and, in the name of the Republic of Panama, undertakes to comply with it faithfully.

IN WITNESS WHEREOF, this instrument of ratification is signed by the Head of Government of the Republic of Panama.

DONE at Panama City, Republic of Panama, this sixteenth day of June 1978.

Omar Torrijos Herrera

(32) Multilateral Discussions with Leaders of Colombia, Costa Rica, Jamaica, Panama, and Venezuela, Held in Panama City June 16–17, 1978: Joint Statement Issued at the Conclusion of the Discussions.[25]

The Presidents of Colombia, Costa Rica, the United States and Venezuela, the Prime Minister of Jamaica,[26] present in Panama City on the occasion of the exchange of the Instruments of Ratification of the Panama Canal Treaties between the Republic of Panama and the United States of America, the culmination of a process with which we have been directly concerned, expressed the belief that the treaties represent an historic step forward in inter-American relations. These treaties symbolize a fundamental respect for sovereignty and a cooperative spirit which can motivate all countries to address the difficult problems which affect all the world.

They believe that the Panama Canal treaties demonstrate how all of us can work together in a new spirit of cooperation to shape the future in accordance with our ideals and to resolve all areas of friction in the region by peaceful means. They are determined to build on this example so that attention can be focused on economic cooperation and integration in order to promote socio-economic development and thereby strengthen solidarity among the peoples of the Americas.

Accordingly, they pledge to work actively and in cooperation with each other and with other states.

To promote world peace, they pledge:

[25]Text from *Presidential Documents,* 14: 1123–5.
[26]Identified at note 16 to Document 31a.

—To work to bring into effect the Treaty of Tlatelolco banning nuclear weapons from Latin America and the Caribbean.

—To strengthen the peacekeeping machinery of the Organization of American States and the United Nations.

—To work toward an effective regional limitation of conventional armaments based on cooperation among suppliers and purchasers to put an end to their acquisition for offensive purposes. They are deeply concerned about the waste of resources to purchase arms and are therefore encouraged by the decision of the countries which signed the Ayacucho Declaration[27] to renew their determination to find a new agreement to limit purchases of weapons. They also hope that the Ayacucho example will be expanded to include all Latin American countries, and perhaps to other regions as well.

—To use their good offices and cooperation to encourage the solution of international disputes and to reduce areas of tension in the hemisphere. They hope that the patience and mutual respect which led to the successful negotiation of the canal treaties will help countries to resolve such problems and points of controversy in a mutually helpful way.

—To consult on a regular and continuous basis on a wide range of international issues in order to reduce the differences between national policies and increase the likelihood of reaching mutual agreement.

To promote greater respect for human rights and to widen the scope of international action in the defense of human dignity, they pledge:

—To strengthen the autonomy and capabilities of the Inter-American Commission on Human Rights.

—To work to bring the American Convention on Human Rights into effect in this year,[28] the 30th anniversary of the Universal Declaration of Human Rights. The leaders viewed with sympathy the offer made by Costa Rica for San Jose to be the site of a proposed Inter-American Court on Human Rights, conscious of the advantages of this site.

—To speak out for human rights and fundamental freedoms everywhere and to work to eliminate repression.

—To facilitate the development of conditions that would promote democracy with popular and effective participation. In

---

[27]Representatives of Argentina, Bolivia, Colombia, Cuba, Ecuador, Panama, Peru, and Venezuela, signed the Declaration at Lima Dec. 9, 1974, expressing, *inter alia,* their commitment toward the limitation of arms in the hemisphere. Details in *Keesing's* (1975): 26923.

[28]The convention entered into force July 8, 1978.

particular, they express gratification that the will of the people of the Dominican Republic was freely expressed in elections last month, and they reiterate their hope and understanding that the electoral commission in the Dominican Republic will adhere faithfully to the integrity of the democratic process.[29]

—To work through international organizations to strengthen the juridical foundations of political, social, and economic rights.

To move forward toward a more just and equitable international economic system and to insure that ongoing multilateral negotiations, including those on the Common Fund and debt, are pursued expeditiously with the goal of bringing concrete and significant results for the benefit of all countries, and to help raise the living standards of the world's poor, they pledge:

—To help alleviate hunger and poverty by emphasizing food production and studying the implications of rapid population growth.

—To complete the work of the Multilateral Trade Negotiations in Geneva and thereby reduce trade barriers and increase the participation of developing countries in an improved world trading system.

—To seek ways to improve the efficiency, growth, equity and stability of commodity markets, and to seek to bring into effect the International Sugar Agreement, the International Coffee Agreement, and other commodity agreements which will have the purpose of establishing fair prices for the products of developing countries. In particular, they consider that the achievement of equitable agreements of this character will strengthen political stability and promote regional solidarity and will benefit both producers and consumers of such products.

—To support fully the work and capital replenishments of the Inter-American Development Bank and the World Bank.

—To give full support to the Caribbean Group for Cooperation in Economic Development[30] and in other ways to encourage the economic development of the region.

They also wish to express their strong support for negotiations in the United Nations toward the conclusion of a treaty prohibiting bribery and illicit payments in international transactions.

In pledging themselves to these objectives, they invite all states to join with them in this spirit of cooperation to work actively for

[29]Cf. Introduction at note 117.
[30]The Caribbean Group for Cooperation in Economic Development held its first meeting in Washington on June 19–24, 1978 and agreed to establish a Caribbean Development Facility (CDF).

peace, human rights, participatory government, and a just and equitable international economic system.

(33) Eighth General Assembly of the Organization of American States, Washington, June 21–July 1, 1978: Address by President Carter to the Opening Session, June 21, 1978.[31]

Mr. Chairman, Mr. Secretary General,[32] *distinguished Foreign Ministers—I believe with 100-percent attendance—Ambassadors, delegates and observers to this General Assembly, and friends:*

In the brief time that I have been President of our country, I have enjoyed a very close relationship with the Organization of American States. Historic events have occurred here in this building, and some have even suggested that I move my office over here because I visit so often. But the importance of your deliberations and the past actions that have occurred here are recognized throughout our own country.

I want to welcome you here to open the Eighth General Assembly of the Organization of American States.

Five days ago, I went to Panama. I went there to celebrate new treaties which permit the United States of America and the Republic of Panama to operate and to defend the canal on the basis of partnership and not paternalism. I went there to fulfill a pledge that I made before you in this Hall of the Americas a little more than a year ago. I went there to explain what the treaties mean to me and to other North Americans. More than simply a fulfillment of a pledge, they are the beginning of a new era of inter-American understanding, reflecting a new spirit of commitment and cooperation.

In the process of reaching agreement, our two nations—and the many others of you who supported us—breathed new life into some old principles, principles of nonintervention, mutual respect, partnership, and multilateral cooperation. What we have accomplished together will make it easier to apply these same principles to the overriding concern of our hemisphere: peace, human rights and dignity, and economic development.

Last year on Pan American Day, I outlined the approach[33] which my own administration would take towards Latin America and the Caribbean. Slogans would no longer suffice to describe the diversity of the Americas, nor would a single formula be helpful when

---

[31]Text from *Presidential Documents,* 14: 1141–6.
[32]Foreign Minister Indalecio Liévano Aguirre (Colombia) and Alejandro Orfila (Argentina) respectively.
[33]Address of Apr. 14, 1977: 328–34.

our individual and our common interests are so clearly global in scope. The problems of the world require that we in the Western Hemisphere think and act more broadly.

That is what I pledged to you last year on Pan American Day. That's what I committed our Nation to do. Our goals still remain the same: to promote world peace, to discourage international intervention and aggression, to foster an international environment in which human rights and dignity are respected by all, and to end repression and terrorism, and, finally, to move toward a more just and equitable international economic system.

These are the most basic goals of the community of nations throughout the world—and therefore of our hemisphere as well. No one nation can do this job alone—not the United States, nor any other. Only by cooperation among the nations of this hemisphere and throughout the world will we have a chance to see these goals fulfilled.

We can advance toward peace with many small steps, as we remove the causes of dispute which have plagued our hemisphere in the past.

The resolution of the Panama Canal issue should be a good omen that other disputes in our hemisphere can also be settled peacefully. Let us approach other problems, such as Bolivian access to the sea, the Honduras-El Salvador border dispute, the future of Belize, in the same spirit of accommodation and friendship.

Just as the nations of this hemisphere offered support to Panama and the United States during the canal negotiations, I pledge today my Government's willingness to join in the effort to find peaceful and just solutions to other problems.

In 1 year's time, it will be a century since the War of the Pacific. We should view this anniversary, this occasion, as an opportunity to reaffirm our commitment to harmony in this hemisphere and to avoid conflict.

The difficult decisions in their region can only be made by Bolivia, Peru, Chile. But we stand ready with the Organization of American States, the United Nations, and other countries to help find a solution to Bolivia's land-locked status that will be acceptable to all parties and will contribute to the permanent peace and development of the area.

In this same spirit, we should work together to bring into effect the farsighted Treaty of Tlatelolco, which bans nuclear weapons from Latin America. It was in this hall last year that I pledged to do my utmost to bring this treaty into effect and to sign Protocol I of that treaty. And on May 26, last year I signed it.[34] Since then, due to the encouragement of the countries that pioneered the treaty, the

Soviet Union has ratified Protocol II,[35] and Argentina has now agreed to ratify the treaty.

All but one of the countries in the hemisphere eligible to sign [Cuba] have now signed the Treaty of Tlatelolco. This precedent-setting treaty represents a dramatic advance for the cause of nuclear nonproliferation, and we should not rest until it is complete. I also support the efforts of those who want to extend the spirit of Tlatelolco to other areas of the world and to conventional arms sales, as well.

I believe that restraint in conventional arms sales is also central to the cause of peace. The United States has adopted a policy, unilaterally, which seeks to reduce the overall sale of weapons each year, especially the most sophisticated, lethal, and expensive weapons. We will not introduce an advanced weapons system into a region. And we are encouraging the Soviet Union, the French, and others to join with us in a multinational control of the sale of conventional weapons throughout the world.

As a major arms salesman, the United States bears and accepts a heavy responsibility for limiting this trade, but we cannot succeed alone. Our efforts will depend upon the active participation of other arms sellers and, obviously, on the participation of those who buy weapons.

I might point out that we have a better record in this hemisphere than is generally recognized. Four other nations of the world sell more weapons in Latin America than does the United States. And we need your help and the help of other countries to continue this progress toward another example of hemispheric peace and the control of weapons of destruction that might be observed and emulated by other regions of the world.

Discussions among supplier nations and providing nations have already begun. As we make our efforts, we draw inspiration from the truly historic initiative that Venezuela and other signatories of Ayacucho[36] are making to remove the causes of insecurity from their region and thereby to reduce the pressures that make nations buy weapons, because they fear their neighbors.

As the Ayacucho nations prepare for another meeting this week, I reaffirm my own country's conviction that their work is bringing us closer to lasting peace, and I express my hope that their efforts can be expanded to other weapons, both purchasers and suppliers.

We can also reduce the pressure for armaments and for regional violence by ensuring that all nations respect the territorial integrity of others. The intrusion of foreign military forces into local disputes can only undermine this cause. We support improvements in

[35]On May 18, 1978; cf. *AFR, 1977:* 82, note 116.
[36]Note 27 to Document 32.

the peacekeeping and dispute-settling machinery of the Organization of American States and the United Nations.

I'd like to say just a word about human rights. The rights and dignity of human beings concern us all and must be defended and enhanced. I'm convinced that the peoples of the Americas want a world in which citizens of every country are free from torture, from arbitrary arrest and prolonged detention without trial, free to speak and to think as they please, free to participate in the determination of their own destiny.

My Government will not be deterred from our open and enthusiastic policy of promoting human rights, including economic and social rights, in whatever ways we can. We prefer to take actions that are positive, but where nations persist in serious violations of human rights, we will continue to demonstrate that there are costs to the flagrant disregard of international standards.

Above and beyond any actions we take ourselves, we believe multilateral action can be the most effective means of encouraging the protection of human rights. Last year's Organization of American States General Assembly demonstrated our common interest in this important commitment.[37] It set the stage for this year's events.

During the past year, the Inter-American Commission on Human Rights, one of our region's most important instruments, has grown stronger. Its budget was tripled, and it was invited by more Governments to investigate and report on conditions. We consider this not an intrusion into internal affairs of countries but a mechanism by which those countries that stand condemned, perhaps erroneously, by the rest of the world, might clear their good name and prove to us and to the rest of the world that human rights indeed are not being violated.

This is a very good encouragement for us in the United States to set a good example, and I hope we'll retain our commitment to this principle so vividly that every day, every head of state in the whole world has before his or her consciousness a concern about "How are we doing to enhance human rights in our own country?"

We have had, I believe, good progress so far, and I commend the reports that have been submitted to this General Assembly and urge that their recommendations be fulfilled.

In the past year, six countries have joined Costa Rica and Colombia in ratifying the American Convention on Human Rights. Three more countries must ratify it for it to come into force. I signed the convention on June 1[1977], a long-overdue action on the part of the United States. I signed this while my wife was in San José, and I pledged my own efforts to bring about the United States ratification as soon as possible.

---

[37]Cf. *AFR, 1977:* 342.

I hope that every nation represented around this table will make every effort expeditiously to sign and to ratify this American Convention on Human Rights without delay.

We should use this General Assembly to plan for the moment when the convention enters into force. We share the view that the present Commission will continue to carry out its mandate until a new Commission is functioning.

The governments whose leaders visited Panama for the ceremonies this past weekend have been at the forefront of the movement for human rights and democracy. A few weeks ago, several of our countries spoke out in support of the democratic election process in a neighboring country.

Now, we realize that the path from authoritarian rule to democratic rule can be difficult and demanding. During such a transition, and in the midst of the electoral process, my Government pledges not to intervene nor to show favoritism toward particular individuals or particular parties. But we will continually support and encourage political systems that allow their people to participate freely and democratically in the decisions that affect their lives.

This past year has seen a measure of progress. In many countries, political prisoners have been released, states of seige have been lifted, or constraints on freedom of the press have been loosened. In the coming year, we hope for more progress. For many in Latin America, the struggle has just begun. But the direction of history toward the expansion of human rights is clear. Where basic human rights are concerned, all of our governments must be accountable not only to our own citizens but to the conscience of the world.

The economic system: We must also devote our common energies to economic development and the cause of social justice. Benefits of the world's economy must be more fairly shared, but the responsibilities must be shared as well.

In many ways, economic issues will be our most important foreign policy concerns in the coming year. We plan to give increased emphasis, much more than we have in the past, to those economic issues which most directly affect the developing countries, particularly trade and aid.

We have not moved far enough or fast enough in the United States Government in the past. Many of you have not been aggressive enough in alleviating economic disparities and abuses in the system which we help to control. We've not spoken often enough nor candidly enough with each other. We must take every opportunity to work with all nations on these fundamental issues, and we must find new ways to discuss them, not through public confrontation, through the news media, but through quiet, substantive, determined negotiation to bring about steady progress designed to reach common goals.

Trade policy will become more and more important as your economies continue their transformation, which is inevitable, with manufactured goods making up a larger and larger proportion of your production and exports.

I have fought hard to resist protectionism, a subject which the President mentioned a few minutes ago, and I will continue to do so. Within the Organization of [for] Economic Cooperation and Development, the OECD, we've urged the healthier economies to grow faster so as to expand markets for your exports. In the multilateral trade negotiations, we seek to reduce barriers to those exports. In return, we ask you to join with us in negotiating a reduction of tariff and nontariff barriers.

Many of your countries whose voices could be heard and could be of great influence do not play an active role in negotiating the reduction of those very tariffs which work against the best interests of the people whom you represent. We ask you to join with us in negotiating a reduction in tariffs and non-tariff barriers.

The middle-income developing countries, some of you, have a special responsibility, along with us, a very powerful, economically developed country, to help widen world trade by opening your markets to exports from other developing and industrial countries.

Some of your economies are now large and dynamic enough to provide for both domestic consumption and exports at the same time. By giving priority to creating jobs, you can alleviate poverty while stimulating your own economies.

The industrial countries should help to stimulate this growth. As one step to this end, we propose to create a foundation for technological collaboration, which will help to develop and share the skills which are needed for economic and social growth. The challenge of economic development is to help the world's poor lift themselves out of misery. We need to assist governments which find themselves in financial crisis, if and when they are willing to make sound measures of self-help.

We need to support regional and sub-regional cooperation and integration through such organizations as the Caribbean Group for Cooperation in Economic Development, which is meeting this week in Washington[38]—I think 30 countries.

The recent decision by several Andean countries to establish a balance of payments support fund is a welcome contribution to regional financial stability. The little-noticed increase in intraregional trade credits and cooperation among central banks testifies to the maturity and the integration of Latin America.

Finally, let me say this: We set for ourselves an ambitious program last year. Much has been accomplished, but much more remains to be done.

The Organization of American States can play an important role in addressing and solving our common problems. It's become particularly effective in the areas of human rights and the keeping of the peace. It can and must become still more effective as its internal administrative and financial structure comes to reflect the greater equality in our relationships.

I believe that the mutual respect which characterized the negotiations, debate, and conclusion of the Panama Canal treaties can become the basis for new relations in this hemisphere and the world. With trust and cooperation, even the most difficult and serious disputes can be settled.

The other nations in this hemisphere, all of you, are increasingly important to my country and to the world. I do not expect that our views will always coincide, but I know that we do share the same basic values. Working together in a spirit of mutual respect and trust, we can achieve our common goals: a more just economic system, enhanced human rights and dignity, and permanent peace for us all.

Thank you very much.

7. ASIAN "ARC OF CRISIS"

(34) The Central Treaty Organization: Statement by Secretary of State Vance at the Opening of the 25th Session of the CENTO Council of Ministers, held in London April 19–20, 1978. [1]

This ministerial meeting reaffirms the commitment of CENTO members to enduring and important common interests. [2] As in the past, the United States remains committed to the central objective of CENTO—protecting the independence and territorial integrity of member states. My country remains committed as well to working with each of you on a number of critical issues which are of special interest to CENTO members because they have a direct or indirect impact on the stability and security of the CENTO region.

U.S. Defense Policies

The United States has recently completed a major review of its national defense strategy. The guiding principles which emerged from this study were first stated a month ago when President Carter spoke at Wake Forest University. [3] They are worth restating today. President Carter said:

We will match, together with our allies and friends, any threatening power through a combination of military forces, political efforts, and economic programs. We will not allow any other nation to gain military superiority over us.

We shall seek the cooperation of the Soviet Union and other nations in reducing areas of tension. We do not desire to intervene militarily in the internal domestic affairs of other countries nor to aggravate regional conflicts. And we shall oppose intervention by others.

[1] Text from *Bulletin,* June 1978: 24–6. Opening paragraphs omitted.
[2] The communiqué of this meeting was not distributed by the Department of State. A summary appears in *Survey of Current Affairs* (New York: British Information Services), May 1978: 151–2.
[3] Document 3.

While assuring our own military capabilities, we shall seek security through dependable, verifiable arms control agreements wherever possible.

We shall use our great economic, technological, and diplomatic advantages to defend our interests and to promote American values.

This statement of American policy indicates more than our concern for our own military strength; it indicates our readiness to act in concert with others to achieve a more peaceful and more stable world. This is why my country's association with CENTO is of fundamental importance to us.

While we maintain our military strength, we are also working for peace in a number of areas. These problems remain as challenges which must be addressed directly and in common. The fact that they are on our agenda this year, at last, indicates their complexity and suggests the difficulty we will face in achieving their resolution. But in each case, the stakes are so high that we cannot fail to do all we can to help the parties to disputes to find just resolutions.

Middle East

A just and lasting peace in the Middle East remains today of crucial importance to the United States and to the world. The past year has brought some progress. Working with the parties, we have been able to move from general concepts to a precise identification of areas of concern on which agreement must be reached. We have witnessed a narrowing of the gap, and with the historic visit of President Sadat to Jerusalem we have seen the initiation of direct contacts between Egypt and Israel. We strongly support these contacts, and we will continue to encourage and assist the parties to resolve their outstanding problems together.

We continue to believe that three basic issues must be addressed if a lasting settlement is to be achieved. These are:

* True peace, based on normal relations among the parties;
* Withdrawal by Israel on all fronts from territories occupied in 1967 and agreement by all parties on secure and recognized borders in accordance with U.N. Resolutions 242 and 338; and
* A just resolution of the Palestinian problem in all its aspects. The resolution must recognize the legitimate rights of the Palestinian people and enable the Palestinians to participate in the determination of their own future.

These are complex and difficult questions. The progress made in the first has, unfortunately, not been matched in the other two areas. Nevertheless, the United States remains committed to a continuation of the peace process. Statesmanship and perseverance will yield compromise—and compromise will open the door to a resolution of the conflict. One thing is clear: If the process of peace remains deadlocked, the inevitable regression toward conflict will be difficult to halt—with the most profound consequences for us all.

The United States will continue to assist and encourage the parties to resolve their differences. We are unwilling to let slip an historic opportunity to achieve a just and lasting peace when it may be within our grasp.

Africa

Another area of great concern to all of us is Africa. We are deeply concerned that the Soviet Union and Cuba are unwilling to recognize the fundamental principle often stated by African nations that they can solve their own problems without the use of external force.

The presence of large numbers of Cuban combat forces and Soviet personnel in the Horn of Africa does not promote stability.

The United States strongly supports the territorial integrity of all states in the region, including particularly Ethiopia, Djibouti, Somalia, and Kenya.

We seek the withdrawal of all foreign forces from Ethiopia and a peaceful resolution of the Eritrean dispute. It is clear to us that if the Eritrean issue is determined through the use of force by foreign troops, bloodshed and suffering will increase, no enduring solution will be found, and tensions in the region will only be heightened.

Now that Somali forces have withdrawn from the Ogaden and the territorial integrity of Ethiopia is not threatened, there is no legitimate rationale for the maintenance of external combat forces in that country. We will continue to consult actively with you as to ways we can work together to reduce tensions in the Horn, in support of the efforts of the Organization of African Unity.

In southern Africa, my country has been working closely with the United Kingdom, nations of the region, and others to help bring about a prompt and fair transition to independence and majority rule without further bloodshed in Rhodesia and Namibia.

Foreign Secretary Owen and I have just completed talks on the Rhodesian problem with the patriotic front and the parties in Salisbury.[4] We are convinced that we must keep the negotiating door open. Otherwise the parties will have no alternative to escalating conflict with the danger of increasing outside involvement. The front-line states and Nigeria have worked closely with us.

I believe our recent trip to Africa was well worthwhile. The patriotic front did not accept all the Anglo-American proposals. They

[4]Apr. 14–15.

did agree to attend further talks at which all parties would be represented. There was also real progress on issues that are central to assuring free and fair elections; there was general agreement on U.N. involvement in peacekeeping and observing elections; and, contingent on agreement on other issues, they accepted the executive authority of a neutral resident commissioner in the areas of defense and internal security.

Our talks in Salisbury and Pretoria were at least as positive as we had hoped. South Africa appears to understand the importance of achieving an early, internationally acceptable settlement which will bring peace. And while the Salisbury parties had said before our visit that they would reject an all-parties meeting, they are now willing to give it serious consideration. At least some realize that if they close the door to negotiations, they will further hurt their standing in the international community and will find it difficult to achieve the cease-fire that is so important to the holding of free and fair elections.

Our primary aim is to achieve a settlement among all the parties that will end the conflict. We remain committed to the Anglo-American proposals as a workable basis for a settlement. We also will continue to try to bring the parties together in roundtable talks.

In our talks on the Namibian question with the South Africans, there was recognition of the importance of a settlement which would have international acceptance. The South Africans have requested clarification of several of the proposals of the contact group. Foreign Secretary Owen and I agreed to discuss these matters with our colleagues in the contact group and to make a prompt reply so that both South Africa and SWAPO may respond soon to the contact group's proposals. A fair settlement in Namibia would do more than protect the people of that territory; it would also help to establish a sense of progress in southern Africa that would assist our efforts in Rhodesia.

Eastern Mediterranean

With respect to another important regional issue—that of Cyprus—my country remains fully committed to helping the parties and the Secretary General of the United Nations in the search for a solution that will permit the two Cypriot communities to live peacefully together within one independent and sovereign nation. We are committed to this goal because a divided Cyprus will continue to be an impediment to good relations between two important friends and allies—Turkey and Greece.

The United States views both Turkey and Greece as essential to the collective self-defense of the free world. The United States pledges its determined efforts to strengthening its ties in this vital region which is so crucial to the long-term interests of CENTO, and of NATO as well.

Persian Gulf

We remain deeply interested, too, in the security of the Persian Gulf region. The cardinal importance of this region is underscored by the world's increasing reliance on its energy resources and by the growing role which the Persian Gulf states have to play in supporting the stability and prosperity of other areas. The United States places great importance on its relationship with Iran—a CENTO partner—and with Saudi Arabia and the other gulf states.

Iran, buttressed by steadily growing economic and defensive strength, remains of fundamental importance as a strategic partner within the CENTO framework. Iran is playing a most valuable role in promoting regional progress and security.

Pakistan, too, can contribute much to the stability of the region. We have noted its significant role in normalizing relations among the countries of the South Asian subcontinent.

Economic Progess

While the swift resolution of disputes necessarily can demand the most urgent of our diplomatic efforts, we recognize that the peace and stability we seek will ultimately elude us unless we are willing to join with others in promoting global economic progress.

We have indicated our willingness to work with others to increase capital flows to the developing world; to build a fairer and more open system of world trade; to work to moderate disruptive movements in commodity prices; to cooperate on energy conservation and development; and to strengthen the technological capabilities of developing nations. We are pursuing each of these policies through bilateral and multilateral channels.

We believe that policies which promise economic equity are strongly linked to the prospects for protecting political human rights more fully. My country will continue to work with others who believe that common security, though dependent upon a strong defense, must be founded as well on the far-sighted pursuit of economic and political justice.

The world is changing. Diplomacy becomes more complex. The agenda of issues expands. Increasingly, no nation acting alone can resolve its problems. In such a world, the close relations and cooperation among the nations represented in this room becomes all the more important. Our security depends not only on our mutual trust and military strength but also on our ability to work together in addressing the problems that affect us all.

(35)   The United States and India: Remarks by President Carter before the Indian Parliament, New Delhi, January 2, 1978. [5]

Mr. Vice President, Mr. Prime Minister, Mr. Speaker, [6] *distinguished leaders of the Republic of India:*

I stand before you in this house, the seat of one of the world's greatest legislatures, with feelings of profound friendship and respect.

I bring with me the warm greetings and good wishes of the people of the second largest democracy on Earth, the United States of America, to the people of the largest democracy, the Republic of India.

Not long ago, both of our people's governments passed through grave crises. In different ways, the values for which so many have lived and died were threatened. In different ways, and on opposite sides of the world, these values have now been triumphant.

It is sometimes argued that the modern industrial state—with its materialism, its centralized bureaucracies, and the technological instruments of control available to those who hold power—must inevitably lose sight of the democratic ideal.

The opposite argument is made even more frequently. There are those who say that democracy is a kind of rich man's plaything, and that the poor are too preoccupied with survival to care about the luxury of freedom and the right to choose their own government.

This argument is repeated all over the world—mostly, I have noticed, by persons whose own bellies are full and who speak from positions of privilege and power in their own societies.

Their argument reminds me of a statement made by a great President of the United States, Abraham Lincoln. He said, "Whenever I hear anyone arguing for slavery, I feel a strong impulse to see it tried on him personally."

The evidence, both in India and in America, is plain. It is that there is more than one form of hunger, and neither the rich nor poor will feel satisfied without being fed in body and in spirit.

Is democracy important? Is human freedom valued by all people?

India has given her affirmative action and answer in a thunderous voice, a voice heard around the world. Something momentous happened here last March—not because any party in particular won or lost, but rather, I think, because the largest electorate on Earth freely and wisely chose its leaders at the polls. In this sense, democracy itself was the victor in your country.

[5] Text from *Presidential Documents,* 14: 5–11.
[6] Vice-President B.D. Jatti, Prime Minister Morarji R. Desai, and Speaker of the House of the People K.S. Hegde.

Together, we understand that in the field of politics, freedom is the engine of progress. India and America share practical experience with democracy.

We in the United States are proud of having achieved political union among a people whose ancestors come from all over the world. Our system strives to respect the rights of a great variety of minorities, including, by the way, a growing and productive group of families from your own country, India.

But the challenge of political union is even greater here in your own country. In the diversity of languages, religions, political opinions, and racial and cultural groups, India is comparable to the continent of Europe, which has a total population about the same size as your own. Yet India has forged her vast mosaic of humanity into a single great nation that has weathered many challenges to survival both as a nation and as a democracy. This is surely one of the greatest political achievements of this century or any other century.

India and the United States are at one in recognizing the right of free speech—which Mahatma Gandhi called "the foundation-stone of *Swaraj*" or self-government—and the rights of academic freedom, trade union organization, freedom of the press, and freedom of religion.

All these rights are recognized in international covenants. There are few governments which do not at least pay lip service to them. And yet, to quote Gandhi once more, "No principle exists in the abstract. Without its concrete application it has no meaning."

In India, as in the United States, these rights do have concrete application, and they have real meaning, too. It is to preserve these rights that both our nations have chosen similar political paths to the development of our resources and to the betterment of the life of our people.

There are differences between us in the degree to which economic growth is pursued through public enterprise on one hand and private enterprise on the other hand. But more important than these differences is our shared belief that the political structure in which development takes place should be democratic and should respect the human rights of each and every citizen in our countries.

Our two nations also agree that human needs are inseparable from human rights; that while civil and political liberties are good in themselves, they are much more useful and much more meaningful in the lives of people to whom physical survival is not a matter of daily anxiety.

To have sufficient food to live and to work; to be adequately sheltered and clothed; to live in a healthy environment and to be healed when sick; to learn and to be taught—these rights, too, must be the concerns of our governments. To meet these ends orderly economic growth is crucial. And if the benefits of growth are to reach those whose need is greatest, social justice is critical as well.

India is succeeding in this historic task. Your economic challenges are no secret, and their seriousness is well understood in the West.

But what is far less well understood is the degree to which Indian social and economic policy has been such a success. In the single generation since your independence was gained, extraordinary progress has been made.

India is now a major industrial power. Your economy ranks among the 10 largest in the whole world. You are virtually self-assured and self-sufficient in consumer goods and in a wide variety of other products, such as iron and steel.

There have been notable increases in production in nearly every important sector of your economy—increases which reflect an economy of great technological sophistication. This kind of growth is doubly important to try to reduce trade barriers and to promote both bilateral trade and mutual responsibility for the whole world's trading system.

But most important are the advances in human welfare that have touched the lives of ordinary Indians. Life expectancy has increased by 20 years since your independence. The threat of major epidemics has receded. The literacy rate in your country has doubled. While only a third of Indian children went to school in the years just after independence, nearly 90 percent of primary-age Indian children now receive schooling. Nine times as many students go to universities as they did before.

I mention these gains that we tend to overlook in our preoccupation with the problems that quite properly face and engage our attention.

India's difficulties, which we often experience ourselves and which are typical of the problems faced in the developing world, remind us of the tasks which lie ahead.

But India's successes are just as important, because they decisively refute the theory that in order to achieve economic and social progress, a developing country must accept an authoritarian or a totalitarian government with all the damage to the health of the human spirit which comes with it.

We are eager to join with you in maintaining and improving our valuable and mature partnership of political and economic cooperation.

It's a sobering fact, for instance, that in a nation of so many hundreds of millions of people, only a few American business leaders are now involved, on a daily basis, in the economic and commercial life of your country.

We need to identify more areas where we can work together for mutual benefit and, indeed, for the benefit of the whole world.

In the area of development, I am deeply impressed with the creative direction that the Government of India has taken in the new

economic statement. You have committed your nation unequivo-
cally to rural improvement and the creation of rural employment.
This policy now faces a test of implementation and, especially, the
test of bringing its benefits to the very poorest areas of your rural
population. The seriousness and the determination, however, of
your commitment is a cause for optimism.

We want to learn from you and to work with you however we
can.

In agriculture, there are also exciting new areas of technology on
which we can work together. After a decade of importing grain, India now stands with a surplus of nearly 20 million tons. This is a
tribute to the growing productivity of your agriculture and the
competence, also, of your administrative services.

We applaud the grain reserve program that you've begun, and we
would welcome the opportunity to share with you our resources
and our experience in dealing with storage problems that surpluses
bring with them.

Our countries must be in the forefront of the effort to bring into
existence the international food reserve that would mitigate the fear
of famine in the rest of the world. At the same time, we must recognize that today's surpluses are likely to be a temporary phenomenon. The best estimates indicate that unless new productive capacity is developed, the whole world with its rapidly growing population may be facing large food shortages in the mid-1980's.

The greatest opportunities to increase agricultural productivity
exist here in India and elsewhere in the developing world. These opportunities must be seized not just so that Indians can eat better,
but so that India can remain self-sufficient and, perhaps, even continue to export food to countries with less agricultural potential
than you have.

In the past, America and India have scored monumental achievements in working together in the agricultural field. But there is still
a vast, unrealized potential to be tapped.

I would like to see an intensified agricultural research program
aimed both at improving productivity in India and at developing
processes that could then be used elsewhere. This program could be
based in the agricultural universities of our two countries, but would
also extend across the whole frontier of research. And beyond research, I would like to identify joint development projects where
research can be tested and put to work.

Perhaps Prime Minister Desai and I may now instruct our governments to focus on these matters and to come up with specific
proposals within the next few months.

One of the most promising areas for international cooperation,
which I have already discussed with your Prime Minister, is in the
regions of eastern India and Bangladesh, where alternating periods

of drought and flood cut cruelly into food production. Several hundred million people live in this area. They happen to be citizens of India, Bangladesh, and Nepal.

Great progress has already been made between your nations in resolving questions concerning water. And we are prepared to give our support when the regional states request a study that will define how the international community, in cooperation with the nations of South Asia, can help the peoples of this area use water from the rivers and the mountains to achieve the productivity that is inherent in the land and the people.

Sustained economic growth requires a strong base in energy as well as in agriculture. Energy is a serious problem in both our countries, for both of us import oil at levels that can threaten our economic health and expose us, even, to danger if supplies are interrupted. American firms are already working with Indians in developing the oil-producing area off the shores of India, near Bombay.

We also have a long record of cooperation in the development of nuclear power, another important element of India's energy plans. Our work together will continue in this field, as well. This is a cold, technological subject. But Prime Minister Desai and I had warm and productive discussions about this field. We have notified him that shipments of nuclear fuel will be made for the Tarapur reactor.

And because of an accident that did occur in your heavy water production plant, we will make available to India, also, supplies from our reserves of heavy water.

Additionally, we stand ready to work with you in developing renewable energy resources, especially solar energy. There is no shortage of sunlight in India. And the lack of a massive, existing infrastructure tied to fossil fuel will make the application of solar and solar-related energy vastly easier here than it will be in my own country, where we are so heavily dependent upon other sources of energy. However, the inherently decentralized nature of solar energy makes it ideal as a complement to your government's stress on developing self-reliant villages and communities.

The silent void of space may seem remote from these challenges. But the intricate electronics of a space satellite can be as useful to earthbound farmers as a new plow.

The Indian and American Governments will tomorrow exchange diplomatic notes confirming that the United States will program its LANDSAT Earth resources satellite to transmit data directly to a ground receiving station that India will own and operate.

This satellite service will provide India with comprehensive topographic and minerals information and timely data on the ever-changing condition of weather, agricultural, water, and other natural resources. Under the terms of the agreement, India will make available to neighboring countries any information that affects them.

Also, India has already reserved space on board the American space shuttle in 1981 to initiate a domestic communications satellite system, using a satellite designed to Indian specifications.

We are very pleased that our space technology, together with India's superb space communications capacity, will serve the cause of practical progress in your country.

Our scholarly exchanges have already enriched the lives of Americans who participated in them. And I hope the same has been true of Indian participants. In matters of culture and the arts, we know how much we have to gain. Not only India but also the rest of Asia and Africa and the Middle East have much to offer us. I hope to expand the opportunities for our own citizens to appreciate and to enjoy the strong and varied culture in the nations of your part of the world.

In global politics, history has cast our countries in different roles. The United States is one of the so-called super powers; India is the largest of the nonaligned countries. But each of us respects the other's conception of its international responsibilities, and the values that we do share provide a basis for cooperation in attacking the great global problems of economic justice, human rights, and the prevention of war.

This pursuit of justice and peace and the building of a new economic order must be undertaken in ways that promote constructive development rather than fruitless confrontation. Every country will suffer if the North-South dialog is permitted to founder.

Because India is both a developing country and also an industrial power, you are in a unique position to promote constructive international discussion about trade, energy, investment, balance of payments, technology, and other questions. I welcome your playing this worldwide leadership role.

I know that there will be times when we will disagree on specific issues and even on general approaches to larger problems. But I hope and believe that our shared interests and our common devotion to democratic values will help us to move toward agreement on important global and bilateral issues.

But neither of us seeks to align with the other except in the pursuit of peace and justice. We can even help each other to alleviate differences which might exist between ourselves and other nations.

Our two countries are part of a democratic world that includes nations in all stages of development, from Sweden and Japan to Sri Lanka and Costa Rica.

We share many common problems. But we also share an obligation to advance human rights—not by interfering in the affairs of other nations, not by trying to deny other nations the right to choose their own political and social system, but by speaking the truth as we see it and by providing an admirable example of what democracy can mean and what it can accomplish.

The danger of war threatens everyone, and the United States is trying to help reduce that danger—in the SALT negotiations with the Soviet Union, in talks aimed at a comprehensive ban of the testing of all nuclear explosives anywhere on earth, and in our own policy of restraint on conventional arms transfers. We are also working hard to restrict the proliferation of nuclear explosives.

We are seeking to help the process of peace in Africa and the Middle East. And we are taking steps to forestall, along with the Soviets, great power rivalry and the escalation of military presence in your own Indian Ocean.

India is pledged to peaceful cooperation with your neighbors, and India is an important part of almost any United Nations peacekeeping force. India is a present and frequent member of the Security Council and has been in the forefront of campaigns against colonialism and against apartheid.

The motto of my country is "In God We Trust;" India's is *Satyameva Jayte*—"Truth Alone Prevails." I believe that such is the commonality of our fundamental values that your motto could be ours, and perhaps our motto could also be yours.

Our nations share the goals of peace in the world and human development in our own societies. And we share, as well, the conviction that the means that we employ to reach these goals must be as much in keeping with the principles of freedom and human dignity and social justice as are the goals themselves.

This affinity of belief is as strong a tie as there can be between any two nations on Earth. The values that Americans and Indians share have deeply affected my own life. I come to you, as a national leader, yes, in the hope that my visit will mark a new and a higher stage in the steadily improving relations between our two countries.

But in a more personal sense—a sense that is very close to my own heart—I come also as a pilgrim.

This morning I had the honor of laying a wreath on the memorial to Mahatma Gandhi. In that sacred place, so simple and so serene, I recalled anew the ways in which Gandhi's teachings have touched the lives of so many millions of people in my own country.

When I was growing up on a farm in the State of Georgia, in the heart of the Southern United States, an invisible wall of racial segregation stood between me and my black classmates, schoolmates, playmates, when we were old enough to know what segregation was. But it seemed then as if that wall between us would exist forever.

But it did not stand forever. It crumbled and fell. And though the rubble has not yet been completely removed, it no longer separates us from one another, blighting the lives of those on both sides of it.

Among the many who marched and suffered and bore witness against the evil of racial prejudice, the greatest was Dr. Martin Luther King, Jr. He was a son of Georgia and a spiritual son of Mahatma Gandhi.

The most important influence in the life and work of Dr. King, apart from his own religious faith, was the life and work of Gandhi. Martin Luther King took Gandhi's concepts of nonviolence and truth-force and put them to work in the American South.

Like Gandhi, King believed that truth and love are the strongest forces in the universe. Like Gandhi, he knew that ordinary people, armed only with courage and faith, could overcome injustice by appealing to the spark of good in the heart, even, of the evil-doer.

Like Gandhi, we all learned that a system of oppression damages those at the top as surely as it does those at the bottom. And for Martin Luther King, like Mahatma Gandhi, nonviolence was not only a political method, it was a way of life and a spiritual path to union with the ultimate.

These men set a standard of courage and idealism that few of us can meet, but from which all of us can draw inspiration and sustenance.

The nonviolent movement for racial justice in the United States, a movement inspired in large measure by the teachings and examples of Gandhi and other Indian leaders—some of whom are here today—changed and enriched my own life and the lives of many millions of my countrymen.

I am sure you will forgive me for speaking about this at some length. I do so because I want you all to understand that when I speak of friendship between the United States and India, I speak from the heart as well as the head. I speak from a deep, firsthand knowledge of what the relationship between our two countries has meant in the past and how much more, even, it can mean for all of us in the future.

For the remainder of this century and into the next, the democratic countries of the world will increasingly turn to each other for answers to our most pressing common challenge; how our political and spiritual values can provide the basis for dealing with the social and economic strains to which they will unquestionably be subjected.

The experience of democracy is like the experience of life itself—always changing, infinite in its variety, sometimes turbulent, and all the more valuable for having been tested by adversity.

We share that experience with you, and we draw strength from it. Whatever the differences between my country and yours, we are moving along the path of democracy toward a common goal of human development. I speak for all Americans when I say that I am deeply grateful that you and I travel that road together. Thank you very much.

(36)   The United States and Japan: Address by Dr. Brzezinski before the Japan Society, New York, April 27, 1978.[7]

I would like to speak to you this evening about U.S. relations with Japan. I shall begin with a few remarks about the Administration's broader intentions in foreign policy, for this defines the context of our bilateral relationship. Our approach reflects both substantial continuity with the policies of our predecessors and some important nuances of change.

- We seek wider cooperation with our key allies. Close collaboration with Japan and Western Europe has long been the point of departure for America's global involvement; however, we are also seeking to broaden these patterns of cooperation to include the new "regional influentials," thus responding to changes over the last 15–20 years in the global distribution of power.
- We are seeking to stabilize the U.S.-Soviet relationship, pursuing through a broader range of negotiations a pattern of detente which is to be both comprehensive and genuinely reciprocal. At the same time, we are expressing cautious but more explicit American interest in Eastern Europe.
- We intend to maintain sufficient military capabilities to support our global security interests. Above all, we shall maintain an adequate strategic deterrent; preserve, along with our NATO partners, the conventional balance in Europe; and develop a quick-reaction global force available for rapid redeployment in areas of central importance to the United States, such as Korea.
- Politically we shall remain engaged in all regions. In the Asia-Pacific area, we shall preserve a strategic and economic presence consonant with our large and growing stake in the region. Above all, this requires a widening of our cooperation with Japan and an expansion of our relationship with China. We shall enhance our collaboration with the moderate states in Africa in the cause of African emancipation. No longer tied to only a regional approach, we shall strengthen our bilateral ties with the nations of Latin America while cooperating with them more fully on their global concerns. We shall continue to pursue a genuine settlement in the Middle East while expanding our relationship with the moderate Arab countries.
- We shall increase our efforts to develop constructive and cooperative solutions to emerging global issues. Above all, we need to head off any drift toward nuclear proliferation.

[7]White House Press Release; text from *Bulletin,* June 1978: 1–4.

- We shall seek to sustain domestic support for our policies by rooting them clearly in our moral values. We believe that our devotion to human rights is responsive to man's yearning everywhere for greater social justice.

This is an ambitious agenda. We shoulder the responsibilities it imposes on us willingly. But obviously we cannot shoulder them alone. Success will require greater cooperation, above all with our closest friends.

Centrality of U.S.-Japan Relations

Japan is clearly such a close friend. We have been impelled toward a special relationship with Japan by the force of history and by strategic and economic imperatives. The members of this Society have long recognized the basic proposition I wish to affirm this evening: Close partnership between the United States and Japan is a vital foundation for successful pursuit of America's wider objectives in the world. If relations between America and Japan are strong, we benefit and the world benefits; when we run into difficulties, we suffer and others suffer with us.

Our alliance not only protects the security of Japan and America; it has also become a central element in the equilibrium in the Pacific, which all the major powers share a stake in preserving.

Japan is our largest overseas trading partner; trade between us exceeded $29 billion in 1977. Economic cooperation confers benefits on each of us; it also sustains the prosperity of the Pacific basin and the stability of the international trade and payments system.

Effective responses to pressing global issues—whether the development of alternative sources of energy, expanding food production, assuring equitable access to the riches of the ocean area, or stemming nuclear proliferation—demand active collaboration between us.

In short, we are mutually dependent. No relationship in our foreign policy is more important. None demands more careful nourishment.

While cooperation between the United States and Japan is indispensable, it is not automatically assured. Managing our relationship has become more challenging as our links have grown more numerous and more complex and as each nation's policies have come to have a more direct impact on the welfare of the other's people. Moreover, most of the problems we face are bigger than both of us—they are not susceptible to bilateral resolution, and they arise most frequently in multilateral forums.

It is scarcely surprising, therefore, that our relations have not been entirely free of difficulties. Over the last year, for example, our approaches to nuclear reprocessing diverged to some extent, and we experienced a large trade imbalance.

In each case we consulted closely. We devised arrangements for managing these problems which reflected both our respective concerns and the broader interests of the international community. We demonstrated that the test of effective ties between societies as dynamic as ours and economies as competitive as ours is not the absence of problems but the spirit in which we confront them and the competence with which we resolve them.

Current Challenge

Our interests and Japan's require that we broaden and deepen our ties, adapting our relationship to an era in which our policies have a global impact. This imposes on each of us an obligation to take each other's interests and perspectives carefully into account on a wider and wider range of issues.

Japan's extraordinary economic growth has challenged it to define a wider vision of its role in the world—in Asia and beyond. Japanese decisions, which once would have been considered domestic in character, now impinge directly on the interests of distant nations. Japan's capacity to promote global economic development, to aid its neighbors, to promote a constructive North-South dialogue, to encourage the reconciliation of former rivals, and to provide for its own defense have grown. So have the expectations of Japan on the part of the international community. A commitment of Japan's political and economic capabilities to the achievement of major global goals is essential to a strong U.S.-Japanese relationship.

In recent years the United States has placed its relationship with Japan primarily in a setting of collaboration among the advanced democratic countries. This is entirely appropriate. It is important that we remember, however, that while Japan is an industrial power, it is also an Asian nation, acutely interested in the continuity of America's role in the Pacific. Uncertainties about our Asian intentions have inevitably arisen in the wake of our disengagement from Indochina and our planned ground force withdrawal from Korea. A strong American role in the Pacific remains essential for the protection of our own strategic interests. It is also an important factor in our relationship with Japan. We must adjust our relationship to accommodate these concerns.

Broadening Cooperation

In the economic field, the world has had to accommodate to Japan's growing strength, even as Japan has been adapting its own policies to shoulder the responsibilities which strength confers.

Neither we nor the Japanese have adjusted policies quickly enough in recent years to avoid major difficulties. Consequently our economic relations have been marked over the past year by a growing Japanese current-account surplus, sharp imbalance in our bilateral trade, a huge U.S. balance-of-payments deficit, and currency disorders. These structural problems arise particularly out of the dramatic growth in U.S. oil imports in recent years and from Japan's transition to an era of lower economic growth. They have global consequences.

Only through concerted action by all the advanced industrial democracies can we deal effectively with our common problems. We will all go forward together to lower trade barriers, or succumb together to protectionism. That is why we must assure a continued expansion in world trade through the successful conclusion of the multilateral trade negotiations (MTN) in Geneva this summer. The United States has taken the lead by presenting a forthcoming tariff offer which we expect other strong economies to match.

The United States and Japan must bear special responsibilities for actions which will not only reduce barriers to trade through a fair and balanced MTN agreement but also promote continued economic recovery, check disorderly exchange rate movements, encourage energy conservation and the development of alternative sources, and increase the transfer of resources to promote growth in the economies of the developing nations. We cannot afford to pursue beggar-thy-neighbor policies, export our domestic problems to others, or look for scapegoats. We have a mutual responsibility to deal with the fundamentals of these problems.

The United States must take decisive action in several areas:

- The implementation of an effective energy program is the most important step. We must substantially reduce our oil imports if we are to reduce our current-accounts deficit, diminish pressures on the dollar, and stabilize international money markets.

    The Administration presented an energy bill to the Congress more than a year ago. We need action, and if Congress does not act, then the executive branch must. While the United States has the largest problem in this respect, the question of how to take joint action to conserve and develop alternative sources of energy must engage the efforts of all advanced nations as well— and particularly those like Japan which experience extraordinary dependence on external sources of supply.
- We must bring inflation under control not only for domestic reasons but also to bolster our competitiveness in international trade.
- We must devote more effort to the promotion of American exports. In the months to come the Administration shall look

not only for ways to encourage exports but to reduce or eliminate current governmental practices which reduce our competitiveness and discourage our business community from searching out overseas markets.

These adjustments are required not only to underpin our economic position in the world but to enhance the stability and growth of the international economy and thus fortify our economic ties with Japan. Japan must make comparable structural adjustments for it has become too large an economy to rely on export-led growth.

The Japanese Government recognizes the need for such adjustments and has begun actions designed to achieve sharp reductions in its current accounts surplus in 1978; an economic growth rate of 7% this fiscal year; an MTN agreement assuring the U.S. of reciprocal and roughly equivalent access to the Japanese market; and expanded long-term capital flows to the developing countries. These measures are essential to the vitality of the world economy as well as the continued health of our bilateral relations. We must be decisive in action and patient in awaiting the results.

If one looks beyond current economic problems, there is a remarkable consonance of view between the United States and Japan on virtually all major international issues. We intend to sustain this confluence in our approaches toward the major Communist powers, toward Asian issues, toward the North-South dialogue, and toward major international negotiations. We look for Japan to play a more active political role in dealing with such matters. It is neither necessary nor possible to preserve identical policies on such issues, but the development of compatible approaches to common problems should be an objective for us both.

America's Role in Asia

Close cooperation between us is especially important in Asia. There have been recurrent suggestions that the United States is withdrawing from Asia. These suggestions are untrue. The United States will maintain a strong and diversified military presence and an active diplomacy in the Asian-Pacific region to support our growing economic and political stakes in the area.

- Above all, we shall sustain the Treaty of Mutual Cooperation and Security with Japan. For Japan this treaty offers strategic protection and firm moorings for its diplomacy. For the United States, alliance with a Japan steadily improving its self-defense capabilities provides the anchor for our position in East Asia and extends the reach of our strategic and political influence in the Pacific. Beyond these reciprocal benefits, our alliance contributes to the stability of Northeast Asia and the Pacific, and it threatens no one.

- We will manage ground combat force withdrawals from Korea in a prudent fashion and help build up South Korea's capabilities in order to assure that there is no weakening of its defenses.
- We shall preserve the strength of the 7th Fleet and our air units in the Pacific while improving them qualitatively.
- We shall strengthen our ties with our traditional allies in Australia and New Zealand.
- We shall seek to assure our continued access to military facilities in the Philippines through arrangements which take full account of Philippine sovereignty over the bases.
- We shall deepen our bilateral relations with the non-Communist states of Southeast Asia and encourage the growing cohesion of the Association of South East Asian Nations. And we shall persevere in our measured efforts to develop constructive relationships with Indochina.
- In recent years Asian nations have come to depend more heavily upon U.S. trade and investment as a result of our strong and steady growth and the comparatively greater access Asian producers of manufactured goods enjoy in our market. We expect that to continue.
- The American-Chinese relationship is a central element of our global policy. We shall endeavor to expand our relations with the People's Republic of China. It is important that we make progress in normalizing relations with China, and we shall consult with the Chinese on major international matters that are of importance to us both.

The steady implementation of these policies is required by our own interests and should converge with Japanese interests.

Our defense cooperation, specifically, is excellent. Japan is strengthening its air and naval defenses. Cooperation between our uniformed services is growing. Base issues arise less frequently and are resolved amicably. Last fall Japan agreed to help with some of the expenses associated with our military presence.

We look for these trends to evolve further, even as Japan continues to remind the world that security cannot be achieved through military strength alone. Through such measures as Prime Minister Fukuda's trip to Southeast Asia last summer, Japan has undertaken to expand its role in Asian development, speed the development of a strong regional grouping in Southeast Asia, and discourage the emergence of polarization between two antagonistic blocs in that area. These are constructive steps, and we welcome their vigorous implementation.

In the weeks ahead, there will be visible evidence of our resolve to intensify America's diplomatic efforts in Asia.

Vice President Mondale will depart April 29 for Southeast Asia and the Southwest Pacific. He will visit the Philippines, Thailand, Indonesia, Australia, and New Zealand on a mission which we consider of great importance. Important changes are taking place in that region. The Vice President will be assessing the force and direction of those changes in order to offer recommendations on how we can continue to play a constructive role commensurate with our significant stake in the prosperity and security of that area.

On May 3 Prime Minister Fukuda will visit Washington for consultations with President Carter. We welcome this chance to harmonize our approaches to key issues in advance of the Bonn summit in July. The two leaders know and respect each other; I know personally that they work well together.

On May 18 I will embark on a trip to Northeast Asia. In Peking I will discuss global issues of parallel concern with Chinese leaders. Subsequently I will visit Tokyo and Seoul to hold consultations with the leaders of Japan and the Republic of Korea.

Conclusion

The relationship that has developed between the United States and Japan is uniquely significant. Despite differences in our national situation and national styles, we have fashioned ties that are rooted in shared interests and common values—our commitment to democratic procedures, civil rights, the market system, a free press, and open societies.

The attributes of the Japanese people and nation are formidable. As a people and a nation, we have come to respect, admire, and often learn from Japan—even as we compete. This is the essence of our interdependence which has been built carefully with trust, vitality, and common purpose.

Looking back at what we have created over the past 30 years, we can assert with confidence that we have established a permanent partnership of value not only to ourselves but to the entire world community. We shall work to assure its durability.

(37) America's Role in Southeast Asia and the Pacific: Address by Vice-President Mondale at the East-West Center, Honolulu, May 10, 1978.[8]

My discussions with the leaders of the Philippines, Thailand, In-

[8]Text from *Bulletin,* July 1978: 22–5. Introductory paragraphs omitted.

donesia, Australia, and New Zealand were held at the request of President Carter in order to help define clearly America's role in the region. I want to report to the American people on this mission and on the new role for our nation in the Pacific community.

For nearly a decade, our involvement in Southeast Asia touched not only every corner of the region but ultimately every family in America. When that era ended 3 years ago, many Americans understandably wanted to turn their attention away from Southeast Asia. Our military presence in the region declined. Aid levels dropped. And for several years high-level American visitors were few. These developments induced deep concern that the United States would abandon the area.

All the non-Communist countries of the region want America to maintain a visible presence. They value our security role and the deployment of U.S. naval and air forces. They want stronger economic ties with us and welcome an active American diplomacy.

The problem that challenged the Carter Administration was to fashion a policy toward Southeast Asia that advanced American interests in a setting of rapidly changing circumstances. We must define a sustainable level of American involvement in the region, one that accommodates local concerns; one that is less colored by past traumas. And our new role requires emphasis on America's new foreign policy concerns—such as human rights and arms transfer restraints. This is not an easy task. But we believe we have begun.

In each capital I visited, I reaffirmed one central proposition: America is unalterably a Pacific power. This is a natural condition of history and geography, as well as a conscious choice. The State of Hawaii and various American territories are located in the Pacific. America has extensive political, economic, and security interests in Asia. Our ties with Asian nations are central to the success of our global policy.

Our key Asian alliances contribute to regional stability and a favorable global balance of power. We will preserve them.

- The freedom of the sealanes in the Pacific are vital to the security and well-being of the United States and all maritime powers. We will protect them.
- Our trade with the Pacific basin nations—which is larger and growing faster than with any other region—is crucial to the health of our own economy. We will expand it.
- Our relationship with the People's Republic of China contributes to a stable balance in the Pacific. We will strive to deepen it.
- Our lives, our art, our sciences are enriched through cultural exchanges of peoples and ideas across the Pacific. We will strengthen them.

We will not cling to past patterns of involvement in the Pacific. We will shape our future involvement to assure a balance between preserving security and promoting constructive change, between government actions and private enterprise. We will meet necessities of power and fulfill the claims of principle.

I saw a vastly different Southeast Asia when I last visited the region in 1966. For many Americans, at that time, Southeast Asia meant violence, instability, and corruption. Ideological conflict tore Southeast Asia apart. The economic outlook was uncertain. Regional cooperation was a mere aspiration. China inspired fear in its neighbors. Japan pursued a diplomacy dominated by commercial interests. Most of the small non-Communist states in the region were deeply dependent on the United States, and the very size of our presence invited excessive involvement in their internal affairs.

Hopeful Trends

What I have seen in the past 10 days reveals dramatically how far Southeast Asia—and we, the American people—have traveled in a few short years. The United States is at peace in Asia, and the region is relatively tranquil. Old ideological struggles have lost their force, nationalism has triumphed over all competing ideologies, and the most intense regional rivalries now pit Communist nations against each other.

The Pacific basin has become the most dynamic economic zone in the world. Its prosperity is shared by all except those nations that have rejected the market system. The era of great power dominion has given way to a more mature and equitable partnership. Regional cooperation is no longer a slogan; ASEAN has moved into a period of substantive accomplishment. Economic issues are now the prime concerns of most governments in the area.

Japan's economy continues to provide an engine of growth for the Pacific basin, and the Japanese are defining a wider vision of their political role in the region through the expansion of their economic assistance, their support for ASEAN, and their efforts to discourage the emergence of antagonistic blocs in Southeast Asia.

China has become an increasingly constructive force in the region and is pursuing policies in Southeast Asia which in some respects parallel our own.

These are hopeful trends. They offer the prospect of new and promising relationships with the nations of the Pacific. They encourage me to believe we can combine our traditional concerns about security with an imaginative response to a new agenda—assuring adequate food supplies for Asia's growing population, solving trade and commodity problems, developing alternative sources of energy, promoting patterns of regional cooperation and reconciliation, and promoting wider observance of basic human rights.

Security Commitments

All these objectives require that America remain strong in the Pacific. If we do so, our security everywhere will be enhanced. If we do not, the consequences will not be confined to Asia alone. Yet the nature of our security role is changing. Our willingness to maintain a U.S. military presence must be balanced by the growing self-reliance of our friends.

Our security concerns are sharpest in Northeast Asia where the interests of all the major powers directly intersect. But we cannot draw a line across the Pacific and assume that what happens in Southeast Asia will not affect Japan and Korea. Moreover, the area is of great intrinsic importance.

- It is rich in resources and offers the United States a large and growing market.
- It sits astride sealanes through which Middle East oil flows to Japan and to our own west coast.
- Access to Philippine bases enhances our strategic flexibility, and our ANZUS ties contribute to the stability of the Southwest Pacific.
- The friends and allies we have in the area strengthen our global positions; their independence and well-being remain important to us.

Perhaps most significant of all are the human ties: ties of kinship, of comradeship and sacrifice in war, of shared dreams for peace.

Fortunately, Southeast Asia is no longer a theater of large-scale armed struggle. But our friends there continue to have serious and legitimate security concerns. Many states in the region remain plagued by internal conflicts. Vietnamese ambitions in the area remain unclear. Armed clashes between Communist states and Sino-Soviet competition generate growing pressures and uncertainties.

The non-Communist nations continue to look to the United States for help. They do not seek our direct military involvement, which they consider neither desirable nor necessary. But they do want us to sustain a military presence to serve as a deterrent and a source of psychological reassurance. They want us to be a reliable source of essential defense equipment, thus avoiding the need to establish wasteful and inefficient local defense industries. They want diplomatic support in their efforts to avoid being drawn into the rivalries of other great powers.

These desires are reasonable and consistent with our interests. I affirmed at each stop our intent to maintain America's multilateral and bilateral security commitments and preserve a balanced and flexible military posture in the Pacific. Our friends want this; our potential adversaries expect it; our interests require it.

- In the Philippines I discussed with President Marcos amendments to our existing Military Base Agreement which can stabilize our continued use of these key military facilities on terms that fully respect Philippine sovereignty over the bases.
- In Indonesia and Thailand I emphasized our intent to remain a reliable supplier of defense equipment even as we attempt to encourage greater restraint in the field of arms transfers. I confirmed our willingness to deliver F-5 aircraft to Thailand and A-4 aircraft to Indonesia. These systems permit our friends to enhance their self-reliance without threatening their neighbors.
- In Australia and New Zealand I reaffirmed our commitment to ANZUS and made it clear that any Indian Ocean arms limitations arrangements we may negotiate with the Soviets will not impair our ability to support these commitments—as evidenced by our decision to hold joint naval exercises from time to time off the west coast of Australia.
- To those who are concerned with putting the Vietnam war behind us, I pointed out that we have made a fair offer to the Vietnamese—that we are ready to establish diplomatic relations without preconditions. But Hanoi is still demanding a prior commitment of American aid, something which the American people cannot accept.
- To all those with whom I spoke, I repeated our determination not to intervene in the internal affairs of Southeast Asian Nations.

We threaten no nation. But we shall express in a tangible way our resolve to contribute to the security of the area.

Addressing the New Agenda

All of the Asian leaders with whom I met emphasized that national resilience, economic growth, social justice, and regional cooperation—rather than military strength alone—provide the essential foundation of security. I conveyed President Carter's desire to support their efforts to help themselves—particularly in developing their economic potential.

As in the security field, our economic involvement is undergoing rapid change. It is difficult to overstate America's economic stake in the Pacific. Two-way trade with the East Asian Pacific nations reached $61 billion last year. Our investments in the Pacific now exceed $16 billion and yield high returns. Forty percent of our imports of manufactured goods come from the Pacific. And the region offers a rich source of energy and raw materials. Our trade and investment with Southeast Asia have matured. We buy more than we sell; our private capital transfers exceed our aid; and our imports include a growing proportion of manufactured goods rather than raw materials.

The concerns I encountered focused less on aid than on business—our regulatory processes, our incentives for private investment, and the fear of possible protectionism in the United States. Conversely, the issues I raised dealt with the need to work together to increase Southeast Asian agricultural productivity, develop alternative energy supplies, expand trade, and promote more equitable growth.

In the future the following tasks must claim our priority attention.

We must assure the continued expansion of our trade with the Pacific nations—and others—through the successful conclusion of the multilateral trade negotiations. Agriculture is an essential element of this negotiation. All of us will benefit if tariff and nontariff barriers to trade are reduced; all of us will suffer if the negotiations do not succeed. The time to make progress is this year. We have put forward a generous offer in Geneva. We expect other developed countries—like Japan and the European Community—to match it.

We must help the Asian nations overcome deficiencies in their agricultural productivity. The Pacific basin has special assets for dealing with this issue. The three largest grain exporters in the world—the United States, Canada, and Australia—border on the Pacific. So, too, do several of the largest grain importers—especially Japan and Indonesia. While rapid population growth is increasing food requirements in Southeast Asia, its nations also have considerable potential for expanding productivity, which we must encourage.

I emphasized our determination to undertake a comprehensive assault on this problem by:

- Expanding our long-term P.L. 480 and other forms of aid to food-deficit countries like Indonesia if they will take practical steps to increase agricultural productivity;
- Offering the use of Landsat[9] satellites to help assess regional ecological problems;
- Focusing our bilateral aid in Southeast Asia on rural development; and
- Improving international food security by helping to create an international system of nationally held food reserves to meet international shortages.

We must promote the development of alternate sources of energy.

[9]Formally called Earth Resources Technology Satellite.

Southeast Asian countries—apart from Indonesia—have only modest proven oil reserves, but they possess abundant supplies of natural gas, coal, uranium, and geothermal resources. Their rapid development will enhance our energy security and that of our friends while slowing the upward pressure on oil prices. We must find new ways to use our technology to assist local development of indigenous energy resources.

In the course of my trip I offered to send technical teams from our Department of Energy to help assess regional energy resources, strengthen energy planning, and identify new areas for collaboration. I made clear our interest in expanding cooperation in the development of conventional and nonconventional fuels. We can learn much from nations such as New Zealand, which have had long practical experience with geothermal energy production.

- I responded positively to the idea of a formal consultative mechanism to facilitate deeper energy cooperation with ASEAN.
- I emphasized that the American private sector remains the most skillful in the world at developing new sources of oil and natural gas.

We must preserve Asia's access to capital on favorable terms. Our bilateral assistance programs remain crucial to the Philippines, Thailand, and Indonesia as each tries to deal with staggering problems of rural poverty, hunger, and unemployment. These development priorities reflect the new directions in our own aid program. We shall work with other donors and recipients to see that these objectives are met.

Meanwhile, we will continue to increase our development assistance to multilateral institutions such as the Asian Development Bank. During my visit to the Bank headquarters in Manila, I confirmed President Carter's decision to contribute $445 million to the 1979-82 replenishment program. This will help assure adequate financing for development plans in the region.

We shall encourage the increasingly influential role of the U.S. private sector in promoting Asian development for our mutual benefit. When I met in Jakarta with representatives of American business in Asia, my message was simple: We want our business community actively engaged in the Pacific; we want its role to grow and our companies to prosper. The Administration is developing a comprehensive strategy for increasing American exports. We will give priority to reforming or eliminating governmental practices that undercut America's competitive position in Asia.

We will continue to promote the cohesion of ASEAN—the Association of South East Asian Nations. One of the most encouraging developments in Southeast Asia is the emergence of the ASEAN regional group. This association of nations is developing greater economic cooperation and acquiring the habit of consulting closely on political issues.

We have long enjoyed close relations with the individual members of ASEAN. We now seek stronger ties with the organization itself. In all of my talks with Southeast Asian leaders, I emphasized our willingness to host U.S.-ASEAN consultations at the ministerial level in Washington later this year. It is up to ASEAN's leaders to define the future patterns of regional cooperation. For our part, we are ready to support their initiatives.

Human Rights

In addition to maintaining security and strengthening our economic ties, our new role in Southeast Asia and the Pacific requires the affirmation of the basic values for which our nation stands. As President Carter said in his inaugural address, "Because we are free we can never be indifferent to the fate of freedom elsewhere. Our moral sense dictates a clear-cut preference for those societies which share with us an abiding respect for individual human rights."[10]

If our foreign policy is to be credible and effective, it must be based on these principles: the right to live without fear of cruel and degrading treatment, to participate in the decisions of government, to achieve social justice, and to seek peaceful change. We can take justifiable pride in our military strength and our economic prowess, but the greatest source of American influence is the power of our example.

The promotion of wider observance of human rights is a central objective of the Administration's foreign policy. In Southeast Asia, there is no more profound test of our government's commitment to human rights than the way in which we respond to the rapidly increasing flow of Indochinese refugees who deserve our admiration for their courage and our sympathy for their plight. My trip has convinced me that we and others have underestimated the magnitude of the refugee problem. The flow of refugees is rapidly increasing. Vietnam's immediate neighbors are hard-pressed to handle the growing numbers of "boat cases" as well as large numbers of land refugees, and the burden of coping with these increased numbers falls disproportionately upon Thailand.

No single country can manage this problem alone. Given our legacy of involvement in Vietnam, we bear special responsibilities, and

[10]*AFR, 1977:* 155–6.

we are prepared to meet them. The United States must take the lead in developing a broader international effort to handle the refugee problem. I informed Southeast Asian leaders that the United States will exercise parole authority to accept an additional 25,000 refugees from Southeast Asia annually. We will expedite the processing of refugees destined for the United States by stationing additional Immigration and Naturalization Service personnel in Bangkok.

I extended to Thai authorities an offer of up to $2 million to support their development of longer term plans for handling the Indochinese refugees. And I made clear that once such plans are developed, the United States will be prepared to offer more substantial assistance, in concert with others, to finance the permanent settlement of refugees in Thailand and elsewhere. In short, we shall do our part to find permanent homes for the refugees; we will urge others to do theirs.

There is no human rights situation in Asia, or indeed the world, which cries out for more attention than the tragedy still continuing in Cambodia. We have little leverage with which to affect the harsh, brutal, repressive nature of the regime in Cambodia, but we will continue to try to focus the world's attention on the horror of what is happening there.

Some critics suggest that the preservation of security and the promotion of human rights are mutually exclusive objectives. They are not. Only in an environment of security can human rights genuinely flourish. Yet, no government which fails to respond to the basic human needs of its people or which closes off all channels of dissent can achieve that security which is derived from the consent of free citizens.

The security we seek is not an end in itself, and it cannot be divorced from the question for social and economic justice. This poses for us a diplomatic challenge of extraordinary delicacy, for we must pursue both our interests and our ideals; we must avoid both cynicism and sentimentalism; we must shun both callous indifference to suffering and arrogant intrusion into others' internal affairs. And if we are to succeed:

- We must concern ourselves with achieving results rather than claiming credit;
- We must combine frankness in our private diplomacy with forbearance in our public statements; and
- We must remember that our example is our most potent weapon.

I am confident that we can strike the right chord. During each of my stops, I was able to speak frankly about human rights while enhancing cooperation on security and other matters. I believe we can develop relationships of confidence with the leaders of these nations without forfeiting the opportunity to listen to a wide variety of political opinions. And in several key stops I met with private citizens to hear a wide variety of views. I hope progress is being made. For example, we have received indications that the Government of Indonesia is seriously considering speeding up the phased release of the 10,000 prisoners scheduled to be freed by the end of this year.

Only time will tell whether our efforts will yield genuine and enduring results. But unless we assert our beliefs, we can neither expect the support of our own people nor respond to the yearnings of others. As Archibald MacLeish once wrote, "There are those who will say that the liberation of humanity, the freedom of man and mind is nothing but a dream. They are right. It is. It is the American dream."

Conclusion

The Pacific basin, I am convinced, has begun an unprecedented and exciting era of change and growth. The future promises rapid economic advance and relative political stability, nationalism accompanied by regional cooperation, security without huge defense budgets, effective governmental authority combined with a growing respect for the rights of individuals.

This is what is possible, but this future is not assured. What happens will hinge on the wisdom, vision, and determination of the Asian-Pacific countries themselves, including the United States. Our role is crucial. Our continuing political, security, and economic involvement is indispensable and in our interest. It must continue to adapt to changing realities. But it is not a burden to be borne, it is a challenge that we welcome.

(38) 27th Meeting of the ANZUS Council, Washington, June 7-8, 1978: Final Communiqué.[11]

The ANZUS Council held its 27th meeting in Washington on June 7 and 8, 1978. The Right Honorable Brian Talboys, Deputy Prime Minister and Minister of Foreign Affairs, represented New Zealand; the Honorable Andrew Peacock, Minister of Foreign Affairs, represented Australia; and the Honorable Cyrus Vance, Secretary of State, represented the United States.

The Council members paid tribute to the memory of Sir Robert Menzies.[12] They recalled the leading role he had played in the for-

[11]Department of State Press Release 242, June 8; text from *Bulletin,* July 1978: 48-9.
[12]Former Australian Prime Minister Sir Robert Menzies died May 15, 1978.

mation of ANZUS and his commitment to the closest ties among the ANZUS partners.

The three countries reaffirmed their common commitment to the democratic traditions and practices that provide the enduring foundation for their long and close friendship. They undertook to continue to work together to promote their shared interests.

The Council members expressed their satisfaction with the close ties among the partners. They noted that these had been strengthened in the past year by fruitful visits of the Australian and New Zealand Prime Ministers to Washington[13] and of the American Vice President to Canberra and Wellington.[14]

The Ministers reaffirmed the great importance that each member attaches to the ANZUS alliance as an element in the framework of Western security and a means of maintaining and developing the individual and collective capacity of its members to resist armed attack. Pursuant to these primary concerns the Ministers recognized the central importance of practical cooperative supply and support arrangements within the alliance which would facilitate the expansion of Australian and New Zealand forces in contingent circumstances. The Ministers welcomed the progress made in the planning and conduct of combined military exercises as a means of strengthening military co-operation and testing its effectiveness.

Sharing a special interest in developments in the Asia-Pacific area, the Council members pledged continued efforts to promote peace and stability there. They agreed that ANZUS makes a significant contribution to regional stability and to the prospects for continued peace and economic development in the Asia-Pacific region. The Ministers stressed the particular importance of Japan in regional and global affairs and emphasized the importance of Japan's efforts to increase domestic demand and reduce its trade surplus. The Council noted that the developing relations between the People's Republic of China and many countries of the region enhance the prospects for regional stability. It expressed support for continued efforts to normalize relations between the United States and the PRC. The Ministers expressed the conviction that the important progress made by the Republic of Korea's armed forces would allow them to assume a greater role in the defense of that country with continuing support to be provided by the United States. The Ministers supported the Republic of Korea's call to North Korea for a resumed dialogue as a first step toward peaceful solution of the Korea question.

The Council welcomed the contribution the Association of

---

[13]Prime Ministers J. Malcolm Fraser (Australia) and Robert D. Muldoon (New Zealand) visited the U.S. June 21–23, 1977 and Nov. 9–10, 1977 respectively.
[14]Cf. Document 37.

Southeast Asian Nations (ASEAN) has made to regional economic and social development and expressed confidence that the organization would be of even greater importance in the future. In particular, the Council members supported the expansion of ASEAN's dialogues with non-member countries. The Council saw the continuing moves toward mutual understanding and closer cooperation among Southeast Asian countries as an element in the development of regional stability.

The Council members reaffirmed their intention to continue to play major roles in ensuring the permanent resettlement of the refugees whose flight from the countries of Indochina continues. They expressed their gratification with the role many other nations are playing in this effort and their hopes that national programs for receiving refugees would be expanded. They also expressed their appreciation of the important role being played by the United Nations High Commissioner for Refugees in alleviating suffering and misery; they called on his organization to renew its efforts to achieve improvements in first asylum practices throughout Southeast Asia and to persuade other nations capable of resettling refugees to provide permanent homes for them. During their discussion, the Council members reiterated their deep concern regarding violations of human rights in Kampuchea.

The Ministers commended the continuing steps toward political and economic cooperation being made by the states of the South Pacific and expressed their support for efforts to form a South Pacific Regional Fisheries Agency. They noted that the membership of Australia, New Zealand, and the United States in such an organization would enhance its contribution to regional economic development. The Council members welcomed the impending independence of the Solomon Islands,[15] expressing their confidence that the Solomons would play an important role in South Pacific affairs, as would other states in the region soon to achieve independence.

The Ministers reviewed developments in the Trust Territory of the Pacific Islands and expressed their support for the United States objective of terminating the Trusteeship by 1981. They noted with interest the statement of Principles for Free Association signed by the United States and the Micronesians, the encouraging prospects for the evolution of close relations among the parties on a new basis, and the plan for a July 12 referendum to be observed by the United Nations in which Trust Territory citizens will express their views on the organization of their future government.

The Council reviewed the negotiations between the United States and the Soviet Union aimed at an agreement limiting their military presence in the Indian Ocean that would enhance the security of the

[15]On July 7, 1978.

partners and all countries in the Indian Ocean region. The Ministers agreed that the balance of military presence of the United States and the Soviet Union in the Indian Ocean region should be maintained at the lowest practicable level. They also agreed that an Indian Ocean arms limitations agreement must not detract from the ANZUS alliance.

The Council conducted a frank and full exchange of views on a broad range of other political, economic, and security issues of concern to the ANZUS partners, including efforts to relieve tensions in various parts of the world. The Council particularly stressed the importance of a successful outcome to the strategic arms limitations talks being conducted between the United States and the Soviet Union. The Ministers emphasized the need for continuing efforts to prevent nuclear proliferation. They stressed the desirability of achieving universal adherence to the Non-Proliferation Treaty, of which all three countries are signatories. It was agreed that the early conclusion of a comprehensive test ban agreement prohibiting nuclear testing in all environments by all states would also make a significant contribution to non-proliferation as well as nuclear arms control objectives. The Ministers accorded high priority to the work being undertaken in the International Nuclear Fuel Cycle Evaluation. The Council members also discussed the United Nations Special Session on Disarmament currently being held in New York. They underlined the great importance they attached to its deliberations. They expressed the hope that it would contribute constructively to an intensified program of arms control activities which could lead by progressive steps to a reduction in world tensions, a strengthening of international security, actual disarmament measures, and the release of resources for social and economic progress.

Reviewing developments in the Middle East, the Ministers commended the historic moves of President Sadat of Egypt and Prime Minister Begin of Israel in their efforts to bring about peace.

The Ministers expressed their concern about developments in southern Africa and the Horn, and called upon the Soviet Union and Cuba to refrain from military intervention in African disputes. They expressed their support for the efforts of the peoples of Zimbabwe and Namibia to achieve independence and majority rule; for the Anglo-American efforts to contribute to a peaceful transition to majority rule in Zimbabwe; and for the efforts of the Western five members of the Security Council to assist in bringing about an internationally acceptable basis for independence and majority rule in Namibia.

In reviewing the global economic situation, the Ministers reaffirmed the principle that the economic health of the three partners is of concern to each. They emphasized that a general reduction of barriers to trade and resistance to protectionist pressures were essential and agreed that an early successful completion of the multilateral trade negotiations would be an important element in this process. They stressed the need for those negotiations to reduce substantially barriers to trade in agricultural products. The Council endorsed members' determination to pursue strong national policies aimed at conserving energy, developing conventional and alternative energy sources, and assisting other countries in these fields.

The Ministers reiterated their support for a continued flow of assistance to the countries of the developing world in order to promote economic and social development. They agreed that an equitable and soundly based world economic order was a vital factor in promoting international stability and peace. The Ministers agreed that the June 14–15 OECD Ministerial meeting would provide an important forum for further review of international economic developments.

The Council members agreed to meet again in Canberra in 1979 at a date to be decided.

(39)   Announcements and Statements on Normalization of Relations with the People's Republic of China, December 15, 1978.

    (a)   Radio-television Address to the Nation by President Carter.[16]

Good evening.

I would like to read a joint communique which is being simultaneously issued in Peking at this very moment by the leaders of the People's Republic of China:

[At this point, the President read the text of the joint communique, which reads as follows:]

JOINT COMMUNIQUE ON THE ESTABLISHMENT OF DIPLOMATIC RELATIONS BETWEEN THE UNITED STATES OF AMERICA AND THE PEOPLE'S REPUBLIC OF CHINA

JANUARY 1, 1979

The United States of America and the People's Republic of China have agreed to recognize each other and to establish diplomatic relations as of January 1, 1979.

[16]Text from *Presidential Documents,* 14: 2264–6.

The United States of America recognizes the Government of the People's Republic of China as the sole legal Government of China. Within this context, the people of the United States will maintain cultural, commercial, and other unofficial relations with the people of Taiwan.

The United States of America and the People's Republic of China reaffirm the principles agreed on by the two sides in the Shanghai Communique and emphasize once again that:

—Both wish to reduce the danger of international military conflict.

—Neither should seek hegemony in the Asia-Pacific region or in any other region of the world and each is opposed to efforts by any other country or group of countries to establish such hegemony.

—Neither is prepared to negotiate on behalf of any third party or to enter into agreements or understandings with the other directed at other states.

—The Government of the United States of America acknowledges the Chinese position that there is but one China and Taiwan is part of China.

—Both believe that normalization of Sino-American relations is not only in the interest of the Chinese and American peoples but also contributes to the cause of peace in Asia and the world.

The United States of America and the People's Republic of China will exchange Ambassadors and establish Embassies on March 1, 1979.

Yesterday, our country and the People's Republic of China reached this final historic agreement. On January 1, 1979, a little more than 2 weeks from now, our two Governments will implement full normalization of diplomatic relations.

As a nation of gifted people who comprise about one-fourth of the total population of the Earth, China plays, already, an important role in world affairs, a role that can only grow more important in the years ahead.

We do not undertake this important step for transient tactical or expedient reasons. In recognizing the People's Republic of China, that it is the single Government of China, we are recognizing simple reality. But far more is involved in this decision than just the recognition of a fact.

Before the estrangement of recent decades, the American and the Chinese people had a long history of friendship. We've already begun to rebuild some of those previous ties. Now our rapidly expanding relationship requires the kind of structure that only full diplomatic relations will make possible.

The change that I'm announcing tonight will be of great long-term benefit to the peoples of both our country and China—and, I believe, to all the peoples of the world. Normalization—and the expanded commercial and cultural relations that it will bring—will contribute to the well-being of our own Nation, to our own national interest, and it will also enhance the stability of Asia. These more positive relations with China can beneficially affect the world in which we live and the world in which our children will live.

We have already begun to inform our allies and other nations and the Members of the Congress of the details of our intended action. But I wish also tonight to convey a special message to the people of Taiwan—I have already communicated with the leaders of Taiwan—with whom the American people have had and will have extensive, close, and friendly relations. This is important between our two peoples.

As the United States asserted in the Shanghai Communique of 1972, issued on President Nixon's historic visit, we will continue to have an interest in the peaceful resolution of the Taiwan issue. I have paid special attention to ensuring that normalization of relations between our country and the People's Republic will not jeopardize the well-being of the people of Taiwan. The people of our country will maintain our current commercial, cultural, trade, and other relations with Taiwan through nongovernmental means. Many other countries in the world are already successfully doing this.

These decisions and these actions open a new and important chapter in our country's history and also in world affairs.

To strengthen and to expedite the benefits of this new relationship between China and the United States, I am pleased to announce that Vice Premier Teng has accepted my invitation and will visit Washington at the end of January.[17] His visit will give our Governments the opportunity to consult with each other on global issues and to begin working together to enhance the cause of world peace.

These events are the final result of long and serious negotiations begun by President Nixon in 1972, and continued under the leadership of President Ford. The results bear witness to the steady, determined, bipartisan effort of our own country to build a world in which peace will be the goal and the responsibility of all nations.

The normalization of relations between the United States and China has no other purpose than this: the advancement of peace. It is in this spirit, at this season of peace, that I take special pride in sharing this good news with you tonight.

Thank you very much.

---

[17]Vice-Premier Teng Hsiao-ping's visit took place Jan. 29–Feb. 1, 1979.

(b) Official United States Statement. [18]

As of January 1, 1979, the United States of America recognizes the People's Republic of China as the sole legal government of China. On the same date, the People's Republic of China accords similar recognition to the United States of America. The United States thereby establishes diplomatic relations with the People's Republic of China.

On that same date, January 1, 1979, the United States of America will notify Taiwan that it is terminating diplomatic relations and that the Mutual Defense Treaty between the United States and the Republic of China[19] is being terminated in accordance with the provisions of the Treaty. The United States also states that it will be withdrawing its remaining military personnel from Taiwan within four months.

In the future, the American people and the people of Taiwan will maintain commercial, cultural, and other relations without official government representation and without diplomatic relations.

The Administration will seek adjustments to our laws and regulations to permit the maintenance of commercial, cultural, and other non-governmental relationships in the new circumstances that will exist after normalization.

The United States is confident that the people of Taiwan face a peaceful and prosperous future. The United States continues to have an interest in the peaceful resolution of the Taiwan issue and expects that the Taiwan issue will be settled peacefully by the Chinese themselves.

The United States believes that the establishment of diplomatic relations with the People's Republic will contribute to the welfare of the American people, to the stability of Asia where the United States has major security and economic interest, and to the peace of the entire world.

(c) Remarks by President Carter to News Reporters. [20]

THE PRESIDENT. Well, I wanted to come by and let you know that I believe this to be an extremely important moment in the history of our Nation. It's something that I and my two predecessors have sought avidly. We have maintained our own United States position firmly, and only since the last few weeks has there been an increasing demonstration to us that Premier Hua [Kuo-feng] and Vice Pre-

---

[18] Text from *Presidential Documents,* 14: 2266.
[19] For full listing see Appendix under 1954.
[20] Text from *Presidential Documents,* 14: 2266-8.

mier Teng have been ready to normalize relations. I think the interests of Taiwan have been adequately protected. One of the briefers will explain the details to you.

Our Ambassador there, Leonard Woodcock, has done a superb job in presenting our own views strongly and clearly to the officials of the People's Republic of China. I will be preparing myself adequately for the visit of Vice Premier Teng. We invited him on one day, he accepted the next, without delay, and I think he's looking forward to this trip with a great deal of anticipation and pleasure.

I have talked personally this evening to Prime Minister Ohira.[21] Early this morning we notified the officials in Taiwan, and we have also notified many of the leaders around the world of this long-awaited development in international diplomacy.

I think that one of the greatest benefits that will be derived from this is the continuation of strong trade, cultural relationships with Taiwan, the people of Taiwan, and a new vista for prosperous trade relationships with almost a billion people in the People's Republic of China. This is also, of course, enhanced by the new opportunities for us to understand the people of China, and to work avidly for peace in that region and for world peace.

This afternoon the Soviet Union officials were notified through their Ambassador here, Mr. [A.F.] Dobrynin. And I think the Soviets were familiar with the fact that we were anticipating normalization whenever the Chinese were willing to meet our reasonable terms, and they were not surprised. As you well know, the Soviet Union and People's Republic of China have diplomatic relations between themselves.

My own assessment is that this will be well received in almost every nation of the world, perhaps all of them, because it will add to stability. And the Soviets and others know full well, because of our own private explanations to them, not just recently but in months gone by, that we have no desire whatsover to use our new relationships with China to the disadvantage of the Soviets or anyone else. We believe this will enhance stability and not cause instability in Asia and the rest of the world.

I'm very pleased with it. And I obviously have to give a major part of the credit to President Nixon and to President Ford, who laid the groundwork for this successful negotiation. And most of the premises that were spelled out in the Shanghai Communique 6 years ago or more have been implemented now.

You can tell that I'm pleased, and I know that the world is waiting for your accurate explanation of the results.

Q. How did the congressional leaders take it?

[21] Japanese Prime Minister Masayoshi Ohira.

THE PRESIDENT. With mixed response. Some of the congressional leaders who were there have long been very strong personal friends of the officials in Taiwan. They are not as thoroughly familiar with the officials in the People's Republic of China.

One of the most long debated issues was whether or not we would peremptorily terminate our defense treaty with Taiwan, or whether we would terminate that treaty in accordance with its own provisions. And the People's Republic officials agreed with our position that we would give Taiwan a 1-year notice and that the defense treaty would prevail throughout 1979. I think that alleviated some of the concerns among the Senators.

And another concern expressed by them was whether or not we could continue cultural relationships, trade relationships with the people of Taiwan. I assured them that we could, that the Chinese knew this. And we will ask the Congress for special legislation[22] quite early in the session to permit this kind of exchange with the people of Taiwan. This would include authorization for the Eximbank and OPEC to guarantee and to help with specific trade negotiations.

I think that many of their concerns have been alleviated, although there certainly will be some Members of the Congress who feel that we should have maintained the status quo.

I'll take just one question.

Q. Mr. President, you said the response to your speech would be "massive applause throughout the Nation." What do you think the response to your speech will be in Taiwan?

THE PRESIDENT. I doubt if there will be massive applause in Taiwan, but we are going to do everything we can to assure the Taiwanese that we put at top—as one of the top priorities in our own relationships with the People's Republic and them—that the well-being of the people of Taiwan will not be damaged.

To answer the other question, I don't think this will have any adverse effect at all on the SALT negotiations as an independent matter. And I think that the Soviets, as I said earlier, have been expecting this development. They were not surprised, and we have kept them informed recently. Their reaction has not been adverse, and we will proceed aggressively as we have in recent months, in fact throughout my own administration, to conclude a successful SALT agreement.

Good night.

---

[22]The Taiwan Relations Act (Public Law 96-8) was signed Apr. 10, 1979; Carter signature statement in *Presidential Documents,* 15: 640–41.

(d) Statement by the Government of the People's Republic of China.[23]

As of Jan. 1, 1979, the People's Republic of China and the United States of America recognize each other and establish diplomatic relations, thereby ending the prolonged abnormal relationship between them. This is an historic event in Sino-United States relations.

As is known to all, the Government of the People's Republic of China is the sole legal Government of China and Taiwan is part of China. The question of Taiwan was the crucial issue obstructing the normalization of relations between China and the United States. It has now been resolved between the two countries in the spirit of the Shanghai Communiqué and through their joint efforts, thus enabling the normalization of relations so ardently desired by the people of the two countries.

As for the way of bringing Taiwan back to the embrace of the motherland and reunifying the country, it is entirely China's internal affair.

At the invitation of the U.S. Government, Teng Hsiao-ping, Deputy Prime Minister of the State Council of the People's Republic of China, will pay an official visit to the United States in January 1979, with a view to further promoting the friendship between the two peoples and good relations between the two countries.

(e) Statement by the Government of the Republic of China on Taiwan.[24]

The decision by the United States to establish diplomatic relations with the Chinese Communist regime has not only seriously damaged the rights and interests of the Government and the people of the Republic of China, but has also had a tremendously adverse impact upon the entire free world. For all the consequences that might arise as a result of this move, the United States Government alone should bear full responsibility.

In the past few years, the United States Government has repeatedly reaffirmed its intention to maintain diplomatic relations with the Republic of China and to honor its treaty commitments. Now that it has broken the assurances and abrogated the treaty, the

[23]Text from *New York Times,* Dec. 17, 1978.
[24]Text from *New York Times,* Dec. 17, 1978.

United States Government cannot be expected to have the confidence of any free nation in the future.

The United States, by extending diplomatic recognition to the Chinese Communist regime, which owes its very existence to terror and suppression, is not in conformity with its professed position of safeguarding human rights and strengthening the capability of democratic nations to resist the totalitarian dictatorship.

The move is tantamount to denying the hundreds of millions of enslaved peoples on the Chinese mainland their hope for an early restoration of freedom. Viewed from whatever aspect, the move by the United States constitutes a great setback to human freedom and democratic institutions. It will be condemned by all freedomloving and peaceloving peoples all over the world.

Recent international events have proven that the United States' pursuance of the "normalization" process with the Chinese Communist regime did not protect the security of free Asian nations, has further encouraged Communist subversion and aggressive activities and hastened the fall of Indochina into Communist hands. The Government and the people of the Republic of China firmly believe lasting international peace and security can never be established on an unstable foundation of expediency.

Regardless of how the international situation may develop, the Republic of China, as a sovereign nation will, with her glorious tradition, unite all her people, civilian and military, at home and abroad, to continue her endeavors toward progress in the social, economic and political fields. The Chinese Government and the people, faithful to the national objectives and their international responsibilities, have full confidence in the future of the Republic of China.

The late President Chiang Kai-shek repeatedly instructed the Chinese people to be firm with dignity and to complete the task of national recovery and reconstruction. The Government and the people of the Republic of China have the determination and the faith, which they will exert to their utmost, to work together with other free peoples in democratic countries to conquer Communist tyrannical rule and its aggressive policy. Henceforth, we shall be calm and firm, positive and hard-working. It is urged that all citizens cooperate fully with the Government, with one heart and one soul, united and determined to fight at this difficult moment. Under whatever circumstances, the Republic of China shall neither negotiate with the Communist Chinese regime, nor compromise with Communism, and it shall never give up its sacred task of recovering the mainland and delivering the compatriots there. This firm position shall remain unchanged.

(40) *Relations with the People on Taiwan: Memorandum from President Carter for All Departments and Agencies, December 30, 1978.* [25]

Memorandum for all Departments and Agencies

Subject: Relations with the People on Taiwan

As President of the United States, I have constitutional responsibility for the conduct of the foreign relations of the nation. The United States has announced that on January 1, 1979, it is recognizing the government of the People's Republic of China as the sole legal government of China and is terminating diplomatic relations with the Republic of China. [26] The United States has also stated that, in the future, the American people will maintain commercial, cultural and other relations with the people of Taiwan without official government representation and without diplomatic relations. I am issuing this memorandum to facilitate maintaining those relations pending the enactment of legislation on the subject.

I therefore declare and direct that:

(A) Departments and agencies currently having authority to conduct or carry out programs, transactions, or other relations with or relating to Taiwan are directed to conduct and carry out those programs, transactions, and relations beginning January 1, 1979, in accordance with such authority and, as appropriate, through the instrumentality referred to in paragraph D below.

(B) Existing international agreements and arrangements in force between the United States and Taiwan shall continue in force and shall be performed and enforced by departments and agencies beginning January 1, 1979, in accordance with their terms and, as appropriate, through that instrumentality.

(C) In order to effectuate all of the provisions of this memorandum, whenever any law, regulation, or order of the United States refers to a foreign country, nation, state, government, or similar entity, departments and agencies shall construe those terms and apply those laws, regulations, or orders to include Taiwan.

(D) In conducting and carrying out programs, transactions, and other relations with the people on Taiwan, interests of the people of

[25]Text from *Presidential Documents,* 15: 1-2; filed with the Office of the Federal Register Jan. 2, 1979.
[26]Document 39.

the United States will be represented as appropriate by an unofficial instrumentality in corporate form, to be identified shortly.[27]

(E) The above directives shall apply to and be carried out by all departments and agenices, except as I may otherwise determine.

I shall submit to the Congress a request for legislation relative to non-governmental relationships between the American people and the people on Taiwan.

This memorandum shall be published in the FEDERAL REGISTER.

JIMMY CARTER

[27]The American Institute in Taiwan, as defined in Sec. 6 of the Taiwan Relations Act (Public Law 96-8, Apr. 10, 1979).

8. AMERICA AND THE WORLD ECONOMY

*(41) Survey of International Economic Policy: Annual Message of
the President on the Economic Report, January 20, 1978.* [1]

(Excerpt)

* * *

INTERNATIONAL ECONOMIC POLICIES THAT PROMOTE ECONOMIC
RECOVERY THROUGHOUT THE WORLD

Outside the United States, the world economy has seen a hesitant
recovery from the deep recession of 1974–1975. The rapid pace of
economic growth that was widespread over most of the postwar
years has all but disappeared. Unemployment is high, and in most
industrial countries except the United States it is rising. Inflation is
at high levels and declining only very slowly.

The imbalances in the international economic system continue to
strain the world economy. Because of the surpluses of oil-exporting
countries, many countries have sizable deficits, including the
United States. Some industrial nations are also running large and
persistent surpluses—thus increasing the pressures on countries in
deficit. These imbalances have been a major factor contributing to
disorder in exchange markets in recent months.

The condition of the world economy requires above all that nations work together to develop mutually beneficial solutions to global problems. If we fail to work together, we will lose the gains in
living standards arising from the expansion of world commerce
over the past three decades. If the world economy becomes a collection of isolated and weak nations, we will all lose.

The first priority in our international economic policy is continued economic recovery throughout the industrial world. Growth of
the U.S. economy—the largest and strongest in the world—is of vital importance. The economic program that I have proposed will

[1]Text from *Presidential Documents,* 14: 142-4.

ensure that America remains a leader and a source of strength in the world economy. It is important that other strong nations join with us to take direct actions to spur demand within their own economies. World recovery cannot proceed if nations rely upon exports as the principal source of economic expansion.

·At the same time all countries must continue the battle against inflation. This will require prudent fiscal and monetary policies. Such policies must be supplemented by steps to reduce structural unemployment, measures to avoid bottlenecks by encouraging investment, and cooperation in the accumulation of commodity reserves to insulate the world from unforeseen shocks.

Reducing the widespread imbalances in international payments will require several parallel steps. To begin with, each individual country must ensure that its own policies help relieve the strains. The United States will do its part. In 1977 we had a current account deficit of about $18 billion. While not a cause for alarm, this is a matter of concern. We can take a most constructive step toward correcting this deficit by moving quickly to enact the National Energy Plan.

Countries in surplus should also do their part. Balance of payments surpluses in some countries have contributed to the economic stagnation among their trading partners. Where their own economies have slack, it is appropriate for nations in surplus to stimulate the growth of domestic demand—thereby increasing their imports and improving the prospects for growth in deficit countries. In some countries, lifting restraints on imports from abroad and reducing excessive government efforts to promote exports would be useful. After consultations with the United States, the Japanese have indicated they will take a series of steps toward reducing their large surplus.

The system of flexible exchange rates for currencies also can be helpful in correcting unsustainable imbalances in payments among countries. Since its inception in 1973, this system has operated well under unprecedented strains.

During 1977 the U.S. dollar has fallen in value against several key currencies. The decline in the dollar's value has occurred primarily against the currencies of those nations that have large trade and payments surpluses, and was not surprising in view of our large payments deficit and their surpluses. Late in 1977, however, movements in our exchange rate became both disorderly and excessively rapid. The United States reaffirmed its intention to step in when conditions in exchange markets become disorderly and to work in close cooperation with our friends abroad in this effort.[2]

Under the flexible exchange rate system basic economic forces

[2]Cf. Carter statement, Dec. 21, 1977, in *AFR, 1977:* 451–3.

must continue to be the fundamental determinant of the value of currencies. However, we will not permit speculative activities in currency markets to disrupt our economy or those of our trading partners. We recognize fully our obligation in this regard, and we have taken steps to fulfill it.

Although substantial progress can be made toward a balanced world economy, some imbalances will persist for a substantial period of time. Financing requirements will remain large while adjustments occur. The private markets can and will continue to channel the bulk of the financing from surplus to deficit countries. But it is essential that adequate official financing also be available, in case of need, to encourage countries with severe payments problems to adopt orderly and responsible corrective measures. To meet this critical need the United States has strongly supported a proposal to strengthen the International Monetary Fund by the establishment of a new Supplementary Financing Facility.

The United States also will continue to contribute resources to promote growth in the economies of the developing nations. International assistance efforts—through bilateral aid and multilateral institutions—must continue to expand. We must also keep our doors open to imports from developing countries, so that their economies can grow and prosper through expanded trade.

A keystone of our international economic policy is to work with our trading partners to protect a free and open trading system. The American economy benefits by exporting those products that we make efficiently, and by importing those that we produce least efficiently. An open trading system increases our real incomes, strengthens competition in our markets, and contributes to combating inflation.

The United States will firmly resist the demands for protection that inevitably develop when the world economy suffers from high unemployment. The ensuing decline in world trade would worsen our problem of inflation, create inefficiencies in American enterprise, and lead to fewer jobs for American workers. But international competition must be fair. We have already taken and we will, when necessary, continue to take steps to ensure that our businesses and workers do not suffer from unfair trade practices.

I place great importance on the Multilateral Trade Negotiations now under way in Geneva. I believe our negotiators will bring home agreements that are fair and balanced and that will benefit our economy immensely over the years to come. The importance of these discussions can hardly be overemphasized. The trading system that emerges from the negotiations will set the tone for international commerce well into the 1980s. Our commitment to a successful conclusion to these talks underscores our long-term emphasis on the retention and expansion of open and fair trade among nations.

THE CHALLENGE BEFORE US

In this message I have outlined my fundamental economic goals and the strategy for attaining them. It is an ambitious, but I believe a realistic, agenda for the future. It calls for a broad range of actions to improve the health and fairness of the American economy. And it calls upon the American people to participate actively in many of these efforts.

I ask the Congress and the American people to join with me in a sustained effort to achieve a lasting prosperity. We all share the same fundamental goals. We can work together to reach them.

JIMMY CARTER

January 20, 1978.

(42) Foreign Assistance and U.S. Policy: Address by Secretary of State Vance before the National Convention of the League of Women Voters, Cincinnati, May 1, 1978. [3]

Today I want to discuss with you a subject about which I care deeply because of its importance to our nation. I speak of foreign assistance.

Over the years the League of Women Voters has endeavored to explain and support our foreign assistance programs. You have done this as an essential part of your nonpartisan program of public education. Your interest in and knowledge of foreign assistance has been a key element in making people aware of what their government is trying to achieve with these programs.

The United States has a profound stake in its relationships with the nations and peoples in developing countries. Our response to their problems, needs, and aspirations tests not only the quality of our leadership in the world but our commitment to economic and social justice.

Let me begin our discussion by posing three questions. First, why do we have foreign aid programs? Second, what are these programs designed to accomplish? Third, do they work?

During the past 15 months as the Carter Administration fashioned aid budgets, reorganized aid programs, and discussed aid issues with Congress, we have thought with great care about these three questions. Today, in discussing our conclusions, I want to return to the basic elements of our aid programs.

Why Foreign Aid

Our foreign policy flows from what we are as a people—our his-

³Department of State Press Release 195; text from *Bulletin,* June 1978: 14–17.

tory, our culture, our values, and our beliefs. One reason this nation has a foreign aid program is that we believe we have a humanitarian and moral obligation to help alleviate poverty and promote more equitable economic growth in the developing world.

We cannot be indifferent when half a billion people are hungry and malnourished, when 700 million adults are illiterate, and when one and a half billion people do not have minimal health care. As free people who have achieved one of the highest standards of living in the world, we cannot fail to respond to such staggering statistics and the individual lives they encompass. We can be proud that we are a people who believe in the development of human potential.

The answer to the question of why we have foreign aid programs also goes beyond our system of values and our concern for the less fortunate. Foreign aid is clearly in our national economic and political interest.

The success or failure of developing countries to grow more food, develop new energy supplies, sell their raw materials and products, curb their birthrates, and defend themselves against aggression will matter to Americans.

Our economic health and our security are more closely tied today than ever before to the economic well-being and security of the developing world. Progress there means more jobs and more prosperity for the United States.

- The non-oil–producing developing countries are a major market for American goods, taking a quarter of our total exports last year. About the same share of our total exports goes to Europe and the Communist countries combined.
- Products from less developed countries—including raw materials such as tin, copper, bauxite, and lead—accounted for nearly a quarter of our total imports last year.
- Our nation gained more than $7 billion from our direct private investment in the developing world in 1975. And in 1976 developing countries absorbed nearly $11 billion of our direct foreign investment.
- In the export of our agricultural abundance last year, developing countries purchased half of our exports of cotton, 65% of our wheat, and nearly 70% of our rice.
- Our economy benefits substantially as aid dollars are spent here to buy commodities and services. For example, for every dollar we have paid into such organizations as the World Bank and the regional development banks for Latin America, Asia and Africa, about $2 has been spent in the U.S. economy.

The economic growth of the developing world is taking place primarily as a result of massive efforts by the leaders and peoples of the developing nations. For many, the most critical international factors in their growth and development are our policies toward trade, investment, commodities, and technology. Our economic aid, as well as that provided by other developed nations, also makes a crucial contribution to their well-being. For some countries—particularly the low-income nations—it is the principal source of foreign exchange and technical assistance. But for many others, it serves as an essential complement to other components of their development strategy.

In addition to America's economic involvement in the developing world, our political interests are strongly engaged as well. Developing countries are often key participants in the quest for peace. Regional stability and peace in the Middle East, southern Africa, and elsewhere cannot be achieved without the cooperation of developing nations. Achieving progress on the global issues which directly affect peace—arms restraint and nonproliferation—depends in large measure on strengthening political ties between the industrialized and developing worlds.

Our ties to developing countries are essential in many other areas which affect our national security: in deploying our armed forces and in maintaining access to straits, ports, and aviation facilities.

But the peace and stability we seek in the world cannot be obtained solely through the maintenance of a strong defense in concert with others. The social unrest which breeds conflict can best be prevented if economic growth and an equitable distribution of resources are realized. As Pope John XXIII so eloquently stated: "In a world of constant want there is no peace. . . ."

Foreign Assistance Programs

In view of the stakes involved, our foreign aid goals must be matched by our performance. The Carter Administration is asking the Congress to authorize and appropriate $8.4 billion for our economic, food, security assistance programs, and contributions to the international financial institutions this fiscal year. About 16% of this sum represents government guarantees and will not result in actual spending. We are requesting these sums because we believe that foreign aid can and does work. We believe it can have a direct impact on economic growth and the maintenance of peace.

Let me give you a summary of what we are trying to do.

First, in the area of bilateral economic assistance, we are trying to determine the most effective way to channel this aid to stimulate economic growth and alleviate poverty. In doing so we are implementing a strategy which targets our resources directly on the needs of the poor. Called the "basic human needs" approach, this development strategy seeks to help people meet such basic needs as nutrition, shelter, education, and health care. It is not an international welfare program. It is, instead, an approach to development which gives the poor a chance to improve their standard of living by their own efforts.

- Farmers need good quality seed if they are going to escape subsistence agriculture and grow enough food for their families and to sell at the market as well. Our aid program in Tanzania, for instance, is helping that government establish a seed multiplication project to provide improved seed for the main crops grown there. The impact on the lives of Tanzanian farmers should be large.
- In vast sections of West Africa, people cannot live in potentially fertile agricultural areas because of a terrible disease—river blindness. We are helping to finance efforts to suppress this affliction. Some success has been achieved. Small farmers are already beginning to resettle in areas which had been virtually abandoned.
- Education is critical to human development. In numerous poor countries, our aid goes to training people in rural and urban areas in basic skills which permit them to earn a better living. Education takes place in many ways besides the schoolroom. It can be carried by low powered local radio programs, such as one we fund in Guatemala, or by direct broadcast satellite TV, as in an experiment we assisted in India.

Second, the programs of the World Bank and the regional development banks through which we channel a significant amount of our foreign aid range from large, capital intensive programs, such as dams and roads, to smaller scale programs designed to directly improve the lives of the poor. These institutions can mobilize and coordinate large amounts of capital for development. And they can build consensus between aid donors and recipients on development goals. In performing these roles, they well serve U.S. interests. The work of these institutions is varied.

- In Buenaventura, Colombia—one of the poorest cities in the hemisphere—the Inter-American Development Bank is trying to relocate slum dwellers and provide the city with safe drinking water to reduce disease.
- In the West African country of Benin, the African Development Fund is improving rural health services by constructing dispensaries in remote areas and training people to run them.
- In Burma, an Asian Development Bank loan will increase fish production for domestic consumption, thus raising the low protein intake of the population.

Third, we support the development programs of the United Nations, which finance technical assistance to children, refugees, and other groups in need of particular relief.

- In India, the U.N. Children's Fund is working to restore and improve potable water resources in the areas hardest hit by the November 1977 cyclone and tidal wave.
- In Central America, experts from the U.N. Development Program are working in four countries to develop energy from underground volcanic steam.

I could go on and on, citing projects in various countries aimed at specific problems and particular groups. The point is that when we are discussing aid levels, we must remember we are not talking about abstract statistics: we are talking about whether or not we can fund practical projects that make a difference to people in need.

There is another important aspect of our foreign aid program which I would like to mention very briefly—our security assistance programs.

These programs have three important objectives. First, they are designed to assist our friends and allies to provide for their legitimate defense needs. Second, these programs support our strategic and political objectives of reducing tensions and promoting stability in areas of potential confrontation and conflict. Third, they provide economic assistance to countries which are experiencing political and economic stresses and where U.S. security interests are involved. The vast majority of our security assistance aid goes to support our peace efforts in the Middle East and in southern Africa. In providing assistance to such nations, we help them meet the economic strains imposed by tensions in their regions.

Does Foreign Aid Work?

Do all these programs work?

There is a popular myth that foreign assistance often does not produce results. The record shows otherwise.

It is impossible to separate foreign assistance from other factors that produce development. But foreign assistance has been central in some measure to the following achievements.

- Between 1950 and 1975 the developing countries grew more rapidly than either they or the developed countries had grown in any time period in the past.
- Substantial increases in life expectancy are taking place in many developing countries.
- The number of children in primary schools in the developing

world has trebled since 1950, and the number of secondary students has increased sixfold during the same period.

- The battle against communicable disease has produced significant results. Smallpox is now confined to a small area of Africa, and the numbers of people suffering from malaria has been reduced by 80–90% in the past three decades.
- The yields of rice and wheat in Asia are estimated to be substantially higher today because of the introduction of high-yielding varieties. More than a billion dollars worth of grain each year is ascribed to the new seed.

Beyond these successes, the record reveals countless instances in which projects funded by foreign assistance have improved the lives of people in fundamental ways.

- When a village has clean water, its children are no longer made sick from the water they drink.
- When couples have access to family planning services, there are fewer mouths to feed.
- When a clinic is constructed, modern medicine enters lives for the first time.
- And when a job program begins, the unemployed can find work and have incomes.

Progress has been made. But more has to be done. Over the last 15 months the Carter Administration has made a substantial effort to further improve the management and effectiveness of all of our programs.

Let me report to you on some of the steps we have already taken or will soon implement to achieve this objective.

One of the key problems with foreign assistance over the years has been a lack of adequate coordination between our bilateral programs and our activities in the international financial institutions. Responsibility for these various programs is spread throughout several Cabinet Departments and agencies.

Shortly before his death,[4] Senator Hubert Humphrey introduced legislation which called for a sweeping reorganization of the government's foreign aid programs designed to meet these defects in coordination. The Carter Administration announced its support of the basic purposes of this bill. Although the Congress will probably not consider this legislation in the current session, the Administration is moving to put into place a new interagency coordinating mechanism which we believe will go a long way toward having the executive branch better coordinate its diverse development efforts.

[4]On Jan. 13, 1978.

The Agency for International Development has been reorganized under the leadership of Governor John Gilligan. More authority is being delegated to our AID missions abroad. Tighter controls are now imposed on financial and operational procedures. In addition, AID has eliminated some complex and cumbersome procedures which have slowed our ability to design and implement projects.

The United States has encouraged the multilateral banks to better take into account the lessons of the past—both successes and failures. The Administration has also shared congressional concerns about high salary levels of bank employees. We want the banks to look especially hard at more effective ways to reach poor people directly, as well as to operate in the most cost effective ways.

In our security programs we have tightened management controls and have instituted an interagency committee to provide coordinated recommendations to me and the President on all aspects of our arms transfer and security assistance programs.

Finally, because we recognize that science and technology offer many opportunities for expanding the development process, President Carter has proposed the creation of a new U.S. foundation on technological collaboration. This foundation will support the application of our research to development problems. And it will improve the access of the developing countries to American science and technology.

We will continue to seek ways to improve the management and delivery of our foreign assistance programs. Accountability to the Congress and to the public is an essential element of our approach.

Other Key Issues

There are several other important questions relating to our foreign assistance programs which I would like to discuss.

First, there is a growing belief that we are both giving more aid and at the same time losing control over where it goes. Let me put this issue in perspective.

Clearly, we are not shouldering a disproportionate burden of global aid flows. While in absolute terms the U.S. aid program is larger than that of any other nation, as a percentage of GNP we rank in the bottom 25% of all non-Communist country donors.

Concerning control, we are very active in attempting to steer multilateral assistance in directions we think best for our nation and for global development. We have often been successful in encouraging the types of projects consistent with our desired policies. We will be working closely with Congress to develop procedures which permit the United States to express its views about multilateral lending policies as effectively as possible. But in doing so, we must recognize the damage that would be done if the international character of these institutions were lost.

Second, our foreign assistance programs must be consistent with our determination to improve the conditions of political, economic, and civil rights worldwide. Over the past year we have reviewed all of our aid programs for their impact on human rights. In some cases we have reduced assistance to governments with consistent records of repression. We have also increased aid to others with good or improving human rights policies.

We face a dilemma when applying human rights considerations to foreign assistance. We do not want to support governments which consistently violate human rights. On the other hand, we do not wish to deny our assistance to poor people who happen to live under repressive regimes. We must resolve this dilemma on a case-by-case basis. In general, we have approved aid programs when they would directly benefit the poor since we recognize that people have economic as well as political rights.

Third, there is the question of which countries should receive our aid. The President has decided that our concessional assistance programs should focus primarily but not exclusively on the poorest countries. In the more advanced developing countries we do not want to substitute our own support for the assistance those governments should be giving. On the other hand, we cannot be indifferent to the plight of people who are no less poor because they live in middle income countries and who need our help. We are resolving this problem by insisting that our efforts to mount programs in middle income developing nations be matched by efforts of the host country.

Fourth, it is sometimes argued that we cannot afford to spend large amounts of money to help solve problems abroad when we have many pressing domestic needs. But I firmly believe that it would be a serious mistake to try to trade off international obligations for domestic priorities. Both need to be addressed.

The health of our nation is increasingly dependent on the world economy. If we neglect international progress, we undermine the welfare of our own society. As a nation we have a major concern with improving the lives of poor people. I do not believe this is a credible commitment if made only domestically. And as a percentage of the Federal budget for 1979 our economic assistance is only 1.47%. Adding our security assistance programs does not increase this figure substantially.

We can afford to increase foreign aid expenditures at a reasonable rate, as we must. At the same time, we can afford to increase our domestic education budget, expand programs for the elderly, and fund other critical domestic programs as we are now doing. Helping the children of Pakistan have adequate diets does not mean that we need neglect the children of Cincinnati, Boston or Los Angeles. Helping the farmers of Mali grow more food does not mean we need to abandon the farmers of Texas, Illinois, or Colorado. And helping the nations of the Middle East remain at peace does not mean that we cannot help meet the needs of our cities. We do not have a choice. Both foreign aid and adequate domestic expenditures are essential to the national interest.

Senator Humphrey raised a fundamental issue about foreign aid. He said, "The question we must decide is whether or not the conditions of social and economic injustice—poverty, illiteracy, and disease—are a real threat to our security. I think they are and they require the same commitment of policy, will, and resources as does our conventional national defense."

As someone charged with helping to protect the national security, I agree with Senator Humphrey's assessment of the role of foreign aid in the scheme of our national priorities. I agree with his approach to the tasks of alleviating poverty and working for peace.

He believed in harnessing the energy and creativity of the American people to solve problems which have plagued the world for centuries. I share his faith in our abilities. I share his optimism that we can do the job.

I ask that you help us inform the American people why foreign aid is essential to the nation's economic health, political interests, and preservation of its humanitarian tradition.

(43) The Organization for Economic Cooperation and Development: Meeting of the Council at Ministerial Level, Paris, June 14–15, 1978.

(a) Statement to the Council by Secretary of State Vance, June 14, 1978. [5]

We meet in a time when unemployment remains high, when inflation recedes too slowly, when payment imbalances remain large, and the development problems of poorer countries persist.

The nations represented here have faced adversities in the past and through extraordinary individual and cooperative efforts have overcome them. Even more recently, in a period of unprecedented economic strains, we have done well to keep those difficulties from

---

[5] Department of State Press Release 254; text from *Bulletin,* Aug. 1978: 24-6.

engulfing us. This Organization has contributed significantly to the progress we have made.

The challenge before us now is to go beyond keeping our heads above water, to develop a coordinated program that will return our economies to a pattern of sustained economic growth. Let me emphasize the word "sustained." How we grow is critically important. We must do so together. No one country can hope to attain economic prosperity by actions detrimental to the well-being of others. None of us can sustain healthy growth alone.

That is the critical business before this ministerial meeting and before the complementary meetings next month of the European Council in Bremen and the summit at Bonn—to develop a common framework for common economic progress.

Essential Elements

Let me outline what I believe are the essential elements of such an effort.

First, each nation must do its share. Our situations are different. But progress for each of us requires action by all of us.

- The United States is determined to reduce its dependence on imported oil and to control inflation.
- Countries which have trade surpluses and relatively low inflation should seek to grow faster.
- Others, who have brought their payment deficits and their inflation problems under better control, can now allow some degree of domestic expansion.
- All of us must go beyond merely resisting protectionist pressures to support positive steps to expand trade and strengthen the trading system.

Building on the important analytical work that has been done by the OECD, each of us must act, in a way compatible with our national circumstances but consistent with our shared objectives, to stimulate lagging investment and to provide new job opportunities for our citizens. As the OECD's analyses convincingly demonstrate, concerted action in this regard can reduce risks and increase general benefits.

Second, long-term sustained economic growth requires expanded world trade. Our representatives in Geneva have made progress toward an important new agreement to reduce tariff and nontariff barriers and to establish improved trading rules. Trade liberalization will help stimulate lagging investment. At the same time, staging the liberalization over a period of years will ease adjustment to more open markets.

Success in these negotiations will be an important political accomplishment as well: At a time of economic hardships we will have joined together not just to avoid a retreat toward protectionism but to take a concerted step forward toward a more open trading system. Our efforts to expand world commerce cannot cease, even with successful completion of the Geneva negotiations.

Sustaining the momentum will require constant attention, especially if growth resumes slowly, unemployment remains high, and problems remain in particular sectors of our economies. We must avoid introducing new barriers even as we reduce others. I, therefore, consider the renewal of the OECD trade pledge to be a major accomplishment of this meeting, and I encourage this Organization to continue to explore ways to strengthen the international trading system in the interests of all countries, developed and developing.

Third, trade liberalization must be accompanied by national policies which encourage economies to adjust to changing trade patterns. Older industries must modernize and diversify. And we must ease the adjustment process for workers whose livelihoods are affected by the changing tides of world trade.

We all agree that policies to assist industries in difficulty should not become prolonged protection. This Organization has taken the initiative to develop specific criteria for distinguishing the important dividing line between adjustment policies and protection. If each of us insures that actions to support specific sectors or companies in trouble are reduced progressively; if we link such support with policies to encourage the phasing out of obsolete capacity and the promotion of viable enterprises; if we resist raising prices to protect inefficient producers—in short, if we follow the OECD criteria—we can avoid the danger that adjustment policy will become a disguised form of protection for inefficiency.

We must be careful to prevent consultation on adjustment policies from becoming efforts to divide up the market, thereby limiting the competition on which growth and prosperity ultimately depend. Governments should also avoid trying to substitute their judgments about future growth sectors for those of the market. The Secretariat's work has rightfully focused on how to free the productive capacities of our countries.

Dealing With Causes of Protectionist Pressures

I hope the OECD can expand its role as a forum for discussing all these issues—how to modernize our industry, expand and improve manpower training, and shift resources to growth industries—in short, how to deal with the causes of protectionist pressures.

Sustainable growth requires strong and effective energy programs. Our heavy dependence on imported oil constrains government growth efforts.

Investment is inhibited by uncertainty over the future price and supply of oil. Reducing imports requires action on a broad front: more efficient energy use, better exploitation of conventional fuels, development of nuclear technologies which àre proliferation resistant and environmentally acceptable, and increased emphasis on renewable energy sources.

National programs are important. My own country intends to improve significantly its performance in this area—and to do so soon.

But the problem goes beond the scope of any single government. We must build on the extensive cooperative work already underway—in the International Energy Agency, in the International Nuclear Fuel Cycle Evaluation, and in the efforts to expand energy production in the developing countries.

We must supplement the efforts I mentioned earlier to increase investment in our own individual economies with further work to improve an international environment that promotes freer flow of investment. With three-fourths of all foreign direct investment taking place among its member countries, the OECD has the primary role in this field. OECD members will shortly be entering into an extensive review of the arrangements on investment carefully negotiated in 1976.[6] The United States plans to contribute actively and positively to these efforts. With other OECD members, we will also continue to work toward a positive result in the broader negotiations within the United Nations aimed at elaborating a code of conduct relating to transnational corporations. Efforts to arrive at an international agreement on illicit payments are also important, and we urge that this be given a high international priority.

Developing Countries

It is no longer possible to consider the economic prospects of the OECD members outside the context of economic development in the Third World. Developing nations have a growing role to play in accelerating and sustaining world growth. The expansion of their economies contributes to our own growth prospects. Thus our efforts to liberalize trade, to expand foreign investment, and to increase the effectiveness and level of foreign assistance improve our own welfare, as well as that of the developing world.

We must continue to strengthen our relations with the developing countries, and we must seek to fashion policies in our mutual interest. Priority attention should be given to sharing responsibility for attaining substantial results in the trade negotiations, increasing

---

[6]Cf. *AFR, 1976:* 435.

foreign assistance flows while at the same time enhancing their effectiveness in improving the lives of poor people, expanding cooperation in all aspects of energy development, strengthening the ability of developing nations to produce food, devising effective means to help stabilize fluctuating commodity prices, fostering a favorable climate for private investment and technology transfer, and insuring an adequate flow of capital.

(b) Communiqué and Declaration Issued at the Conclusion of the Meeting, June 15, 1978.[7]

The Council of the Organisation for Economic Co-operation and Development met at Ministerial level on 14th–15th June, 1978, under the co-Chairmanship of Kiichi Miyazawa, Minister of Economic Planning of Japan, and Nobuhiko Ushiba, Minister for External Economic Affairs of Japan.

Agreement was reached on the major components of a broad programme of internationally concerted action by Member countries to achieve more sustained economic growth, and on the respective responsibilities of individual Member countries in contributing to faster growth, greater price stability, better payments equilibrium and strengthened energy policies. Recognising that the maintenance of an open market-oriented economic system is an essential part of this programme, Ministers renewed the Declaration of 30th May, 1974 (the Trade Pledge)[8] and agreed on the general orientations for policies to facilitate the structural adjustments needed to sustain faster economic growth.

Ministers considered the implications of the growing economic interdependence between developed and developing countries for trade and investment. They confirmed their commitment to constructive policies for development co-operation to help developing countries to strengthen and diversify their economies and to improve the welfare of their people. They emphasized that the capacity of developing countries to participate more fully in world economic growth would be strengthened by an increase in the flow of resources, including increased aid, and an improvement in the conditions of world trade.

The Economic Background

Ministers noted that despite the difficult circumstances there has been some improvement in world economic conditions: recession

[7]Text from OECD Observer, July 1978: 4–11.
[8]Text in AFR, 1974: 150–51.

has been replaced by positive economic growth; inflation has been significantly reduced; unemployment has been substantially reduced in the United States and has been mitigated in a number of Member countries, inter alia by special manpower and employment policies; an open trading system has been maintained; some important payments imbalances have been corrected; and international financial markets have helped to alleviate the problems posed by large trade imbalances inside and outside the OECD. Nonetheless, the record of recent years is in many ways disappointing: unsatisfactory growth rates; inflation and unemployment rates that are still too high; periods of disorderly exchange-market conditions; increasing pressures for forms of government intervention which inhibit market forces in general and world trade in particular; and insufficient preparation against future needs in respect of energy. While these developments are harmful to the welfare of all countries, the adverse consequences for the development prospects of the poorer countries are of particular concern.

Ministers recognised the costs and dangers inherent in the continuation of present trends:

- There are increasing economic and social costs of continuing high levels of unemployment, particularly among youths and disadvantaged groups.
- There are growing pressures for protection against foreign competition and for export subsidies, and a growing risk that unilateral trade and other current account measures could touch off chain reactions.
- There has been a tendency for sectoral, regional and manpower policies to shift from action to foster adjustment to structural change to measures of a defensive character that tend to preserve the *status quo*, which thus in important respects have the same effects as protectionist trade measures. Under conditions of high unemployment, some domestic measures to maintain existing employment in sectors or companies in financial difficulty may in certain circumstances be justified in the short run. But their continuation on a large scale would over time undermine the dynamic process which underlies rising productivity and would inhibit sustained non-inflationary growth.
- The task of creating sufficient jobs in some less-industrialised Member countries has been made much more difficult by restrictions on immigration, by the return of migrants due to the recession, and by serious payments difficulties, and their development risks being gravely impeded if it takes place in a climate of depressed world trade and growing protectionism.

Ministers discussed the constraints on economic growth. Many of these are internal to the countries in question: high rates of inflation, low profits, heavy dependence on exports and difficulties in financing large budget deficits without adverse effects on inflationary expectations and concern about the rapid increase in governments' indebtedness. There is also an external constraint on countries with a weak balance of payments. Together, the persistence of high rates of inflation, low levels of profits and capacity utilisation, large international payments disequilibria and periods of disorderly exchange-market conditions have depressed business confidence. A further significant factor has been uncertainties about the future supply and price of energy, resulting in part from delays in the implementation of effective energy policies. Under these conditions, private investment has not responded as expected to the action taken to stimulate aggregate demand.

While recognising these constraints, Ministers reaffirmed the decision they took in 1976 to aim for a moderate but sustained rate of expansion, sufficient to achieve a progressive return to full employment over a number of years, but not so fast as to risk the re-emergence of bottlenecks and an upsurge of inflationary expectations. In line with this strategy, Ministers agreed that there is a clear need to step up economic growth in the OECD area as a whole above the rate experienced over the last 18 months so as to reduce unemployment. While expansionary demand management policies have a role to play, this cannot be achieved simply by injections of additional purchasing power. The difficulties now facing the world economy are inseparable and cannot be looked at in isolation: growth, jobs, price stability, energy, adjustment to structural change, are only individual facets of the overall predicament facing Member countries today. What is needed now, and over the medium term, is a combination of policies to ensure adequate domestic demand and to create the right environment for sustainable growth, which requires less inflation, the maintenance of an open market-oriented economic system, and a recovery in productive investment and profits.

A key feature of the programme of concerted action set out below is that differentiated action on various fronts by each Member country can, taken together, ease the constraints facing each of them individually:

- the continuation and, in some cases, strengthening of anti-inflationary policies in countries with a poor price performance will lessen the risk that faster growth in the OECD area as a whole sets off a renewed burst of inflation;
- action by an important group of countries to achieve faster growth will ease the balance-of-payments constraints on countries in a weak external position;
- by acting together countries will individually need to take

less expansionary action, and incur smaller budget deficits, than if they acted in isolation;
* policies to facilitate adjustments to structural changes will help to ensure that rising demand is matched by increased supply potential; and
* stronger policies to encourage conservation and increase production of energy in countries best placed to do so will improve confidence in all Member countries.

Ministers underlined the fact that successful implementation of this programme depends not only on government policy, but also on the extent to which all concerned pursue responsible attitudes towards the determination of prices and incomes. They stressed their conviction that, with the necessary co-operation from both sides of industry, more sustained and better balanced economic growth can be secured with a further progressive reduction of inflation.

A Programme of Concerted Action

Against this background, Ministers have agreed on the following major components of a programme of concerted action.

Demand Management and Stabilization

Ministers agreed on the respective responsibilities of individual Member countries in contributing to faster growth, greater price stability and better payments equilibrium over the next 18 months:

* *Belgium, Canada, France, Germany, Italy, Japan, Switzerland* and the *United Kingdom* should ensure, by appropriate measures as necessary, that the expansion of their domestic demand is significantly greater than in 1977 or, where capacity is already fully utilised, should ensure that total demand increases in line with productive capacity. The *Netherlands* should consolidate the effects of the boost in domestic demand which was achieved last year. The scale and timing of expansionary action by countries in this group should be determined in the light of their internal and external circumstances; in this respect a particular responsibility lies with countries in a strong balance-of-payments position. Such action should not undermine anti-inflationary policies.
* *All other Member countries,* who are not currently in a position to take explicit action to expand domestic demand beyond what is now in prospect, should concentrate primarily

on reducing inflation and improving their balance-of-payments position. Most countries in this group can accept the faster growth which concerted action will impart through a stronger rise in their exports. But in a few of them, where activity has been increasing briskly and demand pressures are quite strong, increased exports resulting from concerted action should be accompanied by reinforced stabilization policies which prevent any net addition to total demand. It is particularly important that the recent acceleration of inflation in the *United States* should be reversed.

Maintenance of an Open Market-Oriented Economic System

Ministers agreed that firm commitments to maintain an open market-oriented economic system are essential to the success of this programme. To this end, Ministers:

- Reiterated their commitment to an open multilateral trading system and decided to renew the Declaration to this effect of 30th May, 1974, with a new preamble which takes into account developments since then and reflects the spirit in which they intend to pursue its implementation.
- Reaffirmed their determination to bring the Multilateral Trade Negotiations to a successful outcome in the near future.
- Expressed satisfaction that the negotiations for an Arrangement on guidelines for officially supported export credits had been successfully concluded in February. The United States and Canada requested other Participants in it to enter into negotiations for the substantive improvement of the existing Arrangement. Other participants were not in a position to react definitively to this request on this occasion. However, in recalling that the Arrangement had only come into force in April, they noted the provision in it for reviews at regular intervals, starting this autumn, of its operation in practice and that these reviews would provide the opportunity to consider any further suggestions for reinforcing administration of the guidelines.
- Agreed on the general orientations for policies to facilitate the structural adjustments needed to sustain faster economic growth.

Energy

Ministers took note of the decision as adopted by the Governing Board of the International Energy Agency at Ministerial level on

6th October, 1977.[9] They stressed that strengthened energy policies form an essential part of the concerted action programme. While recognising that considerable progress has been made, Ministers underlined the following orientations for energy policies and agreed that they need to be pursued vigorously:

- Countries where energy pricing is still below world levels should pay particular attention to this element in energy policies since the price mechanism is one of the most important instruments for promoting increased efficiency of energy use and for expanding energy supplies.
- More should be done to achieve greater energy conservation, to replace oil by other forms of energy (particularly by expanding coal use, assuring adequate nuclear programmes as appropriate and developing stable and reliable conditions for trade in coal and nuclear fuels and technologies) and to encourage expanded oil and gas exploration and development and intensified research and development for new energy technologies. A key requirement is the need to resolve as soon as possible conflicts which may exist between energy requirements and important environmental, regional, safety and security concerns.

Given its predominant weight as both a consumer and producer of energy and the cost of oil imports to its balance of payments, it is of decisive importance that the United States should complete the adoption of a comprehensive energy policy along these lines as soon as possible. At the same time, other Member countries have, in the aggregate, an equally important contribution to make, and Ministers agreed that in these countries energy policies need to be strengthened further.

Monetary Cooperation

Implementation of policies along the lines described above, particularly if adopted in the framework of a concerted programme, will not only improve the prospects for economic growth, but will also help to reduce existing payments imbalances and thereby contribute to greater stability in foreign exchange markets. Ministers agreed that monetary policy has an important role to play in the achievement of these objectives. While recognising that exchange rates need to reflect underlying economic conditions, Ministers agreed that their countries will continue to co-operate closely and to intervene in exchange markets to counter disorderly conditions.

[9]Cf. *AFR, 1977:* 110.

Greater stability in foreign exchange markets will, in turn, improve confidence and help to achieve sustained economic growth.

Ministers agreed that the prompt implementation of the various components of this programme of concerted action should be followed up in the appropriate bodies of the Organization.

Ministers noted the work undertaken with respect to the Communiqué issued after their last meeting concerning the particular problems of the less-industrialised Member countries, and agreed that the outcome of this work should be reported to the next meeting of the Council at Ministerial level.

Global Interdependence and Relations with Developing Countries

Ministers reviewed relations with developing countries in the perspective of development co-operation and the management of global interdependence. Recognising that the prosperity of the OECD countries cannot be pursued in isolation, they emphasized the importance of strengthened co-operation with the developing countries to advance common interests in efficient global economic management and mutually beneficial changes in the structure and balance of the world economy. They also stressed the need for positive policies for increased and more effective support of accelerated economic and social development of the developing countries. They noted with satisfaction the recent establishment of the United Nations General Assembly Committe of the Whole as a new form of dialogue on global economic issues with the developing countries.[10] They expressed the hope that its work would be developed constructively and affirmed the determination of their governments to work to this end.

Interdependence, Trade and Adjustment

Ministers discussed recent changes in the pattern of world production and trade, with particular reference to the industrial advances made by some developing countries. While, especially under conditions of slower growth, these advances have been a factor in adjustment problems in a limited number of industrial sectors, Ministers agreed that trade with developing countries has brought positive benefits to both parties, and that there is a mutual interest in continued expansion of such trade. Ministers reiterated their commitment to an open multilateral trading system on a world-wide basis and re-affirmed their readiness to adjust to changes in

[10]Cf. same: 479.

the pattern of world production and trade. Renewal of the Trade Pledge, a successful outcome to the Multilateral Trade Negotiations and endorsement of the need for more positive adjustment policies will contribute to this end.

At the same time Ministers noted the advantages which would follow to the world economy in general, including to other developing countries, if developing countries with stronger economies would progressively adapt their trade and other policies in line with their level of development and overall financial strength.

Interdependence and International Public and Private Investment

Ministers noted that increased investment in developing countries would contribute to sustained and more balanced world economic growth as well as enhancing development in the countries concerned. Both developed and developing countries therefore should have a mutual interest in measures to stimulate investment in developing countries on an economic basis. Among the sectors mentioned were energy, food production, raw materials and processing and related infrastructure. In this connection, Ministers noted the importance of current and prospective negotiations to expand the lending capacity of the international and regional development finance institutions. They agreed to examine within the Organisation the utility and feasibility of other measures designed to increase investment flows to developing countries, building on existing institutions and mechanisms. Such measures clearly need to be compatible with the development objectives of the countries concerned and would naturally have to be worked out in close co-operation with the developing countries. These measures, which should also be of a kind to stimulate investment in least developed countries, should be explored in the framework of positive development co-operation including increased aid.

Energy Co-operation

Ministers also emphasized that the energy problems of the future would affect all countries and would need to be tackled by all countries working in co-operation. They reaffirmed their willingness to engage in such co-operation, especially with the developing countries.

Development Co-operation

Ministers agreed on the need for an evolving approach to development co-operation to help developing countries in their efforts to strengthen and diversify their economies, to secure decent conditions of life for their people, and to participate increasingly as more equal partners within the world economy. In particular, stepped-up collaborative efforts are required to help ensure that the basic needs of the world's poor are met and to encourage constructive structural change in international economic relations, leading to a more equitable and stable international economic system. Ministers noted the disappointing overall recent level of aid flows. However, they welcomed the performance of some donors and the statements by a number of other donors on plans for expanding their aid allocations and taking other measures to make their official assistance more effective. Ministers of OECD countries, donors of aid, reaffirmed the intention as expressed by their countries in different fora to increase effectively and substantially their official development assistance and to achieve an improved balance of their efforts in this regard. They agreed to examine further how best to ensure that larger aid allocations are effectively spent.

Other Matters

Illicit payments

Ministers expressed their satisfaction with the substantial progress made this year by the special working party of the United Nations Economic and Social Council in the preparation of a treaty to prevent illicit payments in connection with international commercial transactions. They expressed the wish that subsequent progress would permit that a conference of plenipotentiaries could be convened at the earliest possible date.

DECLARATION (TRADE PLEDGE)[11]

Revised text of the Declaration of 30th May, 1974, adopted by the Governments of OECD Member countries on 15th June, 1978

GOVERNMENTS OF OECD MEMBER COUNTRIES[12]

Considering that though the economic situation is in several respects different from that which prevailed at the time of the adoption of the Declaration in 1974,[13] it is still characterised by the problem of adjustment to higher energy prices and by a number of other serious difficulties such as slow economic growth, high levels of unemployment, under-utilisation of productive capacity in a number

---

[11]Text from OECD Observer, July 1978: 6.
[12]Including the European Communities. (Footnote in original.)
[13]Same as note 8.

of sectors, continuing inflation, serious imbalances in international payments and monetary problems.

Considering that difficulties experienced by certain sectors, often simultaneously in many countries, reflect the continued weakness of demand together with structural changes such as shifts in relative prices, in competitive positions, and in production and trade patterns.

Considering that these difficulties constitute an important source of tension in the trade field and that therefore the risk remains that unilateral trade and other current account measures could touch off chain reactions of protectionism.

Considering that all Member countries are affected by these developments, though in varying degrees.

AGREE:

that the nature and size of these difficulties continue to call for wide co-operative action in the fields of economic, trade, financial, monetary, investment, energy, employment and development policies, designed notably to achieve more satisfactory, sustained and balanced economic growth;

that the financing of international payments deficits remains a difficult problem of certain Member countries and that, accordingly, Member countries will co-operate fully to facilitate such financing and are ready to consider appropriate arrangements which may prove necessary in this respect;

that unilateral trade or other current account measures by one or more Member countries to deal with the current situation would aggravate the problems of other countries without solving the underlying difficulties in a longer term perspective and, if generalised, would be self-defeating and have a depressing effect on the world economy;

that countries have responsibilities both as importers and exporters to avoid disruption of regular trade flows;

that, in the case of sectoral problems, every effort should be made to identify them before they assume critical proportions and that action in this field should bring about adaptations through measures which do not transfer the burden of adjustment to trading partners and which avoid or minimize distortions to trade;

that there is therefore a continuing need for a joint undertaking, having as its objective to prevent unilateral action which may have a detrimental impact on international economic relations;

that the successful outcome in the near future of the Multilateral Trade Negotiations in both industrial and agricultural areas and its implementation will improve and strengthen the open, multilateral trading system;

that, with a view to stimulating mutually beneficial growth of world trade, there is a need to improve the trade relations between industrialised and developing countries.

REAFFIRM THEIR DETERMINATION, in the light of the foregoing and for a period of one year:

* to avoid having recourse to unilateral measures, of either a general or a specific nature, to restrict imports or having recourse to similar measures on the other current account transactions, which would be contrary to the objectives of the present Declaration;
* to avoid measures to stimulate exports or other current account transactions artificially; and, inter alia, abstain from destructive competition in official support of export credit and aim at continuing progress in co-operative action to this effect;
* to avoid export restrictions which would be contrary to the objectives of the present Declaration;
* to consult with each other, making full use of the general procedures of consultation within OECD, in order to assure that the present Declaration is properly implemented;
* to implement the present Declaration in accordance with their international obligations and with due regard to the special needs of developing countries.

(44) . The Bonn Economic Summit, July 16–17, 1978: Declaration Issued at the Conclusion of the Conference.[14]

The Heads of State and Government of Canada, the Federal Republic of Germany, France, Italy, Japan, the United Kingdom of Great Britain and Northern Ireland and the United States of America met in Bonn on 16th and 17th July 1978. The European Community was represented by the President of the European Council and by the President of the European Commission for discussion of matters within the Community's competence.

1. We agreed on a comprehensive strategy covering growth, employment and inflation, international monetary policy, energy, trade and other issues of particular interest to developing countries. We must create more jobs and fight inflation, strengthen international trading, reduce payments imbalances, and achieve greater stability in exchange markets. We are dealing with long-term prob-

[14]Text from *Presidential Documents,* 14: 1310–15.

lems, which will only yield to sustained efforts. This strategy is a coherent whole, whose parts are interdependent. To this strategy, each of our countries can contribute; from it, each can benefit.

GROWTH, EMPLOYMENT AND INFLATION

2. We are concerned, above all, about world-wide unemployment because it has been at too high a level for many years, because it hits hardest at the most vulnerable sections of the population, because its economic cost is high and its human cost higher still. We will act, through measures to assure growth and develop needed skills, to increase employment

In doing this, we will build on the progress that has already been made in the fight against inflation and will seek new successes in that fight. But we need an improvement in growth where that can be achieved without rekindling inflation in order to reduce extremes of balance of payments surpluses and deficits. This will reduce destabilizing exchange rate movements. Improved growth will help to reduce protectionist pressures. We need it also to encourage the flow of private investment, on which economic progress depends; we will seek to reduce impediments to private investment, both domestically and internationally. Better growth is needed to ensure that the free world is able to develop to meet the expectations of its citizens and the aspirations of the developing countries.

3. A program of different actions by countries that face different conditions is needed to assure steady non-inflationary growth. In countries whose balance of payments situation and inflation rate does not impose special restrictions, this requires a faster rise in domestic demand. In countries where rising prices and costs are creating strong pressures, this means taking new measures against inflation.

—Canada reaffirmed its intention, within the limits permitted by the need to contain and reduce inflation, to achieve higher growth of employment and an increase in output of up to 5%.

—As a contribution to avert the world-wide disturbances of economic equilibrium the German Delegation has indicated that by the end of August it will propose to the legislative bodies additional and quantitatively substantial measures up to 1% of G.N.P., designed to achieve a significant strengthening of demand and a higher rate of growth. The order of magnitude will take account of the absorptive capacity of the capital market and the need to avoid inflationary pressures.

—The President of the French Republic has indicated that, while pursuing its policy of reduction of the rate of inflation, the French Government agrees, as a contribution to the common effort, to increase by an amount of about 0.5% of G.N.P. the deficit of the budget of the State for the year 1978.

—The Italian Prime Minister has indicated that the Government undertakes to raise the rate of economic growth in 1979 by 1.5 percentage points with respect to 1978. It plans to achieve this goal by cutting public current expenditure while stimulating investments with the aim of increasing employment in a non-inflationary context.

—The Prime Minister of Japan has referred to the fact that his Government is striving for the attainment of the real growth target for fiscal year 1978, which is about 1.5 percentage points higher than the performance of the previous year, mainly through the expansion of domestic demand. He has further expressed his determination to achieve the said target by taking appropriate measures as necessary. In August or September he will determine whether additional measures are needed.

—The United Kingdom, having achieved a major reduction in the rate of inflation and improvement in the balance of payments has recently given a fiscal stimulus equivalent to rather over 1% of G.N.P. The Government intends to continue the fight against inflation so as to improve still further the prospects for growth and employment.

—The President of the United States stated that reducing inflation is essential to maintaining a healthy U.S. economy and has therefore become the top priority of U.S. economic policy. He identified the major actions that have been taken and are being taken to counter inflation in the United States: Tax cuts originally proposed for fiscal year 1979 have now been reduced by $10 billion; government expenditure projections for 1978 and 1979 have been reduced; a very tight budget is being prepared for 1980; steps are being taken to reduce the direct contribution by government regulations or restrictions to rising costs and prices, and a voluntary programme has been undertaken to achieve deceleration of wages and prices.

—The meeting took note with satisfaction that the common approach of the European Community already agreed at Bremen[15] would reinforce the effectiveness of this programme.

ENERGY

4. In spite of some improvement, the present energy situation remains unsatisfactory. Much more needs to be done.

5. We are committed to reduce our dependence on imported oil.

6. We note that the European Community has already agreed at

[15]July 6–7, 1978.

Bremen the following objectives for 1985: to reduce the Community's dependence on imported energy to 50 percent, to limit net oil imports, and to reduce to 0.8 the ratio between the rate of increase in energy consumption and the rate of increase in gross domestic product.

7. Recognizing its particular responsibility in the energy field, the United States will reduce its dependence on imported oil. The U.S. will have in place by the end of the year a comprehensive policy framework within which this effort can be urgently carried forward. By year end, measures will be in effect that will result in oil import savings of approximately 2.5 million barrels per day by 1985. In order to achieve these goals, the U.S. will establish a strategic oil reserve of 1 billion barrels; it will increase coal production by two-thirds; it will maintain the ratio between growth in gross national product and growth in energy demand at or below 0.8; and its oil consumption will grow more slowly than energy consumption. The volume of oil imported in 1978 and 1979 should be less than that imported in 1977. In order to discourage excessive consumption of oil and to encourage the movement toward coal, the U.S. remains determined that the prices paid for oil in the U.S. shall be raised to the world level by the end of 1980.

8. We hope that the oil exporting countries will continue to contribute to a stable world energy situation.

9. Looking to the longer term, our countries will review their national energy programs with a view to speeding them up. General energy targets can serve as useful measures of the progress achieved.

10. Private and public investment to produce energy and to use it more efficiently within the industrial world should be increased. This can contribute significantly to economic growth.

11. The further development of nuclear energy is indispensable, and the slippage in the execution of nuclear power programmes must be reversed. To promote the peaceful use of nuclear energy and reduce the risk of nuclear proliferation, the nuclear fuel cycle studies initiated at the London Summit[16] should be pursued. The President of the United States and the Prime Minister of Canada have expressed their firm intention to continue as reliable suppliers of nuclear fuel within the framework of effective safeguards. The President intends to use the full powers of his office to prevent any interruption of enriched uranium supply and to ensure that existing agreements will be respected. The Prime Minister intends that there shall be no interruption of Canadian uranium supply on the basis of effective safeguards.

12. Coal should play an increasing important role in the long term.

16May 7-8, 1977; *AFR, 1977:* 419.

13. Joint or co-ordinated energy research and development should be carried out to hasten the development of new, including renewable, energy sources and the more efficient use of existing sources.

14. In energy development, the environment and human safety of the population must be safeguarded with greatest care.

15. To help developing countries, we will intensify our national development assistance programs in the energy field and we will develop a co-ordinated effort to bring into use renewable energy technologies and to elaborate the details within one year. We suggest that the OECD will provide the medium for co-operation with other countries.

16. We stress the need for improvement and co-ordination of assistance for developing countries in the energy field. We suggest that the World Bank explore ways in which its activities in this field can be made increasingly responsive to the needs of the developing countries, and to examine whether new approaches, particularly to financing hydrocarbon exploration, would be useful.

TRADE

17. We reaffirm our determination to expand international trade one of the driving forces for more sustained and balanced economic growth. Through our joint efforts we will maintain and strengthen the open international trading system. We appreciate and support the progress as set forth in the Framework of Understanding on the Tokyo Round of Multilateral Trade Negotiations made public in Geneva, July 13th, 1978, even though within this Framework of understanding some difficult and important issues remain unresolved.

The successful conclusion of these negotiations, the biggest yet held, would mean not just a major trade liberalisation programme extending over the 1980s but the most important progress yet made in the GATT in relation to non-tariff measures. Thus the GATT rules would be brought more closely into line with the requirements of the next decade—particularly in relation to safeguards—in ways which could avoid any weakening of the world trading system and be of benefit to all trading countries developed and developing alike. A substantially higher degree of equity and discipline in the international trading system would be achieved by the creating of new mechanisms in many fields for consultation and dispute settlement. Uniform application of the GATT rules is vital and we shall move in that direction as soon as possible.

In all areas of the negotiations the Summit countries look forward to working even more closely with the developing countries. We seek to ensure for all participants a sound and balanced result, which adequately takes into account the needs of developing countries, for example, through special and differential treatment, and which brings about their greater participation in the benefits and obligations of the world trading system.

At last year's Downing Street Summit we rejected a protectionist course for world trade. We agreed to give a new impetus to the Tokyo Round. Our negotiators have fulfilled that commitment. Today we charge them, in co-operation with the other participants, to resolve the outstanding issues and to conclude successfully the detailed negotiations by December 15, 1978.[17]

18. We note with satisfaction the renewal of the pledge to maintain an open market oriented economic system made by the OECD Council of Ministers[18] last month. Today's world economic problems cannot be solved by relapsing into open or concealed protectionism.

19. We welcome the statement on positive adjustment policy made by the OECD Ministers. There must be a readiness over time, to accept and facilitate structural change. Measures to prevent such change perpetuate economic inefficiency, place the burden of structural change on trading partners and inhibit the integration of developing countries into the world economy. We are determined in our industrial, social, structural, and regional policy initiatives to help sectors in difficulties, without interfering with international competition and trade flows.

20. We note the need for countries with large current accounts deficits to increase exports and for countries with large current accounts surpluses to facilitate increases in imports. In this context, the United States is firmly committed to improve its export performance and is examining measures to this end. The Prime Minister of Japan has stated that he wishes to work for the increase of imports through the expansion of domestic demand and various efforts to facilitate imports. Furthermore, he has stated that in order to cope with the immediate situation of unusual surplus, the Government of Japan is taking a temporary and extraordinary step of calling for moderation in exports with the aim of keeping the total volume of Japan's exports for the fiscal year of 1978 at or below the level of fiscal year 1977.

21. We underline our willingness to increase our co-operation in the field of foreign private investment flows among industrialized countries and between them and developing countries. We will intensify work for further agreements in the OECD and elsewhere.

22. In the context of expanding world economic activity, we recognize the requirement for better access to our countries' markets

[17]The negotiations were concluded Apr. 12, 1979.
[18]Document 43b.

for the products of the developing countries. At the same time we look to increasing readiness on the part of the more advanced developing countries to open their markets to imports.

RELATIONS WITH DEVELOPING COUNTRIES

23. Success in our efforts to strengthen our countries' economies will benefit the developing countries, and their economic progress will benefit us. This calls for joint action on the basis of shared responsibility.

24. In the years ahead the developing countries, particularly those most in need, can count on us for an increased flow of financial assistance and other resources for their development. The Prime Minister of Japan has stated that he will strive to double Japan's official development assistance in three years.

We deeply regret the failure of the COMECON countries to take their due share in the financial assistance to developing countries and invite them once more to do so.

25. The poorer developing countries require increased concessional aid. We support the soft loan funds of the World Bank and the three regional development banks. We pledge our governments to support replenishment of the International Development Association on a scale that would permit its lending to rise annually in real terms.

26. As regards the more advanced developing countries, we renew our pledge to support replenishment of the multilateral development banks' resources, on the scale needed to meet the growing needs for loans on commercial terms. We will encourage governmental and private co-financing of development projects with these banks.

The co-operation of the developing countries in creating a good investment climate and adequate protection for foreign investment is required if foreign private investment is to play its effective role in generating economic growth and in stimulating the transfer of technology.

We also refer to our efforts with respect to developing countries in the field of energy as outlined in paragraph 15 and 16.

27. We agreed to pursue actively the negotiations on the Common Fund to a successful conclusion and to continue our efforts to conclude individual commodity agreements and to complete studies of various ways of stabilizing export earnings.

INTERNATIONAL MONETARY POLICY

28. The erratic fluctuations of the exchange markets in recent months have had a damaging effect on confidence, investment and growth throughout the world. Essentially, exchange rate stability

can only be achieved by attacking the fundamental problems which have contributed to the present large balance of payments deficits and surpluses. Implementation of the policies described above in the framework of the concerted program will help to bring about a better pattern of world payments balances and lead to greater stability in international exchange markets. This stability will in turn improve confidence and the environment for sustained economic growth.

29. Although exchange rates need to respond to changes in underlying economic and financial conditions among nations, our monetary authorities will continue to intervene to the extent necessary to counter disorderly conditions in the exchange markets. They will maintain extensive consultation to enhance these efforts' effectiveness. We will support surveillance by the International Monetary Fund, to promote effective functioning of the international monetary system.

30. The representatives of the European Community informed the meeting of the decision of the European Council at Bremen on 6/7 July to consider a scheme for a closer monetary co-operation. The meeting welcomed the report and noted that the Community would keep the other participants informed.

CONCLUSION

31. It has been our combined purpose to attack the fundamental economic problems that our countries confront.

The measures on which we have agreed are mutually reinforcing. Their total effect should thus be more than the sum of their parts. We will now seek parliamentary and public support for these measures.

We cannot hope to achieve our purposes alone. We shall work closely together with other countries and within the appropriate international institutions; those among us whose countries are members of the European Community intend to make their efforts within this framework.

We have instructed our representatives to convene by the end of 1978 in order to review this Declaration.

We also intend to have a similar meeting among ourselves at an appropriate time next year.

(45) *33rd Annual Meeting of the Boards of Governors of the International Bank for Reconstruction and Development and the International Monetary Fund: Remarks by President Carter at the Opening Session, Washington, September 25, 1978.* [19]

[19]Text from *Presidential Documents,* 14: 1627-9.

Mr. Chairman, Managing Director de Larosiere, President McNamara,[20] *Governors of the Fund and the Bank, and distinguished visitors:*

On behalf of the American people, I want to welcome you to Washington again for your 33rd annual meeting.

We meet as a group, dedicated to the cause of international cooperation. In the political field, you and I share the belief that cooperation among leaders can lead to peace. We've learned that lesson once again in the last few days. And I know that you will join me in saluting the statesmanship and the courage of President Anwar Sadat and Prime Minister Menahem Begin.[21]

Your tremendous influence as leaders in your own nations can contribute greatly to maintaining the momentum toward peace, both in the Middle East and throughout the world. In the economic field, also, cooperation brings large benefits to the people who look to us for leadership.

Three decades of existence of the Fund and the Bank have brought progress and a better life for the people of the world. Like you, I want to build on that record to achieve still further economic cooperation, progress, and a better life. Since your meeting here last year, our countries acting together have made tangible progress on world economic problems.

The issues that remain, as you and I well know, are very difficult. But they, like other difficult questions, are not insoluble.

You assembled in this room are the economic leaders of the world. The task before you is to consolidate past gains and then to push ahead in ways that will foster economic growth in both developing and the industrialized nations.

Our goal is to achieve progress for all peoples, not just a few. The basic strategy has already been agreed. In Mexico City, at the IMF Interim Committee, agreement was reached on the general directions that economic policy should take.[22]

Progress on those agreements has been made. The outlook for improvement is good. We must not falter. A contribution to this strategy is needed from every country represented here, no matter how great nor small, no matter how weak nor powerful.

In this effort, the United States has a major responsibility. Two months ago at Bonn,[23] I made specific promises to our major trading partners about the actions that my country will take to this end.

[20]Tengku Razaleigh Hamzah (Malaysia), Jacques de Larosière (France), and Robert S. McNamara (U.S.).
[21]Documents 18–20.
[22]Cf. Introduction at note 155.
[23]Document 44.

I pledged that the United States will fight inflation, will reduce oil imports, will expand exports.

Let there be no doubt in your mind about how seriously I take these pledges that have been made on my own word of honor and on behalf of the people of the United States. Taken together, they encompass the most urgent priorities of my own administration; my own reputation is at stake as a leader. And they are commitments that I am most fully determined to fulfill.

I've come here today to underline that determination and to describe the next steps that we will take.

I will soon announce the first phase of a long term program to expand American exports.[24] Removing disincentives to exports and encouraging exports are overriding tasks for my own administration. As you know, compared to many nations represented here, the export commitment has not been as great in our own country as it has perhaps among some of you.

I've also intensified my efforts, which were already great, to obtain legislation that will curtail United States imports of oil, imports which are entirely too high.

The United States Senate is scheduled to vote this week, day after tomorrow, on the key bill, natural gas regulation and pricing. This is one of the most complicated and difficult and challenging assignments that the United States Congress has ever faced.

This particular bill is expected to save 1.4 million barrels of imported oil per day by 1985. I am confident that the Senate and then the House of Representatives will do their duty to our Nation by approving this bill. I hope to have other bills comprising a strong package of energy legislation enacted before the Congress adjourns, probably, hopefully, less than a month from now.[25]

This is essential, we know, to a sound American dollar. I intend very shortly to announce a further series of important and specific and tough measures to strengthen our fight against inflation.[26]

These next steps will certainly not be the end of our effort, only the renewed beginning and commitment, part of a sustained effort to control these very serious problems for our own people in this country, and our relationship with your countries as well.

Every nation represented in this room understands how difficult this struggle against inflation is and what sustained commitment it demands. My administration will continue that struggle on a wide variety of fronts until we succeed. There will be obstacles and objections from special groups all along the way. But I will not shrink from the hard decisions and the persistent efforts that are needed.

[24]Document 46.
[25]Cf. Introduction at note 161.
[26]Cf. Introduction at note 166.

I'm determined to maintain a sound dollar. This is of primary importance to us, and I know it is of great interest and importance to you as well. We recognize that our currency plays an international role, and we accept the responsibilities which this involves. Our countries are acting to meet our responsibilities to the system, consistent with the directives set at the IMF meeting in Mexico and as was pledged again by seven of us national leaders at the Bonn Summit. The United States will do the same.

Through programs which I have just described, we will achieve the strong U.S. economy and noninflationary U.S. growth that must underlie a sound dollar and a stable international monetary system.

The outlook for progress is good. Some of the causes of our large trade deficit have already been removed. Others are now being removed. Our current account position should improve significantly next year. The United States will remain an open and vigorous economy, and an attractive place to invest.

Other steps are also required to achieve the economic progress that we all seek. In these steps, the IMF and the World Bank have, of course, a vital role to play. These two institutions are the core and the symbol of the international economic order that was built after World War II. They've shown a high capacity to adapt to new and rapidly changing needs. Strengthening and enlarging them, both institutions, is a prime goal of United States policy.

The United States is firmly committed to a strong International Monetary Fund, exercising effective surveillance over the system and with adequate resources to meet official financing needs. The United States has supported and will continue to support an increase in IMF quotas and a new allocation of special drawing rights.

I'm pleased that legislative consideration of U.S. participation in the supplementary financing facility is nearing completion.[27] I expect final action to be taken shortly.

I might report to you that this year, the attitude of the United States Congress is better than it has been in my own memory toward supporting international financial institutions and toward foreign aid as well.

I trust that our European friends will fashion the proposed European monetary arrangements which were discussed, at least superficially, at Bonn in a way that will also strengthen the international monetary system and that will facilitate growth and trade and investments and also, quite importantly, the continued central role of the IMF.

Current European efforts to these ends are a logical step toward the great European integration which the United States has long supported. We also support proposals to enlarge the resources of

[27]Cf. Introduction at note 158.

the World Bank and its soft loan affiliate, the International Development Association, as we pledged at the Bonn summit.

Again, the Congress has met our expectations. Expanded help to developing countries contributes, we know, to the healthy world economy and to world peace. Last week, the United States Senate, as the House of Representatives had already done, met our Nation's obligations for both multilateral and bilateral aid [28] beyond, I must admit, my own expectations.

I will seek next year to continue this commitment as part of a growing international effort to eliminate the worst aspects of human poverty. The United States Governor for the Fund and the Bank, Secretary of Treasury Mike Blumenthal, will outline our policies for achievement in more detail when he addresses your session tomorrow.

You are gathered in Washington to address formidable challenges in both monetary and development fields. The future of all peoples in both developing and developed countries depends upon the outcome of your deliberations and subsequent action. I reiterate my Nation's commitment to the common effort that is required. I am confident that this effort will succeed.

Thank you very much.

(46) Promoting American Exports: Statement by President Carter, September 26, 1978. [29]

It is important for this Nation's economic vitality that both the private sector and the Federal Government place a higher priority on exports. I am today announcing a series of measures that evidences my administration's strong commitment to do so.

The large trade deficits the United States has experienced in recent years have weakened the value of the dollar, intensified inflationary pressures in our own economy, and heightened instability in the world economy. These trade deficits have been caused by a number of factors. A major cause has been our excessive reliance on imported oil. We can reduce that reliance through the passage of sound energy legislation this year.[30] Another factor is that the United States economy has been growing at a stronger pace in recent years than the economies of our major trading partners. That has enabled us to purchase relatively more foreign goods while our trading partners have not been able to buy as much of our exports. We will begin to correct this imbalance as our trading partners meet

[28]Cf. Introduction at note 157.
[29]Text from *Presidential Documents*, 14: 1631-5.
[30]Cf. Introduction at note 161.

the commitments to economic expansion they made at the Bonn summit.[31]

The relatively slow growth of American exports has also been an important factor in our trade deficit problem. Over the past 20 years, our exports have grown at only half the rate of other industrial nations, and the United States has been losing its share of world markets. Until now, both business and Government have accorded exports a relatively low priority. These priorities must be changed.

The measures I am announcing today consist of actions this administration has taken and will take to:

(1) provide increased direct assistance to United States exporters;
(2) reduce domestic barriers to exports; and
(3) reduce foreign barriers to our exports and secure a fairer international trading system for all exporters.

These actions are in furtherance of the commitment I made at the Bonn summit to an improved United States export performance.

DIRECT ASSISTANCE TO UNITED STATES EXPORTERS

1. *Export-Import Bank.* I have consistently supported a more effective and aggresive Export-Import Bank. During the past 2 years, my administration has increased Eximbank's loan authorization fivefold—from $700 million in FY 1977 to $3.6 billion for FY 1979. I intend to ask Congress for an additional $500 million in FY 1980, bringing Eximbank's total loan authorization to $4.1 billion. These authorizations will provide the Bank with the funds necessary to improve its competitiveness, in a manner consistent with our international obligations, through increased flexibility in the areas of interest rates, length of loans, and the percentage of a transaction it can finance. The Bank is also moving to simplify its fee schedules and to make its programs more accessible to smaller exporters and to agricultural exporters.

2. *SBA Loans to Small Exporters.* The Small Business Administration will channel up to $100 million of its current authorization for loan guarantees to small business exporters to provide seed money for their entry into foreign markets. Small exporting firms meeting SBA's qualifications will be eligible for loan guarantees totalling up to $500,000 to meet needs for expanded production capacity and to ease cash flow problems involving overseas sales or initial marketing expenses.

[31]Document 44.

3. *Export Development Programs.* I am directing the Office of Management and Budget to allocate an additional $20 million in annual resources for export development programs of the Departments of Commerce and State to assist United States firms, particularly small and medium-sized businesses, in marketing abroad through:

—a computerized information system to provide exporters with prompt access to international marketing opportunities abroad and to expose American products to foreign buyers;
—risk sharing programs to help associations and small companies meet initial export marketing costs; and
—targeted assistance to firms and industries with high export potential and intensified short-term export campaigns in promising markets.

4. *Agricultural Exports.* Agricultural exports are a vital component of the U.S. trade balance. Over the past 10 years, the volume of U.S. farm exports has doubled and the dollar value has nearly quadrupled. Trade in agricultural products will contribute a net surplus of almost $13 billion in fiscal year 1978. This strong performance is due in part to this administration's multifaceted agricultural export policy, which will be strengthened and which includes:

—An increase of almost $1 billion (up from $750 million in FY 1977 to $1.7 billion in FY 1978) in the level of short-term export credits.
—An increase of almost 20 percent in the level of funding support for a highly successful program of cooperation with over 60 agricultural commodity associations in market development.
—Efforts in the Multilateral Trade Negotiations to link the treatment of agricultural and nonagricultural products.
—Opening trade offices in key importing nations in order to facilitate the development of these markets.
—Aggressive pursuit of an international wheat agreement, to ensure our producers a fair share of the expanding world market.
—Support of legislation to provide intermediate export credit for selective agricultural exports.

5. Tax Measures. I am hopeful that Congress will work with the administration to promptly resolve the tax problems of Americans employed abroad, many of whom are directly involved in export efforts. Last February, I proposed tax relief for these citizens amounting to about $250 million a year. I think this proposal, which Congress has not approved, deals fairly and, during a time of great budget stringency, responsibly with this problem. I remain

ready to work with the Congress to resolve this issue, but I cannot support proposals which run contrary to our strong concerns for budget prudence and tax equity.

My administration's concern for exports is matched by our obligation to ensure that government-sponsored export incentives constitute an efficient use of the taxpayers' money. The DISC[32] tax provision simply does not meet that basic test. It is a costly (over $1 billion a year) and inefficient incentive for exports. I continue to urge Congress to phase DISC out or at least make it simpler, less costly, and more effective than it is now, and my administration stands ready to work with Congress toward that goal.

REDUCTION OF DOMESTIC BARRIERS TO EXPORTS

Direct financial and technical assistance to United States firms should encourage them to take advantage of the increasing competitiveness of our goods in international markets. Equally important will be the reduction of Government-imposed disincentives and barriers which unnecessarily inhibit our firms from selling abroad. We can and will continue to administer the laws and policies affecting the international business community firmly and fairly, but we can also discharge that responsibility with a greater sensitivity to the importance of exports than has been the case in the past.

1. *Export Consequences of Regulations.* I am directing the heads of all executive departments and agencies to take into account and weigh as a factor, the possible adverse effects on our trade balance of their major administrative and regulatory actions that have significant export consequences. They will report back on their progress in identifying and reducing such negative export effects where possible, consistent with other legal and policy obligations. I will make a similar request of the independent regulatory agencies. In addition, the Council of Economic Advisers will consider export consequences as part of the administration's Regulatory Analysis Program.

There may be areas, such as the export of products which pose serious health and safety risks, where new regulations are warranted. But through the steps outlined above, I intend to inject a greater awareness throughout the Government of the effects on exports of administrative and regulatory actions.

2. *Export Controls for Foreign Policy Purposes.* I am directing the Departments of Commerce, State, Defense, and Agriculture to take export consequences fully into account when considering the

---

[32]Domestic International Sales Corporation.

use of export controls for foreign policy purposes. Weight will be given to whether the goods in question are also available from countries other than the United States.

3. *Foreign Corrupt Practices Act.* At my direction, the Justice Department will provide guidance to the business community concerning its enforcement priorities under the recently enacted foreign antibribery statute. This statute should not be viewed as an impediment to the conduct of legitimate business activities abroad. I am hopeful that American business will not forgo legitimate export opportunities because of uncertainty about the application of this statute. The guidance provided by the Justice Department should be helpful in that regard.

4. *Antitrust Laws.* There are instances in which joint ventures and other kinds of cooperative arrangements between American firms are necessary or desirable to improve our export performance. The Justice Department has advised that most such foreign joint ventures would not violate our antitrust laws, and in many instances would actually strengthen competition. This is especially true for one-time joint ventures created to participate in a single activity, such as a large construction project. In fact, no such joint conduct has been challenged under the antitrust laws in over 20 years.

Nevertheless, many businessmen apparently are uncertain on this point, and this uncertainty can be a disincentive to exports. I have, therefore, instructed the Justice Department, in conjunction with the Commerce Department, to clarify and explain the scope of the antitrust laws in this area, with special emphasis on the kinds of joint ventures that are unlikely to raise antitrust problems.

I have also instructed the Justice Department to give expedited treatment to requests by business firms for guidance on international antitrust issues under the Department's Business Review Program. Finally, I will appoint a business advisory panel to work with the National Commission for the Review of the Antitrust Laws.

5. *Environmental Reviews.* For a number of years the export community has faced the uncertainty of whether the National Environmental Policy Act (NEPA) requires environmental impact statements for Federal export licenses, permits, and approvals.

I will shortly sign an Executive order which should assist U.S. exports by eliminating the present uncertainties concerning the type of environmental reviews that will be applicable and the Federal actions relating to exports that will be affected. The order will make the following export-related clarifications:

—Environmental impact statements will not be required for Federal export licenses, permits, approvals, and other export-related actions that have potential environmental effects in foreign countries.

—Export licenses issued by the Departments of Commerce and Treasury will be exempt from any environmental reviews required by the Executive order.

—Abbreviated environmental reviews will be required only with respect to (1) nuclear reactors, (2) financing of products and facilities whose toxic effects create serious public health risks, and (3) certain Federal actions having a significant adverse effect on the environment of nonparticipating third countries or natural resources of global importance.

Accordingly, this order will establish environmental requirements for only a minor fraction (well below 5 percent) of the dollar volume of United States exports. At the same time, it will provide procedures to define and focus on those exports which should receive special scrutiny because of their major environmental impacts abroad. This Executive order will fairly balance our concern for the environment with our interest in promoting exports.

REDUCTION IN FOREIGN TRADE BARRIERS AND SUBSIDIES

We are also taking important international initiatives to improve U.S. export performance. Trade restrictions imposed by other countries inhibit our ability to export. Tariff and especially non-tariff barriers restrict our ability to develop new foreign markets and expand existing ones. We are now working to eliminate or reduce these barriers through the Multilateral Trade Negotiations in Geneva.

United States export performance is also adversely affected by the excessive financial credits and subsidies which some of our trading partners offer to their own exporters. One of our major objectives in the MTN is to negotiate an international code restricting the use of government subsidies for exports. In addition, I am directing the Secretary of the Treasury to undertake immediate consultations with our trading partners to expand the scope and tighten the terms of the existing International Arrangement on Export Credits.

I hope that our major trading partners will see the importance of reaching more widespread agreements on the use of export finance, to avoid a costly competition which is economically unsound and ultimately self-defeating for all of us. These international agreements are essential to assure that American exporters do not face unfair competition, and this administration intends to work vigorously to secure them.

CONCLUSION

While these initiatives will assist private business in increasing exports, our export problem has been building for many years, and we cannot expect dramatic improvement overnight. Increasing our exports will take time and require a sustained effort. Announcement of my administration's export policy is not the end of our task, but rather the beginning. To ensure that this issue continues to receive priority attention, I am asking Secretary Kreps,[33] in coordination with officials from other concerned Government agencies, to direct the continuation of efforts to improve our export potential and performance.

I will shortly sign an Executive order to reconstitute a more broadly based President's Export Council to bring a continuous flow of fresh ideas into our Government policymaking process. I expect this Council to report to me annually through the Secretary of Commerce.

Increasing U.S. exports is a major challenge—for business, for labor, and for Government. Better export performance by the United States would spur growth in the economy. It would create jobs. It would strengthen the dollar and fight inflation.

There are no short-term, easy solutions. But the actions I am announcing today reflect my administration's determination to give the United States trade deficit the high-level, sustained attention it deserves. They are the first step in a long-term effort to strengthen this Nation's export position in world trade.

(47) *Strengthening the Dollar: Remarks by President Carter and Secretary of the Treasury W. Michael Blumenthal, November 1, 1978.*[34]

THE PRESIDENT. Last week, I pledged my administration to a balanced, concerted, and sustained program to fight inflation.[35] That program requires effective policies to assure a strong dollar.

The basic factors that affect the strength of the dollar are heading in the right direction. We now have an energy program passed by Congress; our trade deficit is declining; and last week I put in place a strong anti-inflation program.

The continuing decline in the exchange value of the dollar is clearly not warranted by the fundamental economic situation. That decline threatens economic progress at home and abroad and the success of our anti-inflation program.

As a major step in the anti-inflation program, it is now necessary to act to correct the excessive decline in the dollar which has recently occurred. Therefore, pursuant to my request that strong action be

[33]Secretary of Commerce, Juanita Kreps.
[34]Text from *Presidential Documents,* 14: 1908-10.
[35]Cf. Introduction at note 166.

taken, the Department of the Treasury and the Federal Reserve Board are today initiating measures in both domestic and international monetary fields to assure the strength of the dollar.

The international components of this program have been developed with other major governments and with central banks. They intend to cooperate fully with the United States in attaining our mutual objectives.

Secretary Blumenthal and Chairman Miller[36] are announcing detailed measures immediately.

Thank you very much.

SECRETARY BLUMENTHAL. In the past few months the United States has taken action to correct the imbalances that have characterized our economy. We have passed an energy bill which will lead to a reduction of our dependence on imported oil. We have implemented a program to enhance exports as a national priority.[37] We have launched a tough and determined anti-inflation campaign. We have taken steps to reduce the Government's preemption of the Nation's financial resources by cutting dramatically our budget deficit. We have also moved decisively toward undoing the overregulation of our great economy. We have enacted a tax bill which will enhance capital formation and improve productivity. More must and will be done, but the prerequisites for improved economic performance are in place.

Recent moves in the dollar exchange rates have not only exceeded any decline related to the fundamental factors but plainly are hampering progress toward the price stability, balance-of-payments improvement, and enhanced climate for investment and growth which these measures are designed to bring about.

The time has, therefore, come to call a halt to these developments. At the President's direction, Chairman Miller and I are today announcing comprehensive corrective actions.

Effective immediately, the Federal Reserve is raising the discount rate from 8½ to 9½ percent, and is imposing a supplementary reserve requirement equal to 2 percentage points of time deposits of $100,000 or more.

In addition to domestic measures being taken by the Federal Reserve, the United States will, in cooperation with the Governments and central banks of Germany and Japan, and the Swiss National Bank, intervene in a forceful and coordinated manner in the amounts required to correct the situation. The United States has arranged facilities totalling $30 billion in the currencies of these three countries, which will finance the U.S. contribution to the coor-

[36]Of the Federal Reserve Board G. William Miller.
[37]Document 46.

dinated market intervention activities of the four participating countries.

That $30 billion in the currencies of these three countries are being raised through a drawing of the U.S. reserve tranche of the International Monetary Fund; through the sale of SDR's to Germany, Japan, and Switzerland; through a substantial increase in the Federal Reserve swap lines with the Bundesbank, the Bank of Japan, and the Swiss National Bank; and through our intention to issue foreign currency denominated securities. Together, this will make up the $30 billion package.

In addition, the Treasury will increase its gold sales to at least 1 ½ million ounces monthly, beginning in December. The currency mobilization measures will be described in more detail, and Under Secretary Solomon[38] is here to answer any questions.

We'll have a brief break so that you can digest this and give you a few minutes, and then we'll go into the details of it.

The fact is that the foreign exchange situation that this program is designed to correct has gotten out of hand. It must end, and it will end. The dollar's deterioration has already led to a rise in import competitive prices, which further fuels inflation and perpetuates a vicious cycle. And the image of the American economy and its leadership is adversely affected by this.

We feel that failure to act now would be injurious to the American and to the world economy. Our economy is strong. Steps have been taken to strengthen it further, and the fundamental economic conditions and growth trends in the four nations that are a party to this agreement are moving toward a better international balance.

Assisted by the actions we have now announced, this will provide an improved framework for a restoration of more stable exchange markets and the correction of the recent excessive exchange rate movements.

Thank you very much.

---

[38]Under Secretary of the Treasury for Monetary Affairs Anthony M. Solomon.

9. LIFE IN THE HUMAN COMMUNITY

(48) The Terrorist Scourge.

(a) Scope of the Threat: Statement by Secretary of State Vance before the Committee on Governmental Affairs, United States Senate, January 23, 1978.[1]

I am pleased to appear before you today to discuss a subject of the greatest concern and urgency: how to defend our citizens and our national interests against threats of terrorism around the world. Congress and the Administration must work closely on this vital issue so that as a government we are prepared to deal with terrorist acts rapidly, decisively, and effectively.

Terrorism is one of the most inhumane phenomena of our time. We must do everything we can to combat this problem. As your first witness, let me present the Administration's position on the overall problem of terrorism and the need for effective legislation.

It is clear from the pending legislation that the Administration and Congress share common goals: to deter terrorist attacks, to discourage other governments from cooperating with or giving refuge to terrorists, to capture and prosecute those who participate in such crimes, and to do this in cooperation with other governments.

Strong legislation can help achieve these goals. It will demonstrate to the world that the American Government and people will not tolerate such violence and that we are prepared to act promptly and firmly. Effective legislation can strengthen our ability to work together with other governments toward this shared goal.

Let me begin by describing the scope of the terrorist threat, as we see it today.

- International airplane hijackings have increased in the past 2 years, after a brief pause in their frequency.
- Worldwide, the number of terrorist attacks—including bombings, assassinations, ambushes, and arson—has been

[1]Text from *Bulletin,* Mar. 1978: 53-5.

higher in the past 2 years than in any previous comparable period.

- There has been a shift away from attacks against U.S. Government officials and property to attacks on American businessmen and corporate facilities. The indications are that these threats on overseas facilities of U.S. corporations and their employees could continue at least at their present level.
- Cooperation among terrorist groups, with totally different goals, appears to be growing. Groups such as the Popular Front for the Liberation of Palestine, the Japanese Red Army, and the Baader-Meinhof Gang increasingly cooperate in lethal attacks against innocent victims regardless of their nationality.

Some terrorist groups find their ideology in a radical nationalism that allows no compromise. Others seek to destroy the political order of their countries, either because they reject all authority or because they seek to intimidate the established authorities. While the motivations of individual terrorists vary, however, it is clear that there is one common thread: They will attack the forms of organized society by all the means they can command.

In their common pursuit of violence, they share information, weapons, money, and, at times, logistical support. In the expression of that violence, they threaten the personal freedom and security of us all.

International Response

Before I talk about what the United States is doing to combat this threat, let me briefly discuss the international response that is emerging, for as much as any other problem we face, the fight against terrorism must be international in scope.

There have been some encouraging developments.

- Hijackers find they can no longer count on landing in countries which once gave them sanctuary. During the recent Japan Air Lines and Lufthansa hijackings, nearly every nation in the Middle East where the hijackers sought refuge turned them away. We must, nonetheless, gain universal acceptance of the responsibility of nations to prosecute or extradite terrorists apprehended within their jurisdiction, as prescribed by the Hague and Montreal Conventions.
- On November 3, 1977, the U.N. General Assembly passed a resolution[2] condemning hijacking and urging the adoption of

[2]Resolution 32/8, Nov. 3, 1977; cf. *AFR, 1977:* 134–5.

effective measures to combat it. The approval of this consensus resolution reflects a growing appreciation by nations throughout the world of the need for more effective action against this form of political violence.

• The successful actions of the Israelis at Entebbe and the West Germans at Mogadiscio demonstrated that terrorists can be defeated by a combination of appropriate rescue capacity, flexible contingency planning, and skillful tactics. We should recognize, however, that such operations entail great risk to the hostages and may not always be feasible.

U.S. Response

For our part, the United States has taken strong actions on a number of fronts.

First, we have made clear to all that we will reject terrorist blackmail. We have clearly and repeatedly stated our intention to reject demands for ransom or for the release of prisoners.

Second, in this and past Administrations, we have strengthened airport security within the United States. There has been only one successful hijacking of a U.S. scheduled air carrier since November 1972. We will continue these essential security measures.

Third, we have improved safety measures to protect U.S. officials and property abroad. We have provided protective armor for official vehicles and mandated security training for all personnel posted overseas. Together with the Department of Commerce, the State Department is advising private corporations and their employees on how to protect themselves and their property against terrorist attacks. In most cases, we have been able to carry out these measures in close cooperation with foreign governments.

Fourth, through action initiated this fall by Secretary Adams[3] at the International Civil Aviation Organization, we have been working to upgrade the international standards for airport security. The primary focus of this effort is to require mandatory preflight inspection of all passengers and accompanying baggage.

Fifth, we have intensified our efforts to move other countries to ratify the Tokyo, Hague, and Montreal Conventions. As you know, these conventions provide for the apprehension, prosecution, and extradition of those who hijack or sabotage commercial aircraft. To date, 62 countries have ratified all three conventions; 55 have ratified none. We are not satisfied with these numbers; worldwide acceptance of these basic principles is essential.

Sixth, we have developed, and are improving, procedures for cooperating and exchanging information among law enforcement

[3]Of Transportation Brock Adams.

agencies around the world. For example, during the hijacking of the Japan Air Lines and Lufthansa aircraft last fall, we provided background information on terrorist groups and their past operations and guidelines for protecting and obtaining the release of hostages.

Seventh, we have made major organizational changes within the executive branch that are designed to improve our ability to combat terrorism. Shortly after assuming office, the President reorganized the structure of the National Security Council (NSC). Among the actions taken was the establishment of the Special Coordination Committee (SCC) to handle, among other matters, crisis management. The Assistant to the President for National Security Affairs[4] chairs this committee; its members are the statutory members of the NSC and other senior officials as necessary.

In a crisis situation, the SCC would convene immediately. This committee insures that necessary decisions will be made at the highest levels of the government.

The Special Coordination Committee supervises a senior-level interagency group to insure coordination among agencies dealing with terrorism. The interagency group has an executive committee consisting of representatives from the Departments of State, Defense, Justice, Treasury, Transportation, Energy, and the Central Intelligence Agency and the NSC staff. It is chaired by the representative of the State Department; the deputy chairman is the representative of the Department of Justice. It has met frequently since it was established in September 1977.

To fulfill our responsibilities within this framework, the State Department has developed its own procedures. Our Operations Center is fully staffed on a 24-hour basis to manage crisis situations. It has instantaneous communications to all parts of the government, direct access to top officials, and prompt communication to all posts overseas. It has performed well in the past, and it will do so in the future.

Our procedures are designed to anticipate terrorist attempts as well as to deal with ongoing incidents. Specialized units in the U.S. intelligence community, as well as other agencies of the Federal Government, place high priority cn the collection and evaluation of necessary intelligence. We are working to improve the effectiveness and promptness with which we exchange this information with friendly agencies abroad.

When U.S. citizens in foreign countries are threatened, we immediately communicate with foreign governments and make available to them our information, advice, and experience to assist them in carrying out their responsibilities.

[4]Zbigniew Brzezinski.

Eighth, cooperation on antiterrorism has become an important part of our bilateral relations with other nations. We are urging other governments to take appropriate steps to combat terrorism and bring terrorists to justice.

Obstacles to effective cooperation among governments remain. Some governments, sympathetic to the asserted cause of particular terrorist organizations, not only provide safe haven but also arm, train, and provide cover. Others shy away from resolute action to avoid jeopardizing relations with countries that support terrorist organizations; still others prefer to avoid the apprehension or prosecution of terrorists for fear of new terrorist attacks aimed at freeing comrades. We will continue to press these governments to assume the full measure of their international responsibilities.

The Administration and this committee have the same goals—stopping terrorism. We will continue to work closely with you as you develop effective legislation.

Legislative Provisions

Let me address the provisions we hope will be embodied in such legislation.

- We are prepared to submit regular reports to Congress on acts of international terrorism that affect American citizens or interests. We suggest that these reports be issued quarterly and in a form that can be made public so that all concerned Americans will have authoritative and current data on terrorist incidents. The Department of Justice will address these reporting requirements in greater detail in its testimony.
- We will appear periodically before this committee to supplement these written reports. I know that the committee will appreciate that much of this information will be sensitive. As a result, we strongly urge that these briefings be in closed sessions and on a classified basis.
- The Administration supports the concept of a public list of countries which aid or abet terrorist actions. Public exposure and condemnation can be effective in discouraging support for terrorist activities. Removal of a country from the list would signal a change toward greater responsibility and restraint.
- We are prepared to support appropriate sanctions against countries appearing on such a list; indeed, we already impose sanctions against certain countries which have been identified with terrorist operations. We believe that any such sanctions should be considered on a case-by-case basis taking into account probable effectiveness; the interests of U.S. citizens living abroad; and our overall political, security, and

economic relationships. In addition, to be effective, sanctions must be fashioned so that they can be altered or lifted in response to evidence of change.
- We suport the objective of publishing a list of airports that are deficient in their security measures. However, we must recognize that there are significant technical constraints on evaluating the security of foreign airports and that we must work together with the responsible government to upgrade these procedures. The Department of Transportation will address this issue in greater detail in its testimony.
- We hope that Congress will enact enabling legislation that will result in full U.S. compliance with the terms of the Montreal Convention on aircraft sabotage. In this connection, we seek provisions for civil penalties to complement the criminal penalties already available under aircraft security legislation.
- And finally, it is our hope that the legislation developed by this committee will be consistent with the NSC-SCC reorganization I have described.

Let me say again that we welcome the action of this committee, and we will cooperate with you fully in the development of legislation that will be effective in dealing with this dangerous threat.

(b) The Bonn Summit: Joint Statement by the Heads of State and Government, Bonn, July 17, 1978.[5]

The heads of state and government, concerned about terrorism and the taking of hostages, declare that their governments will intensify their joint efforts to combat international terrorism.

To this end, in cases where a country refuses extradition or prosecution of those who have hijacked an aircraft and/or do not return such aircraft, the heads of state and government are jointly resolved that their governments should take immediate action to cease all flights to that country.

At the same time, their governments will initiate action to halt all incoming flights from that country or from any country by the airlines of the country concerned. The heads of state and government urge other governments to join them in this commitment.

(49) International Narcotics Control: Statement by K. Mathea Falco, Senior Adviser and Director for International Narcotics Control Matters, Department of State, before the Sub-

[5]Text from *Presidential Documents,* 14: 1308–9. The heads of state and government are listed at the beginning of Document 44.

committee on Foreign Operations of the Committee on Appropriations, United States Senate, March 21, 1978.[6]

I am pleased to be here today to present the Department of State's international narcotics control program appropriations request for FY 1979. Drug abuse has been a serious problem in the United States for over a decade. The Federal Government spends more than $800 million each year for drug control efforts in law enforcement, treatment, and rehabilitation. The international narcotics control program (INC) budget represents less than 5% of that total expenditure. The challenge of reducing the availability of dangerous drugs in the United States cannot be met solely by efforts within our own borders. It must be addressed as well in the developing nations where illicit drug crops, such as opium and coca, are cultivated and refined into heroin and cocaine.

The President's August 2, 1977, drug abuse message[7] marked a significant shift in drug control policy from primarily a domestic focus to truly a global concept. Victim countries are not only those which suffer the devastating health and social consequences of drug abuse but also those whose political, economic, and social integrity are threatened by the illicit drug traffic. To implement this new, broadened perspective, we are working through diplomatic and program initiatives in key countries to curtail illicit drug production and traffic.

Cooperative Efforts

Major cooperative program efforts are under way with nine countries which are the principal sources of illicit drugs coming into the United States. Because of its devastating impact on the health and welfare of our society, heroin is our primary drug of concern. Mexico continues to be the primary source of illicit heroin, although with the increasing success of the Mexican poppy eradication campaign, its prominence as a supplier is decreasing.

Southeast Asian heroin, produced in the Golden Triangle, is becoming an increasingly important source of heroin for the United States and is already flooding the countries of Western Europe. The South Asian countries of Afghanistan and Pakistan also are of serious concern, because large quantities of opium are harvested there in remote, mountainous areas which often are not subject to effective central government control. Although most of this opium currently is consumed within the region, the potential for a massive influx of South Asian heroin into the United States is very real. Increasing amounts of South Asian opiates are now reaching Europe.

---

[6]Text from *Bulletin,* June 1978: 42–6.
[7]Text of message, Aug. 2, 1977, in *Presidential Documents,* 13: 1154–60.

Current levels of cocaine use do not present a significant public health threat in the United States. However, if cocaine use increases, fatalities, overdoses, and other adverse health and social consequences might increase dramatically. The goal of our international policy is to restrict the usage of cocaine through curtailing its availability.

Bolivia and Peru are the world's two largest producers of coca leaf, from which cocaine is derived. Ecuador and Columbia figure prominently in cocaine processing and traffic, and it is in these four countries that our major bilateral cocaine control efforts are presently directed. An estimated 15–17 tons of cocaine reach the United States from South America each year.

Increased emphasis is being placed on working with multilateral and regional organizations to strengthen illicit narcotics production and traffic. Through these international and regional organizations, such as the U.N. Fund for Drug Abuse Control (UNFDAC), the Colombo Plan, and the Association of South East Asian Nations (ASEAN), approaches can be made to countries unresponsive to bilateral overtures by the United States to insure that they do not themselves become victims of the ever-changing patterns of the illicit drug traffic.

U.S. Efforts

During the past year, the Department of State—in conjunction with the President's Strategy Council on Drug Abuse, the White House Office of Drug Abuse Policy, and other domestic drug agencies—has evaluated the complex and difficult issues involved in developing an effective, coherent international drug control policy. As a result of this ongoing evaluative process, the Department has intensified its activities on several different fronts, including expanded diplomatic initiatives, increased emphasis on demand reduction activities, and long-term research. The Department also has undertaken a major reorganization to improve management efficiency, accountability, and coordination of the international narcotics control program.

Pursuant to this reorganization, the Secretary of State has directed that those narcotics control functions previously performed by the Agency for International Development (AID) be consolidated under the Senior Adviser's Office (S/NM) to insure a fuller integration of policy, planning, and implementation. The consolidation in Washington has already taken place; the changes in overseas missions are under way and scheduled for completion by the end of FY 1978. To insure more effective coordination among the principal agencies operating abroad in carrying out programs funded under INC appropriations, liaison officers have been detailed to S/NM from the Drug Enforcement Administration

(DEA), the National Institute on Drug Abuse, and the U.S. Customs Service.

Complementing this organizational consolidation, the Department is implementing a comprehensive effort in the planning of INC activities on a worldwide basis. In collaboration with the regional bureaus within State and other U.S. agencies, multifaceted approaches will be developed to long-term issues critical in the resolution of the worldwide drug problem, such as integrated rural development and alternative crop identification for primary drug-producing areas, and implementation of a strategic poppy-heroin forecasting system. At the same time, we will maintain ongoing initiatives in improving drug control capabilities in key countries through technical and logistical assistance; training, treatment, and rehabilitation demonstration projects; and by encouraging expanded interregional approaches to drug abuse control efforts.

Our program request for FY 1979 to support these activities is $40 million. This amount is allocated on a regional and functional basis in the following manner:

	Total	Opium	Cocaine
Latin America	$21.2	$13.5	$7.7
East Asia	7.8	7.8	—
Near East	1.5	1.5	—
Other	9.5	—	—
	$40.0	$22.8	$7.7

The amount shown as "other" includes U.S. contributions to international organizations, substantial training programs designed and implemented by the Drug Enforcement Administration and U.S. Customs Service, the demand reduction program implemented largely through the National Institute on Drug Abuse, and program development and support costs

Mexico

In assisting the Mexican Government to curtail illicit drug production and traffic, we also seek to strengthen its own long-term narcotics control capability. Both our governments agree on the necessity for joint efforts in eliminating opium production in Mexico and in breaking up major trafficking networks. The Mexican Government wishes to avoid a domestic heroin abuse problem and is acutely aware of the corrosive effects that unrestrained illicit drug trafficking can have on the political and economic stability of

After he first took office, Mexican President Lopez Portillo met with President Carter[8] and affirmed his personal commitment to a greatly intensified effort to curtail illicit heroin production and traffic. President Lopez assigned new narcotics control missions to the Mexican Defense Department in support of Attorney General Flores Sanchez who has overall responsibility for Mexico's narcotics control effort. The Mexican Defense Department is using more than 20,000 troops in the primary poppy growing areas, both to interdict drug traffic and to inhibit planting of the illicit opium poppies.

Dr. Peter Bourne[9] and I met twice last year with the Mexican Attorney General, the Secretary of Defense, and other Mexican officials to review our governments' efforts to curtail illicit narcotics production and traffic. At our most recent meeting last December, the Mexicans discussed with us specific elements of their expanded national narcotics control plan, which calls for an intensified eradication and interdiction effort over the next 3 years.

Since 1973, the United States has provided approximately $50 million in international narcotics control assistance to Mexico. During the past year (FY 1977), approximately 30% of our total program budget, $13.4 million, was committed to assisting the Mexican effort. An additional $16.8 million, to meet immediate program needs, is projected for this fiscal year (FY 1978). This large commitment for 1978 will reduce requirements for FY 1979, and we are, accordingly, requesting $13.5 million for next year.

The Mexican Federal Government estimates that it spends well over $40 million annually in its drug control efforts. This figure does not include personnel and resources committed at the state and local levels. The Mexican Attorney General's office employs about 500 enforcement agents, pilots, mechanics, managers, and administrative personnel on a year-round basis in the narcotics control effort. During spring and fall, when the poppy eradication campaigns are intensified, 70% of the Attorney General's approximately 3,000 personnel are devoted to the program.

The Mexicans have also paid a human toll for their efforts. Scores of Mexican enforcement officials and soldiers have been injured or killed during recent years while carrying out drug control activities. Six Mexican federal judicial agents were killed in 1977, and 12 were seriously injured during eradication operations.

During the 1977 poppy eradication campaigns, approximately 47,000 fields of opium poppies (comprising about 14,000 acres) were destroyed. These figures represent an increase of almost 50%

[8]Feb. 13–14, 1977 in Washington.
[9]Special Assistant to the President for Health Issues; resigned July 20, 1978.

over the previous year's eradication effort. An additional 7,847 poppy fields were destroyed in January and February of this year.

The real success of the Mexican effort can be measured in terms of reduced amounts of heroin reaching the United States. DEA estimates that in 1977 the Mexican eradication program prevented the equivalent of more than 10 tons of heroin from entering the United States. The scarcity of heroin supplies in Mexico has resulted in an upward movement of wholesale prices. According to DEA data, heroin purity on our city streets has dropped to the lowest point since 1973 (5%). The increase in heroin retail prices to their highest point on record ($1.69 per milligram), decrease in purity levels, and the decline in heroin overdose deaths (44% below last year) to the lowest point since 1973 are significant signs of progress.

The Mexican Government is presently reviewing economic and social studies designed to develop alternative sources of income for the remote, poor regions where poppy is grown. The Mexican Government has not sought U.S. assistance for such programs but might turn to international financial institutions or U.N. organizations for necessary support.

Bolivia and Peru

Coca leaf has been grown on the Andean slopes of Bolivia and Peru for thousands of years. Use of the leaf dates from the Inca era when it was chewed by priests during religious ceremonies. It is a deeply ingrained cultural habit which is continued today by perhaps 2 million residents of the region. Although chewing of the leaf is more prevalent in rural, high-altitude areas, coca tea is consumed by virtually all segments of Bolivian society. Bolivia and Peru are the world's two largest producers of coca leaf and both permit legal cultivation.

Bolivia. Bolivia is in the second year of an accelerated program to limit coca cultivation to levels required for legal internal use while strengthening the capability of its enforcement agencies to prevent leakage of the crop to the production of cocaine. Experiments are being conducted with alternative crops to replace coca which will provide the basis for integrated rural development programs in the Yungas and Chapare coca growing regions. Provision of economic alternatives, as well as improvements of existing crops such as coffee and cacao, food processing, and marketing structures will allow Bolivia to implement a phased ban on coca cultivation. As part of this process, Bolivia has recently completed a registry of all coca growers and banned new coca cultivation. We are requesting $1.8 million in FY 1979 to assist Bolivian pilot rural development efforts in primary coca growing regions. In addition, AID will provide $8.5 million in rural development assistance to expand the pilot projects.

The Bolivian National Directorate for Control of Dangerous Substances (DNSP) has demonstrated substantial progress in drug enforcement in the last year, particularly in the seizure of cocaine laboratories. The most recent seizure, in February, immobilized principal elements of an international trafficking network.

The DNSP has also placed narcotics enforcement and intelligence units in coca transit and production areas to enforce the ban on new plantings of coca and to control the movement of leaves and processed coca. For FY 1979 we are requesting $1.7 million to strengthen the DNSP through advisory and training services, communications equipment, vehicles, and a utility helicopter. This will also enable the DNSP to target effectively major trafficking organizations.

Peru. The Government of Peru in early March promulgated a new comprehensive drug law which prohibits plantings of coca in new areas and requires conversion of larger coca fields to other crops within 3 years. Actual conversion of smaller coca plots probably will depend on the government's ability to provide these subsistence farmers with economic alternatives.

Implementation of the new drug law will be entrusted to a new interministerial body assisted by police units. Our Embassy in Lima is working with the Peruvian Government on a number of projects related to licensed coca production and marketing, illicit crop control, and law enforcement. In FY 1979 we are requesting $871,000 for coca crop control. We are also requesting continued support ($566,000) for Peruvian narcotics law enforcement agencies, primarily for training and communications equipment.

Colombia and Ecuador

Ecuador is the receiving point for most of the coca paste headed north from Peru. Much of it arrives overland, carried by all types of conveyances and passengers. Small quantities of the paste are converted to cocaine in Ecuador, but most of it continues to Colombia for further refinement. There it passes into the hands of the professional traffickers. Colombia is the refining and transshipment point for the major portion of cocaine reaching the United States. The income derived by the criminal networks exceeds the national revenue from the export of coffee, Colombia's major source of foreign exchange.

In 1977 the increased commitment of the governments in the major narcotics program countries in the region and a growing professionalism in the better equipped narcotics enforcement agencies resulted in many more significant seizures of illicit drugs and the arrest of key violators. One of the more successful cases in Colombia resulted in the seizure of 1,100 pounds of cocaine base. The Colombian seizures represent a greater quantity of cocaine than the total amount seized in the United States in 1977. Ecuador also showed a substantial rise in cocaine seizures in 1977 over 1976 and a doubling of the amount of processed marijuana seized.

Colombia. In meetings last June, President Lopez[10] of Colombia expressed his personal commitment to joint narcotics control efforts. Last December he established a select narcotics enforcement unit under the Attorney General, for which we are providing training through DEA. In FY 1979 we are requesting $180,000 to strengthen the Attorney General's new narcotics unit. Assistance funds will continue to be programmed to other law enforcement entities in Colombia so long as they continue to have narcotics control functions. For FY 1979 we are asking $830,000 for support of such enforcement organizations.

Three helicopters provided the Colombian Government last September have been effectively used, most notably in an October raid where agents seized 1,100 pounds of cocaine base, an aircraft, weapons, several vehicles, and arrested a key drug trafficker. More recently, the helicopters were used in a raid which netted 165 tons of marijuana. We are requesting $300,000 in FY 1979 for continued maintenance and support of U.S.-provided helicopters, as well as of other aircraft provided by the Government of Colombia.

Ecuador. The United States has provided financial assistance to Ecuador's narcotics enforcement organizations since 1973. Such support has helped that country's antinarcotics effort, and in 1977 drug seizures and arrests by Ecuador's police increased substantially over those in 1976. Beginning in 1978 we have expanded our assistance to include support for the Ministry of Education's campaign to increase public awareness of the drug problem. In FY 1979 we are requesting $436,000 to assist Ecuador's narcotics enforcement units and $100,000 for demand reduction efforts.

Mr. Richard Arellano, Deputy Assistant Secretary for Inter-American Affairs, and I have just returned from Quito. While there, we conveyed the high priority which our government attaches to international narcotics control. We were pleased to receive a firm commitment from the Government of Ecuador to cooperate more closely on narcotics matters, while we assured that government of our continued support for such cooperation.

[10]Alfonso López Michelsen.

In the coming year, regional cooperation in narcotics control will receive added State Department impetus as we seek to encourage Latin American countries to coordinate their narcotics efforts more closely. Areas of potential cooperation include enforcement, crop substitution, demand reduction, and research efforts. As part of this cooperation, a regional narcotics communications network in South America will be completed and a program inaugurated to foster joint planning and coordination of operations against international trafficking networks. In FY 1979 we are requesting $260,000 to support joint regional narcotics enforcement projects in Latin America.

Afghanistan and Pakistan

The cultivation and use of opium poppy is deeply ingrained in the culture of areas of Afghanistan and Pakistan, based on centuries of practice and public acceptance. In contemporary Pakistan, the opium gum is added to tea or processed to a primitive stage and smoked as a relaxant by a large segment of the older peasant classes or used as a medicine. The poppy straw is used for animal fodder and to strengthen the adobe-type building materials. In certain areas of Afghanistan, opium is the only available form of medication, and the oil and seeds of the poppy are used in cooking.

Little or no capability for processing opium into heroin exists in Afghanistan today, and most of the opium leaving the country is smuggled in ton lots across the border into Pakistan and Iran by animal caravans and vehicles. If estimates which place Afghanistan's domestic consumption of opium at around 100 tons a year are correct, as much as 270 tons of Afghan opium will be exported during the coming year.

Afghanistan. The Afghan Government's antinarcotics effort has been largely directed at the traffickers in opium. In 1977, Afghan authorities seized 13 metric tons of opium. However, police units assigned to antitrafficking duties are undermanned, undertrained, and underequipped. The U.N. Fund for Drug Abuse Control, the principal agency through which international narcotics control assistance is channeled to Afghanistan, is assisting in the development of a more effective interdiction capability. We have supplied training through the Drug Enforcement Administration and the U.S. Customs Service.

A joint commission consisting of representatives of the Afghan Government, the United Nations, and the United States has been established in Kabul to coordinate narcotics control activities. A U.S. development expert seconded to the U.N. Fund for Drug Abuse Control has designed an integrated rural development project for the Upper Helmand opium producing area, which will be financed by international donor countries and financial institutions. This project will provide farmers alternatives to opium cultivation and thus allow the Afghan Government to eliminate opium production from the area. We are requesting $500,000 to support selected crop replacement and enforcement activities to complement existing multilateral efforts.

During the past year, AID has used side letters with the Afghan Government to require that AID assistance not be used to foster opium cultivation. We received a report from the Afghan Government that in late January it plowed under 70 hectares of opium poppy discovered in one of the project areas.

Pakistan. Pakistan is estimated to have produced 200 tons of opium during 1977, of which 120 tons were consumed locally. The remaining 80 tons finds its way into Iran, Turkey, Western Europe, and the Persian Gulf. As in Afghanistan, Pakistan's opium poppy fields are concentrated in remote border areas where the central government exercises minimal control. Production is centered in the desolate mountainous regions of the North West Frontier Province bordering Afghanistan, where most of the poppy farmers live at a subsistence level with opium as the only cash crop.

Our narcotics control assistance in Pakistan is directed at helping develop the local capability to keep Pakistan opium and its derivatives from entering the international market and to assist in the development of alternative cash crops to replace opium. We are requesting $850,000 in FY 1979 for the Swabi Tehsil project which will identify economic alternatives to poppy cultivation in that area of the North West Frontier Province. This project will in turn serve as the basis for a large-scale rural development undertaking for which support of other major donor countries will be sought.

Political instability during the past year, which led to the overthrow of the Bhutto government by the military, created conditions which did not allow our bilateral efforts to progress as successfully as we had hoped. As conditions in the country stabilize and the military leadership devotes its attention to the narcotics problem, we expect more vigorous control of both trafficking and production. For FY 1979 we are requesting $150,000 to equip Pakistan's customs service with vehicles and patrol craft to interdict drugs leaving the country through the Karachi seaport and adjacent coast.

Southeast Asia

Southeast Asian illicit narcotics production and traffic have plagued the world for decades. Despite the valiant efforts of law enforcement officers around the world, tightly organized international trafficking groups continue to profit from the misery they bring to others in the form of drug addiction. In Southeast Asia, narcotics control efforts are further complicated by traditional political instability and insurgency, creating situations in which illicit narcotics traffic can flourish. Despite these obstacles, however, progress in reducing Southeast Asian narcotics production and traffic is being made. My January visit to Southeast Asia encouraged me that prospects of curtailing the illicit narcotics traffic in that region are more favorable now than at any time in the past.

We are particularly encouraged by two aspects of recent Golden Triangle narcotics trafficking developments: the flow of raw and refined narcotics and the prices at which they are sold. During the last 6 months, shipments of raw or processed opiates from the northern Shan State to the Thai-Burma border refining areas have declined very sharply, accompanied as well by significant decreases from most other parts of Shan State.

These reductions are a result of the aggressive Burmese narcotics eradication and interdiction program, which has drastically reduced opium production and led to the virtual disappearance of the large narcotics caravans so common in the past. Narcotics delivered to the border have been increasingly handled by relatively small-time traffickers dealing in limited quantities. Moreover, unlike previous years of opium surplus, opiate products now reaching the border area go directly into refineries, bypassing storage sites. Despite the decline in border deliveries, the output of processed heroin has remained high, an indication that large stockpiles which had existed for so long are now being drawn down. If these trends continue, the result will be an inevitable drop in the availability of Golden Triangle heroin.

Also encouraging has been the behavior of narcotics prices in the Golden Triangle in the past year. Border prices for narcotics are at their lowest levels in several years. These low prices are an indication that the large stockpiles which had been cached in the border areas are still sufficient to meet current demand. To understand the significance of the low prices at the border refinery area, they must be compared to the price of finished opiates in Bangkok, where prices are up sharply above 1976 levels. The current price differential per kilogram of heroin is nearly $1,400 between the border refinery areas and Bangkok. This compares with a 1976 price differential of slightly over $700. A price spread of this magnitude indicates the high-risk factor in moving narcotics from the border areas to Bangkok created by aggressive enforcement efforts by Thai police organizations.

Thailand. In Thailand I met with the Prime Minister, the Foreign

Minister,[11] and other government officials responsible for narcotics control. During our several meetings, Prime Minister Kriangsak expressed to me his firm commitment to move against the illicit narcotics traffic which transits his country to reach regional and international markets. An important key to suppression of this traffic is cooperation among countries of the Golden Triangle, particularly Burma and Thailand. During our meetings, Prime Minister Kriangsak pledged personally to pursue close cooperation with the Government of Burma.

On a bilateral basis, the Department of State is exploring possible support for a pilot rural development project for the Mae Chaem watershed—an area which produces approximately one-half of that country's estimated annual 50-ton opium crop—scheduled for implementation this summer. The Agency for International Development has requested $2.2 million for this highland integrated rural development project.

Thailand and the United States have just signed a 5-year agreement under which the United States will provide treatment and rehabilitation assistance for Thai drug addicts. Over the term of the agreement, the Bangkok metropolitan health department addict treatment project will establish detoxification programs at 15 existing public health centers for treating narcotics addicts and will provide training for Thai treatment specialists. The accord marks the first direct U.S. involvement in supporting Thai Government efforts to rehabilitate the estimated 400,000 Thai narcotics addicts.

To assist Thai efforts in FY 1979, we have requested $1,674,000, slightly more than the $1,549,000 allotted for FY 1978. About half of these funds ($866,000) will be used to maintain ongoing cooperative programs with Thai police and customs, particularly in training and communications. A new aspect of our program in Thailand is the Bangkok treatment project mentioned previously, for which we have requested $274,000 in FY 1979. To support crop substitution efforts we have requested $400,000 in FY 1979.

Burma. In January, Deputy Assistant Secretary Oakley[12] and I met with Burmese officials and visited drug abuse prevention and treatment programs in Rangoon. We were particularly impressed with the extensive nationwide preventive education campaign being conducted in Burmese schools at all levels.

Our discussions with Colonel Sein Lwin, Minister of Home and Religious Affairs and Chairman of the Burmese Narcotics Control Board, assured us of the strong Burmese commitment to suppress illicit narcotics cultivation and trafficking. We stressed the import-

---

[11]General Kriangshak Chamanun and Foreign Minister Uppadid Pachariyangkun.
[12]For East Asian Affairs Robert B. Oakley.

ance of cooperation with Thailand to increase the effectiveness of suppression efforts.

From Rangoon, I accompanied several high-ranking Burmese enforcement officials to observe large-scale poppy eradication projects under way in the Shan State. As of February 28, more than 8,000 acres of opium poppies had been destroyed this year, eliminating an estimated potential of 38 tons of opium from the illicit traffic. Fields from which poppies had previously been eradicated were now planted with food crops such as rice, potatoes, and vegetables by the same farmers who had previously grown poppies. The Burmese did not hesitate, however, to show me areas where illicit poppies were still growing. They pointed out that those fields would also be the subject of their eradication campaigns but that resource limitations would delay their destruction.

Our FY 1979 budget request for Burma is $6,050,000, an increase of approximately $1.2 million over FY 1978. This will provide for six helicopters ($3,800,000), communications equipment ($250,000), and aircraft maintenance assistance ($1,940,000) to strengthen the Burmese efforts to curtail illicit narcotics production and trafficking. Three of the requested helicopters will replace those that have crashed. The additional three will strengthen the Burmese capability to locate illicit poppy fields and narcotics refineries.

Malaysia. We have recently agreed to assist the Malaysian Government in a demand reduction project. An American drug adviser will work for a year with Malaysian drug experts to develop a halfway house to rehabilitate addicts after their release from government treatment facilities. At the same time, a three-member training team will work with Malaysian health authorities to train specialists in various aspects of drug treatment and rehabilitation. Our contribution to this program in FY 1978 will be approximately $200,000. Requirements for FY 1979 have not yet been precisely determined, pending results of the initial phase.

U.N. Fund for Drug Abuse Control

As this committee knows, the United States has traditionally been the major financial contributor to the U.N. Fund for Drug Abuse Control. One of the most significant developments this past year was the broadening of the Fund's financial base through major contributions from several countries, particularly the substantial $5.4 million commitment by Norway for crop substitution in Burma. As a result of these pledges, our contribution to the Fund in 1977 represented slightly less than half of the total financial commitments it received. At last month's Commission on Narcotic

Drugs meeting in Geneva,[13] to which I was the U.S. representative, I expressed our government's pleasure at that development and our hope that major contributions from other countries would continue to reduce the U.S. share. In FY 1979, we are requesting $3 million for UNFDAC, the same amount as our 1978 contribution.

In Geneva I noted the increasing recognition that contributions from governmental development aid funds are appropriate for UNFDAC projects, which further the socioeconomic development of primary narcotics producing areas while at the same time eliminating illicit narcotics crops. The increasing availability of such contributions to UNFDAC requires careful, advance planning of projects for submission to potential donors. We have provided the services of a developmental planning expert to assist the Fund in meeting this need, as with the integrated rural development project being developed in the Upper Helmand Valley in Afghanistan.

(50) The Law of the Sea: Statement to the Press by Ambassador Elliot L. Richardson, Special Representative of the President for the Law of the Sea Conference, March 16, 1978.[14]

In less than 2 weeks representatives of 156 countries will assemble in Geneva at the seventh session of the third U.N. Conference on the Law of the Sea to try once again to hammer out a comprehensive treaty.

The last attempt to reach agreement, at the sixth session held in New York last summer, ended in disarray and—from the U.S. point of view—setback and disillusionment.[15] Through the exercise of procedural sleight-of-hand, compromises on the exploration and exploitation of the deep seabed—an issue of paramount import to the United States and a host of other nations—were summarily discarded. These compromises—struck after weeks of painstaking effort and open discussion—were replaced in the negotiating text by provisions developed in secret that are clearly inimical to essential U.S. interests.

Disturbed by this abridgment of due process, and unsure of the advantages of continued participation, I felt constrained to recommend to the President that the United States undertake a searching review of both conference procedures and the substantive matters before it. This review is still in process. It is so advanced, however, that I can now appropriately share with you its principal conclusions which guide our preparations for the forthcoming session.

---

[13]Held Feb. 13–14, 1978 in Geneva.
[14]Text from *Bulletin,* June 1978: 47–9.
[15]Cf. *AFR, 1977:* 131.

The first issue to come under scrutiny was the continued desirability of working toward a treaty. In light of discouraging reverses, did the United States still believe that a treaty was in its national interest? The response to that question remains affirmative. We are still convinced that a new magnitude of global order can emanate from successful negotiations on the law of the sea. A treaty deemed just and equitable by the world community can dramatically enhance the prospects for the rule of law.

But commitment alone carries no guarantee of success. Agreement at the seventh session can come only through an exertion of political will and a determination by all nations to forge an accommodation that leaves no nation with its essential interests impaired.

Deep Seabed Mining

For the United States, success of the conference will depend on unraveling the tangle of conflicts surrounding the deep seabed mining issue. More than our essential interests are at stake in this area; there is opportunity here to establish a precedent which can serve as a blueprint for the development of future international institutions concerned with common resources. The deep seabed beyond areas of national jurisdiction contains vast quantities of nodules that can become a major source of the manganese, nickel, copper, and cobalt needed by an increasingly industrialized world.

We support the concept of an International Seabed Resource Authority that would supervise the conduct of deep seabed mining. We believe that revenues stemming from these mining operations should be shared among the nations of the world. Yet the current negotiating text would discourage entry into the deep seabed by those nations which are both able to extract its minerals and have a growing need for them. The text imposes onerous financial conditions, dictates mandatory transfer of technology as a condition of access, and contains several other features which would combine to deter entrepreneurs from investing the $700–900 million required to bring a single mining site into production.

Our position on mining the deep seabed is clear.

- We accept a dual system of development which will give states and companies, as well as the international Enterprise, reasonable assurance of access to seabed resources. We reject the concept of rigid state centralism projected on a global scale.
- We accept some limitation on production of seabed minerals in deference to the essential interests of land-based producers—but not to the extent that it excessively restricts the availability of resources needed by an expanding world economy.

- We believe that the Authority should be controlled in ways that adequately take into account such factors as production, investment, and consumption—and not be based on the simplistic, ideological platform of one nation, one vote.

There is room for compromise in these positions, but the fundamental concerns they express cannot be ignored. If the final text fails to recognize these concerns, the United States could not become a party to it.

Unfortunately we cannot be confident that we shall be able to achieve our goals. It follows that the United States must stand ready to protect its interests should an unbridgeable split appear in the course of the negotiations.

There is little doubt that mining will begin during the next decade regardless of the outcome of the Law of the Sea Conference. The forces already in motion have an irresistible momentum. The deep seabeds are a new and inviting frontier, ready for exploitation. Technology is becoming increasingly advanced. Should the conference fail to reach agreement on a seabed mining regime, it would be a distortion of the concept of the seabeds as the common heritage of mankind to allow this concept to prevent the development of this important new resource.

On the domestic front, legislation to facilitate the initiation of deep sea mining operations by American corporations is moving through Congress. The Administration favors this legislation—not for use as a club to beat down opposition in Geneva—but in the belief that we must be prepared to provide the necessary encouragement and support to our industry in its development of this new resource whether or not a comprehensive treaty on the law of the sea can be negotiated. I do not, however, anticipate congressional passage of a seabed mining bill until some time after the seventh session closes on May 19th.

Other Major U.S. Interests

Our review has reached certain conclusions regarding other major law of the sea interests.

Navigation and Security Interests. As a global power with extensive interests in the maintenance of high seas freedoms, the United States has placed much emphasis in the negotiations on maintaining those freedoms in the face of unilateral actions that purport to assert national jurisdiction of various kinds over the high seas.

The negotiating text before the conference provides for freedom of navigation through, over, and under international straits by military and commercial vessels and aircraft. It also meets the environmental and safety of navigation concerns of the straits states.

The text makes clear that beyond a 12-mile territorial sea, the high seas freedoms of navigation and overflight and the laying of submarine pipelines and cables and other traditional uses of the sea related to those freedoms shall be fully maintained.

Although our maritime interests and responsibilities would in any case compel us to insist on the exercise of traditional navigational freedoms, it is clear that failure to achieve a comprehensive treaty would entail less stability and higher costs. It is thus our conclusion that a law of the sea treaty which adequately safeguards these freedoms would be clearly preferable.

Fisheries. The United States seeks to secure wide acceptance of international standards for conservation and optimum utilization of marine living resources.

In addition, we have specific and important commercial interests in our own coastal fisheries as well as in salmon, tuna, and species off the coasts of other countries. We are also deeply concerned about the protection of marine mammals. U.S. interests in coastal species within 200 miles are already protected by the Fisheries Management and Conservation Act of 1976.[16] The negotiating text does, however, serve our interests in regard to salmon, tuna, and fisheries off the coasts of other states.

It should be noted, however, that a comprehensive treaty will not of itself fully protect these U.S. interests but rather will foster regional and bilateral agreements. Finally, the negotiating text does promote international recognition of the need to protect marine mammals.

We believe that the understandable and legitimate interests in fisheries of the landlocked and geographically disadvantaged states should be fairly accommodated as part of an overall package.

Continental Shelf. It is estimated that there are significant amounts of exploitable petroleum beneath the continental margin off our coasts. We support the coupling of coastal state jurisdiction over continental margin resources beyond 200 miles with revenue-sharing for the benefit of the developing countries. Although the conference has not yet agreed upon a precise definition of the outer limits of that jurisdiction, we have every reason to believe that such a definition can be negotiated. The open-ended formula now contained in the negotiating text is undesirably vague and might be so interpreted as to lead to excessive claims of jurisdiction.

[16]Public Law 94-265, Apr. 13, 1976; cf. *AFR, 1976:* 100-101.

Without a treaty, the U.S. interest in the resources of the continental margin would nevertheless be protected. A comprehensive treaty, however, would enable us to protect this interest with greater predictability.

Marine Scientific Research. The United States places a high value on the conduct of research on a free and broad basis, accompanied by a maximum flow of information with respect to both the conduct of the research and its results.

Unfortunately, the United States has been unable to find more than minimal support in the negotiations for the creation of a free and open marine scientific regime in the economic zone and on the Continental Shelf. The consequence is that the negotiating text contains undesirably broad provisions requiring coastal state consent for research to be conducted within 200 miles. While the negotiating text introduces a degree of predictability that would make the administration and planning of research easier, it also creates rather complicated conditions for the granting of consent. In weighing the prospective benefits of a comprehensive treaty, therefore, science must be seen as a neutral factor. At a minimum the freedom of research must be maintained beyond the economic zone and on the deep seabed.

Marine Environmental Protection. The United States has a major interest in protecting its coastal areas from all forms of pollution. Regarding vessel source pollution, the negotiating text establishes a mixed system of port state, coastal state, and flag state jurisdiction that, given shipping patterns off our coasts, would afford substantial protection against hazards to the marine environment within 200 miles. It must be noted that the negotiating text gives flag states the right to preempt jurisdiction, albeit with important exceptions. Protection of the marine environment will thus be, in part, a function of the responsible exercise of flag state jurisdiction.

At the same time the negotiating text makes binding on all participating states those standards adopted by the Intergovernmental Maritime Consultative Organization. The treaty also provides protection against pollution from Continental Shelf resource activities, deep seabed mining, and ocean dumping. While a treaty cannot accomplish all of our maritime environmental objectives, it would create a useful framework for safeguarding the marine environment.

Global Order. Our review has recognized that agreement on the large number of issues dealt with by the conference will introduce into the international system a greater measure of stability and predictability and a commitment to peaceful settlement of disputes.

The United States shares with the world community as a whole the aim of avoiding chaos and conflict in the utilization of the world's oceans.

If the conference succeeds in negotiating a treaty that serves the specific interests under discussion, it will have further advanced the goal of the elimination of conflict in international affairs. Moreover, it will have done so largely by the process of consensus, an important precedent in itself.

Alternatives

It follows that the United States must be prepared to protect its interests by other means than a comprehensive treaty if an acceptable treaty proves unattainable. Indeed, it would be irresponsible not to begin consideration of viable alternatives. In the case of deep seabed mining, reciprocal legislation is one such alternative but not necessarily the most desirable. Another possibility—one which might be regarded as more consonant with the concept of the common heritage—would be a multilateral arrangement in which all countries could join and which provided for revenue-sharing with developing countries. In the case of other subjects such as military and commercial navigation, satisfactory alternatives are less obvious, and we have begun an examination of the measures that would become necessary for the protection of these interests should the conference fail to achieve agreement.

Procedural Issues

The law of the sea interests of the United States which I have described can only be served if the conference operates on the basis of open discussion with broad, representative participation. Since the summer of 1977 this objective has been a major concern of a series of intersessional meetings. Although a substantial measure of agreement on these procedural matters has been developed, difficult questions remain to be resolved. For this reason, I and a number of colleagues intend to go to Geneva next week. We will discuss these questions with representatives of the Group of 77, which will be meeting there during the same week, in an effort to find accommodations which will prevent any protracted delay in the conference.

In sum, our review of U.S. positions reinforces our conviction that a comprehensive treaty is the clearly preferable means to promote orderly use of the oceans and to insure responsible and fruitful development of their resources. The world community has before it a singular opportunity to consummate a breakthrough. We are resolved to do everything in our power to make this come to pass.

(51) 33rd Regular Session of the United Nations General Assembly (First Part), New York, September 19–December 21, 1978: Statement by Secretary of State Vance in Plenary Session, September 29, 1978. [17]

A generation ago, the United Nations was created by men and women who shared a vision.

- They saw the need, in the wake of war, to create stronger international institutions that could dampen the flames of conflict and lift nations and people to a new level of material well-being.
- They saw the need to afford self-determination to millions.
- They saw the need for the world community to take a compelling stand against repression, discrimination, and the denial of the rights of man.

The men and women who gathered in San Francisco raised their sights above the differences and divisions of the moment. They dared to see the world as it could be—a world where those who were hungry are fed, where those who were poor have escaped the degradation of poverty, where diplomacy among nations is a pervasive substitute for violence among nations, and where the resources of the world are used effectively and shared equitably.

In the years since, the record of the United Nations in working toward this vision has been one of accomplishment. It has played an indispensable part in the process of peaceful decolonization, in defusing tensions among nations through its peacekeeping missions, and in promoting genuine economic and social progress.

Today, the members of this body still share that common vision. And we understand, far better than ever before, our common destiny—that no nation, acting alone, can assure its people peace and economic security; that the future of each of our nations depends upon the future of all of our nations.

Our challenge today is to summon the political will to act in concert toward the goals we share—to go beyond the rhetoric of interdependence and to begin to recognize its inescapable implications for the national interests of each of us.

We must build a new consensus on this proposition: that in this new era, each nation must weigh more carefully than ever before its long term interest in a healthy global community when making decisions about its immediate concerns. For only through cooperation and compromise in the short run can we assure our longer term future.

[17]Department of State Press Release 376; text from *Bulletin,* Nov. 1978: 45–50.

On crucial issues, the coming months will present turning points of incalculable importance. In negotiations on the Middle East, on southern Africa, on trade, on arms control, and on many other pressing problems, genuine progress has been made. Without continued progress, the gains we have already made can be lost.

This point applies not to any single nation nor group of nations, but to every nation, including my own.

The resolution of dangerous regional disputes and progress in limiting weaponry must always be at the top of the immediate international agenda. I will return to these issues later. But we cannot so concentrate our energies on the political diplomacy of international peace, essential as it is, that we discover too late that international inequities, and poverty and injustice within nations, make peace among nations impossible.

So let me concentrate my comments today on those issues that so centrally touch people's lives around the globe—economic security, equitable development of the Earth's resources, and individual freedom.

International Economic System

Shared economic progress requires a global consensus on the benefits of cooperation among nations. Cooperation and compromise are often difficult.

- The economic problems we share require long term efforts, but we are all constrained by domestic concerns which call for immediate attention.
- The problems we share are so widespread in their impact that solutions cannot be found by a single nation or group of nations.
- These problems require more than general agreements. Application of substantial technical and financial resources are necessary. Debate over sterile texts will neither feed the hungry nor create new jobs for the unemployed. Only common action can be effective. And each must contribute if all are to benefit.

Only 3 or 4 years ago there was extraordinary tension between North and South. Each side was deeply suspicious of the other's motives. Each held sharply different perceptions of global needs and priorities.

But these differences have been narrowed. From the seventh special session, through the U.N. Conference on Trade and Development (UNCTAD) IV, the Conference on International Economic Cooperation, and the meetings of this Assembly—and

through other serious efforts in the Organization for Economic Cooperation and Development (OECD) and the economic summits—
agreement has been achieved on several basic issues relating to a
new international economic order.

- We are agreed on the need to work toward the elimination of
  poverty in all countries. Concessional aid flows have increased. More attention is being devoted to food production.
  Satisfying basic economic needs is becoming a greater priority of the international community.
- We are agreed on the urgent need to accelerate equitable,
  noninflationary growth. The Geneva trade negotiations are
  in their final stages. We are discussing guidelines for international investment. Private capital flows are increasing. The
  facilities of the International Monetary Fund (IMF) have
  been expanded, and discussions are underway to expand the
  facilities of the multilateral development banks.
- We are agreed on the need to reduce economic instability and
  uncertainty. The IMF is playing a major role in providing
  balance-of-payments financing to those most severely affected by recent disruptions in the world economy. We are
  engaged in serious discussions on a variety of commodity
  arrangements, including a system of internationally coordinated national grain reserves.
- We are agreed on the need to facilitate smooth adjustments
  for workers and businesses that have borne the brunt of
  changing economic circumstances. The Bonn summit made
  clear that we must intensify our efforts in this area.

Because we have come far, the road ahead will be even more
challenging, for the most difficult issues remain. To maintain our
progress, we should be guided by three fundamental principles in
the North-South discussions over the coming months.

First, every nation must resist the temptation to solve its own
economic problems at the expense of others. We must fashion our
domestic policies on the basis of global as well as national needs.

Second, all nations which bear their fair share of responsibility
should benefit from a healthy world economy.

Third, all nations must enter international economic negotiations
with a spirit of accommodation.

These principles will not by themselves solve the problems we
face. But without their general acceptance, there can be no genuine

progress. Adherence to them will prevent critical negotiations from turning into polarizing and self-defeating tests of will.

Let me discuss several major issues where the application of these principles can make the difference between success and failure.

Committee of the Whole

One of our most recent collective efforts to address the economic challenges we share was the establishment of the Committee of the Whole.[18] This Committee has the potential to look at economic issues comprehensively and to identify longer term priorities. The United States strongly supports this forum.

The meeting in May[19] made progress in identifying some important areas of agreement between industrial and developing countries. Substantive discussions in the Committee had an important impact on the June ministerial meeting of the OECD and in the Bonn summit.[20] We, of course, shared the disappointment of other delegates that a procedural impasse earlier this month interrupted the Committee's work.

Since the September meeting,[21] we have carefully examined the statements made by others on this issue. We have noted in particular statements by the chairman to the Committee[22] on September 8 and to the press on September 11 and have taken account of subsequent consultations. It is now generally agreed that the Committee would not seek to provide specific solutions to problems outstanding in other bodies. Rather, it would achieve agreed conclusions on fundamental or crucial underlying issues and only to the extent that all members agreed to decide on them.

We are satisfied that on the basis of these statements, sufficient procedural agreement now exists to resume substantive work in the manner suggested by the chairman at the end of the informal consultations on September 6.

Trade

The spirit which must guide our work in the Committee of the Whole applies as well to our policies on trade. The developing world is no longer on the periphery of world trade. Increasingly, growth in the developing countries is important to the health of industrial countries.

---

[18]General Assembly Resolution 32/174, Dec. 19, 1977; adopted without vote; cf. *AFR, 1977:* 136.
[19]Details of the meeting held May 3–13, 1978, in *UN Monthly Chronicle,* June 1978: 40–42.
[20]Documents 43 and 44.
[21]Sept. 5–8; details in *UN Monthly Chronicle,* Oct. 1978: 48.
[22]Idriss Jazairy (Algeria); details in same.

Committment to open trade, however, is extremely fragile. It is tempting for one nation to use trade restrictions to export its economic difficulties. It is often easy to avoid adjustments which are beneficial in the long term but which in the short run present difficult problems for workers and industry.

We must be concerned about rising protectionist pressures, but we should also recognize that world trade has expanded remarkably well in recent years. Despite a deep recession in the early 1970's, we not only avoided the trading wars of the 1930's, we continued negotiations to liberalize and improve the world trading system. Our ability to conclude these trade negotiations successfully this year is a critical test of our commitment to an open trading system. And agreement will stimulate production. It will provide jobs. And it will help reduce inflation.

Beyond our efforts to expand trade, the United States will fulfill our commitment to assist developing nations through differential measures including, where appropriate, special and more favorable treatment. We in turn expect those developing countries which can do so to contribute to trade liberalization by improving access to their markets. Improved access will not only benefit the industrial countries, it will be even more important to many developing countries.

Finally, we believe that in trade, as elsewhere, the developing countries should have a voice in determining the policies which affect them. We have encouraged their full involvement in the Geneva negotiations. We urge developing countries, especially those which play a large role in international trade, to participate actively in the General Agreement on Tariffs and Trade and in the agreements that result from the Geneva negotiations so that their interests are fully represented.

Commodities

An essential element of trade for most developing nations is their export of basic commodities. At UNCTAD IV we agreed to intensify our collective effort to address commodity problems. Progress has not always been as fast as we all would like, but this has generally reflected the technical complexity of commodity issues rather than lack of political will or good faith. We will continue to work for stabilization agreements and other measures that strengthen commodity markets.

Let me affirm also that we believe a soundly designed common fund could play a useful role in alleviating commodity problems. A well-structured fund will provide economic benefits to participating countries. We also recognize that establishment of a fund is of major political importance to the general North-South dialogue.

We will cooperate with others to bring the common fund

negotiations to a successful conclusion. Recent consultations have identified a convergence of views on some issues. All agree that a fund could play a useful role in reducing the overall financial costs of supporting buffer stocks which effectively stabilize prices.

In addition, there is a growing recognition of the importance of encouraging improved productivity and more effective marketing of many commodities. A separate "second window" of the common fund, based on voluntary contributions and operating under agreed guidelines, might be an appropriate mechanism. We are prepared to negotiate flexibly on this issue, as on others, if there is a similar approach on all sides.

While progress has been made on some issues, important differences still remain. Movement on all sides of the conference table will be necessary. But we are convinced that with mutual accommodation a workable agreement can be achieved.

Resource Transfers

As with trade, increased resource flows to the developing world must be part of an international system of shared responsibility.

We ought not think of resource transfers as a sacrifice for donors or a unilateral benefit for recipients. They are an economic investment in the future of all countries. They will contribute to global economic growth, greater trade, and enhanced prosperity for us all.

My country is committed to increasing our contributions both to multilateral and bilateral development efforts. We have done so in the past year: Our multilateral commitments increased 31% and our bilateral program expanded by 20%. And because we are determined that U.S. aid funds will be used effectively, we will concentrate our efforts in countries where programs are aimed most directly at meeting the essential needs of their people.

The United States believes strongly that a key objective of foreign assistance should be to help meet basic human needs. We recognize that nations will have different development priorities in approaching this goal. Whether emphasis is on enhancing the productivity of the poor, increasing food production, improving health, or expanding industry which creates jobs, the critical ingredient in every nation is to have all its citizens—men and women—as active participants and beneficiaries in their nation's growth.

Finally, we recognize the debt problems that many of the least developed countries face. We will soon have authority from our Congress for retroactive adjustment of certain aid terms which would permit us to help those most in need.

Managing Global Resources

As we work together to promote economic development, we

must also assure an equitable sharing of the world's resources. Four issues demand our urgent attention.

Food. Our first urgent priority is assuring adequate food and stable agricultural prices for all people. Four years have passed since the World Food Conference,[23] where we agreed on measures we must take for the future. But despite our efforts, the fundamental problems remain.

- Food production is hardly keeping pace with the growth in population.
- Food deficits in many countries are increasing.
- Negotiations on grain reserves have dragged on without success.

We believe progress must be made.

The United States has created a 9-million-ton farmer-held grain reserve. We have proposed to our Congress the establishment of an international emergency wheat reserve of 6 million tons to provide food for emergency needs in developing countries. We intend to maintain our food aid level at a fair share of the target set at the World Food Conference. We will continue to support the activities of international organizations devoted to food production, such as the International Fund for Agricultural Development. And we intend to make food aid a more effective tool in support of development.

I propose that this Assembly review the world food situation—to identify the current obstacles to progress and to restore a sense of urgency to meeting mankind's most basic need. We must not be lulled by good weather and plentiful harvests. Another tragedy is inevitable unless we act now.

Energy. We must act now to develop new energy resources so that we avoid a harsh transition to the time when fossil fuels will no longer be plentiful. This task has several dimensions.

- There must be an expansion of oil and gas production. And we need to improve our conservation of these energy sources, especially in the United States. The World Bank has expanded its lending to help developing countries increase their fossil fuel supplies. We welcome this, and we also encourage the regional development banks to assist.
- The development of nuclear energy will also be central to the future of many countries. We hope the International Nuclear

[23]Cf. *AFR, 1974*: 428–42.

Fuel Cycle Evaluation will provide a consensus on nuclear technologies free from the serious risk of nuclear weapons proliferation. My government supports the development of safeguardable nuclear power, including assured nuclear fuel supplies. The developing nations should, of course, participate in the design and management of the institutions which form the basis of an international nuclear energy regime.

- Priority attention must be given to the development of renewable energy sources. Many technologies already exist for harnessing solar, wind, and geothermal power. All of us can benefit from these technologies, but a special effort should be made to meet the needs of the poorer countries.

Two opportunities now exist for the United Nations to continue to play an important role.

- The United States supports the proposed U.N. conference on new and renewable energy. It could result in a more coordinated U.N. energy effort and clearer priorities. It could also provide up-to-date information on renewable energy technology and examine the role of the private sector in energy development.
- The U.N. Development Program might also expand its efforts to help nations assess their own renewable energy possibilities, finance the testing of new technologies, and provide training and technical assistance for effective energy management.

The United States is willing to contribute to a major global effort to develop new energy sources. We will intensify our assistance programs in this area. We will increase domestic research which can benefit all nations. And we will expand cooperative energy programs from which we too stand to benefit.

Law of the Sea. We must strive to conclude successfully the Law of the Sea negotiations. At stake is whether this vast expanse of the globe will be an arena of conflict or cooperation.

Considerable progress has been made on a number of issues in these negotiations. These achievements have been obscured, however, by continued stalemate over seabed mining. The basis for an equitable solution already exists and is widely accepted. It permits all sides to benefit fully from seabed mining, with private firms as well as an international enterprise allowed to mine on a competitive basis. A mutually acceptable solution is imperative, and it is possible.

Time is running out for reaching an agreed solution. Without it, seabed mining will inevitably take place but in the absence of an internationally agreed framework. This would be less satisfactory than a widely supported international regime.

Science and Technology. Finally is the critical question of how best to harness technology and science for the benefit of mankind. We hope that the U.N. Conference on Science and Technology for Development[24] will focus attention on how all countries can contribute their knowledge to global development. It will be particularly important to find ways for developing nations to enhance their capacity to generate, select, and apply technology for their own development priorities. We will contribute to the work of the conference, and we hope to benefit from it.

Furthermore to help mobilize the technical talents and knowledge of our nation on behalf of the development of others, we intend to establish during the coming year a new foundation for international technological cooperation.

Enhancement of Human Dignity

The ultimate purpose of all our policies is the enhancement of human dignity. The rights to food, to shelter, to a decent education, to adequate health—the rights which lie at the heart of our approach to economic issues—are hollow without political and civil freedoms—freedom from torture and government mistreatment; freedom to worship, to travel, and to speak without fear; freedom to participate in the affairs of one's government. There is no incompatibility among economic, political, and civil rights, no choice that must be made among them. They reenforce one another.

We commemorate in this Assembly the 30th anniversary of the Universal Declaration on Human Rights.[25] Dag Hammarskjold described the Declaration as a "living document." We have a continuing obligation to keep that document alive in our own nations. And as members of the United Nations, we must strengthen the international machinery that serves to promote the full range of human rights—political and economic.

We have made significant progress in the past year. Concern for human rights is more central to international discourse today than ever before. But more needs to be done.

- This Assembly should review the activities of the various U.N. human rights institutions.

---

[24]Established by General Assembly Resolution 33/192 of Jan. 19, 1979, the conference was scheduled to be held in Vienna Aug. 20–31, 1979; details in *UN Monthly Chronicle,* Feb. 1979: 67–8.
[25]Cf. Documents 5 and 52.

- • We must resolve in this Assembly to make torture alien to the experience of every nation and to conclude an international agreement to outlaw it.
- • We need to insure that we are doing all we can to end conditions which are tantamount to genocide.
- • We must ask what more each of us can do to insure the vitality of the Universal Declaration—to provide amnesty to prisoners of conscience, to assure due process for all, and to advance social justice and equity for our people.

In addition, the plight of one group of individuals—refugees—demands our special compassion. We urge all nations to increase their support for the vital humanitarian work of the High Commissioner for Refugees.

The refugee problem is not confined to any single region. In Africa alone, some 2 million individuals are now outside their native lands. We must do more to offer them sustenance, security, and a realistic hope of resettlement or return to their homelands.

In Southeast Asia, hundreds of new refugees from Indochina appear daily, some risking their lives to cross borders, other challenging the sea in every form of vessel. We urgently need greater efforts to provide them sanctuary. We hope that the High Commissioner will consider convening an international conference in the very near future to seek humane solutions to the desperate plight of these refugees. We propose that consideration also be given at a later date to a general conference on the worldwide refugee problem.

International Peacekeeping

Too often the anguish of the uprooted is grim testimony to our collective failure to achieve international peace. War and strife are the enemies of the fundamental rights I have discussed.

Today my government and many of those assembled here are actively pursuing the path of peace in troubled areas of the world.

Middle East. The accords achieved at Camp David offer hope that at long last a turning point has been reached in the Middle East. The agreement achieved between Egypt and Israel, with active American participation, constitutes a framework for a comprehensive peace settlement. Much remains to be done in ensuing stages of negotiations, but a major step has been taken in resolving the difficult issues that lie at the heart of 30 years of Arab-Israel hostility.

As negotiations are pursued on the basis of the Camp David framework, a dynamic process will be set in motion that can profoundly change attitudes on the issues that remain to be resolved. That process will significantly advance legitimate Arab objectives while protecting Israel's security. It is our hope that the members of this body will lend their full support to the task of building a just and lasting peace upon this framework.

In his recent address before Congress,[26] President Carter reviewed the main elements of the Camp David agreements. As the President said, our historic position on settlements in occupied territory has remained constant. As he further said, no peace agreement will be either just or secure if it does not resolve the problem of the Palestinians in the broadest sense. We believe that the Palestinian people must be assured that they and their descendants can live with dignity and freedom and have the opportunity for economic fulfillment and political expression. The Camp David accords state that the negotiated solution must recognize the legitimate rights of the Palestinian people.

The Camp David accords make a solid start toward achieving these goals for the Palestinians in real terms. In the West Bank and Gaza, the framework provides that Israeli occupation shall end and a self-governing authority shall be instituted. This can be achieved within a few months. Thus, for the first time, the Palestinians have the prospect of governing themselves within the framework that has been agreed.

The Camp David framework also gives the Palestinians a vital role in shaping their destiny by recognizing them as participants in all aspects of the negotiations that determine their future. They will participate in the negotiations to set up their self-governing authority, in those to determine the final status of the West Bank and Gaza, and in those leading to a Jordan-Israel peace treaty. Finally, the agreement on the final status of the West Bank and Gaza will be submitted to a vote of representatives of the inhabitants for either ratification or rejection.

These steps set in motion a political process of the utmost importance to all Palestinians.

The Camp David accords concentrate on the means by which self-government can be established for the Palestinians living in the West Bank and Gaza, but there was also clear recognition by all three leaders at Camp David that the problem of the Palestinians living outside these areas must also be addressed.

We recognize that this problem has political as well as humanitarian dimensions which must be resolved as an integral part of a durable peace settlement. When the Camp David accords call for "...the resolution of the Palestinian problem in all its aspects," they acknowledge and embrace that central fact. As the political institutions of self-government take shape in the West Bank and Gaza through negotiations among the parties, the rela-

[26]Document 19.

tionship between those institutions and the Palestinians living outside the area should be defined, including the question of admission of Palestinian refugees to the West Bank and Gaza.

The framework provides for the establishment of a committee to decide on the modalities of admission to the West Bank and Gaza of persons displaced in the 1967 war. For the first time, the parties to the conflict—Egypt and Israel—have agreed to work with each other and with other interested parties to establish agreed procedures for a prompt, just, and permanent resolution of the refugee problem.

As President Carter stated in his address to Congress, the United States is irrevocably committed to bringing about a satisfactory solution to the problem of the Palestinian refugees. We will play an active role in the resolution of this problem. A solution must reflect the relevant U.N. resolutions relating to these refugees.

We urge the international community to support Egypt and Israel in establishing procedures urgently to address this issue in all its aspects. And the international community should contribute to a program to promote economic development in the West Bank and Gaza as well as to assist those refugees residing elsewhere.

We are determined to achieve a fair and just settlement of the Middle East question in all its parts, and we hope the Palestinian people will seize this historic opportunity. It is our hope that the people of the Middle East will agree that it is imperative to begin the negotiating process now—and not to stand still until every last issue is resolved. We urge the other interested parties to join the negotiations without delay.

As the Middle East peace process moves forward, it is vital to maintain the effectiveness of the U.N.'s peacekeeping role there. It is critical that the mandates of U.N. peacekeeping forces in the Golan Heights and Sinai be renewed this fall. They have thus far helped all sides avoid renewed hostilities; they must now remain to help achieve a stable peace.

Lebanon. In Lebanon, the fighting and tragic loss of life continues. The U.N.'s interim force in southern Lebanon has done much to stabilize the situation in that part of the country, and we call on all to support this effort to help reassert Lebanese authority.

Elsewhere in Lebanon confrontation and tensions continue at a high pitch. President Carter has made clear in his address to the joint session of Congress following the Camp David summit, and again yesterday,[27] his determination to spare no effort to assist in finding a solution to the Lebanese tragedy. As the President said yesterday, it is time for us to take joint action to call for a con-

[27]At news conference, Sept. 28, in *Presidential Documents,* 14: 1658–9.

ference of those who are involved and try to reach some solution. It may involve a new charter for Lebanon.

Namibia. In Namibia, the world community faces a fundamental challenge. I will be commenting on this more fully this afternoon in the Security Council.[28] Let me simply say now that the United States is determined to see Namibia achieve independence in accordance with the contact group proposal and Security Council Resolution 431.[29] We call upon South Africa to cooperate fully with the United Nations so that this critical opportunity for a peaceful settlement will not be lost.

Rhodesia. In Rhodesia, time may be running out for the possibilities of diplomacy. But we will continue to work with the British Government, the governments in the region, and the parties to seek a negotiated solution. We condemn the murder of innocent civilians as a matter of both conscience and reason. The prospects of peace in Rhodesia will diminish if violence increases.

Cyprus. On Cyprus, an opportunity now exists to help the two communities narrow their differences and achieve a just and lasting solution to this long-standing problem. The United Nations has done a commendable job of nurturing an atmosphere which should now make possible productive intercommunal negotiations.

To grasp this opportunity, we would welcome and actively support a renewed effort by Secretary General Waldheim to help the parties reach agreement on a sovereign, bicommunal, nonaligned federal republic of Cyprus which would meet the concerns of the people of Cyprus.

Nicaragua. In this atmosphere, we must respond to the agony of those caught up in the violence and bloodshed of Nicaragua. We and several countries in Latin America have offered to assist in the mediation of Nicaragua's internal crisis. It is our hope and expectation that all parties concerned will accept these offers and agree to a fair mediation process in which all can have confidence. Only a democratic solution in Nicaragua—not repression or violence—can lead to an enduring stability and true peace.

Terrorism. As we work together to find peaceful resolutions to the most dangerous regional disputes, we must also seek at this assembly to strengthen the U.N.'s peacekeeping capability. And while this Organization works to limit violence among nations, we

[28]Substance of Vance address in *UN Monthly Chronicle,* Oct. 1978: 8–9.
[29]Of July 27, 1978; cf. Introduction at note 177.

must not lose sight of the havoc wreaked by those who perpetrate terrorist acts on innocent persons. No single nation, acting alone, can deal adequately with this serious problem. Collective action is essential.

We are beginning to make some progress. Last year the General Assembly adopted a significant resolution on aircraft hijacking.[30] The Bonn Declaration of this July produced a much-needed agreement on the harboring of hijackers.[31] We strongly urge all nations to subscribe to this Declaration.

Arms Control. The pursuit of peace and security must go beyond resolving conflicts and preventing violence. The security of all is enhanced if nations limit the weapons of war through mutually negotiated arms control agreements.

We are engaged with the Soviet Union and other nations in a broad range of arms control negotiations.

- The conclusion of a strategic arms limitation agreement with the Soviet Union is a fundamental goal of the United States. We hope that we may conclude a SALT II agreement before the end of this year.[32]
- The United States hopes that early progress can be made in concluding a comprehensive agreement to end the testing of nuclear weapons.
- Increased efforts are critically needed to prevent the spread of nuclear weapons. It is important to prepare fully for the 1980 Nonproliferation Treaty review conference; to continue to make progress in the International Nuclear Fuel Cycle Evaluation; and to recognize one of the important achievements of the Special Session on Disarmament (SSOD)[33]—the decision by several nuclear powers to pledge, under specific circumstances, to refrain from use of nuclear weapons against non-nuclear states. We suggest that the Security Council take note of these pledges.
- The United States will also work to realize the call in the SSOD Declaration of Principles and Program of Action for restraint in the transfer of conventional arms. We are actively discussing with the Soviet Union how our two nations might encourage restraint consistent with the legitimate right to

---

[30]Cf. note 2 to Document 48a.
[31]Document 48b.
[32]The SALT II agreement was signed by Presidents Carter and Brezhnev at Vienna on June 18, 1979; official texts of treaty documents in *New York Times,* June 19, 1979.
[33]Cf. document 7.

self-defense and international obligations. We are encouraged by the new initiatives already being undertaken to promote restraint on a regional basis in Latin America, and we stand ready to support similar efforts by countries in other regions.

Conclusion

Let me emphasize that on all the issues I have addressed today, what we share is greater than how we differ. We share the same small planet. We share human aspirations—for better lives, for greater opportunity, for freedom and security. And because we share a common destiny, we are compelled to resolve our differences.

If we focus on these common interests, we can begin to find the common ground for global progress. We can, as Jean Monnet said, "put our problems on one side of the table and all of us on the other."

The measure of our progress will not be whether we achieve all of our goals in this generation, for that will surely prove to be impossible; it is whether we can now summon the will to move forward together so that our children may benefit from our efforts and our vision.

(52) The United Nations and Human Rights: Statement by Ambassador Andrew Young, United States Representative to the United Nations, to the General Assembly, December 14, 1978. [34]

The world-awakening to human rights and fundamental freedoms that emerged in 1948 in the adoption of the Universal Declaration of Human Rights has taken on a new urgency in the past few years. For perhaps the first time in history we can truly say that there is a worldwide human rights movement, and it is steadily gaining force.

Mahatma Gandhi in 1921 wrote that every good movement passes through five stages: indifference, ridicule, abuse, repression, and, finally, respect. We know that human rights abuses are usually, when first noted, regarded with indifference. Then will come the ridicule, then the abuse, and perhaps even the repression. This is the path of progress. It has been true in the United States, India, across the African Continent. It is no less true in the East or Middle East than it has been in the West and South. It is part of the process of widening participation in the public dialogue, of expanding the concerns and concepts we use when we develop public and international policy.

There is no room for self-righteousness and self-congratulation in the field of human rights. Each of our nations has people of vision and people of fear, those who create and those who repress and torture. I believe we should identify particular problems and work together toward solving them. It is better to solve one small problem than to engage in political fireworks about the grand issues of our time. We have the potential of a new pragmatism in these halls, and I hope it grows.

Behind this new pragmatism is, I think, the growing realization that we, indeed, have common goals and that if we stop fearing and fighting each other we might find some practical solutions. The task is too serious to waste our effort in nonproductive exercises. We are faced with the necessity of promoting worldwide rapid, peaceful social change if we are to move toward the goals of the Universal Declaration of Human Rights.

In 1967, a few months before his death, Dr. Martin Luther King, Jr., reflected on the next steps of the struggle for full human rights and came to the conclusion that the crisis of the modern world is international in scope and that this is a crisis that "involves the poor, the dispossessed, and the exploited of the whole world."

Today, more than 1 billion people live in conditions of abject poverty—starving, idle, and numbed by ignorance. Life expectancy in the poorest countries is only slightly greater than half that in the industrialized countries.

The sad fact is that most of the people in these countries who were born in the year we adopted the Universal Declaration of Human Rights are not around anymore to celebrate this occasion. And most of those who are still here have very little to celebrate. Three quarters of their number in these countries do not have access to safe water. They cannot read the speeches we make today honoring human rights. They earn less money in a year than most of us in this hall of the United Nations earn in 1 day—and even that is only a figure of speech, since most of them have never been paid at all for their work.

The birthright of these people has been disregarded, denied, and violated, although it was done not by torturers, not by jailers, not by persecution, and not by repressive government. As President Carter reminded us a week ago: "Hunger, disease, poverty are enemies of human potential which are as relentless as any repressive government."[35]

The freedoms from arbitrariness, torture, and cruel punishment are the rights of everyone by the simple fact that he or she is born.

[35]Document 5.

The freedom of thought, speech, religion, press, and participation in public affairs are so fundamental that they enhance the quality of our life and character as individuals. Their exercise cannot be made dependent on any other considerations. But we must understand too that these rights are hollow for any individual who starves to death. Therefore, the human rights struggle is not only a defense of our individual liberty but also a struggle to protect life.

The Universal Declaration of Human Rights is a call for worldwide movements to promote human rights. This call is often heard with alarm by many who believe that there is far more to lose than to gain by encouraging political, economic, and social change. Perhaps, in the short run, there is some cost for those who have special privilege or for those who have an investment in thinking of themselves—as a nation or class or race—as superior or more advanced than others. But the plain lesson of history is that as the circle of participation in society widens, almost everyone profits. They profit not just in a better standard of living for everyone but in the productivity of the economy, in better social services for everyone, in wider political participation, and in more freedom and more protection for human rights.

The process of change entails risks. But change is inevitable. It is not a question of being able to withstand change or even of directing it; it is a question of understanding change and cooperating with it. The change of our time, the basic dynamic of our time, leads to more participation by more people in society. Poverty is the basic obstacle to the realization of human rights for most people in the world today. Where poverty is the problem, participation is the answer, participation in the economic life of the society. Economic growth must be pursued with equity in mind and not just for the profit of the few at the top or for the power of the state and the government. The ultimate goal of economic development must be equity, with broader participation in production and consumption by all as the main objective. Speaking before the opening session of the 8th General Assembly of the Organization of American States,[36] President Carter said: "The challenge of economic development is to help the world's poor lift themselves out of misery."

He called upon that Assembly to join together the concepts of economic development and social justice: "We must also devote our common energies to economic development and the cause of social justice. Benefits of the world's economy must be more fairly shared, but the responsibilities must be shared as well."

To share responsibility is to make more participation possible.

[36]Document 33.

The more participation, the wiser will be the government. Prime Minister Manley[37] made a stirring affirmation of his own faith in democracy when he spoke to us in October. He was, you will recall, urging us to united efforts in the struggle against apartheid. He said: "We believe that any government which has the courage to mobilize its people and tell the truth will receive the overwhelming support of its citizens." I also believe that. We must let our people hear the truth, the whole truth. And we must not be afraid to mobilize our citizens to participate more fully in the political and economic processes.

Expanding participation should not be limited, however, to government initiative. There is an important role for nongovernmental organizations. For the last year the Government of India has been reminding us of the importance of autonomous—and I stress that word—autonomous national human rights institutions.

We need not fear change if we build into it more equity and more participation. Indeed, fear of social change is the thing we need to fear the most. If we are afraid of it and try to preserve that which is already eroding beneath our feet, we will fail, because the dynamic of history is to widen the circle of those who participate in society. Whether the struggle is for medical care for those who do not have it, bread for those who are hungry, freedom from prison for those imprisoned for conscience's sake, freedom of the press to print dissenting opinions, a job for those who are unemployed, the right to self-determination of majorities oppressed by minorities, the rights of workers to organize, the right to speak one's own language in one's own school—all of these are demands for more participation and more dignity.

If we invest just half as much energy and imagination in building a world community of the people as we have wasted in resisting the aspirations of the people, we will overcome.

I believe that we are at the end of the period of cold wars, in the middle of the era of detente, and just beginning to find ways to build the structures of cooperation. Cooperation will demand a different substance and different style than confrontation. It will take a while for us to learn how to change, and I am afraid that we will all carry with us for some years some of the characteristics of confrontational politics. But it is more rewarding for everyone, even if it is more difficult and demanding, to practice the art of building community and cooperation for the common good. I believe that we can get just as excited about building something as we can about protecting something. I believe that cooperation for the common good of humankind can be as powerful an incentive to our im-

[37]Michael N. Manley of Jamaica.

aginations as fear for our survival. Indeed, I submit that cooperation for the common good, for the protection and promotion of human rights, is the way to survival.

Perhaps some neglected methods can be of great help to us in the struggle to promote and protect human rights.

First, an emphasis on autonomous, national institutions. We have not given due credit, nor due attention, to the creative role of independent, private institutions, dedicated to the protection and promotion of human rights. My own experience was with the civil rights movement and the churches of this country, and I know what they were able to do in a few short years. Also, the role of a free and responsible press needs to be recognized. The press can be a guardian of the public interest and a critic of the abuses—where they exist—of public power, and of private power, for that matter.

A second way to promote human rights is the use of the United Nations and of government authority and influence as a catalyst and agent of goodwill in stimulating a process of participation by those who have common interests and concerns. The United Nations and interested nations are doing this in the case of Zimbabwe and Namibia, where the effort is not to impose a solution but to facilitate the building of communication among all the parties which are concerned, so that by talking to one another they learn to formulate their own solutions to their own problems.

This is what the United States has been trying to do in the Middle East; acting not as a judge between Egypt and Israel but as a mediator, trying to be a catalyst in a process of ever-expanding conversation and cooperation. This is what the United States, the Dominican Republic, and Guatemala are trying to do in Nicaragua; not the imposition of an external answer but the strengthening of the process of consultation among all parties involved so they can find their own answers.

I believe we can be even more active in this way than we have been at the United Nations. It is not enough to halt conflicts and to provide buffer or peacekeeping forces. It is not enough to denounce problems or supposed culprits. We must find a positive, creative role, of being the catalyst of change, of promoting the process of wider participation where there are conflicts so that all the parties are involved.

In the struggle to make all people free, we ourselves must become free. Freedom is not some distant state of affairs when there will be no more problems and history will have arrived at some utopia, some paradise, some order of perfect justice. Freedom is solidarity with those who are less free than we are. Freedom is taking the risk of working for social justice for all people.

The United Nations was brought forth as a result of the struggle for freedom against tyranny. There are many forms of tyranny, and none of us are exempt from the temptation to conspire with tyranny against freedom by remaining indifferent to the struggle of others to be free. But our very humanity rests in our capacity to identify with the other and to join in the struggle to make all persons free.

The United Nations is now challenged to take the next steps that can move us forward in the struggle of humankind for peace, justice, and freedom. If we accept this challenge, I believe we will all be free someday.

(53) *Contribution of the Mass Media: Declaration Adopted by the General Conference of the United Nations Educational, Scientific and Cultural Organization (UNESCO), Paris, November 28, 1978.*[38]

(Provisional Text)

Preamble

The General Conference,

1. *Recalling* that by its Constitution the purpose of UNESCO is to "contribute to peace and security by promoting collaboration among the nations through education, science and culture in order to further universal respect for justice, for the rule of law and for the human rights and fundamental freedoms" (Art. I, 1), and that to realize this purpose the Organization will strive "to promote the free flow of ideas by word and image" (Art. I, 2),

2. Further *recalling* that under the Constitution the Member States of UNESCO, "believing in full and equal opportunities for education for all, in the unrestricted pursuit of objective truth, and in the free exchange of ideas and knowedge, and agreed and determined to develop and to increase the means of communication between their peoples and to employ these means for the purposes of mutual understanding and a truer and more perfect knowledge of each other's lives" (sixth preambular paragraph),

3. *Recalling* the purposes and principles of the United Nations, as specified in the Charter,

4. *Recalling* the Universal Declaration of Human Rights, adopted by the General Assembly of the United Nations in 1948 and particularly Article 19 which provides that "everyone has the right to freedom of opinion and expression; this right includes free-

[38]U.N. Press Release UNESCO/2339, U.N. Office of Public Information, Press Section (United Nations, New York).

dom to hold opinions without interference and to seek, receive and impart information and ideas through any media and regardless of frontiers"; and the International Covenant on Civil and Political Rights, adopted by the General Assembly of the United Nations in 1966, Article 19 of which proclaims the same principles and Article 20 of which condemns incitement to war, the advocacy of national, racial or religious hatred and any form of discrimination, hostility or violence,

5. *Recalling* Article 4 of the International Convention on the Elimination of all Forms of Racial Discrimination adopted by the General Assembly of the United Nations in 1965, and the International Convention on the Suppression and Punishment of the Crime of *Apartheid* adopted by the General Assembly of the United Nations in 1973, whereby the States acceding to these Conventions undertook to adopt immediate and positive measures designed to eradicate all incitement to, or acts of, racial discrimination, and agreed to prevent any encouragement of the crime of *apartheid* and similar segregationist policies or their manifestations,

6. *Recalling* the Declaration on the Promotion among Youth of the Ideals of Peace, Mutual Respect and Understanding between Peoples, adopted by the General Assembly of the United Nations in 1965,

7. *Recalling* the declarations and resolutions adopted by the various organs of the United Nations concerning the establishment of a New International Economic Order and the role UNESCO is called upon to play in this respect,

8. *Recalling* the Declaration of the Principles of International Cultural Co-operation, adopted by the General Conference of UNESCO in 1966,

9. *Recalling* Resolution 59 (I) of the General Assembly of the United Nations, adopted in 1946 and declaring

"Freedom of information is a fundamental human right and is the touchstone of all freedoms to which the United Nations is consecrated;
Freedom of information requires as an indispensable element the willingness and capacity to employ its privileges without abuse. It requires as a basic discipline the moral obligation to seek the facts without prejudice and to spread knowledge without malicious intent;

10. *Recalling* Resolution 110 (II) of the General Assembly of the United Nations adopted in 1947 condemning all forms of propaganda which are designed or likely to provoke or encourage any threat to the peace, breach of the peace, or act of aggression,

11. *Recalling* Resolution 127 (II), also adopted by the General

Assembly in 1947, which invites Member States to take measures, within the limits of constitutional procedures, to combat the diffusion of false or distorted reports likely to injure friendly relations between States, as well as the other resolutions of the General Assembly concerning the mass media and their contribution to strengthening peace, thus contributing to the growth of trust and friendly relations among States,

12. *Recalling* Resolution 9.12 adopted by the General Conference of UNESCO in 1968 reiterating UNESCO's objective to help to eradicate colonialism and racialism, and Resolution 12.1 adopted by the General Conference of UNESCO in 1976 which proclaims that colonialism, neo-colonialism and racialism in all its forms and manifestations are incompatible with the fundamental aims of UNESCO,

13. *Recalling* Resolution 4.301 adopted in 1970 by the General Conference of UNESCO on the contribution of the information media to furthering international understanding and co-operation in the interests of peace and human welfare, and to countering propaganda on behalf of war, racialism, *apartheid* and hatred among nations, and *aware* of the fundamental contribution that mass media can make to the realization of these objectives,

14. *Recalling* the Declaration on Race and Racial Prejudice adopted by the General Conference of UNESCO at its twentieth session,

15. *Conscious* of the complexity of the problems of information in modern society, of the diversity of solutions which have been offered to them, as evidenced in particular by consideration given to them within UNESCO as well as of the legitimate desire of all parties concerned that their aspirations, points of view and cultural identity be taken into due consideration,

16. *Conscious* of the aspirations of the developing countries for the establishment of a new, more just and more effective world information and communication order,

17. Proclaim on this . . . . day of . . . . 1978 this Declaration on Fundamental Principles concerning the Contribution of the Mass Media to Strengthening Peace and International Understanding, to the Promotion of Human Rights and to Countering Racialism, *Apartheid* and Incitement to War.

Article I

The strengthening of peace and international understanding, the promotion of human rights and the countering of racialism, *apartheid* and incitement to war demand a free flow and a wider and better balanced dissemination of information. To this end, the mass media have a leading contribution to make. This contribution will be more effective to the extent that the information reflects the different aspects of the subject dealt with.

Article II

1. The exercise of freedom of opinion, expression and information, recognized as an integral part of human rights and fundamental freedoms, is a vital factor in the strengthening of peace and international understanding.

2. Access by the public to information should be guaranteed by the diversity of the sources and means of information available to it, thus enabling each individual to check the accuracy of facts and to appraise events objectively. To this end, journalists must have freedom to report and the fullest possible facilities of access to information. Similarly, it is important that the mass media be responsive to concerns of peoples and individuals, thus promoting the participation of the public in the elaboration of information.

3. With a view to the strengthening of peace and international understanding, to promoting human rights and to countering racism, *apartheid* and incitement to war, the mass media throughout the world, by reason of their role, contribute effectively to promoting human rights, in particular by giving expression to oppressed peoples who struggle against colonialism, neo-colonialism, foreign occupation and all forms of racial discrimination and oppression and who are unable to make their voices heard within their own territories.

4. If the mass media are to be in a position to promote the principles of this Declaration in their activities, it is essential that journalists and other agents of the mass media, in their own country or abroad, be assured of protection guaranteeing them the best conditions for the exercise of their profession.

Article III

1. The mass media have an important contribution to make to the strengthening of peace and international understanding and in countering racism, *apartheid* and incitement to war.

2. In countering aggressive war, racism, *apartheid* and other violations of human rights which are *inter alia* spawned by prejudice and ignorance, the mass media, by disseminating information on the aims, aspirations, cultures and needs of all people, contribute to eliminate ignorance and misunderstanding between peoples, to make nationals of a country sensitive to the needs and desires of others, to ensure the respect of the rights and dignity of all nations, all peoples and all individuals without distinction of race, sex, language, religion or nationality and to draw attention to the great

evils which afflict humanity, such as poverty, malnutrition and diseases, thereby promoting the formulation by States of policies best able to promote the reduction of international tension and the peaceful and the equitable settlement of international disputes.

Article IV

The mass media have an essential part to play in the education of young people in a spirit of peace, justice, freedom, mutual respect and understanding, in order to promote human rights, equality of rights as between all human beings and all nations, and economic and social progress. Equally they have an important role to play in making known the views and aspirations of the younger generation.

Article V

In order to respect freedom of opinion, expression and information and in order that information may reflect all points of view, it is important that the points of view presented by those who consider that the information published or disseminated about them has seriously prejudiced their effort to strengthen peace and international understanding, to promote human rights or to counter racism, *apartheid* and incitement to war be disseminated.

Article VI

For the establishment of a new equilibrium and greater reciprocity in the flow of information, which will be conducive to the institution of a just and lasting peace and to the economic and political independence of the developing countries, it is necessary to correct the inequalities in the flow of information to and from developing countries, and between those countries. To this end, it is essential that their mass media should have conditions and resources enabling them to gain strength and expand, and to co- operate both among themselves and with the mass media in developed countries.

Article VII

By disseminating more widely all of the information concerning the objectives and principles universally accepted which are the bases of the resolutions adopted by the different organs of the United Nations, the mass media contribute effectively to the strengthening of peace and international understanding, to the promotion of human rights, as well as to the establishment of a more just and equitable international economic order.

Article VIII

Professional organizations, and people who participate in the professional training of journalists and other agents of the mass media and who assist them in performing their functions in a responsible manner should attach special importance to the principles of this Declaration when drawing up and ensuring application of their codes of ethics.

Article IX

In the spirit of this Declaration it is for the international community to contribute to the creation of the conditions for a free flow and wider and more balanced dissemination of information, and the conditions for the protection, in the exercise of their functions, of journalists and other agents of the mass media. UNESCO is well placed to make a valuable contribution in this respect.

Article X

1. With due respect for constitutional provisions designed to guarantee freedom of information and for the applicable international instruments and agreements, it is indispensable to create and maintain throughout the world the conditions which make it possible for the organizations and persons professionally involved in the dissemination of information to achieve the objectives of this Declaration.

2. It is important that a free flow and wider and better balanced dissemination of information be encouraged.

3. To this end, it is necessary that States should facilitate the procurement, by the mass media in the developing countries, of adequate conditions and resources enabling them to gain strength and expand, and that they should support co-operation by the latter both among themselves and with the mass media in developed countries.

4. Similarly, on a basis of equality of rights, mutual advantage, and respect for the diversity of cultures which go to make up the common heritage of mankind, it is essential that bilateral and multilateral exchanges of information among all States, and in particular between those which have different economic and social systems be encouraged and developed.

Article XI

For this Declaration to be fully effective it is necessary, with due respect for the legislative and administrative provisions and the other obligations of Member States, to guarantee the existence of favorable conditions for the operation of the mass media, in conformity with the provisions of the Universal Declaration of Human Rights and with the corresponding principles proclaimed in the International Covenant on Civil and Political Rights adopted by the General Assembly of the United Nations in 1966.

APPENDIX:
SELECTED HISTORICAL DOCUMENTS
1945-1977

1945

Charter of the United Nations, opened for signature at San Francisco June 26, 1945 and entered into force Oct. 24, 1945 (TS 993; 59 Stat. 1031).

The IMF Articles of Agreement: Articles of Agreement of the International Monetary Fund, opened for signature at Washington Dec. 27, 1945 and entered into force on the same day (TIAS 1501; 60 Stat. 1401).

1947

The Rio Treaty: Inter-American Treaty of Reciprocal Assistance, opened for signature at Rio de Janeiro Sept. 24, 1947 and entered into force Dec. 3, 1948 (TIAS 1838; 62 Stat. 1681); text in *Documents, 1947:* 534-40.

1948

The OAS Charter: Charter of the Organization of American States, signed at Bogotá Apr. 30, 1948 and entered into force Dec. 13, 1951 (TIAS 2361; 2 UST 2394); text in *Documents, 1948:* 484-502.

The Genocide Convention: Convention on the Prevention and Punishment of the Crime of Genocide, done at Paris Dec. 9, 1948 and entered into force Jan. 12 1951 (not in force for the U.S.); text in *Documents, 1948:* 435-8.

The Universal Declaration of Human Rights: U.N. General Assembly Resolution 217 A (III), adopted in Paris Dec. 10, 1948; text in *Documents, 1948:* 430-35.

1949

The North Atlantic Treaty, signed at Washington Apr. 4, 1949 and entered into force Aug. 24, 1949 (TIAS 1964; 63 Stat. 2241); text in *Documents, 1949:* 612-15.

The Geneva Conventions: Convention for the Amelioration of the Condition of the Wounded and Sick in Armed Forces in the Field; Convention for the Amelioration of the Condition of the Wounded, Sick and Shipwrecked Members of the Armed Forces at Sea; Convention Relative to the Treatment of Prisoners of War; Convention Relative to the Protection of Civilian Persons in Time of War; done (dated) at Geneva Aug. 12, 1949 and entered into force for the U.S. Feb. 2, 1956 (TIAS 3362, 3363, 3364, and 3365; 6 UST 3114, 3217, 3316, and 3515).

1951

The ANZUS Treaty: Tripartite Security Treaty between the Governments of Australia, New Zealand, and the United States, signed at San Francisco Sept. 1, 1951 and entered into force Apr. 29, 1952 (TIAS 2493; 3 UST 3420); text in *Documents, 1951:* 263–5.

1953

The Korean Armistice: Agreement Concerning a Military Armistice in Korea, signed at Panmunjom and entered into force July 27, 1953 (TIAS 2782; 4 UST 234); partial text in *Documents, 1953:* 289–97.

The U.S.-Korean Treaty: Mutual Defense Treaty between the U.S. and the Republic of Korea, signed at Washington Oct. 1, 1953 and entered into force Nov. 17, 1954 (TIAS 3097; 5 UST 2368); text in *Documents, 1953:* 312–13.

1954

Public Law 480: Agricultural Trade Development and Assistance Act of 1954, approved July 10, 1954 (Public Law 480, 83rd Cong.).

The Manila Pact: South-East Asia Collective Defense Treaty, signed in Manila Sept. 8, 1954 and entered into force Feb. 19, 1955 (TIAS 3170; 6 UST 81); text in *Documents, 1954:* 319–23.

The U.S.-Taiwan Security Treaty: Treaty of Mutual Defense between the U.S. and the Republic of China, signed at Washington Dec. 2, 1954 and entered into force Mar. 3, 1955 (TIAS 3178; 6 UST 433); text in *Documents, 1954:* 360–62.

1959

The Antarctic Treaty, signed at Washington Dec. 1, 1959 and entered into force June 23, 1961 (TIAS 4790; 12 UST 794); text in *Documents, 1959:* 528–35.

1960

The U.S.-Japan Security Treaty: Treaty of Mutual Cooperation and Security between the U.S. and Japan, signed at Washington Jan. 19, 1960 and entered into force June 23, 1960 (TIAS 4509; 11 UST 1632); text in *Documents, 1960:* 425–31.

1963

The *"Hot Line" Agreement:* U.S.-Soviet Memorandum of Understanding Regarding the Establishment of a Direct Communications Link, signed at Geneva and entered into force June 20, 1963 (TIAS 5362; 14 UST 1825); text in *Documents, 1963:* 115–16.

The *Nuclear Test Ban Treaty:* Treaty Banning Nuclear Weapon Tests in the Atmosphere, in Outer Space and Under Water, signed in Moscow Aug. 5, 1963 and entered into force Oct. 10, 1963 (TIAS 5433; 14 UST 1313); text in *Documents, 1963:* 130–32.

The *Tokyo Convention:* Convention on Offenses and Certain Other Acts Committed on Board Aircraft, done at Tokyo Sept. 14, 1963 and entered into force Dec. 4, 1969 (TIAS 6768; 20 UST 2941).

International Covenant on the Elimination of All Forms of Racial Discrimination, adopted by U.N. General Assembly Resolution 2106 A (XX) of Dec. 21, 1965 and signed by U.S. Sept. 28, 1966 but not in force for the U.S. as of 1978; text in *Documents, 1966* 399–412.

1966

International Covenant on Economic, Social and Cultural Rights, adopted by U.N. General Assembly Resolution 2200 A (XXI) of Dec. 16, 1966 and entered into force Jan. 3, 1976; signed by the U.S. Oct. 5, 1977 but not in force for the U.S. as of 1978.

International Covenant on Civil and Political Rights, adopted by U.N. General Assembly Resolution 2200 A (XXI) of Dec. 16, 1966 and entered into force Mar. 23, 1976; signed by U.S. Oct. 5, 1977 but not in force for the U.S. as of 1978.

1967

The *Outer Space Treaty:* Treaty on Principles Governing the Activities of States in the Exploration and Use of Outer Space, Including the Moon and Other Celestial Bodies, signed Jan. 27, 1967 and entered into force Oct. 10, 1967 (TIAS 6347; 18 UST 2410); text in *Documents, 1966:* 391–8.

The *Treaty of Tlatelolco:* Treaty for the Prohibition of Nuclear Weapons in Latin America, opened for signature at Mexico City Feb. 14, 1967 and entered into force Apr. 22, 1968; text in U.S. Arms Control and Disarmament Agency, *Documents on Disarmament, 1967:* 69–83.

Additional Protocol I: Done at Mexico City Feb. 14, 1967 and signed by U.S. May 26, 1977, but not in force for the U.S. as of 1978; text in *AFR, 1977:* 334-5.
Additional Protocol II: Done at Mexico City Feb. 14, 1967 and entered into force for the U.S. May 12, 1971 (TIAS 7137; 22 UST 754); text in *Documents, 1968-9;* 392-4.
Protocol of Amendment to the Charter of the Organization of American States, signed at Buenos Aires Feb. 27, 1967 and entered into force Feb. 27, 1970 (TIAS 6847; 21 UST 607); summary in *Documents, 1968-9:* 399-401.
U.N. Security Council Resolution 242 (1967), enunciating principles for peace in the Middle East, adopted Nov. 22, 1967; text in *Documents, 1967:* 169-70.

1968

The Astronaut Rescue Agreement: Agreement on the Rescue of Astronauts, the Return of Astronauts, and the Return of Objects Launched into Space, signed Apr. 22, 1968 and entered into force Dec. 3, 1968 (TIAS 6599; 19 UST 7570); text in *Documents, 1967:* 392-6.
The Nuclear Nonproliferation Treaty: Treaty on the Non-Proliferation of Nuclear Weapons, signed in London, Moscow and Washington July 1, 1968 and entered into force Mar. 5, 1970 (TIAS 6839; 21 UST 483); text in *Documents, 1968-9:* 62-8.

1969

American Convention on Human Rights, opened for signature at San José, Costa Rica Nov. 1969 and entered into force July 8, 1978; signed by U.S. June 1, 1977, but not in force for the U.S. as of 1978; text in *Bulletin,* 77: 28-39.

1970

Declaration on Friendly Relations: Declaration on Principles of International Law concerning Friendly Relations and Co-operation Among States, adopted as U.N. General Assembly Resolution 2625 (XXV), Oct. 24, 1970.
The Hague Convention: Convention for the Suppression of Unlawful Seizure of Aircraft, done at The Hague Dec. 16, 1970 and entered into force Oct. 14, 1971 (TIAS 7192; 22 UST 1641); text in *Documents, 1970:* 350-55.

1971

The Anti-Terrorist Convention: Convention to Prevent and Punish the Acts of Terrorism Taking the Form of Crimes Against Persons and Related Extortion That Are of International Significance, done at Washington Feb. 2, 1971 and entered into force Oct. 20, 1976 (TIAS 8413; 27 UST 3949); text in *AFR, 1971:* 437–41.

The Seabed Arms Limitation Treaty: Treaty on the Prohibition of the Emplacement of Nuclear Weapons and Other Weapons of Mass Destruction on the Seabed and the Ocean Floor and in the Subsoil Thereof, opened for signature Feb. 11, 1971 and entered into force May 18, 1972 (TIAS 7337; 23 UST 701); text in *Documents, 1970:* 69–73.

The Berlin Agreement: Quadripartite Agreement on Berlin Between the United States of America and Other Governments, signed at Berlin Sept. 3, 1971 and entered into force June 3, 1972 (TIAS 7551; 24 UST 283); text in *AFR, 1971:* 166–70.

The Montreal Convention: Convention for the Suppression of Unlawful Acts Against the Safety of Civil Aviation, done at Montreal Sept. 23, 1971 and entered into force Jan. 26, 1973 (TIAS 7570; 24 UST 565); text in *AFR, 1971:* 548–55.

Agreement on Measures to Reduce the Risk of Outbreak of Nuclear War Between the United States of America and the Union of Soviet Socialist Republics, signed in Washington and entered into force Sept. 30, 1971 (TIAS 7186; 22 UST 1590); text in *AFR, 1971:* 110–12.

The Second "Hot Line" Agreement: Agreement Between the United States of America and the Union of Soviet Socialist Republics on Measures to Improve the U.S.A.-U.S.S.R. Direct Communications Link, signed in Washington and entered into force Sept. 30, 1971 (TIAS 7187; 22 UST 1598); text in *AFR, 1971:* 113–14.

1972

The Shanghai Communiqué: Joint Statement issued at Shanghai on the conclusion of President Nixon's visit to the People's Republic of China, Feb. 27, 1972; text in *AFR, 1972:* 307–11.

The Space Liability Convention: Convention on International Liability for Damage Caused by Space Objects, done at London, Moscow, and Washington Mar. 29, 1972, and entered into force Sept. 1, 1972 (TIAS 7762; 24 UST 2389); text in *AFR, 1971:* 555–65.

The Biological Warfare Convention: Convention on the Prohibition of the Development, Production and Stockpiling of Bacteriological (Biological) and Toxin Weapons and on Their Destruction, opened for signature in London, Moscow, and Washington Apr. 10, 1972 and entered into force Mar. 26, 1975 (TIAS 8062; 26 UST 583); text in *AFR, 1971:* 90–95.

The ABM Treaty: Treaty Between the United States of America and the Union of Soviet Socialist Republics on the Limitation of

Anti-Ballistic Missile Systems, signed in Moscow May 26, 1972 and entered into force Oct. 3, 1972 (TIAS 7503; 23 UST 3425); text in *AFR, 1972:* 90–95.

The Interim Agreement: Interim Agreement Between the United States of America and the Union of Soviet Socialist Republics on Certain Measures with Respect to the Limitation of Strategic Offensive Arms, signed in Moscow May 26, 1972; entered into force Oct. 3, 1972 and expired Oct. 3, 1977 (TIAS 7504; 23 UST 3462); text in *AFR, 1972:* 97–101.

Declaration on the Human Environment, adopted by the U.N. Conference on the Human Environment at Stockholm June 16, 1972; text in *AFR, 1972:* 470–75.

1973

U.N. Security Council Resolution 338 (1973), calling for peace negotiations on the Middle East, adopted Oct. 22, 1973: text in *AFR, 1973:* 459.

The War Powers Act: Public Law 93–148, passed by the Senate Oct. 10 and by the House of Representatives Oct. 12, 1973 and repassed over the President's veto on Nov. 7, 1973: text in *AFR, 1973:* 484–90.

The Diplomatic Protection Convention: Convention on the Prevention and Punishment of Crimes Against Internationally Protected Persons, Including Diplomatic Agents, done at New York Dec. 14, 1973 and entered into force Feb. 20, 1977 (TIAS 8532; 28 UST 1975); text in *AFR, 1973:* 586–94.

1974

Declaration on the Establishment of a New International Economic Order, adopted as U.N. General Assembly Resolution 3201 (S-VI), May 1, 1974; text in *AFR, 1974:* 103–7.

The ABM Protocol: Protocol to the Treaty on the Limitation of Anti-Ballistic Missile Systems, signed in Moscow July 3, 1974 and entered into force May 24, 1976 (TIAS 8276; 27 UST 1645) text in *AFR, 1974:* 226–8.

The Threshold Test Ban (TTB) Treaty: Treaty on the Limitation of Underground Nuclear Weapons Tests, signed in Moscow July 3, 1974 but not in force as of 1978; text in *AFR, 1974:* 229–33.

The IEA Agreement: Agreement on an International Energy Program, done at Paris Nov. 18, 1974 and entered into force Jan. 19, 1976 (TIAS 8278; 27 UST 1685); text in *AFR, 1974:* 466–90.

The Vladivostok Statement: Joint statement on the limitation of strategic offensive arms, released in Vladivostok Nov. 24, 1974; text in *AFR, 1974:* 508–9.

Charter of Economic Rights and Duties of States, adopted as U.N.

528   AMERICAN FOREIGN RELATIONS 1978

General Assembly Resolution 3281 (XXIX), Dec. 12, 1974; text in *AFR, 1974:* 528–41.

1975

The Space Registration Convention: Convention on the Registration of Objects Launched into Outer Space, opened for signature at New York Jan. 14, 1975 and entered into force Sept. 15, 1976 (TIAS 8480; 28 UST 695).

The Helsinki Final Act: Final Act of the Conference on Security and Cooperation in Europe, signed in Helsinki Aug. 1, 1975; text in *AFR, 1975:* 292–360.

The Anti-Zionist Resolution: U.N. General Assembly Resolution 3379 (XXX), adopted Nov. 10, 1975; text in *AFR, 1975:* 507–8.

1976

U.S.-Spanish Treaty: Treaty of Friendship and Cooperation between the United States of America and Spain, signed at Madrid Jan. 24, 1976 and entered into force Sept. 21, 1976 (TIAS 8360; 27 UST 3005); text in *AFR, 1976:* 212–15.

U.N. Security Council Resolution 385 (1976), calling for U.N.-sponsored elections in Namibia; adopted Jan. 30, 1976.

The IMF Amendment: Second Amendment of Articles of Agreement of the International Monetary Fund, approved by the IMF Board of Governors at Washington Apr. 30, 1976 and entered into force Apr. 1, 1978 (TIAS 8937).

Peaceful Nuclear Explosions (PNE) Treaty: Treaty between the United States of America and the Union of Soviet Socialist Republics on Underground Nuclear Explosions for Peaceful Purposes, signed in Washington and Moscow May 28, 1976 but not in force as of 1978; text in *AFR, 1976:* 181–6.

Environmental Modification Convention: Convention on the Prohibition of Military or Any Other Hostile Use of Environmental Modification Techniques, adopted by U.N. General Assembly Resolution 31/72 of Dec. 10, 1976 and signed at Geneva May 18, 1977 but not in force as of 1978; text in *AFR, 1976:* 188–93.

1977

The Panama Canal Treaties: Panama Canal Treaty, signed at Washington September 7, 1977 but not in force as of 1978; text in *AFR, 1977:* 345–64.

Treaty Concerning the Permanent Neutrality and Operation of the Panama Canal, signed at Washington Sept. 7, 1977 but not in force as of 1978; text in *AFR, 1977:* 364–9.

INDEX

A

Afghanistan, 2–3, 61, 96, 97, 98–9; Falco reference, 485–6

Africa, 16, 61–79; and Cuban-Soviet involvement, 2, 24–5, 61–2, 68–72, 79, 111; Carter reference (Annapolis, June 7), 209; Carter address (Lagos, Apr. 1), 307–14; Vance statement (May 12), 314–21; Carter statement on Zaire crisis (May 25), 322–3; Brzezinski interview on same (May 28), 323–30; Vance address (Atlantic City, June 20), 330–37; Lake address on South Africa, 337–44; Vance reference (London, Apr. 19), 387–8

African Development Fund, Carter reference (Lagos, Apr. 1), 312; Vance reference (May 12), 316

Agency for International Development (AID), Vance reference (Cincinnati, May 1), 436

AID, see Agency for International Development

Algeria, 13, 58, 79

Ali, Kamal Hassan, 59

Amerasinghe, H.S., 135

American Legion, Brown address (New Orleans, Aug. 22), 169–77

Amoco Cadiz, 135

Andreotti, Giulio, 36, 119

Angola, 24, 61–2, 68, 69–71, 73

Annapolis, Carter address (June 7, excerpt), 204–10

ANZUS, 103, 106–7; Mondale reference (Honolulu, May 10), 407, 408; Council meeting (Washington, June 7–8): final communiqué, 413–17

Arab-Israeli conflict, 1, 16, 17, 31, 46, 48–60; Baghdad summit, 59; Vance reference (Los Angeles, Jan. 13), 154–5; planes for Israel, Egypt, and Saudi Arabia (Feb. 14–May 15): Vance announcement (Feb. 14), 272–3, Vance remarks (Apr. 28), 273–4; Carter letter to Congress (May 12), 274–6; Carter statement (May 15), 276–7

Camp David meetings (Thurmont, Sept. 5–17): Carter, Sadat, and Begin remarks on signing Camp David documents (White House, Sept. 17), 277–82; Carter address to Congress (Sept. 18),

B

C

Chamoun, Camille, 59

Chile, 87, 90, 91, 93

China, People's Republic of, 1, 2, 18, 24, 95, 102, 108–10, 112; and U.S.S.R., 25, 31, 107; Brzezinski visit (May 20–23), 105; Hua visit to Eastern Europe, 45, 107; Brzezinski reference (May 28), 324–5, 326, 328–9; same (New York, Apr. 27), 403; in ANZUS communiqu9 (June 8), 414; Carter address and joint statement on U.S.-China normalization (Dec. 15), 417–19; official U.S. statement, 420; Carter remarks, 420–22; Chinese statement, 423; Taiwan statement, 423–4

China, Republic of, 1, 18, 105, 108; statement on U.S.-China normalization (Dec. 15), 423–4; Carter memorandum on U.S.-Taiwan relations (Dec. 30), 425–6

Chirac, Jacques, 37

Chirau, Jeremiah, 63

Christian Science Monitor, 125

Christopher, Warren M., 46, 110

CIEC, *see* International Economic Cooperation, Conference on

Clark amendment, 70–71; Carter reference (May 25), 323; Brzezinski reference (May 28), 325

Clark, Dick, 16, 70

Colombia, 87, 89, 90, 92, 139; Falco reference, 483–4

Colombo Plan, 132; Falco reference, 479

COMECON/CMEA, *see* Council for Mutual Economic Assistance

Congress (U.S.), 11–13, 15–16, 29; and Panama Canal treaties, 12, 81–6, 345–75; and Middle East, 12, 50, 52–3; and Cyprus, 12, 42–4; and human rights, 17; and nuclear nonproliferation, 21, 100, 120; and SALT, 29; and Turkish embargo, 42–4, 255–6; and Africa, 68, 70–71, 76; and Latin America 86–7; and U.S. forces in Korea, 106; and China, 110, 422–6; and foreign aid, 116, 122; and IMF, 116, 122; and energy, 117, 119, 122, 124; and trade, 119, 127; and terrorism, 130; and law of the sea, 136; and U.N., 138–9

Contreras Sepúlveda, Juan Manuel, 93

Costa Rica, 87, 89, 90, 93

Council for Mutual Economic Assistance (COMECON/CMEA), in Bonn summit declaration (July 17), 458

Crawford, F. Jay, 26

CSCE, *see* Security and Cooperation in Europe, Conference on

Cuba, 79–80, 87, 88, 93, 94–5; *see also* Africa

Cyprus, 12, 16, 42–4, 131; Carter reference (Sept. 26), 255; same, 256; in NATO communiqu9 (Brussels, Dec. 8), 260; Vance reference (London, Apr. 19), 388–9; same (New York, Sept. 29), 508

Czechoslovakia, 25

D

E

J

K

Kenyatta, Jomo, 3, 78
Khalid, King, 6, 56
Khalil, Mustapha, 60
Khomeini, Ruhallah, 97–8
Korea, Republic of, 16, 101–2, 104–5; Carter reference (Wake Forest, Mar. 17), 168; Brzezinski reference (New York, Apr. 27), 398, 400, 402; in ANZUS communiqué (June 8), 414
Kreps, Juanita, 124

L

Lakas Bahas, Demetrio Basilio, 88
Lake, Anthony, 77–8; address on South Africa, 337–44
Laos, 104
de Larosière, Jacques, 121
Latin America, 2, 79–95; multilateral discussions (Panama, June 16–17), 89–90, 375–8; see also OAS; country and topical entries
Law of the Sea, 133–7; Richardson statement (Mar. 16), 490–95; Vance reference (New York, Sept. 29), 503–4
Laxalt, Paul D., 84
Lebanon, 2, 51, 54, 58–9, 131; Mondale reference (New York, May 24), 198; Vance reference (New York, Sept. 29), 507–8
Leonard, James F., 24; statement at U.N. (June 30, excerpts), 200–204
Leone, Giovanni, 36
Letelier, Orlando, 93
Liberia, 64, 65–6
Libya, 58, 68, 79
Liévano, Indalecio, 139
López Michelsen, Alfonso, 89
López Portillo, José, 89, 95
Low, Stephen, 67, 77
Luns, Joseph M.A.H., 34

M

Malaysia, 104; Falco reference, 489
Manley, Michael N., 89

N

O

P

Q

R

S

T

U

Y

Z